The
BOSTON
FOOD
LOVER

Lisë Stern

ADDISON-WESLEY PUBLISHING COMPANY, INC.

Reading, Massachusetts · Menlo Park, California · New York
Don Mills, Ontario · Harlow, England · Amsterdam · Bonn
Sydney · Singapore · Tokyo · Madrid · San Juan
Paris · Seoul · Milan · Mexico City · Taipei

Many of the designations used by manufacturers and sellers to distinguish their products are claimed as trademarks. Where those designations appear in this book and Addison-Wesley was aware of a trademark claim, the designations have been printed in initial capital letters.

Library of Congress Cataloging-in-Publication Data

Stern, Lisë.
   The Boston food lover / Lisë Stern.
     p. cm.
   Includes index.
   ISBN 0-201-40644-6
   1. Grocery trade—Massachusetts—Boston Metropolitan Area—
Guidebooks. 2. Bakers and bakeries—Massachusetts—Boston
Metropolitan Area—Guidebooks. 3. Markets—Massachusetts—
Boston Metropolitan Area—Guidebooks. 4. Food industry and
trade—Massachusetts—Boston Metropolitan Area—Directories.
5. Boston (Mass.)—Guidebooks. I. Title.
HD9321.8.B67S74   1996
381'.456413'002574461—dc20   96-10944
                                        CIP

Jacket design by Suzanne Heiser
Text design by Wilson Graphics
Set in 10-point Garamond by dix!

1 2 3 4 5 6 7 8 9-DOH-99989796
First printing, May 1996

The
BOSTON
FOOD
LOVER

❖

To my boys,
Jeffrey, Gabriel, and Eitan,
with love

❖

CONTENTS

Contents

Contents

ACKNOWLEDGMENTS

*T*HERE are so many people to thank when a book is completed. As this is my first book, I want to acknowledge everyone who has ever had an influence on me. But this is not an autobiography.

First and foremost, I want to thank my husband Jeffrey Robbins. Without his constant support, none of this would have been possible. Special thanks to my sons: Gabriel Stern-Robbins, who offered definitive opinions on foods I sampled, and Eitan Stern-Robbins, who helped consume treats in utero.

Thank you, thank you to Kim Sundik, for everything—for her palate, for her ongoing help with every chapter, especially with meat and seafood, and for her terrific spirit and support.

I also want to acknowledge the following people:

My parents, Joyce and Michael Stern, who have always supported me in my endeavors, and given me the confidence to undertake this book. Thanks also to my in-laws—the best one could ask for—Donald and Esther Robbins, for everything. And to my grandmothers, Leontina "Omi" Stern and Florence "Grandlady" Duran, for their love.

My agent, Doe Coover, who helped me shape the book into what it eventually became; Elizabeth Carduff of Addison-Wesley for choosing to publish it; my editor, Sharon Broll, for her patience and guidance; production editor Beth Burleigh Fuller for turning the manuscript into a book; copy editor Maggie Carr for her sharp eye and organization; and proofreader Barbara Ames for her attention to fine details. Thanks also to food writers and editors, notably Sheryl Julian of *The Boston Globe* and Peter McNamara of *Improper Bostonian*. And to Corby Kummer, the food writer I have known and admired the longest, who inspired me to do what I do.

K.C. Turnbull (maker of the best homemade buttercrunch), Elisa Stark Rifkin, and Stacy Gasteiger, for their friendship and encouragement.

Everyone who helped me with *The Cookbook Review,*

especially my aunt Raya Stern, Victoria Riccardi, Gail Segal, and Lauren Byrne.

Michele Topor offered invaluable North End advice, time, and tours. Mike Loo was a great source for Chinatown information, and Sandy Block's wine expertise was most useful. Anneli Johnson of the Massachusetts Department of Agriculture, along with her staff, offered tremendous help and enthusiasm with all things produce-related.

Special thanks to all the people in the food business, who are dedicated to creating and selling wonderful breads, confections, pasta, pizza, produce, salads, sandwiches, sausages, seafood—everything described in this book. The food business is demanding, hands-on, and very busy, and I greatly appreciate the time everyone spent with me. Without them there would be no *Boston Food Lover.*

INTRODUCTION

SOME people collect stamps, some collect china figurines. I collect food places. From homemade ice cream to fresh pasta, supermarkets and gourmet shops, I collect them, keeping track of who offers what. I love to eat, and I love to cook, and *The Boston Food Lover* will help you do both. The necessity for such a guide became apparent to me whenever I would peruse cookbooks for new recipes. Intriguing dishes would call for flaxseeds, glutinous rice, chipotle peppers. I knew Boston was a large enough city that such items *could* be found here; I just didn't always know where to look. After all, the *Yellow Pages* doesn't categorize stores by the ingredients they carry. It also doesn't indicate the quality of the establishments listed.

I have always been a picky eater (ask my mother), and I think this is why I care so much about food. I know what I like, and I am not happy with culinary compromises. For this reason, I wanted to find the best that Boston has to offer, for everything, be it corned beef, strawberries, or chocolate truffles. *The Boston Food Lover* answers all your where-can-you-find-the-best-food questions.

The Boston area is wonderfully varied, with our own native specialties, as well as the culinary traditions brought by immigrants from around the world. The area has residents from every continent and dozens of countries—England, Italy, Ireland, India, China, Japan, Vietnam, Korea, Mexico, Cuba, Brazil, France, Germany, Russia, Haiti, Jamaica, Trinidad, Guatemala, and more. Boston has its food neighborhoods, such as the Italian North End and Chinatown, and all the towns that are part of Boston, such as Jamaica Plain and Dorchester, have bakeries, eateries, and food stores for their Irish, Caribbean, and Asian populations. Cambridge is notable for both its excellent ice cream and its several health-food stores. Other metropolitan areas, such as Brookline, Somerville, and Newton, are overflowing with wonderful foods. But then there are also surprises, like Everett, home of marvelous Italian specialties, and charming Marblehead and historic Concord, both a gourmand's delight.

Several very successful food companies with national distribution were launched out of the Boston area—Prince Spaghetti, Dunkin' Donuts, Colombo Yogurt, Baker's Chocolate, Boston Market, Au Bon Pain, Fig Newtons, Necco Wafers. The area also has many unique culinary finds, such as Jessica's Biscuit, the largest mail-order cookbook company in the country, a daily selection of incredibly fresh seafood, pick-your-own farms, seasonal ice-cream stands, and award-winning microbreweries. It's obviously an area that inspires food lovers.

To research this guide, I had to establish limits, both categorical and geographical. Categorically, I sought out food businesses that are not restaurants, with the exception of places that specialize in take-out, sandwiches, and pizza. I tried to cover everything food related in Boston—bakeries, butchers, fishmongers, pasta makers, produce stands, gourmet shops, ethnic markets, health-food stores, coffee roasters, juice bars, wineries, breweries, ice-cream makers, and chocolatiers.

The Boston food scene has certainly changed, for the better, since I began working on this book. The most notable developments are in the areas of bread and coffee. Bread is booming. There are some establishments that have been baking bread for years, and, much to my delight, many places have opened within the past two years. Good coffee has long been available in Boston, primarily from Coffee Connection, but in limited areas. In the last couple of years, quality coffee shops have popped up all over the place—on every corner and highway. There are also more take-out operations than ever.

Geographically, I used Route 495 as a boundary, more or less. To the northeast and southeast, the boundary gets vague, and I tried to include every feasible town within reason, in terms of time.

I grew up in a city, and live in a city now, and always felt reluctant to drive more than fifteen minutes for anything. In researching this book, I covered thousands of miles (not to mention calories) exploring towns and neighborhoods I had never been to, and discovering foods I had never heard of, and items worth driving for. In the process I compiled a database of over two thousand establishments. I would visit a place and try something; if it was good, I would try as many other items as possible.

The Boston Food Lover is much more than a listing of which stores offer which goods; rather, it assesses the shops and a range of their goods. A bakery that makes fantastic rye bread may make only mediocre whole wheat; a gourmet shop's take-out potato salad may be to die for, but the pasta salad may be better off dead. *The Boston Food Lover* tells you not only where to find whatever you may be looking for, but also what level of quality to expect.

The book is organized by culinary category into chapters. Within each chapter, listings are organized first by area then by town according to the following list:

BOSTON	NORTH	SOUTH	WEST
Boston	Andover	Abington	Acton
Allston	Beverly	Braintree	Arlington
Brighton	Billerica	Brockton	Belmont
Charlestown	Burlington	Canton	Bolton
Dorchester	Danvers	Chatham	Chelmsford
East Boston	Ipswich	Dedham	Concord
Hyde Park	Lynnfield	Dover	Framingham
Jamaica Plain	Malden	Easton	Gardner
Mattapan	Manchester	Foxboro	Hatfield
Roslindale	Marblehead	Hingham	Haverhill
Roxbury	Medford	Mansfield	Hopkinton
South Boston	Melrose	Milton	Hudson
West Roxbury	Middleton	Norwell	Lexington
	Newburyport	Norwood	Lincoln
	North Andover	Plymouth	Lowell
METROPOLITAN	Peabody	Providence	Marlboro
BOSTON	Revere	Quincy	Natick
	Salem	Randolph	Needham
Brookline	Saugus	Raynham	Sherborn
Cambridge	Wakefield	Sharon	Shrewsbury
Chelsea	Wilmington	Stoughton	Southboro
Everett	Winchester	Walpole	Sudbury
Newton	Woburn	Westport	Waltham
Somerville		Westwood	Watertown
Winthrop		Weymouth	Wayland
			Wellesley
			Weston

I include the business's street address, phone number, and hours of operation. Bear in mind that hours change *all the time;* those indicated here can at least give you an idea of when an establishment is open; it is always best to call before visiting. Mondays and Tuesdays are usually less busy days, and some stores are closed then. Sunday is the most common day businesses are closed. Many places that are usually closed on Sunday are open Sundays during the five weeks between Thanksgiving and Christmas. Establishments often have summer and winter hours. I also indicate if a business offers mail-order service. At the beginning of each chapter I include an alphabetical list of places covered. I offer my picks for "The Bests of the Best" at the end of each chapter. Some chapters deviate from this standard organization; when this is the case, I indicate the format in those chapters.

A word about terminology. Several businesses use the terms *home-baked* and *homemade* rather loosely. *Home-baked* usually means that they got the batter for items such as cookies or muffins from another company and bake it on the premises. *Homemade* can mean made on the premises *or*, well, that *some*-body or company made the item. I use the term *homemade* to mean made on the premises, by that particular business.

No one is infallible, and there are probably many worthwhile places that I missed. The food world is very dynamic —businesses are closing and opening daily. There were some wonderful places that closed after I visited, and others are opening even as I write. If you come across a worthy find, please write and let me know, and I'll include it in a revised edition.

Boston has more than its share of wonderful food finds, and of people dedicated to producing the best quality foods. There are small businesses and large, and behind the best there is someone who cares about great food, someone who probably was, and is, a picky eater.

For them, and for those who have wondered if, indeed, good bread is available in Boston, if there is a source for fresh lemongrass and kefir lime leaves, or where to find homemade turkey sausage, *The Boston Food Lover* will be an invaluable resource.

CHAPTER ONE

THE STAFF OF LIFE

Where to find freshly baked sourdough, rye, white, whole wheat, challah, bagels, French baguettes, Middle Eastern pita, Mexican tortillas, Italian focaccia, and other breads

*A*H, bread. The very word conjures up pleasing images of hominess, comfort, wholesomeness. The smell of bread baking makes everyone happy. I love to bake bread, but there are certain textures and styles of bread that simply can't be made in a home oven, so I look with hope toward a professional bread baker.

For bread lovers, the greatest thing since sliced bread is unsliced bread, round loaves of crusty hearth breads, with chewy, slightly sour interiors, dense rolls filled with raisins and nuts, focaccia covered with fresh rosemary and slivered onions, rectangular loaves made with freshly milled whole wheat flour, egg-rich braided challah, molasses-scented pumpernickel, soft fresh pita, long thin baguettes, bagels sprinkled with sesame seeds, flaky croissants. Bread making is an art, and bread bakeries are the galleries that display these creations.

In the last few years, the bread scene in Boston has expanded dramatically—more than half the bakeries covered in this chapter opened after 1990. For me, the ideal would be a great bread bakery in every town. That has yet to happen, but we're definitely on our way.

1

Boston is the headquarters for the wildly successful Au Bon Pain chain; while not quite France, this company makes surprisingly acceptable baguettes and other breads available all over the area.

There has also been a bagel explosion in the past few years. Fifteen years ago, bagels were heard of, but they were not in demand the way they are today. Some local bakers attempted to expand then, to lukewarm response. Now everyone wants bagels, and it seems that everyone is making them. I describe the area's best bagel bakeries in a separate section. I also include a separate listing for Middle Eastern pita bakeries.

* Described in another chapter.

BREAD

Angel's Bakery and Café	Watertown
*Avenue Bakery	Dorchester
Biga Breads	Charlestown
Big Sky Bread Company	Newton, Waltham
Boschetto Bakery	Boston
Boston Daily Bread	Brookline, Sudbury
The Boston Pretzel Bakery	Jamaica Plain
Brandano's Bakery	Revere
Bread & Circus	Everett
The Bread Shop	Hingham
Breads 'n' Bits of Ireland	Melrose
Breadsong	Newton
Cake Art and Confections	Sharon
Carberry's Bakery and Coffee House	Cambridge
Casal Bakery Co.	Cambridge
Central Bakery	Peabody
*Christian Payen Fine French Pastries	Beverly
Clear Flour Bakery	Brookline
Common Ground Bakery and Café	Dorchester
Diamond Bakery	Newton
*Diane's Bakery	Roslindale
*Gooches Bakery	Roslindale
Greenhills Traditional Irish Bakery	Dorchester
Iggy's	Watertown, Marblehead
Il Panificio	Boston
*Japonaise Bakery	Brookline, Cambridge
Kaplan's Bakery	Providence, RI
Keltic Krust	Newton

*La Patisserie	Winchester
LMNOP	Boston
*Lyndell's Bakery	Somerville
*Manny's Pastries	Roslindale
Maria & Ricardo's Tortilla Factory	Jamaica Plain
*Montilio's Cake Shoppe	Quincy
*Ohlin's Bakery	Belmont
Panini	Somerville
Peter Bread, Etc.	Sudbury
Pomme Frite	Cambridge, Newton
*Quebrada Baking Co.	Arlington, Wellesley
*Salamander Food Shop	Cambridge
*Sally Ann Food Shop	Concord
Spagnuolo's Bake House	Newton
Today's Bread	Jamaica Plain
*Tutto Italiano	Hyde Park, Newton, Wellesley
*Wheatberries of Manchester	Manchester
Wheatstone Baking Company	Boston
*White's Pastry Shop	Brockton

BAGELS

Brooklyn Bagel	Framingham
Eagerman's Bakery	Brookline
Finagle a Bagel	Boston
Katz Bagel Bakery	Chelsea
Kupel's Bagels	Brookline
Rosenfeld Bagel Co. Inc.	Newton
The Ultimate Bagel Co.	Boston, Cambridge, Newton
Zayde's Bagels	Saugus
Zeppy's Baigel Bakery	Randolph

PITA

Droubi Bakery	Roslindale
Lebanon Baking Co.	Boston
Near East Bakery	West Roxbury

❖ BREAD ❖

BOSTON

BOSTON

Boschetto Bakery

158 Salem Street, North End, Boston, MA 02113   (617) 523-9350
Mail order: not available   Hours: Mon.–Sat. 7 A.M.–5 P.M.;
    Sun 6 A.M.–noon

Carmine Bruno has been running Boschetto Bakery for the last thirty years, but the bakery has been in operation here for over a century. That's how old the brick oven is where they bake their great loaves of **Italian bread** and long, thin *grissini* breadsticks. (Boschetto also makes traditional **Italian cookies**—acceptable but not remarkable.) There are four kinds of bread, which come in a variety of shapes and sizes. There's a dense **Tuscany bread with salt,** great for sandwiches. Others are *napoletano,* a flat round bread; *Bostone,* a long loaf; and the slipper-shaped *ciabatta.* **Rosette** are round rolls made with oil; they are airy, with a nice crust.

Il Panificio. See Spagnuolo Bake House, Newton, page 24.

LMNOP

79 Park Plaza, Boston, MA 02116   (617) 338-4220
Mail order: not available   Hours: Mon.–Sat. 7:30 A.M.–7 P.M.;
    closed Sun.

LMNOP is the bakery and take-out branch of Lydia Shire's culinary enterprises. She opened LMNOP just after Pignoli, her second restaurant (Biba is her first). Why a bakery, on top of two busy restaurants? Precisely because of the two restaurants, Shire explains. "We always made our own breads, so it seemed an obvious choice. I wanted to sell the breads retail and wholesale."

The space is tiny, an irregularly shaped corner area off to the side of Pignoli's, but with the unusual decor that characterizes Shire's other establishments. Breads line the back wall, and racks of loaves rest near the side. A display case is filled with pastries; a smaller counter proffers a few salads.

The breads are the best item here. My favorites are the **organic sourdough,** which is crusty and chewy, with a pleasing sour flavor, and *pane rustico,* also chewy, but milder. The **potato**

loaf is on the fluffy side, but it has an appealing potato flavor. The bread used for many sandwiches is **Biba bread,** a cross between a French- and Italian-style loaf. The **focaccia** is good, if a little soft and crumbly, and is available with three different toppings: **tomato, onion,** and **olive.** I like the toothsome, triangular **dinner rolls;** also superlative is the **blue cheese bread.** This is a long rectangular loaf made with the same dense dough as the rolls, with a vein of blue cheese running through the middle.

The take-out items are not extensive. There are the prepared salads, as well as a few entrees and sandwiches. **Egg salad,** that classic comfort food, is served with *mesclun* greens. The lunch items tend to reflect Shire's upscale tastes and flair for unusual combinations, such as **tenderloin of beef with chestnut stuffing** or **white asparagus, avocado, and goat cheese salad.** The **potato Gorgonzola soup** is rich and filling. The LMNOP pizza, called a **pizzette,** is a slice topped with fresh plum tomatoes, yellow peppers, basil, and fontina cheese.

The **pastries** are a mixed bag. Several items were created by pastry chef extraordinaire Rick Katz, former owner of Bentonwood Bakery and Café, and those items are delicious, such as **Rick's chocolate chip cookie.** A **mocha square** is also very good, with a light, crispy layering of meringue filled with mocha cream. The **cranberry cake** is a pleasing contrast of tart berries and sweet streusel topping. Other items were disappointing, overdone, or unremarkable.

Wheatstone Baking Company

96 Peterborough Street, Boston, MA 02215   (617) 247-3566
Mail order: not available   Hours: Mon.–Fri. 7 A.M.–7 P.M.;
Sat., Sun. 7 A.M.–5 P.M.

Specialty bread stores seem to be popping up right and left—which is great. But long before we saw such an abundance of bread in Boston, John Shawb opened Wheatstone. Shawb had a degree in business management and had worked for a couple years in a gourmet store when he decided to open his own business in 1984. "At the time no one else was doing upscale breads," he recalls.

He started in a small, 800-square-foot kitchen with one oven on what was then a desolate street near the Fenway. "I only had a vision of a wholesale business," he says. Now, over a third of his business is retail, and he's moved into much larger quarters.

You can see the kitchen from the street through the plate-glass window. As you enter, there are display cases and a few tables by the window. It's a pleasant place for a sandwich, and Wheatstone makes a variety with classic fillings such as **tuna fish** and **roast beef,** using their own breads.

For plain bread eating, I prefer chewy hearth breads, but as sandwich breads, Wheatstone's are very good. Shawb calls his white bread **anadama,** which is made with honey. It's a good sandwich loaf, although I think it's a misnomer, since anadama bread traditionally is made with molasses. The **dark rye,** which *is* made with molasses, is a good, mild pumpernickel. **Seeded buckwheat** is a popular bread, and it derives a good solid flavor from poppy and sunflower seeds. Pass on the **sourdough.** It's a fine bread, but not a notable sourdough, and there are several places around town doing a better version. The **whole wheat** is good, and the **French** is decent, but my favorite is **herb poppy seed,** which is tasty with a distinct dill flavor. The **focaccia** comes in two flavors, **rosemary** and **garlic-Parmesan;** I found the latter to be more flavorful.

In addition to breads, Wheatstone makes a variety of **baked goods.** The **croissants** are very heavy. The **muffins** are loaded with berries, but the batter does not have much taste. Similarly, the **raisin scone** was bland, its texture spongy. Your best bet for breakfast pastries is the **sticky bun with nuts,** with a pleasant honey flavor. The **brownie** is very good, and the **chocolate chip cookie** is phenomenal—the best one with nuts of all I tasted. It's a large cookie, which I don't usually care for, but the texture is good, and it's thick with nuts and chips. The **almond chocolate chip biscotti** is also good. It is very hard, with only a slight chewiness, and is perfect for dunking in coffee.

CHARLESTOWN

Biga Breads
50 Terminal Street, Charlestown, MA 02129   (617) 242-1001
Mail order: not available   Hours: daily 9 A.M.–3 P.M.

197 8th Street, Charlestown, MA 02129   (617) 242-1006
Mail order: not available   Hours: Mon.–Sat. 7 A.M.–7 P.M.;
Sun. 7:30 A.M.–6 P.M.

Biga Breads was started as a wholesale operation by partners Laurie Brooks and Tracey Bern in a former cotton mill in Charlestown in 1994. The pair met when they were attending the Cambridge Culinary School and formed a catering company after they graduated. According to Chloe Cahill, director of sales, they started making bread when "they couldn't find bread to match their exquisite food."

The word *biga* is the Italian term for "starter dough." All of the breads are leavened using wild yeast, from a sourdough starter, but they are not particularly sour. When I visited, the company was making almost a dozen different breads, as well as **focaccia** and *grissini.* The latter are my favorite of their products: they are terrific crunchy breadsticks twisted with Parmesan cheese, garlic, black pepper, and sesame seeds. On the whole, I like Biga's, breads, but I find them a little bit *too* dense, perhaps owing to the fact that they use durum flour, which is usually used for pasta. The flavors are what makes these breads more interesting. In addition to **classic white** and **peasant,** which uses a blend of whole wheat and rye flour, there are **sour cherry–walnut, black currant–molasses, fig–toasted pine nut,** and **cranberry-pecan.** I like the latter best, but because of the high cost of cranberries during the summer, it's seasonal—available only in the fall and winter.

There are more **savory breads** as well: **Sicilian green olive, herb** (with basil, cilantro, and sage), **spinach and walnut,** and **Second Harvest bread,** which uses the spent grains from Tremont ale (see "Libations," page 478).

The Terminal Street location is a wholesale bakery. Cahill says that they always make extra, and you can stop by during bakery hours to pick up a loaf. It's best to call in advance to find out what's available.

In late 1995, Biga opened a retail store in the Charlestown Navy Yard. There are tables and coffee here, along with **soups** and **sandwiches.** Try Biga's very good **biscotti**—nice and hard—in **almond, orange-fennel,** or **chocolate-walnut.**

DORCHESTER

Avenue Bakery. See "Everything Nice," page 236.

Common Ground Bakery and Café

2243 Dorchester Avenue, Lower Mills, Dorchester, MA 02124
   (617) 298-1020
Mail order: not available   Hours: Mon.–Thurs. 9 A.M.–10 P.M.;
   Fri. 9 A.M.–3 P.M.; closed Sat. and Sun.

It was pouring rain and I was driving down Dorchester Avenue,
looking for a fish market. The Common Ground sign caught my
eye, and I dashed through the rain to enter another world. The
interior of this establishment feels like something from *The Hob-
bit.* New Age music plays in the background. A wooden path
leads to the cashier, where you can buy a selection of homemade
breads. A low wooden fence lines the path, separating you from
the restaurant's heavy wooden tables and booths. Some of the
tables are sheltered by wooden shingles erected to resemble a
cottage roof, and the lighting is warm and muted.

   Common Ground is a business run by the Messianic
Community Church. They celebrate their Sabbath on Friday
night and Saturday, and hence are closed from Friday afternoon
through the weekend. The community has a 120-member branch
in Dorchester, where they've been living communally in three
houses since 1982. They also produce a variety of craft items,
including furniture, clothing, and candles, which are available in
an adjoining shop.

   The Common Ground breads are very good. My favorite
is the **seven-grain,** which is nutty and chewy without tasting *too*
healthy. A close runner-up is the **oatmeal,** toothsome and slightly
sweet. Other breads are **whole wheat, rye, sourdough,** and a
light **sandwich roll,** which is made with eggs. They also make a
whole wheat bagel, which was not good at all—more like a
dinner roll.

   These breads are used for the **sandwiches** served here,
which include variations using **turkey, tuna,** and **tofu**—no red
meat. There is also a **peanut butter, banana,** and **honey** on
whole wheat. Try it with the wonderful **house iced tea** made
with peppermint and lemon tea—great in the summer.

   The **baked sweets** are good, though not as good as the
breads; all are sweetened with honey or maple syrup. The best is

the **oatmeal-raisin** cookie, which a smooth cinnamon flavor. The **cream-cheese pie with blueberry sauce** is a good version of a cheesecake.

Greenhills Traditional Irish Bakery

793 Adams Street, Dorchester, MA 02124   (617) 825-8187
Mail order: not available   Hours: Mon. 6 A.M.–noon;
     Tues.–Sat. 6 A.M.–7 P.M.; Sun. 8 A.M.–noon

Dermot and Cindy Quinn opened this Irish bakery in 1991. Dermot was a chef by trade, working as a bricklayer, and Cindy had been a gold buyer for a jewelry store. Dermot's grandmother used to send the couple brown bread from Ireland, and Cindy learned how to make it for area Irish bars that wanted brown bread for their Irish breakfasts. The Quinns started working out of their house but soon shared a kitchen with a caterer, giving them the courage to open a retail store.

Greenhills' signature products are the Irish pastries, but the Quinns also make a number of other breads and pastries. The **brown bread** is very good, as is the **Irish soda bread.** The **scones** aren't bad, but they are made with margarine, and I prefer the flavor of butter. They are popular, though—several people came and ordered them while I visited. You can order them split and heated up. **Cream slices** consist of layers of puff pastry spread with jam **(apple, strawberry,** or **raspberry)** and whipped cream. I prefer the **eclairs,** which are excellent, among the best I've tried; they are filled with a layer of rich egg custard and a layer of sweetened whipped cream.

The **congo bars** are good, if slightly underdone, consisting of a buttery crust topped with chocolate chips and coconut. But the best pastry by far is the **apple squares.** The crust is thick and flaky, and the filling is great. If you're lucky, you'll be there when these come fresh from the oven. The **apple pie** is made with the same crust. Although the crust is thicker and more biscuitlike than a typical crust, I find this to be the best apple pie I've tried at a bakery. And the pies are cheap, too: when I visited the price was $6 for a ten-inch pie, which seemed incredibly low, given the quality—they use fresh apples, not canned filling.

Greenhills also offers a selection of good **sandwich breads,** including **white, wheat and molasses, basil and garlic, four-grain and honey,** and **cinnamon-raisin.**

HYDE PARK

Tutto Italiano. See "The World in a Jar," page 420.

JAMAICA PLAIN

The Boston Pretzel Bakery

284 Armory Street, Jamaica Plain, MA 02130   (617) 522-9494
Mail order: not available   Hours: daily 7 A.M.–noon

I love soft pretzels, but I am constantly surprised at how bad many of them taste. When made poorly, soft pretzels sit in your stomach like a hard lump. When made well, they are delicious, flavorful, and fun.

The Boston Pretzel Bakery makes them well, very well, and has been doing so since 1985. Linda DeMarco makes her **pretzels** daily in this Jamaica Plain factory, located in part of the old Haffenreffer Brewery near the Boston Brewing Company (as in Samuel Adams beer) and Maria & Ricardo's Tortilla Factory. Each pretzel is twisted by hand.

The pretzels are low in fat, and they taste best the day they are made. They also freeze well. I had a couple that were one and two days old, and they still tasted good. The pretzels come in a few varieties. I like regular **salt** (and pretzels need salt —without it they taste, well, like they need salt) and **salted sesame seed** best. **Onion, garlic,** and **poppy seed** are also available.

You can get the pretzels at the factory; look for the door with a large pretzel hanging over it. There is no storefront, but you can walk in the door and order as many or as few as you want, at wholesale prices. I paid $3 for a loser pretzel at Great Woods; these wonders are under 50¢ wholesale. Pushcarts at the Boston Common and Downtown Crossing sell these pretzels with your choice of mustard or melted cheese.

Maria & Ricardo's Tortilla Factory

30 Germania Street, Building J, Jamaica Plain, MA 02130
    (617) 524-6107
Mail order: available   Hours: by appointment Mon.–Fri. 9 A.M.–2 P.M.

Maria & Ricardo's Tortilla Factory is not generally open to the public. It is located in an industrial park, and there is no salesroom. But they make excellent all-natural tortillas, which you can order and pick up, and this is the source for freshly made *masa*. You can use *masa* to make your own tortillas or to make tamale fillings. The tortillas are also available in area stores.

Tortillas in Boston? This is not an area known for a dense Hispanic population. Before the company opened, there were no commercially made tortillas in Massachusetts, a lack observed by Mexican immigrant Ricardo Barreto, an art historian. Once when he went home on a visit, he casually commented to his cousins Heidi and Ana Hartung, "Boston could use a tortilla factory." In less than two weeks, Heidi was knocking on his door, saying, "When do we start?"

Heidi honed her tortilla skills by working in a Mexican tortilla factory for three months, then moved to Boston. On February 5, 1987, she and Ricardo opened the shop as Maria & Ricardo's Tortilla Factory (Heidi's middle name is Maria, which they decided sounded more authentically Mexican). That same day, Heidi's sister Ana, an architect, arrived in Boston for a kidney transplant. While recuperating, Ana helped out in the tortilla business; she then took over for Heidi when Heidi married and moved to Hong Kong six months later.

Initially, the company made only **white corn tortillas.** "In Mexico, we say the whiter the tortilla, the better the quality," explains Ana. "It's also more authentic—in Mexico we don't eat yellow corn tortillas. Yellow tastes like cornflakes, while white tastes like sweet corn." In response to customer demand, the company started making **blue corn tortillas** too, and developed **white** and **whole wheat flour tortillas** as well.

Corn tortillas are made in a multistep process. Whole dried corn kernels are cooked in slaked lime water, during which process the corn undergoes a compositional change. The husk softens, and the corn's amino acids become more digestible. Next, the corn is rinsed and soaked overnight in water, then rinsed again. The soaked corn is then stone ground into a paste, called *masa*. This is the corn tortilla dough—nothing else is added. The *masa* is rolled between stone rollers, much like a pasta machine, and die cut into tortilla circles. As the tortilla bakes, it puffs up, and then it flattens as it cools, creating a thin pocket between two layers.

An entirely different process is used for the flour tortillas. A dough made from flour and vegetable shortening is rolled into balls, flattened in a tortilla press, and then baked.

In a few short years, Maria & Ricardo's have become the

tortillas of choice in many of Boston's trend-setting restaurants, including Biba's and Boca Grande. Business is booming. The company now grinds 3,000 pounds of corn a week, and produces over two hundred cases of corn tortillas and three hundred cases of flour tortillas.

Sadly, several months after I interviewed her, Ana died of kidney-related complications. Her sister Heidi returned from Hong Kong and continues to run the business.

Ana came a long way from her glamorous architect's job —but she never looked back. "The tortilla factory was a challenge, something I'd never done before, and I wanted to learn how to do it. When you have a clear idea of what you want— quality, authenticity, a healthy product—then the decisions you make for yourself are very easy."

The tortillas are available in area stores, including several Star Markets and Stop & Shops, as well as Bread & Circus and other natural food stores. The *masa* is available at the factory; call in your order in advance.

Today's Bread

701 Centre Street, Jamaica Plain, MA 02130   (617) 522-6458
Mail order: not available   Hours: Mon.–Fri. 7:30 A.M.–6 P.M.;
    Sat. 8 A.M.–5 P.M.; Sun. 8 A.M.–1 P.M.

Today's Bread started in this location in 1980, when there were virtually no other businesses on Centre Street in Jamaica Plain. Owner Terry Bruce acquired the business from two of her sisters in 1984. Everything, from the bread to the salads and sandwich fillings, is made on the premises. There are actually two businesses here operating simultaneously. Today's Bread is the bakery and take-out section; the Water Café is a full-service restaurant.

When Today's Bread started, it was just a bakery with coffee. Bruce points out that her operation was the fourth shop outside of the North End to have an espresso machine, beating the current coffee trend by nearly a decade. And as the name implies, the shop makes bread. They have a repertoire of about thirty breads, and feature four daily. There's the daily special, such as sweet **oatmeal bread,** and the three regular offerings, a crusty **French,** a hearty **whole wheat,** and a **rye** bread.

The breads are all used for **sandwiches,** which are quite good. They include tempting combinations such as **oven-roasted turkey and Havarti, baked eggplant Parmesan and sweet *capi-***

colla, and **Genoa salami, provolone, and roasted pepper.**
Other take-out offerings include great **soups**—I tried a winter
white bean in a tomato broth and a simple **potato-parsley**—
and an assortment of **salads.** The **chicken-curry salad** (also
available as a sandwich filling) is very good, mixed with chutney
and slivered almonds; the chicken salad varies from day to day.
The **carrot–snow pea salad** sounds boring but is remarkably
good. The carrots are blanched perfectly, so they have some
crunch, but not too much, and the dressing is a blend of vinegar,
ginger, and rosemary.

Then there are the **baked goods.** Today's Bread is one
of the few places that makes really, really good muffins. When I
bit into a **cranberry-walnut muffin,** my immediate reactions
were first relief, and then joy. Yay! I thought, a place that makes
good muffins! The **scones** are also pretty good, and are a realistic
size—not the plate-sized monstrosities that many places serve (I
guess many people must like that size, but I'm not one of them).
They are usually filled with fruit, the filling varying from day to
day. There are also **biscuits,** which go well with soups or **chili;**
these have both butter and shortening in them (the scones are all
butter) and are less sweet. My favorite item in the baked-goods
case is the **sacristain,** an oblong of puff pastry threaded with
sliced almonds and sugar. The **biscotti** are good, as are the other
cookies, notably the **butterscotch-oatmeal.**

There's a second case of sweets; these are fancier pastries
and cakes. I tried the **chocolate decadence.** The chocolate
mousse filling was good, but not the best I've tried, and the
cake part was dry. Much better was the super-rich **lemon–white
chocolate tart.** There was not a noticeable white chocolate taste,
but the lemon filling was tangy and creamy.

You can take out or eat in here—there are several tables.
Or you can dine at the Water Café with its separate menu, and
the atmosphere is pleasant for lingering.

ROSLINDALE

Manny's Pastries. See "Goodies to Go," page 198.

Diane's Bakery. See "Everything Nice," page 239.

Gooches Bakery. See "Everything Nice," page 240.

METROPOLITAN BOSTON

BROOKLINE

Boston Daily Bread

1331 Beacon Street, Brookline, MA 02146   (617) 277-8810
Mail order: available   Hours: Mon.–Fri. 7 A.M.–8 P.M.;
  Sat. 7 A.M.–7 P.M.; closed Sun.

505 Boston Post Road, Sudbury, MA 01776   (508) 443-7474
Hours: Mon.–Sat. 7 A.M.–6 P.M.; closed Sun.

Boston Daily Bread was the first bakery in this area to grind their own whole wheat flour. Founder Cindy Flahive-Sobol opened the Brookline store in December 1992 and followed with a second store in Sudbury in 1994. According to Flahive-Sobol, the success of the flour-ground-on-the-premises venture inspired both Great Harvest and Big Sky (see page 21) to approve franchises in the area, which opened here in 1994. Flahive-Sobol sold the Brookline establishment to enterprising brothers Sage and Ramzi Darwish in February 1995. Her book, with recipes, about Boston Daily Bread is due out in 1996.

Boston Daily mills flour from Montana red and golden hard spring wheat. They also mill a seven-grain mix that includes oats, rye, millet, triticale, barley, and four kinds of wheat. The Brookline store is wide open and friendly. The Sudbury store, located in a shopping center, is larger, with tables. In both locations, the counter supports a bread board laden with loaves of bread ready to be sliced for samples and slathered with excellent butter from Pennsylvania.

There are usually twelve to fifteen varieties of fresh-baked bread daily, many made with no added fat. About half are made with the whole wheat flour; the other half use unbleached white flour, which they do not grind themselves. The biggest seller is a wonderful **cinnamon swirl,** which is white-flour based. Other popular breads include **chocolate chip** and **jalapeño-corn.** Not all the breads I tried were terrific—the **sourdough white** is too sweet and soft for sourdough. But the **whole wheat apple-almond** is great, and the **honey whole wheat** is very good. They also make **whole wheat muffins.** I tried a **raspberry,** which was okay but too heavy. The **fat-free banana-pineapple** was better. The **scones** also are good but not great. Normally I prefer chocolate chip cookies to be medium-sized, but these oversize **white- and dark-chocolate chunk cookies** are made with lots of butter and brown sugar, and are *soooo* good.

  Both the butter and the home-ground flour are for sale as well.

Clear Flour Bakery

178 Thorndike Street, Brookline, MA 02146 (617) 739-0060
Mail order: not available Hours: daily 10 A.M.–8 P.M.

I love sourdough bread. When I was ten or eleven, relatives from California brought us a loaf of San Francisco sourdough. It had probably been purchased at the airport and came wrapped in a plastic bag, but it was terrific. Sliced and toasted, it had this great chewy texture and marvelous sour flavor. Subsequently, I was only able to find sourdough bread of that caliber on visits to California.

  Authentic sourdough bread is made without commercial yeast. The leavening comes from a starter, which contains wild yeast. Starter is a liquidy dough, usually the consistency of pancake batter. Bakeries will use the same starter for years, replenishing it with a measure of flour equal to the amount of starter used. Different strains of wild yeast add a distinctive flavor to the bread.

  I tried making my own, but it just didn't have that depth of flavor that the sourdough starters, used and nourished over years, or even decades, can give a loaf of bread. Clear Flour Bakery has been using such a starter since they opened in 1983, and they make absolutely excellent **sourdough** bread. The crumb is soft, yet chewy, and the crust is toothsome and crispy. Perfect.

  Initially, the bakery sold only wholesale. But the smell of baking bread that fills the neighborhood enticed people inside, so Clear Flour began a small retail business. There is no real storefront. A table with a cash register is set up next to racks of bread right by the door, and a few feet away bakers are kneading dough. About 30 percent of the business is retail, and the company is looking to expand that part of its business. They make nine varieties of bread on a daily basis, all of which are also delivered around town to places like Savenor's in Beacon Hill and Barsamian's in Cambridge, as well as several area restaurants.

  The **sourdough French** comes in a **baguette** shape or a **round** and is my favorite of Clear Flour's breads, but then, sourdough is my favorite kind of bread in general. The **dark ryes**—one with raisins, one without—are made with both sourdough culture and yeast. They are very good, somewhere between light rye and pumpernickel. The **buckwheat walnut** isn't bad, but I found the crumb a bit soft, and I wanted a lot more walnuts. Their **focaccia** comes in two flavors: **rosemary,** which is good, and **onion,** which is great, complemented by herbs and a kick of ground black pepper. The **green olive rolls** are tasty, if a little soft, with a subtle kick from hot red peppers. On the weekends, if you get there early enough, try their excellent **morning buns** —sticky buns made with and without walnuts and just a touch of honey. They are among the best sticky buns I've ever had, definitely worth waking up for. Also good are the dense, bready **scones,** large rectangles filled with currants and dried cranberries.

In addition to the regular breads, there is always a daily special. More interesting offerings include Tuesday's **Paris night,** a dense raisin-walnut bread in a rye and whole wheat dough; Friday's **alpine shepherd,** a cracked wheat and potato bread; and the weekend **golden fruit tea bread,** a brioche studded with sultanas and dried pears.

For business reasons (they don't want to be stiffed), Clear Flour will not reserve any breads. It is possible, however, to reserve their breads through shops that carry it, such as Virginia's Fine Foods (see "Goodies to Go," page 171). The prices are extremely reasonable and pretty close to wholesale—the eighteen-inch-long baguettes are only $1.25. The breads are made without preservatives, but they do freeze well.

There is a strong sense that owners, Christy Timon and Abram Faber, are people who really care about what they are doing, and who do not want to compromise their quality. They occasionally travel to France and Italy and to other bakeries around the country looking for inspiration. They sell their experiments as they develop new breads, looking for customer reactions. The popular olive rolls and scones are results of those experiments.

Clear Flour recently added pastries to their repertoire; the free-form **pear cranberry tarts,** individual sized, are wonderful.

Japonaise Bakery. See "Everything Nice," page 244.

CAMBRIDGE

Carberry's Bakery and Coffee House

74–76 Prospect Street, Cambridge, MA 02139   (617) 576-3530
Mail order: not available   Hours: Mon.–Sat. 6:15 A.M.–8 P.M.;
Sun. 7:15 A.M.–8 P.M.

I have always liked the building where Carberry's is located, which was originally built as a Packard dealership in 1951. Other incarnations have included a discount tile store and a Budget rent-a-truck. Matt Carberry and his partners took this shell of a building and turned it into a lively, appealing bakery-café. The space is large, with periwinkle blue and cheerful orange walls. Several tables are accompanied by attractive color-stained wood chairs. In warm weather, wrought-iron tables are set up outside along a brick walk that outlines the building.

Carberry's makes about fifty breads, with mixed results, and they are displayed to the right of the cashier, toward the back wall. There are always baskets of bite-size samples of at least a half dozen breads. My favorite is **pistachio-sourdough.** It's unusual and very good, but unfortunately they don't make it every week. **Garlic-Parmesan** comes in two sizes and is best as a narrower baguette. Carberry's favorite is the **sourdough rye,** studded with sunflower seeds, but I *love* the **mushroom-artichoke focaccia.** The bread itself, flecked with basil, could be a little firmer, but it has a pleasant herbed taste, and the topping is terrific.

Baker "Gusty" Gunnarsson, from Iceland, is constantly developing new breads. In the works is a series of **dark German mountain breads,** dense breads baked slowly at low temperatures.

A variety of breakfast pastries include very good **muffins** (I like the **banana-walnut** best). The daily **bread pudding** is made from leftover muffins along with other breads and flavored with rum extract.

The yeasted pastries are quite good, especially the **Danishes.** These have almond paste kneaded into the dough and come in various traditional flavors such as **cherry** and **cheese.** The **croissants** are also good—not flaky, but with a delicious taste.

One of the display cases features a variety of more unusual yeasted breads, including a **chocolate-orange bun. Icelandis Snüder** is a sweet yeast pastry flavored with cardamom

17

and frosted with chocolate. Classic **cookies** and **bars** are offered here as well. The **coconut macaroons** are good, as is the oversize **Heath Bar crunch,** although it's too soft for my taste. I like their **molasses** cookies best.

Another case contains cakes and fancier pastries. There are three lines: American **(carrot cake, cheesecake);** French, which includes **genoise** with various mousses such as **chocolate** and **raspberry;** and the best and most interesting, the **Scandinavian,** many of which have an almond paste theme, such as the tasty **Napoleon's Hat,** a butter cookie folded into a triangle shape around a ball of marzipan.

In addition to their baked goods, Carberry's provides a selection of **sandwiches** and offers daily **soups** and **salads,** as well as a selection of coffees and teas. Sandwiches can be made on a choice of breads, including **sundried tomato-basil,** which spices up mundane fillings.

The bakery is popular and always busy, and Carberry's has started to wholesale their goods to other businesses. Beans in Brookline and Chestnut Hill, Newton (see "Liquid Refreshment," page 453) and the bakery at New England Meat Market in Cambridge carry their goods. Plans for a second store, with everything to be made on the premises, are in the works.

Casal Bakery Co.

1075 Cambridge Street, Cambridge, MA 02139 (617) 547-6282
Mail order: not available Hours: Mon.–Fri. 4:30 A.M.–6:30 P.M.;
Sat. 4:30 A.M.–5 P.M.; Sun. 6 A.M.–1:30 P.M.

Casal, in business since the late 1950s, specializes in Portuguese breads. A pleasant adjoining café sells a number of breakfast and lunch breads such as muffins and pizza. The bakery makes a small selection of breads, which they supply to all the area Stop & Shops, as well as several Star Markets and Market Baskets. These white breads—**Vienna loaf, scali bread,** and **bulkie rolls**—are fine but unremarkable; come here for the **Portuguese sweet bread.** This is a sweet, eggy bread baked in a large circular pan. Since it is such a soft bread, it's hard to slice—eat it by the chunk instead.

Pomme Frite

18 Eliot Street, Harvard Square, Cambridge, MA 02138
(617) 497-8220
Mail order: not available   Hours: Sun., Tues., Thurs. 11 A.M.–9 P.M.;
Wed., Fri., Sat. 11 A.M.–midnight; closed Mon.

1208 Boylston Street, Newton, MA 02146   (617) 566-9404
Mail order: not available   Hours: Sun., Mon. 10 A.M.–9 P.M.;
Tues.–Thurs. 11 A.M.–10 P.M.; Fri., Sat. 11 A.M.–11 P.M.

Pomme Frite, subtitled "A European Deli," is more of a restaurant than a bread bakery, at least visually. At the Harvard Square location, which came first, you walk through the restaurant to get to the counter to buy the bread. As a restaurant, the specialty is **French fries** (*pommes frites* is French for "french fries"), with a variety of toppings. I was unimpressed with these, disappointed, in fact, because the menu offered many tempting dipping sauces.

The breads, however, are quite good, especially the ***rochbrot,*** a crusty whole wheat. There is an excellent **Russian pumpernickel** (I prefer the raisinless version) and a **bialy,** which is a very good roll, but it should be called something else: It doesn't even resemble a traditional bialy, which is a flat, chewy roll with a depressed center filled with chopped onions. This one is light and airy, with a slice of onion gracing the surface, and a buttery glaze. There are also **onion rolls** with poppy seeds, which are good, but I like the "bialy" better.

On the deli end, the **sandwiches** are very good, if pricey, and all are served on their own breads. The meats are freshly roasted, which probably accounts for the expense. Meaty offerings include **fresh roast Boston brisket** and the **All-American Thanksgiving** on bread—roast turkey, cranberry sauce, and corn-bread stuffing. The **Jungfrau** is filled with layers of turkey, Roumanian pastrami, and melted Gruyère cheese.

The Newton store is larger and is where the breads are made. Sidell has plans for establishing more stores in the area over the next few years.

Salamander Food Shop. See "Goodies to Go," page 177.

EVERETT

Bread & Circus

115 Prospect Street, Cambridge, MA 02139   (617) 492-0070
Mail order: not available   Hours: Mon.–Sat. 9 A.M.–9 P.M.;
   Sun. 11 A.M.–8 P.M.

186 Alewife Brook Parkway, Cambridge, MA 02138   (617) 491-0040
Mail order: available, but limited   Hours: daily 9 A.M.–9 P.M.

15 Westland Avenue, Boston, MA 02115   (617) 375-1010
Mail order: not available   Hours: Mon–Sat. 9 A.M.–10 P.M.;
   Sun. 9 A.M.–9 P.M.

15 Washington Street, Brighton, MA 02146   (617) 738-8187
Mail order: available   Hours: daily 9 A.M.–9 P.M.

916 Walnut Street, Newton, MA 02161   (617) 969-1141
Mail order: not available   Hours: daily 9 A.M.–9 P.M.

278 Washington Street, Wellesley, MA 02181   (617) 235-7262
Mail order: not available   Hours: daily 9 A.M.–9 P.M.

Also "Going Organic," page 434.

In December of 1994 Bread & Circus moved their baking operation to a huge facility in Everett. Chuck Stenson, the general manager of the bakery, has been with the company since 1989. He has worked for over twenty-five years as a baker in a variety of settings, from tiny all-natural businesses to never-touched-by-human-hands Wonder bread factories.

Bread & Circus's bread-baking operation here is impressive. When the California-based Whole Foods chain bought Bread & Circus a few years ago, Stenson says, "They gave us more money for what we needed to do," which included renovating the 12,500-square-foot facility and building a $67,000 brick oven.

They make two kinds of bread—**sourdoughs** and **standard yeast.** The sourdoughs are baked in the brick oven. The regular loaves are fine, but the brick-oven loaves are more impressive and worth buying. The **farm bread** comes in several shapes and sizes; the different shapes affect the flavor and texture of the dough. The **baguette** has a denser texture, but I preferred the **round,** with a medium-sour flavor and a good crust. The **raisin** is chock-full of raisins, but I found it too heavy on the cinnamon. The *paysano* is slightly salty in an appealing way, dense and absorbent. It's good for sopping up sauces.

NEWTON

Big Sky Bread Company

105 Union Street at Piccadilly Square, Newton Centre, MA 02159
(617) 332-4242
Mail order: not available   Hours: Mon.–Fri. 7 A.M.–6:30 P.M.;
Sat. 7 A.M.–5 P.M.; closed Sun.

1077 Lexington Street, Waltham, MA 02154   (617) 891-7222
Mail order: available, but expensive
Hours: Mon.–Fri. 6:30 A.M.–7 P.M.; Sat. 7 A.M.–6 P.M.;
Sun. 8 A.M.–1 P.M.

Big Sky is a bread-baking franchise that is growing rapidly. In June of 1990, Roger and Beth Elkus opened Stone Mill Bread Company in Cincinnati, Ohio. By 1993 they formed the Big Sky Bread Company and started franchising. The Waltham location, owned by Dario Franchetti, and the Newton location, owned by Helene Satz, are the fifth and sixth franchises, with many more planned.

The company's hook is that the bread is made from flour ground on the premises. Franchise owners are trained to make bread as a product, following a formula. As a foodie, I felt skeptical about this process; so many bakers I've talked with opened their operations after extensively researching and experimenting with bread and yeast. I wondered how good a formulaic bread product could be. Well, pretty darn good, actually. "Big Sky" is a nickname for Montana, which is where the wheat used in this bread is grown. Satz claimed that the freshness of the flour makes the bread last longer—that it could stay fresh, in a plastic bag, for seven to ten days. She was right; the loaf actually lasts that long, and still tastes very good. This is important, because these are *large* loaves.

I tried the **honey whole wheat,** the basic loaf, and it is a very good whole wheat bread. I preferred it to **country wheat,** which is sweeter and bland. A best-seller is **three-seed**—not bad, but again on the sweet side. The **unbleached white** is a good, solid white bread, and the **challah** is excellent. The **cinnamon-raisin** is also tasty. In all, each store makes about fifteen different breads. Some are available daily, others once or twice a week.

Big Sky also make **muffins,** whole wheat and heavy, and quick breads, such as **apple-cinnamon,** which are lighter than the muffins. The **cinnamon rolls,** at least at the Waltham location, are undercooked—the dough was actually half raw in the center. Similarly, the **biscotti** are undercooked and too sweet. The other **cookies,** oversized, are made from one oatmeal-based basic recipe with several variations. The **chocolate chip** and **oatmeal-raisin,** both very good, are made with the whole wheat flour, which gives them a kind of earthy taste, but they also have lots of butter and sugar, which makes them delicious.

Both stores offer samples. Several loaves are set on a wooden cutting board, next to a big tub of butter. There are also cut-up samples of the cookies and muffins.

Both locations have tables and are wide open; only a counter separates you from the main kitchen where you can see the flour mill and people making bread.

Breadsong

349 Auburn Street, Auburndale, Newton, MA 02166   (617) 964-4004
Mail order: not available   Hours: Tues.–Fri. 6 A.M.–7 P.M.;
   Sat. 7 A.M.–3 P.M.; Sun. 7 A.M.–1 P.M.; closed Mon.

Martha Sweet always enjoyed baking, but until she worked part-time at Clear Flour Bakery in Brookline, she says, "It never occurred to me that this was something I could get paid to do." She learned the bread business over six years at Clear Flour and then spent a year at Angel's in Watertown, before setting the wheels in motion for Breadsong, which opened in the fall of 1994.

The breads I tried were a mixed bag, though largely good. The **whole wheat sourdough** has an unpleasantly sour taste. The **cinnamon-raisin** has a good flavor, but the loaf I tried was underdone. Much better is the **French,** a nice, chewy loaf. This dough is used as a base for a variety of breads, including a tasty **olive roll** and **mushroom-cheese roll** (which could have used more mushrooms). The **rosemary focaccia,** made with semolina, has a good flavor, although the texture is softer than what I like in a focaccia. My favorite bread by far is the **potato–black pepper,** which is something special. The flavor is wonderful, with a spicy kick from the pepper, the texture is moist and chewy, and it has a pleasing crust.

Sweet also makes **cookies** and **breakfast pastries.** The **blueberry scone** is quite good, and the **muffins** aren't bad, although a little dense. The **chocolate chip** is a classic Toll House recipe. It suffers from the oversize cookie problem—the center is too soft—but it tastes so good that the texture problem didn't bother me. The **oatmeal-raisin** was equally good. The best cookie, though, is the **semolina butter cookie,** with great flavor and a nice crunch from the semolina.

Diamond Bakery

1136 Beacon Street, Newton, MA 02161   (617) 527-3740
Mail order: not available   Hours: Mon.–Sat. 7 A.M.–7 P.M.;
    Sun. 7 A.M.–1 P.M.

Beverly Gagel (née Diamond) and her husband Joe have owned Diamond Bakery since 1972, and Beverly's father started it in 1949. The bakery's specialty is breads, specifically **challah,** and they make a very good version—so popular, in fact, that they make it daily, not just on Fridays for the Jewish Sabbath.

On Thursdays through Saturdays they also make variations on the classic egg challah. There is **cinnamon,** with cinnamon both kneaded into the dough and sprinkled on top; **raisin,** made with golden raisins, because, Beverly says, "They're plumper and not as sweet"; and **onion.** They also make a **no-cholesterol** challah, but Beverly says she doesn't like to promote it. Challah is an egg bread, and challah without egg yolks is white bread. "The only similarity between it and regular challah is that they are both braided," she says.

Diamond also makes a good **rye bread** and offers a selection of **bagels.**

Keltic Krust

1371 Washington Street, Newton, MA 02165   (617) 332-9343
Mail order: not available   Hours: Tues.–Sat. 6:30 A.M.–5:30 P.M.;
    Sun. 7:30 A.M.–2 P.M.; closed Mon.

Irish immigrant David Riney-Gimpsey has been baking since he was sixteen. He baked in Ireland, Spain, and Algiers before coming to Boston in 1988 and starting his own business in Dorchester. "There were no Irish bakeries in Boston then," he recalls. "And I thought there should be." In 1992 Riney-Gimsey moved his bakery to Newton near the Waltham line, the place he describes as the "Irish capital of Boston."

The baked goods here are wonderful, and many are different from those available in the average bakery. The **hot cross buns** are excellent, scented with cinnamon and studded with bits of candied orange peel. The cross on the bun is made from lighter dough—"No silly frosting," Riney-Gimpsey says. The signature **brown bread** is an Irish soda bread made with coarsely ground whole wheat. It is leavened with baking soda but has an almost yeastlike taste, dense and nutty. The regular **soda bread** is also very good. Other unusual offerings include the **boxty,** a flat potato bread the size and shape of an English muffin, made primarily with potatoes and a little flour, and seasoned with onions. While heavy, it is delicious; with a bowl of soup it makes for a filling lunch. Also on the savory end, the **sausage roll,** made with ground pork, potatoes, and spices, is wonderful, with a buttery, flaky pastry. This pastry is also used for the **Cornish pasties,** filled with ground sirloin. A **vegetarian version** is available as well, filled with a mixture of vegetables that includes shiitake mushrooms. The latter was a little too rich, although it tastes good.

The **scones** are good, slightly cakey. Although Riney-Gimpsey started out intending to make only the most traditional Irish baked goods, he has bowed to market pressure to make scones in a variety of flavors. His **chocolate scone,** chocolate batter studded with chocolate chips, is quite a treat. It tastes like a cross between a scone and a chocolate brownie. I could easily eat several. The **chocolate-caramel shortbread** is a lighter butter shortbread covered with a caramel frosting and a bittersweet chocolate glaze. Yum.

The bakery is also a small café, with a few tables and coffee and tea available. Some shelves proffer imported goods from Britain, as well as Italian olive oils.

Pomme Frite. See Cambridge, page 19.

Spagnuolo Bake House
140 Adams Street, Newton, MA 02158   (617) 964-1843
Mail order: available   Hours: Tues.–Fri. 9 A.M.–6 P.M.;
   Sat. 8 A.M.–2 P.M.; Sun. 7 A.M.–2 P.M.; closed Mon.

Il Panificio
144 Charles Street, Boston, MA 02114   (617) 227-4340
Hours: Mon.–Fri. 7 A.M.–10 P.M.; Sat., Sun. 8 A.M.–10 P.M.

The Spagnuolo family has been in the bakery business for three generations. They bought the Magni bakery business in 1986, and they still make the **scali** loaves people have been coming to buy at that location for decades, but their line of hearty European-style loaves are the real stars.

The **pane rustico** is a country white loaf that comes in two sizes. The taste is very good, and the texture just right, with a crunchy crust. **Toscano scruro** is quite good. It's a whole wheat bread made with sour starters and other grains; it's both light and nutty with a pleasing sour flavor. There is also a **pecan-raisin** and a soft **honey whole wheat,** baked in a loaf, which is good for jam sandwiches.

In 1995 the Spagnuolos hooked up with Todd English of Olive's. English had been wholesaling the breads he developed for his restaurant, but the demand had exceeded the space in his kitchen. He was planning to cancel his bread-baking operation altogether when the Spagnuolos contacted him. They licensed the rights to his breads, called Olive's Grateful Bread Company, which are also quite good. A few are made using a Tuscan dough: the **plain** loaf, which is subtly sour and light tan in color, and the **green olive,** which needs more olives—you barely get an olive per slice. The **currant bread,** however, is loaded with fruit. It is made with a white sourdough, as is the **country white.**

Spagnuolo's makes both their own **focaccia** and Olive's. The Olive's version is laden with various vegetables—eggplant, onions, tomatoes; whereas the Spagnuolo's is a simple **rosemary focaccia.** You can buy fresh yeast here, and Spagnuolo's **dough,** which is especially good for making your own pizza.

In 1996, the family opened Il Panificio, an Italian bakery-café, complete with soups, salads, sandwiches, and **homemade pastries.**

SOMERVILLE

Lyndell's Bakery See "Everything Nice," page 260.

Panini

406 Washington Street, Somerville, MA 02143   (617) 666-2770
Mail order: not available   Hours: Mon.–Fri. 7 A.M.–8 P.M.;
    Sat. 8 A.M.–6 P.M.; Sun. 8 A.M.–5 P.M.

After baking bread for other people for ten years, owner Debbi Merriam decided to open her own bread bakery in 1991. Panini makes about a dozen different kinds of bread.

The **sourdough** needs work (it's very sour and is too crusty), but the **plain baguette** is good. I especially like the *ficelles,* which are thick breadsticks or thin baguettes, depending on how you look at it. They come plain and in several flavors, including **sesame, onion, olive, pesto,** and **salt.** Other breads include **wheat walnut** and *cocodrillo,* made with white and durum wheat.

The **focaccia** is great and is available with a variety of toppings: **onion, herb, pesto, tomato,** and an unusual, tasty **fig and onion.** The **pizza** is substantial and creative, with vegetarian toppings varying according to Merriam's whim. These have included **eggplant and crushed olives** and **pesto with fresh mozzarella, onions, and tomatoes.** There are two versions of the bakery's namesake, *panini:* **smoked turkey** and **eggplant-ricotta,** both of which are served with roasted onions, roasted tomato, and watercress.

The grossly oversized **scones,** available in several variations, are immensely popular, but I don't care for them. I find them too dry and too much. The **pound cake** was also dry; thick crusts go well on yeast breads, but not on delicate cakes. Of the cookie offerings, the **cornmeal ginger cookies** are something special. The crunch of cornmeal brings out the butteriness, followed by a kick of ginger.

Panini is also a coffeehouse, with several tables. It is very busy throughout the morning, with tables covered with newspapers and customers spilling over from one table to the next. Coffee is available by the cup or the pound.

NORTH

BEVERLY

Christian Payen Fine French Pastries. See "Everything Nice," page 263.

MANCHESTER

Wheatberries of Manchester. See "Everything Nice," page 264.

MARBLEHEAD

Iggy's. See Watertown, page 33.

MELROSE

Breads 'n' Bits of Ireland

530 Main Street, Melrose, MA 02176   (617) 662-5800
Mail order: not available   Hours: Mon.–Fri. 6 A.M.–5 P.M.;
Sat. 6 A.M.–4 P.M.; closed Sun.

Breads 'n' Bits offers a variety of Irish and American breads and baked goods. Notable is the very good **brown bread,** a sort of whole-wheat soda bread. It contains no yeast yet works well sliced for a sandwich.

The bakery also makes good **scones.** I tried the **regular currant scone** which contains raisins, not currants, but still tastes very good; it is light and fluffy, not dense the way some scones can be. I also like the very nontraditional **orange–chocolate chip scone.** It is excellent, loaded with orange zest and minichips that melt in your mouth.

The **muffins** are unremarkable, but the **cookies** are good, especially the **oatmeal-raisin.** It's one of the best versions of this cookie I've tried—chewy, crispy edges, buttery.

PEABODY

Central Bakery

48 Walnut Street, Peabody, MA 01960   (508) 531-2101
Mail order: not available   Hours: Mon.–Sat. 5 A.M.–6 P.M.;
Sun. 5 A.M.–2 P.M.

Central Bakery has been making **Portuguese** and **Italian breads** and **pastries** for over seventy-five years. The pastries are generally unremarkable, although on Fridays they make **Portuguese tarts,** individual pies filled with custard and coconut, and these are good.

The best bet is the yeasted **corn bread.** It's moist, with a chewy crumb and a crisp crust. The **Portugese sweetbread** has a classic, sweet flavor.

REVERE

Brandano's Bakery

910 Broadway, Revere, MA 02151   (617) 284-9476 and 289-1938
Mail order: not available   Hours: daily 7 A.M.–8 P.M.

Brandano's is now run by the third-generation Brandano, Chuckie. Brandano's looks like a classic Italian-American bakery, and as far as the **pastries** are concerned, it is. But then there's the *Abruzzése* **bread,** an Italian bread that goes through several risings to yield a firm, chewy round with a crisp crust. A close second is the **regular Italian,** as a longtime employee described it, which is a round bread, dense but not as firm as the *Abruzzése.* The **Italian** is more like the traditional fluffy white scali bread.

Brandano's also makes a selection of **flavored breads,** including *Abruzzése* dough with **sun-dried tomatoes** and four rectangular loaves: **garlic and chive, garlic Romano cheese, wheat,** and **semolina.**

WINCHESTER

La Patisserie. See "Everything Nice," page 270.

SOUTH

BROCKTON

White's Pastry Shop. See "Everything Nice," page 273.

HINGHAM

The Bread Shop
107 South Street, Hingham, MA 02043   (617) 741-5223
Mail order: not available   Hours: Tues.–Fri. 7 A.M.–6 P.M.;
    Sat. 7 A.M.–5 P.M.; Sun. 7 A.M.–1 P.M.; closed Mon.

The Bread Shop is a welcome addition to the South Shore, which has few fresh bread bakeries. Barbara and Jeff Hillary opened shop here in 1993, and they offer a spectrum of tasty breads. The **baguettes** are the most popular item; they are good, but very chewy. The **sourdough** bread is good. I like the **seven-grain,** studded with flaxseeds; it has a subtle honey flavor and is appropriate for sandwiches.

The **cinnamon-raisin** bread received mixed reviews in my house. I liked it; a friend thought it was nothing special. We all liked the **sour cream and chive,** which is moist and flavorful.

Other interesting flavors include **sweet pepper and sun-dried tomato** and **Romano-Swiss.**

Loaves come in small and large sizes. The small is very small, a glorified roll. The bakery also makes a few **cookies, scones,** and **croissants,** none of which are noteworthy. The breads are the real draw here.

PROVIDENCE, RI

Kaplan's Bakery
756 Hope Street, Providence, RI 02906   (401) 621-8107
Mail order: not available   Hours: Mon.–Sat. 6 A.M.–6 P.M.;
    Sun. 6 A.M.–4 P.M.

I know Providence is a bit of a drive from the Boston area, but Kaplan's makes the best **seeded rye bread**—called **cisil rye** (*cicil* is Yiddish for caraway seeds)—I've ever had, anywhere. The loaves are huge, often weighing as much as six pounds. You can buy a whole, half, or quarter loaf; you pay by the pound. This rye bread is worth the trip. The **raisin-pumpernickel** is also very good.

QUINCY

Montilio's Cake Shoppe. See "Everything Nice," page 274.

SHARON

Cake Art and Confections
374 South Main Street, Sharon, MA 02067   (617) 784-1290
Mail order: available   Hours: Tues.–Fri. 7 A.M.–6:30 P.M.;
    Sat. 7 A.M.–5 P.M.; Sun. 7 A.M.–1 P.M.; closed Mon.

The name of the place is Cake Art, but what they do best is bread. For cakes, they specialize in wedding cakes; the samples I tried were unremarkable. The breads, on the other hand, are terrific.

Baker Carl Davis is the son of a baker, and he also worked as a kosher caterer for thirty-five years. He ran a bakery/deli in Florida with his stepson Tom Danilchuk for several years, before they came back to Massachusetts and opened Cake Art in 1987.

Davis makes several **rye breads** and several breads using a challah, or egg, dough. The **seeded rye** is very good—one of the best in the Boston area. The **korn rye,** in large round loaves, is wonderful. It takes a few days to make, so it is sold on Saturdays only. There is also **onion rye, plain rye,** and **marbled rye.** There is both a plain **pumpernickel** and a **Russian health bread,** essentially pumpernickel with golden raisins. Different breads are offered different days of the week; the store posts a schedule.

Challah is available every day. The plain variety is good, but I like the variations, especially the **onion pocket.** This is a rectangular roll filled and sprinkled with finely chopped onions and a peppering of poppy seeds. It's delicious as is, and Danilchuk recommends it with knockwurst. The **onion pletzel** or **onion board** is made by rolling the challah dough ultrathin, about a quarter of an inch high, into an eighteen-inch-long, six-inch-wide rectangle. The dough is then spread with an onion-poppy mixture.

A sweet bread is the rich **chocolate *babka,*** a yeast dough covered with streusel and chocolate bits. Richer still is **Carl's chocolate meltaway,** an outrageous creation. Semisweet chocolate bits and pecans are kneaded into a Danish dough. It is then rolled out and topped with more nuts and chocolate. A little bit goes a long way.

The shop has received accolades for their *rugalach* which comes in **raspberry, chocolate chip, apricot-raisin,** and **cinnamon-nut.** I prefer the cinnamon-nut. It is better than most *rugalach,* but it is not amazing.

WEST

ARLINGTON

Quebrada Baking Co. See "Everything Nice," page 278.

BELMONT

Ohlin's Bakery. See "Everything Nice," page 279.

CONCORD

Sally Ann Food Shop. See "Everything Nice," page 282.

SUDBURY

Boston Daily Bread. See Brookline, page 14.

Peter Bread, Etc.
P.O. Box 776, Sudbury, MA 01776   (508) 443-5395
Mail order: not available   Hours: not applicable

I was at the tail end of writing this book when I visited Duck Soup in Sudbury and discovered Peter Bread, Etc. breads, much to my delight. These are among the best breads in the Boston area.

Peter Franklin had owned a bakery café in California for fifteen years before selling it and moving with his family to Massachusetts. He worked as a pastry chef for a few years, but the desire to work and bake for himself led him to start a wholesale bakery in the basement of his home in late 1994. That basement turns out about two hundred loaves of marvelous bread daily.

Many of the breads have potatoes in the base, which gives them a subtle flavor and a lovely moistness. All the herbs Franklin uses are fresh, and the flour is organic. Franklin divides his breads into categories: "standard," "savories," and "a bit sweeter." Standards include **Cayuga multigrain,** very good, and terrific *ficelles* and **baguettes.** I like the savories, with unusual combinations such as **roasted ginger and scallion,** made with fresh ginger. **Roasted garlic and sage** is studded with whole roasted garlic cloves; it is strongly flavored, but delicious. These loaves are *boules,* round; I prefer the long shape of the simply wonderful **Kalamata and caperberry** bread, because it is easier to slice. **Rosemary fig** is unusual, as is **lavender and chive.** When I tried the latter I liked it, but it was too strong on the lavender; Franklin says he is still tinkering with the recipe. Among the bit sweeter breads is a lovely **orange-raisin-pecan;** there is also a version with bits of chocolate added. Another personal favorite is **cranberry-lime with pine nuts.**

Franklin's breads are available at Duck Soup (see "Epicurean Agenda," page 386) and a few other outlets; call the bakery for more information.

WALTHAM

Big Sky Bread Company. See Newton, page 21.

WATERTOWN

Angel's Bakery and Café

51 Main Street, Watertown, MA 02172   (617) 923-8025
Mail order: not available   Hours: Mon.–Fri. 8 A.M.–6:45 P.M.;
    closed Sun.

Angel's, named for owner Angel Alvarez, originally started as a
bakery called Little Star, an offshoot of Stellina's restaurant next
door, where Alvarez worked as a line chef for six years. In 1993
Alvarez, a native of Guatemala, decided to run the bakery himself. Angel's offers breads, baked goods, and take-out items. The
foods here are an eclectic mix, reflecting Alvarez's Central American heritage and his Italian training.

Alvarez makes two kinds of **focaccia,** both of which are
very good. The **regular focaccia** comes in large, thin rounds
about three-quarters of an inch high, nicely salted and sprinkled
with rosemary. The delicious **potato focaccia** has potato in
the dough and is moist and slightly dense. It is thicker than the
regular focaccia and is seasoned with garlic and oregano. The
potato focaccia is also shaped into loaves, which Angel's uses for
sandwiches. The **challah** is also very good, made with eggs, and
is slightly sweet.

The **baked goods** are decent, although not as good as
the breads. Alvarez uses quality ingredients, including only butter
for his **cookies,** but the cookies are a little dry, and the **muffins**
are heavy.

Alvarez's training has all been on the job, and he has
learned well. Although some of his recipes still need work, Alvarez
places a lot of importance on premium ingredients, preferring to
make everything from scratch, including roasted peppers, salsa,
and tortillas. The **sandwiches** are made on his own bread. **Take-
out items** are fresh and very good. Among those I tried were
Spanish rice studded with mixed vegetables; a delicious **tuna
ceviche** marinated in lime juice, mint, and cilantro; **chicken-
vegetable lasagne;** and **rice and beans.** Alvarez produces regular
items and daily specials, with a lot of choices for vegetarians,
such as a pungent **roasted eggplant and garlic soup.** When the

weather is warm, try the **licuados,** a drink made with fresh fruit blended with ice and a touch of sugar.

Iggy's

205-204 Arlington Street, Watertown, MA 02172   (617) 924-0949
Mail order: available   Hours: daily 8 A.M.–8 P.M.
5 Pleasant Street, Marblehead, MA 01945   (617) 639-4717
Mail order: available   Hours: daily 7 A.M.–7 P.M.

Iggy's is everything I want from a bread bakery. Ludmilla (originally from Canada) and Igor (originally from Yugoslavia) Ivonovich met in New York while working for EAT, a bakery-restaurant. They first opened Pain d'Avignon on Cape Cod, with partners, then started Iggy's as their own venture in 1994. Many of Iggy's breads are leavened with sourdough culture; a few have yeast added to help the dough rise. The bread is made slowly, treated gently, with long and multiple risings.

The Ivonoviches try to use organic ingredients whenever possible, and recently they developed an entirely organic **croissant** (Ludmilla acknowledges that it still needs work). They try to buy produce from local farmers, in season.

The Watertown location—the first store and the place where all the breads are made—is slightly off the beaten track, though it is not far from the Armenian markets on Mt. Auburn Street. A banner hanging outside the door attracts attention. The company sells their bread wholesale to stores throughout the area, but the retail outlets are worth a visit. The space is small, but the selection is varied.

Best bets really include everything, and Ludmilla and Igor are constantly experimenting with new techniques and combinations of ingredients. Texture is as important as flavor in these breads. These are not soft, thin-crust loaves, although some are good for rustic sandwiches, like the thicker **onion focaccia,** a softer bread. The **Francese** is great plain or with a sandwich filling, although the crust is tough, so you may not want to eat it in front of anybody. The **multigrain** bread is the best whole wheat bread I've tasted, and I love the **raisin-pecan** bread. For the holidays they also make **dried cranberry–pecan**—great, but very expensive. On weekends you can indulge in a **dried cherry–chocolate bread.**

Some of the doughs come in different shapes and sizes: there's also a **thinner focaccia round, baguettes** and *ficelles,* long thin loaves about an inch and a half wide and two feet long that just seem to disappear.

The Francese dough is used as the crust for excellent **pizza,** with seasonally changing toppings such as **roasted potatoes, caramelized onions, jack cheddar** or **ground garlic, olive oil, broccoli, caramelized shallots, sliced tomatoes.** Iggy's wins the prize for best cold pizza.

One of my favorite items is **snails,** or a swirl of dough filled with sautéed mushrooms, tiny cubes of potatoes, and smoked *rofumo* cheese. Unfortunately, they are not always available. The same cheese is also used in the marvelous cheese **longettes,** a sourdough baguette split and topped with black olive paste, pine nuts, and the cheese.

Iggy's uses leftover breads to make **herbed croutons,** which you can snack on by the handful, although they are a little too generous with the olive oil. A lighter use for leftovers is the **toasts,** thin slices of various breads turned into crisp melba toast. And they make my all-time favorite **granola,** studded with nuts and sweetened with maple.

You really can't go wrong at Iggy's. Try everything.

WELLESLEY

Quebrada Baking Co. See "Everything Nice," page 278.

❖ B A G E L S ❖

Even more bagel shops than bread bakeries have opened in the past few years, seeming to pop up in storefronts in every town in the Boston area. The more established businesses are still the best; listed here are the most notable bagel shops around.

BOSTON

BOSTON

Finagle a Bagel

6 Faneuil Hall Market Place, Boston, MA 02109   (617) 367-9720
Mail order: not available   Hours: Mon.–Sat. 6:30 A.M.–9 P.M.;
Sun. 7 A.M.–9 P.M.

535 Boylston Street, Boston, MA 02116   (617) 266-2500
Hours: Mon.–Fri. 6:30 A.M.–8 P.M.; Sat. 7 A.M.–8 P.M.;
Sun. 7 A.M.–6 P.M.

1 Center Plaza, Government Center, Boston, MA 02108
(617) 523-6500
Hours: Mon.–Fri. 6:30 A.M.–7 P.M.; Sat. 6:30 A.M.–5 P.M.;
Sun. 6:30 A.M.–3 P.M.

Larry Smith, a transplanted New Yorker, was a mechanical engineer for General Electric for seven years before he decided to start his own business. He thought there was a bagel void in Boston, and he set out, as he says, "to produce the best bagels possible. We're fanatics for quality." (Would anyone admit to *not* caring about quality?) He started his company in 1990, and it has grown considerably since then. Finagle provides **bagels** to a number of markets and take-out establishments, including Star Market and Rebecca's Cafes. By mid-1994, Finagle was producing 5,000 bagels in a twenty-four-hour period.

The size is probably what is most distinctive about Finagle's bagels. Their bagels weigh 5 ounces, closer in size to bagels I've had in New York. Most of the other bagels around town are 3.5 to 4 ounces and probably at least an inch smaller in diameter.

But taste is what counts, and although Finagle's bagels are not the best I've tasted, they are very good. The **sesame** could have more seeds than it does, but the **poppy seed** is loaded with them. I liked the **sun-dried tomato–basil,** but the **pumpernickel** was bland, without much flavor. **Chunky veggie** tastes like one of those instant soups, but it's good spread with the matching veggie cream cheese. I did like the **cinnamon-raisin** and the nonconventional **wild berry** made with cranberries, blueberries, and raisins. Finagle also offers a range of cream cheeses. **Blueberry** is abominable, with a totally artificial taste, and **lox** is very salty. All the others are good, especially **cinnamon-raisin-walnut, chive,** and **vegetable.**

The bagels are mixed, formed, proofed, and retarded at

a main plant then sent to each store, where they are boiled and baked. Smith has big plans for expansions, with an anticipated seven or eight stores to open in the Boston Metropolitan Area by the end of 1996.

The Ultimate Bagel Co.

335 Newbury Street, Boston, MA 02116   (617) 247-1010
Mail order: not available   Hours: daily 7 A.M.–7:30 P.M.

1310 Mass. Avenue, Cambridge, MA 02138   (617) 497-9180
Mail order: not available   Hours: daily 7:15 A.M.–6:30 P.M.

118 Needham Street, Newton, MA 02161   (617) 964-8990
Mail order: available   Hours: daily 7 A.M.–6 P.M.

Joseph LaMacchia and his son Kevin opened the Boston Ultimate Bagel Co. in 1990. The Harvard Square location opened in 1992, and the large Newton location opened in 1994; plans for additional stores are in the works.

The bagels here are good, although a little crumbly (not quite the ultimate). Best-sellers are **plain** and **cinnamon-raisin;** the latter is good with **strawberry cream cheese.** A newer flavor is **cinnamon-glazed,** a plain bagel with a glaze of cinnamon and sugar. This has just the right amount of sweetness, and no fat— good for dieters.

There are several **flavored cream cheeses,** as well as a few **flavored low-fat, nondairy spreads,** which are surprisingly good, considering they are made with tofu.

METROPOLITAN BOSTON

BROOKLINE

Eagerman's Bakery

415 Harvard Street, Brookline, MA 02146   (617) 566-8771
Mail order: not available   Hours: daily 7 A.M.–10 P.M.

Mo Eagerman is a third-generation bagel baker. His grandfather baked bagels in Poland, and his father baked bagels in Dorchester. In 1945, his three older brothers opened a bakery that specialized in bagels. He joined them a few years later after he got out of the army. "In the 1950s, Boston was as strong as New York for bagels," Eagerman recalls, "but strictly in the Jewish areas."

Eagerman was, in fact, ahead of his time in estimating

the popularity of bagels. In the early 1980s he had a chain of eight stores, but bagels were not ready to take off then. It would be another decade before bagel mania. "Years ago every corner store was a drug store," Eagerman says. "Now it's a bagel store." Eagerman's has been at this Brookline location since 1979.

Eagerman's **bagels** are very good. They come in the usual selection of flavors. They are certified kosher. Eagerman also makes a selection of kosher pastries and good **rye bread,** including **sissel** (also spelled *cisil*). He also claims that his is the only bakery in town that makes certified **kosher for Passover pastries.**

Kupel's Bagels

421 Harvard Street, Brookline, MA 02146   (617) 566-9528
Mail order: not available   Hours: Sun.–Thurs. 6 A.M.–11 P.M.;
   Fri. 6 A.M.–midnight; Sat. 6 A.M.–1 A.M.

With its late-night and early-morning hours Kupel's is the place to go whenever you are craving a **bagel.**

In addition to classics such as **plain, egg, onion, sesame,** and **poppy seed,** there are lots of creative combinations, including **California health,** a mix of five grains, four seeds, raisins, dates, and honey. It's a little dense, but the blend of textures and flavors is appealing. **Milwaukee seeded** is a plain bagel topped with a blend of seeds, garlic, and onions. **Russian raisin** is a pumpernickel bagel studded with raisins and caraway seeds.

Kupel's blends a wide variety of **cream cheeses** to go with the bagels: **plain, lox, lox and chives, lox and vegetables, dill-horseradish, Spanish olive,** and **raspberry,** to name a few.

The bakery is kosher and also makes a selection of decent, if unremarkable **pastries.** Bagels are the main attraction here.

CAMBRIDGE

The Ultimate Bagel Co. See Boston, page 36.

CHELSEA

Katz Bagel Bakery

139 Park Street, Chelsea, MA 02150   (617) 884-9738
Mail order: available   Hours: Mon.–Thurs. 8 A.M.–6 P.M.;
   Fri., Sat. 7:30 A.M.–2 P.M.; Sun. 7 A.M.–4:30 P.M.

Katz (pronounced *kates,* because that's how it was pronounced in New England, according to owner Richard Katz) makes the best bagels in the Boston area. If you visit on a weekday, don't be put off by the closed-up retail space—you enter through a side door directly into the kitchen. Walk past racks of rising bagels to a table set up in front of the ovens, and buy your bagels. On the weekends you can buy from the tiny store area on the corner, and the place is packed.

Richard Katz, "Bagel Boss," as the title on his business card reads, has been making bagels most of his life. His father Harry started the company in 1941. "My father made *only* bagels," Katz says. "To specialize in one thing is something."

Katz insists that the best bagel is made by hand, although he no longer makes them that way, owing to demand. When his father started the bakery, all bagels were made in a brick oven. "Of course they were better that way," Katz recalls, "but it was inefficient."

Each step in bagel making is very important to the final outcome. "Bake no bagel before its time," Katz declares. "The definition of a bagel is dense crust, chewy inside," he says. "If you don't have to pull it with your teeth, it's not a bagel."

Katz makes a variety of classic and go-with-the-trends **bagels.** I liked the **plain** and the **sesame;** the **raisin** is a little bland. Contradicting my purist tendencies, the **blueberry** is very good—the dough actually has a blueberry flavor. Katz's father invented the **pizza bagel,** which they've been making for over two decades. They flatten a raw bagel dough to remove the hole, then top it with homemade tomato sauce and cheddar cheese. There's also a **bagel dog,** a kosher hot dog baked in bagel dough. **Teething bagels**—popular with the under-ones—are hardened minibagels.

On weekends, you can get sweet, buttery *babka* and **rye bread,** too. There are a few **flavored cream cheeses:** a tasty **Boursin** and an excellent **veggie cream cheese,** loaded with finely chopped fresh vegetables.

NEWTON

Rosenfeld Bagel Co. Inc.
1280 Centre Street, Newton, MA 02159   (617) 527-8080
Mail order: not available   Hours: Tues.–Fri. 7 A.M.–6:30 P.M.;
  Sat. 7 A.M.–7 P.M.; Sun 7 A.M.–5 P.M.; closed Mon.

Mark Rosenfeld, a Patterson, New Jersey, native, started Rosenfeld's bagels when he was a law student at Suffolk University in 1973 because, he felt, there were few good bagels in the Boston area. Peter de Rosa joined him as a master baker a few years later, and the always busy shop has been producing bagels in the same location ever since.

The bakery offers over twenty kinds of **bagels,** from the traditional (and popular) **plain, sesame,** and **poppy seed** to more novel creations. A relatively recent addition is the **potato bagel,** notable for its spicy flavor from ground black pepper. Rosenfeld's is one of the few places to sweeten their bagels with malt syrup, which gives the bagel a slightly different taste. The sweeter bagels, however, use sugar. The **chocolate chip** wasn't nearly as bad as I thought it would be. Actually, it's even good; I was just prejudiced against it on principle: a bagel shouldn't have chocolate chips! But then, I suppose it shouldn't have **cinnamon** and **raisins** in it either, and I like those additions. There are various fruit flavors, including **blueberry, strawberry,** and **banana-walnut.**

Rosenfeld's is one of the few bakeries that makes **bialys.** I've seen them here and there, and no one makes a New York–style bialy. A bialy is about the size of a bagel, but the texture and flavors are totally different. Bialys are not boiled, so they are hard, with a crisper crust. The center is flattened down so that it is very thin; where the bagel hole would be there is an indentation filled with finely chopped onion. Rosenfeld's bialys are the best I've found in this area.

There are homemade **cream-cheese spreads** to put on your bagel, and these vary from traditional to innovative, **lox spread** to **mocha chip.**

The store is down a flight of steps, and the counter and bagels are located at the back. The kitchen is open, and you can see the bagels being made. You pass several refrigerators on the way; these contain the spreads and also a very good selection of smoked salmon, from several areas of the world—Scotland, Norway, and the United States.

The Ultimate Bagel Co. See Boston, page 36.

NORTH

SAUGUS

Zayde's Bagels
120 Broadway (Route 1 North), Saugus, MA 01906   (617) 233-3080
Mail order: not available   Hours: Mon.–Fri. 4 A.M.–9 P.M.;
   Sat. 4 A.M.–7 P.M.; Sun. 4 A.M.–6 P.M.

Bill Schwab's father-in-law has been in the baking business since 1940, but bagels are relatively new for the company. Previously they made an item that was the same shape, but different texture —donuts. In 1976 Schwab anticipated a demand for bagels, and opened Zayde's Bagels. He developed what he considered to be the ideal bagel. "These are not 'Old World' bagels," he told me. "I 90 percent did away with the hole; I think the bagels stay fresher this way." There is a hole, but it is more like a slit; it looks like a belly button, in fact. And these are good-sized bagels, 30 percent heavier than most. Schwab uses very little yeast, and the bagels have a long, slow rising period.

Zayde's are very good **bagels**—among my favorites. He does a lot of wholesale business, producing 1,500 dozen bagels a day, in sixteen varieties. The **plain** and **sesame** are good, and the popular **cinnamon-raisin.** My favorite here is the **spinach.** It is flecked through with bits of green, but the spinach flavor does not come through. What does come through is a real kick from ground black pepper. They also sell **plain** and homemade **flavored cream cheese** to go with the bagels.

The bakery makes other **bakery items—cookies, cakes,** and such—all of which are forgettable. The bagels, however, are memorable.

SOUTH

RANDOLPH

Zeppy's Baigel Bakery
937 N. Main Street, Randolph, MA 02368   (617) 963-7022
Mail order: not available   Hours: Mon.–Fri. 5 A.M.–6 P.M.;
   Sat. 5 A.M.–5 P.M.; Sun. 5 A.M.–1 P.M.

Rochelle Zeprun is the third generation to run Zeppy's, which was started by her Russian grandfather in 1923. *Baigel* is how her grandfather spelled his product, to make sure people would pronounce the word correctly.

The **bagels** are very good, though a little sweet for my taste. They make twenty varieties, both traditional and trendy. Since Zeprun's tenure, they introduced **blueberry, apple-cinnamon, veggie,** and **spinach.** Classics include the best-selling **plain, pumpernickel, raisin** (Zeprun's favorite), and **egg.**

In the retail store they also sell **breads** and **pastries.** The **rye bread** comes in a round or loaf and is great for corned-beef sandwiches. The *rugalach* made with sour cream, is quite good, and the **raspberry nut squares,** made for Passover, consist of a cookie crust spread with raspberry preserves, then topped with slivered almonds and walnuts in a honey caramel. The squares are then half-dipped in chocolate icing.

WEST

FRAMINGHAM

Brooklyn Bagel
957 Worcester Road, Framingham, MA 01701   (508) 820-1200
Mail order: not available   Hours: daily 6 A.M.–10 P.M.

Daniel Lebov grew up in Brooklyn and has long had an affinity for bagels. He remembers weekly childhood trips with his father to Pop Hirshman's in Brooklyn. During high school he took a job making bagels by hand. When Lebov moved to Boston several years ago, he missed the bagels of his hometown, and in 1994 he found the means (money and a partner) to start Brooklyn Bagels.

The bagels are mixed, formed, boiled, and baked on the premises, which Lebov feels is key to fresh-tasting bagels. His are large, 5 ounces, as in New York, and come in some two dozen flavors, including classics such as **plain, egg, sesame,** and **poppy seed.**

The bagels here are very popular: Brooklyn Bagel sold over a million bagels, just retail, during its first eight months. Lebov plans to open another store, also west of Boston, within the next year.

❖ P I T A ❖

BOSTON

BOSTON

Lebanon Baking Co.

1389 Washington Street, Boston, MA 02118   (617) 267-6973
Mail order: available   Hours: Mon.–Fri. 7 A.M.–5:30 P.M.;
 Sat. 7 A.M.–3:30 P.M.; closed Sun.

The Lebanon Baking Company has been baking pita bread in the South End for some forty years. The store is nondescript. You enter a very large room that is lined with a few shelves containing a handful of jarred and canned items such as fava beans and olives. Two refrigerators hold the salads and frozen goods the company makes—**tabouli, hummus,** *mujadarrah,* **baba ganoush.** Behind the counter are vats of olives and various feta cheeses. A doorway leads to the huge baking area, where ovens operate all night, every night, making **pita.** And the pita is what Lebanon does best. The **spinach pies** are too doughy, and the **hummus** and **tabouli** aren't bad, but both are on the salty side. Rounds of bread topped with **broccoli and cheddar, spinach and feta, tomato and mozzarella** were also a bit doughy. But the pita itself is great. It comes in two variations, **white** or **whole wheat,** and in large or small rounds.

Next door, connected to Lebanon, is the company's pastry shop. The pastries are not particularly exceptional, but the prices are extremely low: whole **pies,** such as **apple** or **pecan,** are $5 to $6.50 each. There are also tables in this section, where you can sit and enjoy a cheap luncheon special of soup and salad, or dessert and coffee.

ROSLINDALE

Droubi Bakery

748 South Street, Roslindale, MA 02131   (617) 325-1585
Mail order: not available   Hours: Mon.–Fri. 7 A.M.–6 P.M.;
 Sat. 7 A.M.–5 P.M.; closed Sun.

Droubi Bakery makes a selection of **pita** and other **Middle Eastern breads,** which it primarily wholesales to various markets around town. You can get the pita here as well, but it's best to arrive early in the day; by noon there's only a handful of packages left. The pita comes in several sizes and is very good. Also good are the large **spinach pies,** about six inches long and shaped into an isosceles triangle. The wide storefront is lined with shelves holding a variety of Middle Eastern goods.

WEST ROXBURY

Near East Bakery
5268 Washington Street, West Roxbury, MA 02132   (617) 327-0217
Mail order: available   Hours: Mon.–Fri. 7:30 A.M.–6 P.M.;
    Sat. 7:30 A.M.–4 P.M.; closed Sun.

The first thing that strikes you as you enter Near East is how attractively everything is displayed. It's a spacious store, with a pair of display shelves set diagonally in the center of the rooms, offering various Middle Eastern items such as tahini, pistachio nuts, and olive oils. A tall shelf lines the right wall, displaying more sundries and condiments.

Richard and Laura George bought the Near East Bakery in 1989; they felt it would complement their other business, Homsy's (see "The World in a Jar," page 424), a Middle Eastern market. Near East had been making pita breads for several years, and the Georges expanded the business significantly. Although the store is spacious, it is not huge. But the bakery space is humongous. Down a spiral staircase, the "kitchen" stretches nearly the length of the block, and enormous machines make 40,000 loaves of pita every night.

The breads, the main reason to come here, are displayed in the back of the store—bags of pita in all kinds of variations: **white, wheat, multigrain, onion, garlic, sesame,** and **caraway.** Sizes vary too: **standard, large, small,** and **mini.** They also make, by hand, **pita pizzas,** with toppings such as **broccoli and cheddar** and **spinach and feta.** These are a little doughy. The *lahaamageen* (also spelled *lamejun* elsewhere) has the same pita base and has a topping of spiced ground lamb. This tasty blend, called *sfeeha,* is used as the filling for triangular **lamb pies.**

There is also a sweeter pita creation, topped with **sesame and honey.** An unusual item is the *kaak,* a bagel-shaped bread. Its texture is light, and the taste is slightly sweet and exotic, from *mahaleb,* a spice derived from a black cherry kernel.

To the left as you enter the store is a food counter, where you can get items like an excellent **tabouli,** heavy on the parsley, **falafel,** and **grape leaves.** I especially liked the *imfassakh,* a blend of puréed eggplant and yogurt.

THE BESTS OF THE BEST

Best bread bakery: **Iggy's**
Best baguette: **Clear Flour, Japonaise Bakery**
Best whole wheat bread: **Boston Daily Bread, Big Sky**
Best white bread: **Japonaise Bakery**
Best multigrain bread: **Iggy's**
Best sourdough bread: **Iggy's,** then **Clear Flour** (the only two worth buying)
Best raisin bread: **Iggy's**
Best Italian bread: **Spagnuolo's** and **Brandano's**
Best dark/pumpernickel bread: **Salamander Food Shop**
Best rye bread: **Kaplan's,** then **Cake Arts and Confections**
Best focaccia: **Iggy's, Clear Flour**
Best challah: **Diamond, Angel's**
Best pita: **Near East Bakery**
Best bagels: **Katz,** then **Zayde's**

❖ C H A P T E R   T W O ❖

EARTHLY DELIGHTS

Featuring in-town produce stores, farm stands, pick-your-own farms,
and farmers' markets

*T*HE demand for good, fresh produce has increased in recent years, evidenced by the variety of fruits and vegetables now sold in the average supermarket. The produce selection at many Star Markets and Stop & Shops is much better and more extensive than it was ten years ago. You can now find at least four varieties of mushrooms in most markets, as well as several exotic root vegetables, pencil-thin asparagus, plum tomatoes, and more. But fruit markets and farm stands still have the better selection, and some have better prices.

The Haymarket near Government Center is Boston's most famous produce market, although the quality of the merchandise receives consistently mixed reviews. A North End food purveyor finds the produce inedible; whereas a visiting Harvard professor drives in early every week for boxes of juice oranges. For produce here and at in-town markets, you'll get the freshest items on Mondays and Tuesdays—all the produce for the week comes in to the New England Produce Center on Monday and is then distributed to markets.

Several area farms sell their own fruits and vegetables during the prime growing season, usually June through October

The season starts with lettuce and strawberries and continues through tomatoes, to apples and pumpkins in the fall. Massachusetts is a small state, so it's never a long drive to these farms. Many also offer a pick-your-own option, as well as entertainment, such as festive activities and hay rides.

Some farms are also garden centers, offering supplies such as mulch and manure, as well as seedlings for many varieties of tomatoes, herbs, and other plants. Places like Arena Farms in Concord and Wilson Farms in Lexington are also the best sources for all kinds of herbs; in addition to the familiar basil, dill, and rosemary, you'll find lovage, bee balm, and a dozen varieties of mint. They also offer useful gardening advice.

My favorite sources for produce are farmers' markets. Most markets start in June or July and run through October. The produce available here is very seasonal—you won't find any tomatoes sold in May—only locally grown, and very fresh, often picked that morning. During the rest of the year and for fruits and vegetables grown elsewhere, the in-town markets are the best source.

This chapter is organized into three sections: produce markets, farm stands, and farmers' markets.

* Described in another chapter.

PRODUCE MARKETS

*Arax Market	Watertown
Baby Nat's Fruitland	Roslindale
*Bread & Circus	Various locations
Calore Fruit	Boston
The Country Store	Somerville
The Elegant Farmer	Chelmsford
Fleet Fruit Store	Boston
Fresh Louie's Farm Market	Boston
Fruit Center Marketplace	Milton, Hingham
The Garden Gate	Middleton
*Harvest Cooperative Supermarket	Allston, Cambridge
The Haymarket	Boston
Joe & Josie	Boston
Kay's	Watertown
A. La Fauci & Sons	Boston
Lambert's Rainbow Fruit Co.	Dorchester, Westwood
Murphy's Fruit Mart	Danvers

46

New Deal Fruit	Revere
New England Produce Center	Chelsea
*Preparations	Dorchester
Rosario	Boston
A. Russo & Sons	Watertown
Sandy's Market	Cambridge
Tony's Produce	Boston
Village Fruit	Brookline
Washington Fruit	Boston

FARM STANDS

Allandale Farm	Brookline
Arena Farms	Concord
Barker's Farm Stand	North Andover
Blue Meadow Farm	Sudbury
Boston Hill Farm	North Andover
Brooksby Farm	Peabody
Clark Farm	Danvers
Connors Farm	Danvers
DeVincent Farms	Waltham
Dowse Orchard	Sherborn
The Food Project	Lincoln
Gibney Gardens	Danvers
Goodale Orchards	Ipswich
Hanson's Farm	Framingham
Hutchins Farm	Concord
Idylwilde Farm	Acton
Land's Sake	Weston
Leonhard & Eldred Poultry Farm	North Andover
Lookout Farm	Natick
*Nashoba Valley Winery	Bolton
Ricci Farms	Waltham
Smolak Farm	North Andover
Spence Farm	Reading, Woburn
Sunny Rock Farm Store	Walpole
Sunshine Farm	Framingham
Verrill Farm	Concord
Volante Farm	Needham
Ward's Berry Farm	Sharon
Wilson Farms Inc.	Lexington

FARMERS' MARKETS

ABCD Parker Hill/Fenway Farmers' Market	Boston
Brighton Farmers' Market	Brighton
Brockton/City Hall Plaza Farmers' Market	Brockton
Brockton Fairgrounds Farmers' Market	Brockton
Brookline Farmers' Market	Brookline
Cambridge Farmers' Market/Central Square	Cambridge
Cambridge Farmers' Market/Charles Square	Cambridge
Charlestown Farmers' Market	Charlestown
Chelsea Community Farmers' Market	Chelsea
Codman Square Farmers' Market	Dorchester
Copley Square Farmers' Market	Boston
Dudley Square Farmers' Market	Roxbury
East Boston Farmers' Market	East Boston
Everett Farmers' Market	Everett
Fields Corner Farmers' Market	Dorchester
Framingham Farmers' Market	Framingham
Framingham Farmers' Market on Route 9	Framingham
Franklin Park Community Farmers' Market	Boston
Gloucester Farmers' Market	Gloucester
Hingham Farmers' Market	Hingham
Hyde Park Farmers' Market	Hyde Park
Jamaica Plain Farmers' Market	Jamaica Plain
Lincoln/Codman Community Farmers' Market	Lincoln
Lynn's Downtown Farmers' Market	Lynn
Manchester-by-the-Sea Farmers' Market	Manchester
Marlboro Farmers' Market	Marlboro
Mattapan Farmers' Market	Mattapan
Melrose Farmers' Market	Melrose
Newton Farmers' Market	Newton
Quincy Farmers' Market	Quincy
Roslindale Farmers' Market	Roslindale
Saugus/Cliftondale Square Farmers' Market	Saugus
Scollay Square Farmers' Market	Boston
Somerville Farmers' Market	Somerville
Waltham Farmers' Market	Waltham

❖ P R O D U C E ❖
M A R K E T S

BOSTON

BOSTON

Bread & Circus. See "Going Organic," page 434.

Calore Fruit
Salem Street, North End, Boston, MA 02113   (617) 227-7157
Mail order: not available   Hours: Mon.–Sat. 7 A.M.–6:30 P.M.;
    Sun. 1 P.M.–6 P.M.

The display window at Calore is at sidewalk level. I was first enticed by the absolutely gorgeous portobello mushrooms on display at knee level. Step down a narrow, short staircase, and behold the other fruit here, most of which is very good. Prices vary—those portobellos that seduced me were amazingly cheap that day, but other items can be more expensive.

John Lavita has been running this business since 1971 and is happy to offer culinary advice about the produce he sells. He makes and sells some canned items, including his own **pickled eggplant.**

Fleet Fruit Store
395 Commercial Street, Boston, MA 02109   (617) 227-9073
Mail order: not available   Hours: Mon.–Sat. 8 A.M.–5:30 P.M.;
    Sun. 8 A.M.–1 P.M.

Fleet Fruit shares a parking lot with Bay State Lobster. It offers a variety of produce at very good prices, with an especially good selection of fresh wild mushrooms and fresh herbs. But beware. Some items seemed to be priced higher than elsewhere, and the quality of the merchandise is not uniform: the artichokes may be fresh and firm, while the asparagus is withering. Shop carefully.

Fresh Louie's Farm Market
349 A Newbury Street, Boston, MA 02115   (617) 247-1474
Mail order: not available   Hours: Mon.–Fri. 9 A.M.–8 P.M.;
    Sat. 9 A.M.–7 P.M.; closed Sun.

Fresh Louie's opened in 1992 on produce-starved Newbury Street. Some items seemed tired (especially nonproduce items in the deli section, such as prepared salads), but considering that

Louie's has come to a neighborhood with few sources for good, fresh produce, it offers a decent variety. You can also buy local fresh breads and fish here.

The Haymarket
Blackstone Street between Hanover and North Streets, Boston, MA 02113
Mail order: not available   Hours: Fri., Sat. dawn to dusk

From dawn to dusk every Friday and Saturday, Blackstone Street, located parallel to the Central Artery opposite the entrance to the Callahan Tunnel, near the North End, is transformed from a quiet location for inexpensive butchers to a bustling open-air market. The feel is of a Middle Eastern souk, with prices changing throughout the day and constant haggling over both the prices and the quality of the produce.

According to Joseph Matera, president of the Haymarket Pushcart Association, merchants have been selling produce in this location since colonial times. Farmers used to bring their produce to Quincy Market and the Faneuil Hall area, where vendors would buy the produce to resell to the public on Blackstone Street. A barn nearby housed the hay farmers used for their horses, hence the Haymarket moniker.

During its peak in the 1950s, the Haymarket had over five hundred licensed vendors. They once used pushcarts but, since pushcart hardware is not manufactured anymore, vendors now sell from improvised stands. The Southeast Expressway (Rte. 93), built in the 1950s, sliced right through the middle of the Haymarket, and many feared its demise. The highway certainly changed the character of the market, but it's still going strong. There are now 220 licensed vendors.

The source for most of the Haymarket produce is the wholesale New England Produce Market in Chelsea. The Chelsea market vendors get new shipments of produce every Monday, and whatever they have left at the end of the week is what the Haymarket vendors are selling. Often this is produce that is nearly on its way out.

What attracts many people to the Haymarket are the incredibly low prices—eight kiwis for $1, fifteen limes for $1. But what you see is not necessarily what you'll get. The beautiful red peppers on display are just that—display. The peppers you get will be from a box behind the counter. Try to pick your own and you may get reprimanded. Tell the vendor what you want, and he (and invariably it is a he—I saw no women working among the fruits and vegetables here—and when Matera talked about the business, he said spaces passed from father to son or father to nephew) will fill up a bag for you. Look in your bag before you leave the stand to make sure that what he gave you is acceptable.

The best time to get here is Friday morning before 10 A.M. The prices are highest (by Haymarket standards), because it's the beginning of the business day, but the produce will be significantly better than it will be on Saturday afternoon. Walk along and note the prices; not everyone has the same deals. Identical pints of blueberries were $1.25 at one stand and 50 cents at another. Most stands have similar produce, but a few specialize in more exotic items, such as the stand near the end, at North Street, that has many Caribbean items, including plantains and papayas.

Saturday is the busier day. The crush of people makes meandering difficult. You can find super deals by the end of the day, but bear in mind that whatever produce is left has been sitting out all day, or even for two days, without refrigeration (or, in the winter, too *much* refrigeration), which is hardly good for fruit that is already on its last legs.

In addition to produce, you can get fish at the Haymarket. Hanover Street is lined with four or five fish markets. The quality varies, and I *strongly* recommend that you buy whatever you're going to buy here first thing Friday morning. The fish is on ice, but on a hot summer day, some items, especially the precut steaks and fillets, looked mighty peaked by noon.

The Haymarket generates thousands of tons of refuse annually, which has been an on-again, off-again bone of contention between the vendors and the city of Boston, which in the past has picked up the cost of rubbish disposal (to the tune of $250,000 or more a year). In 1993 the state Department of Agriculture introduced a composting program as a way to recycle the old produce.

Is the Haymarket worthwhile? Yes, as long as you know what you're getting into. This is not a genteel farmers' market or even a wholesale club. The atmosphere is harried, and you have to guard your wallet against pickpockets. But visiting the market is also a fun experience, and the prices are dirt cheap.

Parking is an issue, especially on Saturdays—another argument for getting to the market early. There are nearby lots (you'll have to add the $7 to $10 parking fee to the money you save on produce, unless you find a metered spot), or you can take the T.

Joe & Josie

(in front of Dave's Curtain Shop)
115 Salem Street, North End, Boston, MA 02113   No phone
Mail order: not available   Hours: June–first frost, Sat. 7 A.M.–4 P.M.

There is no sign announcing this produce stand, just produce, displayed on the sidewalk in front of Dave's Curtain Shop. Joe and Josie come from their farm, bringing a wonderful variety of produce. They specialize in Italian-oriented items, with a variety of greens, such as green radicchio, zucchini flowers, and fresh garlic. The prices are very, very good. The earlier you get here the better—they stay until they sell out, which can be as late as 4 P.M. but is often earlier.

A. La Fauci & Sons

46 Cross Street, Boston, MA 02113   (617) 523-1158
Mail order: not available   Hours: Mon.–Sat. 8 A.M.–5 P.M.;
      closed Sun.

A. La Fauci has beautifully displayed fruit that spills out from the store onto the sidewalk. But if you help yourself, beware the wrath of the employees. This is a place where you tell the proprietor what you want, and he picks it out for you. The prices are reasonable, and the quality is generally very good.

Note that the hours are flexible. When I called to check, they answered, "We try to open early, maybe around eight. Probably until five."

Rosario

Parmenter Street, North End, Boston, MA 02113   No phone
Mail order: not available   Hours: Mon.–Sat. 7 A.M.–6 P.M.;
      closed Sun.

There is no name on this store, the street number is not clear (but the street is only one block long), and the boxes in the window are piled up haphazardly. But enter anyway. This is a great place to buy produce. Whatever Mr. Rosario, a diminutive, friendly man, has is of very good quality. I got the first clementines of the season here, and supersweet red Muscato grapes. Other hard-to-find items include cardoons, loquats, and baby artichokes. Prices are very reasonable.

Tony's Produce

268 Shawmut Avenue, Boston, MA 02119   (617) 542-5937
Mail order: not available   Hours: Mon.–Fri. 11:30 A.M.–6:45 P.M.;
  Sat. 9 A.M.–6:45 P.M.; closed Sun.

Tony has been selling fruit in this South End location for over twenty-five years. There are no fancy displays, just boxes of beautiful fruit and vegetables, arranged along tables. You will find no posted prices here. Regular customers theorize that Tony prices his produce on what he thinks you can pay. A recent college graduate, new to the work force, found that no matter what she purchased, the total always came to $3. Tony carries all the usual items, but in more variety. In the summer you might find several kinds of tomatoes, including yellow pear tomatoes, and I've seen a range of mushrooms, including beautiful giant portobellos and very fresh shiitakes.

Washington Fruit

(in front of Woolworth's at Downtown Crossing)
350 Washington Street, Boston, MA 02108   No phone
Mail order: not available   Hours: Mon.–Sat. 7 A.M.–6 P.M.

A family of Haymarket vendors, including Joey "Bananas" ("I'd rather you not use my last name," he told me), approached Woolworth's in 1979 about setting up a produce market in front of the Downtown Crossing store. They've been going strong ever since. The day I visited, the prices were comparable to the Haymarket prices. You can pick out your own produce here from what's on display. "We won't yell at you," Joey said then looked over at his father, an older man chomping on a cigar stub. "Well, *he* might yell. It goes with the image, you know, the cigar and all." The produce I tried was of a reasonable quality.

Harvest Cooperative Supermarket. See "Going Organic," page 431.

DORCHESTER

Lambert's Rainbow Fruit Co.

777 Morrissey Boulevard, Dorchester, MA 02122   (617) 436-3091
Mail order: not available   Hours: Mon.–Sat. 7 A.M.–9 P.M.;
   Sun. 7 A.M.–6 P.M.

220 Providence Highway (Route 1 North), Westwood, MA 02090
   (617) 326-5047
Mail order: not available   Hours: Mon.–Sat. 7 A.M.– 9 P.M.;
   Sun. 7 A.M.– 6 P.M.

I must have passed Lambert's on the Southeast Expressway hundreds of times before visiting it, and it's worth stopping in. In the spring they have flats of vegetables and flowers displayed under tents in their parking lot. Inside at both locations there is a **salad bar** with a reasonable selection of items. To find the produce, follow the aisle down past boxes of bulk candies, nuts, and dried fruit. On the way you'll pass a deli counter with an extensive selection of meats, where they also make **sandwiches.**

      Prices are very reasonable. The quality varies—check the produce offered on special.

Preparations. See "The World in a Jar," page 410.

ROSLINDALE

Baby Nat's Fruitland

606 American Legion Highway, Roslindale, MA 02131
   (617) 524-9877
Mail order: not available   Hours: Mon.–Sat. 7:30 A.M.–8 P.M.;
   Sun. 7:30 A.M.–3 P.M.

Baby Nat's is a true family business. It was started in 1974 and named for the youngest of the owner's four kids, all of whom now work here. The place feels like a small warehouse, and the prices are generally very good, although not everything is sold at bargain-basement prices. The quality of the produce can vary. The items I bought were good, but make sure to check everything. The staff is friendly and helpful.

METROPOLITAN BOSTON

BROOKLINE

Bread & Circus. See "Going Organic," page 434.

Village Fruit
1659 Beacon Street, Brookline, MA 02146   (617) 738-4140
Mail order: not available   Hours: Mon.–Fri. 8:30 A.M.–7 P.M.;
    Sat. 8:30 A.M.–6 P.M.; Sun. 10 A.M.–6 P.M.

Village Fruit is an appealing market, with produce attractively displayed in wooden cases. The prices are reasonable to high, and the quality is always very good.

CAMBRIDGE

Bread & Circus. See "Going Organic," page 434.

Harvest Cooperative Supermarket. See "Going Organic," page 431.

Sandy's Market
1295 Cambridge Street, Cambridge, MA 02139   (617) 492-6960
Mail order: not available   Hours: Mon.–Sat. 8:30 A.M.–8:30 P.M.;
    Sun. 11 A.M.–5 P.M.

From the outside, Sandy's looks like just another convenience store, with maybe a few boxes of fruit. Step inside. There are, in fact, many boxes of very good fruit, with an emphasis on Caribbean and Asian produce. You may find three or four kinds of bananas, as well as plantains and yucca; the prices are reasonable and the quality good. In addition, the store carries a variety of Caribbean and Asian goods, as well as Middle Eastern foods, such as several kinds of dried beans and many spices.

CHELSEA

New England Produce Center
Beacham Street, Chelsea, MA 02150   (617) 889-2700
Mail order: not available   Hours: Mon.–Fri. 5 A.M.–5 P.M.;
    closed Sat., Sun.

The New England Produce Center, also referred to as the Chelsea Market, is the source for almost all the produce that comes into

Boston. It consists of some forty-four businesses, all grouped together in four long buildings in a warehouse area in Chelsea. This is where distributors and wholesalers such as Russo's get their produce, as well as supermarkets and restaurants. The Produce Center is open to the public, although it is not geared to retail business.

The buildings and the wholesale nature of the businesses can be intimidating, but the prices are very good, and the fruit is as fresh as you'll find anywhere. It's worth a visit just to see where most of the produce we eat around here comes from. Each business has a bay or multiple bays that open onto a loading dock, and you have to buy bulk amounts, usually by the bag or case, in cash only.

The Produce Center has been here since 1968. The business used to be located in Quincy Market, but when Faneuil Hall was becoming Faneuil Hall as we know it today, the produce dealers were evicted. So they grouped together and built the Produce Center in Chelsea.

The market opens in the wee, dark hours of the morning, and that is when distributors are here. Although the official hours are until 5 P.M., as posted above, most businesses close up shop by noon or so. Park your car (the Produce Center is not really accessible by any public transportation) in front of one of the bays and explore. The best deal I found here was a three-pound box of shiitake mushrooms selling for $15.

NEWTON

Bread & Circus. See "Going Organic," page 434.

SOMERVILLE

The Country Store
783 Somerville Avenue, Somerville, MA 02144   (617) 625-5576
Mail order: not available   Hours: Wed.–Sun. 7 A.M.–7 P.M.;
   closed Mon., Tues.

The Country Store is a somewhat mysterious hole-in-the-wall located near Porter Square on the Cambridge/Somerville line. It's not totally clear to me exactly when the place is open, but when the weather warms up, a truck appears on weekends outside the store, displaying produce and large signs announcing daily specials. Inside is a crowded space with crates piled with various seasonal fruits and vegetables. The prices can be quite good; the quality of the produce can vary. I've gotten lovely strawberries there, but I've also found other items that needed to be passed over.

NORTH

DANVERS

Murphy's Fruit Mart
17 Elm Street, Danvers, MA 01923   (508) 774-2756
Mail order: not available   Hours: Mon.–Fri. 8 A.M.–5:45 P.M.;
    Sat. 8 A.M.–5:30 P.M.; closed Sun.

The fruit selection is good here, although not spectacular. Murphy's is a good source for produce in the winter when the local farm stands are closed. Most notably, it has an extensive **salad bar** that includes **hot** and **cold prepared items** such as **baked chicken** and **pasta salads.**

MIDDLETON

The Garden Gate
152 South Main Street (Route 114), Middleton, MA 01949
    (508) 777-2250
Mail order: not available   Hours: Mon.–Wed. 9 A.M.–6 P.M.;
    Thurs., Fri. 9 A.M.–7 P.M.; Sat. 9 A.M.–5 P.M.; closed Sun.

The Garden Gate, located next door to Richardson's Ice Cream, has a nice selection of produce, as well as an appealing **salad bar** with **homemade soups.** There's also a take-out section with **prepared foods,** such as **lasagne** and **roast chicken.**

REVERE

New Deal Fruit
920 Broadway, Revere, MA 02151   (617) 284-9825
Mail order: not available   Hours: Mon.–Thurs. 8 A.M.–8 P.M.;
    Fri., Sat. 8 A.M.–9 P.M.; Sun. 7:30 A.M.–6 P.M.

New Deal is a medium-size produce market, with a sideline of Italian goods. The produce varies in quality and price. Some items are offered at great prices, but those same items may also be available at better quality for a higher price, for example, with grapefruit or artichokes.

On one side of the market is a deli counter with very good meats, including several kinds of Italian sausages. There are also imported Italian items, such as canned tomatoes, dried pastas, and olive oils.

SOUTH

HINGHAM

Fruit Center Marketplace. See Milton, below.

MILTON

Fruit Center Marketplace
338 Granite Avenue, Milton, MA 02186   (617) 698-1900
Mail order: not available   Hours: Mon.–Sat. 8 A.M.–9 P.M.;
   Sun. 8 A.M.–6 P.M.

79 Water Street, Hingham, MA 02043   (617) 749-7332
Mail order: not available   Hours: Mon.–Sat. 8 A.M.–9 P.M.;
   Sun. 8 A.M.–6 P.M.

Milton, a largely residential community, is relatively devoid of food finds. Then you come upon the Milton Marketplace in East Milton and find a treasure of options all under one roof. The Fruit Center is the main business, started in 1973 by Don Mignosa; the store moved to the Milton Marketplace when the complex was built in 1983. Other businesses lease space in the same facility, so there is a supermarket feel, with some overlap. Kinnealey Meats is here (see "Where's the Beef?" page 138), along with a nondescript bakery and an overpriced fishmonger. The Fruit Center has its own deli counter, which includes fantastic homemade **marinated olives** seasoned with lemons and hot pepper flakes. There is also a gourmet area with a variety of cheeses, imported pastas, oils, condiments, and cookies. You can get Dancing Deer (see "Everything Nice," page 242) baked goods here and breads from area bakers.

The produce, however, is the star. It's beautifully displayed, and the quality is top rate: the fruit doesn't turn brown, and the lettuce doesn't wilt within a day of purchasing it. The Fruit Center does produce right. It is the best source for wild mushrooms, both fresh and dried. Fresh wild mushrooms are now seen in many markets—shiitake, portobello, cremini—but the mushrooms here are of excellent quality. Dried mushrooms are sold in bulk amounts, premeasured into containers, and I counted nearly a dozen kinds, including chanterelle, black trumpet, and oyster.

One side of another aisle is devoted to an awesome **salad bar,** with over a hundred items. Every kind of vegetable imaginable is available, along with several **mixed salads,** such as three-bean and **pasta.** In addition there are five kinds of lettuce to choose from, and **fruit salad.**

The Hingham store is slightly smaller and is located in the Hingham Marketplace, just off Route 3A near the harbor. There is a salad bar here as well, located in a separate space since the spring of 1995. You can get bag lunches to go, consisting of a **baguette sandwich,** carrot and celery sticks, and a brownie, as well as several **made-to-order sandwiches.** The take-out section has seating for twenty.

The prices here are not cheap, but they are not the most expensive I've seen. The quality is definitely worth it, and the staff is helpful and knowledgeable.

WESTWOOD

Lambert's Rainbow Fruit Co. See Dorchester, page 54.

WEST

CHELMSFORD

The Elegant Farmer
21 Summer Street, Chelmsford, MA 01824
(508) 256-9811
Mail order: not available   Hours: Mon.–Fri. 10 A.M.–7 P.M.;
Sat. 10 A.M.–6 P.M.; Sun. 10 A.M.–5 P.M.

The Elegant Farmer is an appealing produce store in a Chelmsford shopping center called The Marketplace. The produce is attractively displayed, and the employees are proud of the items they sell. As I waited in line, a staffer was unpacking raspberries and displaying them. "These are amazing," he commented, and then he proceeded to hand one to me and to the other customers waiting in line. (It *was* amazing.)

One aisle includes a lengthy **salad bar** with both sliced vegetables and **prepared salads.** Shelves above the produce and in the center of the store feature various gourmet items, from small bulk bins of dried fruits and candies, to all kinds of preserves and condiments. The prices are not cheap, but they are not outrageous either, and The Elegant Farmer has a user-friendly environment for shopping.

WATERTOWN

Arax Market. See "The World in a Jar," page 421.

Kay's
594 Mt. Auburn Street, Watertown, MA 02172   (617) 923-0523
Mail order: not available   Hours: Mon.–Sat. 7:30 A.M.–7:30 P.M.;
  closed Sun.

Located in the Armenian neighborhood in Watertown, Kay's is overflowing with fresh, excellent produce priced to sell. Boxes of oranges, strawberries, and melons stand on display outside, with more inside. The aisles are narrow, with barely enough room for one person—this is not the place to come with a baby stroller, or a wheelchair. You'll find most basic produce here—lettuce, carrots, lemons, apples—along with many less common items such as watercress, clementines, and raspberries. The cilantro here is always very good and comes in huge bunches. All the produce is very fresh, and always very good, and the prices, which are scrawled illegibly on a blackboard behind each of two cash registers, are reasonable to cheap. Kay's also carries bulk green and black olives, nuts (including roasted, skinned hazelnuts), grains, and beans. You can buy Middle Eastern goods such as canned *ful medames* made from fava beans, as well as a variety of cheeses.

The best time of day to come is midmorning or midafternoon on weekdays. After 4 P.M. and on Saturdays the store gets extremely crowded, with very long, winding lines and an atmosphere reminiscent of a chaotic Middle Eastern souk.

A. Russo & Sons

560 Pleasant Street, Watertown, MA 02172   (617) 923-1500
Mail order: not available   Hours: Mon.–Sat. 8 A.M.–6 P.M.;
Sun. 8 A.M.–2 P.M.

Russo's is my favorite produce market in the Boston area. The produce is invariably fresh and beautiful, the selection is extensive, and the prices are inexpensive. What more could you want? How about fresh bread, pasta, gourmet cheeses, nuts, and dried fruit? Those are here too.

Russo's sells both retail and wholesale, throughout the Boston area, which accounts for their cheap prices, and the tremendous turnover of goods is testament to the high quality of the produce. I like to come here without any particular cooking plans in mind and just buy whatever looks good. The produce is beautiful, and invariably tastes as good as it looks. Beware, however, Russo's has a following, especially on Saturdays, when the place is packed, so maneuvering your way through the store can be a challenge. Once you enter, there's no turning back, at least not if you have a cart. During warmer weather there is also produce in a covered area outside at the front of the store. It's always worth shopping here. The quality, the selection, and the prices are the best of anywhere I've been.

WELLESLEY

Bread & Circus. See "Going Organic," page 434.

❖ FARM STANDS ❖

We are very lucky, in the Boston area, to be quite close to farms. Depending on where you live, you need drive only five to thirty minutes to find a farm that grows and sells its own produce. As with farmers' markets, farm stands offer a variety of fruits and vegetables we often can't get at supermarkets, or even at in-town produce markets. Farmers often grow a more extensive variety of tomatoes, potatoes, and apples, for example. There are a few different kinds of farm stands, and they range in size from glorified shacks to spacious barns.

One kind of farm stand is the *year-round farm stand,* typically part of a farm that grows its own produce, but the store also carries produce from all over the country and is open throughout the year. These farms stands also tend to carry a bit more than produce, such as breads, cheeses, and condiments.

A second kind of stand is the *seasonal farm stand.* These farm stands sell primarily their own produce, along with some other locally grown and produced items, for example, maple syrup and apple cider, and are open only during the produce season, usually April or May through November or December.

The third kind is similar to the seasonal farm stand, except that it also has a *pick-your-own* (PYO) option. These farms sell their own produce and have orchards, berry patches, or vegetable plots from which you can pick your own produce, sometimes at a reduced rate.

The most common pick-your-own items are the following, with the harvest season indicated in the parentheses:

apples (late August–early October)
blueberries (July)
pumpkins (late September–early October)
raspberries (early July and sometimes late August and September)
strawberries (June)
vegetables (varies, depending on vegetable)

I recommend calling each pick-your-own farm before visiting; the PYO times are not always the same as the stand hours; some places are only open for PYO on the weekends. Note, however, that farm-stand phones do not always get answered—often you'll just hear a recording. Tuesday is traditionally considered a slow day for produce, and some stands are closed on that day.

The peak season for farm stands is mid-June through August. Those that open in April or May start by selling bedding plants and flowers, and early produce such as lettuce and asparagus. Most farms grow a variety of vegetables. For fruit, berries are most common; fewer places have orchard fruits. Most stands supplement their own produce with other local or national items.

Not many farms are certified organic, since the process can be time-consuming; I've indicated those that are. Many farms claim that much of their produce is technically, if not officially, organic because they do not use chemical pesticides and herbicides. Others follow a program called Integrated Pest Management (IPM), a low-pesticide method that is designed to encourage farmers to use a low level of chemicals and to explore other pest-control options.

Below is a list of area farm stands; when appropriate, I offer a description of the place in addition to the bare minimum facts.

METROPOLITAN BOSTON

BROOKLINE

Allandale Farm
259 Allandale Road, Brookline, MA 02167   (617) 524-1531
Season and hours: April–December, daily 10 A.M.–6 P.M.
Produce grown: a wide variety of IPM fruits and vegetables, including
   berries, corn, peppers
Pick-your-own options: not available

A farm has been in this location for 350 years; the current owners opened the farm stand about twenty-five years ago. In addition to their own produce they sell produce from area growers and offer locally made breads, baked goods, and jams.

NORTH

DANVERS

Clark Farm
163 Hobart Street, Danvers, MA 01923   (508) 774-0550
Season and hours: May–December, daily 9 A.M.–6 P.M.
Produce grown: bedding plants, most vegetables, primarily tomatoes and
   pumpkins, raspberries; no herbicides or pesticides used
Pick-your-own options: raspberries

Connors Farm
30 Valley Road, Danvers, MA 01938   (508) 777-1245
Season and hours: May–October, daily 8 A.M.–6 P.M.
Produce grown: raspberries and strawberries; vegetables including peas,
   lettuce, beets, rhubarb, spinach, zucchini, tomatoes
Pick-your-own options: raspberries, strawberries

Gibney Gardens

15 South Liberty Street, Danvers, MA 01923   (508) 777-4039
Season and hours: May–December, daily 9 A.M.–6 P.M.
Produce grown: vegetables, including lettuce, corn, tomatoes, pumpkins;
   some are organic
Pick-your-own options: not available

IPSWICH

Goodale Orchards

123 Argilla Road, Ipswich, MA 01938   (508) 356-5366
Season and hours: April–December, daily 9 A.M.–6 P.M.
Produce grown: assorted fruits, including blueberries, raspberries,
   strawberries, and apples; herbs, organic vegetables
Pick-your-own options: blueberries, raspberries, strawberries, and apples

Goodale is a fun place to visit. In addition to the produce, the
farm makes **pies** and presses their own **cider**. In the fall you can
buy homemade **cider donuts.** They also make their own **fruit
wines** (see "Libations," page 473).

NORTH ANDOVER

Barker's Farm Stand

1267 Osgood Street, North Andover, MA 01845   (508) 683-0785
Season and hours: April–December, daily 10 A.M.–6 P.M.
Produce grown: apples, sweet corn, flowers
Pick-your-own options: apples

This farm has been in the Barker family since 1633, and the
current Barkers are the third generation to run a farm stand.

Boston Hill Farm

370 Turnpike Street (Route 114), North Andover, MA 01845
   (508) 682-3817
Season and hours: May–October 31, daily 10 A.M.–7 P.M.
Produce grown: vegetables, including corn, tomatoes (fifteen to twenty
   varieties), potatoes, and pumpkins; blueberries and strawberries; some
   items are organic
Pick-your-own options: pumpkins

Boston Hill Farm has been in the Farnum family since the 1600s.
The current owner, Benjamin Farnum, is the twelfth generation
to farm this land.

Leonhard & Eldred Poultry Farm

1000 Dale Street, North Andover, MA 01845   (508) 683-1158
Hours: Mon.–Fri. 8 A.M.–8 P.M.; Sat., Sun. 8 A.M.–6 P.M.
Produce grown: The only produce available are the pick-your-own items, in season. The farm sells its own fresh eggs, year round, "anytime you can find somebody here."
Pick-your-own options: strawberries, raspberries

Smolak Farm

315 South Bradford Street, North Andover, MA 01845
  (508) 682-6332
Season and hours: April–December, daily 7 A.M.–6 P.M.
Produce grown: a variety of IPM vegetables and fruit, including apples, apricots, sour cherries, nectarines, peaches, pumpkins, and sweet corn
Pick-your-own options: apricots, peaches, sour cherries, apples, pumpkins

A farm has been in this location for three hundred years, and Michael Smolak's family has owned the land since the 1920s. It's an idyllic spot, with swans swimming in the pond out front. The family is very active in promoting farming and their produce. A big part of the business is the on-site bakery. **Pies** from scratch are a specialty, using Smolak fruits whenever possible. They sell "a ton of **muffins**," Smolak says, as well as a variety of **breads,** including multigrain and herb. In the fall they make **cider donuts** and construct **gingerbread houses.** They also sell eggs from Leonhard & Eldred Poultry Farm up the street.

Aside from the very good produce—the main reason for visiting a farm stand—Smolak is a good family entertainment destination, with a petting farm, hayrides, and farm tours—call for a schedule—and you can hold birthday parties here too.

PEABODY

Brooksby Farm

38 Felton Street, Peabody, MA 01960   (508) 531-1631
Season and hours: June–July, hours vary; August–February, daily 9 A.M.–5 P.M.; closed March–May
Produce grown: a wide variety of IPM fruits and vegetables, including zucchini, squash, string beans, cucumbers, pumpkins, apples, peaches, pears
Pick-your-own options: strawberries, raspberries, blueberries, apples

This land has been farmed since the seventeenth century. In 1976 the city of Peabody bought the land to save it from being developed. Apples are the specialty here—they grow twenty-five varieties. The stand also sells jams, vinegars, and homemade **cider** and **cider donuts.**

READING

Spence Farm

40 West Street, Reading, MA 01867   (617) 944-1150
Season and hours: April–December, daily 9 A.M.–6 P.M.
Produce grown: strawberries, herbs, and vegetables, including lettuce,
    corn, tomatoes, beans, cucumbers, squash, pumpkins
Pick-your-own options: strawberries

WOBURN

Spence Farm

30 Wyman Street Woburn, MA 01801   (617) 933-4847
Hours: daily 9 A.M.–6 P.M.
Produce grown: strawberries, herbs, and vegetables, including lettuce,
    corn, tomatoes, beans, cucumbers, squash, pumpkins
Pick-your-own options: strawberries

SOUTH

SHARON

Ward's Berry Farm

614 South Main Street, Sharon, MA 02067   (617) 784-6939
Season and hours: April–October, Mon.–Fri. 9 A.M.–7 P.M.;
Sat., Sun. 8 A.M.–6 P.M.; open again in late November–December for
    Christmas trees only
Produce grown: IPM strawberries, raspberries, and peaches; a variety of
    vegetables, including garlic, lettuce, scallions, radishes, zucchini,
    rhubarb, corn, cucumbers, tomatoes
Pick-your-own options: strawberries, blueberries, pumpkins

WALPOLE

Sunny Rock Farm Store

654 North Street, Walpole, MA 02081   (508) 668-3448
Season and hours: April–December, daily 8 A.M.–8 P.M.; January–March,
    daily 8 A.M.–6 P.M.
Produce grown: vegetables, including tomatoes, corn, pumpkins, squash;
    they use very few chemicals
Pick-your-own options: not available

Sunny Rock Farm raises their own eggs, which you can purchase
at the store. The farm has been here for over seventy years.
Initially the business was door-to-door delivery of eggs, with a
small honor-system stand near the farm. But business grew, and
in 1970 John Buttimer built the farm stand, which includes a
kitchen. His daughter makes all the **baked goods,** including
twenty different kinds of **fruited tea breads, pies,** and **cakes.**
There are also **prepared foods,** including **soup, potato salad,**
and **roast chicken.**

WEST

ACTON

Idylwilde Farm

366 Central Street, Acton, MA 01720   (508) 263-5943
Hours: Wed.–Mon. 8 A.M.–7:30 P.M.; closed Tues.
Produce grown: a variety of vegetables, including corn, tomatoes, and
    broccoli
Pick-your-own options: not available

Located in the hills at the edge of Acton, Idylwilde has a new,
large, rough-hewn pine farm building housing terrific, elegantly
displayed produce, gourmet specialty foods, and a garden center.
Idylwilde had been in business long before the erection of this
building; the farm has been in Tom Napoli's family in Acton
since 1979, and in Lexington since the 1920s. In the spring, flats
of herbs and tomatoes, peppers, and other plants line the tables
by the entranceway outside. In the fall, firewood and pumpkins
take their place.

Inside, the food is on one side, and the gardening shop
on the other side of the building. Produce is displayed in a few
wide aisles. The stand is open year round, so produce comes from

all over, but in the summer and fall many of the vegetables are grown at Idylwilde.

Along one wall is a cheese case, with dozens of varieties. Other dairy goods include nonpasteurized milk. Specialty foods such as maple mustard and chipotle salsa line the other walls, and local baked goods, including muffins, scones, and pies from Concord Teacakes, are on shelves near the cash registers. Everything is very clean and very fresh—and a tad expensive. This is not the place to go for bargain deals on fresh produce, but it is a place to find fruits and vegetables that are consistently very good.

BOLTON

Nashoba Valley Winery. See "Libations," page 474.

CONCORD

Arena Farms

Route 2, near the corner of Fairhaven Street, Concord, MA 01742
   (508) 369-4769
Hours: daily 9 A.M.–7 P.M.;
Produce grown: fruits, including strawberries, blueberries, raspberries, Concord grapes; cut and potted herbs (one hundred varieties); vegetables, including asparagus, lettuces (eight kinds), beets, carrots, scallions, rhubarb, tomatoes, potatoes, corn; some items are unofficially organic
Pick-your-own options: not available

The stand sells local breads and cookies. They also have an enticing **salad bar,** featuring as much produce from Arena Farms as possible, and all the produce is always fresh.

Hutchins Farm

754 Monument Street, Concord, MA 01742   (508) 369-5041
Season and hours: May–October, Tues.–Fri. 10:30 A.M.–6 P.M.;
   Sat. 9 A.M.–5 P.M.; closed Sun., Mon. In August, open Sundays, too,
   11 A.M.–6 P.M.
Produce grown: certified organic strawberries, blueberries, watermelons, herbs, and vegetables, including lettuce, cabbage, greens, peas, cucumbers, tomatoes, potatoes, carrots; low-spray apples
Pick-your-own options: not available

Verrill Farm

415 Wheeler Road, Concord, MA 01742   (508) 369-4494
Season and hours: May–December, daily 9 A.M.–7 P.M.
Produce grown: IPM and unofficially organic strawberries, raspberries, and
    vegetables, including asparagus, lettuce, broccoli, spinach, herbs, snap
    peas, tomatoes (twelve to fifteen varieties), corn (twenty varieties),
    potatoes (six to eight varieties), peppers (seventy kinds—forty hot,
    thirty sweet)
Pick-your-own options: lettuce, strawberries, raspberries, peppers,
    tomatoes, summer squash, pumpkins

Steve Verrill is a second-generation farmer and has been farming
for over forty-five years. For years he and his wife, Joan, operated
out of a tent and made the circuit at various farmers' markets. In
1995 they built a winterized farm stand. The Verrills specialize
in unusual produce—note the many varieties of various vegetables they grow. With the help of their daughter, Jennifer, they
also make wonderful **baked goods,** such as buttery **chocolate
chip cookies** and a variety of **muffins.** With the new stand
Jennifer plans to expand the kitchen offerings to include **prepared salads** and **entrées.** If you're lucky, go in the late spring
and they'll have **strawberry-rhubarb punch,** a terrific, refreshing
beverage.

The stand includes a Massachusetts section devoted to
local products, such as cheese, salsas, and jams. During the course
of the growing season, the Verrills sponsor various festivals, featuring corn, strawberries, and pumpkins, with hayrides and food.
You can also find the Verrills at the Cambridge and Mattapan
farmers' markets.

FRAMINGHAM

Hanson's Farm

20 Nixon Road, Framingham, MA 01701   (508) 877-3058
Season and hours: mid-May–October, daily 9 A.M.–5:30 P.M.
Produce grown: a variety of vegetables, including peppers, tomatoes,
    cucumbers, squash, radishes, beets, carrots, scallions; strawberries,
    raspberries, blueberries; some herbs
Pick-your-own options: strawberries, raspberries, pumpkins

Hanson's produce is sold out of a two-hundred-year-old barn.
Tom Hanson's grandfather started the stand in 1908, and it is
now the last working farm in Framingham. They also sell jam,
cheese, and their own **pies.**

Sunshine Farm

135 Kendall Avenue, Framingham, MA 01701   (508) 655-5022
Season and hours: May–October, daily 9 A.M.–6 P.M.;
    reopens in December to sell Christmas trees
Produce grown: IPM strawberries, raspberries, and vegetables, including
    lettuce, broccoli, zucchini, corn (fourteen varieties), pumpkins
Pick-your-own options: strawberries, peas, raspberries, pumpkins

James Geoghegan's grandfather started Sunshine Farm in the
1930s as a dairy farm. At that time the family also opened the
Sunshine Dairy Restaurant next door, which is still going strong.
Ice cream, from Bliss Brothers, is a popular item there, and many
entrées are made using the farm's produce.

LEXINGTON

Wilson Farms Inc.

10 Pleasant Street, Lexington, MA 02173   (617) 862-3900
Hours: Mon., Wed.–Fri. 9 A.M.–8 P.M.; Sat. 9 A.M.–6:30 P.M.;
    Sun. 9 A.M.–5:30 P.M.; closed Tues.
Produce grown: IPM strawberries, raspberries, herbs, and a variety of
    vegetables, including lettuce, radishes, cabbage, leeks, spinach, carrots,
    tomatoes, and corn
Pick-your-own options: not available

The Wilson family has been farming this land since 1884 and
has had a farm stand here since 1957; there are currently eighteen
family members working in the business. In addition to produce,
they carry a variety of breads, condiments, and cheeses. There is
also a wide selection of poultry, including goose, duck, turkey,
and capon, as well as chicken.

LINCOLN

The Food Project

P.O. Box 705 Lincoln, MA 01773   (617) 259-8621

The Food Project has been in business since 1991. It's main
purpose is to grow organic produce for various homeless inns and
soup kitchens in and around Boston. During the growing season
they also instituted a program called Farm to Family. Participants
are called *shareholders;* anyone can participate. This practice is
part and parcel of a wider program some farmers are pursuing,
called Community Supported Agriculture. At the beginning of

the summer, shareholders pay a set fee. Then, every week, they pick up a bag of produce, enough for a family of four for the week. The produce can be picked up in Lincoln (call to find out the exact location), or Dudley Square in Roxbury. Some eight hundred volunteers help keep the farm going.

During the summer, The Food Project sponsors a group of teenagers who work on the farm and help with deliveries for eight weeks. The Food Project's produce is also available at the Dudley Square Farmers' Market.

NATICK

Lookout Farm

89 Pleasant Street, Natick, MA 01760   (508) 651-1539
Hours: daily 8 A.M.–7 P.M.
Produce grown: apples, some vegetables, including zucchini, lettuces, snap
    peas, asparagus, onions, corn; the farm is organic; but not certified yet
Pick-your-own options: apples, peaches, pears, grapes, pumpkins,
    raspberries, strawberries, vegetables

NEEDHAM

Volante Farm

829 Central Avenue, Needham, MA 02192   (617) 444-2351
Season and hours: April–October, Mon.–Fri. 9 A.M.–6:30 P.M.;
    Sat., Sun. 9 A.M.–6 P.M.; December for Christmas trees only
Produce grown: a wide variety of IPM vegetables, including lettuce,
    peppers, beets, carrots, radishes, beans (five varieties), corn, and
    tomatoes; herbs; strawberries

Alfred Volante's family has had a farm since 1917. Although they don't grow any of their own apples, apples are a specialty here. They carry some thirty-nine kinds from Massachusetts and New Hampshire farmers, including both antique and new varieties.

SHERBORN

Dowse Orchard

98 North Main Street, Sherborn, MA 01770   (508) 653-2639
Season and hours: May–January, daily 9 A.M.–6 P.M.
Produce grown: a variety of vegetables, apples, pumpkins
Pick-your-own options: apples, pumpkins

Dowse Orchard has been in Sherborn since 1782, and the family has a record of produce sales from 1892. In December they sell Christmas trees.

SUDBURY

Blue Meadow Farm

118 Nobscott Road, Sudbury, MA 01776   (508) 443-3880
Season and hours: July–August, Tues.–Sun. 8 A.M.–6 P.M.; closed Mon.
Produce grown: blueberries; unofficially organic
Pick-your-own options: blueberries

WALTHAM

DeVincent Farms

378 Beaver Street, Waltham, MA 02154   (617) 894-7342
Hours: Mon.–Fri. 8:30 A.M.–8 P.M.; Sat., Sun. 8:30 A.M.–6 P.M.
Produce grown: bedding plants, strawberries, and vegetables, including
    greens, lettuce, leeks, beans, peas, eggplant, peppers, corn, squash,
    pumpkins
Pick-your-own options: not available

In addition to produce, DeVincent's sells cheeses, breads, dressings, pies, and fresh chicken. There is also a deli counter for **sandwiches.**

Ricci Farms

659 Trapelo Road, Waltham, MA 02154   (617) 893-8599
Hours: Mon.–Fri. 8 A.M.–7:30 P.M.; Sat., Sun. 7:30 A.M.–6 P.M.
Produce grown: rhubarb, tomatoes, herbs

Ricci sells a few of their own homegrown items; but mainly they sell produce from local farmers, in season.

WESTON

Land's Sake

Junction of Newton and Wellesley Streets, Weston, MA 02193
    (617) 893-1162
Season and hours: mid-June–October, daily 10 A.M.–6 P.M.
Produce grown: unofficially organic strawberries, blueberries, and
    vegetables, including sugar snap peas, rhubarb, lettuce, turnips,
    radishes, herbs
Pick-your-own options: strawberries, blueberries, raspberries, assorted
    vegetables in season

Land's Sake, Inc., started in 1980, is a private nonprofit group dedicated to environmentally sensitive land management. They lease land from the town of Weston and work with area schools to teach environmental awareness. They also do forestry work and maintain trails. In addition to their produce, they sell their own **honey** and **maple syrup**.

❖ F A R M E R S ' ❖
M A R K E T S

Farmers' markets are weekly open-air markets, where area farmers come to sell their produce. They are a wonderful resource for fresh, locally grown produce. To round out their offerings, some farmers also carry other local produce.

The prices are not necessarily less than you would pay at the supermarket (and in many cases they are higher), but the quality of what you are buying is invariably better. There is something truly special about buying lettuce, or rhubarb, or ha-bañero peppers from the farmer who grew them.

You can often find items in the farmers' market that you won't see in the supermarket. This is where I discovered Macoun apples, my all-time favorite eating apples. They have a short shelf life and a short season, so farmers' markets and farm stands are the places to get them. Farmers' markets are also where I discovered callaloo, a green most often eaten in the Caribbean that is similar to, yet milder than, spinach. The farmer who grew it was happy to tell me about it and how to cook it.

The Massachusetts Department of Agriculture is doing its best to promote farmers' markets, and the number of towns offering them has increased significantly in the past decade. The first market opened in Fields Corner in 1971. By 1986 there were forty markets; in 1995 there were a hundred. Anneli Johnson, direct marketing specialist and farmers' market coordinator for the Massachusetts Department of Agriculture, is a strong advocate of farmers' markets and works tirelessly to promote them, adding a few more every year.

The markets vary in size. Some, such as the ones in Newton and Brookline, are quite large, with over two dozen farmers participating. Others have only one or two farmers, but all offer most kinds of produce. Each market has a market coordinator, whom Johnson describes as the "locomotive" behind the market. Market coordinators work with the participating farmers at a given site and do what they can to promote the market to the community. All the markets accept food stamps.

Most markets are open from mid-June through October, once a week. Following is a list of the markets as of 1995. The Department of Agriculture publishes an updated list every year. I have included the name and phone number of a site's market coordinator whenever possible.

BOSTON

BOSTON

ABCD Parker Hill/Fenway Farmers' Market
Brigham Circle, Osco Drug parking lot (Green line stop, Business District)
Boston, MA   Contact: Antonio Prieto, (617) 445-6000
July–October
Thurs. noon–3 P.M.
Number of farmers: 3 or 4

Copley Square Farmers' Market
Copley Square, along St. James Street, Boston, MA
Contact: Anneli Johnson, (617) 727-3018 x 175
July–November
Tues. and Fri. 11 A.M.–6 P.M.
Number of farmers: 10

Franklin Park Community Farmers' Market
Franklin Park Road, next to main entrance of the zoo, Boston, MA
Contact: Robert George, (617) 442-2002 x 108
July–October
Sun. 1 P.M.–4 P.M.
Number of farmers: 4 or 5

Scollay Square Farmers' Market
Boston City Hall Plaza (Government Center), Boston, MA
Contact: Anneli Johnson, (617) 727-3018 x 175
July–mid-November
Mon. and Wed. noon–6 P.M.
Number of farmers: 6

BRIGHTON

Brighton Farmers' Market

Bank of Boston parking lot, 5 Chestnut Hill Avenue, Brighton, MA
Contact: Jessie Salvucci, (617) 254-6100
Mid-July–October
Sat. 11 A.M.–6 P.M.
Number of farmers: 3

CHARLESTOWN

Charlestown Farmers' Market

Thompson Square on Main and Austin Streets, Charlestown, MA
Contact: Colleen Justice, (617) 241-8866
Mid-July–mid-October
Wed. 2 P.M.–7 P.M.
Number of farmers: 4

DORCHESTER

Codman Square Farmers' Market

Second Church parking lot, corner of Washington Street and Talbot
   Avenue, Dorchester, MA
Contact: Mary Lynch, (617) 825-9660
Mid-July–mid-October
Wed. 10 A.M.–2 P.M.
Number of farmers: 3

Fields Corner Farmers' Market

Park Street, Purity Supreme parking lot, Dorchester, MA
Contact: Laura Petrucci or Charlie Cloherty, (617) 825-9126
July–October
Sat. 9 A.M.–noon
Number of farmers: 6

EAST BOSTON

East Boston Farmers' Market

London Street Minipark on Tunnel Authority land, East Boston, MA
Contact: Rev. Robert Hennessey, (617) 567-3227
Mid-July–October
Tues. 10 A.M.–3 P.M.
Number of farmers: 4

HYDE PARK

Hyde Park Farmers' Market
Cleary Square at the corner of Harvard Avenue and Winthrop Street,
  Hyde Park, MA
Contact: Diane Grey, (617) 364-0202
July–October
Thurs. noon–5 P.M.
Number of farmers: 4

JAMAICA PLAIN

Jamaica Plain Farmers' Market
Bank of Boston parking lot, Centre Street, Jamaica Plain, MA
Contact: Robert Ashley, (617) 522-1892
Mid-July–October
Tues. noon–6 P.M.
Number of farmers: 4

MATTAPAN

Mattapan Farmers' Market
In front of Church of the Holy Spirit, 525 River Street, Mattapan, MA
Contact: Robin Rice, (617) 727-3018
Late June–mid-October
Thurs. noon–5 P.M.
Number of farmers: 3

ROSLINDALE

Roslindale Farmers' Market
Taft Court, Roslindale Village or at the MBTA Station, Roslindale, MA
Contact: Marna Persechini, (617) 325-4714
Mid-July–October
Sat. 9 A.M.–2 P.M.
Number of farmers: 4

ROXBURY

Dudley Square Farmers' Market

Nuestra Comunidad Development Corporation
391 Dudley Street, Friendship Garden (Jarden La Amistad)
   Roxbury, MA
Contact: Evelyn Friedman-Vargas or Wanitta Blodget, (617) 427-3599
Mid-July–mid-October
Tues. noon–6 P.M.
Number of farmers: 3 or 4

METROPOLITAN BOSTON

BROOKLINE

Brookline Farmers' Market

Coolidge Corner, Harvard Street, municipal parking lot,
   Brookline, MA
Contact: Dorothy Esterquest, (617) 739-1228
Mid-June–October
Thurs. 1:30 P.M.–dusk
Number of farmers: 25

CAMBRIDGE

Cambridge Farmers' Market/Central Square

Parking lot at Norfolk and Bishop Allen Streets, Cambridge, MA
Contact: Oakes Plimpton, (617) 648-5117
Mid-May–mid-November
Mon. noon–6 P.M. (not open Memorial Day)
Number of farmers: 11

Cambridge Farmers' Market/Charles Square

Front of Charles Hotel at Harvard Square, Cambridge, MA
Contact: Martha Sullivan, director, (617) 864-1200
Mid-June–mid-November
Sun. 10 A.M.–2:30 P.M.
Number of farmers: 8

CHELSEA

Chelsea Community Farmers' Market

Chelsea Square, in front of the police station, Chelsea, MA
Contact: Soavia Soeung, (617) 889-8266
Late June–early October
Sat. 10 A.M.–2 P.M.
Number of farmers: 4

EVERETT

Everett Farmers' Market

Everett Square, Osco parking lot, Everett, MA
Contact: Bill Norton or Ann Mulry (617) 387-3175, (617) 394-2246
Mid-July–October
Fri. 10:30 A.M.–4 P.M.
Number of farmers: 2

NEWTON

Newton Farmers' Market

Cold Spring Park, Beacon Street, Newton Highlands, Newton, MA
Contact: Judy Dore, (617) 552-7120
Mid-July–October
Tues. 2 P.M.–6 P.M.
Number of farmers: 25

SOMERVILLE

Somerville Farmers' Market

Davis Square, Day and Herbert Streets, parking lot, Somerville, MA
Contact: Oakes Plimpton, (617) 648-5117
Mid-June–October
Wed. noon–6 P.M.
Number of farmers: 11

NORTH

GLOUCESTER

Gloucester Farmers' Market

St. Peter's Park or Groton's property on Rogers Street, downtown
 Gloucester, MA
Contact: Maggi Stoddard or Susan J. MacNeil, (508) 283-7874
Mid-July–October
Tues. 11 A.M.–3 P.M. or 3 P.M.–7 P.M.
Number of farmers: 5

LYNN

Lynn's Downtown Farmers' Market

MBTA Garage, corner of Market and Broad Streets, Lynn, MA
Contact: Ann Marie Leonard, (617) 598-4000
July–October
Thurs. 11 A.M.–3 P.M.
Number of farmers: 3

MANCHESTER

Manchester-by-the-Sea Farmers' Market

Rear of R. R. Station parking lot, Manchester, MA
Contact: Roberta Sorbello-Luongo, (508) 388-4470
June–mid-October
Mon. 1 P.M.–5 P.M.
Number of farmers: 3

MELROSE

Melrose Farmers' Market

City Hall parking lot on Main Street, Melrose, MA
Contact: Sally Frank, (617) 324-9648
Late June–mid-October
Thurs. 10 A.M.–3 P.M.
Number of farmers: 8

SAUGUS

Saugus/Cliftondale Square Farmers' Market
Cliftondale Square exit off Route 1, Saugus, MA
Contact: Peter A. Rosetti, Jr., (617) 231-4142, or
   J. Johnson, (617) 233-1855
Mid-July–mid-October
Tues. 10 A.M.–3:00 P.M.
Number of farmers: 4

SOUTH

BROCKTON

Brockton/City Hall Plaza Farmers' Market
City Hall Plaza, Brockton, MA
Contact: Michael McGlone (508) 824-3554
July–mid-October
Fri. 8:45 A.M.–3 P.M., or until sold out
Number of farmers: 6

Brockton Fairgrounds Farmers' Market
Brockton Fairgrounds, Brockton, MA
Contact: Henry Rose, (508) 678-8180
Mid-July–mid-October
Sat. 10 A.M.–3 P.M.
Number of farmers: 2 or 3

HINGHAM

Hingham Farmers' Market
Station Street parking lot, near Hingham Harbor, Hingham, MA
Contact: David Sturgis, (617) 749-4643
Late May–October
Wed. and Sat. 10 A.M.–2 P.M.
Number of farmers: 10

QUINCY

Quincy Farmers' Market
John Hancock parking lot, Quincy Center, across from the Court House, Quincy, MA
Contact: Karl Johnson, (617) 479-1601
Mid-June–October
Fri. 11:30 A.M.–5 P.M.
Number of farmers: 12

WEST

FRAMINGHAM

Framingham Farmers' Market
St. Tarcisius Church parking lot, Framingham, MA
Contact: Joe Pratt, (508) 435-4147
Late June–mid-October
Wed. 3 P.M.–6 P.M.; Sat. 9 A.M.–noon
Number of farmers: 6

Framingham Farmers' Market on Route 9
Caldor's & Ken's Steak House parking lot, Shopping Mall, Route 9 West, Framingham, MA
Contact: Charles Touchette (413) 731-8820
May–mid-October
Thurs. noon–5 P.M.
Number of farmers: 4

LINCOLN

Lincoln/Codman Community Farmers' Market
Corner of Lincoln and Codman Roads, Lincoln, MA
Contact: Dave Hardy, (617) 259-0456
Mid-June–September
Sat. 9 A.M.–1 P.M.
Number of farmers: N/A

MARLBORO

Marlboro Farmers' Market
Parking lot, corner of Bolton Street and Route 20, Marlboro, MA
Contact: H. Schultz, (508) 365-5926
Mid-June–October
Thurs. 2 P.M.–6 P.M.
Number of farmers: 6

WALTHAM

Waltham Farmers' Market
Fleet Bank parking lot, Main and Moody Streets, Waltham, MA
Contact: Jennifer Rose, (617) 899-5344, or
   Marc Rudnick, (617) 893-0361
Mid-June–mid-October
Sat. 10 A.M.–3 P.M.
Number of farmers: 9

THE BESTS OF THE BEST

Best produce source: **A. Russo & Sons** and **Fruit Center Marketplace**
Best farmers' market: **Newton,** then **Brookline**
Best farm stand: **Smolak Farm** and **Verrill Farm**
Best pick-your-own: **Verrill Farm** and **Land's Sake**
Best organic source: **Hutchins Farm**

CHAPTER THREE

LOTSA PASTA

*Homemade spaghetti, linguine, fettuccine, ravioli, tortellini, and gnocchi
—and their accompanying sauces*

F RESH pasta has long been available in Boston. With the large Italian population here, there's always been a demand. Dried pasta also has a Boston history. Prince, one of the country's larger pasta companies, is located in Lowell. It wasn't always referred to as *pasta,* however. "I hate the word *pasta,*" declares Genevieve Trio, of Trio's in the North End. "We called it macaroni, and ravioli—never this *pasta!*"

Whatever you call it, this staple of Italian cuisine is available in abundance in fresh and dried forms all over the Boston area. Several stores sell imported Italian dried pasta in various shapes and flavors. Although the dried pastas are good, I prefer fresh pasta, especially when I'm cooking tortellini and ravioli. I list sources for fresh, homemade pasta in this chapter. For flat pasta, many shops will cut your pasta to order, taking a rectangle of dough, rolling it through a machine until it is ultrathin, and cutting the width to your specifications—linguine, fettuccine, and so on.

Fresh pasta can be made in two ways, sheeted (also called rolled) or extruded, and each method has its followers. Pasta purists prefer sheeted pasta; this is how fresh pasta has traditionally been made. The dough is moister, and it is generally made with a lot of eggs. The dough is mixed and kneaded, usually with an electric mixer, then put through a sheeter, a machine with rollers that flatten the pasta into increasingly thin sheets.

Extruded pasta is made in pasta machines, industrial versions of the electric pasta machines made for home kitchens. In order to work in the machines, the dough must be very dry and crumbly, so the dough is made using a smaller proportion of eggs to flour. The dough is mixed in one part of the machine. Then, when the dough is ready to be extruded, a corkscrew mechanism pulls it along and pushes it through the die that is needed to achieve whatever shape is called for. This may be flat pasta such as lasagne sheets or linguine, or hollow pasta such as macaroni or penne. The latter can be made only in extruders.

Italophiles and pasta purists I know eschew extruded pasta; I find that I like both versions, depending on the sauces I'm using. Sheeted pasta often tastes better by itself and may not even need sauce.

When it comes to ravioli, there are also handmade and machine-made versions. With the latter, because of the way the machine deposits the filling onto the ravioli, the filling must be very smooth. Handmade ravioli can have chunkier fillings.

There are several excellent pasta makers around town. Some produce the traditional basics—egg and (maybe) spinach pasta and cheese ravioli. Others go for experimental recipes, with pasta flavors ranging from simple tomato to chipotle pepper, and ravioli fillings such as lobster, roasted red peppers, and wild mushrooms. There are a few businesses that make tortellini and potato gnocchi.

In Chinatown, there are a handful of businesses that specialize in Asian noodles, a different kind of pasta experience. I found no retail outlet for noodles, but there are a couple of establishments that specialize in Peking ravioli.

The quality of dried pasta varies significantly from brand to brand. The best dried pasta is imported from Italy. See "The World in a Jar," Italian markets, page 416, for good dried pasta sources.

---

*Described in another chapter.

PASTA

Alfredo Aiello Italian Pasta Store	Quincy
Bella Ravioli	Medford
Biagi	Boston
*Bob's Imported Food and Fine Catering	Medford
Capone Foods	Somerville
China America Food Manufacture	Boston
Chinese Spaghetti Factory	Boston, Roxbury
*Cremaldi's	Cambridge
*Formaggio's Deli	Cambridge
*II Pastificio	Everett
*The Italian Express	Newton Highlands
Italo-American Pasta	Charlestown
La Pasta Place	Concord
Lilly's Gastronomia Italiana Inc.	Everett
Nonna Fresh Pasta	Roslindale
Noodles	Somerville
Pasta Bene	Brockton
Pasta Etc.	Framingham, Wellesley
Pasta del Palato	Brighton
Pina Pasta	Waltham
Sabella's Ravioli	Revere
Serino's Italian Food Manufacturing Co.	Hyde Park
Trio's Fresh Pasta and Sauces Factory Outlet Store	Chelsea
Trio's Ravioli Shoppe	Boston
*Via Lago	Arlington, Lexington

BOSTON

BOSTON

Biagi

143 Richmond Street, Boston, MA 02113   (617) 227-5295
Mail order: not available   Hours: Wed. 8 A.M.–1 P.M.;
    Thurs. 8 A.M.–3 P.M.; Fri., Sat. 8 A.M.–2 P.M.

Do not rely on Biagi's posted hours. Owner Joseph Memmolo keeps his own time. To call Memmolo and his wife, who is the daughter of the Biagi who started the store in 1930, reticent would be an understatement. The last interview Memmolo was willing to give was in 1975. He showed me the article, which is where I learned his name. Now he says there is no reason to talk, as he will be retiring within the next year and a half. But I am including him anyway, because his pasta is simply superb.

A sign on the wall in the back of the large room looks as if it has been there for fifty years. It says, "Biagi leads the way. Our product is manufactured with fresh eggs and is guaranteed to be absolutely pure under any chemical analysis." Another sign declares, "When better ravioli are made, we will make them."

In this day of flavored pastas and ravioli with myriad fillings, Biagi's is for purists. The only flavor is **egg pasta,** which can be cut into several widths. A tin box displays twelve possible cuts, numbered from one to fifteen (there's no nine, eleven, or thirteen). Indicate the number width you want, and Memmolo or his wife will run a folded sheet of pasta through a hand-cranked machine, the likes of which I have seen only here. (All other cut-to-order pasta places use an electric machine.) The pasta is thicker than usual, and works better with thinner cuts, such as **linguine** or **angel hair.** The egg pasta also comes dried as *cavatelli,* which must be kept refrigerated or frozen. The ingredients are simple, but Biagi's pasta is so good, I found it didn't even need sauce. They also have **chicken tortellini,** unavailable when I was there, and wonderful fresh **cheese ravioli.**

China America Food Manufacture

81 Tyler Street Boston, MA 02111   (617) 426-1818
Mail order: not available   Hours: daily 8 A.M.–4 P.M.

China America Food Manufacture makes all kinds of Chinese wrapped foods, which the company sells frozen to restaurants and supermarkets. Manager Stanley Young took over the space from the former Peking Ravioli Factory in 1993. The shop is a wholesale business. There is no appearance of a retail operation, but you can buy their products here. When you descend the steps, you'll find yourself in the middle of a kitchen, surrounded by people rolling dough for **Peking ravioli, spring rolls, egg rolls,** and the like.

Everything made here is sold frozen. The **raviolis** come with **pork** and **vegetable** fillings. Fillings are similar, but the wrappings for various items differ. Young says that they have vegetarian versions of most items. There is also **sushi—Califor-**

nia roll, *shumai,* **and scallion pancakes.** Young was vague about minimum requirements for purchases at this factory outlet store; some items are available in smaller quantities than others.

Chinese Spaghetti Factory

22-A Oxford Street, Boston, MA 02114   (617) 542-0224
Mail order: not available   Hours: daily 7 A.M.–4 P.M.

83 New Market Square, Roxbury, MA 02118   (617) 445-7714
Mail order: not available   Hours: daily 7 A.M.–4 P.M.

The name of this business does not describe its product. No noodles are made here. The Chinese Spaghetti Factory makes **Peking ravioli.** They make thousands of these dumplings daily, supplying restaurants all over town. The ravioli is primarily made in the New Market Square location, and you can buy it here by the case; a case weighs about fifteen pounds. Don't be intimidated by the lack of a formal entrance to the warehouse. Climb up on the loading dock and enter one of the doors.

If you want to purchase a more manageable amount of ravioli, go to the Chinatown location on Oxford Street. Not much English is spoken here, but the product line is not extensive. There are three types of **ravioli: pork, pork and leek,** and **vegetable.** The ravioli comes in two sizes and is sold frozen. The larger size has a thicker skin because it is made by hand. The smaller Peking ravioli is bite-size and has a thin skin. Both are appealing.

Trio's Ravioli Shoppe

222 Hanover Street, Boston, MA 02113   (617) 523-9636
Mail order: available   Hours: Mon.–Sat. 9 A.M.–6 P.M.;
Sun. 9 A.M.–1 P.M.

The Trios are a coal-mining family from Pennsylvania. In Boston, Tony and his son Louie dug tunnels, while matriarch Genevieve worked in an army boot factory. One day twenty-three-year-old Louie, impressed with his mother's cooking, suggested, "Let's sell macaroni." In 1960 the Trios opened their first shop, in Cambridge, and later moved to the North End. Word of mouth is the only advertising they've ever used, and it's been very effective.

Trio's is a narrow store with a plain façade shaded by a red awning. A wooden bench sits on the sidewalk in front of the display windows. When you enter Trio's, there's not much to see. A counter runs down the length of the store on the right, across from metal shelves stacked with gallon jars of dried herbs and spices. The simplicity of the displays is misleading. Trio's makes both excellent **pasta** and the best **tomato sauce** you're likely to find. Any pasta tastes great with this vegetarian sauce, which is available by the pint and the quart. The store goes through about three hundred quarts daily. The sauce bubbles on the stove in the back kitchen, filling the air with a wonderful smoky-rich smell that greets you as you enter.

Trio's makes both sheeted and extruded pasta; the best bet for **flat pasta** is the sheeted pasta, cut to order. The pasta dough comes both **plain** and **flavored.** The flavors are assertive —not merely colors. The **red pepper** is spicy hot, and the **garlic and herb** barely needs sauce.

The extruded pasta is good for shapes like ziti and macaroni. The **ravioli,** made using sheeted pasta, is also very good. It comes both **fresh** and **frozen;** unusual flavors, such as **pumpkin,** are more likely to be sold frozen. The **cheese ravioli** is always available fresh, and, good as frozen can be, it can't beat fresh ravioli, cooked and eaten soon after it's made.

In 1987 the Trios signed a licensing agreement with Original Italian Pasta Products Company (see Chelsea, page 92) to reproduce their recipes on a large scale, so now you can buy the Trios' sauces in supermarkets around town and across the country. Since they began to work with Original Italian Pasta Products, most of the **tortellini** the Trios sell in their North End shop is made in the factory. This includes my favorite, **hot pepper pasta with three-cheese filling.** Occasionally, Genevieve will make **pumpkin tortelloni** or some other flavors, and these she makes by hand. She also makes **potato gnocchi** and **ricotta gnocchi** by hand. And if there is a specific filling you want in a tortellini or ravioli, Trio's will make it for you.

In 1995 Trio's introduced **Trio's Tomato Sauce Kit,** which contains three cans of the tomatoes they use along with Genevieve's special blend. Combine all the ingredients and cook the sauce for an hour, and you will end up with a gallon of very good sauce. It's not quite the same as the one you can get from the source, but it's a happy alternative.

BRIGHTON

Pasta del Palato

579 Washington Street, Brighton, MA 02135   (617) 782-7274
Mail order: not available   Hours: Mon.–Fri. 9 A.M.–6 P.M.;
closed Sat., Sun.

Current owner Gary Bemis bought Pasta del Palato from founder
Jimmy Burke (owner of the Tuscan Grill), after many years of
working as a chef. Bemis makes pasta in a variety of flavors for
several area hotels and restaurants, and he will cut it to order
for anyone who comes into his store, which he calls a "factory
outlet."

When you enter the store, you feel almost as if you have
walked into a factory kitchen (albeit a small one). Then you
notice the rows of antique radios lining one wall, and the old
movie advertisements posted along another. A table to the right
holds thick rectangles of pasta ready to be rolled thin; to the left
are sacks of durum flour and drying racks. Bemis explains that
his hand-rolled pasta is so moist that it needs to dry slightly
before it can be rolled thin and cut. A refrigerator near the back
holds more pasta sheets and frozen sauces. Bemis makes a very
good, buttery **pesto** and a tasty **tomato sauce.**

For pasta purists who eschew extruded pasta (and for
any pasta lover), Pasta del Palato is your place. The dough is rich
with eggs—three or four to a pound of extra fancy durum flour.
(Bemis also makes a plain **no-cholesterol pasta** using egg whites
only.) Bemis makes no ravioli or filled pastas—just straightforward **sheet pasta** cut to order in four widths: **fettuccine, tagliatelle, linguine,** and **angel hair.** You can buy the pasta by the
sheet if you want to make your own filled pasta.

The pasta comes in about a dozen flavors, with **plain
egg** being the best-seller. There are a handful of basic flavors—
spinach, tomato, egg—and about a dozen more exotic items. I
especially like the **lemon** and **chipotle pepper** varieties. Also
good are **scallion, mushroom,** and **roasted garlic.** The pasta is
only sold fresh and has a refrigerator shelf life of ten days. It can
be frozen but, as Bemis points out, the point of this pasta (aside
from its great taste and texture) is to eat it fresh.

CHARLESTOWN

Italo-American Pasta

50 Terminal Street, Charlestown, MA 02129   (617) 241-8787
Mail order: not available   Hours: Mon.–Fri. 8 A.M.–4 P.M.;
   Sat. 8 A.M.–noon; closed Sun.

Italo-American Pasta has been in business since 1947; the store
was opened by current owner Ralph D. Matarazzo's father, Ralph
F. Matarazzo. Ralph F. initially had a business selling peeled
potatoes; the M.I.T. grad invented a solution that keeps peeled
potatoes white. He later moved into the pasta business, specializing in ravioli. Ralph D.'s entire family—his wife and five kids—
now works in the factory, which moved to its current location
in 1993. They sell partially cooked, frozen **ravioli** primarily to
restaurants, but you can buy a minimum of six or eight pounds
(depending on the pasta) here. There is no storefront. Italo-
American Pasta is located in a large warehouse building. By the
side entrance, there is a sign listing all the businesses there—just
go up to their floor, knock on the door, and place your order in
the business office.

   I admit I was skeptical about how good partially cooked,
frozen ravioli would be, but it's actually quite good. Right from
the freezer it cooks in just two or three minutes. I was also
impressed with the quality of the products. The pasta is egg-based
and is sheeted. They offer a variety of ravioli **fillings,** from the
more unusual, like **broccoli, chicken, and prosciutto** or **mushroom and sun-dried tomato in wine** to the standard **cheese** and
spinach. The ricotta cheese Italo-American Pasta uses is from
Purity in the North End (see "An Epicurean Agenda," page 390);
it's an excellent cheese. The ravioli comes in large and small sizes,
both square and round.

   Italo-American Pasta also makes their own **tortellini,**
with a **cheese** filling, or **meat, mascarpone and sweet basil,** and
creamy Gorgonzola. Both the tortellini and the ravioli come
frozen, either partially cooked or uncooked. There are also sheets
and cuts of **flat pasta** in about eighteen flavors, including **ginger**
and **jalapeño.**

   Six pounds may seem like a lot of pasta, but if you have
room in your freezer, it's definitely worth having the partially
cooked ravioli on hand for a quick, tasty dinner. It's best to call
in advance to see if the flavor you want is available.

HYDE PARK

Serino's Italian Food Manufacturing Co.

883 Hyde Park Avenue, Hyde Park, MA 02136   (617) 361-5000
Mail order: not available   Hours: Mon.–Sat. 9 A.M.–6 P.M.;
closed Sun.

Guy Serino started his career in the food business as a restaurateur in 1965. A year or two later he closed his restaurant and got
into the wholesale pasta business.

There are display cases set up at Serino's, but you do feel
as if you are walking into the middle of a kitchen. All the pasta
is frozen. The **ravioli** comes with **meat, cheese, vegetable,** or a
nice **wild mushroom filling.** The **spinach gnocchi** is cooked
well. The sauces are not as good as the pastas. The **pesto** tastes
oily, and the tomato sauce is unremarkable.

In addition to the pastas, Serino's makes several prepared
foods. The **eggplant Parmesan** is very good. It comes in foil
pans, ready to be heated through; both refrigerated and frozen
versions are available, in a variety of sizes. They also offer **soups,**
including **pasta and bean** and **minestrone.** And for dessert, they
sell **cannoli** filled with sweetened ricotta cheese.

ROSLINDALE

Nonna Fresh Pasta

Gooches Bakery Inc.
4140 Washington Street, Roslindale, MA 02131   (617) 325-3928
Mail order: not available   Hours: Mon.–Fri. 9 A.M.–9 P.M.;
Sat. 9 A.M.–6 P.M.; Sun. 10 A.M.–3 P.M. (note: Sunday hours vary, and
if it's a nice day, they might be closed.)

Robert Mazza has been making pasta for twenty-five years, but
he only started making his Nonna Pasta in 1994. He had worked
as a chef and a caterer for many years, and had been making
pasta for his business, when one day, when he was making pasta,
his then ninety-seven-year-old grandmother, Nonna, came into
the kitchen. "That's not how you do it," she said. She then
proceeded to tell Mazza how she made ravioli when she was
seven, and he started writing down her recipes. A few years later
he began to make them. In mid-1995 he moved into his cousin
Dominic Candella's kitchen at Gooches Bakery (see "Everything
Nice," page 240), and he now makes a selection of absolutely

excellent ravioli by hand. The texture of the sheeted pasta is just right. Nonna's family recipe—her parents had a bakery and ravioli shop in Italy in 1892—calls for durum, semolina, and bread flour, as well as eggs.

The **cheese ravioli** is delicious, seasoned with parsley. The **spinach ravioli** is excellent. It's quite different from most spinach ravioli, which is usually a blend of cheese and spinach— almost spinach-flavored ricotta cheese. Mazza's recipe calls for spinach, and lots of it, with barely any cheese; each ravioli has one and a half ounces of fresh spinach. Other ravioli fillings include **broccoli and cheese** and **ground sirloin.** The **garlic, white bean, and zucchini** was less interesting, almost bland. Mazza is experimenting with gluten-free pastas, using white bean flour and rice flour.

ROXBURY

Chinese Spaghetti Factory. See Boston, page 87.

METROPOLITAN BOSTON

CAMBRIDGE

Cremaldi's. See "Goodies to Go," page 173.

Formaggio's Deli. See "Goodies to Go," page 203.

CHELSEA

Trio's Fresh Pasta and Sauces Factory Outlet Store
124 Second Street, Chelsea, MA 02150   (617) 887-1202
Hours: Mon.–Wed. 11 A.M.–5 P.M.; Thurs., Fri. 11 P.M.–7 P.M.;
    Sat. 10 A.M.–5 P.M.; closed Sun.

The Original Italian Pasta Products Company has been producing sauces and pastas based on Genevieve and Tony Trio's recipes since 1987 (see Boston, page 87). Trio's Fresh Pasta and Sauces Factory Outlet Store opened adjacent to the company's warehouses in Chelsea. I think Trio's is the best commercial **tomato sauce** available, and the pastas are excellent as well. The factory outlet sells what they call "short-dated" items: these are pastas and sauces that have an expiration date coming up too soon for the company to ship the items to markets. Most of the pastas have a refrigerated shelf life of 45 days, and the sauces have a shelf life of 120 days. The pastas you're going to be getting here are not the absolute freshest, but they taste fine and are significantly discounted—at least 50 percent off the suggested retail price.

All the pasta is extruded, a process that the company literature claims yields a "more tender, lighter pasta." I don't agree; sheeted pasta can be very light. However, their pasta does taste good. The **flat pasta** is available as **linguine** (in **hot red pepper** and **garlic and herb**), **angel hair** (**plain** and **lemon**), and **fetuccine** (**cracked black pepper**). The flavored pastas are used to wrap **three-cheese tortellini,** made with romano, Parmesan, and provolone. Other pasta flavors include **spinach** and **jalapeño.** I especially like the **mushroom tortelloni. Ravioli** is also available made from various pasta doughs, including **Sonoma Valley dried tomato;** all ravioli are filled with cheese. The company recently introduced a line of **low-fat tortellini** and **ravioli,** made with egg-free pasta and low-fat cheeses.

Trio's Fresh Pasta and Sauces has significantly expanded on the Trio family's **sauces.** The company continues to make the wonderful **traditional tomato** and has added a tasty **low-fat** version. There's also **thick and chunky tomato sauce,** with a satisfying **nonfat version, vegetable primavera sauce, classic mushroom, Alfredo** (and a forgettable **low-fat Alfredo),** and **pesto.**

EVERETT

Il Pastificio. See "Everything Nice," page 254.

Lilly's Gastronomia Italiana Inc.

208 Main Street, Everett, MA 02149   (617) 387-9666
Mail order: not available   Hours: Mon.–Fri. 9 A.M.–5 P.M.;
    Sat. 10:30 A.M.–3 P.M.; closed Sun.

Lilly d'Alelio came to Boston from Italy in 1986 specifically to make and sell pasta. "I grew up with a *big* passion for pasta," she says.

Lilly makes traditional pasta—**fettuccini, linguine,** and such—but her specialties are flavored pastas with unusual fillings, such as **asparagus-filled ravioli** made with **lemon-cilantro pasta.** The **vegetable ravioli** is made with nine vegetables (but no cheese) including butternut squash, eggplant, mushrooms, and red peppers. Seafood raviolis are her specialty, especially **lobster.**

Lilly's business is primarily wholesale. She supplies a number of area hotels and restaurants, as well as markets that repackage her products as their own. You can walk into Lilly's at any time, though, and purchase whatever Lilly has on hand. The space does not appear to be retail, and Lilly prefers it that way. A retail-oriented business is another kind of business, and it would require that she stick to specific hours. (The hours listed above are approximate; it's worth calling in advance to be sure Lilly's is open.) You walk into a large room containing desks and a few freezers (all the pasta is frozen). If there is a specific kind of pasta you want, order in advance. Otherwise, experiment and buy whatever is on hand. There is usually a wide selection of flat and filled pasta.

The pasta itself is very good, but the fillings are mixed. The **cheese** and the **basil-ricotta** are very good, but I wanted more Gorgonzola in the **Gorgonzola.** The **cracked pepper linguine** has a nice kick to it. My absolute favorite item here is the **potato gnocchi,** the best I've ever tasted. Lilly is very particular about how she makes gnocchi, and proudly claims, "My company is the only company in America that makes potato gnocchi with real potatoes, not flakes." (Maybe that is true about large companies; I did find some smaller manufacturers that say they use fresh potatoes.) And Lilly is particular about her potatoes. "For good gnocchi," she says, "the potatoes have to be a little old, from last season. It's best if they are a little dry, so you use less flour." Gnocchi can often be heavy and sticky; these are light and ethereal. The **sweet potato and sage gnocchi** are also very good.

SOMERVILLE

Capone Foods
14 Bow Street, Somerville, MA 02143   (617) 629-2296
Mail order: not available   Hours: Wed.–Fri. 1 P.M.–5 P.M.;
    Sat. 10 A.M.–5 P.M.; closed Sun.–Tues.

Capone Foods carries a variety of gourmet items, such as olive oils and imported cheeses, but the main reason to come here is for the pasta. Owner Albert Capone has been in the specialty foods business since 1968, and in this location since 1985. His family had a dried pasta factory in Buenos Aires, Argentina, before they moved to the United States. In the early 1980s they started making specialty pastas. "We were among the first to do lemon pasta, garlic, wine," Capone claims. In all, Capone makes some two dozen flavors of flat pasta, all with the base of durum and semolina flours and eggs, made using an extruder. The 11-by-16-inch sheets can be bought whole if you're making your own lasagne or ravioli, or in four cuts, to order: **vermicelli, linguini, fettuccine,** and **pappardelle. Plain egg** is the most popular, but I like to buy the more unusual flavors Capone sells, such as **red wine,** which is terrific with mushrooms. **Rosemary-garlic** is also very good, and **garlic and parsley.** The **wild mushroom** is good, but with a slightly musty taste.

Capone makes thirteen kinds of **ravioli** and five varieties of **potato gnocchi,** all sold frozen. Good bets are the **mixed mushroom** and the **roasted red pepper ravioli.** The **black pepper gnocchi** are truly spicy.

Capone also makes eleven types of sauces, including five different **tomato-based sauces;** I like *puttanesca,* with capers and olives. The **marinara** is good but a little thick. The **cream sauces** include *bergamo,* with sausage, and **Newburg,** with sherry and paprika.

In addition Capone's sells a selection of imported cheeses. It was here that I first encountered aged farmer's Gouda —Albert Capone's personal favorite cheese, and now one of my top faves. It's dry, tangy, slightly crumbly, yet creamy; a cheese to crave, and I like it all by itself, with apple slices on the side.

Noodles
414 Washington Street, Somerville, MA 02143   (617) 492-1770
Mail order: not available   Hours: Mon.–Sat. 11 A.M.–8 P.M.;
    closed Sun.

David Jick has been making wholesale fresh pasta since 1983. "I didn't really know what I was doing then," he laughs. "I had worked in restaurants and knew I wanted to go into business for myself." At that time there were few wholesale fresh pasta companies, so Jick found his niche, on Lake Street in Arlington, making his Via Lago pastas, all sheeted. A few years later he opened a retail outlet around the corner with his brother Alan, and he continued his wholesale business. Alan then opened a Via Lago in Lexington (see "Goodies to Go," page 193) and carried David's pasta. A few years ago David sold the Arlington store, so he could concentrate on the wholesale business (both Via Lagos continue to carry his pasta) and on preparing to open Noodles, which he describes as a "pasta café."

Jick chose the name *Noodles,* he said, "because I like it." His new store offers some pasta and broth items, but the focus is more Italian than Asian. "There are already two Via Lagos, with different owners and different focuses, so I thought it would be silly to have a third. And I always liked the name Noodles."

Noodles offers a selection of his fresh pastas. Fresh **ravioli** comes with **spinach, basil,** and **ricotta** fillings, all of which are delicious, among the best I've tried. There are also more exotic flavors, such as a flavorful **wild mushroom** and **creamy artichoke mascarpone.** The ravioli comes in two sizes, large (twelve to a pound) and small (thirty to a pound); I prefer the small ones. **Sheets** of **spinach, plain,** or **tomato pasta** can be cut to order as **linguine** or **fettuccine. Sauces** are available as well, including **Amatriciana,** a tomato sauce made with *pancetta;* **pesto;** and the Jick family's **meat sauce,** which is spectacular (you can find it at Via Lago in Lexington too; David says it's his mother's recipe). I'm also fond of the *puttanesca* with Kalamata olives, capers, and anchovies, which is great on fettuccine. The ravioli is flavorful enough that it doesn't need sauce.

In addition to the fresh pasta, there's a menu of **prepared pasta dishes,** to take out or to eat there in the small seating area. Daily specials and regular items are offered, including a generous portion of excellent **wild mushroom lasagne.**

NORTH

MEDFORD

Bella Ravioli
365 Main Street, Medford, MA 02155   (617) 396-0875
Mail order: not available   Hours: Mon. 10:30 A.M.–6 P.M.; Tues.–Sat.
   8:30 A.M.–6 P.M.; Sun. 8 A.M.–1 P.M.

Bella Ravioli is a tiny storefront; most of the narrow space is taken up by the kitchen. There's room for just two or three customers by the counter. Owner Michael DePasquale learned to make pasta from his late father, who was a licensed pasta maker in Naples. The two of them started the store in 1981, making a variety of traditional filled and flat pastas, at downright cheap prices. The **ravioli** is made daily, filled with fresh ricotta cheese as well as Parmesan and Romano; it is available fresh or frozen. The **chicken tortellini**—traditional for soup, DePasquale instructs—are filled with a blend of chicken, ham, and mortadella, and the toothsome **beef** filling includes ham, pork, prosciutto, and Parmesan.

There are also tasty **ricotta *cavatelli*,** and both **ricotta** and **potato gnocchi.** All kinds of shapes are sold frozen, including **rotini, penne,** and **macaroni. Fettuccine, linguine,** and **lasagne** sheets, in **spinach** or **plain** dough, can be cut to order; this dough is sheeted, and the shaped pasta is extruded. DePasquale makes his own good **tomato sauce,** and sells his mother's **meatballs.**

Bob's Imported Food and Fine Catering. See "The World in a Jar," page 416.

REVERE

Sabella's Ravioli

910 Broadway, Revere, MA 02151   (617) 286-0820
Mail order: not available   Hours: Tues.–Sat. 7 A.M.–6 P.M.;
   Sun. 7 A.M.–4 P.M.; closed Mon.

Vinnie Sabella has been involved with pasta since he was eleven years old. His uncle owned Louise's, a wholesale pasta manufacturer that was eventually sold to Heinz, and Sabella worked there. After Louise's was sold and relocated, Sabella decided to open his own place. His pasta is both sheeted and extruded. Shapes, such as **ziti** and **fusilli,** are extruded, and the sheeted egg pasta is used for flat cuts like **fettuccine.**

The pasta does not come in many fancy flavors. You'll find mostly the traditionals here, such as **cheese ravioli,** both square and round. There is fresh-frozen **tortellini;** the **spinach-cheese** is good. My favorite of the pastas I tried is the assertively spiced **black pepper–garlic *cavatelli*.** There are three **tomato** sauces: **plain, meat,** and **mushroom.** Good sauce is hard to find. I tried the plain, and it is excellent.

SOUTH

BROCKTON

Pasta Bene

1041 Pearl Street, Brockton, MA 02402   (508) 583-1515
Mail order: not available   Hours: Mon.–Fri. 10A.M.–6 P.M.;
    Sat. 10 A.M.–2 P.M.; closed Sun.

Pasta Bene is not exactly easy to find. It is outside downtown Brockton, off the main drag, after a series of strip malls, and you may feel as if you are coming to the back entrance. But persevere and you'll be rewarded with terrific, hand-rolled pasta.

Joyce Spillane has been making her Pasta Bene pasta since 1979, when she opened the business with her brother and sister. The flavors are standard—**spinach** and **plain egg** for pasta, cut to order. Filled pasta is frozen. The **spinach and cheese ravioli** and the **meat tortellini** are excellent; there is also **lobster ravioli.** All raviolis are hand-filled.

Accompanying **sauces** include a hearty **tomato** and a lighter **marinara,** as well as **Amatriciana** (made with *pancetta),* **Alfredo,** and **white clam.**

Since they moved to their current location in 1991, Pasta Bene has also been making a selection of prepared foods to take home. These change daily, but I tried a simple yet delectable **fresh mozzarella with balsamic vinegar** and a robust **chicken cacciatore.** Other offerings include **chicken with broccoli, white beans with vegetables,** and **veal and mushrooms** seasoned with balsamic vinegar.

QUINCY

Alfredo Aiello Italian Pasta Store

8 Franklin Street, Quincy, MA 02169   (617) 770-6360
Mail order: not available   Hours: Mon.–Fri. 9 A.M.–6 P.M.;
    Sat. 8:30 A.M.–5 P.M.; Sun. 9 A.M.–noon

Lino Aiello's father started his self-named company in 1967 with his wife. Lino's mother made the pasta, and his father sold it to restaurants and supermarkets. Since then, the business has expanded considerably, and the second generation has taken over. Lino is vice president of operations, his brother, Peter, is president, and his sister, Rosanne, runs the retail store. For years the store was located in front of their production facilities, where large machines churn out *cavatelli,* **tortellini,** and **ravioli.** Retail has accounted for only about 10 percent of the business, but shortly after I visited, the company moved the retail operation around the corner, so that end of business may increase.

Lino describes the new store as "pasta heaven." The Aiellos still sell the pasta made at the factory, which is available both fresh and frozen. The **cheese ravioli** is terrific. The **cheese tortellini** is good, although there is not much filling compared to the amount of pasta. The tortellini comes tricolored (**egg, spinach, tomato),** but there is virtually no taste difference between the three colors. Other ravioli fillings include **meat, vegetable,** and **mushroom.**

In addition, they make **sheeted pasta** at the store. This is a much smaller operation—a ravioli machine makes two at a time—but this way they can make more varieties. There are now different shaped **ravioli,** and creative fillings, such as **prosciutto and spinach.** Fresh flat pasta includes **linguine, fettuccine, angel hair,** and **lasagne** sheets.

They sell both **meat** and **plain tomato sauce.** The sauce is not remarkable; it tastes slightly acidic, as if the canned tomatoes barely had anything done to them.

The store carries a full line of pasta-related items. There are small pasta machines, durum flour, pasta dishes, pots, and pans. There are also several imported Italian dried pastas, as well as Italian tomatoes and olive oils. The store just opened in mid-1995, so the Aiellos were still establishing a routine when I spoke with Lino. He said the store offers occasional pasta demonstrations, such as how to make tortellini by hand.

The freezer contains a variety of **heat-and-serve frozen dinners** made by the Aiellos. These include classic Italian dishes, such as **lasagne, eggplant Parmesan, stuffed shells and sauce,** and **chicken cacciatore.** You can also buy refrigerated **pizza dough** here.

WEST

ARLINGTON

Via Lago Pasta. See "Goodies to Go," page 193.

CONCORD

La Pasta Place
105 Thoreau Street, Concord, MA 01742   (508) 371-7428
Mail order: not available   Hours: Mon.–Fri. 9 A.M.–7 P.M.;
    Sat. 9 A.M.–6 P.M.; closed Sun.

Andrew and Nancy Massucco bought La Pasta Place in 1993, but Nancy had been making pasta for years before that. She has worked at Romagnoli's restaurant and Via Lago. When the opportunity to buy La Pasta came up, she and Andrew decided to go into business for themselves.

La Pasta makes both extruded and sheeted pasta. The **extruded** is egg-free, and comes in four shapes: **ziti, fusilli, spaghetti,** and **fettuccine.** If you're not worried about cholesterol, the **sheeted pasta** is the more worthwhile. You can get **flat pasta** cut to order, in a variety of flavors, including **garlic-parsley, lemon-basil, tomato, spinach,** and **black pepper.**

Ravioli also comes extruded or sheeted; the **sheeted ravioli** is handmade. Fillings include **cheese, basil-ricotta, spinach-ricotta, porcini mushroom, meat,** and **artichoke.** Andrew says that they are very flexible: they'll be happy to fill ravioli with anything you want. Tell them the ingredients you like or give them a recipe, and they'll make it.

In addition to pasta, La Pasta offers a variety of **take-out items,** such as **eggplant Parmesan** and **lasagne.** The Massuccos are among the few proprieters I've met who also offer **low-fat** versions of these and other items—they use egg-free pasta, nonfat ricotta, and low-fat mozzarella. These items are also available frozen. The Massuccos will make dishes in your own pans if you prefer ("I know several people who pass these off as their own," says Andrew).

The **submarine sandwiches** here are quite good. Most of the items are standard, but the Massuccos use good quality meats. They also roast their own **red peppers,** which makes for a wonderful vegetarian sandwich: **roasted red peppers, fresh mozzarella, and basil.**

There is limited seating at La Pasta. A selection of Italian goods, such as imported pasta is also for sale.

FRAMINGHAM

Pasta Etc.

855 Worcester Road, Framingham, MA 01701   (508) 875-3347
Mail order: not available   Hours: Mon.–Fri. 8 A.M.–7 P.M.;
  Sat. 10 A.M.–5 P.M.; Sun. 10 A.M.–3 P.M.

200 Linden Street, Wellesley, MA 02181   (617) 431-2300
Mail order: not available   Hours: Mon.–Fri. 8 A.M.–8 P.M.;
  Sat. 9 A.M.–5 P.M.; closed Sun.

Pasta Etc. is a family business started by Paul Croatti with his father, brother, uncle, and cousin in 1987 at the Framingham location; in 1991 they opened the Wellesley shop.

"Our family has always had good cooks," Croatti explains, "so we decided to have a retail shop, just pasta and sauce. But then the lunch business really took off." They got repeated requests for **prepared foods,** so they prepared them—items such as **lasagne** and a tasty cold **pasta salad.** Then they added several tables and a **salad bar.** Their pasta and sauces are also available cooked, and there is always a pasta of the day. **Nonpasta entrées** include dishes such as **roast** *porchetta,* slow-roasted pork with fennel; or **rotisserie chicken** and **Italian roast potatoes,** potatoes roasted with succulent chicken drippings. The rotisserie chicken is used for the very good **chicken salad.**

The pasta is extruded; it is fine although not exceptional. All pasta is sold refrigerated or frozen, prepackaged. They offer standard **cheese ravioli** and **fettuccine** and **linguine** in a variety of flavors, including **spinach, black pepper,** and **Parmesan peppercorn.** There are also shaped pastas such as **ziti** and **rigatoni.** The most interesting offering is *passatelli;* Pasta Etc. is the only place where I've seen it made. Paul Croatti's family originally came from Rimini, and he says that *passatelli* is a traditional dish there. It is pasta made from bread crumbs, cheese, eggs, and spices, and the dough is put through a meat grinder so that it comes out in fat strands. Croatti says that the pasta is usually served in a mild chicken broth. It's delicious.

The **sauces** are all family recipes. **Meat** and **marinara** are good, if unexceptional. The best bet, again an item I haven't seen elsewhere, is the **broccoli and cauliflower with ricotta sauce,** liberally seasoned with garlic. It's a creamy white sauce, but lighter than an Alfredo because it uses ricotta cheese instead of cream.

LEXINGTON

Via Lago Gourmet Foods. See "Goodies to Go," page 193.

NEWTON

The Italian Express. See "Goodies to Go," page 181.

WALTHAM

Pina Pasta

573 Main Street, Waltham, MA 02154   (617) 899-6065
Mail order: not available   Hours: Mon.–Fri. 9 A.M.–6 P.M.;
    Sat. 10 A.M.–5 P.M.; closed Sun.

In 1989 Marco Aismondo and his sister Carmela Velella decided to help their mother Pina, then sixty-two, fulfill a lifelong dream —to have her own pasta store. Her mother and grandmother had run a store in Naples, and she wanted one of her own.

The pasta here is made in an extruder and contains no eggs. Some may prefer the richness and texture eggs provide, but pasta *is* less fattening made this way. I found that it cooks well and has a good, slightly chewy texture. Marco says that they will make egg dough on request, as a special order.

Prices are a little high for plain pasta. The filled pastas are more interesting here; they are made by hand. When I visited, Pina was busily spooning squash filling into large round ravioli. I especially liked the **squash *agnoletti*** and the **sweet potato ravioli.** You won't see these unusual pasta posted in the menu behind the counter; that list just includes the traditionals. But the freezer is filled with all kinds of tempting filled pastas— **prosciutto, veal, sun-dried tomato, lobster, scallop.** Call in advance to see if they have what you want; what is in stock varies from day to day.

Pina Pasta is one of the few places I found that makes

their **tortellini** by hand. They'll make any filling to order; they have **cheese, spinach, meat,** and **chicken** fillings on hand. They also make their **potato gnocchi** by hand, using fresh potatoes.

You can also buy **ravioli scraps**—the bits of extra dough collected from the cut ravioli shapes—to use in soups. Again, this item isn't posted; just ask.

For several years the store offered a selection of **prepared foods,** including a robust **chicken cacciatore, pasta with a spinach pesto, marinated green beans,** and very good Italian antipasto of **marinated mushrooms and artichokes.** In early 1995 they stopped offering these items on a daily basis in their display case. They still have an extensive menu, but they make everything to order only. Also to order, they sell Pina's homemade **Italian bread,** a pricey loaf ($8) that takes twenty-four hours for them to prepare. "It's a special loaf," Marco says. "My mother makes it exactly the way her grandmother did. You don't have this bread every day. Save it for Sunday dinner. And it tastes better as it gets older."

WELLESLEY

Pasta Etc. See Framingham, page 101.

THE BESTS OF THE BEST

Best traditional flat pasta: **Biagi** (which may not be around for too much longer), then **Noodles**
Best exotic flat pasta: **Pasta del Palato**
Best traditional filled pasta: **Pasta Bene** and **Noodles**
Best exotic filled pasta: **Noodles,** then **Capone**
Best pesto: **Noodles**
Best spinach ravioli: **Nonna Pasta**
Best potato gnocchi: **Lilly's**
Best tomato sauce: **Trio's Ravioli Shoppe;** close second **Sabella's**
Best meat sauce: **Noodles**

CHAPTER FOUR

SOME THINGS FISHY

*Where to get the freshest flounder, super salmon, luscious lobster,
as well as other seafood delights*

BOSTON is a seafood lover's paradise. A major northeastern port, it is a gateway to the cold waters of the Atlantic Ocean. Extremely fresh fish is always available—there is no reason to suffer with frozen versions here.

In most places, the seafood comes from Atlantic waters, and you can also find fish flown in on ice from the Pacific or other waters. Supermarkets have reasonable fish selections, although those in the seafood industry recommend against buying fish at the supermarket, since the freshness can be questionable. Seafood markets are your best bet, both for selection and for freshness. Key to keep in mind when you go to a fish market: You shouldn't smell fish. Fresh fish doesn't smell. Only as it begins to age does it release a characteristic fishy smell.

The Boston area is a great source for lobster, and the fish markets closest to the sea seem to have the liveliest of these critters. If you go to a port town such as Marblehead or Gloucester, you may be able to buy lobster directly from a lobsterman. Wander around the docks, and you may see handpainted signs advertising great prices. Inquire and they'll pull up their catch—right from the ocean. If you are feeling less adventurous, try one of the markets that specializes in lobster. The primary areas for business in the seafood industry are Boston, Gloucester, and New Bedford.

You can get fresh fish from all over the world in Boston, but the freshest seafood will be from local waters. In addition to lobster, this includes clams, mussels, sand crabs, and sea scallops, along with cod, dogfish, flounder, gray sole, haddock, hake, monkfish, ocean catfish, pollock, and skate. The famous Boston scrod is actually not a fish but a term used to describe either a small cod, or any fresh local white fish, including haddock or pollock.

Summer is a great time for fish, and migratory fish that come to our waters include bluefish, mackerel, shark, striped bass, swordfish, and tuna. Summer is also a fabulous time for fresh bay scallops. Note that fish names vary from place to place —one man's steak fish is another man's pollock.

* Described in another chapter.

FISHMONGERS

Bay State Lobster	Boston
Boston Fish Market	Dorchester
Boston Fish Pier	Boston
Boston Harbor Fisheries	Boston
Cape Cod Shellfish and Seafood	Boston
Fraser Fish	Boston
Great Eastern Seafood Inc.	Boston
Ideal Seafood	Boston
John Mantia & Sons Co. Inc.	Boston
Jordan Brothers Seafood	Boston
Point Judith Shellfish Co.	Boston
Puritan Fish Co.	Boston
Sousa Seafood	Boston
*Boyajian Boston	Newton
*Cheng Kwong Seafood Market	Boston
Cherry Street Fish Market	Danvers
Choe's Fish Market	Weymouth
Court House Fish Market	Cambridge
Fernandes Fish Market	Cambridge
The Fishmonger	Cambridge
Frank A. Giuffre & Sons Fishmarket	Boston
*The Haymarket	Boston
James Hook & Co.	Boston
JP Seafood	Jamaica Plain
Legal Sea Foods Market Place	Allston, East Boston, Newton

Lexington Lobster and Seafood	Lexington
Marblehead Lobster Co.	Marblehead
Morse Fish Co.	Boston
New Deal Fish Market	Cambridge
Roslindale Fish Market	Roslindale
Rowand Fisheries	Beverly
Spence & Co., Limited	Easton
Tony's Daily Fish Market	Roxbury
Turner's Seafood Grill & Market	Melrose
Wulf's Fish Market	Brookline

BOSTON

BOSTON

Bay State Lobster

379–395 Commercial Street, Boston, MA 02109   (617) 523-7960
Mail order: available   Hours: Mon.–Thurs. 8 A.M.–6 P.M.;
    Fri., Sat. 7 A.M.–6 P.M.; Sun. 7 A.M.–1 P.M.

Bay State Lobster lives up to its name by carrying lots of fresh lobster. They also carry several other shellfish, including clams and mussels. You'll find all the standard fish here as well— salmon, swordfish, haddock, halibut.

The space is vast. Lobster tanks line the right wall as you enter, and aisles of coolers run horizontally down the center of the store. The coolers are filled with fish-related prepared food, made by Bay State, such as **clam chowder, baked stuffed lobster, finnan haddie,** and all kinds of sauces—**cocktail, lobster, tartar,** and **scampi.** There are also several kinds of smoked fish, including salmon, trout, and eel. Freezers contain frozen seafood, such as shrimp and buckets of fish sticks.

The quality of the prepared foods varies, but it's worth experimenting, and prices here are reasonable.

Boston Fish Pier

Northern Avenue, Boston, MA
See individual addresses, below

My first trip to the behind-the-scenes Boston Fish Pier was several years ago, when I was searching the town for five pounds of monkfish in November. I called around and nobody had any— except Boston Harbor Fisheries, located on the Boston Fish Pier.

The Boston Fish Pier is a place tourists don't go, a group of fish outlets near the World Trade Center. There are close to two dozen businesses here. Boston Harbor and the other fisheries are primarily wholesale establishments, catering largely to restaurants and hotels. You pull up your car to a loading dock; stairs are located every fifty feet or so. The Fish Pier addresses indicate the bays where the businesses are located. The signs with company names are often unobtrusive and easy to miss.

At Boston Harbor Fisheries the small entranceway has a window to an office, where you pay, and a door leading into the main room, where about half a dozen people are busy cleaning fish. There are no showrooms, no display cases, just tubs of ice holding cleaned fish. They had been holding my five pounds of monkfish when I arrived, and a young man obligingly severed the weighty spine bone from the meat and wrapped my purchase for me. Generally, Boston Harbor doesn't do fine-tuning filleting, though. The prices at the Fish Pier businesses are dirt cheap, sometimes half that of retail stores. And the fish is incredibly fresh—it all comes straight off the boat into the fishery.

Most of the Boston Fish Pier businesses sell only wholesale. Following are names of establishments that will also sell to individuals. It is best to call in advance and reserve your order. Some places specialize in what are called *ground fish;* this includes most fin fish, such as haddock and monkfish. Others focus on shellfish, and others offer both. Some places will gut and fillet your fish; others just sell it as is. The three fisheries I like best are Boston Harbor Fisheries, Jordan Brothers Seafood, and Sousa Seafood, primarily because they are the friendliest and the most helpful.

The area surrounding the Fish Pier is undergoing major construction. The Boston Fish Pier will remain, but nearby improvements are underway. Portions of the massive transportation project are encroaching on this area, a courthouse and a couple of hotels are being built, and a new T stop is in the works.

Boston Harbor Fisheries

29–31 Boston Fish Pier, Boston, MA 02210   (617) 423-2696
Mail order: not available   Hours: Mon.–Fri. 7 A.M.–5 P.M.;
     Sat. 7 A.M.–noon; closed Sun.

Cape Cod Shellfish and Seafood
33–35 Boston Fish Pier, Boston, MA 02210   (617) 423-1555
Mail order: available   Hours: Mon.–Fri. 6 A.M.–4:30 P.M.;
closed Sat., Sun.

Fraser Fish
4 Boston Fish Pier, Boston, MA 02210   (617) 426-4374
Mail order: available   Hours: Mon.–Fri. 7 A.M.–3 P.M.;
closed Sat., Sun.

Great Eastern Seafood Inc.
37–45 Boston Fish Pier, Boston, MA 02210   (617) 423-3666
Mail order: not available   Hours: Mon.–Fri. 8 A.M.–4 P.M.;
closed Sat., Sun.

Ideal Seafood
21–23 Boston Fish Pier, Boston, MA 02210   (617) 482-9160
Mail order: not available   Hours: Mon.–Fri. 6 A.M.–4 P.M.;
closed Sat., Sun.

John Mantia & Sons Co. Inc.
32–34 Boston Fish Pier, Boston, MA 02210   (617) 542-1076
Mail order: available   Hours: Mon.–Fri. 6:30 A.M.–5 P.M.;
closed Sat., Sun.

Jordan Brothers Seafood
1 Boston Fish Pier, Boston, MA 02210   (617) 261-9797
Mail order: available   Hours: Mon.–Fri. 6 A.M.–3 P.M.;
closed Sat., Sun.

Point Judith Shellfish Co.
2–4 Boston Fish Pier, Boston, MA 02210   (617) 482-1474
Mail order: not available   Hours: Mon.–Fri. 7:30 A.M.–3:30 P.M.;
closed Sat., Sun.

Puritan Fish Co.
16 Boston Fish Pier, Boston, MA 02210   (617) 426-9264
Mail order: not available   Hours: Mon.–Fri. 7:30 A.M.–3:30 P.M.;
closed Sat., Sun.

Sousa Seafood
9 Boston Fish Pier, Boston, MA 02210   (617) 428-6976
Mail order: available   Hours: Mon.–Fri. 7 A.M.–5 P.M.;
Sat. 10 A.M.–2 P.M.; closed Sun.

Cheng Kwong Seafood Market. See "The World in a Jar," page 395.

Frank A. Giuffre & Sons Fishmarket
71 Salem Street, Boston, MA 02113   (617) 227-6429
Mail order: not available   Hours: Mon.–Sat. 7 A.M.–7 P.M.;
    closed Sun.

The fish in this North End market is very fresh, and the proprietors are friendly and helpful. They occasionally have hard-to-find offerings, such as fresh sardines and eels.

The Haymarket. See "Earthly Delights," page 50.

James Hook & Co.
15 Northern Avenue, Boston, MA 02210   (617) 423-5500
Mail order: available   Hours: Mon–Thurs. 6 A.M.–5 P.M.;
    Fri. 6 A.M.–6 P.M.; Sat. 6 A.M.–3 P.M.; Sun. 8 A.M.–1 P.M.

James Hook & Co. is an excellent source for lobster. This third-generation company has been selling lobster since 1925 and has been at this prime location at the corner of Atlantic Avenue and Northern Avenue for many years. I had passed it hundreds of times before I finally went in.

There are two things going for Hook's lobster. First, since Hook is primarily a wholesale business, they buy a tremendous amount of lobsters frequently, directly from Maine, so the lobster is very fresh. Second, they keep their lobster in tanks filled with fresh seawater, which co-owner Al Hook says greatly improves the flavor. "We have a constant circulation of new water all the time," he says. "We pump water in from the ocean, through a filter, into the tanks, and back out again." The tanks that most fish markets have are closed systems, filled with fresh water to which sea salt has been added. In the coldest part of the winter the water streaming out the side of the building freezes into a lovely sea-green waterfall.

You may notice that a lot of restaurants have lobster specials in the summer. This is not simply because summer is beach season and lobsters taste good in the warm weather. It is because summer is lobster season. It is also when lobsters have soft shells; this is when they molt, shedding their old shells, and the new shells take a few months to firm up. Al Hook says he prefers soft-shelled lobster, also called *shedders,* because he finds the meat sweeter and juicier. However, others find this meat loose and watery; one cookbook author advises that you avoid shedders. These lobsters do have less meat than their hard-shelled counterparts, and are cheaper, because they weigh less.

In addition to whole, live lobsters, Hook sells fresh **cooked lobster meat.** This is significantly more expensive; it takes five to six pounds of live lobsters to make one pound of meat. There are four kinds of meat. The premium, most expensive, meat is straight tail, followed by tail and claw, knuckle, and salad meat, which is made from broken pieces.

Hook sells mainly shellfish; in addition to lobster they have fresh steamers, cherrystones, littlenecks, oysters, mussels, and scallops, and a few prepared items such as stuffed clams; they don't make the prepared foods themselves, and it's not worth buying the ones they offer. They also have fin fish, such as scrod, salmon, and swordfish, which they buy from the piers down the street.

Morse Fish Co.

1401 Washington Street, Boston, MA 02118   (617) 262-9375
Mail order: not available   Hours: Mon.–Thurs. and Sat. 8 A.M.–6 P.M.;
     Fri. 8 A.M.–7 P.M.; closed Sun.

This company, which also sells wholesale to restaurants, has been in business for over ninety years. You can sit at tables and order a selection of items such as **fish and chips** or **fried clams,** but the reason to visit Morse is the raw fish. It's incredibly fresh, and the pieces are downright cheap—similar to what you might find on the piers, but you don't have to buy in bulk. The prices reflect the availability, and they fluctuate, but on a recent visit I found absolutely beautiful fresh tuna steaks for around $6 a pound.

ALLSTON

Legal Sea Foods Market Place

33 Everett Street, Allston, MA 02134   (617) 787-2050
Mail order: available, call 1-800-477-LEGAL
Hours: Mon.–Fri. 9 A.M.–7 P.M.; Sat. 9 A.M.–4:30 P.M.; closed Sun.

Logan Airport, East Boston, MA 02118   (617) 569-4622
Hours: Mon.–Sat. 6:30 A.M.–9:30 P.M.; Sun. 10 A.M.–9:30 P.M.

43 Boylston Street, Chestnut Hill, Newton, MA 02167   (617) 277-0404
Hours: Mon.–Thurs. 9 A.M.–8 P.M.; Fri., Sat. 9 A.M.–9 P.M.;
     Sun. 10 A.M.–8 P.M.

Legal Sea Foods restaurants are famous for featuring straightforward preparations of dozens of fish and seafood. At this writing, there are ten restaurants in the Boston area, and three fish markets. The market in Allston is adjacent to Legal's headquarters. The selection is not extensive; on an average visit there may be a dozen kinds of seafood available, most of it familiar—salmon, tuna, swordfish, halibut, rainbow trout, shrimp, scallops, live lobster. The prices are average to high. The helpfulness of the staff varies depending on who is waiting on you. Some can answer any preparation questions; others shrug and look at you blankly. But the fish is very fresh and very good, and you get a free lemon with every seafood purchase.

You can also get prepared food here, including salads and Legal's deservedly famous creamy **fish chowder.** Several sandwiches are made to order. The **tuna salad** is predictable, but the **smoked-bluefish salad** is something special.

The Allston market has a warehouse feel to it, the no-frills atmosphere that was characteristic of Legal Sea Foods when it first started. Chestnut Hill is the largest market; it is fancier, with more take-out foods available.

For those on their way out of town via Logan Airport, there is a raw bar, and you can get frozen fish chowder and live lobsters for that taste of Boston.

Legal also makes excellent ice cream; see "Frozen Delights," page 300.

DORCHESTER

Boston Fish Market

1484 Dorchester Avenue, Dorchester, MA 02122   (617) 272-2980
Mail order: not available   Hours: Mon.–Fri. 8:30 A.M.–7:30 P.M.;
  Sat. 8:30 A.M.–7 P.M.; closed Sun.

Boston Fish Market is a wide, airy store with a good selection
of standard fish shop fare—haddock, tuna, swordfish, scallops,
shrimp. They also carry a selection of harder-to-find fish, and
even print a list titled "Have You Heard of These Fishes?" These
include cusk, tautog, fluke, shark, and eel. The fish is very fresh,
and you can order anything you see and have it **broiled** or **fried,
with chips.**

JAMAICA PLAIN

JP Seafood

620 Centre Street, Jamaica Plain, MA 02130   (617) 522-0528
Mail order: not available   Hours: Mon.–Sat. 10 A.M.–8 P.M.
  (until 7 P.M. in winter); closed Sun.

JP Seafood is a little intimidating from the outside—the windows are clouded over, and you can't really see inside. But step
in. The seafood here is very fresh and appealing, and the staff is
helpful and accommodating.

  The store also does a lot of take-out business, and makes
inexpensive **dinners to go** from all kinds of fish, including **rainbow trout, gray sole, red snapper, whiting,** and **bluefish.** The
seafood plate includes shrimp, scallops, clams, and fish of the
day served with fries, onion rings, and cole slaw.

ROSLINDALE

Roslindale Fish Market

39 Poplar Street, Roslindale, MA 02131   (617) 327-9487
Mail order: not available   Hours: Mon.–Sat. 9 A.M.–7 P.M.;
  closed Sun.

Roslindale Fish Market is as much a Greek market as it is a
seafood source. The first items that greet you as you enter are
produce, displayed on a table in the center area. The fresh fish
section is by the opposite wall, with good-looking fish. Fresh
sardines are occasionally available. There is also a selection of

Greek cheeses, including five kinds of feta, kasseri, *mannoliri,* and *kefalotiry.*

Though the produce selection is not huge, what is there is very fresh and well priced. A freezer lining one side of the long, narrow store, contains various frozen items such as octopus and quail; the shelves opposite offer various Greek and Middle Eastern items.

ROXBURY

Tony's Daily Fish Market

2249 Washington Street, Roxbury, MA 02119   (617) 227-6429
Mail order: not available   Hours: Mon.–Sat. 8 A.M.–6 P.M.;
  closed Sun.

From the outside, this Dudley Square shop does not look like much. The windows are painted with an amateurish mural, and the sign is smudged and hand-lettered. But when you enter, you are greeted by a noticeably nonfishy smell. The fish here is extremely fresh, and there is a huge selection. Tony Silva, originally from Portugal, first opened his shop in 1987 on the fish piers, before moving to this location. Because most of his clientele are from Caribbean countries, he specializes in fish popular in those areas, and he keeps his prices low. For that reason, you won't find pricier items such as salmon and swordfish here. You will find parrot fish, porgies, croakers, and some two dozen other hard-to-find fish. There's also doctor, whiting, stonebass, kingfish, sea trout, bahoo, butterfish, bluefish, mackerel, mullet, freshwater catfish, jack fish, dogfish, Florida grunt, goi, and a host of others. Silva is knowledgeable, and can tell you about the fish he offers and how to prepare it. The shop will clean, gut, and fillet your fish to order; most fish is kept whole for display.

METROPOLITAN BOSTON

BROOKLINE

Wulf's Fish Market

407 Harvard Street, Brookline, MA 02146   (617) 277-2506
Mail order: not available   Hours: Mon.–Fri. 6 A.M.–5:45 P.M.;
  Sat. 6 A.M.–4:30 P.M.; Sun. 8 A.M.–1 P.M.

Wulf's, you may notice from the posted hours, opens *very* early in the morning. "That's when the fish arrives," said one of the employees. "We have to get up early to find the best fish and the most variety, and we open the store as soon as the fish gets here."

All the fish sold at Wulf's are displayed on flat tables, on ice. The selection is extensive, with several unusual choices. On a given day, you might find red snapper, crayfish, and frogs' legs alongside the more common salmon and haddock. Whenever I enter the store, the two or three older men who work here tend to continue talking amongst themselves without looking up, but as soon as I have a question, one man will break from the group and offer helpful advice. The prices here are on the high end, but the quality and selection are excellent.

CAMBRIDGE

Court House Fish Market
484 Cambridge Street, Cambridge, MA 02141   (617) 878-6716
Mail order: not available   Hours: Tues., Wed., Sat. 8 A.M.–6 P.M.;
    Thurs., Fri. 8 A.M.–7 P.M.; closed Sun., Mon.
Restaurant hours: Mon. 10:30 A.M.–6 P.M.; Tues.–Sat. 10:30 A.M.–8 P.M.;
    closed Sun.

Court House Fish Market has been selling very fresh fish since 1920. They have a seafood restaurant next door that does a heavy take-out business.

The window to your right as you enter contains whole fish, or large pieces of fish, that look very fresh. Inside, a display case stretches to the back of the store. Most of the fish here is in plastic pans, already cut and cleaned. An exception is the conch; this is one of the few places I've seen conch in the shell. Across from the fish are shelves of Portuguese goods—breads, cookies, pudding mixes, jams.

Next door, you can taste how fresh the fish is by ordering any of the **dinners** or **plates.** The menu lists **sea scallops, scrod, haddock, salmon,** or **blue fish,** to be **fried, broiled,** or **baked.** A sign on the door states that if you don't see a fish you want on the menu, you can pick one you like from the store, and they will prepare it for you.

There is also homemade **fish** and **clam chowder** and **seafood rolls** with various fillings, including **lobster, crab,** and **fried clams.**

Fernandes Fish Market

1097 Cambridge Street, Cambridge, MA 02141   (617) 576-1993
Mail order: not available   Hours: Mon.–Fri. 8 A.M.–7 P.M.;
    Sat. 8 A.M.–6 P.M.; closed Sun.

It almost seems as if "Fish Market" is a required moniker for shops on Cambridge Street—at least three places are so designated. Fernandes is as much an ethnic market as a fish market. In fact, when I visited, there was fresh-looking fish displayed in the small window, but nowhere else. On the counter there is **fried fish:** plates of a small, sardinelike fish called *sticokle,* with strips of red pepper; large chunks of tuna; pieces of batter-dipped scrod. There are also chunks of pork.

The display cases to your left and right as you enter the narrow store contain cheeses and fruit. There are several Portuguese cheeses, including *queijo vaquinha, bom petisco,* and *fromage serra.* There are also rounds of fresh white cheese, wrapped in plastic and kept in tubs of wheylike liquid, alongside tubs of salt pork.

A shelf in the middle of the store holds various Portuguese breads and baked goods, and the shelves along the wall contain grains, beans, and condiments.

The Fishmonger

252 Huron Avenue, Cambridge, MA 02138   (617) 661-4834
Mail order: not available   Hours: Mon. 11 A.M.–6:30 P.M.;
    Tues.–Fri. 10 A.M.–6:30 P.M.; Sat. 10 A.M.–5:30 P.M.; closed Sun.

The Fishmonger is a Huron Avenue institution, known for its fresh fish and creative take-out fish preparations. Current owner Cheryl Williams worked here for three years before she bought it in 1991.

The fish is extremely fresh, and Williams will tell you what's best. When I visited, she was impressed with the incredible freshness of a carton of bluefish; indeed, this was some of the best bluefish I have tasted.

The store has a menu of seafood creations, including seventeen **soups** and **chowders.** There are the standard **clam** and **fish chowders,** which are simple and creamy, complemented with chunks of potatoes. Then there are more interesting recipes. **Smoky fish chowder** is made with finnan haddie (smoked haddock). This haddock is also used to flavor **smoky corn chowder.** The most popular soup is the **Provençal fish soup,** flavored with fennel and saffron. Two are great in the summer: **shrimp gazpacho** and **cool cucumber and salmon soup,** with a buttermilk base.

There are also several cold salads, all with some kind of seafood theme. The most popular is **Pad Thai,** available on Thursdays only. Rice noodles are tossed with ground peanuts, lime, cilantro, and shrimp. Shrimp appears in most of the salads, including **shrimp and artichoke hearts** and **black bean with smoked shrimp.** There is also a **calamari and artichoke salad.**

There are several **entrées,** such as a **seafood lasagne** with tomato sauce and mussels, clams, shrimp, and scallops. **Mushroom lasagne** is rich, with a béchamel sauce and mushroom sauce covering layers of scallops and sole. There are several kinds of **fish cakes,** including **bluefish,** with corn and red peppers; **codfish,** with potatoes and both salt and fresh cod; **crabcakes, shrimp and scallop,** with shallots and lime; and **yam 'n salmon,** seasoned with dill.

New Deal Fish Market

622 Cambridge Street, Cambridge, MA 02141   (617) 876-8227
Mail order: not available   Hours: Tues.–Sat. 10 A.M.–7 P.M.;
    closed Sun., Mon.

New Deal is a serious fish market. There is fish on ice in the window, in plastic containers on the floor, and in a display case. Everywhere, the fish is whole, or in large hunks; there are no precut steaks. Some of the chunks of fish aren't exactly eye-catching, since they have not been gutted or filleted yet. "That keeps it very fresh," says owner Sal Fantasia. And he is a reason to come to the store. He is friendly, accommodating, and very knowledgeable when it comes to fish. Want to know the French name for *red mullet?* How about the Greek, or the Italian? Fantasia knows *(rouget, barboúni,* and *triglia,* respectively).

There is variety here as well. You'll find cod, salmon, tuna, and swordfish, which are common to most fishmongers. But then there are fresh sardines and delicate fresh anchovies, skate, red snapper, red comba. There is lobster, but not in a tank, so this is not the best source for lobster.

The store is also filled with goods from Portugal and Italy—olive oils and pastas, beans, many bags of Portuguese breads and pastries, and sturdy-looking cookies and cakes.

NEWTON

Boyajian Boston. See "An Epicurean Agenda," page 381.

Legal Sea Foods Market Place. See Allston, page 110.

NORTH

BEVERLY

Rowand Fisheries

2 Cabot Street, Beverly, MA 01915   (508) 927-1871
Mail order: not available   Hours: Mon.–Sat. 8 A.M.–6 P.M.;
Sun. 9 A.M.–5 P.M.
201 Essex Street, Beverly, MA 01915   (508) 922-7977
Mail order: not available   Hours: Tues., Wed., Sat. 10 A.M.–6 P.M.;
Thurs. 10 A.M.–6:30 P.M.; Fri. 9 A.M.–6:30 P.M.; Sun. noon–6 P.M.;
closed Mon.

Rowand's Cabot Street location is the main branch, and it is slightly larger than the Essex Street store. It's located right next to the Salem–Beverly bridge in Beverly, at the very beginning (or end, depending on where you're coming from) of Cabot Street. There has been construction going on here for years, and it can be difficult to pull into the lot, especially during rush hour. But persevere for fine, fresh fish.

Every Tuesday, the shop makes fresh **fish, clam,** and **seafood chowder.** It is sold both fresh and frozen, and it's best fresh, the day it is made. On alternate Mondays Rowand makes their own **fish stock** from haddock bones, which they use in their chowders. You can buy quarts of the stock **fresh** the day it is made, or **frozen.**

Rowand has a lobster tank, and they also sell cooked lobster. They are known for their **lobster roll.**

DANVERS

Cherry Street Fish Market

26 Hobart Street, Danvers, MA 01923   (508) 777-3449
Mail order: available   Hours: Mon.–Thurs. 10 A.M.–6 P.M.;
Fri., Sat. 9 A.M.–6 P.M.; closed Sun.

As the name implies, this fish market began in a small building on Cherry Street, but after several years they outgrew their space and moved over to Hobart Street. There's lots of parking and a big wide room that holds a good-sized lobster tank. Some of the lobsters swimming around are enormous; manager Lyle Smith says places such as Las Vegas casinos will order these multipounders to give away as door prizes.

Smith and owner Darryl Parker go to Gloucester every day at 5:30 in the morning as the boats unload. The result: a wonderful selection of very fresh fish. They also make a few prepared items, including a perfect **lobster roll**—fresh lobster meat, moistened with just enough mayonnaise to hold it together, offered at this writing for a reasonable $5.50. For lobster lovers who don't like cooking lobster, the store will cook a lobster of your choosing to order. They also make wonderful **haddock pies,** rich with cream and a traditional Ritz Cracker topping; these are available fresh or frozen.

MARBLEHEAD

Marblehead Lobster Co.
Beacon and Orne Streets, Marblehead, MA 01945   (617) 631-0787
Mail order: available   Hours: daily 9 A.M.–5:30 P.M.;
    January–mid-May closed Sun.

Lexington Lobster and Seafood
6 North Hancock Street, Lexington, MA 02173   (617) 862-7630
Mail order: available through the Marblehead store
Hours: Mon.–Sat. 9 A.M.–6 P.M.

Hugh Bishop grew up as a fisherman and a lobsterman. He describes the 1970s as a peak time for lobster. "When they discovered lobsters out in the canyons of the Continental Shelf off of Cape Cod, it was like the Gold Rush," Bishop recalls. "You could make a lot of money in the business. But for those of us going out in smaller boats, like I was, it was very dangerous. I'm lucky to be alive here today; I probably used up eight out of nine lives." Because of the danger involved in offshore lobstering, Bishop decided to buy Marblehead Lobster Co. in 1979.

Initially, lobster constituted 90 percent of the store's business. After a few years he and his sister and partner, Brenda Booma, branched out, and now they carry a wide variety of seafood. Marblehead probably has just about the freshest seafood around. Whereas the fish on the Boston Fish Pier comes in fresh off the boat; the fish Bishop gets is from both "day boats" and "trip boats." Trip boats go out to sea for a week or more. The fish they catch is put on ice, possibly for several days. Some of the fish at Marblehead comes from trip boats. But all the native fish comes from "day boats," boats that go out fishing and bring back their catch the same day. Bishop himself is a day fisherman; Marblehead Lobster Co. is the only fish market I visited where the owner catches fish for the store. Other day boats also supply the store. The lobster is local Marblehead lobster, brought in by area lobstermen. Booma runs the store while Bishop is out fishing.

Bishop's lobster is kept in tanks pumped with ocean water, although he thinks the salted fresh water used by other establishments doesn't affect the lobster's flavor. He and his sister use the ocean water because the store is right on the ocean, and it is easier. Bishop, like Al Hook of James Hook, prefers soft-shell to hard-shell lobster. He feels that soft-shell lobster is significantly sweeter. He also notes that although you get less meat, the shell is also lighter, so you're paying for less shell. You can also buy very good-quality fresh **cooked lobster meat** here; it ranges in price from $20 to $30 a pound, depending on the season. It takes five to six chicken, or 1-pound, lobsters to produce a pound of meat. Marblehead cleans their meat, removing the intestine and any cartilage.

In 1992 Bishop and Booma bought Lexington Lobster and Seafood in Lexington, which has a large kitchen. The Marblehead store cuts all the fish sold in both stores, and the Lexington store makes all the prepared food. They make several items, such as **fish, clam,** and **seafood chowder, lobster bisque,** and **seafood salad.** There is usually a **dinner entrée,** either already cooked and ready to be reheated, such as the **seafood lasagne;** or ready to be cooked, such as the **spinach-stuffed flounder** and the **sole stuffed with lobster and shrimp.** It is best to buy these dishes the day they are made; they will be fresh, in the refrigerated case. After a day they are frozen, and frozen fish just doesn't taste as good as fresh fish. The **soups** and **chowders** are sold hot at lunchtime, but also cold and frozen. Although they freeze reasonably well, they are still better eaten fresh. The two stores also offer side dishes such as **potato salad** and **green bean salad with feta.**

MELROSE

Turner's Seafood Grill & Market

506 Main Street, Melrose, MA 02176   (617) 662-0700
Mail order: not available   Hours: Tues.–Thurs. 9 A.M.– 9 P.M.;
  Fri., Sat. 9 A.M.–10 P.M.; Sun. 3 P.M.–9 P.M.; closed Mon.

From the 1950s until the mid-1980s, Turner Fisheries was a
well-known, reputable wholesale seafood processing plant. So
reputable, in fact, that when the Westin Hotel in Boston opened
its restaurant, they chose to name it after Turner Fisheries. The
processing plant went out of business in the mid-1980s, and the
Turners then moved to Gloucester and opened a new processing
plant, called J. Turner Seafood. Turner's Seafood Grill & Market
is a spin-off of that business. Co-owner Chris Turner says, "We
felt that after supplying restaurants for so long, we had a good
idea of what we needed to do for the area."

   The restaurant occupies the bulk of the space here, and
everything on the menu is available to go. The market area is to
your right as you enter. It is small but complete, with strikingly
fresh fish, and reasonable prices. You'll find the standards—all
kinds of white fish (cod, haddock, pollock), swordfish, salmon,
yellowfin tuna. There will also be fish such as mahimahi (dol-
phin), sturgeon, and tilapia. There is a lobster tank and a variety
of shellfish.

   The market also offers some **prepared items,** such as all
sizes of **cooked shrimp,** a pricey **lobster pie, fish** and **crab
cakes,** and **stuffed clams.**

SOUTH

EASTON

Spence & Co., Limited

719 Washington Street, Easton, MA 02375   (508) 238-0099
Mail order: available   Hours: Mon.–Fri. 8 A.M.–5 P.M.;
  closed Sat., Sun.

I first tried Spence & Co.'s smoked salmon at a seafood show. Of
the dozen smoked salmons I tried, Spence's was by far the best.

   Alan Spence started his company in this area in 1990.
He hails from Scotland originally and has been working in the

fishing industry "my whole life," he says. He has been smoking fish—a common practice in Scotland—since he was eleven. Spence has a wealth of information on smoking; he has even put together a booklet describing the history of the art. He explains that other countries would preserve fish by drying it, but because the air is so moist in Scotland, people would hang fish for drying by the fire—hence the smoky flavor. With the advent of refrigeration it was no longer necessary to smoke fish to preserve it, so smoking became merely a method of preparation, for taste.

Spence uses exclusively farmed Atlantic salmon, noting that Atlantic salmon is best. When the gutted fish arrives, each one is covered with salt, to draw out the moisture. They are rinsed and then smoked in a high-tech $120,000 smoker that controls the humidity and produces the most consistent results. The fish is smoked with bones intact. These and the surface skin are removed after smoking. Spence emphasizes that no part of the **smoked salmon** you buy in his packages has been in direct contact with the smoke, so the fish has a smooth, buttery texture. The areas that were directly smoked, while tasty, can be tough and dry; Spence uses these bits to make his rich, creamy **smoked salmon pâté.**

The salmon is cold-smoked, which means that the texture is like that of raw fish. Spence also hot-smokes a few fish, including **mackerel** and **trout.** The smoked trout is good, but not that flavorful, especially when compared to the smoked salmon, which is wonderful. Also quite good is the **Gravlax,** which is a cured salmon. When I visited, Spence was in the process of perfecting another cured salmon, **pastrami salmon.** He also makes a boneless **finnen haddock.** This smoked haddock is named for the Scottish village Findon; the name is often further mutated to *finnan haddie.*

The Easton location is a wholesale plant, but you can purchase fish here. You can also buy the fish in area health-food and gourmet shops, including Bread & Circus, Cardullo's, and the Fruit Center.

WEYMOUTH

Choe's Fish Market

409 Washington Street, Weymouth, MA 02188   (617) 331-2901
Mail order: not available   Hours: Mon.–Wed. 9:30 A.M.–9 P.M.;
  Thurs.–Sat. 9:30 A.M.–10 P.M.; Sun. 9:30 A.M.–8 P.M.

Choe's is a small ethnic market–seafood store located on a busy
street. On one side is a small but in-depth selection of Asian
goods, including rice vinegar, noodles, and various condiments.
On the other side is the fish market, including a lobster tank,
with good-looking, fresh fish.

WEST

LEXINGTON

Lexington Lobster and Seafood. See Marblehead, page 118.

THE BESTS OF THE BEST

Best fish market: **Marblehead Lobster Co., New Deal Fish Market,** and
   Morse Fish Co.
Best lobster source: **Marblehead Lobster Co.**
Best lobster roll: **Cherry Street Fish Market**
Best prepared food: **The Fishmonger**

CHAPTER FIVE

WHERE'S THE BEEF?

Area butchers who offer beef, pork, lamb, veal, and poultry,
as well as homemade sausages and wild game.
Also, sources for halal and kosher meats.

BEFORE the advent of supermarkets, neighborhood butchers were common. But today most people rely on supermarkets as their source for meat, and neighborhood butchers are few and far between. The Hilltop, a well-known landmark in Saugus and Braintree, seemed to recognize this and developed, essentially, a supermarket butchery. But a butcher is still the best source for meat. A good butcher, like a good baker, is an artist, and the meat you get will invariably be superior. The butchers I visited are devoted to their craft. Many are second- or third-generation butchers; some underwent European apprenticeships to hone their skills.

Unlike bread baking or pasta making, butchering is not a romantic skill. People like to think of meat magically appearing in the case or package, skinned, cut, and ready to grill. The butcher does the dirty work. I visited one butcher who was preparing a leg of lamb, which he had just severed from the animal, the rest of which was hanging from a hook in the ceiling. He trimmed sinew and fat, turning a carcass into a piece of palatable meat.

Sausage making is another skill; several area butchers make their own sausages, with varying degrees of success. There are all kinds of sausages; the most common is plain pork, followed by Italian hot and Italian sweet. There are other ethnic sausages around—kielbasa and other Polish blends, Irish links, and German bratwurst. There are also a few butchers who blend the sausage idea with the healthier eating idea to create chicken or turkey sausages.

Two religions have certain dietary laws attached to meat consumption—Jewish kosher meat and Muslim halal meat. Both require that certain procedures be followed during the slaughtering process. Pork is forbidden to both groups. There are only a handful of kosher and halal butchers in the Boston area, and I list them here.

For the freshest poultry, there are a few places that let you pick out a live chicken, which they will then slaughter and butcher. There are also a few turkey farms; you need to order these birds several weeks in advance of the holidays.

Most butchers carry the usual—beef, pork, lamb, veal, chicken, and turkey—all available fresh. Other, more unusual meats—such as rabbit, venison, duck, and goose—are generally sold frozen and are available by special order. A few places specialize in the truly exotic, such as alligator, buffalo, and lion.

Beef is classified into several grades. Out of a hundred cows, only three or four at most will be labeled prime. Most are graded choice, the next level.

Small butchers will cut meat to order; often they also have precut, or portion-cut, meat. The prepackaged meat comes in two forms—wrapped in plastic or vacuum-sealed (also called Cryovacked). The plastic-wrapped meat will last two or three days in the refrigerator, while the vacuum-sealed will last two or three weeks; both will last several months in the freezer.

Prices at a butcher may be higher than at a supermarket, but it is well worth finding a butcher you like. Once you establish a relationship you can order special cuts and gain valuable culinary advice such as how best to store meat or how to prepare an unfamiliar cut.

My friend Kim Sundik was an invaluable asset to this chapter. Her knowledge of meat is thorough, and she has been a sausage connoisseur for years.

MEAT

Abruzzese Meat Market	Boston
H. Averbuck & Company	Newton
The Danvers Butchery Inc.	Danvers
De Pasquale's Market	Newton
John Dewar & Co.	Newton
Di Paolo & Rossi Meat Market	Boston
J. P. Meat Market	Chelsea
Karl's Sausage Kitchen	Saugus
Kinnealey Meats	Milton
Mayflower Poultry	Cambridge
Moran's Butchers	South Boston
Nappi Meats & Groceries	Medford
New England Meat Market	Peabody, Cambridge
Owen's Poultry Farm	Needham
Paesani Meat Market	Boston
Previte's	Quincy
The Prime Shoppe	Boston
Salett's	Newton Highlands
Savenor's	Boston
Smokehouse	Norwell
Sulmona Meat Market	Boston
Tony's Meat Market	Roslindale

HALAL SOURCES

Blackstone Halal Market	Boston
Brighton Meat Market and Grocery	Brighton
Cambridge Halal Meat Market & Grocery Store	Cambridge
Cheema's Supermarket	Brighton
Haymarket Bargain Basement	Boston
Khyber Halal Meat Market	Burlington
New Halal Meat & Grocery Store	Boston
Pak Halal Meat & Groceries	Brighton
Quality Meat Market	Roslindale

KOSHER SOURCES

American Kosher Products Co.	Mattapan
The Butcherie	Brookline
The Butcherie II	Canton
Gordon & Alperin Inc.	Newton
Hurwitz Kosher Meat Market	Framingham
Levine's Kosher Meat	Peabody
Randolph Kosher Meat Market	Randolph

❖ MEAT ❖

BOSTON

THE NORTH END

The North End has the highest concentration of butchers anywhere in the Boston area. Following are some excellent butcher shops.

Abruzzese Meat Market

94 Salem Street, Boston, MA 02113   (617) 227-6140
Mail order: not available   Hours: Tues.–Sat. 6:30 A.M.–6 P.M.;
    closed Sun., Mon.

Di Paolo & Rossi Meat Market

56 Salem Street, Boston, MA 02113   (617) 227-7878
Mail order: not available   Hours: Mon.–Thurs. 8 A.M.–6 P.M.;
    Fri. 8 A.M.–7 P.M.; Sat. 7 A.M.–6 P.M.; closed Sun.

Paesani Meat Market

120 Salem Street, Boston, MA 02113   (617) 523-8507
Mail order: not available   Hours: Mon.–Sat. 6:30 A.M.–6:30 P.M.;
    closed Sun.

Sulmona Meat Market

32 Parmenter Street, Boston, MA 02113   (617) 742-2791
Mail order: not available   Hours: Tues.–Sat. 8 A.M.–6 P.M.;
    closed Sun., Mon.

Sulmona is a small butchery that sells excellent meat. Everything is cut to order—even the ground beef. There is a display case, but almost nothing is on display—just a few items wrapped up, waiting for customers to pick them up. You'll know you've come to the right place, however, because there is almost always a long line of people.

Three kinds of **sausage** are available daily—**Italian sweet, Italian hot,** and **liver,** made with garlic and orange peel (intriguing, but an acquired taste). Sulmona carries choice beef, lamb, and pork, but they are known for their veal, which is wonderful, especially the **osso buco.** They also have excellent fresh rabbit.

BOSTON

The Prime Shoppe
104–112 Faneuil Hall Marketplace, Boston, MA 02109
  (617) 523-1206
Mail order: available   Hours: daily 9 A.M.–9 P.M.

Faneuil Hall of today seems an unlikely spot for a butcher, but this is where you'll find The Prime Shoppe, a source for very good meat.

The main meats here are beef and poultry, and some lamb; everything is fresh and vacuum-sealed. The poultry includes fresh chicken, turkey, and duck. Other cuts and meats available are New York strip steak, **filet mignon wrapped with bacon,** boneless prime rib, prime rib, smoked goose, and smoked pheasant.

According to Prime Shoppe owner Branko Pishev, prime beef should age for twenty-five to thirty days for maximum flavor. While the beef here is very good, poultry in recent years has been the best-seller, especially turkey. The Prime Shoppe sells more than seven hundred **roasted turkeys** (not stuffed) for Thanksgiving.

If you want to try the meat before buying a few pounds, order a **sandwich**—all are made from the store's meats, cooked on the premises. Try the succulent **prime aged filet mignon sandwich** with mushrooms, onions, and peppers. Other sandwiches include a **marinated chicken breast, prime roast beef,** and **roast turkey.** There is also good homemade **pork sausage,** sometimes available on a stick. For the diet-conscious, the **turkey burgers** are a popular item.

Savenor's
160 Charles Street, Boston, MA 02114   (617) 723-MEAT (6328)
Mail order: available   Hours: Mon.–Fri. 9 A.M.–8:30 P.M.;
  Sat. 9 A.M.–8 P.M.; Sun. noon–7 P.M.

Savenor's was started in Cambridge in 1939 by Abraham and Dora Savenor as a gourmet market; their son Ronnie Savenor helped establish the shop's reputation for quality and exotic meats, and was known as neighborhood resident Julia Child's butcher. Then, in 1992, the store suffered an unexpected, devastating fire. But by the end of the year, son Ronnie had opened Savenor's in a new location, at the foot of Beacon Hill. The new digs are significantly smaller—the Cambridge store was the size of a small supermarket—which makes its specialty, meat, that much more noticeable. The back of the store is devoted to a butchery, where knowledgeable butchers will cut your meat to order. The store also makes excellent homemade **meatballs** and **Italian sausage,** and portion-cut meat is available along one of the store's two aisles.

The quality of meat here is superb. Talk to owner Ronnie Savenor for a few minutes and you'll get an education in butchery. The beef is all prime, the top grade, but pork is the true specialty here. Savenor's buys whole pigs from a farm in New Hampshire, and they sell all cuts. They make their own **head cheese** and smoke their own **bacon** and **ham.** The lamb and veal are also excellent.

In addition to quality traditional meats (which you do pay for—the prices here are high), the store specializes in both common and obscure game meats. There's a whole line of game birds (squab, quail, goose, and partridge, to name a few) and meats such as venison, goat, rabbit, and wild boar. Depending on the season, these items are available fresh or frozen. For the adventurous, there are all kinds of exotic meats, including lion ($21.99/pound), bear, and llama. The store also sells a selection of fresh and smoked seafood.

Meats are Savenor's main attraction, but the store also offers a wide selection of gourmet items, including breads from area bakeries such as Clear Flour and Iggy's; rich cakes and pies from Creative Gourmet and Sweet Endings; and a variety of imported cheeses. They have a selection of flavored fresh pastas, in creative flavors such as red wine, ginger, and Spanish saffron. Various condiments and teas line the shelves, and there is a small produce section.

ROSLINDALE

Tony's Meat Market
4253 Washington Street, Roslindale, MA 02131   (617) 323-7313
Mail order: not available   Hours: Tues.–Sat. 8 A.M.–5 P.M.;
    closed Sun., Mon.

Tony deBenedictis has been a butcher since 1963, and in this location since 1969. He specializes in fresh meat, cut to order, primarily lamb, beef, pork, and veal. "I didn't know anything about meat when I started," deBenedictis confesses. He had bought the business with his father and brother-in-law. When they discovered that the previous owner had been a gambler and the business was failing deBenedictis's father wanted to sell. "But I said no. I wanted to prove I could do it."

When a butchery in Roslindale came up for sale, deBenedictis decided to go into business for himself and buy it. The meat cutter, who had been there for forty years, was still employed there, and deBenedictis arranged to have him stay on for a few weeks to teach him more about the business. "Two weeks turned into fifteen years," deBenedictis recalls. "He stayed with us until he died. He's the one who taught me how to make sausage." DeBenedictis now runs the business with his wife, Sarah.

The long narrow store has a wooden floor that stretches to the back. Shelves line the walls, filled with imported Italian goods, such as pastas, confections, olive oils, vinegars, and cheeses. These are a little on the pricey side, but it's convenient to have such items available when you're purchasing meat.

The store offers deBenedictis's own **sausage, hot** and **sweet,** which is very good. For holidays such as Easter, deBenedictis sells baby lamb and goat, and fresh rabbit is often available. In addition, there is a full selection of Italian deli meats.

SOUTH BOSTON

Moran's Butchers

472 West Broadway, South Boston, MA 02127   (617) 464-2406
Mail order: not available   Hours: Mon.–Sat. 9 A.M.–7 P.M.;
    closed Sun.

The display windows at Moran's are more than nondescript; they are empty. You have to walk down a length of store before finally reaching anything for sale. But once you reach the butchery at the back, you'll be glad you stuck it out. The specialty here is Irish meats, including rashers of bacon and boiling bacon, which is similar to corned beef in texture. Owner Billy Moran makes **Irish pork sausage** (a breakfast sausage) a few times a week; the time to get it is Thursday mornings. He also makes **blood pudding,** and at Christmas and Easter you can get **Irish hams,** which are boiled and then baked.

In addition to meats, Moran's has assorted produce and a small selection of Irish goods—cookies, candies, and jams.

METROPOLITAN BOSTON

CAMBRIDGE

Mayflower Poultry

621 Cambridge Street, Cambridge, MA 02141   (617) 547-9191
Mail order: not available   Hours: Mon.–Thurs. and Sat.
   7 A.M.–4:15 P.M.; Fri. 7 A.M.–5 P.M.; closed Sun.

As its name implies, Mayflower Poultry specializes in poultry, especially chicken. The spacious room behind the small entranceway features fresh chicken, already cut in every way imaginable—roasters, fryers, whole, half, parts, legs, drumsticks, wings, and so on. You can buy the already cut chicken at very reasonable prices, or you can check out the live chickens in a back room, which can be killed to order.

In addition to chicken, Mayflower stocks fresh turkey, capon, rabbit, and frozen Long Island duck, squab, pheasant, quail, and goose. They also sell eggs.

New England Meat Market. See Peabody, page 134.

CHELSEA

J. P. Meat Market

108 Chestnut Street, Chelsea, MA 02150   (617) 884-0421
Mail order: not available   Hours: Tues.–Sat. 8 A.M.–6 P.M.;
   closed Sun., Mon.

Frank Pietkiewicz's father started J. P. Meat Market in the 1930s, when there was a significant Polish population in Chelsea. The population has changed over time, but J. P. continues to produce Polish specialties, including very good **kielbasa,** both **fresh** and **smoked,** and an intriguing *kabanosy,* a dried sausage. Other meats in the deli case are from Kayem, whose factory is right down the street.

In addition to meats, J. P. carries a variety of eastern European–style goods, from stuffed cabbage (mediocre) in the freezer to their own bottled **horseradish.**

If you're lucky, you'll catch Pietkiewicz on a good day; otherwise he and the woman who works with him can be on the dour side. But it's worth tolerating if you like kielbasa, and only a handful of butchers around town make their own.

NEWTON

H. Averbuck & Company

547 Commonwealth Avenue, Newton, MA 02159 (617) 527-4110
Mail order: available Hours: Mon.–Fri. 8 A.M.–6 P.M.;
Sat. 8 A.M.–5 P.M.; closed Sun.

The Averbuck family has been in the food and meat business since 1931. Harold Averbuck's father and uncle had a butchery in Dorchester before moving to this location. Averbuck had run a grocery store for several years before opening his own butchery here in 1983. It is located in a Jewish neighborhood and specialize in kosher-style meat—traditional cuts that are not actually kosher. (Averbuck notes that there is not much demand for pork here.)

In addition to the cut-to-order prime and choice meat and poultry, Averbuck and his son make several prepared foods. Their **corned beef** is excellent, one of the best around. The **turkey Italian sausage** is also very good.

Knishes are a specialty, made with flaky puff pastry instead of the heavier dough frequently used for these stuffed pastries. Fillings include the traditional **meat, potato,** and **kasha,** plus a newfangled **spinach and cheese** (made with four cheeses) and **turkey,** made with homemade roast turkey and onions.

Other prepared foods included sweet-and-sour **stuffed cabbage** and **Krispy Duck by Averbuck,** a whole duck roasted on the rotisserie. There are also sauces and side dishes such as **rice pilaf** available.

De Pasquale's Market

325 Watertown Street, Newton, MA 02158 (617) 244-7633
Mail order: not available Hours: Tues.–Fri. 10 A.M.–5:30 P.M.;
Sat. 10 A.M.–4 P.M.; closed Sun., Mon.

241 Adams Street, Newton, MA 02158 (617) 332-1384
Mail order: not available Hours: Mon.–Fri. 7 A.M.–7 P.M.;
Sat. 7 A.M.–5 P.M.; closed Sun.

De Pasquale's specialty is **sausage,** and for years that is all the store sold. Maria De Pasquale's grandfather started the business as an Italian grocery; in 1969 her father, Peter, realized he was selling more sausage than anything else, so he decided to make that his business. Maria took over when he passed away in 1984; incidentally, she is the only female butcher I encountered in researching this book. She sold the business to her cousin Steven in 1990. He added a few other meats and Italian pastas, but Maria still makes the sausages.

I've heard many people rave about the **sausages,** and they live up to their good reviews. There are just two varieties— **Italian hot** and **Italian mild.** The sausages are made in the Watertown Street location; the Adams Street store sells the sausages, but it is more of a convenience store.

John Dewar & Co.
753 Beacon Street, Newton MA 02159   (617) 964-3577
Mail order: available   Hours: Mon.–Sat. 9 A.M.–5:45 P.M.; closed Sun.

John Dewar and Frank Donovan started John Dewar & Co. in 1981 to provide quality meats to the community. Within six months, their wholesale business outgrew the small Newton Center retail space, so they opened a separate wholesale operation in Roxbury. The Newton store's manager Harry Wedge has been with the store since 1983 and knows a lot about meat. Any questions you have about a certain cut—be it beef, pork, lamb, fowl, or game—Wedge can answer, and he will offer cooking instructions as well. The poultry is from Bell & Evans—the best, according to Wedge, and the beef is Angus and prime.

Dewar's is a good source for items such as **rack of lamb** and homemade **honey-baked ham,** and they make their own excellent **Italian sausage.** They offer other **prepared fresh meats,** such as a choice of **marinated chicken breasts** in several styles, including **French** (dill and basil), **Greek** (with spinach), and **Italian** (vinaigrette with sliced peppers and pine nuts). Just take the chicken breasts home and bake them. There's also a buttery **stuffed veal roast,** rolled with olive oil, garlic, pine nuts, three kinds of sweet peppers, and basil. There are also some frozen options, such as venison and buffalo patties, and duck and rabbit sausage.

In addition to meat, which is the primary focus of this store, several cheeses are available, some of which are hard to find, like a French Pyrené and *Bleu de Verne*. They also carry breads from Clear Flour, Iggy's, and Biga, (see pages 15, 33, and 6), and there's a selection of olive oils and condiments.

The meat at Dewar's is of amazing quality—but be prepared to pay for it. These are not bargain prices.

Salett's

170 Needham Street, Newton Highlands, MA 02161   (617) 527-6100
Mail order: available   Hours: Mon.–Fri. 8:30 A.M.–5:30 P.M.;
    Sat. 8:30 A.M.–3 P.M.; closed Sun.

Salett's has been in business since 1952, and the bulk of its sales have always been wholesale. This is not a huge store, but it is clean, and everything is nicely displayed. Open freezers line all the walls; the meat here is all vacuum-sealed and flash frozen, and so is the small amount of fish sold here.

Owner Seymour Salett is defensive about the fact that he sells only **frozen food,** and he gives a good argument for freezing his meat, noting that Salett's was "one of the pioneers of vacuum sealing." If you are going to freeze your meat anyway, it is better to get it flash frozen, because it will retain more of its flavor. The flash frozen meat is cut, wrapped, and frozen in about an hour. If you buy fresh meat and then freeze it, it can take several hours or even up to a day to freeze, and it loses flavor along the way.

The meat is good, and Salett's carries a range of cuts for beef, lamb, veal, and pork, as well as poultry. There are marinated items—**lemon-pepper** is popular—which are also frozen (I question how much meat can marinate after it's been frozen).

NORTH

DANVERS

The Danvers Butchery Inc.

10 Donegal Lane, Danvers, MA 01923   (508) 777-3000
Mail order: not available   Hours: Mon.–Wed. and Sat. 9 A.M.–6 P.M.;
    Thurs., Fri. 9 A.M.–8 P.M.; closed Sun.

The Danvers Butchery is an attractive, airy butchery. It, along with a sister shop in Newbury, has been in business for over fifty years. Portion-cut meat, vacuum-sealed, is displayed in open cases in the center of the store. In addition to items such as tenderloin, boneless rib eye, and top sirloin, there is a variety of packaged, marinated meats. These are good but not remarkable. The **lemon-pepper chicken** we tried had good meat, but the marinade was bland. On the other hand, a **teriyaki beef marinade** was tasty, but the meat was fatty. You are better off buying the meat by itself here.

Both large and small cuts of chicken, pork, beef, lamb, and veal are available. There is also an area of the store devoted to custom cutting—while you wait or if you order in advance. The refrigerated areas on the side walls hold **prepared foods.** The recommended **chicken salad,** is only mediocre, although the meat used was tender and moist.

MEDFORD

Nappi Meats & Groceries
370 Salem Street, Medford, MA 02155   (617) 391-7900
Mail order: not available   Hours: Tues.–Sat. 8:30 A.M.–6 P.M.;
    Sun. 9 A.M.–1 P.M.; closed Mon.

Joe and Anne Nappi have been cutting meats and making their own sausages since 1988. They make almost a dozen different kinds of **pork sausages,** from a mildly spiced, very juicy **plain pork** to a tangy **vinegar pepper.** But they sell more of their **chicken sausages,** which come in half a dozen flavors, including **garlic-cheese-wine** and **pineapple.** The sausages are all made fresh daily, and are sold fresh, not frozen. There are usually just two or three kinds available at any one time, so call ahead and see what the sausages of the day are.

Nappi's also provides a variety of meats available cut to order, including, on occasion, fresh rabbit. In addition to meats, Nappi has an extensive selection of imported Italian goods, including pastas, rice, canned tomatoes, olive oils, cookies, and other goods.

PEABODY

New England Meat Market
62 Walnut Street, Peabody, MA 01960   (508) 531-0846
Mail order: not available   Hours: Mon., Tues. 8 A.M.–6 P.M.;
    Wed.–Fri. 8 A.M.–7 P.M.; Sat. 8 A.M.–6 P.M.; Sun. 8 A.M.–3 P.M.

468 Broadway, Cambridge, MA 02138   (617) 547-2334
Mail order: not available   Hours: Mon.–Sat. 8 A.M.–9 P.M.;
    Sun. 11 A.M.–8 P.M.

New England Meat Market is one of the friendliest butcheries
I've visited. Charles Bougas's grandfather opened the Peabody
store in 1919, at the same location. When Bougas's father ran the
business, meat was definitely a part of the business, but not a
major part; it was as much a grocery store as a butchery. When
Charles took over from his father in 1985, he took on a partner,
Charles Silva, who had been working at the store for many years.
The two Charleses have put the emphasis on the meat business
over the past decade.

About a third of the meat they sell is marinated—there
are a total of about twenty marinades—and Bougas and Silva are
constantly experimenting with new flavors. The **marinated
meats** include **boneless chicken breast, chicken wings, beef
sirloin tips, pork cutlets, pork ribs,** and **lamb chops.** Both the
teriyaki sirloin tips and the **honey-barbecue chicken** are very
good. The **lemon-pepper chicken** is good, but the lemon juice
does affect the texture of the chicken to a certain extent. The
absolute best is their **marinated lamb,** cut for shish kabob and
marinated in a Greek-style blend of olive oil, lemon juice, garlic,
and rosé wine. This item is so popular you can get it both fresh
from the case or vacuum-sealed. Try the **lamb lollipops,** sliced
from a rack of lamb, which are fantastic. The **homemade sausage**
is also very good.

The Peabody store is like a large grocery store as well
as a butchery. You can find all sorts of items, from breads to
canned goods and produce. The store also carries a variety of
imported Greek and other ethnic specialties, such as olives and
feta cheese.

Bougas and Silva opened the Cambridge store in December 1994, and they find that the clientele of the two stores
differs significantly. They sell a lot more red meat in Peabody and
more chicken in Cambridge.

The butchered meats are the same in both places—
available cut to order and portion-cut and vacuum-sealed. The
quality of the meat is excellent, be it lamb, beef, pork, veal, or
poultry. They have actual **osso buco**— not renamed veal shanks.
And the store is happy to meet special requests; they'll supply
items such as baby lamb, suckling pigs, and goat to order. There

is also a small seafood section; the quality is good, but the selection is limited.

The Cambridge store has an extensive deli section. The long lines at lunchtime are testament to the popularity of the **sandwiches.** Along with the sandwiches are a few dozen **salads,** sold by the pound. Bougas notes that the **chicken salad** is very popular in Cambridge, and they supply several kinds, including **pesto chicken salad,** flavored with basil, Romano cheese, pine nuts, pecans, and anchovies. The **bacon chicken salad** is a much requested item. There are a variety of nonmeat items as well, from various **pasta salads** and **potato salads** to a **seafood medley** with lemon and pepper and a vinegary **broccoli salad** made with raisins, onions, and cheddar cheese.

A bakery recently opened in the Cambridge store has breads from area bakers and sweets from Carberry's (see page 17). They also make their own tasty **baklava.**

Of key importance to both Bougas and Silva is service. Whenever I've gone into either store, the staff has always been extremely courteous, patient, and helpful. If you have any questions about meat preparation, they will be happy to help you.

SAUGUS

Karl's Sausage Kitchen
142 Broadway, Saugus, MA 01942   (617) 233-3099
Mail order: not available   Hours: Mon.–Thurs. and Sat. 9 A.M.–6 P.M.;
  Fri. 9 A.M.–7 P.M.; closed Sun.

Michael Engel's father is the Karl who started this sausage-lover's heaven in 1958. Karl's grandfather was a butcher in Germany, and Karl learned his trade there before coming to this country. Karl's Sausage Kitchen is, as the name implies, a source for sausages; no regular cuts of meat are sold here; there simply isn't room.

The **Italian sweet** and **hot sausages** are very good, but that isn't why you come here; you can find good Italian sausages at many butchers. Karl's specialties are the German sausages. The **fresh sausages** are made every Wednesday; come on this day or Thursday for the best selection. There are several kinds of **bratwurst—fresh fine** (with finely ground pork), **fresh coarse** (with pork and veal), **smoked,** and **roasted,** also called **Thuringer,** which is ideal for grilling.

Smoked sausages include *Landjaeger,* a wonderful all-beef creation that is sort of a cross between beef jerky and a soft salami. It is cured and smoked, then seasoned with rum and caraway. This sausage is labor-intensive to make, so it is not cheap, but it is a very popular item, and I can understand why.

There are several **deli meats,** and Engel makes most of them. Most are pork-based, sometimes blended with veal or beef, as with the excellent **veal loaf** (also called *Leberkäs*), which is mildly spiced with nutmeg and paprika. There are two kinds of **salami,** a **mild** version and a **garlic** version. I recommend the latter, which is spiced with black peppercorns. Both are lean, not fatty, and much less salty than salami usually is. The **bologna** is homemade; I'm not a big fan of bologna, but this is a very good version. The *Jagdwurst* is more interesting; it is essentially bologna spiked with mustard seeds.

The **liverwurst** is very popular; Engel's sister, Susan, who also works in the store, says that people will remove the casing and serve it as pâté. It is creamy and very spreadable. It does have a strong liver taste. Karl's also has a homemade **frankfurter,** made from pork, beef, and veal, plus "Karl's gourmet frankfurter seasoning." Whatever is in it, this is one of the better pork hot dogs you're likely to find. There is also fresh and smoked **kielbasa.**

Engel smokes several meats, including **bacon,** both **slab** and **ready-to-eat.** The latter is cured and smoked three times, and you can eat it like salami. It has a strong flavor and is good to use in cooking to flavor a dish such as rice or potatoes. The **roast beef** is rare and buttery.

Karl's carries several deli meats that they do not make, but all are good. The turkey breast is flavorful, smoky without being salty. There are a few kinds of ham, including a Black Forest ham that is unbelievable—moister than prosciutto, but with a prosciutto-like taste. Black ham is another delicious pork preparation.

To accompany their deli meats, Karl's makes the best **potato salad** I've ever had. It is German-style, which means there is no mayonnaise, just oil and vinegar, and it tastes refreshing and is great for a picnic, midnight snack, lunch—anytime.

In addition to the meats, Karl's carries a big selection of

German and other European goods. Chocolates, candies, and sweets occupy several shelves, and during the holidays, the store carries stollen imported from Germany. There are also jams and condiments, smoked fish, herring fillets, smoked eels, and German pickles. There are sugar cones—literally a conical chunk of sugar—used for a heated holiday wine drink called *Feuerzangen Bowle*. Spiced wine is poured over the cone and slowly heated; the sugar gradually melts into the drink (ask Susan to describe how it's made). There are juices from Germany, including my favorite, sour cherry juice; there is also sour cherry syrup.

The shelves near the door usually contain dozens of breads. There are huge, ten-pound loaves of rye bread from two bakeries in Toronto, cut into chunks, and normal-size loaves from Alice's Home Bakery, a wholesale bakery in South Boston. Karl's stocks several loaves from Mestemacher and Schlünder, two German companies. I visited the store in July, and the bread offerings were scant; Susan said that Alice's was on vacation for the month. Deliveries normally come in late Wednesday; Thursday is probably the best day for breads here, but call and see what has arrived. When the shelves are full, there may be as many as two dozen different kinds of rye breads.

Susan and the other employees here are very helpful.

SOUTH

MILTON

Kinnealey Meats
6 Bassett Street, Milton, MA 02126   (617) 696-2260
Mail order: not available   Hours: Mon.–Sat. 8 A.M.–8:30 P.M.;
    Sun. 8 A.M.–6 P.M.

For over fifty years, Kinnealey Meats has supplied quality meats to food services and restaurants in New England, New York, and Bermuda. In 1985, when the Milton Marketplace opened, Kinnealey added a retail operation.

The meat is available both cut to order and portion-cut and vacuum-sealed. The quality of the meat is excellent. We had filet mignon tips that were amazingly tender when we cooked them. Since they are tips and not whole pieces, the price for this item is quite good. The prices for other cuts aren't as cheap, but they are reasonable. Kinnealey's has some fancier meats, such as crown roasts of lamb and a few prepared items. The **sausage,** either **hot** or **sweet,** is good but unremarkable. The fist-sized **meatballs,** a blend of beef, pork, cheese, and eggs, are delicious, and understandably popular.

NORWELL

Smokehouse
340 Washington Street, Norwell, MA 02061   (617) 659-4824
Mail order: not available   Hours: Mon.–Fri. 10 A.M.–6 P.M.;
     Sat. 9 A.M.–5 P.M.; closed Sun.

When he graduated high school, Dave Nosiglia decided he wanted to be a butcher. His father, Victor, attributes this desire to one time when Dave shot a deer and had trouble butchering it. But the butchers in the Boston area, Victor felt, "don't really teach you to cut meat." So Dave went to Germany to participate in a three-year apprenticeship program. When Dave returned to the States, he went into business with his father. First they bought a sausage place in Hyannis. "But," Victor said, "we found that Hyannis is not the sausage hub of the universe." So they moved to Roxbury (wholesale only; not listed here) and started selling sausage wholesale to hotels and restaurants. They then opened a retail outlet in Norwell.

The Smokehouse now makes over sixty kinds of sausage, from traditional **Italian sweet** and **hot** to **kielbasa,** to a variety of excellent **chicken sausages.** There are three variations: **chicken and apple, chicken and rosemary,** and **spicy chicken.** Dave is constantly experimenting with new combinations of ingredients and flavors. When I visited, **prosciutto–red pepper** was the newest product. In addition to the sausage, Dave smokes several meats. In the summer he prepares 1,500 pounds of **barbecued ribs** a week. The **smoked turkey breast,** which is excellent, is understandably a best-seller. There's also **smoked duck breast** and **duck halves.** Their **beef jerky** is a treat. Making it is an elaborate process, during which the beef is trimmed, then frozen, sliced, and marinated overnight; it is then hung from racks, cooked, then smoked.

The bulk of the Smokehouse business is wholesale, and all the meats are prepared in the Roxbury location, but many items are available in the Norwell retail store.

QUINCY

Previte's

72 Summer Street, Quincy, MA 02169   (617) 472-9830
Mail order: not available   Hours: Mon.–Fri. 9 A.M.–6 P.M.;
Sat. 8 A.M.–5 P.M.; closed Sun.

It's hard to just stumble across Previte's, which is located on a small side street in Quincy. But find this place and you'll experience some of the best sausage in the Boston area.

The meat counter runs along one side of the store, adjacent to a deli counter. The deli meats are fine, but Previte's does not prepare them, so they aren't particularly special. The meats themselves—precut or cut to order—are, and include beef, pork, and veal. There are also **"grill-ready" marinated items,** such as **Italian chicken, oriental beef tips,** and **Chinese ribs.**

But **sausages** are where owner Joe Previte excels. He makes six kinds. The **Italian sweet** and **Italian hot** are the best of the best, but all varieties are good. There is also **stuffed pepper-mushroom-onions, garlic–imported provolone,** and **liver sausage.** The latter is for liver fans only, but it is intriguing, seasoned with orange zest and garlic. On the more low-fat end, there is **chicken sausage,** with fennel, garlic, and marsala wine.

In addition to meats, Previte's offers a variety of **prepared foods** made to order, such as **sausage cacciatore,** the ever popular **chicken, ziti, and broccoli,** and **baked lasagne.** A good portion of the store is devoted to shelves of Italian goods—imported pastas, canned goods, olive oils, grains, and cookies.

WEST

NEEDHAM

Owen's Poultry Farm

585 Central Avenue, Needham, MA 02194   (617) 444-1861
Mail order: not available   Hours: Mon.–Sat. 8 A.M.–5:30 P.M.;
closed Sun.

Douglas Owen's father started this chicken and turkey farm in 1935. The store, with its own kitchen, is on a busy street, overlooking the farm. Initially everything sold was raw, but since the 1970s the bulk of the meats Owen's sells are **cooked, prepared**

foods, made from the birds Douglas raises. **Turkey** with all the trimmings is available year round. Trimmings include **green bean casserole, baked butternut squash, real mashed potatoes, stuffing,** and **gravy.** In November turkey is the lion's share of the business: during the three days preceding Thanksgiving, Owen's sells three thousand turkeys. At holiday time, order your bird well in advance.

As Christmas approaches, Owen's sells a lot of ducks and geese. The rest of the year **chicken** dominates, both raw and prepared. You can get eggs here—and turkey eggs too. They make their own **chicken soup** and **turkey soup,** good for what ails you, **stuffed boneless chicken breast,** and homemade **apple, pumpkin,** and **blueberry pies.**

❖ HALAL SOURCES ❖

Halal meat is meat that has been slaughtered in accordance with Muslim dietary laws. The following are sources for halal meat.

BOSTON

BOSTON

Blackstone Halal Market

96 Blackstone Street, Boston, MA 02109   (617) 367-6181
Mail order: not available   Hours: Mon.–Thurs. 9 A.M.–7 P.M.;
    Fri., Sat. 6 A.M.–8 P.M.; Sun. 10:30 A.M.–5 P.M.

You'll see few meats on display when you ascend the steps into Blackstone Halal. At first glance it appears to be a Middle Eastern market with rows of spices and dried beans in plastic bags, canned goods from Mediterranean countries, and Arabic music playing in the background. There is a refrigerated display case, but, at least when I visited, it was empty. Then I noticed the whole skinned lamb hanging from a ceiling hook behind the case. The meat sold here is entirely cut to order, and you have to order in advance. Everything is halal, including the chicken, beef, lamb, veal, and goat.

Haymarket Bargain Basement

96A Blackstone Street, Boston, MA 02109   (617) 367-0099
Mail order: not available   Hours: Mon.–Thurs. 8 A.M.–6 P.M.;
   Fri., Sat. 6 A.M.–7 P.M.; Sun. 11 A.M.–4 P.M.

The meats here are inexpensive and not the greatest cuts; much of the meat is frozen. A small section of the store features a handful of Middle Eastern goods, such as rose syrup and rice.

New Halal Meat & Grocery Store

14 Blackstone Street, Boston MA 02109   (617) 720-3833
Mail order: not available   Mon.–Thurs. 8 A.M.–7 P.M.;
   Fri., Sat. 6 A.M.–8 P.M.; Sun. noon–6 P.M.

New Halal is the new kid on the Blackstone Halal block, having just opened in 1994. Beef, chicken, lamb, and goat are available, and New Halal makes their own *mergez* sausage links from ground lamb. The store is reminiscent of a Middle Eastern open-air market. On tables outside the store are uncovered containers proffering spices, olives, nuts, and dried fruit. The space inside is small and filled with canned beans, pepper pastes, oils, sauces, and other condiments.

BRIGHTON

Brighton Meat Market and Grocery

567 Washington Street, Brighton, MA 02135   (617) 254-2424
Mail order: not available   Hours: Mon.–Sat. 10 A.M.–8 P.M.;
   Sun. noon–4 P.M.

Cheema's Supermarket

562 Cambridge Street, Brighton, MA 02135   (617) 783-9800
Mail order: not available   Hours: daily 7 A.M.–11 P.M.

Pak Halal Meat & Groceries

600 Washington Street, Brighton, MA 02135   (617) 782-5333
Mail order: not available   Hours: daily 10 A.M.–8 P.M.

Pak Halal carries lamb, goat, beef, and poultry. In a kitchen to the side, a butcher busily cuts and wraps halal meat. Pak Halal also carries Indian and Pakistani goods. The items are not well displayed; you feel as if you are standing in a storage room rather than the display area of a store.

ROSLINDALE

Quality Meat Market

13 Corinth Street, Roslindale, MA 02131   (617) 469-5632
Mail order: not available, but they do deliver
Hours: Mon.–Wed. and Sat. 9 A.M.–9 P.M.; Thurs., Fri. 9 A.M.–10 P.M.;
   Sun. 11 A.M.–6 P.M.

METROPOLITAN BOSTON

CAMBRIDGE

Cambridge Halal Meat Market & Grocery Store

2374 Mass. Avenue, Cambridge, MA 02140   (617) 491-5568
Mail order: not available, but there is free delivery
Hours: Tues.–Sat. 9:30 A.M.–7 P.M.; Sun. 10 A.M.–4 P.M.; closed Mon.

The Cambridge Halal butchery is in the back of the store; as with most halal places, little meat is on display. They make their own Algerian *mekarnek* and *mergez,* sausages, made from beef and lamb with spices. They also carry halal cold cuts, including hot dogs, bologna, and salami. There is also a nice selection of Middle Eastern and Pakistani goods in two aisles, including big bags of basmati rice.

WEST

BURLINGTON

Khyber Halal Meat Market

274 Cambridge Street (Route 3A), Burlington, MA 01803
   (617) 229-9177
Mail order: not available   Hours: Mon.–Sat. 10 A.M.–7 P.M.;
   Sun. noon–6 P.M.

❖ KOSHER SOURCES ❖

Kosher meat is meat that has been slaughtered in accordance with Jewish dietary laws. The following are sources for kosher meat.

BOSTON

MATTAPAN

American Kosher Products Co.

1188 Blue Hill Avenue, Mattapan, MA 02126   (617) 296-5605
Mail order: not available   Hours: Mon.–Fri. 8 A.M.–4 P.M.;
Sun. 8 A.M.–noon; closed Sat.

When Leon Weiner's father opened American Kosher in 1955, Mattapan had a large Jewish population. Although most Jews have left that neighborhood since, the store remains. Their kosher meats are available both wholesale and retail, but finding the business is a little tricky. There's a large sign over the window, but you'll have to walk through a West Indian take-out restaurant, Ali's Roti (see "Goodies to Go," page 169), to get there. Ask the folks at Ali's, and they'll point you in the right direction. Walk down a hallway, through a door and another door, and then you'll find yourself in the small space where the business does retail. To the left are huge refrigerated rooms where sides of beef hang.

Weiner, the current owner, says that American Kosher is the only kosher wholesaler in the New England area. But they also do retail, and it's worth finding your way if just for the **corned beef,** which they make on the premises. This lean corned beef is quite simply the best I've ever tasted. It's dry, not greasy, delicately flavored and not too salty. Weiner or one of his employees will make a sandwich for you if you ask. There are no fancy trimmings here, but they will pile on the corned beef on a bulkie roll for you. They also make a fantastic **pastrami,** which even tastes good cold. Other homemade deli meats include **spiced beef** and **rolled beef.** The deli meats are available in some area stores, including the Butcherie and Gordon & Alperin (this chapter, pages 145 and 146) and Rubin's Kosher Deli (see "Goodies to Go," page 199).

Knishes are available frozen, in both **beef** and **potato;** they are good if you like knishes, but I've never been a big fan of this heavy pastry. I did like the potato better than the beef. If you want the knishes fresh, not frozen, come on a Wednesday, which is when they are made.

In addition to the deli meats, American Kosher carries a whole line of kosher cuts of beef, veal, lamb, and poultry.

METROPOLITAN BOSTON

BROOKLINE

The Butcherie
428 Harvard Street, Brookline, MA 02146   (617) 731-9888
Mail order: not available   Hours: Mon., Tues. 6:30 A.M.–6 P.M.;
    Wed., Thurs. 6:30 A.M.–8 P.M.; Fri. 6:30 A.M.–2 P.M.;
    Sun. 6 A.M.–4 P.M.; closed Sat.

Butcherie II
15 Washington Street, Canton, MA 02021   (617) 828-3530
Mail order: not available   Hours: Mon.–Wed. 7 A.M.–6 P.M.;
    Thurs. 7 A.M.–7:30 P.M.; Fri. 7 A.M.–3:30 P.M.; Sun. 7 A.M.–2 P.M.;
    closed Sat.

The Butcherie is more than a meat market; it is also a kosher grocery store that carries a good selection of items imported from Israel. Most meat is precut and wrapped in plastic but there is also a cut-to-order section. A deli case features kosher meats from several sources, including regular and extralean corned beef from American Kosher at relatively reasonable prices. There are **rotisserie chickens** and other prepared foods, such as homemade real Jewish **chicken soup**—available with **matzo balls** during Passover.

The meat is good here, but you may find that the market is more rewarding as an ethnic market. There are several cheeses from Israel, including a tasty *fromage blanc,* also called, simply, white cheese. This is a sour cream–like dairy item that is lighter, with a more subtle flavor. There are also several **kosher cheeses.** Among their canned fruit is one of my personal favorites, Israeli pink grapefruit. The aisles are crammed with all kinds of products, from frozen dinners to crunchy cookies, mango juice to kosher wine.

Of the two stores, I prefer the Brookline location; it is cleaner and has a more extensive selection of goods.

NEWTON

Gordon & Alperin Inc.

552 Commonwealth Avenue, Newton, MA 02159   (617) 332-4170
Mail order: available; delivery also available
Hours: Mon.–Wed. 7 A.M.–5 P.M.; Thurs. 7 A.M.–6 P.M.;
   Fri. 7 A.M.–2 P.M.; Sun. 8 A.M.–11:30 P.M.
   (closed Sun. in the summer); closed Sat.

Gordon & Alperin, a kosher butchery, has been in business for over seventy years. Current owner Murray Kessel took over in 1989, after running a nonkosher butchery in Marblehead for many years.

The store is tiny, but the quality of the meat is superb. This is the best kosher meat around. Kessel takes great pride in his store and in his products. You can buy meats cut to order, as well as meats on display in a case to your right as you enter, ready to be cut and wrapped. On the left there is a shelf of Jewish cookbooks. They aren't for sale, but feel free to peruse them—Kessel encourages people to look through them for recipe ideas.

Kessel is a foodie, and his enthusiasm for cooking is apparent in the prepared foods he sells. There are frozen, home-made **turkey sausages,** modeled after Italian hot and Italian sweet sausage, and they are excellent. They are also expensive —costing more than twice as much per pound as most pork sausages.

There are **rotisserie chickens,** and you can also get a variety of homemade **frozen dinners,** such as several **soups, stuffed cabbage,** and **kugel.** Kessel prides himself on his non-meat offerings as well. The store carries a small line of kosher condiments, oils, and other foods.

NORTH

PEABODY

Levine's Kosher Meat

134 Newbury Street (Route 1 South), Peabody, MA 01960
  (617) 884-1406
Mail order: available; delivery also available
Hours: Mon.–Thurs. 8 A.M.–6 P.M.; Fri. 8 A.M.–3 P.M.;
  Sun. 8 A.M.–noon; closed Sat.

Larry Levine first worked as a butcher in Providence. Then he opened his own kosher butchery in Chelsea in 1975. Over the past two decades the neighborhood changed, and a kosher butcher needs to be near kosher customers, so Levine moved to Peabody.

In addition to offering good kosher meat cut to order, Levine's has a variety of prepared foods. They are famous for their **barbecued chicken.** A sign in the freezer proclaims, "You haven't lived till you've had a Larry Burger," and the all-beef **hamburgers** are quite good, especially on the grill. Larry's son Todd works here now, and also his wife, Mindy, who makes the **meatballs.** They make their own **corned beef,** which is okay, and their own **roast beef,** which is very good.

SOUTH

CANTON

Butcherie II. See Brookline, page 145.

RANDOLPH

Randolph Kosher Meat Market

41 N. Main Street, Randolph, MA 02368   (617) 961-2931
Mail order: not available, but they do deliver
Hours: Mon.–Thurs. 9 A.M.–6 P.M.; Fri. 9 A.M.–1 P.M.;
  Sun. 8 A.M.–1 P.M.; closed Sat.

Randolph Kosher is a small market with a good selection of meat, all cut to order. They also make their own **barbecued chicken** and carry a few groceries and frozen Empire dinners (these are dinners made by Empire, a company that specializes in Kosher meats).

WEST

FRAMINGHAM

Hurwitz Kosher Meat Market
326 Concord Street, Framingham, MA 01701   (508) 875-0481
Mail order: not available, but they do deliver
Hours: Mon.–Wed. 7 A.M.–6 P.M.; Thurs. 7 A.M.–7 P.M.;
    Fri. 7 A.M.–3 P.M.; Sun. 7 A.M.–noon; closed Sat.

Hurwitz is a small kosher butchery, carrying primarily precut, plastic-wrapped items. Most meats are available cut to order. They carry American Kosher corned beef, and make a selection of **deli sandwiches.**

THE BESTS OF THE BEST

Best overall meat market: **New England Meat Market**
Best upscale meat market: **Savenor's** and **Dewar**
Best pork source: **Savenor's**
Best veal source: **Sulmona Meat Market**
Best lamb source: **New England Meat Market**
Best beef source: **Dewar**
Best poultry source: **Mayflower Poultry** and **Owen's Poultry Farm**
Best pork sausage: **Previte's**
Best chicken sausage: **Smokehouse**
Best kielbasa: **Karl's Sausage Kitchen**
Best turkey sausage: **Gordon & Alperin**
Best kosher butcher: **Gordon & Alperin**
Best halal butcher: **Blackstone Halal Market**

❖ CHAPTER SIX ❖

GOODIES TO GO

*Choices for take-out foods, from rotisserie chicken to swordfish kabobs,
potato salad to lasagne, as well as sources for pizza and sandwiches, from
roast beef to falafel, tuna salad to veggie melts*

*T*AKE-OUT foods let you eat out while eating in. There is
little preparation time involved, few dishes to wash, and
you can have a terrific, multicourse meal in the comfort
of your home, usually for significantly less than the cost of eating
out at a restaurant. The options range from the casual and inexpensive to the elaborate and pricey. Prepared meals might be
anything from pasta salad and barbecued spare ribs to bouilla-
baisse and ginger-peanut noodles.

Several different kinds of establishments offer foods to
go. There are stores that specialize in this area—several business
owners told me that they feel that prepared foods are the wave of
the future; then there are markets that include a deli counter
with salads and heat-at-home entrées; finally, there are take-out
restaurants.

Nearly every restaurant around town will package menu
items for takeout. With a few exceptions, I chose to focus on
establishments that *specialize* in takeout, where takeout consti-
tutes at least half of the business, if not more. Some of these
establishments have several tables but no table service—you place

your order at the counter. Others are sit-down restaurants with a separate take-out store.

This chapter is divided into three sections: takeout, sandwiches, and pizza. The takeout section features establishments that offer a variety of prepared foods, from soups and salads to entrées and desserts. If they offer sandwiches, I describe those offerings in this section.

The sandwiches section focuses on establishments that specialize in sandwiches. Some places in this section do make other items, but they are unremarkable compared to the sandwiches. Both this and the takeout section are organized geographically.

Pizza is available at a few different venues. There are restaurants that include pizza on a menu with several items. Then there are pizza restaurants, sit-down establishments that do all kinds of creative things with pizza dough, sauce, and cheese. And finally there are pizza joints, where you can get a slice of pizza to go. Some of the other take-out places listed in this chapter make very good pizza, and I mention the pizza there. There are hundreds of places to get pizza. I've included a small selection of the absolute best.

Very few of the establishments in this chapter offer mail-order services, but several do offer catering, so I have added this category along with the other information at the beginning of each entry.

* Described in another chapter.

TAKEOUT

Ali's Roti Restaurant	Mattapan
*Angel's Bakery and Café	Watertown
Baci	Boston
Baker's Best	Newton
*Barsamian's	Cambridge
*J. Bildner & Sons	Brookline
*Bob's Imported Food and Fine Catering	Medford
Bo Shek	Boston
Boston Common Foods	Newton
J & S Brandi's	Marblehead
*Bread & Circus	Boston, Brighton, Cambridge, Newton, Wellesley

Caffé Gianni	Boston
Calla Lily Café	Cambridge
Chicken Etc.	Hingham
Codman Square Bakery	Dorchester
*Court House Fish Market	Cambridge
Cremaldi's	Cambridge
Dudley Pastry & Restaurant	Roxbury
*The Earth Food Store	Andover
*The Fishmonger	Cambridge
*Formaggio Kitchen	Cambridge
*Harvest Cooperative Supermarket	Allston, Cambridge
Harvest Express	Cambridge
Healthy Heart Café	Framingham
The Italian Express	Newton, Woburn
Jake & Earl's Dixie BBQ	Cambridge
*La Pasta Place	Concord
*Legal Sea Foods Market Place	Allston, Boston, Newton
*Lexington Lobster and Seafood	Lexington
*LMNOP	Boston
*Marblehead Lobster Co.	Marblehead
*Maryam's Famous Cuisine	Dorchester
*Massis	Watertown
Mex	Boston
*Middle East Restaurant	Cambridge
Moka	Boston
*Morse Fish Co.	Boston
*The Natural Gourmet	Concord
*Near East Bakery	West Roxbury
*Noodles	Somerville
*J. Pace & Son Inc.	Boston
*Pasta Bene	Brockton
*Phoenicia Market	Brockton
Picante	Somerville, Cambridge
Pic-a-Pasta	Brighton
Rebecca's Bakery	Boston
Rebecca's Cafe	Boston, Cambridge
Rustica	Belmont
Salamander Food Shop	Cambridge
*Sally Ann Food Shop	Concord
*Salt & Pepper	Somerville
Savoury Lane	Acton
*Sevan's Bakery	Watertown
*Sorelle Bakery and Café	Charlestown
Stephanie's on Newbury	Boston

Tapa's Corner	Beverly
A Taste of Italy	Canton
Tastebuds	Beverly
*Today's Bread	Jamaica Plain
To Go	Boston
Truffles	Marblehead
*Turner's Seafood Grill & Market	Melrose
*Tutto Italiano	Hyde Park, Newton, Wellesley
*Via Lago Gourmet Foods	Lexington
Via Lago Pasta	Arlington
*Vicki Lee Boyajian	Needham
Virginia's Fine Foods	Brookline
*Wheatberries of Manchester	Manchester

SANDWICHES

Artu's	Boston
*Bentonwood Bakery and Café	Newton
Dagwoods	Hingham
Darwin's Ltd.	Cambridge
David's World Famous 1st Class Eateries	Woburn, Burlington
The Five Corners Deli	Marblehead
Formaggio's Deli	Cambridge
Garden of Eden	Boston
Kravings	Norwood
Manny's Pastries	Roslindale
The Oasis Grille	Somerville
Provizer's	Newton
Rami's	Brookline
Rosetti's Italian Market	Revere
Rubin's Kosher Delicatessen & Restaurant	Brookline
Salumeria Italiano	Boston
Season's Harvest	Somerville
Shawarma King II	Brookline
Stuff-It	Cambridge
West End Strollers	Boston

PIZZA

Bella Luna	Jamaica Plain
Bertucci's	Wakefield, Somerville
Bianchi's Pizza	Revere
Bluestone Bistro	Brighton, Waltham

Café Vesuvius	Marblehead
Café Fiorella	Belmont
Figs	Boston
Il Panino	Cambridge, Boston
John's Pizza	Chelsea
Mario's Trattoria	Dorchester
Pino's Pizza	Brookline
Pizzeria Regina	Boston
Santarpio's Pizza	East Boston

❖ T A K E O U T ❖

BOSTON

BOSTON

Baci

61 Massachusetts Avenue, Boston, MA 02115   (617) 266-2200
Mail order: not available   Catering: available
Hours: Mon.–Thurs. 7 A.M.–9 P.M.; Fri. 7 A.M.–11 P.M.;
    Sat. 8 A.M.–11 P.M.; Sun. 8 A.M.–9 P.M.

Baci is a beautiful store, with high ceilings of pressed tin, wide tiles on the floor, granite counters, and mahogany trim and shelves. The shape of the space is a little odd; it's half a block wide but less than twenty feet deep. Part of the store is a take-out operation, with some tables; the other part is a gourmet food and wine shop.

The latter is less interesting—it seems almost lost in the space, although there are some nice items, and occasional wine tastings. Takeout is the draw here. The place opened in 1994 and is owned by a brother-and-sister team, Carlo and Gina Petruzziello. Carlo is precise about the food he likes to cook. There are many successes and some items that need work.

There are several **salads;** the best is a **citrus salad,** a mix of bitter greens with fresh orange, in a lemon dressing that has the barest hint of lime. It's refreshing and sunny. The **black bean salad** also has a lemony dressing and a subtle sweetness from corn. The hot **potatoes with tarragon and vinegar** were less successful—the potatoes were overcooked, and the seasonings were *too* subtle. Carlo calls the rich gazpacho **white gazpacho**— even though it is pale red—because it lacks tomatoes. He uses roasted red peppers, as well as a little chili, for this unusual cold soup.

The crust of the **quiche** needs work; it has an odd, spongy texture. The fillings, which change daily, are very good, however, with a creamy custard. I tried **asparagus-onion.** A popular item is the **savory pie,** a tall layering of roasted red peppers, spinach, provolone, and Black Forest ham, surrounded by a crust. There are also **hot entrées,** such as **chicken in a reduced wine sauce.**

Some baked goods come from outside sources, including Dancing Deer (see "Everything Nice," page 242), and Carlo makes several treats as well. The **muffins** are good, although some had a slightly off taste, as if something was wrong with that batch of batter. The **banana–chocolate chip muffin** is an elegant treat, not exactly light breakfast fare. Carlo uses chopped imported bittersweet chocolate, and it tastes wonderful. The **lemon-raisin scone** could use a lighter touch with the lemon; the texture is rich and crumbly, but it has a bitter aftertaste. For breakfast, go for the **coffee cake,** with its streusel topping. The **strawberry–sour cream tart** had the same spongy crust problem as the quiche, but the frangipane filling is tasty. The best item is the **brownie.** The texture is a little cakey, which may not appeal to fans of gooey, sticky brownies, but it is the most chocolatey brownie I've tasted. A real bittersweet chocolate flavor makes this an excellent brownie.

Baci always has **pizza** in two styles. The Petruzziellos' father owns Pino's Pizza in Brookline (page 216), and they grew up making the stuff. There is a **thick-crusted pan pizza** and a **thinner crust round pizza;** both are good, topped with creative toppings such as **mushroom and grilled summer squash** or **breaded eggplant,** and a good **tomato sauce.** You can order a variety of **sandwiches;** a deli case contains an assortment of meats and cheeses. The ***Baci*** is popular—prosciutto, fresh mozzarella, and tomatoes—but you can create any combination you like. "We're very accommodating," Carlo says. "Tell us what you want, and we'll make it for you."

Bo Shek

61–63 Beach Street, Boston, MA 02111   (617) 482-4441
Mail order: not available   Catering: not available
Hours: daily 9 A.M.–6 P.M.

If you wander around Chinatown, you will notice a few prepared meat shops, notable for the whole roast ducks and chickens hanging from racks in the window. Bo Shek is the best of these.

The format is simple. Everything for sale is displayed in the window, and it's all cooked and ready to eat. The Chinese are very fond of pork; they eat pretty much the whole pig. Some items may be less appealing to the average American palate, such as the bright orange **pig's intestines** or the **barbecued pigs feet.** Other items will definitely please, such as the **roast pork.** Often a whole or half roasted pig will be hanging in the window. Enter the door to the left of the window and tell the employees what you want; they will slice off the pork or weigh out some **barbecued spareribs** or **pork strips.**

The duck and chicken are sold whole or in halves. The **roast duck** is fabulous, juicy, with complex flavors. The accompanying sauce features star anise. They cut the duck, bones and all, into several pieces. You'll need to use your fingers to eat, and you'll want to—to get every last scrap.

The roast duck and roast chicken have dark skin; the baked salty chicken and duck are pale, with coarse salt on the skin.

Bread & Circus. See "Going Organic," page 434.

Caffè Gianni

500 Boylston Street, Boston, MA 02116   (617) 262-0200
Mail order: not available   Catering: available
Hours: Mon.–Fri. 7 A.M.–6 P.M.; Sat. 10 A.M.–5 P.M.; closed Sun.

Caffè Gianni was started by restaurateur Michela Larson's (of Rialto) brother, Gianni, in 1989. He left the business to go into venture capital, and Michela now owns it. Given its downtown location, Gianni caters to the lunchtime office crowd, offering a wide selection of **prepared foods. Pizza** is available by the slice; I had a slice that looked like it had been sitting out for a while, and it still was quite good—with decent crust and terrific tomato sauce. You can also order a whole pizza.

There is a selection of homemade **baked goods,** none of which are very good (heavy **scone,** dry **cookies**). Stick to the **salads.** A salad plate is relatively inexpensive, available in a few sizes, and you can try as many different salads as you like for one price. **Black-and-white bean salad** is very good; the chickpeas in the **curried chickpeas** were undercooked. The **roasted vegetables** are tasty.

There are also daily **entrées** and **warm salads,** such as blackened chicken with Southwestern vegetables and flank steak with ginger, which is tossed with green beans and assorted vegetables. There is a hot pasta bar with a choice of two pastas and three sauces—always marinara; other choices might include grilled vegetable, Bolognese, and Alfredo.

In the winter, there are two hot soups daily, and in the summer one hot and one chilled. The gazpacho is good, and the curried cucumber is unusual. Hot choices include minestrone, escarole, and chicken noodle; usually one of the soups offered is vegetarian.

You can get traditional sandwiches to order—such as turkey, roast beef, tuna salad. More interesting are the focaccia sandwiches, made on Gianni's very good homemade focaccia. There is always a cold tomato, basil, and fresh mozzarella, and a second, hot sandwich. The fillings include portobello mushrooms and provolone, prosciutto and asparagus, and marinated flank steak and watercress with spicy red-pepper mayonnaise.

Legal Sea Foods Market Place. See "Some Things Fishy," page 110.

LMNOP. See "The Staff of Life," page 4.

Mex

312 Shawmut Avenue, Boston, MA 02118   (617) 338-5675
Mail order: not available   Catering: not available
Hours: daily 11 A.M.–3 P.M.; 5 P.M.–10 P.M.

Jim Mercer worked in the space Mex now occupies when it was the kitchen for East Meets West To Go. When that business was sold, he took over this space and turned it into a small restaurant serving primarily takeout. "I looked around the neighborhood to see what was needed," he says. "I asked myself, 'What don't we have?' A Mexican restaurant."

Mercer proceeded to research Mexican cooking in depth, because he wanted to avoid being just another taco stand; he referred to Diana Kennedy's books extensively. In May of 1995 he opened Mex.

He succeeds in his goal: the food here is terrific and different. The menu is short, and the shop was just beginning to offer lunches when I visited. There are no dessert items. A few items here are found elsewhere, but Mercer's interpretation makes them unique. **Tacos** are made with blue corn tortillas (all the tortillas came from Maria & Ricardo's Tortilla Factory in Jamaica Plain; see "The Staff of Life," page 10) and filled with **grilled chicken.** Dishes all come with sides of **Mex rice** and **black** or **pinto beans;** these are disappointingly bland. The rice is fine, a good brown rice, but little is done to flavor it. Both kinds of beans could benefit from a few grains of salt.

Mex's variation on *quesadillas* is great. Three flour tortillas are layered with cheese and a choice of three fillings: **zucchini and fresh corn, potato and herb,** and **grilled chicken and black bean.** This dish is served with a side of spicy, vinegary *adobo* **sauce,** made from pureed chili peppers, garlic, and spices. The quesadilla plate is one of the best deals on the menu—you get a lot of food.

As an appetizer try the *garnacha,* a rich tart made with a cornmeal crust and filled with a mixture of goat cheese and fresh corn, and topped with kidney beans and ancho chili peppers. Delicious.

I love the **gazpacho,** another unusual rendition of a common item. It contains fresh corn and whole coriander seeds, which give it an unexpected sweetness. You can order the soup topped with either strips of corn tortillas or croutons made from corn bread. This is a seasonal item. It's worth coming here in the summer just for this.

Burritos are the most popular item; they are available with four fillings: **chicken,** *carnitas* (shredded pork), **fresh spinach,** and **squash and mushroom.** The fillings are packed in, and the burritos even taste good cold.

Moka

130 Dartmouth Street, Boston, MA 02116   (617) 424-7768
Mail order: not available   Catering: available
Hours: Mon.–Fri. 7 A.M.–11 P.M.; Sat., Sun. 8 A.M.–11 P.M.

Sherry Kozlowski has worked in restaurants, did a stint as a professional bodybuilder, then worked as a bartender before opening Blue Wave restaurant. She then opened Moka, a combination take-out/sit-down restaurant and bakery. Both savory and sweet are good here. Take-out offerings include a variety of soups, sandwiches, and salads. The **salads** invariably include a **fruit salad** made with whatever fruit is in season, a **vegetarian**

pasta salad, and a few other offerings. I tried a decent **chili chicken salad** and a very good **sesame wild rice chicken salad.** On the chicken front, the **chicken soup** is excellent, with a full-bodied chicken aroma and good-sized chunks of meat and vegetables—perfect for a winter's day. All the soups are made from scratch. Others of note include a tomato-based **minestrone** and a hearty **black bean chili.**

The **sandwiches** are good, served on a tasty, although light, homemade **focaccia.** (I like focaccia to be a little chewier.) The choices are creative, with plenty to appeal to both carnivores and vegetarians, and include **Brie, fresh pear, and chicory** and **smoked turkey, mushroom and leek duxelle, alfalfa sprouts, and Swiss cheese.** There are individual-sized **pizzas,** also in creative combinations, such as **bacon, olive, tomato, feta, and mozzarella.** *Quesadillas,* similar to the pizza but with a flour tortilla crust, include **chicken with tomato, roasted eggplant, and red onion.**

The **desserts** are far from light. They are all substantial, and most benefit from not being overly sweet. **Carrot cake,** frosted with walnut buttercream, is a good choice. My favorite is the **key lime cheesecake** with coconut—refreshing and light, even though it is a cheesecake. Cheesecake flavors vary with the season and the whim of owner Kozlowski. The **chocolate mousse cup,** a chocolate genoise covered with a rich, yet feathery ganache, is an elegant dessert, one of the more delicate offerings. Heartier is the substantial **deep-dish apple-fig pie.**

Cookies, brownies, muffins, and **scones** are all very big here, each the size of two or three elsewhere. Bigger is not always better; the brownies and cookies are a bit much. The **muffins** are good. There are always fat-free flavors available, and these are impressive—good in their own right. The plate-sized **scones,** available **plain** or in one of seven **fruit flavors,** such as **raspberry,** are pretty good, although too large for my taste.

Kozlowski intended Moka to be a California-style restaurant in Boston, and the atmosphere is whimsical, with decor that includes kitschy-clad mannequins and a beach mural. Moka works as an early-morning breakfast stop, a lunch-on-the-go takeout joint, and a late-night hangout.

Morse Fish Co. See "Some Things Fishy," page 110.

J. Pace & Son Inc. See "The World in a Jar," page 417.

Rebecca's Bakery

70 Charles Street, Boston, MA 02114   (617) 742-9542
Mail order: not available   Catering: available
Hours: Mon.–Fri. 7 A.M.–10 P.M.; Sat., Sun. 8 A.M.–10 P.M.

My first introduction to Rebecca's was through its muffins. In the early 1980s Rebecca's restaurant on Charles Street had a tiny adjacent bakery and take-out operation, and they made the best muffins ever. I worked in the Back Bay and probably purchased a muffin at least once a week.

Since that time, Rebecca's has gone through many changes. Rebecca's is owned by Rebecca Carras, who has been in the food business for a long time. She started out catering then worked as the chef for Kevin White when he was mayor. From there she opened a gourmet take-out place in Cambridge and then opened her eponymous restaurant in 1978, with the attached bakery and take-out counter. Carras says that baking is not her forte, and that her mother, "a phenomenal cook," set up her bakery. In 1985 she took on a partner and developed a chain of Rebecca's Cafes, which she sold in 1990. Do not confuse the Rebecca's Cafes (see page 161) you see all over town (there are ten) with Rebecca's Bakery on Charles Street, located down the street from the restaurant. There are two different owners.

The bakery and the cafes do carry some similar stuff. The **muffins,** unfortunately, are not what they once were. Carras told me when I visited that her baker of ten years had left recently, and certain recipes were adjusting to new bakers. On a later visit, they were better, and I hope they'll be back to excellence soon. The **currant scones** are quite good, although they have a noticeable baking soda aftertaste. There are also **ham-and-cheese scones.** The oversized **cookies** are mixed, but the good ones are great. Rebecca's has one of the best **peanut butter cookies** around. It is chewy, with a great flavor, and studded with whole peanuts. The **mocha chip** is a chocoholic's dream come true. It's better than any brownie, crisp on the edges, chewy in the center, with a chocolate flavor that will knock your socks off. A little bit goes a *long* way. I like the **congo bars;** Rebecca's version is what others might call a *seven-layer bar,* with a graham-cracker crust and a filling of coconut, nuts, chocolate chips, and sweetened condensed milk. Also excellent are the **fruit tarts.** There are large ones and individual ones, topped with **raspberries, strawberries,** or **blackberries.** The amount of fruit on each one is generous, the custard filling is great, and the crust is perfect, firm and buttery. A true winner.

The **cakes** are eye-catching, such as a **chocolate cake** covered with huge shavings of chocolate, and a similar **white chocolate** counterpart. Most taste as good as they look, but it's worth checking with Carras to see if the baked goods are back to normal.

Rebecca's Bakery is as much about savories as it is about sweets. There is always a selection of **salads,** and these remain fairly constant, changing occasionally with the seasons. The **Greek tomato-feta,** with cucumbers, is refreshing and perfectly seasoned. I love the **green bean salad.** Whole string beans are tossed with fried shiitake mushrooms in a vinaigrette. The mushrooms are a little greasy, but they taste *so* good. The **Oriental noodles** are also a little oily, and also very good, with a sesame-soy dressing and a mélange of vegetables, including red and yellow peppers and water chestnuts. Also delicious is the **roasted potato salad,** with rosemary and an emulsified grainy mustard vinaigrette.

Rebecca's Bakery offers a choice of **entrées** every day, along with several savory pies. These include a conventional **quiche** and a less conventional *torta rustica,* a mammoth yeasted pastry filled with layers of mushrooms and other vegetables and ricotta and fontina cheeses. The **salmon pie,** made with fresh salmon in a pastry crust, is also a huge wedge. This sounds promising but it is ultimately disappointing, rather heavy and bready. I like the **spinach pie,** made with a filo pastry. Unlike most spinach pies, this one is baked in a pie pan and cut into wedges; the spinach filling is two inches high and is flavored with feta and Swiss cheese. There are several vegetarian entrées to go, including **stuffed eggplant, twice-baked potato,** and **lasagne.** Carnivores will be happy too, with dishes such as **stuffed chicken, paella,** and huge **swordfish kabobs.**

There is a variety of **sandwiches** available, made to order, including **grilled chicken, roast turkey,** and **smoked ham,** served on a variety of breads.

Although I always liked the food at Rebecca's, the service

can be mixed, and less than friendly. The last time I visited it was noticeably better. I hope this trend will continue.

Rebecca's Cafe

75 State Street, Boston, MA 02109   (617) 261-0022
Hours: Mon.–Fri. 7 A.M.–7 P.M.; closed Sat., Sun.

18 Tremont Street, Boston, MA 02108   (617) 227-0020
Hours: Mon.–Fri. 7 A.M.–7 P.M.; Sat. 8 A.M.–3 P.M.; closed Sun.

56 High Street, Boston, MA 02110   (617) 951-2422
Hours: Mon.–Fri. 7 A.M.–7 P.M.; closed Sat., Sun.

411 Brookline Avenue (Longwood), Boston, MA 02215
(617) 731-1300
Hours: Mon.–Fri. 7 A.M.–7 P.M.; closed Sat., Sun.

560 Harrison Avenue, Boston, MA 02118   (617) 482-1414
Hours: Mon.–Fri. 7 A.M.–4 P.M.; closed Sat., Sun.

112 Newbury Street, Boston, MA 02116   (617) 267-1122
Hours: Mon.–Fri. 7 A.M.–8 P.M.; Sat. 7:30 A.M.–8 P.M.;
Sun. 9 A.M.–6 P.M.

Prudential Center Food Court, Boston, MA 02116   (617) 266-3355
Hours: Mon.–Fri. 7 A.M.–9 P.M.; Sat. 8 A.M.–9 P.M.; Sun. 9 A.M.–7 P.M.

Jordan Marsh, First floor, Downtown Crossing, Boston, MA 02110
(617) 357-3866
Hours: Mon.–Sat. 9:30 A.M.–6:30 P.M.; closed Sun.

75–101 Federal Street, Boston, MA 02110   (617) 482-0066
Hours: Mon.–Fri. 7 A.M.–7 P.M.; closed Sat., Sun.

Kendall Square, 290 Main Street, Cambridge, MA 02142
(617) 494-6688
Hours: Mon.–Fri. 7 A.M.–7 P.M.; closed Sat., Sun.

All stores: Mail order: not available   Catering: available

Rebecca's Cafes started as a partnership with Rebecca Carras of Rebecca's restaurant and Bakery (see page 159). She parted ways with her partners in 1990, but the Cafes still maintain some of the original terrific recipes, including the **muffins,** especially the **blueberry muffins.** So few bakeries make really good muffins, and these are great. A central commissary mixes the batter for the muffins and the cookies, and they are baked in each store.

Vice president of sales and marketing Suzanne Woolston says that the company's hope is to provide the convenience of McDonald's with high-quality restaurant food. On many fronts they succeed. A board above the counter lists all the regular items, and a blackboard has the daily specials. There are soups, salads, sandwiches, entrées, and pastries. The soups are great, with several dozen recipes, and the offerings change daily. Every day there is one **soup** in each of three categories—**cream, broth,** and **vegetarian**—as well as a mild **chili.** I tried **cream of spinach,** which is fantastic. It is not overly rich and contains bits of spinach, leeks, and potatoes. The **chicken soup with rice** is strong tasting—too chickeny—and the **harvest vegetable** is good, hearty, but a little salty.

The **salads** remain the same every day. My favorite two are the **green bean and feta,** with crunchy string beans and bits of tomato and feta cheese in a vinaigrette. The similar-sounding **Greek tomato salad** has a lemon dressing, which gives it a nicely different taste. Both are refreshing, and both are best-sellers. Also popular is the **roasted red potato salad,** but the quality of the potatoes was mixed. Some were mealy, and others spurted oil when I bit into them. **Rebecca's famous chicken salad** has a creamy dressing made from a tasty blend of sour cream and mayonnaise. Chunks of light and dark meat are tossed with red and green grapes and tiny bits of walnut. It tastes good, but I prefer all white meat. The **tuna salad** is good, a classic blend of white-meat tuna and mayo—and no relish.

There is a variety of made-to-order **sandwiches,** including the tuna and chicken salads. Other fillings are **roast turkey, chicken,** and **beef,** as well as a tasty **egg salad.** This comfort food seems to be showing up on menus all over town, and Rebecca's does a great version. Beware; it includes raw chopped onions, but they add a lot of flavor. When I visited, the company was promoting their **pannini.** These are sandwiches that are premade, served on homemade **focaccia.** The focaccia itself is much too yeasty, but the fillings all sound tempting, such as **smoked turkey,** with roasted leeks, roasted red peppers, and Swiss cheese, or **roast beef,** with marinated plum tomatoes, caramelized onions, cheddar cheese, and garlic mayo.

Every day the **entrées** change; there are four categories to choose from. The **Healthy option entrées** derive less than 30 percent of their calories from fat. The **hoisin chicken,** for example, is lightly spiced bite-size pieces of chicken breast in marinade-like sauce, served on top of rice. The meat is good, although this dish will make you feel a little virtuous. **Blue Plate Special** items are at the opposite extreme of the dietary chart, including **country fried chicken, meat loaf, boiled dinner,** and other diner fare. **Pasta** is the third category, and it is also highly caloric.

Baked cheese tortellini tastes very good, but the tortellini is baked in a tomato cream sauce and topped with cheese. Cholesterol anyone? There are not many veggie options in entrées, and not much seafood. The fourth category is **Rebecca's Special,** and this could be anything from **chicken enchilada** (which is really more of a burrito, since it is that size, and uses a flour, not a corn, tortilla) to an excellent **beef Stroganoff.**

The company prints a monthly schedule of its daily specials, so you can plan your month accordingly. There are also hot-line numbers you can call to hear a recording of the daily specials.

Everything is made at Rebecca's Cafes' central commissary, so all items will be consistent from store to store. I think one reason the company is able to maintain the quality they do —not everything is great, but many items are—in what is essentially an upscale fast-food joint is that the upper-tier kitchen staff has remained the same for many years. Executive chef Hubert Wittich has been there for several years, and pastry chef Alan Fezzini has been with the company from the start.

The **baked goods** are top quality. As I mentioned, the **muffins** are good, especially that blueberry. They also make the trendy **muffin tops;** these are muffins baked in a very shallow pan so that they are 90 percent muffin top—everyone's favorite part of a muffin. I think real muffin tops taste better—they have all that muffin underneath to give them moistness. The **scones** are not good. The texture is right, but the baking soda taste dominates everything else—the butter, the cream, the currants, the blueberries. The **pecan twist,** although made by Rebecca's, has a commercial flavor to it. Stick with the muffins for breakfast. Or go for the **mile-high apple pie.** It's excellent. A dozen Granny Smith apples go into each double-crusted pie, which bulges in the display case. The apples are perfectly cooked, redolent of cinnamon with a hint of orange, and the crust is flaky and delicious. The **cookies** are also excellent, especially the **mocha chip.** It tastes almost exactly like the one at Rebecca's Bakery; it's deep, dark, and chocolatey. The **chocolate chip** is also very good, even though it is an oversized cookie. There are lots of chips, as well as nuts. The **hermit** tastes like a gingersnap with raisins, and I like gingersnaps, so I like it. There is always a fourth cookie, which changes each month. When I visited, it was **white chocolate–pecan,** and I hope they make this one a regular. The cookie is flavored with cinnamon and has a great crispy edge and a chewy center texture. The **brownie** is good too, but not worth getting as long as the mocha chip cookie is around. The **fruit tart** has good fruit, but the crust is too crumbly, and the custard filling has a chemical aftertaste. There are several fancy **cakes,** including the popular **chocolate paradise.** This is a **flourless-style cake** with a raspberry filling, coated with a milk chocolate and dark chocolate ganache and garnished with fresh raspberries. It tastes as good as it sounds, although the piece I tried was too gooey and underdone in the middle. The edges were delicious, though, and my four-year-old chocolate connoisseur inhaled it.

Stephanie's on Newbury

190 Newbury Street, Boston, MA 02116   (617) 236-0990
Mail order: not available   Catering: available
Hours: Mon.–Sat. 8 A.M.–midnight; Sun. 8 A.M.–9 P.M.

Stephanie Sidell had never cooked until she was a young bride living in New York City in the mid-1970s. "I didn't even know what a whisk was," she recalls, "but I was blown away by Dean & DeLuca and Zabars." A next-door neighbor taught Sidell to cook, which inspired her, when she moved back to Boston, to take a year of cooking classes with Madeleine Kamman. She then met Bob Sassy, whom she describes as "an amazing chef," and went into business with him. They ran a catering company, Sidell & Sassy, which became Sidell & Co. when Sassy moved to Florida. Sidell catered for some fourteen years, including the meals for the U.S. Trust corporate dining room (where her father, Jack Sidell, was president and CEO). But in the back of her mind, Sidell always planned to open the kind of business Stephanie's on Newbury is: a restaurant-café-take-out-bakery-gourmet shop.

Indeed, Stephanie's is an impressive operation of hyphenates. It opened at the end of 1994, in the space that was the Harvard Bookstore Café for many years. Sidell transformed it, and the interior is a pleasing mix of wood, metal, and stone. The best items here are the prepared foods, which include a wide range of **salads.** There are daily specials, but regular items include a simple yet great **egg salad** (and I never was a big fan of egg salad), made with traditional mayonnaise and bacon. Big chunks of chicken are the base of **roasted chunky chicken salad,** which also includes capers and slivered almonds. The **salmon salad** is made with tender, moist fresh salmon. One of my favorites is the **French potato salad,** made with caramelized onions. I love caramelized onions. A best-seller is the **Chinese chicken salad,** made with napa cabbage, fried wonton skins, roasted peppers, and sweetened walnuts—a pleasing combination of flavors and textures. The **roasted garlicky tomatoes and fresh mozzarella** is a wonderful version of this traditional Italian combination. The tomatoes are slow roasted so that they are almost sweet; I could eat indefinite amounts of this salad. The **marinated mushrooms** are also addictive.

In addition to the salads, there are several entrées to go, including **glazed ham, grilled chicken breast, grilled salmon,** and the popular **turkey burgers.** There are also sandwiches, with tempting descriptions, but these are quite pricey—$8.95 for an **old-fashioned turkey club,** served on brioche; $11.95 for **rotisserie-roasted tenderloin.** The soups are terrific, especially the flavorful **chicken–wild mushroom** and the heady **roasted garlic soup.**

I was generally disappointed by the **baked goods,** which looked much better than they tasted. Some are made on the premises, some are made at Pomme Frite (owned by Sidell's father; see "The Staff of Life," page 19), and some come from other sources. The **cranberry muffin** is heavy, and the **gingerbread** is too sweet. The *babka* has a delicious caramelized nut topping, but the cake is slightly oily. Then I tried the *marjolaine,* which is delicious, simultaneously light and rich. Chocolate buttercream, praline buttercream, and fresh raspberries are sandwiched between three layers of hazelnut meringue. Also good are the rich, buttery **brownies** and **chocolate chip shortbread.** The **honey cookies** taste like graham crackers, with a pleasantly chewy texture. The **Hungarian walnut torte** is double-crusted, with a dense honey-caramel-walnut filling; it is unusual and delicious. There are also breads made by Pomme Frite.

Because of space constraints, Sidell was in the process of shrinking down the gourmet shop items, which included dried pastas, coffees, loose teas, and various oils and condiments.

To Go

312 Shawmut Avenue, Boston, MA 02118   (617) 482-1015
Mail order: not available   Catering: not available
Hours: Mon.–Sat. 7 A.M.–6 P.M.; Sun. 7 A.M.–3:30 P.M.

This tiny takeout used to be the take-out arm of East Meets West caterers, and was called East Meets West To Go. In 1995 East Meets West caterers was bought by Rebecca's Cafes, and the take-out business was bought by Rene Roberts. The name became simply To Go.

To Go is as much a bakery as a take-out establishment. The space is tiny, with a kitchen smaller than most apartment kitchens; the catering kitchen got turned into Mex, another take-out business (see page 156). There are a couple of tables inside and more outside when the weather is nice. The staff emphasized how much of a neighborhood establishment this is, and they know many customers by name.

To Go goodies include a selection of **salads,** usually a couple **pasta,** a couple **vegetable,** and a **fruit salad.** Summertime is slow, so the selection is more limited then. Jerry Pond, the general manager, says that there are very few items that they have all the time. There is always **tuna salad** and **chicken salad** for **sandwiches,** which are roll-ups on Syrian bread. The **tuna** is excellent—the best I've tried. I don't care for mayonnaise, and To Go uses a very light hand with the stuff; the fish is flecked with bits of fresh herbs and vegetables. The **chicken salad** is also low on the mayo, but it is not that interesting—it could use something to spice it up.

Other salads change all the time. To Go encourages creativity in the kitchen. If they don't have something you like, ask for it; Pond says they are open to requests. Put in a word for **spicy Tex-Mex bean and corn** (terrific, flavored with smokey chipotle chilies). I love the **lemon pasta with broccoli, tomatoes, and beans;** it's refreshing with bits of lemon zest tossed with linguine. **Jicama black bean salad** is very clean and fresh tasting.

There are four daily **pizzas** with creative toppings, such as **salami and *pepperoncini*** or **pasta and corn** (yes, pizza topped with tubular spirals and corn). The **pan pizza slices** are huge, and not cheap ($3.50 a slice), but they are about twice as big as pan pizza slices usually are. These are thick-crust pizzas, quite a meal. I like them, but the crust is a little strong on the yeast.

As a bakery, To Go makes terrific **cookies.** They are all huge (and I prefer smaller cookies), with mixed results. My favorite is the **gingersnap,** which has just the right balance of spices and molasses, and a great texture, with a sugary top. The **choco-**

late-spice cookie, however, is dry and crumbly. The **peanut butter cookie** is good, but not very peanut-buttery—it is more like a sugar cookie with peanuts in it. They call the **chocolate chip** Toll House, but it is unlike any Toll House recipe I've tried. They used finely chopped chocolate, as opposed to chips or chunks, and the effect is a marble swirl of chocolate. They taste good, though.

The shop is open early, for breakfast, and the **muffins** are quite popular. There are always good **blueberry muffins,** laced with cinnamon. Then there are three other variations daily, and the rule of thumb is anything goes. Combinations have included **cherry–white chocolate, banana–butterscotch chip,** and **zucchini-orange-cherry-spice.** Although these are creative combinations, some of the muffins filled with a lot of stuff tend to be underdone and overly moist.

Pond told me that To Go had changed the original **scone** recipe from the scone I had first tasted here a few years ago. This is unfortunate. That other scone may have been "greasy" (I would call it rich), made with butter and cream cheese, but it had a better texture and flavor than the revised version does, and I considered it one of the best in the area. Other baked goods include beautifully decorated **cakes,** such as **chocolate bundt with buttercream, chocolate caramel torte,** and various **pound cakes** and **pies.** The store also sells Iggy's breads (see "The Staff of Life," page 33).

ALLSTON

Harvest Cooperative Supermarket. See "Going Organic," page 431.

Legal Sea Foods Market Place. See "Some Things Fishy," page 110.

BRIGHTON

Bread & Circus. See "Going Organic," page 434.

Pic-a-Pasta

435 Faneuil Street, Brighton, MA 02135   (617) 789-4555
Mail order: not available   Catering: not available
Hours: Mon.–Sat. 11 A.M.–10 P.M.; Sun 4 P.M.–8 P.M.

I first encountered Pic-a-Pasta several years ago, near the rotary in Revere. I ate there once, and then it seemed to have disappeared, until I found it again in Brighton.

Co-owners Dan Howe and James Meagher met when responding to an advertisement for a business opportunity placed by the owner of the original Pic-a-Pasta. The pair bought the business, made changes, and opened the Brighton Pic-a-Pasta in the fall of 1994. At this writing, there is just the one store, but the partners have high hopes for a chain of stores and possibly franchises. The name appears on the menu as "The Original Pic-a-Pasta of Brighton."

The concept is appealing for fast food: you have a list of **pastas, sauces,** and **add-ins,** and you make your picks from each list. And how is the food? Surprisingly good, if you stick to the pasta. They also have **sandwiches,** which are mediocre, and I found the **garlic spears,** which the menu called "a must" to be oily and bland. But the **pasta** was cooked just right, not overdone as I had feared. I had low expectations because of the fast-food appearance of the place—bright colors, Formica counter, fluorescent lighting. Howe says that they were actually aiming for the "franchise look"; he is pleased when people have that impression, since it is in keeping with their goals. The menu is simple yet varied.

The pasta portions come regular or large with three elements: **Pic-a-Pasta, Pic-a-Sauce,** and **Pic-a-Topping.** Pastas include **spaghetti, fettuccine, rotini, linguini, angel hair, rigatoni, shells.** There are seven sauces: **marinara** (decent), **pesto, ricotta** (a lighter version of a white cream sauce), **lemon-butter, natural** (olive oil, garlic, and cracked pepper), **Bolognese** (tomato with ground beef), and **chopped tomato.** You get a choice of toppings, such as carrots, chick peas, **meatballs,** or chopped clams.

CHARLESTOWN

Sorelle Bakery & Café. See "Everything Nice," page 235.

DORCHESTER

Codman Square Bakery

521 Washington Street, Dorchester, MA 02124   (617) 436-2554
Mail order: not available   Catering: not available
Hours: Mon.–Sat. 7:30 A.M.–6 P.M.; closed Sun.

Codman Square Bakery makes three kinds of turnover-style pastries, called **patties: beef, chicken,** and **vegetable.** Beef is by far the best, spicy and smooth. The other two taste good, but we couldn't figure out which was which; this doesn't say much for the amount of chicken used. Both were bready, like stuffing, but nicely flavored. They also make **sweets,** including **coconut drops,** a praline-like candy that could have benefited from more ginger, and a pudding-like **banana bread,** redolent with nutmeg.

Maryam's Famous Cuisine. See "Everything Nice," page 237.

HYDE PARK

Tutto Italiano. See "The World in a Jar," page 420.

JAMAICA PLAIN

Today's Bread. See "The Staff of Life," page 12.

MATTAPAN

Ali's Roti Restaurant

1188 Blue Hill Avenue, Mattapan, MA 02126   (617) 298-9850
Mail order: not available   Catering: available
Hours: Mon.–Thurs. 11 A.M.–9 P.M.; Fri., Sat. 11 A.M.–10 P.M.;
    closed Sun.

Ali's Roti was one of the first Caribbean restaurants to open in the area, in 1988. Today, many of the Caribbean restaurants around town are Jamaican-based; Ali's is Trinidadian. The food here is like a cross between East Indian and Caribbean, with some African influences. The spices used include African seven-pot or Congo peppers and Trinidadian cilantro, which co-owner Julie Ali says is more pungent than conventional cilantro.

Ali's Roti serves **dhalpouri roti,** a homemade West Indian flat bread that is used as a wrapper for a variety of fillings. The roti dough is filled with spices and ground yellow split peas, then baked on a griddle; the bread is slightly thicker than a flour tortilla. It is then wrapped around the filling of your choice. All are curries, including **chicken, beef, goat, oxtail, red snapper,** and **shrimp,** as well as vegetables. The food is spicy, filling, and very good—and the prices are reasonable.

In addition to roti, there are small flat breads, called pies, filled with various vegetables. These include *bougani,* with eggplant; *sahena,* with spinach; and *aloo,* with potatoes. The pies are served with a mild **tamarind chutney** or a fiery **mango chutney.** To cool your palate, you can try a Trinidadian beverage. Drinks include **sorrel,** which is in the hibiscus family and tastes like citrusy punch. *Mauby* is made from carob tree bark and is flavored with anise; it has a woody taste. **Sea moss** is a strange concoction, made from kelp that has been cooked extensively, then combined with milk, lime, and sugar. I like the sorrel best.

Ali's is the restaurant that is in front of American Kosher Products Co. (see "Where's the Beef?" page 144). There are a few booths, but much of the business is takeout.

ROXBURY

Dudley Pastry & Restaurant

52 Warren Street, Roxbury, MA 02119   (617) 427-7620
Mail order: not available   Catering: available
Hours: Mon.–Sat. 10 A.M.–10 P.M.; closed Sun.

I was impressed by the number of customers who flowed through Dudley Pastry as I was contemplating the menu. Atmospherically, there's nothing here. There are no tables, just a space to stand off to the side. The counter is chest-high, and the cashier calls to the kitchen through a small opening cut into a wooden wall. To get change, she pushes money through that hole, and a hand pushes the change back.

Everyone seemed to be ordering **beef patties on coco bread,** so that's what I tried. It's an intriguing combination. Patties are actually turnovers, pastry with beef filling (sometimes they also have vegetable). Homemade **coco bread** is a thick, soft bread, rectangular and about the length of a submarine roll. It seemed redundant to try a pastry on bread, but it was actually quite good. You can get it with or without **cheese,** the cheese being of the Velveeta persuasion. The patties here are great, among the best I subsequently tasted. The beef is finely ground to an almost creamy consistency, flavored with a Jamaican blend of spices, which have some fire.

There are also a variety of **curries** to go—including **goat, oxtail, steak, cowfoot, chicken,** and **vegetable**—served on a bed of spiced rice. I tried the latter two, and they were very good. The curries come in three sizes, ranging in price from $4 to $7.50; the small is a hefty serving for one.

In keeping with the pastry part of the establishment's name, there are a handful of made-on-the-premises **baked goods.** Most are not particularly tempting—variations on **yellow cakes** with different frostings. I tried a **hot cross bun,** which was good, soft and sweet. My favorite Caribbean sweet is a candy, **coconut drops,** and Dudley does a great version. These look like pralines, but they have chunks of coconut jutting out of a brown-sugar base. Good coconut drops should have a definite bite from generous amounts of fresh ginger, and Dudley's do. They're bad for the teeth, but so tasty.

WEST ROXBURY

Near East Bakery. See "The Staff of Life," page 44.

METROPOLITAN BOSTON

BROOKLINE

J. Bildner & Sons. See "An Epicurean Agenda," page 375.

Virginia's Fine Foods

8A Cypress Street, Brookline, MA 02146   (617) 566-7775
Mail order: not available   Catering: available
Hours: Mon.–Fri. 8 A.M.–6 P.M.; Sat. 8 A.M.–5 P.M.;
   Sun. 8 A.M.–3 P.M. (closed Sun. in August)

Virginia's Fine Foods, in business since 1986, was bought in 1991 by three graduates of the Culinary Institute of America, who met while working at the Charles Hotel. Owners Michael Spirdione, Helene Lustgarten, and Mark Wissman found that it was easier to buy an existing business than to start one from scratch. Virginia's main focus is take-out items and sandwiches, both of which they do very well.

Virginia's makes several **spreads,** which you can buy in containers or enjoy on one of their **sandwiches.** Among the spreads is a very good **Boursin,** which I tried on a sandwich with **eggplant and sun-dried tomato spread,** along with lettuce, tomatoes, and cucumbers on Clear Flour Bakery's sourdough bread. It was great. Another cream cheese–based spread is the **roasted red pepper and olive spread. Sandwiches** are available with various deli meats, complimented by these spreads. There are two rich **mousses: chicken liver** and **smoked salmon.**

Virginia's always has three **"protein entrée items,"** such as a robust **Mediterranean chicken ragout** or **traditional chicken salad,** as well as four or five **vegetable** and **starch dishes.** The **spicy peanut noodles** are great, perfectly flavored and not drowning in sauce. Also good are the **spicy cucumber-celery salad,** the light **pasta primavera,** and the **orzo with feta and lemon vinaigrette.**

Virginia's carries a variety of baked goods from Vickie Lee Boyajian and Bentonwood Bakery and Café (see "Everything Nice," pages 283 and 257). They do make their own **scones** and **muffins.** Pass on the below-mediocre **regular scones** and go for the fantastic **oatmeal scones,** rich with butter and studded with currants. Definitely the best oatmeal scones I've tried. There are two muffins daily—a changing special and **low-fat bran,** surprisingly good even to me. (I generally disdain bran muffins, no matter how much fat they have in them.) You can order Clear Flour's focaccia here—they'll reserve loaves for you—but the markup is steep.

CAMBRIDGE

Barsamian's. See "An Epicurean Agenda," page 377.

Bread & Circus. See "Going Organic," page 434.

Calla Lily Café
92 Kirkland Street, Cambridge, MA 02138   (617) 492-2545
Mail order: not available   Catering: available
Hours: Mon.–Sat. 8 A.M.–8 P.M.; closed Sun.

Calla Lily started as a catering business and expanded to a retail operation in this location in 1994. Partners Marsha Tarrh, Rob Pelletier, and Jim Carr run a nice operation offering tasty, appealing food. The atmosphere is great, with walls painted a deep sienna with white trim. There are several tables, with cloth tablecloths decorated with a floral print.

Salads, sandwiches, soups, and entrées change daily; all those I tried were quite good. Most of the breads come from outside sources, but they do make their own **focaccia**. The **focaccia with caramelized onions, goat cheese, yams, and red bliss potatoes** is very good. It went well with the simple, hearty **black bean soup.** There is always some kind of **chicken salad,** the recipe changing daily. *Sam bok* uses Thai seasonings, and there is also a **Cuban chicken and bean salad. Saffron rice with peas** is nicely flecked with cilantro, and the **Greek salad** is light and refreshing.

The **sandwiches** are creative; even the old standbys have a refreshing twist. For example, **roast beef** is served with Boursin, caramelized onions, and Dijon mustard. **Grilled chicken** comes with roasted peppers and pesto.

Calla Lily also makes a variety of **breakfast pastries** and classic **cookies.** The **muffins** aren't bad, and the **scones** are very good, crumbly and rich. The **chocolate almond biscotti** has a subtle orange flavor that is pleasing, although I would prefer a tougher texture. Raisin lovers will appreciate the **oatmeal-raisin cookie,** which seems to have as many raisins as will fit in a cookie. Other cookies are **pecan chocolate chip,** which has a distinctive pecan flavor in the batter, and **chocolate chocolate chip,** which is chewy and chocolatey. The **peanut butter cookie** has a very good flavor and texture.

Court House Fish Market. See "Some Things Fishy," page 114.

Cremaldi's

31 Putnam Avenue, Cambridge, MA 02139   (617) 354-7969
Mail order: not available   Catering: available
Hours: Mon.–Sat. 10 A.M.–7 P.M.

Cathy Cremaldi, daughter of Genevieve and Tony Trio of Trio's in the North End (see "Lotsa Pasta," page 87) worked in her parents' store for several years before opening her own Italian market with her husband Cosmo in 1984. Cremaldi's started as an Italian gourmet market, but it has evolved into a café with sandwiches and take-out dinners.

Cremaldi has a gift when it comes to food—everything she makes tastes great. "I have a fascination and love of food," she sighs. "I just adore it." Cremaldi learned to cook from her parents, but "I believe there's a special gene for cooking," she says. "You have to be a natural." And Cremaldi is. You know it when you sip her **Mexican carrot soup** flecked with fresh coriander. Or grill her amazing **basil–pine nut sausages** made with ground pork and stuffed in real casings. For sausage lovers, the **sweet Italian** and the **hot Italian sausages** are also excellent.

For lunch, there are packaged **salads,** such as a lightly dressed **Caesar,** sometimes topped with strips of grilled chicken. Five or six **sandwiches** are available daily, served on Tuscan or sourdough bread. These include combinations such as **Italian with the works** (mortadella, salami, provolone, *prosciuttini*, vinegared peppers, hot peppers, tomato, and lettuce) or **fresh mozzarella with tomatoes and roasted red pepper.** There's also a **pasta** offering and **pizza,** but they tend to run out of these items by the early afternoon.

For dinner Cremaldi's specializes in take-home **refrigerated entrées,** which you can reheat. While these, like everything at Cremaldi's, are not cheap (dinners go for about $15; sandwiches tend to be $8), each entrée serves two to three people. The quality keeps you coming back for more, with offerings such as **lobster Newburg, chicken with five mushrooms,** and **vegetable lasagne.** In season, Cremaldi's offers delicious, huge **stuffed artichokes** filled with seasoned bread crumbs and cheese. As an hors d'oeuvre, try the spicy **marinated olives,** made with several kinds of olives and fresh rosemary.

Cremaldi's has homemade **pasta,** cut to order as *cappalini,* **spaghetti, linguini, fettuccine,** *pappardelle,* and **lasagne;** it comes in **basil, spinach,** and **egg.** They also carry a range of filled pastas from Trio's. Fillings for tortellini, tortelloni, ravioli, and agnolotti include mushroom and Gruyère, lean beef, radicchio, and veal and spinach. There are over a dozen **sauces,** including **lemon-scallop, anchovy-nut,** and **ginger-vermouth,** as well as the more traditional **tomato, Alfredo,** and **white clam.**

Cremaldi's is also a gourmet Italian market (with gourmet prices) where you can get all kinds of dried pastas and imported Italian baked goods. Cremaldi's does not make their own desserts, but they carry a selection of fancy decorated cakes and pies, as well as crunchy biscotti, cannoli shells, and *pizzelles*. At the center of the store is a wooden cart topped with a huge umbrella and laden with various fresh vegetables and breads from local bakers. Tables fill the floor to the left and right. Counter service is not the speediest, but the food is always worth the wait.

The Fishmonger. See "Some Things Fishy," page 115.

Formaggio Kitchen. See "An Epicurean Agenda," page 380.

Harvest Cooperative Supermarket. See "Going Organic," page 431.

Harvest Express

44 Brattle Street, Cambridge, MA 02138   (617) 868-5569
Mail order: not available   Catering: available
Hours: Mon.–Fri. 9 A.M.–6:30 P.M.; Sat. noon–5 P.M.; closed Sun.

The Harvest Restaurant is an institution in Harvard Square. It has had its ups and downs, and it seems to be on an up since Patrick and Jane Bowe bought it in 1993. Harvest Express, the take-out branch of the restaurant, started around 1988. It's not exactly easy to find, even though it's attached to the restaurant. If you've never been to the restaurant, that's not easy to find either. The Harvest is located in a building on Brattle Street that is behind another building. Walk down some steps in a wide space between Ann Taylor and Crate & Barrel, and you'll soon see the restaurant on your left. Keep walking the length of the restaurant, and you'll see another door on the left, with a neon sign proclaiming Harvest Express.

The shop is small—a narrow counter lines the outside wall, with a couple of stools. **Sandwiches** can be made to order; if you're in a hurry, there are several prepackaged sandwiches. I tried a prepackaged **roasted eggplant with roasted plum tomatoes and marinated fresh mozzarella** on homemade **focaccia.** It was pretty good, although the vinegar of the marinade dominated. Other sandwiches are generally gourmet variations on traditional themes, such as **Virginia baked ham with a spicy dried cherry mustard** and **tuna salad with dill mustard mayonnaise and celery seed.** If you're not in a hurry, the sandwiches are best made to order, otherwise the bread can get soggy. Some less common combinations include **Italian meats with provolone cheese and roasted red pepper relish** and **grilled vegetables with herbed goat cheese and olive spread.**

The **soups** here are quite good, and there are always three or four options. Many contain tomatoes, but they're used in different, creative ways. The vegetarian **spicy curried lentil soup** is nicely seasoned; the tomatoes are used more as a flavoring than as a base. The **chicken mushroom** is filled with chunks of meat and tomatoes.

The display case holds the salads. Tomatoes are used in the dressing for the **Thai noodle salad.** They are puréed with garlic, lime, and sherry, then tossed with pasta, cilantro, carrots, and ground peanuts to create an intriguing combination of flavors. **Tortellini with asparagus** had a very different roasted tomato vinaigrette. A nice side to the sandwiches is the **coleslaw,** which is seasoned with caraway seeds.

Harvest carries a variety of simple **baked goods.** There are **muffins** and bland, heavy **scones.** Of the **cookies,** I like the **gingersnaps** and the **raspberry crunch bars.**

Jake & Earl's Dixie BBQ

1273 Cambridge Street, Cambridge, MA 02139   (617) 491-7427
Mail order: not available   Catering: available
Hours: daily 11:30 A.M.–11 P.M.

Jake & Earl's is a meat lover's paradise. It is a teeny-tiny take-out joint, located next to sister business East Coast Grill. Owner Chris Schlesinger had wanted to pursue a longtime interest in pulled pork and the art of barbecue, and he offers it up here, with the help of chef Ken "Jake" Jacobs. Like Schlesinger's other establishments, Jake & Earl's is fun, and the food is fun. It's meaty, spicy, sweet and sour, and great for a picnic.

Most items can be bought in a sandwich, served on a hamburger bun or Kaiser roll, or by the pint or pound. **Burnt ends** are fabulous strips of smoked brisket, great with homemade **barbecue sauce;** they smoke for about nine hours. The **pulled pork,** made from pork butts, smokes for sixteen hours. **Memphis dry rubbed ribs** are seasoned with a blend of dry spices that are rubbed onto the meat before it is cooked.

The **West Indies hot hot sausage sandwich** is for the true chili head. The **jerk-rubbed half chickens** are spicy as well as moist and delicious, but the **barbecued birds** are disappointingly dry. Daily specials might include **baby back ribs** or **Tennessee tube steak** (barbecued bologna, which tastes like, well, strips of bologna with barbecue sauce).

If you order a sandwich or a plate, such as nine ounces of the ribs, it comes with a side of creamy **coleslaw,** terrific **baked beans,** and watermelon for dessert.

Among the **side dishes** are homemade **corn bread** (which is good and moist, although a tad sweet), **potato salad** (very good), and **sweet potato salad** (excellent). **Sweet mash** is a wonderful purée of sweet and white potatoes that will make your mouth happy. Pass on the **applesauce,** though—it's way too sweet. **Sweets** in general are unremarkable here, although Husbands says they sell well, especially the **Rice Krispie treat** and the **six-layer bar.** The peanut butter pie from The Blue Room, however, is great, with a chocolate cookie crust and a chocolate glaze.

Middle East Restaurant. See "Everything Nice," page 249.

Picante. See Somerville, page 182.

Rebecca's Cafe. See Boston, page 161.

Salamander Food Shop

1 Athenaeum Place, Cambridge, MA 02142   (617) 225-2121
Mail order: not available   Catering: available
Hours: Mon.–Fri. 7:30 A.M.–5:30 P.M.; closed Sat., Sun.

Salamander is known primarily as a wonderful upscale restaurant, run by Stan Frankenthaler since the fall of 1994. But, as Michela's did in this space before Frankenthaler moved in, Salamander also has a terrific take-out section. It offers a variety of sandwiches and prepared foods, excellent breads, and baked goods.

Everything is very good, but I was impressed most by three of the **breads.** The **barley malt bread** is a basic peasant loaf, with a dense texture and excellent flavor. The **mixed grain** is slightly salty, moist, and chewy, flecked with bits of walnut. The crust is just right—crisp and tasty. The dark **Russian bread with dried fruit** is complex, sweet with a molasses taste. The **focaccia** and **baguettes** are also good, but less impressive.

Scone flavors change daily. I tried **almond** and **tart**

cherry; they weren't bad, but I like a more crumbly texture for scones. In lieu of muffins, there's always a **breakfast cake,** which changes daily. Recent offerings included **sour cream–nut, angel food, coconut mango,** and **apricot date.** There is no one item available all the time; baked goods change daily. The **coconut macaroons** are huge and moist, with a base dipped in very good dark chocolate. These are available at least once a week, usually on Fridays. Also available weekly is an **almond-apricot-oatmeal cookie.** This has a great crunchy texture and butter flavor, although it could benefit from a dash of salt. The **chocolate truffle cake** is a must for chocoholics, or any dessert lover; it's simply excellent.

Salads change daily, and these offerings tend to be off the beaten track. **Asian rice noodles with julienned vegetables in soy vinaigrette** is terrific. The vegetables in this dish include haricots verts, carrots, and red peppers, and the dressing is spiced with sesame and chili oils. The **grilled vegetables,** often served with a **Greek salad with lamb,** are excellent. As a side, instead of potato chips, try the homemade **veggie chips,** made using beets, sweet potatoes, and regular potatoes.

Sandwiches are divided into two categories—**Traditional** and **Funky**—and the featured sandwiches change daily. Given the descriptions of each, the distinction is not always clear, except that Traditional sandwiches are a dollar less than Funky ones. All are tempting. When I visited, **Traditional** included **grilled eggplant with roasted red pepper mayo, tomatoes, onions, and crumbled feta cheese. Funky** was the **pastrami with horseradish slaw, sliced apple, grainy mustard, and Jarlsberg cheese.** Yum, yum.

Frankenthaler has plans to expand the food shop to include a variety of produce and meats, including some of the more exotic items he uses on his menu.

NEWTON

Baker's Best

27 Lincoln Street, Newton Highlands, MA 02161   (617) 332-4588
Mail order: not available   Catering: available
Hours: Mon.–Fri. 7:30 A.M.–8 P.M.; Sat. 7:30 A.M.–6 P.M.; closed Sun.

Given his name, it almost seems as if Michael Baker *had* to choose a career in the food business. In 1984 he and his wife

Sandy opened Baker's Best across the street from the current location. The space there was tiny, and they stayed there for ten years. In 1994 they moved to this spacious, comfortable setting. The business is primarily take-out, but there are several tables.

The food is attractively presented in display cases and on the counters. A case of **salads** greets you as you enter, followed by plates of **entrées** and more salads. **Baked goods** are next. Baker says he is proud of his **Caesar salad,** and deservedly so. It is quite good, with just the right amount of dressing (Caesar salads tend to be overdressed). There are several **chicken salads. Chicken salad with red grapes** is nice, but I prefer the **grilled chicken salad,** which has an appealing marinade. There is also a **Southwestern turkey salad,** with red peppers and avocados; and a **tuna niçoise,** with green beans and new potatoes.

Baker's sells **spreads,** packaged into containers. These are a blend of cream and other cheese. The **Boursin** is actually too herby. I prefer the **spinach,** which is mild and good in a sandwich with vegetables. The best is the **cheddar horseradish,** with an assertive and spicy taste.

Entrées vary from day to day. There are lots of **chicken** offerings, such as **herb-marinated chicken breast, chicken pot-pie,** and the always popular **chicken with broccoli and ziti.** There are several other **pasta dishes,** including both a **white lasagne,** with béchamel sauce, and a **lasagne marinara.**

The **sandwiches** are served on breads from Iggy's, Wheatstone, and Clear Flour. The **turkey** is roasted on the premises and carved to order. It's very good with the cheddar-horseradish spread. Other meats include Black Forest ham, salami, corned beef, **chicken salad,** and **chopped liver.** There are always daily specials, such as **chicken piccata,** a chicken breast with a lemon-caper sauce, and **pork loin** served with caramelized onions. For vegetarians there is the **grilled vegetables with mozzarella sandwich**—delectable.

A freezer in the back holds frozen hors d'oeuvres. Of note are the excellent **potato latkes,** the best nonhomemade version I've tasted.

Baker's Best is also a bakery, although the **baked goods** generally aren't as good as the salads and entrées. When I visited they were in the process of hiring a new pastry chef, so this may change. Cookies and muffins are made there, but fancier desserts are not.

The **muffins** are good but not great; they come in several flavors. The best **cookie** is the **almond macaroon,** which is moist and chewy and delicious. Also good are the **fruit tarts,** with a pleasing assortment of seasonal fruit, such as **kiwi, blueberries, strawberries,** and **raspberries.** Of the **squares,** the **lemon** aren't lemony enough and the crust is too soft, and the **blondies** are undercooked. The **cream-cheese brownie** is best, with a very good flavor. I like the **snickerdoodles;** Baker's makes a classic version of these cinnamon sugar cookies.

Boston Common Foods

447 Centre Street, Newton, MA 02158   (617) 964-7878
Mail order: available   Catering: available
Hours: Mon.–Sat. 6:30 A.M.–11 P.M.; Sun. 8 A.M.–11 P.M.

Frank La Verdi opened Boston Common Foods in 1994. "I'm offering American comfort food to people who are meal shopping," he says. "And while they are here, they can pick up other items." The store is a combination upscale small supermarket and take-out shop.

There are a variety of made-to-order **sandwiches,** including a breakfast **egg on a muffin** with **bacon** or **ham** and a choice of **cheeses.** You can also get a bagel. Sandwiches come on sliced bread or submarine rolls, and include the usual assortment of meats. The **hot sandwiches** are more tempting, like **sirloin tips** and **hot turkey meatloaf.** There are five **Uptown sandwiches,** including **tarragon chicken salad with cheddar cheese** and **hand-carved turkey with herb mayonnaise, cranberries, stuffing, and gravy.**

Entrées change daily, and include **roast loin of pork, slow-cooked pot roast,** and **fresh roasted turkey.** You can buy all the **side dishes** as well—green beans, mashed potatoes, peas and carrots, and so on. The produce department includes a nice **salad bar.**

You can get supermarket sundries here such as detergent, milk, and canned tuna, as well as fresh produce. I visited when the store had barely been open a month, and La Verdi says expansion is planned.

Bread & Circus. See "Going Organic," page 434.

The Italian Express

2-4 Hartford Street, Newton Highlands, MA 02161   (617) 332-6210
Mail order: not available   Catering: available
Hours: Mon.–Fri. 7:30 A.M.–7:30 P.M.; Sat. 7:30 A.M.–6 P.M.;
   Sun. 8:30 A.M.–3 P.M.

600 W. Cummings Park, Suite 1950, Woburn, MA 01801
   (617) 933-5156
Mail order: not available   Catering: available
Hours: Mon.–Fri. 7:30 A.M.–3:30 P.M.; closed Sat., Sun.

Marcello Rafaella has been in the food business since he was nine, and he wanted to have his own place for a long time before he opened Italian Express in 1991. The Newton location is a double storefront, two businesses joined at the hip. There is a bakery on one side, with tables. A collection of paperbacks is on hand for you to peruse while you enjoy a cup of coffee. **Bakery items** are good, though not striking. The **almond horn** is very nice—a large, crescent-shaped almond macaroon with the ends dipped in chocolate. And the **glorious muffin** is decent, a morning pastry loaded with carrots, raisins, and apples.

The items that live up to the store's name are on the other side. There is a wide array of **Italian prepared foods,** including half a dozen kinds of **lasagne.** "We're known for our lasagne," Rafaella notes. And it's good stuff, filling, layered with lots of cheese and homemade tomato sauce. Fillings include **vegetables, spinach, meat, cheese, sausage,** and **eggplant.** There are several other pasta dishes as well, including **baked ziti, stuffed shells,** and **spaghetti and meatballs.** Rafaella makes his own **pasta** and uses it in these dishes. The **marinara sauce,** which you can get by the pint, is good—flavorful and not too acidic.

There are several **salads,** with pasta again a dominant theme, all presented in a display case. There are both Italian inspirations like **pasta primavera** and others, such as **Pad Thai** and **ginger-peanut noodles.** Of the **sandwiches,** the Italian-inspired sandwiches are more interesting, including three **parmigianas: chicken, veal,** and **eggplant.** The **sausage sandwich** uses fresh Italian sausage and homemade sauce. There are also several Italian cold cuts, including mortadella, prosciutto, and Genoa salami.

Shelves across from the display cases contain various imported Italian goods, such as olive oil, tomatoes, and dried pastas. The Newton store is the commissary for the Woburn store, which caters mostly to office workers. There is no bakery there.

Legal Sea Foods Market Place. See "Some Things Fishy," page 110.

Tutto Italiano. See "The World in a Jar," page 420.

SOMERVILLE

Noodles. See "Lotsa Pasta," page 95.

Picante

217 Elm Street, Davis Square, Somerville, MA 02144
   (617) 628-MEXI (6394)
Mail order: not available   Catering: available
Hours: daily 11:30 A.M.–11 P.M.

735 Massachusetts Avenue, Cambridge, MA 02139
   (617) 576-MEXI (6394)
Mail order: not available   Catering available
Hours: Mon.–Thurs. 11 A.M.–11:30 P.M.; Fri., Sat. 11 A.M.–11 P.M.;
   Sun. 11 A.M.–10 P.M.

Picante is a Mexican take-out place with good clean flavors and some items that are a little bit different. Everything is heavy on the cheese; I find that the fillings are flavorful enough that most don't need cheese. You can order the standard Mexican food wrappers—**burritos, tacos, enchiladas,** and **quesadillas.** For fillings you have a choice of **grilled steak, grilled chicken,** and a vegetarian **grilled squash and mushroom.** Everything is very good, often served with a side of *arroz Mexicano,* lightly seasoned rice, and delicious **black beans.**

    There is a **salsa bar,** usually featuring three or four different kinds. Take some home in one of the small take-out containers. My favorite is *pico de gallo,* loaded with tomatoes, onions, cucumbers, and cilantro. It complements the tacos and burritos nicely. There is also a smoky **chipotle salsa.** The best thing to drink with these dishes is the homemade **limeade**—tart, perfectly sweetened, always refreshing. It does not stay fresh-tasting for more than a few hours, however; at the Cambridge store, the manager has declined to serve a batch on occasion in the mid-afternoon, recommending that I wait for a new batch.

Salt & Pepper. See "Everything Nice," page 262.

NORTH

ANDOVER

The Earth Food Store. See "Going Organic," page 440.

BEVERLY

Tapa's Corner
284 Cabot Street, Beverly, MA 01915   (508) 927-9983
Mail order: not available   Catering: available
Hours: Mon.–Thurs. and Sat. 7 A.M.–9 P.M.; Fri. 7 A.M.–10 P.M.;
closed Sun.

Tapa's Corner is, in fact, located on a corner, and it is an appealing mix of gourmet and earthy. There's a selection of **soups** and **salads.** The regular **tomato-lime tortilla soup** is very good. Soups and salads come small or large, and a small here is really small. A small **field of greens**—a mix of arugula, watercress, and radicchio—is a bare taste.

The **sandwiches** are more filling and come in four formats and prices: a **burrito** is a twelve-inch flour tortilla, "folded envelope-style," according to the menu; a **roll-up** is a nine-inch flour tortilla spread with filling and rolled into a cylinder—this is the best one for eating and walking; a **soft taco** is a six-inch flour tortilla, served open-face; and a **taco** is a folded, crisp corn tortilla. The wrappers may be Mexican, but the fillings generally are not. There is **bean,** a toss of black, kidney, and pinto. Some combinations work better than others. **Curry chicken and rice** and **Brie and avocado** are good, but **peanut butter and jelly** is best on regular sliced bread. House specialties include **roasted eggplant** with balsamic vinaigrette and pan-seared **Cajun catfish.**

Tapa's **siesta bowls** are essentially stews served over rice—good cold-weather items. There's a hearty **seasoned ground beef** and **sautéed portobello mushroom.** Vegetarian offerings include **hummus, tabouli,** and **baba ganoush.** Tapa's Corner reflects eclectic influences.

There is a handful of tables and chairs, and a counter with stools in the middle of the store, if you want to eat there. There's also a selection of baked goods.

Tastebuds

151 Hale Street, Beverly, MA 01915   (508) 922-0151
Mail order: not available   Catering: available
Hours: Mon.–Fri. 7:30 A.M.–6:30 P.M.; Sat. 8:30 A.M.–5 P.M.;
   Sun. 8:30 A.M.–3 P.M.

You're driving along Route 127 in Beverly, nary a store in sight, when all of sudden, on the southern side of the street, a tiny little house with a flowered banner bearing the name Tastebuds beckons promisingly. Here it is, a gourmet take-out shop, virtually in the middle of nowhere. There's a choice of several **salads,** including seven different **chicken salads,** such as the popular **chicken and green grape** and a tasty **chicken mango.** Other salads include an appealing **Indonesian rice.** "We are famous for our roll-up bread!" proclaims the menu, and this is how sandwiches are made here: the filling is spread on a round of Syrian bread, which is then rolled tightly into a cylinder. Among the combinations is the **Montserrat,** roast turkey and stuffing spread with cranberry mayonnaise. The **Endicott** is popular, a combination of roast turkey, ham, dilled Havarti cheese, and Russian dressing.

Tastebuds offers **large platters** and **items to go** that can serve eight to twenty people, including items such as **shepherd's pie, meat loaf,** and a selection of **soups, pastas,** and **salads.**

The store also has a variety of baked goods, including muffins, cookies, pies, and cakes made by area bakers. There are several gourmet items, such as condiments and preserves.

MANCHESTER

Wheatberries of Manchester. See "Everything Nice," page 264.

MARBLEHEAD

J & S Brandi's

7 Bessom Street, Marblehead, MA 01945   (617) 631-5040
Mail order: not available   Catering: not available
Hours: Mon.–Fri. 9:30 A.M.–7:30 P.M.; Sat. 9 A.M.–6 P.M.; closed Sun.

John and Sue Brandi had both worked in the food business for several years before opening their appealing self-named establishment in 1989. "We realized how busy people are these days," Sue

Brandi explains. "The kids get out of school, and there is no time to make dinner. We wanted to provide restaurant-quality food, without the tables." Sue's forte is the front of the house—service —and John's is the kitchen.

Service is very important to Sue, and, indeed, when I visited, everyone working behind the counter was not only help-ful, but genuinely friendly toward the customers. There were obviously many regulars.

The business has grown significantly, and the Brandis now have a commissary nearby for all their food preparation. There are two display cases. One contains **salads,** the other contains **entrées.** These are all sold cold, to be reheated; with each item you purchase, the price label prints out baking instructions.

The foods are homey, not too fancy, although there are many creative combinations. A best-selling entrée is the *pollo alla Salerno,* a boneless chicken breast cooked with wine and topped with mozzarella and mushrooms. Also popular is the **chicken salad;** this is a classic version, heavy on the mayo. I prefer the **low-fat chicken salad** because it is more interesting—spicy and flecked with diced carrots, peppers, and onions.

Fat content is a concern to the Brandis, and they even hired a nutrition consultant to help develop recipes lower in fat. There is lots of chicken, prepared all different ways. **Chicken Roosevelt** is marinated with basil, scallions, and olive oil. The **herb-roasted rotisserie chicken** is the most appealing; it is sold hot and will taste the freshest. Another popular dish is the **roasted pork loin with caramelized onions.**

A delicious (and not low-fat) side dish is **corn on the cube,** a cross between corn bread and corn pudding. It is great on its own, or accompanying the pork or a chicken dish. Also good is the vegetarian **stuffed zucchini,** filled with a blend of rice, cheese, and vegetables.

The refrigerator and freezer case includes a variety of homemade **soups** and **dips,** and appetizers made by a local com-pany. There are some desserts, like a custardy *tiramisù.* Other **baked goods** are near the cash register. The quality of these varies —all are individually plastic-wrapped, and some items were stale. Ask when the cookies were made. The **muffins** aren't bad; they are loaded with fruit such as blueberries. The **oatmeal cookies** are very good, and the **peanut butter** ones include peanut butter chips. The best dessert is the outrageous **Caribbean bar** (the reason for the name is unclear), a sort of candy-cookie. This consists of a base of ground Hydrox cookies and butter topped with white chocolate chips, chocolate chips, pecans, and mini-marshmallows.

Marblehead Lobster Co. See "Some Things Fishy," page 118.

Truffles
114 Washington Street, Marblehead, MA 01945   (617) 639-1104
Mail order: not available   Catering: available
Hours: Mon.–Fri. 10 A.M.–7 P.M.; Sat., Sun. 10 A.M.–6 P.M.

Truffles is located on the very charming Washington Street, in the heart of old Marblehead, a few blocks up from the ocean. They make a variety of terrific **salads** and **entrées,** as well as **sandwiches.** Items offered change with the seasons, but there are always various vegetable combinations, pasta, and starches. A popular item is the **chicken salad with grapes and walnuts**— excellent, among the best chicken salads I've tasted. The **sesame noodles,** also popular, are too mild for my taste, but the **grilled vegetables** are terrific—they are really grilled. I've found that most places simply oven roast vegetables and call them grilled. These have a true smoky flavor; they are thinly sliced and delicious.

Truffles has a cheese case, with various domestic and imported cheeses. They also make several unique **cheese spreads** based on a cream cheese and sour cream blend. Tempting combinations include **artichoke-garlic spread** and **black-olive spread,** made with hand-pitted olives blended into a paste. There are several glass containers of **olives** sitting on the counter, with half a dozen varieties of both black and green, with some marinated in an herbed marinade.

The **soups** are usually vegetable-based—the shop has a large vegetarian clientele. The offerings change daily. I tried an unusual **mushroom with spinach soup,** a refreshing change from the ubiquitous cream of mushroom or mushroom-barley soups.

The **sandwiches** are creative and very good. Goat cheese, olive spread, and roasted peppers—a combination I love—comprise the **McElroy.** The **Buddha** is grilled chicken breast with a wonderfully spicy Thai peanut sauce. **Peppet's Pride** is Black Forest ham, Brie, scallions, and Pommery mustard.

Truffles does catering, and they sell a line of their **appetizers** and **hors d'oeuvres,** frozen. These include items such as **sundried tomato and feta tart** and **artichoke and shrimp puffs.**

They carry Biga's focaccia and baked goods from various bakeries, including Delphin's Gourmandise (see "Everything Nice," page 265). Pamela Marvin recently bought the shop, and she is expanding Truffles' line of homemade baked goods. Homemade items include **scones, chocolate killer cake,** and **lemonblueberry cake.**

There are a handful of tables here, and you can buy a variety of gourmet items such as oils and condiments.

MEDFORD

Bob's Imported Food and Fine Catering. See "The World in a Jar," page 416.

MELROSE

Turner's Seafood Grill & Market. See "Some Things Fishy," page 120.

WOBURN

The Italian Express. See Newton, page 181.

SOUTH

BROCKTON

Pasta Bene. See "Lotsa Pasta," page 98.

Phoenicia Market. See "The World in a Jar," page 426.

CANTON

A Taste of Italy

520 Washington Street, Canton, MA 02021   (617) 821-1231
Mail order: not available   Catering: available
Hours: Tues.–Sun. 10 A.M.–9 P.M.; closed Mon.

It was at the end of a rainy day in April when I came across A
Taste of Italy. I wasn't optimistic—it looked like the business was
a restaurant. There is a display case as you enter, but the choices
were not extensive. But no matter. What is there is very, very
good. The **potato-pepper-onion frittata** is worth driving for; it
is simply excellent. The peppers used are homemade vinegared
peppers; they balance the potatoes and egg nicely. After a taste, I
promptly bought two pounds. This dish is good both hot and
cold. It goes well with their equally excellent **tomato salad.** The
tomatoes are dressed with imported extra-virgin olive oil, balsamic vinegar, and capers; celery is thrown in for crunch. I also
like the **caponata.** It is sweet and sour (a tad more on the sweet
side), but meltingly good.

The shop also makes a variety of **sandwiches.** In addition to the standard **ham-and-cheese** and **turkey,** there is
chicken Parmesan and **veal Parmesan.** There are several **heat-
and-serve dishes,** including a variety of **pastas.** These tend to be
rich, like **lasagne** or **fettuccine Alfredo.** You can also buy **sauces**
by the pint, including **pesto, white clam,** and **Taste of Italy,** a
very good marinara.

HINGHAM

Chicken Etc.

69 Water Street, Hingham, MA 02043
(617) 740-4344 or (800) 585-2473
Mail order: not available   Catering: available
Hours: Mon.–Fri. 11:30 A.M.–8 P.M., Sat., Sun. noon–7 P.M.

Roger Westhaven opened Chicken Etc. in 1989 as a counterpart
operation to his Bear Cove Gourmet take-out and catering business; the latter is now Dagwoods (see "Sandwiches," page 209).
This is one of the best **rotisserie chicken** places I've seen; the
quality of the meat and the side dishes is excellent. You can get a
whole, half, breast quarter, or **leg and thigh.** The side dishes
are delicious, especially the **real mashed potatoes.** Also good are

the **garlic mashed potatoes,** although they aren't that garlicky. One version is puréed smooth, the other is lumpier, with the skin kept on. the **butternut squash** is sweet and buttery. Other sides include cold **Mexican corn salad** and **rice pilaf.**

The rotisserie chicken is the best chicken preparation, but you can also get **chicken fried, grilled,** in **soup,** and chopped into **chili** or **chicken salad.**

WEST

ACTON

Savoury Lane
256 Arlington Street, Acton, MA 01720   (508) 263-8743
Mail order: not available   Catering: available
Hours: Mon.–Sat. 10 A.M.–9 P.M.; closed Sun.

I used to frequent Savoury Lane when I worked in West Concord. At that time they were located on Great Road in a house that was over a hundred years old—an anomaly on a highway of strip malls. But, says Rick Gordon, who has owned the place since 1985, the house was falling apart, and the landlord wasn't interested in renovating. So Gordon and his wife Paula built the new Cape-style building from the ground up at a new site and moved in in January of 1995. There are now many more seats, and business is as much eat-in as take-out.

Savoury Lane specializes in creative **sandwiches** and **salads.** The latter are primarily pasta-based. **Deb's pasta** is a refreshing mix of shells, peppers, scallions, and peas in a dill dressing. **Low-fat chicken ziti** is tossed with broccoli, red peppers, garlic, and Parmesan. Nonpasta salads include **shrimp and copy crab;** *copy crab* is one third crab and two thirds pollock, and not particularly interesting. The **New Delhi chicken salad** is better, seasoned with curry and studded with raisins and, yes, a bit of pasta.

The menu lists over forty **sandwiches.** There are the usual deli meats, as well as items such as **Cajun meatloaf, cream cheese and olive,** and **chicken liver.** Several sandwiches are grilled; I always like Savoury Lane's **grilled tuna melt** made with Havarti. They make a very good **Reuben.** House specialty sandwiches have names such as the **Actonian** (corned beef, pastrami, bacon, Swiss, lettuce, and tomato with Russian dressing on dark rye) and the **Gourmet special** (Pâté de Campagnon on French bread).

To top off your meal, Savoury Lane makes a handful of **baked goods,** including **chocolate chip cookies** and **killer brownies.**

ARLINGTON

Via Lago Pasta. See Lexington, page 193.

BELMONT

Rustica
30 Leonard Street, Belmont, MA 02178   (617) 489-6333
Mail order: not available   Catering: available
Hours: Mon.–Wed. 11:30 A.M.–9 P.M.; Thurs., Fri. 11:30 A.M.–10 P.M.;
   Sat. 9:30 A.M.–10 P.M.; closed Sun.

The atmosphere of Rustica is lovely. The room is an irregular-shaped corner space, with plate-glass windows lining the front. Squares of earthy tiles cover the floor, and there are several tables of various sizes and styles to the left as you enter. Maiolica pottery, with its lovely, rustic designs, is displayed around the store, and you can purchase the various bowls, cups, and plates. Italian goods—boxed tomatoes, olive oils, dried pastas, and vinegars—line the floor-to-ceiling shelves on the right. The path leads to the food counters, which display **salads** and other **prepared foods,** as well as **baked goods.**

The prepared food is the main reason to come to Rustica, because it is very, very good. Owner Robert G. Goodman takes obvious pride in his recipes as he describes the preparation of various dishes. I have a lot of favorites here. I could eat the vegetarian **crisped saffron risotto cakes** daily. They are simultaneously chewy, creamy, and crunchy; they taste divine served with a **roasted tomato sauce.** The **spaghetti torta** is wonderful, a rich layering of spaghetti, eggplant, and roasted red peppers topped with a sun-dried tomato aioli. My mouth waters just thinking about it.

Salads change daily, but the popular **flash-grilled calamari and vegetable salad** is always available, as is the **roasted**

chicken salad with roasted vegetables. This delectable chicken is rubbed with coarse kosher salt and pepper and infused with garlic and herbs. It marinates overnight then is quickly grilled in a 600°F pizza oven. The **roasted chicken** is also available whole or as part of an entrée and is incredibly tender and moist. It's served with addictive **roasted mushrooms** that have been tossed with olive oil and thyme.

Most of the breads come from Panini or Iggy's (see "The Staff of Life," pages 25 and 33), but Rustica does make a **Tuscan bread,** a good, chewy loaf. Grilled slices come with most entrées. The homemade **focaccia** is made with potatoes and is soft, with a crisp crust. The **pizza** crust is an entirely different recipe, one that includes both semolina and cake flour. The pizza is very good here. Rustica is one of the few places in the area to make the Italian sweet bread **panettone,** which they bake in coffee cans. It has a slightly yeasty flavor but is quite good nonetheless, studded with raisins and other dried fruit and pine nuts.

A few of the **baked goods** need work, but most of them are very good, and some are fantastic. In the latter category is the **almond-brandy torte with brandy crème anglaise,** which Goodman said was experimental; I strongly recommended that he make it a regular item. It's one of those desserts that you keep tasting until all of a sudden, it's gone. Less good are the **biscotti,** which are too soft. The **orange amaretti cake** is good for dieters; essentially it's an angel food cake.

I like the subtly sweet **pear almond tart.** The **lemon risotto teacake** is like a rice pudding in a cake form. Like the savory risotto cakes, it's a pleasing mélange of chewy and creamy textures, with a hint of sweetened lemon. The **maple pecan butter cookie** has an indiscernible maple flavor, but as a butter cookie it's great. Of the cookies, **chocolate amaretti meringues** are one of the best, crisp on the outside, chewy within. The soft almond flavor marries well with the bits of chocolate that pepper the cookie.

Goodman originally planned Rustica to be a take-out restaurant with seats. Customers repeatedly requested table service, however, so the place now functions as a restaurant as well, serving lunch and dinner.

CONCORD

La Pasta Place. See "Lotsa Pasta," page 100.

The Natural Gourmet. See "Going Organic," page 445.

Sally Ann Food Shop. See "Everything Nice," page 282.

FRAMINGHAM

Healthy Heart Café
1645 Concord Street, Framingham, MA 01701   (508) 877-6577
Mail order: not available   Catering: available
Hours: Mon.–Sat. 7 A.M.–6 P.M.; closed Sun.

Healthy Heart Café is the take-out offshoot of Pure & Simply Gourmet, a catering business started by Barbara Wilson in 1985. As the name implies, the foods tend to be lower in fat than your average take-out items. Before starting her catering company, Wilson had worked as a nurse. A few years ago, her husband had to go on a low-cholesterol diet. "I realized that take-out food is very high in fat," Wilson says. "Everything in the café is low-fat, but you wouldn't know it." Indeed, the items I tried were very good. A low-fat diet should have between 20 and 30 grams of fat a day, and that is what Wilson aims for in these dishes.

The menu lists eight **salads,** but the company makes several more, and these rotate daily. One listed item is the **Mandarin curry chicken pasta salad,** with a creamy-tasting dressing. A special is the **roasted red pepper tortellini;** this is less successful than the other salads I tried. Frankly, tortellini doesn't work well cold, in my opinion—the filling gets firm and clammy. Rotini and penne work much better in pasta salads, as in the **Greek penne,** which has bits of spinach, feta, and toasted pine nuts. Some of these ingredients may sound rich, but Healthy Heart uses them in smaller amounts to flavor a dish. My favorite salad is a regular item, **nine-spice chicken with roasted vegetables.** The chicken is subtly spiced, and the vegetables include wonderful potatoes, thinly sliced and full of flavor.

There are a number of **hot entrées** that change daily. I tried a **vegetable lasagne,** which was good, but not remarkable. There are several filling **sandwiches,** including a **grilled turkey breast,** served with cranberry salsa on focaccia. The **Mediterranean roll-up,** with cucumbers, red onions, sun-dried tomatoes, and feta is good, but a little odd in that it is rolled up in a flour tortilla, as opposed to pita bread, which would complement these ingredients better.

The **low-fat muffins** are very popular and very good. I tried **blueberry** and **blueberry-raspberry.** Fat-free muffins tend to be too sweet, and you end up gaining calories from the extra sugar. These low-fat muffins are not overly sweet, and they use nonfat yogurt and enough oil to give them a nice crumb. Other **low-fat desserts** change daily, and include **coffee cake, brownies,** and **cheesecake.**

LEXINGTON

Lexington Lobster and Seafood. See "Some Things Fishy," page 118.

Via Lago Gourmet Foods
1845 Mass. Avenue, Lexington, MA 02173   (617) 861-6174
Mail order: not available   Catering: available
Hours: Mon.–Fri. 8 A.M.–7 P.M.; Sat. 8 A.M.–6 P.M.; Sun. 8 A.M.–3 P.M.

Via Lago Pasta
212A Mass. Avenue, Arlington, MA 02174   (617) 643-6644
Mail order: not available   Catering: available
Hours: Mon.–Fri. 10 A.M.–6 P.M.; Sat. 8 A.M.–6 P.M.; closed Sun.

David Jick started Via Lago in Arlington making wholesale fresh **pasta** in 1982. He opened the Arlington store in 1988 with his brother Alan, primarily as a take-out shop and an outlet for his pasta. Alan then took over the business and also opened the Lexington location, selling the Arlington store to its manager Karen Andrew in 1994.

The pasta is still made by David Jick, at Noodles, his new business (see "Lotsa Pasta," page 95), and it's great. There is both fresh **(spinach, basil,** and **ricotta)** and frozen **ravioli** (some twenty kinds, including **sun-dried tomato** and **Swiss chard). Sheets of pasta** can be cut to order as **linguine** or **fettuccine.** There are also ten **sauces** available. The regular **tomato sauce** is very good, but the **meat tomato sauce** is fantastic. An Italian friend who eschews any sauce that's not homemade said she would buy this sauce. Sauces are available in pint and quart containers to go.

There is also a variety of **frozen dinners,** reasonably priced, such as **Thai shrimp curry over rice, lamb ragout over couscous,** and **spinach** or **meat lasagne.**

The **sandwiches** are very good. Via Lago uses bread from Clear Flour and Iggy's (see "The Staff of Life," pages 15 and 33); they also sell whole loaves. Among the offerings is the **Via Lago Italian,** a layering of prosciutto, mortadella, salami, hot *cappicola,* roasted red pepper, and provolone. The **tuna salad** is tasty, made with homemade **mayonnaise,** scallions, and celery.

The take-out **salads** are generally good, although some could have used more flavor. It's worth asking for a taste before buying. The best I tried were **broccoli rabe** with olive oil and pine nuts; **Mediterranean pasta salad** with tomatoes and feta cheese; and **chicken orzo salad.** An unusual item is **garden tomatoes and English cucumbers with Brie in a light balsamic dressing.**

The two shops have different owners, so the focus differs slightly. Most of the recipes are the same in both places. Lexington was remodeled recently and is doing more prepared dinner entrées. Arlington sells prepared foods and raw ingredients, such as porcini mushrooms and sun-dried tomatoes.

Via Lago in Lexington carries a variety of **baked goods;** they aren't bad, but none I tried were remarkable.

NEEDHAM

Vicki Lee Boyajian. See "Everything Nice," page 283.

WATERTOWN

Angel's Bakery and Café. See "The Staff of Life," page 32.

Massis. See "The World in a Jar," page 425.

Sevan's Bakery. See "Everything Nice," page 284.

WELLESLEY

Bread & Circus. See "Going Organic," page 434.

Tutto Italiano. See "The World in a Jar," page 420.

❖ S A N D W I C H E S ❖

BOSTON

BOSTON

Artu's

6 Prince Street, North End, Boston, MA 02113   (617) 742-4336
Mail order: not available   Catering: available
Hours: daily 11 A.M.–11 P.M.

89 Charles Street, Boston, MA 02114   (617) 227-0499
Mail order: not available   Catering: available
Hours: Mon.–Sat. 11 A.M.–11 P.M.; closed Sun.

Donato Frattoroli comes from a restaurant family: his family runs Lucia's on Hanover Street and Filippo's by the Charlestown Bridge. But in 1992 Frattoroli decided to go out on his own with Artu's. Lucky for sandwich-lovers, and foodies in general. There are several tables here for sit-down service, but the restaurant also does a tremendous amount of take-out business. Their inexpensive ($6) **rotisserie chickens** are very popular but are a little dry. The **antipasto** platters are always a good bet here, consisting, among other things, of thinly sliced grilled eggplant, marinated peppers, and roasted carrots.

But ah, those **sandwiches.** The **roast pork** is awesome: a halved loaf of Italian bread is buried under what seems like over half a pound of thinly sliced, juicy meat. Likewise with the **roast lamb.** One sandwich could easily feed two hungry people. The classic **fresh mozzarella, tomato, and basil sandwich** is great here. The tomatoes are diced and tossed in a garlicky marinade. You can also get a variation with prosciutto. When you order the sandwiches, be sure to get a side of the **grilled eggplant.** It's sliced paper-thin and has a meaty feel and taste to it. The **marinated peppers** are okay, but they have a tinny taste.

Note that most items are prepared at the North End location and taste fresher when bought there.

Garden of Eden

577 Tremont Street, Boston, MA 02118   (617) 247-8377
Mail order: not available   Catering: available
Hours: Tues.–Fri. 7:30 A.M.–7 P.M.; Sat., Sun. 8 A.M.–6 P.M.; closed Mon.

Garden of Eden is a very tiny, very attractive shop and café. The walls are painted with twirling vines and adorned with hanging silks. You can sit on a wicker and iron chair at one of seven copper tables decorated with terra-cotta pots and attractive flower arrangements. The atmosphere is refined and relaxed.

Kelly Brown, who owns the store with her husband Oliver Desnain, says the concept of the store came to her in a dream. "It really did," she says. "I dreamed the store, that it was a safe place to go to that felt like a sheltered garden in a thunderstorm."

Atmosphere is important, but it is the food that anchors Garden of Eden. The menu has evolved since the store opened in 1991, in part owing to the lengthy time it took to get various licenses. The store, Brown says, is now what she envisioned.

Brown and Desnain do not make any of the items in the display cases; foods from baked goods to fresh pastas are made by various "friends" from around the state and New England. The couple has a knack for ferreting out the best, and the unusual. They do make sandwiches, and serve coffee and tea.

The **sandwiches** are excellent and many feature cured Russian and Polish meats, among other fillings. The **Dartmouth** includes Ukrainian ham, which is not at all salty and has a buttery aftertaste; the sandwich is layered with endive, Swiss cheese, and fresh dill, and heated in a sandwich press to melt the cheese. The press is used for several of the sandwiches, which are served warm. Heating the sandwiches gives them a pleasing texture—and they don't fall apart as you eat them. Viennese rolled chicken breast is the centerpiece of the **Union Park;** it is complemented by cucumbers, parsley, and mustard vinaigrette and served on a dense raisin-pecan bread. The sandwich breads, which come from area bakers, are also available by the loaf. The store's namesake sandwich, the **Garden of Eden,** is an excellent vegetarian offering, among the best veggie sandwiches I've tried. *Mesclun* greens are tossed with a tangy vinaigrette and sandwiched in a crusty baguette with thin slices of apple and crumbled blue cheese.

Fresh **pasta** and **pasta sauces** are next to the assorted cheeses. My favorite sauces are the **Romesco,** rich with ground toasted almonds and tomatoes, and the **sun-dried tomato and mozzarella.** There is also a decent **pesto** with pine nuts and walnuts and a vinegary olive oil–based **olive and herbs,** made with crushed green olives. There is a delicious frozen **garlic and parsley ravioli with wild mushroom and walnut filling.**

Baked goods include **buttery croissants** and **pecan buns,** as well as elegant, French-style desserts.

Salumeria Italiano

151 Richmond Street, Boston, MA 02113   (617) 523-8743
Mail order: not available   Catering: not available
Hours: Mon.–Thurs. and Sat. 7 A.M.–6 P.M.; Fri. 7 A.M.–7 P.M.;
    closed Sun.

Salumeria Italiano in the North End is the place for great food at decent prices. They are well known for their **sandwiches** (although owner Erminio Martignetti says, "Our main focus is selling the cold cuts and cheeses for people to make their own sandwiches, though we do make samples"). There's a wonderful selection of potential sandwich fillings in the deli case at the back of the store. To get there, you pass a table full of breads from Iggy's (see "The Staff of Life," page 33) and from a New Jersey bakery. A good selection of imported dry Italian pasta is to the left, and shelves of olive oils and artisan balsamic vinegars is to the right. There are intriguing imported items here, such as whole baby anchovies in hot oil, and pickled garlic cloves from Spain.

The deli case is filled with tempting items: beautiful salamis, three kinds of prosciutto—*cotto* (boiled), *crudo de Parma* (cured), and *fumicato* (smoked)—and *bresaola* (air-dried beef). Cheeses include buffalo-milk mozzarella, mascarpone, and *stracchino.* They'll gladly give you a taste of any item you're curious about. There are jars of olives, including big, crunchy green *cerignola, gaeta,* tiny Niçoise, purple Alfonso, and fennel–hot pepper Calabrese.

West End Strollers

200 Faneuil Hall Marketplace, Boston, MA 02109   (617) 720-6020
Mail order: not available   Catering: available
Hours: Mon.–Thurs. 9 A.M.–9 P.M.; Fri., Sat. 9 A.M.–10 P.M.;
    Sun. 9 A.M.–6:30 P.M.

Johnny Bistany has had a business in Faneuil Hall since 1987. Bistany's, down the hall from West End Strollers, offers an average selection of coffees and candies. But West End Strollers, open since 1993, is much more notable. I'm not sure who coined the term *stroller* to describe a sandwich rolled in a large, flat pita bread, but that's what strollers are.

West End's **strollers** come with a variety of Middle Eastern fillings. The **falafel** is good, although a little dry; it needs
tahini and tabouli for moistness. The **grilled chicken** is wonderful. Before cooking the chicken they marinate it in wine, garlic,
and olive oil for two days. **Kibbeh** is a mildly spiced blend of
cracked wheat and ground beef. The aroma that will entice you
here comes from the **beef** and **chicken shawarma,** meat stacked
and slow-roasted on a vertical broiler.

The **baklava** is delicious, buttery, crisp, not cloyingly
sweet, and it's made with pistachios. The other Middle Eastern
pastries, including **finger** (filo dough rolled to a cigar shape with
a cashew filling) and *basma* (a semolina dough flavored with
rosewater and pistachios), are also quite good. West End is one
of the best sources for Middle Eastern pastries I've tried.

ROSLINDALE

Manny's Pastries

633 Hyde Park Avenue, Roslindale, MA 02131   (617) 325-2718
Mail order: not available   Catering: not available
Hours: Mon.–Sat. 7 A.M.–5 P.M.; Sun. 10 A.M.–5 P.M.

Manny's is a bakery, featuring some nice sweets, but the reason
to come here is for the **Cuban sandwich.** The elements are
simple: bread, pork, ham, Swiss cheese. But it's the quality of the
elements that makes the difference, and Manny's are excellent.
They make their own **Cuban bread,** a long loaf, wide and softer
than a French baguette, yet with a crisp crust.

Owner Manuela Lopez roasts the **pork.** First she rubs it
with her blend of spices; then she wraps it first in plastic, then
aluminum foil, which in effect steams the meat as it roasts for
almost four hours. The result is pork with a texture almost like
that of ham.

Once roasted, the pork is thinly sliced and layered with
smoked ham and Swiss cheese on the split Cuban bread. The
sandwich then goes in a sandwich press, which melts the cheese
and melds the flavors. Terrific.

Manny's also has a small selection of **sweets.** The best is
the *guayaba empanada,* a turnover with a homamade guava
filling. The pastry is made with cream cheese and is delicious.
There are other flaky pastries with guava and other fillings called
de hojas. As I was about to leave, Lopez convinced me to try

both the **rice pudding** and the **vanilla pudding.** They looked pretty plain, packaged in clear plastic cups covered with plastic wrap. But boy, are these good puddings! Simple, creamy, inhalable.

The place was originally named for Lopez's nephew, who is no longer involved with the business. Lopez's son said that they may be changing the name to Panificadoro la Sisegoza, after bakeries the family ran when they lived in Cuba.

METROPOLITAN BOSTON

BROOKLINE

Rami's

324 Harvard Street, Brookline, MA 02146   (617) 738-3577
Mail order: not available   Catering: not available
Hours: Sun.–Thurs 10 A.M.–10 P.M.; Fri. 10 A.M.–2:30 P.M.; closed Sat.

Rami's prepares **glatt kosher** Middle Eastern **sandwiches.** They make very good **falafel** and **hummus,** but the best item here is the **grilled chicken.** Strips of boneless, skinless chicken breast are sautéed on the grill with onions and spices then scooped into pita bread and drizzled with tahini and hot sauce. There is a choice of two sauces. The **green sauce** includes cilantro. Beware: it looks mild, but it packs a wallop. The *amba* is also spicy, made with mangos and curry. I prefer the chicken to the **shawarma,** which is turkey slow-cooked on a vertical rotisserie. The turkey can be tough and fatty. The **kabob beef** is tasty. This consists of ground beef mixed with parsley, onions, and spices.

The meats and falafel are all served either as **sandwiches** or as **platters,** which means they come with a little more food as well as a salad. Rami's also carries *bourekas,* flaky yet heavy savory pastries filled with **meat** or **spinach.** You can accompany your meal with one of their juices imported from Israel; my favorite is mango juice.

Rubin's Kosher Delicatessen & Restaurant

500 Harvard Street, Brookline, MA 02146   (617) 731-8787
Mail order: available   Catering: available
Hours: Mon.–Thurs. 10 A.M.–8 P.M.; Fri. 10 A.M.–3 P.M.;
   Sun. 9 A.M.–8 P.M.; closed Sat.

Larry Grupp's grandfather and great-uncle started Rubin's in 1927 as a strictly kosher delicatessen. It is the area's classic Jewish deli, with the best **deli sandwiches** around. Grupp does all the cooking and says that maintaining a single location enables him to maintain quality; he has been asked repeatedly over the years to open more Rubin's restaurants. He and his father bought the business from his great-uncle in 1974 and were the first in the area to bring kosher deli meats from New York to the Boston area. "I hate to say it," he says, "but New York meats are better —and I'm not a lover of New York. When we brought them in, people went wild over the way the meats were cured."

But the food is also expensive, since kosher meats are pricey. My husband's long-standing favorite combo, the **Number 12,** is a layering of American kosher corned beef, hot Roumanian pastrami, and excellent chopped liver. It costs $8.55 for a large and $10.55 for an overstuffed (these are Rubin's sandwich classifications; there are no smalls here, perhaps so you will feel better about paying these prices).

This is a full-service restaurant, and invariably there are lines and lengthy waits for tables. But the sandwich-to-go service is speedy. The **sandwiches** are definitely the reason to come here; the **hot entrées** never tempt me. There are a dozen combos. The **Number 2** is an appealing mix of turkey breast, spiced beef, and tongue. **Creative Eating** consists of two potato pancakes topped with your choice of hot corned beef (my favorite), tongue, or brisket.

There are also lots of cold and hot single-item sandwiches, including **turkey pastrami, bologna,** and **meat loaf;** I prefer the combos, or the **extralean corned beef.** Hot items include juicy **hamburgers** and **hot dogs.** You can also create your own combinations.

Several traditional side dishes include **potato** and **meat knishes,** *kasha varnishkes,* and **stuffed cabbage.** Grupp also makes a heart-warming **chicken-noodle soup.**

Shawarma King II

1383 Beacon Street, Brookline, MA 02146   (617) 731-6035
Mail order: not available   Catering: available
Hours: daily 11 A.M.–midnight

Ale Hacham and Hassam Kassab opened Shawarma King in Boston in 1989 and followed it with Shawarma King II in Brookline in 1992. In 1995 they closed the Boston space, which was take-out only; they plan to reopen it with full table service within the next year.

Shawarma King II has tables and is self-service. It features an extensive Middle Eastern menu, with items seen in few other places. As the restaurant's name implies, the main dish here is **shawarma,** which consists of beef, lamb, or chicken breast that is marinated for two days then skewered and roasted on a vertical rotisserie. The tender, juicy meat is then sliced and put into a pocket sandwich. *Kefta,* ground spiced beef or lamb, is served in two ways: as *arayes* it is spread on pita bread and broiled, then served with hummus; as **kabob** it is formed into balls, skewered, and broiled. Three other kinds of kabob are available—chunks of **chicken, beef,** or **lamb.** All meat is halal, cut by Kassab, who trained as a butcher.

Kibbeh is cracked wheat mixed with ground beef or lamb, or puréed pumpkin for vegetarians, formed into two layers, and filled with pine nuts and onions. For **sandwiches** it is sliced and rolled into a pita with lettuce, tomatoes, and cucumber pickles and then drizzled with tahini. It is unusual and delicious.

Among the several **vegetarian offerings** is *labne*—yogurt cheese topped with black olives and seasoned with mint and thyme. You can combine any of the sandwich ingredients on the menu with other items—**grape leaves with baba ganoush** or **falafel with hummus,** for example.

Shawarma King also makes savory pies. *Zaatar* is an oregano-like herb spread on pita with sesame seeds and olive oil; it's a pleasing accompaniment to salads, such as the lemony **tabouli.** *Lamejun* is an ultrathin dough topped with ground spiced lamb or beef and diced tomatoes and onions.

The restaurant makes its own fresh **juices,** extracted to order. These include **banana,** mixed with milk and honey, **carrot,** and **coconut.** There are also combinations, such as **cocktail juice,** a blend of mango, guava, and strawberries. For dessert try a piece of the homemade **baklava.**

CAMBRIDGE

Darwin's Ltd.

148 Mt. Auburn Street, Cambridge, MA 02138   (617) 354-5233
Mail order: not available   Catering: available
Hours: Mon.–Sat. 6:30 A.M.–9 P.M.; Sun. 7 A.M.–5 P.M.

When Steve and Isabel Darwin opened Darwin's in 1993, the neighborhood welcomed them with open arms. A convenience store had long been in this space, but the previous incarnation had been a pit. The Darwins cleaned up the space considerably, painted it, and gave it a fresh face. The store is now a combination upscale convenience store and deli. A deli was what the couple had planned to start with, and the neighbors told them what else they wanted. You can buy shampoo, Iggy's breads, soda, and fresh produce from Russo's (See "Earthly Delights," page 61). When I visited, a customer stopped me and said, "You know what makes this place so great? Steve and Isabel."

The couple provides service—and great **sandwiches,** which they have named after area streets. You can choose any of these combinations or create your own with the assortment of cheeses and quality Boarshead meats that are available. The **Chapman** features "awesome" egg salad and roasted red peppers, and it is excellent egg salad. (It converted me to this comfort food, which I had never cared for.) Against the advice of the sandwich maker, I tried it on one of Iggy's baguettes (because I love Iggy's baguettes; see "The Staff of Life," page 33). The server was right: the filling squeezes out all over the place. This filling is best on peasant white or honey whole wheat sliced breads, sandwich breads that come from Boston Daily Bread (see "The Staff of Life," page 14). Smoked Gouda and smoked ham, spread with honey mustard, go into the **Lowell,** and the **Gibson** includes salami, provolone, and a homemade marinated artichoke and olive salad.

You can get **side salads.** Darwin's makes their own, and there are usually two or three choices available daily, such as **shrimp Creole pasta salad** or **saffron rice salad,** made with chicken, red peppers, and pine nuts, then tossed with a tangerine vinaigrette. They also make their own **tabouli,** which isn't bad, but I like the Middle Eastern versions that are primarily parsley; Darwin's is primarily bulgur. It is served with good **hummus** as part of the **Lakeview** sandwich.

The shop also carries scones and slices of low-fat cakes, which are light and surprisingly good.

Formaggio's Deli

81 Mount Auburn Street, Cambridge, MA 02138   (617) 547-4795
Mail order: not available   Catering: available, but limited
Hours: Sun.–Thurs. 8 A.M.–9 P.M.; Fri., Sat. 8 A.M.–10 P.M.

Formaggio's Deli opened in 1976 and was originally owned by the same person who started Formaggio Kitchen on Huron Avenue (see "An Epicurean Agenda," page 380). Carlo Ferrante bought the Harvard Square shop in 1986. I had been coming to this sandwich shop for years, and I watched it decline.

Then, in the early 1990s, Ferrante renovated Formaggio's, totally redesigning the space; I thought it must be under new ownership. For me, the change was welcome, although the facelift was extreme. Gone was the funky early seventies atmosphere. Gone also was the dowdiness. The new look was streamlined: black and white tiles, bright lights, and more seating.

But the **sandwiches** are still very good, and they are the main attraction. The fillings are not that unusual, but they are generous. The breads are sliced over half an inch thick and are laden with deli meats such as **roast beef, smoked turkey,** and **honey ham.** There are two **tuna salads,** both of which are departures from the usual. **Tuna Niçoise** includes marinated artichoke hearts and black olives, and **tuna curry** is studded with apples, almonds, and raisins. I have always been fond of the **Scottish smoked salmon sandwich;** it's good with a bit of the homemade **Boursin.**

Ferrante says a lot of his customers are vegetarian; the **veggie menu** is posted behind the counter. There are various vegetarian sandwich combinations, too. **Veggie I** includes vegetables, a choice of cheese (Havarti, Swiss, provolone, American) and a peppery Parmesan dressing. **Veggie II** is the same, with a sour cream–dill sauce. There are also other **spreads** you can have with your choice of cheese and vegetables on a sandwich. The **hummus** is okay; it could use some tahini to lend it more flavor. I like the **smoked mozzarella and sun-dried tomato spread.** it's great on a baguette with fresh spinach and tomatoes. It's also good with smoked turkey.

True to his Italian roots, Ferrante offers a variety of Italian dishes, made by his mother, Luciana. These include **chicken Parmesan** and **eggplant Parmesan,** served as an **entrée** or on a **sandwich.** There is usually a **hot pasta entrée,** such as

lasagne or **pasta with chicken, broccoli, and tomatoes.** Ferrante makes all his own **pasta,** and uses it in the **hot entrées** and in the **cold salads,** such as **spinesto,** spinach pasta with pesto, or **primavera,** with fresh vegetables. You can also buy the pasta by the pound; try it with Luciana's very good **tomato sauce.**

There are several **soups** available; these change daily. Popular recipes include **chicken soup, lentil,** and **minestrone.**

Ferrante's wife makes the **baked goods,** which are fine. The best choices are the **carrot cake** and the **cheese cake.**

Stuff-It

8½ Eliot Street, Cambridge, MA 02138   (617) 497-2220
Mail order: not available   Catering: not available
Hours: daily 10 A.M.–11 P.M.

Stuff-It has been making **rolled sandwiches** in Harvard Square for many years. They started in the Garage and then moved to their current location a few years ago. The space is a little odd, and not accessible to those with wheelchairs or strollers, unfortunately. You go up a short, steep flight of steps to order, then down a second flight of stairs to tables. But persevere: these are very good rolled sandwiches, with some unusual vegetarian fillings. All sandwiches come with lettuce, tomatoes, carrots, sprouts, Swiss cheese, and tamari dressing. They always ask if you want onions. The makings are placed on flat pita bread and rolled into a sandwich.

The various fillings are added to this basic structure. They include a variety of deli meats—**turkey, chicken, roast beef**—but there are also a few Middle Eastern items, including **falafel, tabouli,** and **hummus.** I like the **lentil and brown rice** filling, which tastes healthy and good at the same time. Pass on the **avocado;** it is puréed until it is ultrasmooth. I prefer the texture of sliced avocado. There are four kinds of **tofu: plain, curried, salsa,** and **solar,** a mysterious spice concoction that is pretty good.

Stuff-It also makes a few **baked items,** and they are excellent—exceeding my expectations for a place that is not a bakery. The **brownies** are very good and come in a few variations. The **chocolate chip cookie,** oversized but not gigantic, is delicious and buttery and has crisp edges and a chewy center. Best of all is the **walnut bar,** which is very rich and fantastic.

NEWTON

Bentonwood Bakery and Café. See "Everything Nice," page 257.

Provizer's

549 Commonwealth Avenue Newton, MA 02159   (617) 527-4333
Mail order: not available   Catering: available
Hours: Mon.–Sat. 7 A.M.–5:30 P.M.; Sun. 7 A.M.–2 P.M.

Provizer's is a Newton institution, specializing in deli sandwiches since 1936; Katherine Whitestone has owned it since 1983. The meats used are very good, and some are even kosher, such as the corned beef from American Kosher (see "Where's the Beef?" page 144). Some **sandwiches** come in two sizes; most are about $4.25 for a small and $5.95 for a large. These include **roast beef, hot brisket,** and **turkey,** all baked on the premises. Provizer's **Reuben** is made with both corned beef and excellent Roumanian pastrami, but they zap it in a microwave to melt the cheese, and it's just not the same as having it grilled.

The shop makes a variety of **meat** and **fish salads,** all with traditionally liberal amounts of mayonnaise. These include **egg salad, tuna, turkey, seafood, chicken,** and **chopped liver.** Provizer's also makes a variety of **hot soups** and **entrées to go.**

SOMERVILLE

The Oasis Grille

255 Washington Street, Somerville, MA 02143   (617) 666-5122
Mail order: not available   Catering: available
Hours: Mon.–Thurs. 11 A.M.–9 P.M.; Fri., Sat. 11 A.M.–10 P.M.; closed Sun.

The Oasis Grille specializes in Armenian and Middle Eastern fare and happens to make the best **falafel** around. It is tasty, lemony, not too salty, with spicy undertones of cumin. It is also significantly less greasy than falafel often can be, because it is grilled rather than fried. Falafel purists may object to this practice, but the falafel tastes great, especially rolled in a **pita sandwich.**

Oasis is a full-service restaurant with several tables and a counter with stools, but they do a lot of take-out business as well. The **tabouli** is tasty, with the unusual addition of red and green peppers. The **baba ganoush** is very good, if heavy on the garlic.

Owner Genie Melkonian makes her own yogurt for a **hot yogurt soup,** and for *labane,* a yogurt cheese. In a sandwich, the labne is rolled with black olives, lettuce, and tomato.

Oasis makes both **beef** and **chicken shawarma,** served with tahini sauce. Both are spicy and very tasty. There are four kinds of **kabob—beef, chicken, lamb,** and *losh* (which is ground sirloin mixed with onions, parsley, and spices)—all of which are broiled and then rolled in Syrian bread with marinated onions and homemade pickled turnips.

For dessert, the **baklava** was disappointing. More unusual, and delicious, are the **Armenian braided cookies,** made with butter and honey.

Season's Harvest
52 Broadway, Somerville, MA 02145   (617) 628-1182
Mail order: available   Catering: not available
Hours: Mon.–Fri. 8 A.M.–4 P.M.; closed Sat., Sun.

Season's Harvest is a wholesale business specializing in natural **sandwiches.** In the late 1960s Iseti and Ademar Reis were involved with a macrobiotic community in Brazil and then in Los Angeles, where they started making sandwiches. They came to the macrobiotic community in the Boston area and started their sandwich business here in 1975, supplying all the area's health-food stores.

The couple are no longer macrobiotic, but the dishes they prepare are free of additives and preservatives. They make very good **chicken salad** and **tuna salad sandwiches,** but the vegetarian items are the true draw here.

The Reises make their own **vegetarian meatballs,** a pleasing mix of tofu, brown rice, soy flour, onions, green peppers, and walnuts. I would hardly confuse them with beef meatballs, but they are tasty and good on a sandwich. You can buy packages of these meatballs to use in your own cooking. There are also several varieties of **veggie burgers. California dream** has a tofu and brown rice base, with a variety of vegetables and sesame seeds. The **vegetable patty** includes cracked wheat and rolled oats along with mushrooms and potatoes.

Season's Harvest makes eight kinds of **burritos,** all wrapped in a whole wheat chapati, which is like a flour tortilla. These are generally good, although I like some fillings better than others, and I prefer burritos heated up (the sandwiches are good hot or cold). The **Mexican burrito** includes kidney beans, salsa, and cheddar cheese. I like the **black bean burrito** with fresh green peppers and tomatoes.

In addition to sandwiches, the business makes a variety of very good **salads** and **spreads.** Iseti says that they were the first to package **hummus** for health-food stores. Their **beet salad** is quite good and refreshing, seasoned with wine vinegar and lemon juice.

The operation is primarily wholesale, but you can stop in and pick up any items they have on hand. They usually make extra, and there is no minimum purchase required. Different items are made on different days, so it's best to call in advance. Although Season's Harvest is open on Wednesdays, they make very little that day, so it's not the best day to visit.

NORTH

BURLINGTON

David's World Famous 1st Class Eateries. See Woburn, page 209.

MARBLEHEAD

The Five Corners Deli

2–4 School Street, Marblehead MA, 01945   (617) 631-6707
Mail order: not available   Catering: not available
Hours: Mon.–Thurs. 7 A.M.–10 P.M.; Fri., Sat. 7 A.M.–11 P.M.;
    Sun. 7 A.M.–9 P.M.

As the store name implies, Five Corners is located at the intersection of five streets. There are two parts to this sandwich shop, with separate entrances—the to-go counter and the sit-down restaurant. The place has been in business since 1983, and current owner Andrew Dixey bought it in 1993 after working there for half a dozen years. He describes himself as a "lifetime Marbleheader," with very deep roots in this town. His family were Adamses, and they were one of Marblehead's three founding families, some 375 years ago.

Five Corners has **soups** and **chili** to go, but the specialty is **sandwiches,** available in a variety of creative combinations.

While the ingredients aren't totally gourmet, this is a few steps above the average sub shop. Sandwiches are classified as **Classics** and **Specials.** One of the **Classics** I find unusual is the **avocado and Brie BLT**—a great combination of textures. There is also the kid-friendly **Fluffernutter,** peanut butter and marshmallow fluff.

There are several **cold club sandwiches,** including the meaty **Corner Club,** a generous layering of ham, roast beef, turkey, and provolone on wheat toast. The hot **Dixie Header** includes smoked turkey, Muenster, and pesto on a French roll. There are also several vegetarian combinations, such as the hot **Mushroom Header,** a French roll laden with mushrooms, broccoli, tomatoes, Havarti, and cheddar cheese. There are **salads,** including a **salad bar,** and homemade **soups,** all available to go.

The restaurant side of the business is worth a stop, especially for breakfast, when they make **pancakes** and all kinds of **egg dishes.**

REVERE

Rosetti's Italian Market
313 Park Avenue, Revere, MA 02151   (617) 284-0075
Mail order: not available   Catering: available
Hours: Mon.–Fri. 8 A.M.–8 P.M.; Sat. 8 A.M.–6 P.M.; Sun. 8 A.M.–1 P.M.

I came to Rosetti's for the **steak and cheese sandwich,** which had come highly recommended. If not for the recommendation, I would have passed this place by. The market is on a busy street but not in an area with many shops. There is a parking lot in front but not much to tempt you to stop in. Even inside, it could be just another sub shop. But it's not. It's a very, very good sub shop. The sandwich is made with good-quality grilled steak, and lots of it, topped with melted mozzarella cheese.

Several other **submarine sandwiches,** both hot and cold, are available. There is **chicken and cheese** and **Cajun** versions of both the steak and the chicken. The hot **sausage sub** is made with homemade **sausage.**

In addition to sandwiches, Rosetti's makes various **pastas** and **chicken** and **veal dishes.**

WOBURN

David's World Famous 1st Class Eateries

30 Commerce Way, Woburn, MA 01801   (617) 935-1555
Mail order: not available   Catering: available
Hours: Mon.–Fri. 7 A.M.–3 P.M.; closed Sat., Sun.

164 Middlesex Turnpike, Burlington, MA 01803   (617) 229-8786
Mail order: not available   Catering: available
Hours: Mon.–Fri. 7 A.M.–3 P.M.; closed Sat., Sun.

David's came recommended to me by my editor, and they make great **sandwiches**. Most are unusual, creative combinations, such as **Chinese duck breast** served with pea pods, bean sprouts, and hoisin sauce. I love duck, and this is one of the few places I've seen that puts it into a sandwich. The **blackened Cajun fish** sandwich is made with swordfish, topped with homemade honey mustard. David's makes a few homemade **spreads,** which you can have on any sandwich. Among them are **creamy horseradish** and **curry apple.**

The **tuna salad** is a classic rendition, made with Hellman's mayonnaise, celery, and grated carrots. The **Southwestern vegetarian** is very good, with chunky guacamole, salsa, tomatoes, and cheddar cheese. Complete your meal with **hand-cut French fries** or yummy **sweet potato fries.** David's also makes five different **Caesar salads—traditional** or topped with **grilled shrimp, grilled chicken, chicken salad,** or **tuna salad.** I like it plain.

SOUTH

HINGHAM

Dagwoods

69 Water Street, Hingham, MA 02043   (617) 740-4373
Mail order: not available   Catering: available
Hours: Mon.–Fri. 11 A.M.–8 P.M.; Sat. 11:30 P.M.–7 P.M.;
  Sun. noon–6 P.M.

Roger Westhaven opened Chicken Etc. and Bear Cove Gourmet in 1989, two businesses joined at the hip. In 1993 he changed Bear Cove to Dagwoods, a terrific **sandwich** joint. The flagship sandwich is named in honor of the shop's namesake, the comic hero Dagwood, creator of enormous sandwiches. The **Dagwood Sr.** is a mound of ham, turkey, roast beef, coleslaw, and Swiss cheese on marble rye.

There are some three dozen creative combos, as well as traditional deli meats. All the meats are cooked on the premises, such as **roast beef, lamb, turkey,** and **chicken.** The **chicken salad** is tender, complemented with the crunch of almonds.

Other combos are named for Dagwood's costars. **Mr. Dithers** is chicken breast, roasted red pepper, arugula, and garlic mayonnaisse on focaccia. **Blondie** has a blond filling—Swiss, Havarti, and provolone—with Russian dressing. I like the **Tina,** smoked mozzarella with sun-dried tomatoes, arugula, and Parmesan vinaigrette. It's served on French bread, which was a little undercooked.

Amy's Hero is a daily special that should be a regular item. Grilled spiced lamb is layered with balsamic caramelized onions, tomatoes, cucumbers, and lettuce then drizzled with minted yogurt. Another special is the **Caribbean Fitzroy,** a spit-cooked pork loin topped with papaya-mango chutney.

You can also order your own combination from a variety of meats, cheeses, and extras. These include **marinated fresh mozzarella, radicchio, hummus,** and **roasted peppers.** Condiments and spreads include **onion** and **tomato chutney, roasted garlic mayonnaise,** four kinds of mustard, and scallion cream cheese.

A freezer stores all kinds of **prepared soups** and **dinners to go.** The countertop holds a variety of good but not great **baked items,** such as **brownies, lemon squares,** and **chocolate chip cookies.**

NORWOOD

Kravings
91 Central Street Norwood, MA 02062   (617) 762-4567
Mail order: not available   Catering: available
Hours: Mon. 7 A.M.–3 P.M.; Tues.–Fri. 7 A.M.–5 P.M.; Sat. 7 A.M.–noon; closed Sun.

The original owners of Kravings were sisters named Kathi and Kristine, hence the *K* in the store name. Bill Walsh, who had worked as a cook there, bought the business in 1994. A high-school football player with a B.A. in English, Walsh had always felt drawn to restaurants and enjoyed working in the food business.

Kravings offers a delicious assortment of **sandwiches, salads,** and **baked goods.** There are half a dozen tables in this corner location, and everything is available to go. The original owners were Lebanese, and the menu still offers a handful of Middle Eastern items, such as an excellent **tabooleh** (their spelling), with lots of parsley and lemon. It's great in the **Middle Eastern roll,** with **hoomus** (again, their spelling) and romaine lettuce. Other sandwiches include an excellent **Southern-style chicken salad,** made with buttermilk and dill mayonnaise. The **roast turkey breast** is served with Brie and honey mustard. Hot sandwiches include a **steak sandwich,** made using grilled strips of London Broil complemented with horseradish cream and Havarti cheese.

The **baklava** is very good—you can tell it's made with real butter. Other baked goods are homey and American. Almost all are **squares,** including four different **brownies,** all good. My favorites are the **Mounds bar brownie,** made with coconut and sweetened condensed milk, and the **chocolate fudge with white chocolate chunks.** And I love the **Reeses squares,** a layer of peanut butter cookie topped with chocolate. It's like a cross between a cookie and a candy. The **oat squares** are an oatmeal, butter, and brown sugar concoction, topped with either fruit preserves or caramel sauce. The **muffins** are pretty good. I tried **cranberry-lemon** and **sour cream streusel.**

❖ P I Z Z A ❖

Pizza places are a dime a dozen. One baker I spoke with said that it costs less than a dollar to make a pizza, so it's a very high-profit food field. This may explain why there is a pizza parlor on practically every block in and around Boston.

To choose pizza places from the plethora in the area, I went almost exclusively by word of mouth. I would ask for recommendations from every person in the food business I talked to, and then I'd check out the place myself.

Pizza restaurants come in a variety of styles. There are the pizza joints, places that offer pizza by the slice and have some or no seating, and no atmosphere. Then there are places where you can order pizza whole, no slices, but nothing fancy either. Then there are those that have elevated pizza to a new art, spending time developing the perfect dough and sauce, and offer myriad elaborate toppings. There are various styles of pizza. Thin crust, thick crust, deep-dish, lots of cheese or just a sprinkle, lots of sauce or just a dab. I like thin-crusted pizza with a crispy bottom, a fair amount of sauce, and not too much cheese.

Some of the take-out and sandwich establishments above make very good pizza, notably Baci, Caffé Gianni, Moka, and To Go (all in Boston), Cremaldi's (Cambridge), and Rustica (Belmont). Iggy's (see "The Staff of Life," page 33) makes the best cold pizza.

Several places deliver, but delivery is primarily within the immediate area; pizza does not travel well. I have indicated whether each place delivers and whether the pizza is available by the slice.

BOSTON

BOSTON

Baci. See "Takeout," Boston, page 153.

Caffé Gianni. See "Takeout," Boston, page 155.

Figs
42 Charles Street, Boston, MA 02104   (617) 742-FIGS (3447)
Delivery: not available   Slice: not available
Hours: Mon.–Fri. noon–3 P.M. and 5:30 P.M.–10 P.M.;
    Sat. noon–10 P.M.; Sun. noon–9 P.M.

Figs on Charles Street is Todd English's latest culinary endeavor and his first attempt at serving lunch. English owns Olives and Figs in Charlestown, which are open only for dinner. **Pizza** is the focus at Figs on Charles Street, and it's fantastic—the best I've tried. It's baked at 700°F in a brick oven, which the restaurant had custom-built. The oval-shaped pies come in two sizes; the large, enough to fill up two or three people, is available only at dinnertime; the small, a generous serving for one, is served only at lunchtime.

I like the plain **Oliver's**—tomato sauce with a pleasing garlicky kick, mozzarella cheese, and topped with fresh basil leaves. It is a perfect balance of flavors. The crust is ultrathin— just thick enough to support the toppings. As per the Olive's mode of cooking, the toppings are very creative. **Fig and prosciutto** has a rosemary crust topped with fig and balsamic jam, prosciutto, and Gorgonzola. **Fresh asparagus** includes red onions and fontina cheese. There are also two **Napoletana** pizzas, with thicker crusts. One is a simple tomato sauce and mozzarella; the other features baby artichokes, mascarpone, and prosciutto. You pay for the toppings, though. This pizza is not cheap, but it's worth the price.

At lunch you can get a variety of excellent **sandwiches,** too, which change seasonally. *Pollo* is made with smoked chicken, arugula, and green-olive relish on **focaccia. Maine crab** is made with fresh crab, fennel, avocado, and aioli.

Figs has table service, but the place is always very busy. If you want pizza, your best bet is to order it to go. It's good cold, too.

Il Panino. See Cambridge, page 217.

Pizzeria Regina

11½ Thatcher Street, Boston, MA 02113   (617) 227-0765
Delivery: not available   Slice: lunchtime only
Hours: Mon.–Thurs. 11 A.M.–11:30 P.M.; Fri., Sat. 11 A.M.–midnight;
   Sun. 11 A.M.–11 P.M.

The Polcari family has been making pizza at this location since 1926, in the same oven. That is one reason the Regina's pizza is best at this location. There are seven other stores, but the North End location is consistently the best of the bunch. Many people I asked concurred. This is classic **thin-crust pizza,** with traditional toppings such as mushrooms, peppers, pepperoni, and sausage. You can go for the grease and try it with extra oil. When it comes to pizza, I like plain cheese, and it's very good here.

Two years ago Regina's bought Bel Canto's in Wellesley and Lexington. The toppings there are different from Regina's, but the crust recipe is the same.

BRIGHTON

Bluestone Bistro

1799 Commonwealth Avenue, Brighton, MA 02135 (617) 254-8309
Delivery: available   Slice: not available
Hours: Mon.–Thurs. 5:30 P.M.–11 P.M.; Fri. 5:30 P.M.–midnight;
   Sat. 10 A.M.–midnight; Sun. 10 A.M.–11 P.M.

663 Main Street, Waltham, MA 02154   (617) 891-3339
Delivery: available   Slice: not available
Hours: Sun.–Thurs. 5:30 P.M.–10:30 P.M.; Fri., Sat. 11 A.M.–11:15 P.M.

When Lisa Flashenberg opened the Bluestone Bistro in 1987 in Brighton, pizza was not the main focus of the menu. But it proved to be so popular that it now makes up some 70 percent of the Brighton location's business. Pizza is a smaller percentage of the Waltham business, which Flashenberg opened with her brother Dave in 1994.

Their **pizza** is very good, although it is not exactly my style. It is for fans of thicker crusts, but it is not at all bready. The bottom of the crust is coated with lots of cornmeal, giving it a nice subtle crunch. The crust comes in **regular white,** which I prefer, or **whole wheat**—it's a very wheaty-tasting whole wheat. There is also a choice of sauces: **regular,** which is slightly spicy, and **tomato basil.** Both are good.

Bluestone's pizza is also for people who like lots of cheese —they are very generous with the mozzarella. (I like a minimal amount.) There are a number of creative topping combinations. **Wild mushroom** is a white pizza (no sauce) with Gouda and Asiago cheeses and wild mushrooms. **Southern Comfort** in-cludes sweet potato, corn, and red onion. Fresh tomato salsa is used in place of sauce in the **Mexican** pizza, which also contains black olives and jalapeños. You can create your own combo from a choice of forty toppings, including andouille sausage, carrots, scallops, and walnuts (I love walnuts on pizza, with mushrooms). The pizza comes in three sizes: personal, medium, and large.

The restaurant also offers a variety of **appetizers** and **pastas,** as well as very cheesy **calzones,** which come with a variety of fillings that can be combined with any of five cheeses (**ched-dar, mozzarella, Parmesan, ricotta,** and **Romano**), for example, **prosciutto–red pepper** and **chicken-pesto.**

DORCHESTER

Mario's Trattoria

789 Adams Street, Dorchester, MA 02124   (617) 436-1993
Delivery: available   Slice: available
Hours: Mon.–Wed. 11 A.M.–10 P.M.; Thurs.–Sat. 11 A.M.–11 P.M.;
    Sun. 1 P.M.–9 P.M.

When I visited, Mario's had the feel of a typical pizza joint—a counter, a couple of Formica tables, no atmosphere. Owner Mario San Filippo has since expanded and renovated the place, adding more tables and giving the place more of a restaurant feel.

Mario's has very good **pizza,** with a light, crisp crust, good sauce, and just the right amount of cheese. They also make a variety of good **sandwiches,** and several **Italian specialties.** The *arancine* is very good. A ball of ground beef is surrounded by rice and deep-fried—although the meat at the center was a bit cold. I love the *panzarotti,* which I have yet to see elsewhere. These are oblongs of mashed potatoes mixed with onions, parsley, and mozzarella cheese, deep-fried, and served with tomato sauce. So good!

EAST BOSTON

Santarpio's Pizza

113 Chelsea Street, East Boston, MA 02128   (617) 567-9871
Delivery: not available   Slice: not available
Hours: Mon.–Sat. 11:30 A.M.–12:30 A.M.; Sun. 1 P.M.–12:30 A.M.

Ask most Bostonians who makes the best pizza around, and two out of three will invariably say Santarpio's. Pizza is not available by the slice, but you can order it whole to eat there or to take out. The atmosphere is pure smoky bar, and the menu includes **pizza** and excellent **shish kabob.**

The **pizza** is just right. The crust is thin and crispy, the sauce is flavorful and not sticky or sweet, and they use the perfect amount of mozzarella. The toppings here are nothing fancy: peppers, onions, mushrooms, sausage, pepperoni, anchovies, and garlic—and the mushrooms are canned. Your best bet is **plain** or **sausage.**

The pies are cheap and come in one size only, starting at $5.50 for a plain. This is enough pizza to feed two very hungry and three moderately hungry people.

To pick up pizza to go, enter through a side door labeled "Take-out" around the corner from the main entrance. Don't be intimidated when you find yourself in the middle of the kitchen, next to a counter where a cook is kneading dough; this *is* where you order and pick up your pizza.

JAMAICA PLAIN

Bella Luna
405 Centre Street, Jamaica Plain, MA 02130   (617) 524-6060
Delivery: available within Jamaica Plain   Slice: not available
Hours: Sun.–Wed. 11 A.M.–11 P.M.; Thurs.–Sat. 11 A.M.–midnight

Bella Luna is great on ambience. The tables are painted creatively, there is original art on the walls, and the kitchen is open, right there behind the counter. The **pizza** comes in small, medium, or large and is good. The crust is a little spongy, but the sauce is tasty, and the toppings are varied and fun. The menu lists two dozen creations, such as the tempting **La Sophia,** with pesto chicken and artichokes, and the multicultural **City Year Pizza (very inclusive),** with black olives, ricotta, roasted red peppers, and cheddar cheese. Some combos are more interesting than tasty, for instance, the **Harry Belafonte,** with shrimp, banana, and bacon. You can also create your own pie from a list of four dozen items, including asparagus, baby corn, jalapeño peppers, shiitake mushrooms, and Canadian bacon.

METROPOLITAN BOSTON

BROOKLINE

Pino's Pizza
1920A Beacon Street, Brookline, MA 02146   (617) 566-6468
Delivery: available   Slice: available
Hours: Mon.–Sat. 11 A.M.–1 A.M.; Sun. 11 P.M.–midnight

Pino's Pizza was initially recommended to me by a cousin of the owner, and then simply by fans. It's in Cleveland Circle, and double parking seems to be the norm at this very busy location. There is ample seating here, with booths, and ample takeout as well.

As with anything that comes too highly recommended, I was dubious. And I was not impressed with the first bite. By the third bite, I *was* impressed. Although the crust is a little tough, there is something addictively delicious about Pino's **pizza.** The amount of cheese is just right and tastes good, and the sauce is just plain yummy. I was surprised to find that restraint was in order as I finished my second piece and hankered for a third.

CAMBRIDGE

Il Panino

1001 Massachusetts Avenue, Cambridge, MA 02138   (617) 547-5818
Delivery: not available   Slice: available
Hours: Mon.–Sat. 11 A.M.–10 P.M.; Sun. 3 P.M.–10 P.M.

11 Parmenter Street, North End, Boston, MA 02113   (617) 720-1336
Delivery: not available   Slice: available
Hours: daily 11 A.M.–10 P.M.

There are lots of tables at both Il Paninos, but there's no table service. Place your order at the counter. The **pizza** here is good enough to get again and again with tasty sauce and a toothsome crust. The restaurant also makes very good **sandwiches** and excellent **calzones.** These are huge, individual calzones that could easily serve two. I like the **spinach calzone,** made with tons of fresh spinach and cheese.

CHELSEA

John's Pizza

8 Central Avenue, Chelsea, MA 02150   (617) 884-2617
Delivery: available   Slice: available
Hours: Mon.–Sat. 10 A.M.–midnight; Sun. 4 P.M.–midnight

John's is a classic pizza joint with no atmosphere, a few tables, and very good **thin-crust pizza** with a flavorful sauce.

SOMERVILLE

Bertucci's. See Wakefield, page 218.

NORTH

MARBLEHEAD

Café Vesuvius

18 Bessom Street, Marblehead, MA 01945   (617) 639-8120
Delivery: available   Slice: available
  Hours: Sun.–Thurs. 6 A.M.–9 P.M.; Thurs.–Sat. 6 A.M.–10 P.M.

Café Vesuvius makes very good **pizza,** available by the slice or in different sizes. The sauce is chunky and tasty. The crust is a little thick, but crispy on the bottom. This is also a bakery; that is why the café is open so early in the morning.

REVERE

Bianchi's Pizza

322 Revere Beach Parkway, Revere, MA 02151   (617) 284-9472
Delivery: available   Slice: available
  Hours: Sun.–Thurs. 10:30 A.M.–midnight; Fri., Sat. 10:30 A.M.–1 A.M.

Bianchi's has been making and selling pizza across the street from Revere Beach for over forty years. After Santarpio's, this was one of the pizza places most frequently recommended to me. And the **pizza** is great. The sauce is nicely spiced and plentiful, and the crust is thin and crispy on the bottom. Toppings include the usual. Slices are priced on the high end for pizza joints—$1.75 compared to $1.25 at most places, but these are big slices.

There are no tables here, just a sidewalk counter where you order. Pick up a slice, cross the street, sit on the beach wall facing the ocean, and enjoy.

WAKEFIELD

Bertucci's

Headquarters and test kitchen, 14 Audubon Road, Wakefield, MA 01880
  (617) 246-6700
Hours: Mon.–Fri. 9 A.M.–5 P.M.; closed Sat., Sun.

197 Elm Street, Somerville, MA 02144   (617) 776-9241
Delivery: available   Hours: Mon.–Thurs. 11 A.M.–11 P.M.;
  Sat. 11 A.M.–midnight; Sun. noon–11 P.M.

Joey Crugnale's first independent culinary venture was Joey's Ice Cream in Teale Square, Somerville. I remember it in the early 1980s for its creative sundae bar. Crugnale went on to buy Steve's

218

Ice Cream and turn it into a multimillion dollar franchise operation. He bought it for $80,000 and sold it a few years later for $4.5 million.

The original Steve's was located on Elm Street in Somerville. Noticing the long lines, Crugnale saw an opportunity for another food business—selling pizza. He opened Bertucci's & Bocce next door in 1981. It was great pizza—one of the Boston area's first gourmet pizzerias, offering creative toppings. What distinguished it in particular was the wood-burning brick ovens, which gave the crust a terrific crispness and flavor. The pizza cost a bit more, but I always felt it was worth it. The bocce part of the operation was fun; the restaurant had two levels, and there was an actual bocce court on the ground level, complete with sand and balls. You could play while you waited for your pizza.

Crugnale did not open a second store until 1985, and then the business grew quickly. Along the way, bocce was dropped, and the menu was expanded to include **pasta, appetizers,** and **sandwiches.** As of mid-1995, the company had seventy-four stores in twelve states and the District of Columbia, with several more planned for the next year.

Has the quality survived the expansion? Sometimes. When there was just one and then a few stores, the **pizza** was consistently great. These days, it is inconsistent: sometimes the pizza is drastically underdone, with a soggy or doughy crust; other times it is still very good. Generally, Bertucci's is one of the better pizzas available, another often recommended pie.

The menu includes all the traditional pizza toppings, as well as lots of specialty items. There are a number of, combinations, such as the **Marengo,** roasted peppers, sliced tomatoes, and grilled chicken seasoned with red pepper, white wine, and lemon. With the **Quattro Stagioni** the pizza is divided into quadrants, with a different topping in each section: artichoke hearts, green peppers, mushrooms, and prosciutto. **Formaggio** has four cheeses and no sauce. You can also choose your own toppings from a list of over twenty items, including broccoli, clams, eggplant, caramelized onions, and sun-dried tomatoes.

The original Somerville store still has bocce, and just pizza, with some **salads.** The Wakefield address is the company headquarters and test kitchen. This is where you can taste new items and give them your feedback as well. There are more than two dozen Bertucci's in the Boston area; call the main office to find the one nearest you.

WEST

BELMONT

Café Fiorella

263 Belmont Street, Belmont, MA 02178   (617) 489-1361
Delivery: available   Slice: available
Hours: Mon.–Sat. 11 A.M.–10 P.M.; closed Sun.

Café Fiorella is a pleasant pizza spot. You place your order at the counter, but the place has a nice atmosphere for eating in. **Pizza** comes small, medium, and large, as well as by the slice. It's baked in a brick oven, which gives it an appealing flavor. The crust is not superthin, but it's tasty and has a good texture. There are the usual toppings and then some. There is a variety of combinations available, such as the **Anita,** with fresh mushrooms and pitted olives. Two are called **Anchovy**—one with cheese, and the other without, substituting oregano and olive oil. **Chicken eggplant Parmesan pizza** is a meal—diced chicken breast and battered slices of eggplant. The place also makes very good **calzones, sandwiches, pasta,** and **salads.**

WALTHAM

Bluestone Bistro. See Brighton, page 214.

THE BESTS OF THE BEST

Best salads: **Virginia's Fine Foods** and **Stephanie's on Newbury**
Best vegetarian takeout: **The Natural Gourmet**
Best overall takeout: **Rustica**
Best meat sandwich: **Artu's** and **Jake & Earl's Dixie BBQ**
Best vegetarian sandwich: **Garden of Eden**
Best burritos: **Mex**
Best falafel: **The Oasis Grille**
Best Middle Eastern sandwiches: **Shawarma King II**
Best roasted eggplant sandwich: **Bob's Imported Food and Fine Catering**
Best overall sandwiches: **Dagwoods**
Best chicken salad: **Kravings** and **Truffles**
Best tuna salad: **To Go**
Best egg salad: **Darwin's Ltd.** and **Rebecca's Cafe**
Best deli: **Rubin's Kosher Delicatessen & Restaurant**
Best pizza: **Figs** and **Santarpio's Pizza**
Best cold pizza: **Iggy's**

✦ CHAPTER SEVEN ✦

EVERYTHING NICE

Featuring cakes, cookies, muffins, pastries, pies, scones, tarts, tortes, and
other bakery sweets, plus Boston's best donuts

*O*KAY, I admit it. I love baked goods. Especially cookies. Perhaps it's because baking cookies was my introduction to cooking, but cookies are, to me, the perfect sweet. Of course, I won't turn down cakes or pies, either, and I tasted hundreds of them while researching this book (just a taste, of course, a teeny, tiny taste).

Baked sweets come in all different forms. There are about a million things you can do with butter, sugar, eggs, and flour. ("It's all cookies," my husband is fond of saying about sweets.) Most bakeries have a few categories of items. There are breakfast goods—muffins, donuts, Danishes, and scones. Then there are what I call the comfort sweets, primarily cookies and brownies, pies and tea breads—easy to eat, nothing fancy. Fancy goes with the fancy desserts—elaborately decorated cakes, tarts, mousses, and the like.

There are literally hundreds of bakeries in the Boston area. This was by far the largest category I researched for this book. I looked for places that offer something special and that do an excellent job with the items they produce. There are all kinds of bakeries listed here—from Chinese, Japanese, and Middle Eastern to French, Italian, and Colombian. Some have been in business for nearly a century; others opened just in time to be described in this book. A few are standouts in every category, and others have a single specialty worth buying.

Long before I conceived of this book, I had undertaken the arduous but important task of seeking out the perfect chocolate chip cookie. Perfection, of course, is subjective, but for me chocolate chip cookies should be crisp around the edges and chewy in the center, without tasting undercooked. The chips should be good, dark chocolate but shouldn't overpower the dough, which should have a noticeable buttery flavor. The ideal size is about three to four inches across; any bigger (and humongous cookies seem to be popular) and the texture becomes too soft. I make an excellent cookie, but I love to try others'. After all, Massachusetts is the birthplace of this ubiquitous confection: the first Toll House cookies were created and sold in Whitman.

I have also been searching for the perfect muffin, which should be slightly dense, heavier than cake, with a moist crumb. Making a good muffin is a challenge, and only on rare occasions have I been able to bake one I feel is perfect. And only a handful of the hundreds of places that bake muffins make muffins worth buying.

Scones have flourished in the last few years. For decades, you could hardly find a scone this side of the Atlantic; now *everybody* carries them. As with muffins, few are worth buying twice. Many are just too big to taste good—and a scone is too big if it is the size of a large person's open hand from wrist to fingertips. I prefer smaller, more manageable palm-sized choices. They should be buttery, yet light; crumbly, yet firm enough to be spread with jam. Preparing scones requires a delicate touch; otherwise, they turn out like hockey pucks.

Donuts are a separate category—they even have their own heading in the Yellow Pages (under *Doughnuts*), and a donut shop is different from other types of bakeries. Massachusetts is the country's donut headquarters, home of Dunkin' Donuts in Randolph and Honey Dew Donuts in Plainville, two very large chains.

These days all kinds of baked sweets worth their weight in calories are available in Boston. My search for the best in each category is a lifelong project.

* Described in another chapter.

BAKERIES

Alden Merrell Cheesecake Co.	Newburyport, Brookline, Newton, Salem, Sudbury, Wellesley
*Angel's Bakery and Café	Watertown
Avenue Bakery	Dorchester
*Baker's Best	Newton
*Barsamian's	Cambridge
Bentonwood Bakery and Café	Newton
Boston Brownies	Boston
The Boston Chipyard	Boston
Boston Coffee Cake Co.	Woburn
*J & S Brandi's	Marblehead
*Bread & Circus	Boston, Brighton, Cambridge, Newton, Wellesley
*Breads 'n' Bits of Ireland	Melrose
*Breadsong	Newton
Buns of Boston	Newton
*Café au Lait	Boston
*Café Paradiso	Boston, Cambridge
Cakes to Remember	Brookline
*Calla Lily Café	Cambridge
*Carberry's Bakery and Coffee House	Cambridge
*Central Bakery	Peabody
Chinatown Bakeries	Boston
Eldo Cake House	
Kam Lung Bakery & Restaurant	
Mix Bakery	
*The Chocolate Box	Arlington, Cambridge
Christian Payen Fine French Pastries	Beverly
*Codman Square Bakery	Dorchester
Concord Teacakes	Concord
Dancing Deer	West Roxbury
Daniel's Bakery	Brighton
Delphin's Gourmandise	Marblehead, Brookline
Diane's Bakery	Roslindale
*Dudley Pastry & Restaurant	Roxbury
*Eastern Lamejun	Belmont
El Dorado Bakery	Chelsea
The Gingerbread Construction Co.	Winchester
Golden Bakery	Cambridge
Gooches Bakery	Roslindale

*Greenhills Traditional Irish Bakery	Dorchester
Hana Pastry	Cambridge
*Healthy Heart Café	Framingham
Icing on the Cake	Newton
Il Pastificio	Everett
*India Foods & Spices	Cambridge
*The Italian Express	Newton
Jacqueline's Pasticceria	Everett
Japonaise Bakery	Brookline, Cambridge
Joseph's Bakery	South Boston
*Keltic Krust	Newton
Kilvert & Forbes Ltd.	Boston
Konditor Meister	Braintree
*Kravings	Norwood
Lakota Bakery	Arlington
*LMNOP	Boston
Lolly's Bakery	East Boston
Lucky Duck Fortune Cookie	Everett
Lyndell's Bakery	Somerville
*Manny's Pastries	Roslindale
Maria's Pastry Shop	Boston
Maryam's Famous Cuisine	Dorchester
The Meridien Chocolate Bar	Boston
Middle East Restaurant	Cambridge
Modern Pastry Shop	Boston
*Moka	Boston
Montilio's Cake Shoppe	Quincy
My Grandma's Coffee Cake	Dedham
New Paris Bakery & Candy Shop	Brookline
Ohlin's Bakery	Belmont
Pan Delis Bakery	Brighton
*Panini	Somerville
Panini's at the Blacksmith House Bakery	Cambridge
Party Favors	Brookline
La Patisserie	Winchester, Andover
Peach's & Cream	East Boston
Piqueteadero y Cafetería La Orquidea	Chelsea
Quebrada Baking Co.	Arlington, Wellesley
*Rebecca's Bakery	Boston
*Rebecca's Cafe	Boston, Cambridge
Rosie's Bakery	Cambridge, Boston, Newton, Burlington
*Rustica	Belmont
*Salamander Food Shop	Cambridge

Sally Ann Food Shop	Concord
Salt & Pepper	Somerville
Savoy French Bakery	Brookline
Sevan's Bakery	Watertown
Sorelle Bakery & Café	Charlestown
*Stephanie's on Newbury	Boston
*Stuff-It	Cambridge
Tabrizi Bakery	Watertown
Teahouse Floreal	Wakefield
This Takes the Cake	Quincy
*To Go	Boston
Vicki Lee Boyajian	Needham, Belmont
*Virginia's Fine Foods	Brookline
Vouros Pastry Shop	Roslindale
*West End Strollers	Boston
Wheatberries of Manchester	Manchester
*Wheatstone Baking Company	Boston
White's Pastry Shop	Brockton

DONUTS

Cottage Bakers Inc.	Brighton
Dandy Doughnuts	Norwood
Donut Junction	Needham
Gail Ann Coffee Shop	Arlington
Golden Brown Doughnut Co.	Quincy
Mike's Donuts	Everett
Pauline's Doughnut Shoppe	Medford
Verna's Coffee and Doughnut Shop	Cambridge
West Concord Donut Shoppe	Concord
Ziggy's Donuts	Salem

❖ B A K E R I E S ❖

BOSTON

CHINATOWN

There are several bakeries in Chinatown. Chinese pastries differ considerably from American pastries, using ingredients Americans generally do not use, such as rice, bean paste, and even ham. They also make many savory pastries, breads with various fillings. Generally, I find Chinese pastries are not to my taste—since my palate has been trained in the butter-and-cream school of pastries. Nonetheless, these are very interesting. I like the savory pastries the best. For sweets, I tend to like the items that are closer to American baked goods. The following establishments are worth a visit, especially for those who like to experiment with new foods.

Eldo Cake House

36 Harrison Avenue, Boston, MA 02111   (617) 350-7977
Mail order: not available   Hours: Mon.–Sat. 7 A.M.–6:30 P.M.;
  Sun. 8 A.M.–6:30 P.M.

You can't miss the Eldo Cake House: its façade is painted a bright kelly green. Inside, one display case features several **cakes** decorated with flowers, messages, or swirls of colorful pink, green, and yellow decorations. Avoid these. They taste like standard bakery cakes with Crisco frosting. Instead, go over to the other display case, the one with the Asian pastries. The **coconut cakes,** in palm-size rounds, are slightly gelatinous yet deliciously creamy, like a cross between a custard and a cake. I can't leave without purchasing at least one individual **egg custard.** Although these are not exactly Chinese, they are really good. Eldo also makes **savory pastries** with flaky crusts holding finely chopped **chicken and ham, sliced beef and vegetables,** and other combinations. The *Ma yung bao* are steamed buns with a sweet bean filling; this combination might seem unusual to a Western palate, but try them—they are tasty and filling. Beans and rice flour figure prominently in other sweets. All go well with a cup of **green tea,** which you can order in Styrofoam cups and consume while sitting at one of a handful of tables. Not much English is spoken here, so don't expect answers to queries regarding ingredients or details about unfamiliar pastries. You'll just have to taste your way through the display case.

Kam Lung Bakery & Restaurant

77 Harrison Avenue, Boston, MA 02111   (617) 542-2229
Mail order: not available   Hours: daily 6 A.M.–8 P.M.

David Shu and his brothers have owned Kam Lung for nearly twenty-five years. The pastries here are very attractive. The Chinese year has several festivals, and various pastries are associated with each one. August has the moon festival, during which **moon cakes** are consumed. Shu says that this item is so popular that they carry it throughout the year. Moon cakes are round pastries that come with a variety of fillings. The dough is made from a lemon-infused sugar syrup, mixed with flour and oil. The pastry is fitted into a mold, the filling is inserted, and the top is decorated with molded symbols; each filling calls for different symbols. Fillings include **black bean,** which is rich and sweet with a slight peanut taste; **lotus seed,** also with a peanut flavor; and **mixed nut.** Oddly sweet and savory, this is a chewy blend of walnuts and sesame seeds seasoned with tiny bits of ham. Another **nut cake,** in a flatter shape, is seasoned with preserved bean curd, giving this item a sweet, pickled flavor. This is not my kind of treat, but it's definitely intriguing.

There are oval cakes made with a flakier pastry that is pale white and decorated with Chinese characters in red. The **melon cake** has a winter-melon filling that is sticky and chewy and tastes like bubble gum. The **yellow bean cake** is sweet and slightly beany.

Rice flour is used to make wrappers for various items. The **black-bean donut** is a ball of rice-flour dough fried, coated with sesame seeds, and filled with a sweetened black-bean paste. To my Western palate it is weird, but I liked this item more than others. The items I tended to like are more borderline. My favorite item at Kam Lung is the **coconut-butter roll,** a moist yeast bread with a wonderful coconut filling. I also like the **crispy roll,** a sweet bread topped with an almond batter that tastes like Chinese almond cookies.

The savory items are best. The **steamed dumpling** is a thin, sticky rice flour pastry filled with a mix of onions, pork, and dried shrimp. The same filling is used in the greasy **fried dumpling.** The *chong* is an unusual pastry. The dough is made from sticky rice; it is formed into a triangular shape, filled with boiled peanuts, salty pork, Chinese sausage, and egg yolk, then wrapped in layers of bamboo leaves and boiled for four hours. You can eat it at room temperature, but it tastes best heated up.

If you are lucky, Shu will be available when you visit. He speaks English well and can explain the different items Kam Lung makes.

Mix Bakery

36 Beach Street, Boston, MA 02111   (617) 357-4050
Mail order: not available   Hours: daily 7 A.M.–7 P.M.

When you enter Mix Bakery you'll first be struck by the dense cloud of cigarette smoke. This is also a coffee shop, often filled with people getting ready to go to work at various area Chinese restaurants. The fact that most of the clientele is Chinese is apparent by the lack of English labels by the pastries: everything is in Chinese. But owner Grace Kwong speaks fluent English, and she's happy to explain the contents of various items.

Mix Bakery has **moon cakes.** A popular filling for them is **roasted pickled egg yolks,** often duck egg yolks. You can buy the cakes with **one yolk** or **two,** or **no yolks.** I tried a **coconut moon cake** with one yolk; it's definitely an acquired taste. There is an odd mix of sweet surrounding the briny taste of the yolk. The *ki ji pan* (these are my transliterations of what Kwong called various items) is a Chinese ginger cookie, a sticky patty of ginger, honey, sesame seeds, walnuts, melon seeds, and peanuts. It sounded promising, but it, too, seems to be flavored with ham, giving it an odd sweet and savory taste. *Yea hun so,* also called *pillow pastry,* is a rice flour ball rolled in coconut.

Again, I prefer the **savory pastries.** There is a triangular pastry made from sticky rice, filled with pork and chicken, then wrapped in a lotus leaf. The **steamed dumpling** is best—a large round of steamed bread dough filled wtih vegetables and pork. Their **sticky rice roll** is filled with scallions, ham, and vegetables.

BOSTON

Boston Brownies

Faneuil Hall Marketplace, Boston, MA 02109   (617) 227-8803
Mail order: available   Hours: Sun.–Thurs. 8:30 A.M.–9 P.M.;
    Fri., Sat. 8:30 A.M.–11 P.M.

Brownies are not my favorite kind of baked good, but I know what I like. I like brownies to be chewy, not cakey, with a strong chocolate flavor, and I don't like them to be fudgy or gooey, because then they taste undercooked. However, there are a whole bunch of people who like dense, fudgy, moist brownies, and if you are one of them, then Boston Brownies are for you.

Owner Laura Palmer started the company in 1981 and now makes some eighteen varieties of **brownies.** There are several classic flavors, including **old-fashioned fudge, frosted fudge,** and **butterscotch.** The chocolate flavors work better than the nonchocolate: butterscotch tasted too raw, and **oatmeal-raisin** had a downright foul taste. The best is **cheesecake.** It is a fudge brownie, very chocolatey and rich, with a very good cream-cheese topping. I also liked the **German chocolate** and the **English toffee. Heavenly hash** is for the candy lover. It's a fudge brownie topped with M&Ms, Reeses, and various other nuts and chocolate chips.

If you are totally throwing calorie caution to the wind, you might want to try **Laura's special,** which consists of layers of brownie, fudge buttercream, and melted chocolate chips. Egads!

The Boston Chipyard

Faneuil Hall Marketplace, Boston, MA 02109   (617) 742-9537
Mail order: available   Hours: Sun.–Thurs. 10 A.M.–10 P.M.;
    Fri., Sat. 10 A.M.–2 A.M.

In 1976 three Newport Beach, California, teenagers set out to make and sell the perfect **chocolate chip cookie.** Brothers Michael and Mitchell Hurwitz and Frank Beaver opened their business in a shack and were immediately successful—so much so that the Hurwitz's father, Mark, an attorney, decided to open another store, and he thought that Faneuil Hall Marketplace would be the right place. The Boston Chipyard opened in 1977 as the flagship store of a company-owned chain that ultimately grew to fourteen stores.

Today Michael is a surgeon and Mitchell is a television producer and writer (his credits include *The Golden Girls, Empty Nest,* and *The John Larroquette Show*), and the Faneuil Hall store is the only one left; the company sold the other stores a few years ago. Mark Hurwitz is now the president of the company, and Dana Joly manages the store.

The Chipyard makes about half a dozen flavors, and the **traditional chocolate chip cookie** is great. It is the best chocolate chip cookie I've tasted (other than my own, of course).

Ignoring the trend of making dinner plate–size cookies, the Chipyard continues to make small cookies, barely two inches across, and I think this size makes for a better texture. These cookies have just the right crispness around the edges, they're chewy inside without tasting underdone, and they have a great butter-and-brown-sugar flavor. I liked the **traditional** best, but the other flavors are good too, including **macadamia nut–chocolate chip, peanut butter–chocolate chip,** a very rich **chocolate-fudge chocolate chip,** and a decent but not great **oatmeal-raisin.** Joly says that they make chocolate chip cookies with any kind of nut, including cashew and pecan.

If you want to make Chipyard cookies at home, you can buy the dough to go—$8.50 will get you two pounds. And note the late weekend hours: if you crave a midnight snack on Saturday, this is the place to go.

Bread & Circus. See "Going Organic," page 434.

Cafe au Lait. See "Liquid Refreshment," page 451.

Café Paradiso. See "Frozen Delights," page 296.

Kilvert & Forbes Ltd.
200 Faneuil Hall Marketplace, Boston, MA 02109   (617) 723-6050
Mail order: available
Hours: Mon.–Fri. 8 A.M.–9 P.M.; Sat. 8 A.M.–10 P.M.; Sun. 8 A.M.–7 P.M.

Kilvert & Forbes was opened in Faneuil Hall at the end of 1979 by K. Dunn Gifford, now of the Oldways Preservation & Exchange Trust, and Senator John Kerry. Current owner Linda Klein and her husband bought it less than two years later purely as an investment. "Then I started working here," Klein says, "and I fell in love with it."

The business has three parts: cookies, chocolates, and a New England section. The latter includes a selection of touristy items—maple syrup, Boston Harbor Tea, and so on. Most of the chocolates are not made by Klein, but they do make their own **pet truffles,** which are truffles for kids. They have a sweet milk-chocolate center with coatings of various colors, decorated to look like pigs, cows, and other animals. They're cute and fun.

The baked goods are the real draw here, though, especially the **brownies.** These are damn good brownies, among the best I've tasted. They have a good buttery flavor, as well as a rich chocolatey taste. They are fudgy without tasting raw and are studded with chocolate chips. I prefer them plain, but they also come frosted, with vanilla or chocolate buttercream. To me, frosting on a brownie is overkill, but the buttercream frostings are quite tasty. The **congo bar,** a butterscotch brownie with nuts and chocolate chips, is also quite good.

Of the cookies, my hands-down favorite is the **pecan-butterscotch,** a chewy, lacy oatmeal cookie. The **macaroons,** both plain and dipped in chocolate, are popular, although they weren't particularly special. I preferred the **dark chocolate decadence** and the **peanut butter cookie,** studded with bits of chopped peanuts.

LMNOP. See "The Staff of Life," page 4.

Maria's Pastry Shop

46 Cross Street, Boston, MA 02113   (617) 523-1196
Mail order: available   Hours: Mon.–Sat. 6:30 A.M.–6 P.M.;
     Sun. 6:30 A.M.–1 P.M.

Maria's is easy to miss—the display window is cloudy, and the pastries inside are hard to see—but it's worth venturing inside. Owner Maria Merola has been making traditional Italian pastries here for almost thirty years.

A number of traditional Italian pastries are available here, including *sfogliatelle,* a triangular-shaped layering of crisp, flaky dough surrounding a creamy filling flavored with flecks of candied citron. These taste best fresh out of the oven, still warm. Another traditional item is *zuccharadi,* a pastry the shape and size of a bagel. I don't particularly care for this item (neither does Maria), but it is different. It is slightly sweet and sprinkled with sesame seeds, and the texture is as hard as a week-old bagel. Good for teething. The **marzipan** is overly sweet, but the *torrone* and *chocolate torrone—torrone* being a nougat made with egg whites and honey—are delicious.

Italian **cookies** are different from American cookies; they tend to be sturdier, made without butter, and less sweet. They are not, in fact, my favorite kind of cookies, but that's only my personal taste. Maria's cookies are all very good. I prefer the **almond biscotti,** chock-full of nuts. The **almond macaroons** are also quite good. The *osso di morta* are sweet, crunchy sticks, like extrafirm meringues.

There's a great variety of pastries here, and it's fun to try all the different items.

The Meridien Chocolate Bar

Meridien Hotel, 250 Franklin Street, Boston, MA 02110
  (617) 451-1900
Mail order: not available   Hours: October–May, Sat. 2 P.M.–4 P.M.

The Meridien Chocolate Bar, an all-you-can-eat chocolate buffet (at this writing, $15.50), is a must for chocolate lovers. There are always certain constants, but individual chefs will also add their signature dishes and style. The chocolate menu changes every few months, so I suggest that you return to the bar several times a year and try new treats each time.

Over two dozen cookies, cakes, candies, and other desserts are featured here. The chocolate quotient ranges from mild hint-of-chocolate delights to deep, dark, full-blown chocolate fantasies. As I walked by the bar, I overheard someone say, "I'd like to meet the chef who created all these—he's a *god!*"

The desserts range from the forgettable to the formidable. Of the items that are always there, the **île flottante with chocolate crème anglais** is very good. This dessert is common in France but seldom seen here. It consists of pillows of soft poached meringue floating in a pool of milk-chocolate custard sauce. The **chocolate croissant bread pudding** is also wonderful, a sophisticated version of the traditional comfort food. The **chocolate chip cookies** are okay, as are the **brownies**—not bad, but spend your calories on other things. The **truffle cake,** another constant, is poor. The mousse filling has an unpleasant aftertaste, surprising, because the regular **chocolate mousse** is quite good, light yet rich, and not sticky.

An **ice-cream station** includes Häagen-Dazs ice cream with **hot fudge sauce,** as well as the Meridien's very good **chocolate sorbet.**

Other desserts change, and it's fun to try everything, even what you may not like. Take a taste anyway and move on. Unfortunately no doggy bags are allowed, so come prepared to pig out and enjoy.

Modern Pastry Shop

257 Hanover Street, Boston, MA 02113   (617) 523-3783
Mail order: not available   Hours: Mon.–Thurs. 8:30 A.M.–8:30 P.M.;
   Fri.–Sun. 8:30 A.M.–9:30 P.M.

A funky, but hardly modern neon sign juts out above the door of Modern Pastry, announcing its storefront location. Two display windows on either side hold trays of candies and marzipan, not particularly artfully arranged. But this is *the* place to come for Italian pastries in the North End. Owner Johnny Picarillo's uncle started the bakery in 1931, and his family was in the business back in Pulea, Italy. Picarillo took over Modern in 1963.

Although this is primarily a bakery, the candies here are impressive. Picarillo's daughter makes the oversized **peanut butter cups.** More interesting, though, are the trays displaying candy bar–shaped *torrone,* a confection made with honey nougat and roasted almonds. Picarillo makes a tempting variety—**regular, chocolate, chocolate covered,** and **chocolate-and-caramel covered;** try slices of each.

Italian cookies are not my favorites, but Modern's are the best, classic versions of everything. These **cookies** tend to be hardier and less sweet than American cookies. The **biscotti** are good, as are the *mostaccioli,* a honey-molasses cookie. There are also refrigerated **whipped-cream rum cakes**—rich and moist with rum syrup. These are fine—they use real whipped cream— but to me rum cakes just feel soggy. The *sfogliatelle* is flaky and rich, best warm from the oven. The **marzipan** is very good, as is the *cassata*—a pastry with a filling of ricotta cheese and chocolate bits. The **florentines** disappear fast—by midafternoon they are usually gone.

Moka. See "Goodies to Go," page 157.

Rebecca's Bakery. See "Goodies to Go," page 159.

Rebecca's Cafe. See "Goodies to Go," page 161.

Rosie's Bakery. See Cambridge, page 251.

Stephanie's on Newbury. See "Goodies to Go," page 164.

To Go. See "Goodies to Go," page 165.

West End Strollers. See "Goodies to Go," page 197.

Wheatstone Baking Company. See "The Staff of Life," page 5.

BRIGHTON

Bread & Circus. See "Going Organic," page 434.

Daniel's Bakery
395 Washington Street, Brighton, MA 02135 (617) 254-7718
Mail order: not available Hours: Mon.–Fri. 6 A.M.–6 P.M.;
Sat. 6 A.M.–5 P.M.; closed Sun.

On the surface, Daniel's looks like a typical fine-but-not-remarkable bakery. But there is a wide selection of items here, some of which are real treats. The simple **molasses cookie** was very good. This is a hardy kind of cookie, slightly tough in texture, but I like that. It is great with a cup of hot cider. The predominant flavor is molasses, not ginger. Also good is the **peanut butter–coconut-pecan bonbon.** The chocolate coating is forgettable, but this candylike confection is very good, with creamy peanut butter and a crunch from toasted coconut and pecans. I liked the **Swedish shortbread,** which is simple and buttery, and the paper-thin **florentine** laced with oatmeal and almonds. Pass on the **sour cream dainty**—a real misnomer. The flavor is okay, but the pastry was overcooked and heavy tasting.

Pan Delis Bakery
228 Market Street, Brighton, MA 02135 (617) 787-5747
Mail order: not available Hours: Mon.–Sat. 8 A.M.–1 P.M. and
5 P.M.–9 P.M.; closed Sun.

Pan Delis is the only Guatemalan bakery I found in the Boston area. When I visited they told me the hours, but they don't stick to these times religiously. And you'll be lucky if you find someone who speaks English here.

After tasting several items, I concluded that Guatemalan pastries aren't my cup of tea, but they are intriguing nonetheless. The item I liked best is the *cachito,* a wide oblong with three diagonal holes. This is a sweet roll that is best heated. The *hojaldra* is a long, thin oval, essentially a sugar cookie, good for dunking in coffee. The same dough, made with butter and eggs, is used for other **cookies** formed into different shapes and given different names, such as the flat circle *champurrado* and the sunburst *orosca.* The *cubiletes* is a square that tastes like a cross between a biscuit and quick bread; it is flavored with sesame seeds.

CHARLESTOWN

Sorelle Bakery & Café
1 Monument Avenue, Charlestown, MA 02129   (617) 242-2125
Mail order: not available   Hours: Mon.–Fri. 7 A.M.–5 P.M.;
    Sat. 8 A.M.–3 P.M.; Sun. 8 A.M.–1 P.M.

Sorelle first opened in 1987, and current owners Mark Sills and Marc Perelman bought it in 1990. This is one of those hyphenated places—bakery-takeout-sandwiches-café. Both partners have been in the restaurant business before, and they make almost everything they serve from scratch.

Their baked goods, especially their cookies, are good. The **negative chip** is a cross between a truffle and a cookie, although it could have used a few more white chocolate chips. The **peanut butter cookie** is a classic version, not overly large, with the traditional crisscrossed fork marks across the top. There are several **bars;** my favorite is the **turtle square,** which has a thick crust made with brown sugar and butter that is topped with pecans and semisweet chocolate. The **brownie square** is topped with a delectable cream-cheese frosting. Since **biscotti** are so common, Sorelle goes for the unusual flavors: **orange-walnut and black pepper, cappuccino with hazelnuts and chocolate chips, toasted fennel with almond,** and the relatively common **chocolate almond.** These are very good biscotti—nice and hard, the way I like them.

I was less impressed with the **scones,** which Sills says are very popular. They are oversized and laden with fruit. I tried cranberry-apple and found it to be doughy and underdone. The **black raspberry coffee cake** is good, as are the **muffins,** which come in a variety of flavors, including **mixed berry, lemon-blueberry,** and **walnut–raisin bran.** The **croissants** are slightly dense but have an excellent flavor of true butteriness.

The **prepared foods** are very, very good. A popular item is the classic comfort food, all-beef **meat loaf.** Based on a family recipe, it's clean and pure tasting. Particularly good is the **chicken**

cutlet sandwich, which has a unique flavor. A tender pounded chicken cutlet is fried then served with a great basil-pesto mayonnaise. Other meats are also prepared on the premises: Sills and Perelman roast their own **turkey breast** and **roast beef.** The **sesame noodles,** which seem to be available at every take-out place, are nonetheless quite good here. Other **pasta salads** change daily; the one I tasted was mild and unremarkable. But the dressing served with a basic **green salad** is delicious. It's a **balsamic vinaigrette,** flavored with a touch of Dijon mustard.

The business at Sorelle's is largely takeout, and the place is small and bustling, especially at lunchtime. There are several tables, and it's pleasant to sit there during off-peak hours.

DORCHESTER

Avenue Bakery

988 Dorchester Avenue, Dorchester, MA 02125   (617) 265-5504
Mail order: not available   Hours: Tues.–Sat. 6 A.M.–6 P.M.;
   Sun. 6 A.M.–3 P.M.; closed Mon.

Avenue Bakery has been in business since 1908. Current owner Joe Svelnis has owned the shop since 1978. Svelnis learned his trade from his father, who had a bakery in South Boston specializing in European rye breads.

The bakery has many fine offerings. They are known for their **brown bread** and **Boston baked beans,** made with salt pork, both of which are available only on Friday and Saturday. **Fish cakes,** another specialty, are available only on Fridays. Svelnis also prides himself on his **cupcakes.** "We don't use paper liners," he says. "We butter the pan and put the batter right in." The cupcakes are available every day, as is the **Irish soda bread.** This comes in **loaves** as well as in **rolls,** if you just want a taste. It's a nice, flavorful version, flecked with bits of candied fruit and caraway seeds. Avenue also makes pretty good **donuts** and **apple dumplings.** My favorite item here is the *mezzarine,* a cupcake with almond filling that is simply delicious—it's light and not too sweet.

Avenue has an adjacent coffee shop, which is also open on Monday, but it is smoky and unappealing.

Codman Square Bakery. See "Goodies to Go," page 169.

Greenhills Traditional Irish Bakery. See "The Staff of Life," page 9.

Maryam's Famous Cuisine

310 Bowdoin Street, Dorchester, MA 02122   (617) 825-9226
Mail order: not available   Hours: Mon. Sat. 8 A.M.–9:30 P.M.;
   Sun. 10 A.M.–9 P.M.

Maryam's is run by a brother-sister team, Nick and Maryam. The space is primarily a restaurant.

The bakery section, a glass case by the cash register in the first section of this multi-storefront restaurant, contains a handful of items. Pass on the cookies. They are baked on the premises, but the batter is made by Otis Spunkmeyer—they aren't that great. Go for the **bean pie.** This is a sweet pie made with puréed navy beans; it is reminiscent of pumpkin pie. Nick prides himself on his **muffins,** and they are very good. The flavors vary, but regular offerings include **blueberry, pineapple, apple-spice,** and **banana-nut.** Maryam's also has a simple **yellow cake** that is nice and moist with a subtle lemon flavor. The homemade **challah** is good.

My favorite items here, though, are the **beverages.** They make their own **ginger beer,** a sweet beverage made with fresh ginger root. It can be quite spicy because of the ginger, and Maryam's version is potent: a small sip goes a long way. They also make **sorrel,** a tangy punchlike drink made from a tropical flower, and fresh **carrot juice.**

Nick and Maryam also offer several **sandwiches.** A popular item is the **come back,** a sandwich of **fried chicken** or **fish** served on a homemade long **sub roll** and topped with lettuce, tomato, and a sweetish special secret sauce. They gave the sandwich this name, Nick explains, because people always want to come back for more. The menu also includes several Caribbean specialties.

EAST BOSTON

Lolly's Bakery

158 Bennington Street, East Boston, MA 02128   (617) 567-9461
Mail order: not available   Hours: Tues.–Sat. 6 A.M.–5 P.M.;
    Sun. 6 A.M.–1 P.M.; closed Mon.

Lolly's is a tiny hole-in-the-wall bakery. It's easy to pass by, but step inside. Between the display case counter and the built-in display case there is barely room for two people, but it's worth coming here for two items. The **spinach pie,** kept in the cloudy window, is a huge round double-crusted pie. You buy it by the wedge, and a slice is about an inch and a half thick, with a filling of spinach and cheese. It is good both at room temperature and warmed in the oven. The other item of interest is the **filled cookies.** These are half-moons with a variety of **fruit jam fillings.** They taste great.

Peach's & Cream

69 Bennington Street, East Boston, MA 02128   (617) 561-4725
Mail order: not available, but delivery is available for cakes
Hours: Mon.–Fri. 6 A.M.–6 P.M.; Sat. 8 A.M.–6 P.M.; Sun. 10 A.M.–1 P.M.

Dave Peach learned pastry making on the job, but he came to the bakery business indirectly after working in other areas of the food trade first. He waited tables, tended bar, and worked as a cook on oil rigs before he landed a job working at the Hotel Meridien pastry shop. "The pastries there were really pretty, but too strong for American tastes," Peach says. The European cakes were often steeped in alcohol, and Peach believes Americans just don't want that kind of taste. When he opened his bakery in 1989, he set out to achieve a European look using American-style cakes and flavors.

    There's a catalog of cakes Peach makes, including his signature **peaches and cream cake,** a tasty golden cake layered with peaches and whipped cream. For those who don't want to order a whole cake, there's a pastry case full of temptations. Items with whipped cream are sure winners here. The **almond slice** is a flaky pastry—Peach makes his own very good puff pastry from scratch—layered with raspberry jam and whipped cream and topped with slivered almonds. Whipped cream tops the **English trifle,** a cup filled with very good pastry cream, ladyfingers, peaches, and strawberries. It's refreshing and not overly sweet.

Pâte à choux, or cream puffs, are the base for **nuns,** a double layer of cream puffs filled with a wonderful ricotta cream then coated with dark chocolate and decorated with white buttercream.

The **truffles** are not so hot. They tasted too strongly of alcohol and had a grainy texture. The **dark-and-white-chocolate mousse cup** was also disappointing. The **pecan-pie tart,** however, is quite tasty, as are the **eclairs.**

A second case holds pretty good **muffins** and a variety of **cookies.** My favorite are the **sugar cookies,** or, as Peach describes them, "chocolate chip cookies without the chocolate chips." They have a pleasing taste and a slightly chewy texture. The **chocolate chip cookies** are good, too. I also love the **florentines,** which are small and crisp, with a subtle ginger flavor. The **spritz cookies,** Peach's version of Italian butter cookies, are actually made with butter and are very good. The best version is the one that sandwiches a **raspberry filling** and is half-dipped in chocolate.

Peach also makes very good **biscotti.** Both the **dried fruit with hazelnut** and the **chocolate-hazelnut** have a good, crisp texture.

ROSLINDALE

Diane's Bakery

9 Poplar Street, Roslindale, MA 02131   (617) 323-1877
Mail order: not available   Hours: Mon.–Sat. 7 A.M.–5:30 P.M.;
    closed Sun.

Diane's is one of those bakeries that at first glance seems typical, but on closer inspection turns out to be quite good. **Danishes** are a specialty here, some made with all butter, some with a mix of butter and shortening. I prefer all butter. They come in several flavors, including **raspberry, cherry,** and **marshmallow.** The **blueberry Danish** is very good, with some of the blueberry filling kneaded into the rich dough. I also liked the **butter pecan square,** a pastry crust filled with nuts, brown sugar and coconut and glazed with a pineapple icing. The **cannoli** was a bust, though—the filling had gone bad. The **Boston cream pie,** available in several sizes, is a good classic version. Diane's makes an unusual, good **soda bread.** Usually soda bread is leavened with baking soda, hence the name; here both baking soda and yeast are used for a lighter texture. There are also several **yeast breads.**

The round **cinnamon swirl** is tasty and light and makes good French toast.

Gooches Bakery

4140 Washington Street, Roslindale, MA 02131   (617) 325-3928
Mail order: available   Hours: Mon.–Fri. 9 A.M.–9 P.M.;
  Sat. 9 A.M.–6 P.M.; Sun. 10 A.M.–3 P.M. (Sunday hours vary:
  if it's a nice day, they might be closed)

In 1976 Dominic Candella began making his **sugar-free, salt-free cookies** as a treat for his mother, who was diabetic. She suggested that he try to sell them, and Gooches, named for Candella's cockatoo, was born. The cookies are all-natural, sweetened with barley malt, which, Candella says, the body can break down more efficiently than it can sugar. I've found very few bakeries that don't use sugar as a sweetener. Gooches is the only one that uses barley malt exclusively.

Most of Gooches's business is wholesale. You can find his packaged cookies in most health-food stores around town. Candella also delivers his cookies to hundreds of stores in New York City.

The bakery feels like a wholesale operation. There are no windows in the front—just boards. When you enter, you are immediately in front of the counter. The rest of the room is the kitchen, where racks of cookies cool, and an employee feeds finished cookies into a packaging and labeling machine.

The taste of the cookies varies. All taste healthy, and I like health-food–style desserts. They are obviously different from traditional butter, egg, and sugar creations (Gooches's cookies have no butter either, or chocolate). The best cookie by far is the **wheat-free carob chip macaroon,** made with oatmeal and coconut. Also good is the **oatmeal-raisin,** moist and flavorful. I thought the **carob-walnut brownie** was the epitome of a blah carob dessert, but my four-year-old chocoholic son loved it. Some cookies I would avoid. The **wheat-free banana-raisin** is flavored with banana extract and has an unpleasantly artificial taste. The **tahini squares** are mouth-puckeringly dry. Other better options include the **peanut butter cookies,** with a peanut butter filling, the subtle **almond cookies,** and the **lemon-sesame cookies** laced with coconut.

Candella also makes bread; the **apple swirl** I tried was

delicious. He also sells Nonna's pastas made by his cousin (see "Lotsa Pasta," page 91).

The prices here are wholesale, about half what you'd pay at area health-food stores. It's worthwhile to drop by if you're in the neighborhood.

Manny's Pastries. See "Goodies to Go," page 198.

Vouros Pastry Shop

4252 Washington Street, Roslindale, MA 02131   (617) 323-5068
Mail order: not available   Hours: Tues.–Sat. 8 A.M.–8 P.M.;
    Sun. 10 A.M.–5 P.M.; closed Mon.

Vouros has been making Greek pastries since 1978, and current owners Maria and Chris Petropolis have run the shop for the last decade or so. All the classic Greek pastries are here, and they are pretty good. The **baklava** is made with butter, and it is on the overly sweet side. I liked the *bougatza* best, a kind of custard sandwiched between layers of buttery filo dough. A similar custard is used in the *galakabouriko,* a custard pie. The *finike* is a dense, sticky walnut cookie, and *gianiotiko* is a nutty pastry made with shredded wheat.

Vouros also makes some **Italian cookies.** These are mediocre, so stick with the Greek pastries.

ROXBURY

Dudley Pastry & Restaurant. See "Goodies to Go," page 170.

SOUTH BOSTON

Joseph's Bakery

258 K Street, South Boston, MA 02148   (617) 269-2182
Mail order: not available   Hours: Mon.–Sat. 5 A.M.–7 P.M.;
    Sun. 5 A.M.–3 P.M.

Joseph Masciave started his bakery in 1969, and now his four daughters are in the business. They offer a slew of **Italian butter cookies;** none of these are great, so skip this case and go for the larger pastries. The **ricotta pie** is delicious, light and not too sweet. Best is the **raspberry chocolate chip pastry,** a sophisticated treat. A cream-cheese pastry is rolled with raspberry jam and chocolate chips. The **almond macaroons** are good here, crispy on the outside and moist inside. Pass on the ***tiramisù***—it's too sticky and gelatinous. Joseph's makes a variety of **Danishes.** Both the **apple-raisin** and the **nut,** which is a twisted oblong, are tasty.

There are a few **savory pastries,** including a variety of filled **calzones. Spinach and cheese** is very good. Their light, flavorful **Italian garlic and tomato breadsticks** go nicely with a plate of spaghetti.

One side of Joseph's is a bakery; the other is a take-out service, with a variety of **Italian specialties,** such as **lasagne** and **eggplant Parmesan.**

WEST ROXBURY

Dancing Deer

5197 Washington Street, West Roxbury, MA 02132   (617) 469-2021
Mail order: available   Hours: Tues.–Sat. 8 A.M.–4 P.M.;
    closed Sun., Mon.

Suzanne Lombardi learned to cook while she was an art student. She also assisted *Boston Globe* columnist Sheryl Julian in testing recipes and food styling before starting her wholesale baking company. Seeing coffee shops opening up all over the Boston area, she knew that many would need quality baked goods. That's what she provides. When I spoke with her, she had just opened a small retail outlet in the bakery.

Dancing Deer makes several breakfast pastries. The **blueberry scone** is not that exciting, but the **lemon-cornmeal scone** is delicious. It's crumbly with a little crunch from the cornmeal, complemented with lemon zest. Her yeasted **breakfast breads** are like light Danishes and are available with a variety of toppings, such as a wonderful, tangy **orange–poppy seed** and a cheesy **wild blueberry streusel.** I would have preferred more topping.

Another good breakfast pastry is the **sour-cream nut cake,** with a swirl of cinnamon and nuts through the center. Other cakes include a rich, moist **chocolate-orange-spice cake.**

There are a variety of large **cookies,** including **mocha-walnut drops,** which have a wonderful dark chocolate flavor. **Peanut butter–honey** cookies have slivered almonds in them, an unusual touch.

The two best items are **breads.** The **sweet fruit bread** is fantastic. The sweet yeast dough is lightly rubbed with a citrus-infused cream-cheese mixture and rolled with dried cherries, fresh wild blueberries, and golden raisins. Their **stuffed bread snails** are savory pastries—large buns rolled with a mixture of vegetables, cheeses, and herbs. The **spicy white bean and tomato** is terrific. One makes a great lunch.

Dancing Deer baked goods are also available at a number of stores and coffee shops around town; call the bakery for other locations.

METROPOLITAN BOSTON

BROOKLINE

Alden Merrell Cheesecake Co. See Newburyport, page 267.

Cakes to Remember
248 Cypress Street, Brookline, MA 02146   (617) 738-8508
Mail order: not available   Hours: by appointment

Ellen Bartlett, an art major from Brown University, says, "I always knew that whatever I was going to do, I wasn't going to need a résumé." She may not need a résumé to sell you on her beautiful cakes, but it helps to look through her impressive album, a portfolio of the gorgeous cakes she has created.

Bartlett's early professional experience was working for the Silver Palate gourmet shop in New York. She created most of the dessert recipes for the well-known *Silver Palate Cookbook.* Her cakes do more than look good—they taste delicious. Her business is by appointment only, and she specializes in wedding and occasion cakes. In addition to the traditional tiered and flowered cakes, she has created swimming pools, a mountain ski slope, an armadillo, a crouching weimaraner, and a gingerbread house representing the turreted St. Basil's Cathedral in Russia.

Bartlett makes an impressive variety of cakes, frostings, and fillings. I tasted several, and all were very good. I tried three very different chocolate fillings: **mousse,** light and flavorful; **truffle,** dark and intense; and **buttercream,** fluffy and good as a frosting. The **lemon curd** is great, especially with a buttery **lemon zest cake.** The **raspberry buttercream,** which has a lovely rose color, is also good with the lemon zest cake. I also tried the

orange–poppy seed cake. There are over twenty-five different cakes, plus seven kinds of chocolate cake. I tried a dense **chocolate fudge** and a lighter **devil's food.**

Wedding cakes are never cheap, but Bartlett's, which are among the best I've tasted, are priced competitively.

Delphin's Gourmandise. See Marblehead, page 265.

Japonaise Bakery
1020 Beacon Street, Brookline, MA 02146   (617) 566-7730
Mail order: not available   Hours: daily 7 A.M.–7 P.M.
1815 Mass. Avenue, Cambridge, MA 02140   (617) 547-5531
Mail order: not available   Hours: daily 11 A.M.–7 P.M.

Japonaise is one of the best bakeries in the Boston area, primarily because owner Hiroko Sakan, a native of Japan, is an absolute perfectionist. She had no formal training—she learned her craft through books—but she obviously has a lot of talent. The bakery makes two main categories of goods: breads and other yeasted pastries and elegant desserts.

Sakan describes the style here as "European with a Japanese twist." This twist is apparent in items such as the **azuki cream,** a flaky pastry filled with sweet azuki-bean paste and slightly sweetened whipped cream. The cream Sakan uses comes from local farms and tastes somehow richer and creamier than regular whipped cream. The **yeasted pastries** are more traditionally French. The **croissants** are the best in town—the butteriest, flakiest, best-tasting croissants in the area, bar none. My favorite pastry is the **Danish crisp,** a twist of buttery Danish dough crispy with sugar. It's simple but fantastic.

The list of "bests" here goes on and on. Try something new every visit. Sakan's partner Yoshi Inada is in charge of all the **breads,** in addition to the yeasted pastries. Among the breads are a classic **French baguette,** a very good **seven-grain bread,** and a terrific **raisin *pan*** made with sultanas. The signature bread, however, is the area's best **white bread,** modeled after a style popular in Japan. There are two kinds: *shoku pan* and cream *shoku pan.* Both are rich with butter and eggs; the latter also has heavy cream. There are also great soft, flavorful **butter rolls,** which are used as the base for a **tuna roll** and a **ham roll,** a kind of sandwich with the filling baked in.

Japonaise makes three kinds of donuts: *an,* filled with

sweet azuki-bean paste; **twist,** a plain donut sprinkled with sugar; and a **curry savory,** including vegetables sautéed with ground beef and chutney. Other savory offerings include three different **vegetarian sandwiches**—classic **egg salad;** *yaki soba,* with an intriguing filling of ginger-sauced soba noodles (my favorite); and **croquette,** a potato-based patty imported from Japan.

Then there are the fine **pastries.** Sakan's primary complaint about American pastries is that they are too sweet. Her desserts strike a perfect balance of sweetness and flavor. The most popular items are the **African Queen,** consisting of layers of chocolate genoise, chocolate buttercream, and thinly sliced banana; and the **strawberry shortcake,** made with almond genoise, whipped cream, and strawberries. **California Dream** is light and delicious genoise layered with a Bavarian cream made with yogurt and studded with orange sections. I wasn't crazy about the **Japonaise,** but that is probably owing more to my Western tastes than to the quality of the dessert. This is a green-tea sponge cake layered with green-tea mousse. Interesting. **Lemon Divine** is an excellent lemon cream pastry, nice and tart. Again, try everything. Japonaise makes about a dozen cakes, and all are good.

Sakan is in the process of opening a branch in Belmont Center.

New Paris Bakery & Candy Shop

10 Cypress Street, Brookline, MA 02146   (617) 566-0929
Mail order: not available
Hours: Sept.–June, Mon.–Fri. 8 A.M.–6 P.M., Sat. 9 A.M.–5:30 P.M.;
    July, Mon.–Fri. 8 A.M.–4:30 P.M., Sat. 9 A.M.–4:30 P.M.;
    closed Sun. and during August

New Paris has been at this location since 1929, and current owners James and Roula Kappas have owned the bakery since 1987. James worked here as a baker before buying it.

They say **eclairs** are their specialty, and they make an acceptable version. I never saw the great appeal of eclairs, and these are not the ones to convert me. Better bets are the **cookies,** most of which are French. I've not seen their like in many places. Check when they were made, however, because some I tried tasted stale. Those using almonds are best. The **almond square** is a tiny cake with a sweet, subtle flavor. The **glazed macaroon** and the **almond macaroon** are both very good, and I liked the **raspberry sandwich cookie.** The **brownie** (which I know is not a unique offering) is very good here.

In addition to cookies, New Paris makes their own **chocolates.** The **almond-buttercrunch** is great, and I also liked the **coconut candy.** The **orange-acorn** is a knob of orange-scented marzipan dipped in dark chocolate, and **King Tut** is a square of milk chocolate, caramel, and pecans. Also very good is the **peanut crunch.**

Party Favors

1356 Beacon Street, Coolidge Corner, Brookline, MA 02146
  (617) 566-3330
Mail order: not available   Hours: Mon.–Sat. 9:30 A.M.–7:30 P.M.;
  Sun. noon–6 P.M.

From the outside, Party Favors looks like what its name implies —a store selling party decorations such as streamers and wrapping paper. But inside, alongside the paper goods, you'll find an impressive selection of festive baked goods.

Of the **cookies,** the **butter cookies** are best. They come in a variety of flavors, including **orange** (very good), **lemon,** and **mocha.** Some tasted very stale, so ask when the cookies were made before you buy them. There is also a case of **candies** which includes a variety of fun **molded chocolates,** such as a smiling crescent moon on a stick. During the holidays owner John Pergantis makes **truffles,** but most of the time he does not make the chocolates available here.

What Pergantis does make, year round (in addition to the cookies), are cheerfully **decorated cakes.** My preschool son, who loves frosting, especially enjoyed the **fruit-basket cupcakes.** The cake itself is tasty, in **chocolate** or **golden,** and the frosting, made primarily with butter, is also good. The fruit basket decor contains about as much frosting as cake, with brightly colored three-dimensional renderings of apples, grapes, and bananas perched atop the cake. It is also available as a full-sized **cake.** Other decorative patterns include a bird's nest and flowers.

There are always several **cakes** available off the shelf, in the refrigerator, but to avoid staleness or a refrigerator taste, I recommend ordering your cake ahead of time for special occasions.

In addition to cakes, there are several **tarts.** Especially good is the **apple tart** and the very rich **white chocolate–cinnamon mousse tart.** Tarts are available in individual sizes and larger.

Savoy French Bakery

1003 Beacon Street, Brookline, MA 02146   (617) 734-0214
Mail order: not available   Hours: Tues.–Fri. 7:30 A.M.–6:30 P.M.;
Sat. 8 A.M.–6:30 P.M.; Sun. 8 A.M.–2 P.M.

Carol Pollak and Gerard Jones started Savoy French Bakery in 1983, after working together at the Meridien Hotel. Initially they also offered savory lunch items, but now they concentrate on **baked goods.** There is not a huge selection, but what they do make is good, and reasonably priced. The best item I tried is a simple **almond macaroon.** It has just the right crunchy-chewy texture and delicate almond flavor. The **brownies,** large and laden with pecans, are dense and chocolatey. Chocoholics will also appreciate the **chocolate-mousse tart.** The crust is dipped in dark chocolate, and the bittersweet mousse is incredibly creamy, but not overly sweet. The fresh **fruit tarts** are also tasty, more homey than elegant. The **chocolate chip cookies,** although a little dry, are very good, heavy with pecans and chocolate and flavored with touches of coffee and coconut.

There are two **muffins, blueberry** and **raspberry-blackberry;** both are quite good. The bread, **baguettes** in various sizes, is okay—not bad, but not worthwhile considering the many better loaves now available around the city. The **croissants** are also average.

Virginia's Fine Foods. See "Goodies to Go," page 171.

CAMBRIDGE

Barsamian's. See "An Epicurean Agenda," page 377.

Bread & Circus. See "Going Organic," page 434.

Café Paradiso. See "Frozen Delights," page 296.

Calla Lily Café. See "Goodies to Go," page 172.

Carberry's Bakery and Coffee House. See "The Staff of Life," page 17.

The Chocolate Box. See "Sweet Indulgences," page 338.

Golden Bakery

403 Cambridge Street, Cambridge, MA 02141   (617) 864-7860
Mail order: not available, but they do deliver
Hours: Mon.–Fri. 6:30 A.M.–8 P.M.; Sat. 6:30 A.M.–6 P.M.;
  Sun. 7 A.M.–2 P.M.

Golden Bakery makes a variety of standard bakery items. Pass on their **cookies** and **muffins** and go for the **Portuguese specialties.** These include a variety of plain-looking tarts called *kueijadas.* In fact, these are delicious, although very sweet. They are baked in individual pans, about three inches across, and come in eight variations. My favorite is the **molasses tart,** which tastes like a buttery Indian pudding. The *cintra* is unusual, made with a white cheese and cinnamon. The sweet **white bean** is popular, as is the tasty **plain custard.** The **almond,** however, is disappointing. Although full of almonds, it lacks almond extract and does not have much flavor. Almond lovers should go for the **almond slice pie,** a rich almond cream covered with toasted almond slices. It is delicious.

Golden also makes **milk bread,** a mildly sweet roll, which they use for sandwiches.

Hana Pastry

1815 Mass. Avenue, Cambridge, MA 02140   (617) 661-4996
Mail order: not available   Hours: Mon.–Sat. noon–9 P.M.;
  Sun. noon–7 P.M.

Jun Kikuchi is a professional musician who loves to cook. He learned pastry making on the job when he bought Hana Pastry in 1992. The shop is teeny-tiny, next to a run of Japanese restaurants and noodle shops in the Porter Square Exchange building. One display case offers ice cream in unusual flavors; the other has the pastries.

Good things come in small packages. Everything here is great. The **desserts** are less sweet than desserts often are, and they taste just right.

One item has become an unexpected favorite—**coffee jelly.** I never was a fan of Jello, but this very simple dish, made of ever-so-slightly sweetened fresh-brewed coffee gelatin, topped with slightly sweetened whipped cream, is so good. The **green-tea cake** is tasty, an unusual dessert. Genoise is layered with sweetened azuki-bean paste and a green-tea mousse. A popular item is the **strawberry shortcake.** It is also made with genoise, topped with whipped cream and fresh strawberries.

The *tiramisù* is different from traditional Italian versions, yet appealing anyway. In this version a round of genoise is topped with a blend of cream cheese, whipped cream, and eggs. Another pudding-like dish is the **crème caramel**—classic and very good. I also liked the simple **chocolate cake,** which is very light yet has an intense dark chocolate flavor. Kikuchi's favorite item is the **cheesecake.** It is delicious, but, again, it is not a traditional version. It is a small, individual-sized round. The inclusion of a small amount of flour yields a texture in between a cheesecake and a regular cake.

The ice creams, which Kikuchi does not make, are notable for their unusual flavors. Some are made by Sedutto in Detroit; others are made for Hana Pastry by Ice Cream Works (see "Frozen Delights," page 311). I liked **afternoon tea ice cream,** which tastes like tea with lots of milk in it, with an underlying rosewater flavor. It's quite different from the more assertive **green tea.** The **red bean** is too unusual for me, but I like the refreshing **nonfat ginger yogurt.**

India Foods & Spices. See "The World in a Jar," page 413.

Japonaise Bakery. See Brookline, page 244.

Middle East Restaurant

472 Massachusetts Avenue, Cambridge, MA 02139   (617) 492-1886
Mail order: not available   Hours: Sun.–Wed. 11 A.M.–1 A.M.;
    Thurs.–Sat. 11 A.M.–2 A.M.

The Middle East is primarily a restaurant, a personal favorite that I've been patronizing for over a decade. They've been in business since 1974, and I'm including them here because they make the best **baklava** I've had, anywhere.

All the recipes are from Amalia Sater, mother of co-owners Nabil and Joseph Sater, who hail from Lebanon. This baklava, made with pure butter, is less sweet and sticky than most. It has a walnut filling and pistachios sprinkled on top. The other **Lebanese pastries** are also quite good. For the **bird's nest,** filo dough is rolled into a tube and formed into a crisp circle, surrounding a center of sweetened walnuts and pistachios. The ingredients and flavor are similar to those of baklava, but the texture is quite different; it is also superb. The third filo pastry is the **ladyfinger,** which the Middle East makes as a thick cylinder filled with a ricotta-cheese custard scented with rosewater. The ladyfingers are generally made on Friday and Saturday and are best when fresh—the filo soon gets soggy. They serve two **cakes.** The **saffron cake** is not too sweet, topped with a crust of sesame seeds. It's not bad, but it's less interesting than the other pastries. The **carrot cake** is not like American carrot cake; it is more like a cross between a cake and a pudding.

The Middle East has several entrances, for various sections of the restaurant. To get to the bakery, walk through the entrance at the corner of Brookline Street and Mass. Avenue and head toward the back. There is a bar on the left, and just before you get to the bar is the nondescript pastry case with the finest Middle Eastern pastries around. These pastries taste best the day they are made, although the baklava keeps well. Check and see when the items were made.

Panini's at the Blacksmith House Bakery

56 Brattle Street, Cambridge, MA 02138   (617) 354-3036 and
    876-2725
Mail order: available on request   Hours: Mon.–Sat. 8 A.M.–6 P.M.;
    Sun. 11 A.M.–3 P.M.

The Blacksmith House Bakery opened in 1939 as a place for World War II refugees to work. It was first called the Window Shop. The name changed to the Blacksmith House when the business moved to its current historic location in 1946. The Cambridge Center for Adult Education bought the business in the 1970s. In 1996, Panini (see "Staff of Life," page 25) leased this space and changed the name. Panini breads are now available here. The future of the pastries is uncertain, but I hope my favorites here will continue.

Many of the original Blacksmith bakers were European; thus many of the pastries are too. The bakery is known for its *linzertorte,* which is a decent version of this pastry: a nut crust filled with raspberry jam. I like a firmer crust, and this one is a little crumbly, but it has a flavor that grows on you, and I ultimately liked it very much. I was not crazy about the *sachertorte.* It has a tasty, very tart apricot filling, but the chocolate genoise has no discernible chocolate flavor; all I could taste was apricot. The **emperor** is the best of the **European tortes.** A half-inch of a dark chocolate buttercream is sandwiched between two layers of light hazelnut genoise then topped with a slightly grainy chocolate glaze.

I prefer the **cookies** and **bars.** There are many combinations I haven't seen anywhere else. My favorite is the **orange nut bar.** A buttery crust is covered with ground nuts then finished with an orange glaze. Nuts abound in Blacksmith's cookies. The **four-nut cookie** is like a classic Russian teacake, a confectioner's sugar–coated ball. The **chocolate-pecan cookie,** not too sweet, is riddled with chopped pecans, and it has the texture of a classic icebox cookie—nice to have with a cup of coffee. The **Ischler cookie** consists of two nutty wafers spiced with ginger and other sweet spices, sandwiching **raspberry** or **apple jelly,** then coated in chocolate. I like the raspberry best.

Check when the cookies were made, because some I tried tasted stale. On one visit, a **madeleine** was missing something; on another, I tried a lemon version fresh from the oven, and it was lovely, a light cake with a pleasing flavor from lemon zest.

Blacksmith makes several **breakfast pastries.** The **muffins** have a good flavor but are too cakey in texture—more like cupcakes than muffins. The **croissants** are forgettable—not very buttery or flaky. The **scones** are the best breakfast item here. If you're getting several, try the **Irish soda cake,** which is lighter and more crumbly than traditional soda *bread.* It's studded with currants and is very good—light, crumbly, buttery. The **cheese scones** are wonderful, rich and cheesy and light in texture.

Blacksmith also is a restaurant, with thirty tables in the winter and ninety in the summer, because of the patio seating. They do catering and **wedding cakes** as well.

Rosie's Bakery

243 Hampshire Street, Inman Square, Cambridge, MA 02139
  (617) 491-9488
Mail order: not available   Hours: Mon.–Wed. 7 A.M.–10 P.M.;
  Thurs., Fri. 7 A.M.–11 P.M.; Sat. 8 A.M.–11 P.M.; Sun. 8 A.M.–10 P.M.

2 South Station, Boston, MA 02110   (617) 439-4684
Mail order: not available   Hours: Mon.–Sat. 7 A.M.–8 P.M.;
  closed Sun.

Burlington Mall, Burlington, MA 01806   (617) 229-0093
Mail order: not available   Hours: Mon.–Sat. 8 A.M.–10 P.M.;
  Sun. 10:30 A.M.–6 P.M.

9 Boylston Street, Chestnut Hill, Newton, MA 02167
  (617) 277-5629
Mail order: not available   Hours: Mon.–Thurs. 7:30 A.M.–10 P.M.;
  Fri., Sat. 7:30 A.M.–11 P.M.; Sun. 8:30 A.M.–10 P.M.

When it comes to sweet treats, Rosie's literally takes the cake. A self-confessed dessert addict ("I'm always dieting," claims the diminutive owner), Judy Rosenberg started baking as an art project. "I decided to decorate Valentine's cookies," she recalls. "I merchandised them in satin boxes, and they weren't really edible after all the decorations." She brought her cookies to the now defunct Baby Watson bakery in the Garage in Harvard Square, "and they flew out of there." A career began.

From the beginning, Rosenberg had a sense of presentation. Her **cakes** and **cookies** look as luscious as they taste. Not everything is perfect: the **scones** and **muffins** are unremarkable, but most of Rosie's goods range from really good to amazing. Really good are the **poppy-seed pound cake,** the oversized **chocolate chip cookies,** and the **pecan sandies.** The **brownies** are popular, especially the **chocolate orgasm,** a fudgy brownie with too-sweet chocolate frosting. The **fudge-nut brownie** is the best classic brownie around. But for a chocolate treat, I prefer the **Soho Glob,** a dark, soft, chewy cookie with a not-too-sweet coffee-chocolate flavor.

The *rugalach,* made with a sour-cream pastry and an apricot-walnut filling, are amazing. They aren't cheap, but they are the best *rugalach* I've had, anywhere. The **walnut dream bars** live up to their name. They are made with a butter crust covered with a brown sugar–walnut filling. The pecan pie is perfect.

Rosie's excels when it comes to cakes. The **deep dark raspberry fudge cake** is a chocoholic's nirvana, a sophisticated, dense creation. Lighter, but moist and delicious, is the **sour-cream chocolate cake,** which comes in a variety of forms, with **bittersweet fudge frosting, raspberry filling,** or **mocha buttercream.** All are great. Pick your fancy. Cakes are available in a range of shapes and sizes, including wedding cakes.

Salamander Food Shop. See "Goodies to Go," page 177.

Stuff-It. See "Goodies to Go," page 204.

CHELSEA

El Dorado Bakery

18 Congress Avenue, Chelsea, MA 02150   (617) 884-9039
Mail order: not available   Hours: daily 6 A.M.–9 P.M.

El Dorado Bakery has been baking Colombian specialties since 1990. Many pastries include a white cheese, similar to mozzarella, incorporated into the dough, such as the *pan de queso*. El Dorado's version is less sweet than that of nearby Piqueteadoro y Cafetería La Orquidea (see below). *Buñelos* are cheese balls, a deep-fried, yummy concoction that is 80 percent cheese mixed with cornstarch, flour, and eggs. The *pan de bono* is also made with cheese, using primarily tapioca flour. Yucca flour is the featured ingredient of the *pan de yucca,* which looks like a horseshoe and has a popover-like texture, buttery and chewy; this tastes best warm from the oven. Also best warm is the *churro,* a fried pastry with a crisp crust and tangy guava filling.

Pass on the *lengues* (tongues). These are long, flat cookies that are kind of dry, overdone, and sweet. I didn't care for the *pan de ros,* cookies made with rice flour that crumble into starchiness when you bite into them. I grew to like the *galletas de montequillo* the more I tasted them; these are simple butter cookies, not too sweet and good with coffee. The **black cake** is not chocolate; it gains its color from molasses and from raisins and prunes steeped in red wine. There is also a tasty *trenza bread,* a braided loaf rich with butter and eggs.

El Dorado offers a slew of Colombian beverages. These include all kinds of tropical fruit juices—**papaya, guanábana, mango.** Hot drinks are made with sweetened grains, like **Aveno,** made with oatmeal, and *mazatto,* made with rice.

There are also several **savory dishes,** including **roast chicken, empanadas** (meat-filled pastries), and **fried plantains.** You can get anything to go or sit at one of a handful of tables.

Piqueteadero y Cafetería la Orquidea

109 Central Avenue, Chelsea, MA 02150   (617) 884-3381
Mail order: not available   Hours: daily 7 A.M.–8 P.M.

For several years la Orquidea was primarily a restaurant. In January 1995 they became a bakery as well, specializing in **Colombian and Puerto Rican pastries.** There are items here you'll find in few other places. You'll get by better here if you speak Spanish; the staff speaks little English. *Pan de queso* is a cheese bread. It comes both in loaves and in bagel-shaped rolls. The rolls are unusual, rich, and slightly sweet, laced with cheese—a white cheese sold in area Hispanic markets—which is kneaded into the dough and melts as it bakes. *Torta Colombiana* is a kind of spice cake, studded with candied fruit, with a light, appealing taste.

Caramelized sweetened condensed milk, called *rojo,* is used in a few pastries. While it sounded like it would be good, the pastries made using this ingredient were disappointing. In the *arequipe* the *rojo* is used as the filling between two powdery cookies redolent of shortening. More successful is the *rollo Colombiano,* a sponge cake spread with *rojo* and rolled, jelly roll– style. It is a little dry but has a homemade taste. Intriguing is the *pastel breves arequipe,* a pastry filled with dried figs. I liked the simple *cacaita polvorosa,* a flat coconut cookie, less sweet than macaroons usually are.

There are also **savory turnovers,** called *empanadilla.* I like the **pizza** filling; also available are **meat** and **meat and potatoes** fillings.

Note that the store hours are flexible. An employee said that they may close earlier if it's a slow day.

EVERETT

Il Pastificio
328 Broadway, Everett, MA 02149   (617) 387-3630
Mail order: not available   Hours: Tues.–Sat. 10 A.M.–7 P.M.;
    Sun. 9 A.M.–2 P.M.; closed Mon.

Il Pastificio offers three taste treats in one: pastries, gelato, and pasta. A husband-and-wife team runs the store. Alberta Dello-Iacono prepares all the pastries, decorating the elaborately trimmed cakes, and she makes the ravioli. Antonio makes the rest of the pasta, and the gelato.

The **Italian pastries** here are the best I tried—yes, even better than the ones in the North End. The selection is huge, and Alberta apologized for the paltry offerings on the day I was there, saying that the weekend is the time to come. If you visit during the middle of the week you might only have three dozen items to choose from.

There is a wonderful variety of **almond-based cookies.**

The absolute best is *pasta di mandorle,* balls of ground almonds flecked with grated chocolate and ground coffee. The **almond macaroons** are dry and come in a few flavors. I like **plain** almond best, but there is also **strawberry, sambucca,** and an artificial-tasting **tangerine.** *Brutti ma buoni* (ugly but good) are chewy balls of ground almonds studded with chopped hazelnuts (my favorite). You get a mouthful of pine nuts in the *pinolatta,* which is an almond cookie filled with pine nuts inside and topped with more on the outside. There are also crunchy **amaretti.**

The non-almond creations are also pleasing. A clover-shaped butter cookie sandwich is filled with apricot jam and dipped in white chocolate. The **chocolate butter cookie** is dry and uninteresting, but the *giandùia chocolate square* a chocolate cookie crust with a hazelnut cream, is rich and fulfilling.

In addition to the myriad cookies, there are several **Italian cakes.** These are subtly sweet, with unusual flavors. I like the **rice cake,** studded with raisins and candied fruit. The **cappuccino cake** is a sponge cake layered with coffee cream and topped with coffee mousse. Antonio's specialty is the *cassatina,* a sponge cake brushed with sambucca and layered with dried fruit, chopped chocolate, marzipan, ricotta, and whipped cream. The **lobster tails** here are flaky and big, filled with a blend of whipped cream, boiled cream, and ricotta, and spiked with Strega liqueur.

When you choose your pastries, the employees place them on a cardboard tray, which they then wrap in colorful paper and tie with a ribbon—a lovely method of presentation that Alberta says is common in Italy.

To the left of the extensive pastry case is the wonderful **gelato**—fresh, flavorful, delicious. Flavors vary daily, and include *baci,* made with hazelnuts, chocolate, and rum; *tiramisù* made with mascarpone cheese and with ladyfingers soaked with coffee and brandy stirred in; the *torroncino* is reminiscent of *torrone* nougat candy, flavored with honey and hazelnuts. For the less adventurous, more common flavors are available, including **pistachio, vanilla,** and **chocolate.**

The fresh fruit **sorbets** change with the seasons: **apple** is available in the fall, **strawberry** in the summer. There is an unusual **cucumber** and a super **apricot.** They also come packed into frozen, hollowed-out fruit—very decorative.

The **pasta** is less successful than the pastry and sorbet. Some I tried were excellent, notably the **ravioli with pheasant**

and morel mushrooms. But the **lobster ravioli** was fair, and I could not discern any asparagus in the **asparagus-mascarpone ravioli.** Much better was the simple **fusille,** which is hand-twisted into long strands, and the **black pepper fettuccine.** The DelloIaconos also make **sauce;** the **plain tomato** is not bad, but the *puttanesca,* with capers and olives, is excellent.

Jacqueline's Pasticceria

27 Norwood Street, Everett, MA 02149   (617) 387-3666
Mail order: not available   Hours: Mon.–Fri. 7 A.M.–3 P.M.;
     Sat. 7 A.M.–2 P.M.; closed Sun.

Jacqueline Hazeo only baked at home until she worked as a pastry chef at the now-closed Bayside Hotel in Lynn. That job inspired her to open her own bakery in 1993. Her baked goods are known for their consistent quality. Item after item tasted *really* good. The **scones** are simply great, among the best I've tasted. They are oversized and frosted, which I usually don't care for, but the texture and flavor is just right, and the icing, with a hint of lemon, complements them well. My favorite is **mixed berry,** but they are all good. Other flavors include **apple, orange-currant,** and **lemon–poppy seed.** Jacqueline's is one of the few places that makes **devil dogs,** and they taste just like the snack I remember from childhood lunches—oblongs of slightly dry, dense chocolate cake with a very good buttercream filling.

The **chocolate chip cookies** were a tad underdone but otherwise yummy, a twist on traditional versions. They include a little bit of oatmeal and coconut and are laced with minichips. I liked the **sugar cookies,** which are used as the base for a **raspberry heart**—a cookie sandwich with raspberry jam. The **biscotti** were the only disappointment: the **almond** ones were very chewy, and the **anise,** while nice and crunchy, had an overwhelmingly artificial aftertaste.

In additional to cookies, **breakfast pastries** (including a great **coffee cake** with a tasty streusel), and **tea cakes,** Jacqueline's makes a number of to-die-for **cheesecakes,** the best I've tasted. They come in fun flavors such as **Snickers** (which is actually too much—a brownie crust and cream-cheese cake studded with chopped candy bars) and **banana Kahlua,** which has a banana-bread crust and a flavor of fresh bananas. Several of the **tortes,** as Jacqueline's calls them, are to my mind variations on cheesecake, although the cream-cheese base is different from what she uses in her cheesecakes. The incredibly rich and good **peanut butter torte** has a nutty graham-cracker crust and a cream-cheesy peanut butter filling, topped with a smooth chocolate ganache. The *tiramisù* here is excellent.

Jacqueline makes most of the cakes for the wholesale side of her business. You'll need to call in advance to see what's available. The cakes are generally sold whole, rather than by the slice.

Lucky Duck Fortune Cookie

305 Main Street, Everett, MA 02149   (617) 389-3583
Mail order: available   Hours: Mon.–Sat. 7 A.M.–5:30 P.M.; closed Sun.

Lucky Duck makes fortune cookies, and nothing but. The business is primarily wholesale, but you can enter a door that opens on top of a fortune-cookie machine (made in Framingham) and buy bags of fortune cookie seconds for about a dollar. *Seconds* usually means that the cookies aren't folded perfectly or that they are broken.

For significantly more money, you can order custom fortune cookies. The minimum is fifty cookies for $23, but the price per cookie drops if you order more.

NEWTON

Alden Merrell Cheesecake Co. See Newburyport, page 267.

Baker's Best. See "Goodies to Go," page 178.

Bentonwood Bakery and Café

47 Langley Road, Newton, MA 02159   (617) 527-5830
Mail order: not available   Hours: Mon.–Fri. 7 A.M.–7 P.M.;
   Sat. 8 A.M.–5 P.M.; Sun. 9 A.M.–3 P.M.

When I first visited Bentonwood, founder Rick Katz was still there, and I was impressed by the quality of everything I tried. He was a true perfectionist, making literally *everything* in the place, including the wonderful **jams** served with scones and **ketchup** for the sandwiches. But after four years in the business, Katz sold the place in 1995 to Clive Minihan. At this writing it is too soon to tell what changes will take place, but without Katz at the helm, I wonder how long his recipes will survive intact. That said, everything I tried here is wonderful, and Minihan continues to make many of Katz's specialties.

Bentonwood is the kind of place where you can't go wrong, no matter what you order, and whenever I think about the place, I yearn to drive over there and stock up. The individualized **Boston cream pie** is awesome, with a rich custard and bittersweet glaze. The **lemon bars** are the best around as well, tart and very lemony. Another best is the **chocolate chip cookie,** really good, with a perfect texture. The **brownies** are very good as well. Coffee lovers will like the **mocha chip cookies,** laced with ground espresso. When Katz was there, he made a marvelous **macaroon** using freshly grated coconut, and the staff told me that it is still made the same way. If they continue with the recipe, Bentonwood's is the best macaroon around. The **fresh fruit tarts** are lovely, and the **crème caramel** is rich and creamy.

On the savory end, Bentonwood offers a selection of breads, including **baguettes,** and **cinnamon-raisin bread.** The **focaccia** is used as the base for individual made-to-order **pizzas,** available with delectable combinations such as **roasted red pepper, oven-dried tomato, sautéed mushroom, mozzarella, and provolone.** The **sandwiches** are also creative. I loved the **eggplant, roasted peppers, spinach, and hummus sandwich.** Other combinations include **tuna and pickled beets, roasted turkey with Russian dressing and watercress,** and **Jamaican-jerk chicken salad with mixed greens and jicama, pineapple, and tamarind dressing.**

Everything, including **soups** and **salads,** is available to go, but there are also several tables, so you have the option of eating in.

Bread & Circus. See "Going Organic," page 434.

Breadsong. See "The Staff of Life," page 22.

Buns of Boston
45 Kenneth Street, Newton Highlands, MA 02161   (617) 965-9100
Mail order: not available   Hours: Mon.–Fri. 9 A.M.–5 P.M.;
    closed Sat., Sun.

Meri Bond owned a gourmet take-out shop for seven years, called Bond and Burkhart (where Bentonwood is now located). She closed that shop in 1990 and looked for another business, finally deciding to market her trademark sticky bun, which she had sold at her store. Buns of Boston **Sticky Wicked Buns** are, quite simply, the absolute best **sticky buns** around. Oh, others are very good, but these are perfect. They are made using a butter-rich croissant dough, and they come in a variety of flavors. **Pecan** is the standard, with a noticeable honey flavor. Others include **cinnamon-raisin, cranberry-orange,** and, my favorite, **apricot-almond.** One bite and you'll say, "Wow!" When I last spoke with Bond, she was developing a great **Hooper Bun,** which includes the delectable combination of cranberries, apricots, coconut, and ginger. She was also perfecting a **maple-walnut bun** with a real maple-syrup glaze.

Buns of Boston also makes **scones.** These are mixed. I wasn't crazy about the basic flavors—**cinnamon-currant** and **cranberry-orange.** The **lemon-ginger,** speckled with bits of crystallized ginger, is better. But best of all is the **maple-oatmeal scone,** a different creation entirely. Buns of Boston is among the first—and only one of a few at this writing—to make **savory scones,** laced with various cheeses, and these taste great. Flavors include **cheddar-dill** (made with aged Canadian cheddar), **spinach-feta,** and **Italian herb,** made with Parmesan and Romano. The best is **Southwestern corn,** seasoned with chipotle pepper, scallions, and pepper jack cheese. A meal in a scone.

Bond makes some very good **cookies,** especially the **coconut** and the **almond macaroons.** I also like the cinnamony **oatmeal-raisin** cookies.

Buns of Boston started as a wholesale business, and the buns, scones, and cookies are available in coffee shops and gourmet stores throughout Boston. At this writing, Bond was working on developing a retail store; the hours posted above are what she planned. Call to verify, and to see which places near you carry the goods.

Icing on the Cake

212 Adams Street, Newton, MA 02158   (617) 969-1830
Mail order: not available   Hours: by appointment, and
Tues.–Fri. 9 A.M.–5 P.M.; Sat. 11 A.M.–2 P.M.; closed Sun., Mon.

Icing on the Cake is not particularly noteworthy from the outside, and even once you step inside, you may not be sure you've come to the right place. But stay. The shop specializes in decorated cakes, and their portfolio boasts everything from traditional flower designs to elaborate cake-and-frosting sculptures, such as a banana split, an eighteen-wheeler truck, or the State House.

But it's what's inside that counts, and the **cakes** taste delicious. I tried a very good **double chocolate** and a delicious **golden Amaretto**—buttery golden cake laced with Amaretto liqueur. I was less impressed with the **carrot cake**—it was a little too sweet. For filling, the **white-chocolate mousse** is quite good; it tasted of real white chocolate, a subtle yet distinctive flavor.

Owner Paula Kiran worked at the Icing on the Cake for five years before she bought it with coworker Chris Staff. They bake the cakes to order, in small batches, and specialize in birthday and wedding cakes. If you want to order one, schedule a visit so you can taste samples and see which combination you like best. The cakes are not cheap, but they are very good, and very attractive.

The Italian Express. See "Goodies to Go," page 181.

Keltic Krust. See "The Staff of Life," page 23.

Rosie's Bakery. See Cambridge, page 251.

SOMERVILLE

Lyndell's Bakery
720 Broadway, Somerville, MA 02144   (617) 625-1793
Mail order: not available   Hours: Mon.–Sat. 7 A.M.–6 P.M.;
   closed Sun.

Lyndell's has been operating continuously since 1887, under just three different owners. The current owners, Herman and Janet Kett, have had the bakery since 1971 and have worked here nearly twice as long. Janet worked at Lyndell's during high school when Herman was the baker, and that's how they met. This is a full-service bakery, making everything from breakfast items to birthday cakes, cookies, and breads.

At first glance, Lyndell's looks like a standard bakery, nothing remarkable. But it is more than that. It's a very good bakery, which Janet describes as "full-line American with German overtones." The **butter cookies** here are made with butter. The **bismarcks**—a cream-filled donut lined with raspberry jam—are filled with real whipped cream. Janet is a trained nutritionist, and, although her husband is the baker, she knows exactly what goes into every item. If you have a nut allergy or a question about fat content, ask Janet.

The **honeycomb-graham bread** is a signature item, and it is a great whole wheat bread. It gets its name from the texture of the bread, which resembles a honeycomb. The bread has no added fat, although, Janet points out, the pan used to bake it is heavily greased, since the batter is very wet. There is no actual honey in the bread; its sweetness comes from molasses. This loaf lasts a long time in the fridge and makes great sandwiches, especially grilled cheese. The holiday **stollen** is an opposite of this bread: it's filled with butter and candied fruit and thickly coated with powdered sugar.

Most of what I tried here was very good. I prefer butter-based baked goods, but for those who don't, Lyndell's also makes standard shortening-based bakery fare, such as **cakes** with white shortening-based frosting. This frosting is used as the **whoopie pie** filling. There is a slight twist: the pink frosting available on the cupcakes gets its color from crushed strawberries, not food coloring. I liked most of their **cookies.** The **pecan** is buttery, really special; the **chocolate chip** has a good flavor. The **date square** was slightly underdone, but tasted delicious; this is an item not many bakeries make. The **apple square** consists of a butter-cookie crust covered with sliced fresh apples and raisins then topped with sweetened farmer's cheese; it has an old-world flavor. The *linzer* **cookie** is a best-seller, one the Ketts made as an experiment after a visit to the Midwest. Raspberry preserves are sandwiched between two thin, buttery hazelnut wafers. Raspberry jam is also used in what they call **florentines.** These are different from the lacy round cookies of this name that most bakeries sell; they are squares, a layer of cookie crust spread with the jam and topped with a caramel-almond coating and drizzled with chocolate. Yum. Also yummy is the **cream puff,** made with real whipped cream.

In fact, most items I tried here ranged from good to terrific. The **macaroons** come in **plain** or **chocolate**—flavored, not dipped. I prefer the plain, which has a good flavor, although the chocolate is very good, sure to be appreciated by chocolate lovers, with a candy bar–like flavor and texture. The prices are quite reasonable.

Panini. See "The Staff of Life," page 25.

Salt & Pepper

81 Holland Street, Somerville, MA 02144   (617) 666-1376
Mail order: not available   Hours: Mon.–Thurs. 6:30 A.M.–8:30 P.M.;
    Fri., Sat. 6:30 A.M.–10 P.M.; Sun. 6:30 A.M.–4 P.M.

Salt & Pepper started as a tiny storefront in Arlington, a publicity vehicle for owner Robin Peevey's catering business. In 1994 they moved to these much larger digs, a double storefront at the edge of Davis Square. The place is light and airy, with golden yellow walls and pressed tin ceilings. A high ledge on the wall behind the bakery counter holds a collection of the shop's namesake salt and pepper shakers.

There are two sections, joined in the middle: the bakery and the savory section. On the bakery side, the featured item is **biscuits**—not to be confused with scones—a nod to Peevey's southern heritage, and the recipe is based on her grandmother's. There are several flavors, the most popular being **sweet potato and ham.** These biscuits are big, and heavy; I preferred **peach,** slathered with jam and eaten with a mug of tea.

The **muffins** come in unusual flavors, such as **cranberry–poppy seed.** The **blueberry-corn** is very good. Other breakfast pastries include **brioche, sticky buns,** and *kolaches,* a Czech pastry filled with fruit and cream cheese and similar to a Danish. The **cherry** is delicious, but pass on the **lemon**—it has an odd flavor.

The **cookies** here are also slightly off the beaten track. Among the more ordinary there is the ubiquitous **chocolate chip,** oversized and good. The flavor of the **biscotti** is good—I tried **pecan-praline**—but the texture is too tender for a biscotti. They should be rock-hard and need to be dunked in something (coffee, wine) to soften them slightly. The **maple shortbread,** shaped like a maple leaf, is buttery, with a crisp glaze. **PB&Js** are subtly flavored peanut butter cookies with a drop of raspberry jelly. There is a choice of **coffee cakes,** including a very good **blueberry–poppy seed;** the **plum** was good but too dense, perhaps from the moisture in the fruit. There are always several **pies;** the southern **pecan pie** is sweet and delicious.

The **savories** include a selection of food to take out or to pick up at the counter and eat at one of the tables. There are a variety of **salads** and **prepared goods;** Peevey says she wants the food to be "interesting and fun—but not *too* gourmet, not *too* far-out." She succeeds. The **moussaka** is delicious, made with multilayers of mashed potatoes, ground lamb, eggplant, and tomatoes. There are always **vegetarian offerings,** such as a great **Asian noodles** with sesame and **creamy fusille and mixed peppers** in a mustard vinaigrette. There is always a **meaty chili,** and a variety of **soups.** I tried a very good **winter squash** and a wonderful, smoky **chicken-turkey soup.**

NORTH

ANDOVER

La Patisserie. See Winchester, page 270.

BEVERLY

Christian Payen Fine French Pastries

36 West Street, Beverly, MA 01915   (508) 922-6612
Mail order: not available   Hours: Mon.–Fri. 7 A.M.–5 P.M.;
    Sat. 7 A.M.–4 P.M.; closed Sun.

Christian Payen is a third-generation baker—although the first of his family to bake in this country. His parents had shops in Paris. Payen takes great pride in his **French bread** and won't discuss how it's made for fear of giving away secrets. The **baguette** is very good, but not amazing; it tasted slightly salty. The **croissants** are a little heavy, but they taste delicious and are even a little flaky. They come **plain** or with various fillings, including **raspberry, chocolate, raisin,** and **almond,** as well as savory **spinach and cheese** and **ham and cheese.**

Payen makes over thirty different **tarts** and **cakes,** but few items are on display (there are maybe a dozen desserts in the case). *L'Erreur* is a delectable blend of pastry cream and marzipan. *Tarte au citron* is *very* lemony, and rich. I prefer it to the *tarte aux pommes.* This is good too, with thinly sliced apples with a perfumey taste, perhaps from rosewater, but the crust is thick. the *mousse au chocolat* is very good, served in an individual cup and topped with an apricot glaze.

The bakery makes **mousse cakes,** with a genoise base; these are kept frozen. Tell Payen what size you want, and what flavors, and he'll frost and decorate your cake the way you like it.

BURLINGTON

Rosie's Bakery. See Cambridge, page 251.

MANCHESTER

Wheatberries of Manchester

10 Summer Street, Manchester, MA 01944   (508) 526-8011
Mail order: available   Hours: Mon.–Fri. 7 A.M.–7 P.M.;
   Sat. 7 A.M.–6 P.M.; Sun. 8 A.M.–4 P.M.

Wheatberries is a wonderful bakery-café, opened by John and Gina Fettig in 1990. Gina is self-taught and worked in several area food businesses for fifteen years before opening Wheatberries. The atmosphere here is relaxed and friendly. You will pass several marble-topped tables on your way to the food. A wall is painted with a lavender rendition of fields. On your left is a table stacked with loaves of bread, both **yeast** and **quick breads.** The yeast breads change daily. I tried an appealing **sesame-cornmeal,** which has a nice crunch from the cornmeal. The **multigrain** is good, but it does not taste that different from the **old-fashioned white,** which is moist without being doughy—great for sandwiches. The **mocha tea bread** is very good, moist and bittersweet. The **cakes** change daily and use seasonal ingredients; there's **strawberry-peach** in the summer.

Next to the breads is a glass cookie case. The quality of the **cookies** varies. The **chocolate chip cookies** are very good, chock-full of chips and crispy—almost too crisp, but without the mushiness common to oversized cookies. The **oatmeal-raisin** is homey, with a great taste from rolled oats and tons of raisins. The **milk-chocolate shortbread** is too heavy and studded with milk-chocolate disks—fine if you are a milk-chocolate fan. The **molasses crinkles** were disappointing; usually this is a cookie I like. These are too thick and soft, and the molasses flavor is too strong. Better are the *linzertorte* **cookies,** made with finely chopped hazelnuts and excellent raspberry jam. The **biscotti** tastes good but isn't hard enough. The **almond biscotti** have a nice toasted taste, and the **mocha pistachio** are unusual.

Bar cookies and **cakes** are displayed in a refrigerated case, and some suffered from a stale taste. Before buying any of these, check when they were made. But this case has some wonderful treats. **Apricot brown bars** consist of a butter crust spread with apricot jam then topped with a brownie and chopped hazelnuts. The **lemon squares** are good; they could be more lemony, but they have a delicate, crisp crust and a tender texture. The crème de la crème here is the **eclair**—the best I've ever tasted. The pastry is good, and the custardy filling is divine. Top that with a pure chocolate ganache. Wow.

Next to the pastries are the **savory items.** These change daily, and there are several **vegetarian options,** and creative **chicken preparations.** I tried a hearty **black-bean casserole** and a terrific **fresh tomato and wild mushroom lasagne. Mexican chicken–saffron rice salad** is a light offering, but the **almond-chicken tenderloins** are more filling. There are also **sandwiches,** made using Wheatberries bread. They include creative combinations such as **roast beef with herb cream cheese** and **roast turkey with cranberry mayonnaise.**

MARBLEHEAD

J & S Brandi's. See "Goodies to Go," page 184.

Delphin's Gourmandise
258 Washington Street, Marblehead, MA 01945 (617) 639-2311
Mail order: not available Hours: Tues.–Thurs. 7 A.M.–4 P.M.;
  Fri., Sat. 7 A.M.–6 P.M.; Sun. 7 A.M.–noon; closed Mon.

1336 Beacon Street, Brookline, MA 02146 (617) 731-0005
Mail order: not available Hours: Mon.–Fri. 7 A.M.–7 P.M.;
  Sat. 7 A.M.–6 P.M.; Sun. 7 A.M.–5 P.M.

Delphin Gomes, a native of France, has been practicing the art of pastry making since he began an apprenticeship at the age of fourteen in the Dijon region of France. In France, they take pastry making—and all aspects of food preparation—very seriously. Gomes was the eldest of seven, and he saw pursuing a career in pastry as preferable to working in a factory, as many of his peers were doing.

The pastry apprenticeship is a three-year course, during which students learn how to make ice cream, candy, and pastries. In Burgundy, out of 1,500 students who began the program, 600 made it to the end, and only 200 passed the weeklong examination and received a diploma. Gomes was third in his class. After graduating, he found work in Paris, worked and studied at Le

Nôtre, and then was offered a job as pastry chef at L'Hermitage in Los Angeles. He was there for three years. "I hated L.A.," he says. "I was ready to go back to France, but then I met my wife, who was from Peabody. I visited here and said, 'Okay, I'll stay.' " The Gomeses decided to go into business for themselves—his wife is the manager of their store—and they live above their Marblehead storefront, which they opened in 1986.

Gomes's desserts are truly beautiful, and unique. The cakes—*gâteaux,* as Delphin calls them—are not sold by the slice, but by the cake, in either large or individual sizes. The individual sizes are rounds, miniatures of a large cake, and are beautiful as well as delicious. They generally consist of layers of genoise and various mousses and fruit. There are about a dozen regular *gâteaux,* as well as seasonal specials. Being a caramel fan, I enjoyed the **Triomphe,** a walnut cake covered with caramel mousse and caramel glaze. The popular **Megador** is also good. The chocolate genoise is soaked with raspberry juice, spread with raspberry jam, then topped with an awesome chocolate mousse and a raspberry glaze. The mousse is very rich—a small amount of these treats goes a long way.

The **tarts** vary with the season, but there is usually a **Catalane tarte.** This is different from the usual tart with custard filling and topped with fresh fruit. The crust is a flaky pastry, and the filling is made with browned butter, baked with fruit—I especially like the **sour cherry**—and more crust.

Gomes makes huge **croissants,** and the flavor is excellent, but they are not as flaky as I want a croissant to be. The fillings, especially **almond,** are very good. There is also a handful of **French cookies.** The **meringues** are unique. They consist of two hemispheres of egg-white meringue mixed with ground almonds joined together by a spread of flavored buttercream. When you bite into one, you get a wonderful swirl of flavors and textures—crunchy, creamy, sweet. There are three flavors: I like the **coffee** best by far; the **chocolate** is a little too sweet; the **lemon** isn't lemony enough. Their *palmiers,* while a little on the heavy side, are deliciously buttery and crunchy from sugar.

Delphin's Marblehead operation is where everything is made. The pastries are driven to the Brookline location every morning.

Because so many of the items are so good, they're apt to

disappear by lunchtime. If you want a specific item, reserve it in advance.

MELROSE

Breads 'n' Bits of Ireland. See "The Staff of Life," page 27.

NEWBURYPORT

Alden Merrell Cheesecake Co.
4 Graf Road, Newburyport, MA 01950   (508) 462-4495
Mail order: not available   Hours: Mon.–Thurs. and
  Sat. 8 A.M.–6 P.M.; Fri. 8 A.M.–7 P.M.; Sun. 10 A.M.–5 P.M.
43 Central Street, Wellesley, MA 02181   (508) 431-9530
Mail order: not available   Hours: Mon.–Sat. 8 A.M.–7 P.M.;
  Sun. 10 A.M.–5 P.M.
1361 Beacon Street, Brookline, MA 02146   (617) 734-5573
Mail order: not available   Hours: Mon.–Sat. 8 A.M.–8 P.M.;
  Sun. 10 A.M.–5 P.M.
34 Langley Road, Newton, MA 02159   (617) 965-1090
Mail order: not available   Hours: Mon.–Sat. 8 A.M.–7 P.M.;
  Sun. 10 A.M.–5 P.M.
Pickering Wharf, Salem, MA 01970   (508) 744-2820
Mail order: not available   Hours: Mon.–Wed. 8 A.M.–6 P.M.;
  Thurs.–Sat. 8 A.M.–7 P.M.; Sun. 10 A.M.–5 P.M.
447 Boston Post Road, Sudbury, MA 01776   (508) 443-7517
Mail order: not available   Hours: Mon.–Thurs. 9 A.M.–6 P.M.;
  Fri., Sat. 8 A.M.–7 P.M.; Sun. 10 A.M.–5 P.M.

I admit to a prejudice against chain stores; I have low expectations when it comes to the food they offer. So Alden Merrell certainly exceeded my expectations. This Newburyport-based chain started selling cheesecakes from a small stand on Plum Island in 1977. And the **cheesecake** is good; it is available in a few fruit varieties, including **cherry, blueberry,** and **pineapple.**

But cheesecakes are not the draw of this bakery. The best two desserts are the **carrot cake,** frosted with a light cream-cheese frosting; and the **Chambourd torte,** a chocolate cake misted with raspberry Chambourd liqueur, containing a thin filling of cheesecake, and frosted with bittersweet chocolate and chocolate glaze. I prefer it to the popular **triple-chocolate truffle cake,** which is more sweet than chocolatey. The **lemon cake,** with a lemon cream-cheese frosting is pretty good but not amazing. The prices of the cakes are extremely reasonable. All cakes are available in a variety of configurations—from loaf to round to sheet cakes, and the stores will decorate them to order.

The company also makes a variety of **pies.** I generally like the fillings, especially that of the creamy **cappuccino silk pie,** but the cookie crusts tended to be underdone. The **Boston cream pie,** made with golden cake and custard, is very good.

For lighter sweets, the company makes **muffin tops**— flat muffins that are primarily crusty top. The **blueberry** was okay but underdone, as was the **Morning Glory,** a variation on a carrot muffin. The **banana bread** was the most disappointing —much too sweet. The **brownies,** however, are very good— fudgy, with a dense chocolate flavor.

PEABODY

Central Bakery. See "The Staff of Life," page 27.

SALEM

Alden Merrell Cheesecake Co. See Newburyport, page 267.

WAKEFIELD

Teahouse Floreal
55 Albion Street, Wakefield, MA 01880   (617) 245-1023 or
  (800) 698-1023
Mail order: not available   Hours: Mon.–Sat. 7 A.M.–6 P.M.;
  Sun. 8 A.M.–4 P.M.

Patricia Quinn and David Tsypkin met while working at La Patisserie (see page 270). In the summer of 1995 they decided to go into business for themselves and bought Teahouse Floreal; a bakery has been in this location for more than half a century. Teahouse Floreal specializes in European baked goods. Tsypkin is from Russia and has added his influence and training to several of the pastries offered. The most notable one is not sweet—the savory **piroshkis.** These are oval-shaped rolls made with a rich soft dough and filled with various items; the fillings change daily. I tried a wonderful **chicken, onion, and pepper piroshki.**

The pastries are generally very good. Some of these offerings are not seen elsewhere. The **almond cookie** is very simple, yet very good, with subtle hints of lemon and rum. I especially like the *trier*, a square with a short bread base topped with a mélange of raisins, almonds, and honey, scented with lemon. The **Bakewell tart** is intriguing, a large sort of cookie-cake about five inches in diameter. It's crispy on the outside, yet both airy and chewy inside, with an almondy interior. They also make their own **Milano cookies,** delicate ovals of cookie flecked with orange zest sandwiching bittersweet chocolate and edged with chopped nuts. The **pecan diamonds** are delicious. I prefer them to the thick-crusted **florentine bars,** which have a honey-almond filling.

The specialty cookies are significantly better than the classic-style ones. The best is the **chocolate chip cookie,** which is riddled with tiny bits of chocolate, oatmeal, and walnuts. The **English toffee** cookie I tried was unpleasant-tasting, and the **brownie** is nothing special.

Teahouse Floreal also makes attractive **cakes,** beautifully assembled. The **raspberry mousse** filling is okay, and the **strawberry mousse** is delicious. They also make a few **breads.** I especially like the **raisin bread,** which is both light and rich with butter and eggs, almost like a raisin-studded brioche. The tasty **cheddar cheese bread** is also delicate and rich. The sweet **cinnamon buns** are simple and very good. The **croissants** taste good, but the texture is too heavy.

Quinn and Tsypkin had just taken over the business when I visited, and they still seemed to be getting their bearings. Based on what I sampled, Teahouse Floreal has a promising future.

WINCHESTER

The Gingerbread Construction Co.

562 Washington Street, Winchester, MA 01890   (617) 729-7700
Mail order: available   Hours: Mon.–Fri. 6 A.M.–6 P.M.;
   Sat. 6 A.M.–5 P.M.; Sun. 6 A.M.–2 P.M.

John and Janet D'Orsi started the Gingerbread Construction Company by making and selling gingerbread houses out of their basement in 1987. The houses proved popular, so the D'Orsis soon opened shop in this converted gas station at the corner of a busy intersection in Winchester. The shop itself is cute—it looks like a slate-roofed, brick version of a gingerbread house.

As the name implies, **gingerbread houses** are the focus here, and they are available in three sizes. You can get the confection already decorated or as a do-it-yourself kit. With the kit you buy the house already assembled, and it comes with frosting and candies for decorating—lots of fun for kids.

But gingerbread houses are a seasonal business, so the store carries other items as well, namely muffins and cookies. John D'Orsi worked as a product developer for Dunkin' Donuts; he developed their muffin recipe. He has applied his expertise to his own business. These are very good **muffins,** and they come in several fun flavors. My favorite is the **gingerbread muffin.** I prefer it to the **gingerbread boys** and **girls,** the decorated cookies the store makes. This muffin has a cream-cheese filling and is delicious. Also good is the **orange-almond muffin,** filled with slivered almonds and mandarin orange segments. The **carrot muffin** is popular; it comes frosted with the same tasty cream-cheese frosting.

The **cookies** are also very good, especially the **white chocolate–macadamia nut.** I also like the **peanut butter–chocolate-chunk,** studded with whole peanuts and chunks of semi-sweet chocolate. Pass on the **sugar cookies**—pretty but not much flavor—and the doughy tasting **oatmeal raisin.** The **chocolate chunk with pecans** is delicious. At this writing, the D'Orsis were in the process of opening a second location, in Wakefield.

La Patisserie

30 Church Street, Winchester, MA 01890   (607) 729-9441
Mail order: available   Hours: Mon.–Sat. 7 A.M.–9 P.M.;
   Sun. 7 A.M.–6 P.M.

63 Park Street, Andover, MA 03811   (508) 475-4445
Mail order: available   Hours: Mon.–Thurs. 6:30 A.M.–8 P.M.;
   Fri., Sat. 6:30 A.M.–9 P.M.; Sun. 6:30–5 P.M.

La Patisserie has been in Winchester since 1982 and in Andover since 1988. The store is like a French *patisserie,* offering a wide array of pastries, truffles, croissants, and breads. The pastries are mixed: several **cookies** and **truffles** I tried tasted stale. I did like the **peanut butter–filled cookie.** This is a half-moon–shaped chocolate cookie with a peanut butter filling and half-dipped in chocolate. The similarly shaped **apricot-filled cookie,** with a butter cookie base, was much less appealing. The **almond crois-**

sant was very good, with a flaky texture and a buttery taste. I also liked the **almond** *linzertorte.* It consists of layers of soft chocolate cookie and marzipan. The **raspberry** *linzertorte* is also made with a chocolate crust, but it was too crumbly.

The best items here are the **breads.** The **multigrain bread** is very good, and the **rye bread** is one of the area's best. There are some beautiful large round, flattish loaves that are decorated with different seeds and grains, such as poppy seeds, sesame seeds, and oatmeal, arranged in a wedge pattern. You'll need to order these in advance.

WOBURN

Boston Coffee Cake Co.

16 Henshaw Street, Woburn, MA 01801   (617) 938-4450
Mail order: available   Hours: Mon.–Fri. 5 A.M.–5:30 P.M.;
    closed Sat., Sun.

Mark Forman worked as a hotel food and beverage director before going into business with his brother Bruce in the niche market of wholesale coffee cakes. They started the business in 1992, with their **cinnamon-walnut coffee cake.** It proved popular, and they've added five more flavors since then. The original cake is a moist sour-cream cake with a tasty swirl of cinnamon and walnuts. All the cakes get an appealing moistness from sour cream and eggs, but they do not contain butter (I think butter would enhance the taste).

Two flavors were disappointing. The **Applicious** is the original cake with apples, but the apple content is scant, and the texture is drier than the original. **Blueberry Blizzard** has a generous but not overwhelming amount of blueberries and is topped with powdered sugar. It, too, is on the dry side. The cakes come in two sizes, and the larger cake (38.5 ounces) is moister; some of the smaller cakes (21 ounces) were overcooked, which made them dry. The best flavor is the **Chocolate Razamataz,** which is laced with just the right amount of chocolate chips and bits of raspberries. It's topped with a grainy but chocolatey icing. A close second is the **Lemon Burst,** which has an appealing lemon flavor and speckles of poppy seeds.

The bakery is a wholesale operation located in an office park, but you can come in any time during the week and pick up whatever cakes are on hand. If you want a specific flavor, call and order it in advance.

SOUTH

BRAINTREE

Konditor Meister

32 Wood Road, Braintree, MA 02184 (617) 849-1970
Mail order: not available Hours: Mon.–Sat. 10 A.M.–5 P.M.;
Sun. 11 A.M.–1 P.M.

Gunther Mösinger is from the Black Forest area of Germany, and he learned his craft as a pastry chef there. When he moved to the States, he worked as the pastry chef at the Ritz-Carlton for several years before opening his own business with his wife, Rebecca Smith. At the Ritz, a colleague had occasionally called Mösinger *konditor meister,* which is German for "master pastrymaker," so the couple chose that as the name for the business.

Konditor Meister specializes in wedding cakes, and in providing cakes and pastries for hotels and large functions. When I visited, kitchen workers were frosting dozens of cakes and decorating still more small pastries, which are sold primarily wholesale. You can buy the smaller items, but you have to buy a minimum of a dozen.

The quality of the **small pastries** varies. The **fruit tart** is mediocre—too much crust in relation to the amount of filling. Similarly, the tasty **cheesecake** has too much crust. The **eclairs** with chocolate mousse filling are rich and chocolatey. The filling in the **lemon tart** is deliciously lemony, and the crust is coated with a thin layer of dark chocolate. The **chocolate châpeau,** a nutty meringue filled with chocolate mousse and dipped in chocolate, is an appealing blend of textures. There are **chocolate cups,** a shell made of dark chocolate and filled with various mousses. The **orange** has an artificial aftertaste, but the **raspberry** tastes quite good, although I would prefer no seeds. The **pecan tart** is yummy, with finely chopped nuts.

Their **cakes,** available as wedding cakes or to celebrate other occasions such as birthdays, come in a variety of combinations. A popular one is **strawberry Grand Marnier.** A light golden cake is brushed with Grand Marnier and raspberry jam then spread with white chocolate mousse and fresh strawberries. The whole thing is covered with buttercream frosting. Also good, but slightly sticky, is the **Schokolade,** a moist chocolate cake layered with chocolate mousse and white buttercream. The **carrot cake,** a Ritz recipe laden with nuts and pineapple, is quite good, containing layers of apricot jam and a cream-cheese frosting.

If you are interested in the **pastries,** it is a good idea to call in advance to see what is available. Before ordering a wedding cake, it's best to set up a tasting appointment.

BROCKTON

White's Pastry Shop

1041 Pearl Street, Brockton, MA 02401   (508) 584-5100
Mail order: not available   Hours: Mon.–Fri. 7 A.M.–6 P.M.;
    Sat. 7:30 A.M.–6 P.M.; Sun. 7:30 A.M.–5 P.M.

White's Pastry Shop is right next door to Pasta Bene (see "Lotsa Pasta," page 98). It's hard to find both establishments, since the location feels like a rear entrance. But pull off the road into a parking space and check it out. The baked goods are largely Italian and American, with some interesting variations. One of these is a **cardamom bread,** a braided eggy sweetbread that is simply delicious—worth making a special trip. I tried a variety of standard **cookies—oatmeal, peanut butter,** and **almond macaroon**—and all were pretty good.

White's makes a variety of creative, tempting **cakes.** Among them is a **cappuccino torte** made with chocolate cake layered with cappuccino and chocolate buttercream. The *tiramisù* **torte** is a chiffon cake brushed with espresso and layered with mascarpone cheese. There are a few fresh whipped cream cakes—the best are the fruit cakes ordered in season—**strawberry** or **peach shortcake.** There are also a number of inexpensive but good **pies,** including a classic **custard, mincemeat** (which few places make), and both **pumpkin** and **squash.**

DEDHAM

My Grandma's Coffee Cake

231 Bussey Street, Dedham, MA 02026   (800) 847-2636
Mail order: available   Hours: Mon–Fri. 9 A.M.–6 P.M.;
    closed Sat., Sun.

Bob Katz sold paper goods and chemical cleansers to organizations for several years, and one of his customers was My Grandma's Coffee Cake. Katz fell in love with the cakes and found that his sales went up when he included a cake as a gift to his clients. So in 1993 Katz bought the company, expanded the product line, and moved to larger digs. The cakes do have preservatives, so they last, but they also have things that make coffee cake delicious: sour cream and eggs. The flagship flavor, **cinnamonwalnut,** is very good, but my favorite is a toss-up between **Granny Smith apple** and **golden raspberry.** The cake is rich and moist, with a swirl of nuts, fruit, and cinnamon, and topped with more of the same. The **cappuccino** is less appealing, with a bitter coffee aftertaste. Otherwise, this is really good coffee cake. Katz is a definite salesman, but he loves his product and is both accommodating and convincing. The large cakes are large, serving twelve to fourteen generously. They aren't cheap, but they aren't outrageous either. The coffee cake can last up to two years in the freezer, but once you dig into one, it probably won't last long.

The cakes are available at the bakery and at several outlets around town.

NORWOOD

Kravings. See "Goodies to Go," page 210.

QUINCY

Montilio's Cake Shoppe

638 Adams Street, Quincy, MA 02169   (617) 472-5500
Mail order: not available   Hours: Mon.–Thurs. 6 A.M.–9 P.M.;
    Fri., Sat. 6 A.M.–10 P.M.; Sun. 6 A.M.–8 P.M.

George Montilio's father started Montilio's in downtown Quincy in 1947. The business was immensely successful for many years, ultimately growing to twenty-seven stores throughout New England. But, says George, eventually rent began to exceed profitability. The company began to downsize, and now the Quincy store, which moved to this location in 1988, is the only one left. But George is upbeat, believing that his product is better done on this smaller scale, although he continues to do a large wholesale business in addition to retail.

The **cakes** are a specialty, especially decorated cakes—often enormous ones. Loose-leaf notebooks offer a portfolio of cakes that Montilio's has made over the years, such as a life-size upright piano, all cake, made for Jimmy Durante; a huge globe cake; and a twenty-six-foot tall tower cake that fed 10,000 for Faneuil Hall's birthday celebration.

The cakes come in standard flavors—**white, golden, chocolate,** and **carrot.** There are a variety of tasty fillings, such as **Swiss chocolate** and **French buttercream.** The **pastry cream** is custardy and very good. Montilio's makes about two dozen cake and filling combinations, such as a **Doboschtorte**—seven layers of golden cake spread with chocolate buttercream and topped with a chocolate glaze. The **German chocolate cake** has a filling that is a blend of honey, brown sugar, coconut, and pecans.

Montilio's also offers many standard bakery items, most of which are good. The **cheesecake** is in the classic **New York** style, dense and rich. The **bramble** is a pastry filled with lots of fruit; I especially like the **raspberry.** Montilio's is one of the few traditional bakeries that makes **chocolate chip cookies** using butter (not shortening), and that makes all the difference. These cookies are oversized and hence slightly soft, but the flavor is great. I also liked the **oatmeal cookies,** which have an unusual touch of molasses in them. The **coconut brownie** is a pleasing combination of chocolatey brownie and coconut macaroon. My favorite cookie of all is the *quaresimale.* George claimed that the ones I tasted were overdone and not good, but I loved them. Several Italian bakeries make these cookies, which are similar to biscotti, but Montilio's are best. They are hard and crunchy, with a hint of orange, and laden with toasted almonds and hazelnuts.

In 1992 Montilio's started making **breads** because, George says, there was a demand. They make *scali* and **Vienna,** and a good, though slightly soft **abruzzi.** Their bagels and rye breads come from Zeppy's in Randolph (see "The Staff of Life," page 40).

This Takes the Cake

764 Hancock Street, Quincy, MA 02170   (617) 773-2253
Mail order: not available   Hours: Tues.–Sat. 10 A.M.–6 P.M.;
    closed Sun., Mon.

Regina Kelly-O'Brien started This Takes the Cake with no intention of opening a retail bakery. "Whenever someone in an office would have a birthday, and we needed a cake, there would be the drudgery of having to pick one up. I decided to start a business delivering quality cakes to Boston offices," Kelly-O'Brien explains. Before launching the business in 1985, she had previously worked in an office and had never decorated cakes before. So she hired a pastry chef and went to work. But the demand for the cakes themselves made continuing the delivery business difficult, so Kelly-O'Brien stopped that after a year. Then she took over as pastry chef and began creating terrific cakes.

This Takes the Cake makes only a few cake flavors, but the ones they make are great. I tried **golden,** which is a classic cake, rich with butter and eggs and very moist. The **chocolate** is also very moist and delicious. **Lemon** and **carrot** cakes are available as well. You have a choice of buttercream fillings (all of which are made with butter), including **raspberry, apricot, peach, strawberry, chocolate,** and **mocha.** Or you can also choose a filling of **chocolate ganache** or **mousse.**

In addition to these cakes, This Takes the Cake offers **ice-cream cakes,** made with Kelly-O'Brien's cakes and ice cream from the Ice Creamery in Randolph (see "Frozen Delights," page 324). Since the cake itself is so good, these are some of the better ice-cream cakes around.

The cakes are beautifully decorated. The basic package includes a floral cascade decoration, but you can choose from several other designs as well. The shop makes lots of wedding cakes, but these cakes are terrific for birthdays too.

WEST

ARLINGTON

The Chocolate Box. See "Sweet Indulgences," page 338.

Lakota Bakery

1373 Massachusetts Avenue, Arlington, MA 02174   (617) 646-0121
Mail order: not available   Hours: Tues.–Fri. 8:30 A.M.–6 P.M.;
    Sat. 10 A.M.–6 P.M.; closed Sun., Mon.

Lakota Bakery started out as the bakery arm of The Chocolate Box (See "Sweet Indulgences," page 338), located next door. Current owner Barbara Wyne had worked at the business for seven years before buying the bakery part in 1991. Wyne originally hails from South Dakota, home of Native Americans called either Lakota or Dakota—the source for the name of her business. Wyne's bakery started primarily as a wholesale business, but people kept popping in, so the bakery sells retail now as well. When you enter the small shop, you step right into the kitchen; there are no display cases, just racks of cooling cookies.

Cookies are the specialty here, and Wyne has a true flair for them; nothing is mediocre, just good to amazing. You may notice some of the cookies appear similar to those at The Chocolate Box, reflecting the shared roots, but many are different. The cookies are rich with butter and not too sweet, which makes them taste more sophisticated. They are also lovely to look at.

Chocolate appears in most items, either as the main flavor or as a decoration. The most intense chocolate item is the **almond macaroon.** An almond macaroon base is covered with a mound of chocolate ganache, then finished with a bittersweet chocolate coating. A small bite goes a *long* way. The macaroon base is delicious by itself, too.

Florentines are wonderful here. These are big, lacy cookies, very flat and candy-like brittle, threaded with oatmeal and sliced almonds. The bottom half of the cookie is coated with dark chocolate. (I also like these with no chocolate.) The **coconut macaroon** is similarly candy-like, almost a reverse Almond Joy. The sweet coconut is studded with disks of dark chocolate the size of a quarter, which are also used in the **chocolate chip cookie,** a different version of this classic confection. It is quite good: rich chocolate surrounded by a delicate, buttery dough threaded with finely chopped walnuts.

277

Holiday cut-outs are excellent shortbread cookies, the best I've tasted. The shapes change with the season and are half dipped in dark chocolate (you can order them plain, too). The **gingerbread men** are also the best around. At this writing, Wyne makes them only from Thanksgiving through Christmas, but I encourage her to make them year round. The taste is nice and gingery, and the texture is perfect—not too hard, not too soft. Two kinds of *linzer* **cookies** are sold here. A dough containing ground almonds surrounds a generous filling, either apricot, which is decorated with drizzles of dark chocolate, or raspberry, which is decorated with white chocolate. The jam filling is very fruity.

There are two sandwich cookies. The **mint sandwich** is two tasty wafers of dark chocolate cookie surrounding a peppermint buttercream; it is too minty for me, but I overdosed on mint twenty years ago and still haven't recovered. The **mocha sandwich** consists of two butter cookies holding together a strong coffee buttercream; the cookie is then half-dipped in dark chocolate.

Lakota makes excellent **brownies;** the **frosted brownies** are covered with the knockout bittersweet ganache. Wyne also uses the ganache to frost made-to-order cakes, such as the very good **chocolate cake.** To balance this richness, Wyne recently started a line of **low-fat fruitbreads,** in **banana, blueberry,** and **cranberry-orange.**

Quebrada Baking Co.

208 Mass. Avenue, Arlington, MA 02174   (617) 648-0700 or
    648-0100
Mail order: not available   Hours: Sun.–Thurs. 6 A.M.–8 P.M.;
    Fri., Sat. 6 A.M. –10 P.M.

272 Washington Street, Wellesley, MA 02181   (617) 237-2111
Mail order: not available   Hours: Mon.–Fri. 6 A.M.–7 P.M.;
    Sat., Sun. 6 A.M.–6 P.M.

Kay Wiggin started Quebrada in Arlington in 1977, after spending a year working for Judy Rosenberg of Rosie's. She spun off on her own to start a line of all-natural baked goods, and she started out as a wholesaler of whole wheat bread, sweet rolls, and muffins, which she called *hooters*. Six years later she opened a branch in Wellesley, turned Arlington into a retail store, and closed the wholesale business.

The original line of bakery goods used organic whole wheat flour and no sugar; the muffins were sweetened with honey and maple syrup. My favorite is one of the originals, the **maple-nut hooter.** It has a definite maple taste, which I love, and the top is studded with thick walnut halves.

As Quebrada grew, its product line expanded. "We brought in white flour and sugar, so we could make cookies and other good things," Wiggins says. One of the early white-flour creations was a **croissant** line, but they also make **whole wheat croissants** in a variety of flavors including **raspberry, chocolate, spinach,** and **ham and cheese.** The pastry of the croissants is very good and rich, but it's not flaky enough. The regular are better than the whole wheat. The **sticky buns,** covered with pecan halves, are great—not too rich and with a good crunch from the nuts. Most of the **cookies** are softer than I like, although the flavor is good. The best is the **molasses-ginger cookie,** with pieces of candied ginger surprising your tongue. The smallish **cheese Danish** is also tasty.

Quebrada makes three kinds of **bread.** The **challah** is delicious; it uses two thirds white flour and one third whole wheat, so it has a pleasing nutty flavor. There is also an **oatmeal** and a **honey white bread.**

In 1994 the Arlington Quebrada expanded into space next door and opened a full-service coffee shop. They use Shapiro's coffee, and offer it iced in the summer. They also make fresh **lemonade.** All the bakery items are available to eat in or take out. There are also fancier items, such as a yummy **chocolate cake with sour-cream chocolate frosting** and excellent **cappuccino cream puffs,** filled with a terrific coffee cream. The same custard, in vanilla, fills the homemade **eclairs,** which are topped with an intense chocolate glaze.

BELMONT

Eastern Lamejun. See "The World in a Jar," page 422.

Ohlin's Bakery

456 Common Street, Belmont, MA 02178   (617) 484-0274
Mail order: not available   Hours: Mon.–Sat. 7 A.M.–6 P.M.;
   Sun. 7 A.M.–1 P.M.

Ohlin's is a long-established family bakery. It's been at its current Belmont Center location since 1915 and has had only two owners: the original Ohlin's, and now the Klemm family. Current manager Paul Klemm is the fourth of nine siblings, and various other brothers and sisters work in the bakery.

Ohlin's is an all-purpose bakery, making everything from **cookies** and **birthday cakes** to **quiches** and **yeast breads.** They make excellent **donuts,** all kinds, both **cake** and **raised,** hand-cut. The **honey-dip, sugar,** and **jelly donuts** are among the best I've tasted. Another star is the **apple flip,** a hefty yeast dough formed into an appealingly sloppy free-form shape, filled with fresh-cut cinnamon apples. In fact, most things Ohlin's makes with apples are very good, since they don't use canned fillings. Their **apple fritters** are yummy, too.

A popular item is the **TV snack.** It consists of a slab of chocolate cake covered with a sort of Twinkie-like "creme" made with sugar and shortening, then glazed with a sweet, not very chocolatey glaze. I didn't care for it. The **apple scone** is pretty good, considering that it is made with margarine (me being the butter purist that I am), and the inexpensive **brownie** is decent as well.

There are several options for diabetics, including **sugarless cookies** and **fruit turnovers,** made with NutriSweet. The Klemms make their own regular **muffins** and use a mix for the **nonfat variety.**

Ohlin's makes a number of **breads.** The round **cinnamon loaf** is very good.

Rustica. See "Goodies to Go," page 190.

Vickie Lee Boyajian. See Needham, page 283.

BURLINGTON

Rosie's Bakery. See Cambridge, page 251.

CONCORD

Concord Teacakes

59 Commonwealth Avenue, Concord, MA 01742   (508) 369-7644
Mail order: available   Hours: Mon.–Fri. 7 A.M.–5 P.M.;
  Sat., Sun. 8 A.M.–5 P.M.

Several years ago I worked in West Concord, which at the time was virtually a culinary wasteland. One lunch hour I was wandering through a warehouse area when I saw a beckoning sign for Concord Teacakes. I followed the arrow up a few steps through a door that opened into a huge room with a small table set up by the entrance. A harried-looking woman came over as I entered. "We're closed," she apologized. "I'm very sorry." She looked around, concerned, then opened a nearby refrigerator. "But here's a brownie for your trouble. Come back Friday morning!" The **brownie** was very good, and I did indeed return that Friday.

The woman turned out to be the owner Judy Fersh, baker of the world's best **scones.** They are perfectly textured, crumbly without being dry, rich and buttery, yet flaky and light. **Plain, cinnamon,** or with **currants,** they taste fantastic and don't even need jam. They come in two sizes: **miniature** and **regular.** The regular is a good size, smaller than the palm of your hand, which I prefer to the popular oversized creations. To me, scones were not meant to be humongous, and Concord Teacakes' are perfect. They are available **plain,** with **currants,** or **cinnamon.**

In addition to scones, the company makes a variety of baked goods, including **pies, cakes,** and **muffins.** These are all homey sweets—no elaborate tortes or fancy desserts. The **oatbran muffins** are delicious, made with finely chopped walnuts and enough butter to counteract any cholesterol-lowering affects the oat bran might have. The **cranberry, blueberry,** and **cranblue** muffins are fine but not exceptional—they are too cakey for my taste. The **chocolate chip** and **oatmeal cookies** are unexceptional. The **fruit pies** are wonderful, especially the **cherry** made with frozen Michigan sour cherries, and the fantastic **strawberry-rhubarb,** which, I admit, became a dinner for two on more than one occasion.

Fersh started the company with three **tea cakes** in 1984, and they're still popular today: **almond-lemon, chocolate-chocolate,** and the **Emily Dickinson fruitcake,** made from the poet's recipe. The **coffee cakes,** topped with **plain streusel, cran-**

berry, or **blueberry,** are great: brunch guests will thank you profusely if you serve one of these.

Since I first encountered Concord Teacakes, the bakery has expanded—there now is a retail shop on the main street, with regular hours, so these scones and coffee cakes are now much easier to find.

Sally Ann Food Shop

73 Main Street, Concord, MA 01742   (508) 369-4558
Mail order: not available   Hours: Mon.–Sat. 6:30 A.M.–5:30 P.M.;
    Sun. 7 A.M.–noon

The sweets at Sally Ann's are both simple and fancy. The **pecan caramel square** is for honey lovers: a butter crust supports a thick layer of chopped pecans in a honey filling. It differs from the **pecan square,** which is more like pecan pie. The brownie part of the **mocha-frosted fudge brownie** is very moist and very sweet; the frosting has a barely discernible coffee flavor. The **lemon square** has a tasty lemon filling, but the crust is much too underdone. Of the **cookies,** I liked the **oatmeal-raisin,** which is chewy, buttery, and loaded with cinnamon and raisins. The **chocolate chip cookie** is too soft and floury tasting, but the **white-chocolate chunk** is great. This is a chocolate cookie with a great flavor and perfect texture—crunchy, chewy, just right.

Their **cakes** come in several sizes, from seven inches to a full sheet. There is **vanilla** and **carrot,** as well as three kinds of chocolate: **classic, chocolate carrot,** and **fudge.** The cakes can be frosted with flavored **French buttercream, fresh whipped cream,** or **cream-cheese frosting.** There are also several classic combinations, such as *sachertorte,* made with chocolate cake, apricots or raspberries, and chocolate ganache. **Tarts,** such as **key lime** and **fresh fruit,** come in individual or large sizes.

Don't miss the **sandwiches.** They make their own **roast turkey** and an intriguing **curried tuna.** There are usually six sandwiches daily, and they change. I like the **melted Brie and Granny Smith apples.** The sandwiches are all made on Sally Ann's **breads.**

There are two categories of breads. **Enriched breads,** baked on Tuesdays, Thursdays, and Saturdays, are made with eggs, oil or butter, and milk. They include **anadama,** made with cornmeal and molasses; **herb,** made with dill, parsley, and scallions; and traditional **white. Unenriched breads,** baked on Mondays, Wednesdays, and Fridays, are made using no added fat, and they are quite good. I liked the popular **cracked wheat,** a white bread with cracked wheat kneaded into the dough, which gives it a pleasing crunchiness. Other unenriched breads are **caraway rye** and **pumpernickel; whole wheat** is available daily. On Fridays you can get **cinnamon-raisin bread** and **challah,** the Jewish-style egg bread.

FRAMINGHAM

Healthy Heart Café. See "Goodies to Go," page 192.

NEEDHAM

Vicki Lee Boyajian

1019 Great Plain Avenue, Needham, MA 02192   (617) 449-0022
Mail order: not available   Hours: Tues.–Fri. 8 A.M.–7 P.M.;
    Sat. 8 A.M.–5 P.M.; Sun. 9 A.M.–2 P.M.; closed Mon.
105 Trapelo Road, Belmont, MA 02178   (617) 489-0077
Mail order: not available   Hours: Tues.–Sat. 7 A.M.–7 P.M.;
    Sun. 9 A.M.–3 P.M.; closed Mon.

Vicki Lee Boyajian's bakery-café is a beautiful large room with a bar counter and several tables on one side and pastries and take-out items displayed on the other.

    The **cakes** are beautiful, and distinctive. The **strawberry charlotte** is a signature dish. Strawberry Bavarian cream is encased in slices of raspberry roulade, and the presentation is impressive. **Chocolate regal torte** is an elegant, dark-chocolate creation garnished with candied violets. The **fruit tarts** are very good, although the crust is a little thick. The pastry cream has an unusual almond-rum flavor that goes nicely with the fresh fruit.

    The fancy desserts are all very nice, but I really like the homier ones, and Boyajian makes some terrific **cookies.** The best —the **Anzak**—is a major gustatory thrill. This is a cookie of Australian origin, made with Lyle's Golden Syrup, a sweet syrup made in England, plus nuts, oatmeal, and coconut. The cookie's texture is perfect—crispy on the edges, chewy in the middle. The **chocolate street cookie** also has a great texture, and just the right amount of chocolate, enhanced by chunks of walnuts. The **Toll House cookie** is disappointing. The flavor is great, nice and buttery, but the texture is too floury; also it is made with nuts, and I like the **chocolate chip cookie with no nuts** better. The **lemon bars** are excellent, among the best I've tried. Also excellent are the **coconut macaroons**—another best. They are not like most coconut macaroons: they are a little more cookielike, with an appealing butter flavor, and they contain walnuts. They may be nontraditional, but they are *so* good. The **almond macaroons** are also delicious.

But don't leave until you've tried the **muffins.** One bite of the **blueberry** and I wanted more, more, more. Then I tried the **lemon–poppy seed** and felt the same way. These are perfect muffins, the standard to which all other muffins should aspire.

There is also an extensive menu of **take-out items** and **sandwiches.** A trademark product is the **Aram sandwich,** a tribute to Boyajian's Armenian roots. Armenian flat bread is spread with herbed cream cheese and a choice of meats **(roast beef, ham, turkey).** It is then rolled and sliced into spirals. While these look attractive, I found the taste unremarkable. Other items are more appealing. I'd rather have the meat, which is good quality, as a **Bistro sandwich,** on thick slices of good bread.

Boyajian's offers several **salads** and **spreads,** including an excellent garlicky **hummus.** The **stuffed grape leaves** are tangy with lemon. The **chicken salads** vary. I tried a **peppered chicken salad,** which is very rich, but delicious. I also liked the spicy **coleslaw,** flecked with poppy seeds. The **linguini with sun-dried tomatoes and chicken** was bland, but the **lemon** *tagliatelle* is refreshing and good. Also refreshing is the **tomato-feta salad,** a nice blend of flavors and textures.

SUDBURY

Alden Merrell Cheesecake Co. See Newburyport, page 267.

WATERTOWN

Angel's Bakery and Café. See "The Staff of Life," page 32.

Sevan's Bakery
598 Mt. Auburn Street, Watertown, MA 02172   (617) 924-3243
Mail order: not available   Hours: Mon.–Sat. 8 A.M.–8 P.M.;
    closed Sun.

Sevan's has been in business since 1970, and current owners Margaret and Kapriel Chavushian have owned the bakery since 1975. They are Armenians originally from Istanbul, and some of the items they make have a Turkish twist.

The pastries here are all Middle Eastern. There are several **filo pastries,** including **baklava,** formed into various shapes. I like the **rose** best, which is a square of filo leaves folded over a filling of whole pistachios. There are three cuts of **baklava;** the **walnut diamond cut** is best, with the most nuts. The **walnut triangle cut** has a good buttery flavor, but it and the **folded baklava**—a rectangle shape, folded over pistachios—are low on nuts. The **bird's nest,** a cylinder of filo pastry encircling a walnut filling was very sweet, and soggy from the syrup used. I prefer the **ladyfinger,** a thin cylinder of filo filled with chopped walnuts. This item had the best taste and texture.

There are several other pastries which I have only seen at a few places. *Mamoul* is a filled butter cookie made with crunchy semolina and scented with rosewater. There are three different fillings: **puréed date, walnut,** and **pistachio** (my favorite). This is better than the too-hard *kourabia,* a butter cookie that tastes mainly of confectioner's sugar.

I hadn't thought of **coconut macaroons** as particularly Middle Eastern, but Margaret assured me that they are. Sevan's version is quite good—light and crispy brown on the outside, tender and moist on the inside, and not too sweet. Other cookies also fall into the pleasingly not-too-sweet category. There's the *barazy,* a flat, round cookie studded with whole pistachios, then topped with sesame seeds and honey; and the **crescent** cookie, with walnuts and currants.

Simit is a name given to three pastries and a bread. Two of the pastries are the same, but they come in different shapes—a **ring** and a **small twist.** These are salty, sprinkled with kalonji seeds, which look like black sesame seeds but have a very different and unique flavor. The **sweet simit** is a small four-inch-long twist. It is flavored with orange zest and sprinkled with sesame seeds. The **simit bread** is a large ring coated with sesame seeds.

Sevan's also makes several other **breads** and **savory pastries.** Their **Armenian pita bread** is an inch-high flat bread, not a pocket bread. When the same dough is shaped into an oval shape, it is called *laghanis. Cheoreg* is a sweet roll, made primarily for Easter. The **tahini bread** is also sweet; yeast dough is rolled with a sweetened tahini paste to make a flat, flaky bread.

Sevan's makes their *lamejun* with ground beef (elsewhere you can get it with lamb or chicken). This is a very flat bread topped with the spiced beef. Spiced ground beef is also used as a filling in the *mantee,* tiny frozen rectangles of dough similar to ravioli, which you put in soup. There is also a triangular **turnover,** made with a yeast dough and filled with **beef;** other fillings include **spinach, spinach and cheese, spinach-tahini-walnut,** and **three cheese.** The turnovers are made with a yeast dough.

In addition to all the baked goods, Sevan's makes a variety of Middle Eastern **spreads.** There is *taramasalata* a blend of fish roe, bread crumbs, and olive oil, that has a pleasing fishy saltiness. The **tabouli** is terrific—full of chopped parsley and refreshing lemon juice. The **hummus** is a bit heavy on the tahini, but otherwise good. The *muhammara* spread, made with ground walnuts, red peppers, pomegranate, molasses, and pine nuts, is quite good, with a little kick from hot peppers. The **stuffed grape leaves** are the best I've seen sold anywhere. The flavor is terrific, and the tomatoey rice filling includes both currants and pine nuts. Very yummy.

Sevan's is also a complete Middle Eastern market, with goods imported from several countries. You can buy all kinds of nuts and grains in bulk, and items such as candy-coated chickpeas and roasted, salted peas. The store is not huge, but the selection is.

Tabrizi Bakery

56 Mt. Auburn Street, Watertown, MA 02172   (617) 926-0880
Mail order: available   Hours: Mon.–Sat. 10 A.M.–8 P.M.;
   Sun. noon–7 P.M.

Mouhamed Tahmili jokes that his bakery is part of an international franchise—of two. His father has the other Tabrizi Bakery, in Tehran, which has been in operation for over forty-five years. Tahmili, who owns the Watertown franchise with his cousin Zohra Tabatabei, says that the city of Tabriz is well known in Iran for its good food and pastry.

Iranian pastries are different from most other pastries. There are some that are similar to Greek pastries, notably **baklava,** but the flavorings used are different. Tahmili makes both a **Greek-style baklava,** with walnuts, cinnamon, cloves, and honey, and an **Iranian-style** one, with almonds, pistachios, cardamom, and rosewater. Butter is not used here, and the baklava, to my tastebuds, would benefit from it. Other items are very distinctive. It is worth trying an assortment just for the experience, then settling on personal favorites. The **almond macaroons,** while good, lack the characteristic almondy flavor; Tahmili grinds his own almonds and uses no almond extract. I prefer the excellent, unusual **walnut macaroons** made simply with ground walnuts, egg white, and sugar. Light and chewy, they are as addictive as potato chips.

His *zolbi* are translucent, crunchy swirls, made from a batter of cornstarch and yogurt drizzled into hot corn oil, then drenched with a honey-sugar syrup. The *bami,* which Tahmili says took him several tries to perfect in America, are also fried, but they are ball-shaped and made from an egg-based batter. Cardamom flavors the tiny, sandy *nohodi,* which are made from chickpea flour. Also tiny are the *berengi,* made with rice and wheat flour, rosewater, and poppy seeds. The same flaky dough is used for three different cookies, with subtly different results. The *zabon,* tongue-shaped, is only slightly sweetened; it's good with a cup of coffee for breakfast. The *nazok* is a narrow rectangle, the flaky pastry layered with a shortbread dough (this would also benefit from butter, in my American opinion). It's thin, glazed lightly with honey, and sprinkled with sesame seeds. The *popyon* is lighter in feel and bow-tie shaped.

Tahmili also sells a **Napoleon** made with flaky layers of pastry and sweetened whipped cream, and a delicacy he does not make, called *sohun. Sohun* is made from ground wheat sprouts, oil, sugar, pistachios, rosewater, and cardamom, and is unlike anything I've tasted. It comes in a large, cookie-sized round, which you can break into pieces. The flavor is definitely uncommon, and the texture is like a cross between buttercrunch and a cookie. *Sohun* is strangely addictive; I offered it on small plates at a dinner and, while people commented on the oddity, there was none left at the end of the evening.

Bástany is a Persian ice cream Tahmili makes, an excellent blend of milk, cream, saffron, and rosewater. It is light, a mix of enticing flavors on your tongue. Go on step further and try a shake made with the ice cream and carrot juice or blended with cantaloupe. More unusual still is the *faludem,* rice noodles mixed with sugar water and frozen, then scooped into a bowl and topped with lemon juice or sour-cherry syrup.

There are a handful of tables here, so you can eat at the bakery and enjoy a cup of coffee or tea. Tabrizi also carries a variety of bulk nuts, dried fruit, and a few imported Iranian foods.

WELLESLEY

Alden Merrell Cheesecake Co. See Newburyport, page 267.

Bread & Circus. See "Going Organic," page 434.

Quebrada Baking Co. See Arlington, page 278.

❖ D O N U T S ❖

Donut shops have a unique atmosphere. They are often smoky, and a popular stop for truckers and others who work through the night. Many close by midafternoon, since they open early, often at five or six in the morning. They do not tend to do mail order.

This was a difficult category to report on, since there are so many places that make donuts. Whenever I would see a donut shop, I would hop out of the car and buy a few. To judge, I tried a honey-dip raised donut and a cake donut, either plain, sugar, or cinnamon. I also often tried butternut because I like it, and occasionally jelly donuts and chocolate donuts.

In recent years, many donut shops have also made other baked goods, but you don't go to a donut shop for their cookies. Few I visited had anything worth buying other than donuts. And the quality of the donuts ranged tremendously. I figured I could use Dunkin' Donuts as a benchmark; if you get Dunkin's fresh they are not bad, especially if you're hungry. What could be worse? I thought. A lot, I discovered. Many are about the same. Below is my list of the top donuts in the Boston area.

Note that some of the bakeries listed in the previous section also make very good donuts.

BOSTON

BRIGHTON

Cottage Bakers Inc.
533 Washington Street, Brighton, MA 02135   (617) 254-9144
Hours: daily 5 A.M.–1 P.M.

METROPOLITAN BOSTON

CAMBRIDGE

Verna's Coffee and Doughnut Shop
2344 Mass. Avenue, Cambridge, MA 02140   (617) 354-4110
Hours: Mon.–Fri. 5:30 A.M.–5 P.M.; Sat. 5:30 A.M.–3 P.M.; closed Sun.

EVERETT

Mike's Donuts
127 Broadway, Everett, MA 02149   (617) 389-9415
Hours: Mon.–Thurs. twenty-four hours a day; Fri. until midnight;
   Sat. 6 A.M.–midnight; Sun. from 6 A.M.

NORTH

MEDFORD

Pauline's Doughnut Shoppe
453 High Street, Medford, MA 02155   (617) 396-2388
Hours: daily 5:30 A.M.–1 P.M.

SALEM

Ziggy's Donuts
2 Essex Street, Salem, MA 01970   (508) 744-9605
Hours: Mon.–Fri. 6 A.M.–3 P.M.; Sun. 6 A.M.–noon; closed Sat.

SOUTH

NORWOOD

Dandy Doughnuts

528 Washington Street, Norwood, MA 02062   (617) 551-0571
Hours: Mon.–Sat. 4:30 A.M.–3 P.M.; Sun. 4:30 A.M.–1:30 P.M.

QUINCY

Golden Brown Doughnut Co.

36 School Street, Quincy, MA 02169   (617) 472-9560
Hours: Mon.–Fri. 6 A.M.–2 P.M.; Sat. 6 A.M.–noon;
  Sun. 6 A.M.–12:30 P.M.

WEST

ARLINGTON

Gail Ann Coffee Shop

10 Medford Street, Arlington, MA 02174   (617) 648-9584
Hours: Mon.–Fri. 5 A.M.–6 P.M., Sat. 5 A.M.–5 P.M., Sun. 6 A.M.–1 P.M.;
  July and August, Mon.–Sat. 5 A.M.–3 P.M., Sun. 6 A.M.–12:30 P.M.

CONCORD

West Concord Donut Shoppe

1335 Main Street, Concord, MA 01742   (508) 369-8737
Hours: Mon.–Sat. 5:30 A.M.–2 P.M.; Sun. 6 A.M.–2 P.M.

NEEDHAM

Donut Junction

35 Chapel Street, Needham, MA 02192   (617) 444-5506
Hours: Mon–Fri. 5 A.M.–5 P.M.; Sat. 5 A.M.–2 P.M.; Sun. 5 A.M.–1 P.M.

THE BESTS OF THE BEST

Best bakery: **Rosie's Bakery** and **Japonaise Bakery**
Best chocolate chip cookie (without nuts): **The Boston Chipyard**
Best chocolate chip cookie (with nuts): **Wheatstone Baking Company**
Best chocolate cookie: **Sally Ann Food Shop, Rosie's Bakery,** and **Vicki
  Lee Boyajian**

Best oatmeal cookie: **Formaggio Kitchen, Big Sky in Newton,** and **Breads 'n' Bits of Ireland**

Best peanut butter cookie: **Sorelle Bakery & Café** and **Rebecca's Bakery**

Best ginger cookie: **Carberry's Bakery and Coffee House, Quebrada Baking Co.,** and **To Go**

Best gingerbread: **Lakota Bakery**

Best sugar cookie: **Peach's & Cream**

Best coconut macaroon: **Bentonwood Bakery and Café** and **Vicki Lee Boyajian**

Best almond macaroon: **Savoy French Bakery** and **Vicki Lee Boyajian**

Best cookie: **Vicki Lee Boyajian:** *Anzaks* and **Bread & Circus: maple cream pie**

Best biscotti: **Sorelle Bakery & Café** and **Modern Pastry Shop**

Best *quaresimale:* **Montilio's Cake Shoppe**

Best Italian cookies: **Il Pastificio**

Best shortbread: **Lakota Bakery**

Best brownie: **Rosie's Bakery** and **Kilvert & Forbes Ltd.**

Best apple pie: **Greenhills Traditional Irish Bakery**

Best pecan pie: **Rosie's Bakery**

Best lemon dessert: **Japonaise Bakery**

Best fruit tart: **Rosie's Bakery, Japonaise Bakery,** and **Rebecca's Bakery**

Best chocolate cake: **Rosie's Bakery, Alden Merrell Cheesecake Co.,** and **This Takes the Cake**

Best Boston cream pie: **Bentonwood Bakery and Café** and **Alden Merrell Cheesecake Co.**

Best golden cake: **This Takes the Cake**

Best fancy cakes: **Japonaise Bakery, Delphin's Gourmandise,** and **Vicky Lee Boyajian**

Best wedding cake: **Cakes to Remember**

Best coffee cake: **Concord Teacakes**

Best cheesecake: **Jacqueline's Pasticceria**

Best eclair: **Wheatberries of Manchester**

Best traditional scone: **Concord Teacakes**

Best scone with stuff in it: **Jacqueline's Pasticceria** and **Keltic Krust**

Best muffins: **Vicki Lee Boyajian**

Best sticky buns: **Buns of Boston**

Best donuts: **Ziggy's Donuts**

Close second donuts: **Ohlin's Bakery**

Best baklava: **Middle East Restaurant**

Best *tiramisù:* **Café Paradiso** and **Jacqueline's Pasticceria**

Best cannoli: **Maria's Pastry Shop** and **Modern Pastry Shop**

Best lobster tails: **Maria's Pastry Shop** and **Modern Pastry Shop**

CHAPTER EIGHT

FROZEN DELIGHTS

*A choice of hundreds of flavors of ice cream, sorbet, gelato, sherbet,
and frozen yogurt*

ONE of the first kinds of food places I collected was ice cream shops, starting when I was about sixteen. Anyplace I would go, I would sample the ice cream. Metropolitan Boston was then, and is now, a mecca for ice-cream connoisseurs. New Englanders are known for their love of ice cream. They consume more per capita in the winter months than some people of other states do during the summer.

Somerville was home to Steve's, which became famous in the 1970s for its premium ice cream and creative flavors. Its popularity led to a proliferation of premium ice creameries in the area. Farther afield, there's another New England specialty—seasonal ice-cream stands. These are large roadside buildings, often with no indoor seating, that make lots of fresh ice cream and serve it in generous portions when the weather is warmer. There are a few ice-cream chains in the area as well. Friendly's and Brigham's are based in Massachusetts; Baskin Robbins, Ben & Jerry's, and Häagen Dazs are national chains or franchises. I don't include the chains here; I was more interested in smaller places that make their own ice cream. With the fresh-made ice cream so widely available locally, it just isn't worth going out for the mass-produced stuff.

There are over a hundred so-called homemade ice-cream operations in the Boston area. Several of these places do not actually make their own ice cream; rather, they get it from some of the larger homemade ice-cream businesses. I've chosen to concentrate on places that actually make their own ice cream.

Frozen yogurt enjoyed a spell of popularity in the early 1970s, died out, and was resurrected with a vengeance in the late 1980s. I do like frozen yogurt, as long as we don't pretend that it's a substitute for real ice cream. Several chains sell it, but few stores make their own from scratch; often they use a mix. Common brands sold in area frozen-yogurt parlors include Colombo and Stonyfield Farm. The shops that make their own are the best. For low-fat frozen items, I prefer sorbet, although only a handful of places make it. Sherbet is also a tasty option found in a few more places. Both of these generally come in fruit flavors and are especially refreshing in the summer.

A relatively new option with fat-free yogurt is soft-serve yogurt flavors prepared to order. Blocks of vanilla nonfat yogurt are placed in a machine with any ingredients you choose then blended together to a soft-serve consistency. Several establishments now offer this option, and I found it makes for better flavors. Fresh fruit is generally used, so these soft-serve flavors taste superior to many of the premixed yogurts.

I always used to wonder about the significance of getting a hand-packed versus a prepacked pint or quart of ice cream: what's the big deal? The big deal is you get more ice cream in a hand-packed container, and usually it will be denser and creamier. *Poured* ice cream means that the container is filled as the ice cream is being dispensed from the ice-cream machine. Ice cream is beaten as it goes from a liquid mixture to a solid frozen state, and during the process air gets mixed in, increasing the volume of the ice cream—this is also called *overrun*. For example, if the ice cream has 100 percent overrun, this means it is double the quantity of the liquid mix—that is, two gallons of mix will yield four gallons of ice cream. That may sound fluffy, but I've had many delicious 100 percent overrun ice creams. When you scoop frozen ice cream into a container, it gets packed down. So the poured quarts will be fluffier; in the hand-packed quarts the ice cream gets pressed down and packed into the container, so it is denser. Hence places that offer both prepacked and hand-packed containers will charge a higher price for the hand-packed, since it is heavier.

Those of us who have lived and eaten ice cream in Massachusetts for a while know the difference between *milkshakes* and *frappes*. A milkshake is milk mixed with flavored syrup. A frappe is ice cream, milk, and syrup blended together.

More than any other business, ice-cream store hours vary from summer to winter, with many places open only during the warmer months. Call and check the hours before visiting. For obvious reasons, I have not included mail-order information in this chapter.

* Described in another chapter.

Aljay's Homemade Ice Cream Shoppe	Winthrop
Bon Santé	Boston
Cabot's Ice Cream	Newton
Café Paradiso	Boston, Cambridge
Cherry Farm Creamery	Danvers
Christina's Homemade Ice Cream	Cambridge
Crescent Ridge Dairy	Sharon
The Dairy Barn	Randolph
Dick & June's Ice Cream	Beverly
Emack & Bolio's Ice Cream	Cambridge, Boston
Furlong's Cottage Candies and Ice Cream Co.	Norwood
*Hana Pastry	Cambridge
Herbie's Ice Cream	Sudbury
Herrell's Ice Cream	Allston, Cambridge, Boston
Hilliard's House of Candy	Easton
The Ice Creamery	Randolph
Ice Creamsmith	Dorchester
Ice Cream Works	Newton, Brookline
*Il Pastificio	Everett
JP Licks Homemade Ice Cream	Jamaica Plain, Brookline, Boston
Kimball's at Bate's Farm	Westford, Carlisle
Legal Sea Foods Market Place	Allston, Newton
Maddie's Ice Cream	Dedham, Norwood
Meletharb Ice Cream	Wakefield
Puleo's Dairy	Salem
Purdy's Ice Cream Parlor	Quincy
*Putnam Pantry	Danvers

Rancatore Ice Cream	Belmont
Richardson's Ice Cream	Middleton
Richie's Slush	Everett
Ron's Gourmet Homemade Ice Cream	Hyde Park
Scoops	Beverly
Skip's Ice Cream Stand	Chelmsford
Sully's Ice Cream Stand	Chelmsford
Sweet Scoops	Salem
Toscanini's Ice Cream	Cambridge
Treadwell's Ice Cream	Danvers, North Andover, Peabody
Tuesday's Ice Cream	Brookline
Welcome Farm Ice Cream	Weymouth
White Farms	Ipswich
White Mountain Creamery	Newton, Wellesley

BOSTON

BOSTON

Bon Santé

Corner of Washington and Franklin Streets, Boston, MA 02108
(617) 451-1153
Hours: Mon.–Fri. 11 A.M.–6 P.M.; Sat., Sun. noon –5 P.M.

The company literature describes Bon Santé as a premium low-fat ice cream, "son of the Goddess of Indulgence and the God of Health and Nutrition." The product was developed by Health Management Resources (HMR), a company that makes nutritional products, including a high-protein shake. HMR also runs medically supervised weight-loss programs. Bon Santé was introduced in 1993, in various cafeterias; this shop opened in the summer of 1995.

This **ice cream** is similar to frozen yogurt, and the selling point seems to be its nutritional content: A four-ounce serving provides 7 grams of protein and 25 percent of the recommended daily allowance for many vitamins and minerals. It is low in fat and has only 101 calories. To keep the calories down, the mix is sweetened with a blend of fructose and aspartame (as in Nutra-Sweet).

The shop, in Downtown Crossing next to the entrance to Filene's, consists of windows where you place your order—

there is no inside area here. I tasted this soft-serve ice cream the day the shop opened. There were four classic flavors available, all with souped-up names. The **vanilla bean** (with no specks of vanilla bean) was pretty good. **Chocolate truffle** is the best of the four flavors although it is mild chocolate, lacking the intensity promised by the name. The **mountain strawberry** tastes totally fake, and the **gourmet coffee** is so subtle in flavor, you wouldn't know it was coffee. You can mix pairs of flavors. While I am not ready to forgo regular, high-fat ice cream, I do like Bon Santé better than many soft-serve frozen yogurts.

Café Paradiso

255 Hanover Street, North End, Boston, MA 02113   (617) 742-1768
Hours: daily 7 A.M.–2 A.M.

1 Elliot Square, Cambridge, MA 02138   (617) 868-3240
Hours: daily 7 A.M.–midnight

Gelato is actually significantly less fattening than American ice cream, with about 8 percent butterfat, as compared to the 14 to 16 percent butterfat content of most area ice cream. Yet gelato tastes terrific, and Oscar DeStefano makes very good flavors. He makes much more in the summer, and this is the best time to try it. When I had some in the early spring, some of the less popular flavors tasted old.

DeStefano's parents started the business at the North End store. The gelato has been made there since 1978. The Harvard Square location has been here since 1985. **Gelato** is softer than American ice cream, because it is stored and served at a slightly warmer temperature. You don't get scoops of gelato, more like shmears; a flavor is sort of smoothed into a serving cup. **Amaretto,** which often tastes strong and artificial, has a subtle almond flavor that is quite good. Similarly, both **hazelnut** and *bacio* (chocolate hazelnut) taste of the nuts and not of artificial flavoring. The **espresso** tastes like a shot of the coffee, and the **pistachio** tastes like pistachio. In the winter DeStefano colors it green ("People want it green," he shrugs), but in the summer he goes through so much he doesn't have time to dye the pistachio. The **lemon,** which is dairy-free, is wonderful and very refreshing, nice and tart. DeStefano goes through gallons of it during the summer.

Paradiso has several **pastries.** Most are made elsewhere,

but some are house specialties. The ***tiramisù*** is great. Ladyfingers are brushed with just the right amount of *millefiore* liqueur. The **Delìzia** is a rum-brushed sponge cake covered with a layer of almond paste. The **ricotta pie,** flavored with lemon zest, is light and tasty.

There is also a store in the Financial District, but it does not carry gelato. The Harvard Square store also offers **salads** and **sandwiches.**

Emack & Bolio's Ice Cream. See Cambridge, page 306.

Herrell's Ice Cream. See Allston, below.

JP Licks Homemade Ice Cream. See Jamaica Plain, page 303.

ALLSTON

Herrell's Ice Cream

155 Brighton Avenue, Allston, MA 02134   (617) 782-9599
Hours: 7 A.M.–midnight; Sun. 8 A.M.–midnight

15 Dunster Street, Cambridge, MA 02138   (617) 497-2179
Hours: Sun.–Thurs. 11 A.M.–midnight; Fri., Sat. 11 A.M.–1 A.M.

350 Longwood Avenue, Boston, MA 02115   (617) 731-9599
Hours: Mon.–Fri. 11:30 A.M.–9 P.M.; Sat., Sun. noon–8 P.M.

Herrell's is the child of the famous Steve's. It was a thrill for me to speak with THE Steve Herrell, the man who had single-handedly forever changed the face of ice cream in America.

Steve Herrell opened Steve's ice cream near Davis Square in Somerville in 1973. Because he was a conscientious objector during the Vietnam War, he needed to earn some money while fulfilling his community service duties. He rented some space at a former dry cleaner and went into the ice-cream business.

Ice cream was hardly unheard of in Massachusetts at the time; there were already ice-cream institutions such as Brigham's, Bailey's, and Friendly's, as well as scores of seasonal ice-cream stands. But Herrell did a few things differently.

There are two factors that contribute to the creaminess of Steve's premium ice cream. The first is butterfat, and the second is overrun. Most ice-cream establishments use a commercially produced *base,* or *mix.* Local dairies such as Hood, Rosev, and West Lynn Creamery make the ice-cream bases used by most area ice-cream makers. The base has a certain percentage of butterfat; regular ice cream has a 12 percent butterfat content; ice cream with 14 percent butterfat is now classified as premium, and Herrell did much to popularize that; superpremium is ice cream with 16 percent butterfat.

When ice cream is made, a certain amount of air gets beaten into it. This is called *overrun.* A lower overrun makes for a denser, creamier ice cream; ice cream with a high overrun is fluffy and less rich. Steve's ice cream had a low overrun.

Another eye-catching thing Herrell did was to make the ice cream in the window, in full view of customers. The third innovation was his creation of *mix-ins.* (At Herrell's, these are called *smoosh-ins;* the company that owns Steve's trademarked the term *mix-ins.)* The ice-cream server would scoop your choice of ice cream, plop it on a marble slab, sprinkle it with your choice of candies, nuts, or crushed cookies, and mix them into the ice cream with a couple of spoons. Herrell attributes this idea to a suggestion made by a housemate of his at the time who recalled seeing such a thing at an ice-cream parlor in Miami. Herrell tried it at home and then introduced it at the store. It was a hit (and a contributing factor to the long lines at Steve's—it took time to mix in the items).

The first day, Herrell made thirty gallons of ice cream in five flavors, and he sold out by midafternoon. From then on Steve's was immensely popular. Winter or summer, lines would lead out the door and down the block.

After four years, Herrell decided to quit the business and become a piano tuner in Northampton. "I wanted to homestead in western Mass.," he told me. "I thought piano tuning would be a good portable trade." He sold the store to Joey Crugnale, founder of Bertucci's (see "Goodies to Go," page 218).

Herrell bought land in the Berkshires, but the homestead idea never happened. "I got lonely," Herrell recalls. "I missed the ice-cream business." In 1980 he decided to return to the business, so he opened Steve Herrell's in Northampton. When he attempted to open a store of the same name in Harvard Square, Crugnale sued him over the use of the name *Steve.* The *Steve* was dropped, and Herrell's was opened as a franchise in Harvard Square in 1982, by Jessica Leahy. Marc Cooper opened the Allston store in 1984, and the Boston shop in 1988.

In the meantime, Crugnale sold Steve's, and the Steve's today has nothing to do with the original recipes that Steve Herrell created. Sadly, it is now ice cream to be avoided.

Herrell's, however, is simply some of the finest ice cream around. Flavor after flavor is great—full of taste but no aftertaste. Steve Herrell is a master of creating flavors that taste exactly the way you want them to taste. He now has over seventy flavors, with more in the works—some take years to get just right. When I spoke with him, he was working on a cherry flavor that he said he has been tinkering with for twenty-two years.

He makes the absolute best **maple cream** and **maple walnut** ice cream I've tried, anywhere, ever. The maple ice creams have a real maple syrup taste, not too sweet, and are sublime. **Malted vanilla** was one of the earlier flavors he created, and it is great; there is also **malted chocolate.** The shop specializes in **coffee** and **chocolate flavors,** with a variety of each offered. Chocolate lovers will swoon over **chocolate pudding,** a deep, dark, intensely chocolate ice cream. Others in this category include a delicate **milk chocolate** and a sophisticated **Dutch orange-chocolate.**

The **coffee** ice cream, along with all its variations, is excellent. I love the **cappuccino,** made with cinnamon, and the subtle **cafe au lait.** The **espresso** is strong without tasting bitter.

I'm not usually a fan of the **cookie dough ice cream** fad, but Herrell's makes a very good version, using real cookie dough from a local chocolate chip cookie maker. I always like the simple **sweet cream,** the most basic flavor.

In keeping with the trends, Steve's makes **frozen yogurt,** in a variety of configurations: **nonfat sugar-free** (pass, if you have a choice), **nonfat,** and **low-fat.** The latter tastes best. The yogurts come in the same flavors as the ice cream. There is also **sorbet** and **No-Moo,** a nondairy creation.

The ice cream is pricey, but worth the money. You can get all the usual combinations—frappes, sundaes, and such. You can still get candies smooshed into your ice cream, or sprinkled on top.

The homemade **hot fudge** is excellent, one of the best around. Marc Cooper has been marketing a jarred version of the stuff from his stores. He also makes **bonbons,** bite-size pieces of chocolate-covered ice cream, using Merckens chocolate (see "Sweet Indulgences," page 353). These are good but I still prefer a plain scoop of coffee ice cream.

Each of the three stores has a different feel. The Harvard Square store is in a former bank, and you can eat your ice cream in a converted vault, painted with an aquatic motif. A jungle mural decorates the main room. In 1995 Cooper renovated the Allston store and changed the name to Herrell's Renaissance Café. They have coffee, as well as breakfast pastries in the morning. The ceiling is painted with a coffee-themed Sistine chapel motif, and takeoffs of original paintings with ice-cream themes decorate the walls.

Legal Sea Foods Market Place

33 Everett Street, Allston, MA 02134   (617) 787-2050
Hours: Mon.–Fri. 9 A.M.–7 P.M.; Sat. 9 A.M.–4:30 P.M.; closed Sun.

43 Boylston Street, Chestnut Hill, Newton, MA 02167
  (617) 277-7300
Hours: Mon.–Thurs. 9 A.M.–8 P.M.; Fri., Sat. 9 A.M.–9 P.M.;
  Sun. 10 A.M.–8 P.M.

Also: "Some Things Fishy," page 110.

News flash: Legal Sea Foods makes their own **ice cream,** and it's great. Legal never really made desserts, but around 1987, Roger Berkowitz, president and CEO, decided he wanted to put ice cream on the menu. The range of flavors is not extensive, or complicated; they are basically Berkowitz's take on the four most popular New England flavors: vanilla, coffee, chocolate, and chocolate chip. The base used is 15 percent butterfat. The **vanilla bean** is perfect, the best vanilla I've tasted, anywhere. It is made with vanilla beans and is flecked with tiny specks of flavor. The texture is rich and creamy, and the flavor is pure and delightful. The **cappuccino,** which Berkowitz describes as "coffee for grown-ups," came highly recommended. I like it, although it is on the strong side. There is coffee in it, as well as ground coffee beans. The **double chocolate** is a must for chocoholics; it tastes like a cross between classic chocolate ice cream and chocolate mousse. The **Famous Amos** uses that brand of chocolate chip cookies mixed into a sweet cream base, and the flavor of the cookies permeates the ice cream. It tastes great.

Legal also makes **sorbets.** There is always **pear,** which has a perfumy, real pear taste—quite good. Other flavors are seasonal, such as **boysenberry,** which has a brilliant purple-red color and a just right sweet-tart balance.

You can get Legal's ice cream for dessert at any of the ten Boston-area restaurants. The Chestnut Hill and Allston markets carry it in prepacked half-pint containers. It ain't cheap—a pint is about $4—but it is so very good.

DORCHESTER

Ice Creamsmith

2295 Dorchester Avenue, Dorchester, MA 02124   (617) 296-8567
Hours: March–November, daily noon–10 P.M.;
    closed December–February

David and Robin Mabel opened Ice Creamsmith in 1976. "There were not that many homemade ice-cream places at the time," Robin says. "David was looking for a job and saw an ad for used ice-cream equipment. So he created a job." Ice Creamsmith is a small store, with seating for about twelve, located at the very beginning of Dorchester Avenue, across from the old Baker's Chocolate factory, near the Milton line.

During a time when most ice-cream makers are going all out creating new and sometimes outrageous flavors, the Mabels have always kept things simple. They have about a dozen flavors available at any one time, as well as a couple of **frozen yogurts.** The ice cream is 14 percent butterfat. Most flavors are the usual, but there are also seasonal items—the store makes a lot of fruit flavors; **peach** and **blueberry** in the summer, **pumpkin** and **cranberry** in the fall. I like the **pineapple sherbet** in the summer; it is light and refreshing. **Coconut pineapple** is fruity and very rich-tasting, and the **banana** has a pleasing fresh banana taste. **Sweet cream** is an understated flavor that is surprisingly good. The naturally sweet flavor of cream comes through; Ice Creamsmith does a great job with this one. They also make a great, clean-tasting **vanilla.** The **chocolate** is a lighter chocolate, the way I like it; if you prefer deep, dark chocolate ice cream, this one is not for you. The **mocha chip** had a good coffee-to-chocolate balance.

The Ice Creamsmith is probably the only ice-cream place I visited that does not make Oreo ice cream. They do, however, offer **Oreos** as a **mix-in,** along with various other items, such as coconut and **raisins.** Any ice cream you like can also be turned into a **cake.** Cakes here are all ice cream and decorated by David with buttercream frosting. The store is also notable for its prices —about the lowest of any place I visited, and the servings are very generous.

HYDE PARK

Ron's Gourmet Homemade Ice Cream

1231 Hyde Park Avenue, Hyde Park, MA 02136   (617) 364-5274
Hours: Mon.–Sat. 8 A.M.–11 P.M.; Sun. 9 A.M.–11 P.M.

It was a sunny Friday afternoon when I pulled up to Ron's Ice Cream and bowling. I was skeptical. A bowling alley with ice cream? Inside, the place was mobbed. To the right are ten candle-pin lanes, and to the left is the ice cream.

"Is your ice cream homemade?" I asked the guy behind the counter.

"Yep," he said, scooping some onto a cone.

"You make it here?"

"Yep. Everything's made here." The man turned out to be owner Ronald Covitz, and the ice cream is wonderful.

Covitz's father opened the bowling alley in 1952, with a pool hall downstairs. When Ron took over the business he says, "I couldn't get along with the pool players. I needed another business to support the bowling alley." He started serving soft-serve ice cream, until one day Hood, who supplied the base he used, sent over the wrong mix, and Ron learned how to make hard ice cream. This was in 1980. "It wasn't supposed to work," Covitz says. "It's a candlepin lane. Ice cream doesn't go with bowling. But it works."

I think Ron's works because the ice cream is so good. Covitz uses quality ingredients to flavor his ice creams. He says he spent two and a half years developing his **Irish coffee**—the basic coffee. Coffee is my favorite flavor of ice cream and this is a very good coffee. **Coffee Madness** uses the Irish coffee as a base for Oreos, chocolate chips, and almonds. A lighter coffee flavor is the **Kahlua chip.** The **rum-raisin** has Myer's rum in it, and the rum flavor has a real kick. The popular **Grape-nut** tastes like comforting Grape-nut custard. The **brownie nut** is vanilla ice cream with fudgy homemade brownies. For candy lovers, **Snickers** is vanilla ice cream studded with lots of chopped Snickers bars. I especially liked the **coconut,** a flavor Covitz's daughter Jennifer suggested. It's creamy, subtly flavored, and great in a sundae. The **banana** is fair, but the **black raspberry** is nice and fruity. Another personal favorite is **peanut surprise,** a light milk chocolate with a swirl of peanut butter running through it.

The prices are quite reasonable as well—lower than most places I've visited.

You can also get **ice-cream cakes.** Covitz's wife Patricia makes the **golden** or **chocolate cake** base, and you can top it with your choice of ice cream.

And then you can go bowling.

JAMAICA PLAIN

JP Licks Homemade Ice Cream

674 Centre Street, Jamaica Plain, MA 02130   (617) 524-6740
Hours: daily 11:30 A.M.–midnight

311-A Harvard Street, Brookline, MA 02146   (617) 738-8252
Hours: daily 11 A.M.–midnight

352 Newbury Street, Boston, MA 02115   (617) 23ᴜ-1666
Hours: daily 11:30 A.M.–midnight

JP Licks ice cream is made from a 14 percent butterfat base, and the flavors are generally very good. **Oreo,** the store's most popular flavor, has a good balance of cookies to ice cream. The regular **coffee** is not so great; it has a bitter molasses taste. But the **white coffee,** made by infusing whole coffee beans in the cream, has a delicious brewed-coffee flavor. I like the clean, pure taste of the **sweet cream,** and the **banana** is great. The **mint chip** is refreshing and not too strong. The **French chocolate hazelnut,** however, is very strong, with both an artificial flavor and the taste of alcohol. The **Kahlúa** is also alcoholic, but with a much better taste. The **chocolate brownie,** which uses Alden Merrell brownies (see "Everything Nice," page 267), is very good. Some flavors, such as the latter two, are considered "exotic" and cost a little more per scoop. Servings at JP Licks are generous, but the prices are not cheap.

In addition to ice cream, JP Licks offers **sorbet.** The **lemon sorbet** is excellent—tart and lemony, with pieces of zest. The **apple cider** is also good. The **frozen yogurt** is pretty good; it comes in both hard and soft renditions. The hard yogurt **chocolate chip cookie** is good, and the soft **chocolate** and **Oreo** (in which the cookies are totally puréed into the ice cream, coloring it an almost unappetizing gray) are best.

Owner Vince Petryk stresses that service is extremely important to him, and this is reflected in each shop. Many employees have worked there, part-time or summers, for several years, and they are helpful and friendly.

METROPOLITAN BOSTON

BROOKLINE

Ice Cream Works. See Newton, page 311.

JP Licks Homemade Ice Cream. See Jamaica Plain, page 303.

Tuesday's
30 Station Street, Brookline Village, Brookline, MA 02146
   (617) 566-8190
Hours: vary

Tuesday's, so named because that's the day of the week on which it opened in 1977, is a friendly kind of hangout place. The floors are wooden, and the ceilings are cavernously high. Several tables are scattered at the front of the store; ice cream and baked goods are at the back. Over the years, owner Cindy Spindler has developed over 250 flavors. Although only nine are listed on the blackboard, dozens more are available in the back freezer; if you have a favorite flavor and it's not listed, just ask for it.

The ice cream is very good—the flavors are clean and appealing. The **drumstick,** vanilla ice cream with peanuts and chocolate—tastes like the frozen chocolate-and-nut-covered cone you used to get from the ice-cream truck. **Coconut-almond cream** has subtler overtones of coconut and almond; it's delicious with hot fudge. I like the **lemon** and **ginger.** The **chocolate** is very fudgy and reminiscent of a Fudgsicle, and the **vanilla** has a pronounced vanilla taste.

Of particular note is the **low-fat frozen yogurt.** Most frozen yogurts use a prepared yogurt base; Cindy uses regular yogurt, which gives the flavors a slightly tangy taste that goes especially well with fruits. Spindler adds no sugar to her frozen yogurt, which she initially developed for diabetics. The **Oreo** is unpleasantly tangy, but the fruit flavors are great, among the best around, especially the **peach, strawberry,** and **banana.** For those who are lactose-intolerant, Spindler developed a great **mixed fruit sorbet.** I prefer this dairy-free treat to ice cream during the hottest summer days.

In the cooler months, Tuesday's also offers a variety of homemade **baked goods.**

CAMBRIDGE

Café Paradiso. See Boston, page 296.

Christina's Homemade Ice Cream
1255 Cambridge Street, Cambridge, MA 02139   (617) 492-7021
Hours: Sun.–Thurs. 11:30 A.M.–11:30 P.M.; Fri., Sat. 11 A.M.–midnight

When you first walk into Christina's, you may be overwhelmed by the incredible number of ice cream flavors available. Owner Ray Ford says he has a repertoire of some seventy-five flavors, and usually forty-five to fifty will be available on a given day—and this does not include frozen yogurt. When I visited on a December day, forty-eight flavors were offered.

More impressive, however, is that the ice cream tastes great. Christina's offers quantity and quality. They have all the classics—**chocolate, vanilla, strawberry, coffee**—as well as a variety of very creative flavors. Some are more appealing than others. I could never bring myself to try **clam chowder.** For chocolate fans, Christina's offers over a dozen variations, from **white-chocolate fudge swirl,** with a distinctive taste of white chocolate, to **orange-chocolate, Mexican chocolate** (with a hint of cinnamon), and **chocolate mousse.**

I judge an ice-cream parlor by its coffee ice cream, and Christina's wins here. The **white coffee,** contrary to what the name might make you think, is pale only in color. Coffee beans are steeped in the cream, and the ice cream has a perfect, earthy coffee flavor. The regular **coffee** is also excellent. The **pistachio** uses real pistachios (some places use almond flavoring, color the ice cream green, then fill it with almonds or walnuts), and is chock-full of them. The **ginger** is the best version of this flavor I've tasted; it's made with fresh ginger and not too strong. This is one of the store's "premium" flavors—flavors that cost a little more than those on the regular list. Other creative offerings in this category include *khulfee,* based on an Indian frozen dessert made with evaporated milk and cardamom, and **Black Forest—** kirsch-flavored chocolate studded with black cherries and devil's food cake. Try the ice cream in homemade **waffle cones.**

Ford, who hails from England and has a master's degree in criminology, fell in love with American ice cream while working summers at Christina's. When the owner was ready to sell, he was ready to buy.

Christina's homemade creativity extends to their **sauces** as well. The cream is whipped in a standard mixer, and they make their own **marshmallow, hot fudge,** and **butterscotch sauces.** You can also get dry **mix-ins,** such as Heath Bars, Oreo crumbs, or (my favorite) chopped-up Reeses Peanut Butter Cups.

If you decide to forgo the calories offered by Christina's rich ice creams, you can still enjoy refreshing frozen desserts with yogurt. The **hard yogurt,** in a dozen flavors, is very good. Most flavors are not fat-free, so frozen yogurt won't save you that many calories over the ice cream. The **soft serve** is **nonfat,** and they will custom-blend a flavor from a vanilla base, using a variety of flavorings. The fresh fruit works best, especially **raspberries** and **strawberries.**

Emack & Bolio's Ice Cream

1726 Mass. Avenue, Cambridge, MA 02140   (617) 354-8573
Hours: Mon.–Sat. noon–10:30 P.M.; Sun. 2 P.M.–10:30 P.M.

290 Newbury Street, Boston, MA 02116   (617) 247-8772
Hours: daily 11 A.M.–midnight

Emack & Bolio's has gone through ups and downs since they first opened in 1975 in Brookline. Bob Rook, an attorney, named the store for a couple of his clients. He claims to be the inventor of Oreo ice cream, although some might disagree. The ice cream proved to be very popular, notable for its creative flavors. In the early '80s they had several stores in the Boston area and began franchising. Then came the downs: a class action suit was brought against the company concerning the franchising.

Today there are two stores in the Boston area and several more in other states. Rook says they are not franchises; rather, each store is individually owned and agrees to buy the ice cream he makes in Attleboro.

Controversies aside, Emack & Bolio's makes good ice cream. The **Vanilla Bean Speck** is tasty—with actual bits of vanilla bean. **Java** is a good coffee flavor. I was disappointed with the famous **original Oreo,** however; the ice cream tasted a little thin and not that creamy. The **strawberry** also is nondescript. But the **Chocolate Moose** is very good, a rich chocolate flavor. The creative flavors are the better ones here. The **Bavarian Creme Raspberry Truffle** is a sweet cream with a raspberry ripple, studded with bits of chocolate truffle. The **Cosmic Crunch** is fun; it's vanilla packed with caramel, pecans, and chocolate flakes. The **coffee-fudge-pecan-praline** is also good. I like the **chocolate–peanut butter,** which is a chocolate ice cream blended with peanut butter.

Emack & Bolio's also makes **nonfat frozen yogurt** that I don't care for—it's watery and very sweet. You can get **sundaes** and a full array of **add-ins** mixed into or sprinkled on your ice cream. The store makes their own gourmet **waffle cones**—waffle cones dipped in semisweet chocolate and rolled in a variety of toppings, such as **crushed candies, coconut,** and **nuts.**

The store also makes fresh **juice drinks.** They don't extract juices; instead they make blends using fresh orange juice. I tried a **fresh fruit smoothie,** which consists of orange juice blended with two kinds of fruit. It wasn't bad, but it was warm. I would recommend refrigerating the fruit so that it would be refreshing on a hot summer day. A **cooler** is a drink made with sorbet or sherbet, fresh fruit, and sparkling water. Their **health shake** is a fruit smoothie with protein powders added. You can also get items such as **bee pollen** and **wheat germ** added into a drink.

The ice cream is not made on the premises, but at a central location. Their prices are among the highest around.

Hana Pastry. See "Everything Nice," page 248.

Herrell's Ice Cream. See Allston, page 297.

Toscanini's Ice Cream

899 Main Street, Cambridge, MA 02139   (617) 491-5877
Hours: Sun.–Thurs. 8 A.M.–11 P.M.; Fri., Sat. 8 A.M.–midnight
MIT Student Center, Mass. Ave., Cambridge, MA 02139
    (617) 494-1640
Hours: Mon.–Thurs. 8 A.M.–11 P.M.; Fri. 8 A.M.–midnight;
    Sat. 10 A.M.–midnight; Sun. 10 A.M.–11 P.M.

Gus Rancatore opened Toscanini's in 1981 during the Harvard Square ice-cream heyday. Its location in Central Square is far from the tourist haunts, and when it first opened prices were about a third less than those found in Harvard Square, and the servings were larger. Those of us who ventured into Central Square shared the conspiratorial feeling of having made a secret discovery, for Toscanini's ice cream was and is among the best. It's extremely rich and creamy, and there are a number of creative flavors, including **Vienna Fingers** and **gingersnap molasses,** a subtle molasses ice cream threaded with crushed gingersnaps. I am not crazy about the **coffee,** however; it has a certain bitterness that coffee ice cream can sometimes have. Similarly, the **espresso** is just too strong. But the **pistachio** is mild but assertive, loaded with the green nuts. The **banana-walnut chip** has an excellent banana taste. The **French vanilla** is very good. There are a few chocolate options. I like the **Belgian chocolate,** which is a lighter chocolate ice cream. The **dark chocolate** is a classic version. The **cocoa pudding** is almost more chocolatey, but with a definite cocoa overtone. My favorite is **caramel chocolate chip,** with a tantalizing burnt sugar taste.

The **frozen yogurt** is available in the same flavors as the ice cream, and it is good frozen yogurt, probably because it is **low-fat,** as opposed to nonfat.

Toscanini's also makes excellent **sorbet,** but the flavors aren't always posted. Just ask. Rancatore supplies several area restaurants with custom ice creams and sorbets, and he may have small amounts of certain flavors left over. The **mango jalapeño** is, well, interesting. The **strawberry margarita** is great, as is **tangerine.**

I prefer my ice cream unadorned, but for sundae lovers, Toscanini's makes intense, extravagant **sauces.** The **hot fudge** is rich and dark, and the **butterscotch** is sweet and caramelly. Not for the faint of heart. You can also get coffee and a choice of cookies and muffins from area bakeries.

You can't hide a great thing forever, and Toscanini's is now quite popular. The prices are very high, and the servings seem to be portion-controlled. But the ice cream is still excellent.

EVERETT

Il Pastificio. See "Everything Nice," page 254.

Richie's Slush

2084 Revere Beach Parkway, Everett, MA 02151   (617) 389-6407
Hours: April–October, daily 10 A.M.–10:30 P.M.;
   closed November–March

Richie's Slush. You see it everywhere—pushcarts, airports, fairs, convenience stores. So much that I thought it was a product of some anonymous large company. Not so. There was and is a Richie, and Richie's Slush is a family-owned business, another culinary surprise based in Everett.

The current owner is Richie Cardullo, son of the late Richie Cardullo who started the company in 1956. Cardullo had worked with his father since he was nine. "My father grew up in the North End," Cardullo recalls. "He used to work for some old-timers, making slush. One guy got older and gave my father his recipe that he had brought with him from Italy. My father brought it over to the Parkway and started making slush."

What is *slush,* exactly? Different places may have different definitions, but Richie's is a smooth, icy concoction that is midway between something you drink with a straw and something you eat with a spoon. There is no milk in slush, and for that reason, Cardullo says, it can be challenging to come up with flavors. Of the twenty-one flavors, most are artificial, but the citrus flavors use natural lemon oils. I like the **lemon** best, and it and the **watermelon** are best-sellers. **Blue vanilla** is a kid-oriented flavor—a vanilla syrup combined with blue coloring. The Everett store also offers flavors such as **mango, tangerine, sour apple,** and **almond.**

Richie's is available in outlets all over New England, but the family has just the one store in Everett, since much of the business is wholesale. The store, run by Cardullo's sister Valerie, offers all twenty-one flavors. Cardullo says that the company is in the process of developing individual prepackaged servings. These would be frozen hard, more the consistency of Italian ice.

NEWTON

Cabot's Ice Cream

743 Washington Street, Newton, MA 02160   (617) 964-9200
Hours: Sun. and Tues.–Thurs. 9 A.M.–11 P.M.;
  Fri., Sat. 9 A.M.–11:45 P.M.; closed Mon.

Cabot's specialties are **sundaes,** lots of sundaes. I first encountered the place as a teenager when I was visiting my cousin in
Watertown. I remember noise, crowds, and mounds of ice cream,
sauce, and whipped cream.

Joe Prestejohn owns the business and runs it with his
mother and sister; he has worked here since he was ten. Prestejohn's parents had had a restaurant in Boston that was destroyed
by fire. When his late father bought Cabot's in 1969 it was an
ice-cream parlor and diner, and the Prestejohns focused on the
food. Cabot's continues to serve good diner fare. (The company
takes its name from this area of Newton, which, Prestejohn says,
was once referred to as Cabot.)

At a certain point making their own ice cream proved to
be too much, so the Prestejohns looked for a source, and found
it in Richardson's Ice Cream (see page 317). "We were their first
wholesale account," Joe Prestejohn claims, and the dairy makes
several flavors just for Cabot's. Richardson's is very good ice
cream, so Cabot's makes very good sundaes.

Cabot's exudes fun, and reading the menu is part of the
experience. A five-page menu outlines all the various sundae
combinations. The top of the first page proclaims, "Welcome to
our world—the crazy world of ice cream, and you're in the
middle of it now! So enjoy!"

The basic **"big"** sundae comes with a choice of eight
hot toppings or eighteen cold toppings. There are five different
hot fudges. I like the **hot peanut butter fudge** and the **hot
bittersweet fudge.** The **lite fudge,** which is fat-free, is not bad
for what it is. Cold toppings include **Florida orange-pineapple,
ginger, Brazilian coffee,** and **maraschino cherry.** They also
make **party sundaes,** which can have from ten to sixty pints of
ice cream in them.

There's a choice of forty-two ice cream flavors. There is
also **low-fat** and **nonfat frozen yogurt** and **dairy-free tofu ice
cream,** all of which can be blended with your choice of flavorings, such as **banana, granola,** and **Snickers.**

A page of the menu is devoted to **ice cream drinks;** in addition to a variety of **frappes** and **malteds,** there are refreshing **freezes,** fruit sherbet blended with fruit soda.

Personally, I prefer my ice cream naked; I would rather have a sampler of a few different flavors than vanilla with a blob of sauce. But sundaes are what Cabot's is all about.

Ice Cream Works

28 Lincoln Street, Newton, MA 02159   (617) 969-6256
Hours: daily 10 A.M.–11 P.M.

1663 Beacon Street, Brookline, MA 02146   (617) 731-6256
Hours: Mon.–Thurs. 11 A.M.–11 P.M.; Fri.–Sun. 10 A.M.–11 P.M.

Ice Cream Works has been in business since 1984, and they make tons of flavors. Owner Barry Gradwohl estimates that he has a recipe list of 160 different flavors. There are usually 30 to 35 flavors available. The quality varies. The **vanilla,** made with vanilla beans, is quite good, and I preferred its clean taste to the custardlike **French vanilla.** But the **hazelnut** is awful, with a totally artificial taste. The **banana-fudge nut** is disappointing, and the **cappuccino fudge** has a strange aftertaste. I liked the mildly spiced **pumpkin** and the **strawberry.** My favorite flavor I tried here is the **Snickers,** a butterscotch ice cream rippled with chocolate fudge and peanuts. The store also makes ice creams for hotels and restaurants around town.

Ice Cream Works could more accurately be called **Frozen Works,** because when it comes to frozen sweets, Gradwohl makes the works. Because of a problem he had with high cholesterol, Gradwohl spent a lot of time developing his **nonfat frozen yogurt** recipes. There are some 28 flavors available at any one time —4 to 7 are **soft serve** and the remainder **hard frozen yogurt.** There is also **Perfect Ten,** frozen yogurt that is both **fat-** and **sugar-free** (made with aspartame). I prefer the regular yogurt— no matter how you disguise it, aspartame is always so sweet that it is jarring. There are also a few **sherbets,** made with low-fat milk, and some very good **sorbets.** I especially like the **lemon sorbet,** which is pleasantly tart.

Legal Sea Foods Market Place. See Allston, page 300.

White Mountain Creamery

19 Commonwealth Avenue, Newton, MA 02167   (617) 527-8790
Hours: daily 10 A.M.–midnight

552 Washington Street, Wellesley, MA 02181   (617) 239-0676
Hours: Sun.–Thurs. 11 A.M.–11 P.M.; Fri., Sat. 11 A.M.–11:30 P.M.

The ice cream here is generally very good, although the quality varies from flavor to flavor. It's always worth tasting a flavor of ice cream before you buy it, since flavors can differ so widely from shop to shop. The White Mountain **coffee ice cream** is very good, and I also liked the **cinnamon-coffee.** I like the cookies in **Oreo** ice cream to be well crushed, and these are; some schools of Oreo ice-cream makers believe in using big chunks, almost whole cookies. The **chocolate chip** is good, but it has too many chips for my taste. At the Newton store, there are sometimes two chocolates. The regular **chocolate** is good, dark chocolate with a rich flavor; I preferred the light, hint-of-chocolate taste of the **chocolate mousse.** The **rum** is very alcoholic tasting, unpleasantly so; conversely, the **Kahlua** didn't seem to have much flavor at all. The **Butterfinger** is good—it tastes just like the candy bar.

You can get several toppings—crushed candies and cookies, a decent hot fudge sauce, a too-sweet hot butterscotch. You can also eat your ice cream from one of their homemade **waffle cones.**

WINTHROP

Aljay's Homemade Ice Cream Shoppe

29 Crest Avenue, Winthrop, MA 02152   (617) 846-7499
Hours: Mon.–Sat. 6 A.M.–9 P.M.; Sun. 7 A.M.–9 P.M.

Aljay's, in business since 1984, makes a variety of dependably good flavors of ice cream. The ice cream is creamy and smooth. The **banana** is very good. It tastes like fresh bananas and is great in a hot fudge sundae: it's like a built-in banana split. Pass on the fake-tasting **pistachio**—the nuts are there, but the ice-cream flavor isn't—and the mediocre **French vanilla.** The regular **vanilla** is better. **Decadence** is a fun flavor if you like stuff in your ice cream; it is loaded with chocolate chips, brownies, almonds, the works. The **chocolate** is rich and fudgelike. Aljay's also makes **muffins** and other **breakfast pastries** and serves **sandwiches;** they are also known for their **pies.**

NORTH

BEVERLY

Dick & June's Ice Cream

294 Elliott Street (Route 62), Beverly, MA 01915   (508) 921-0433
Hours: April–October, Mon.–Fri. 11:30 A.M.–10 P.M.;
    Sat., Sun. 11 A.M.–10 P.M.; November–March,
    Wed.–Sun. noon–8 P.M., closed Mon., Tues.
550 Ober Street, Beverly, MA 01915   (508) 921-4707
Hours: Memorial Day–Labor Day, daily 11 A.M.–8 P.M.;
    closed September–May

Dick Williams was a firefighter in Beverly who wanted to have a side business, so he started making ice cream with his wife June in 1968. The Williamses now make ice cream for their two stores in their own factory, and they supply wholesale ice cream to area stands.

This is a good, 14 percent butterfat ice cream, and it's available in about thirty flavors. The Ober Street location is on the beach and is a concession stand; it usually offers just ten flavors. The Elliott Street location carries most flavors. There are no seats inside (orders are generally taken at the outside window), but a picnic table sits by the adjacent parking lot.

Notable flavors include **Mississippi Mud Pie,** a great coffee ice cream with Oreos and fudge. The plain **coffee bean** is very good, too. I especially like the **peanut butter fudge**—peanut butter ice cream with a swirl of fudge; it's delicious. The **coconut-almond chip** is terrific, with a toasted coconut flavor. Pass on the **French vanilla,** though; it's only mediocre. The **cookies 'n' cream** is a little different, made with both Oreos and a swirl of fudge.

All the chocolate flavors are good. I like the **Bavarian chocolate–raspberry,** with bits of raspberry and a raspberry swirl. The **Swiss chocolate–almond** is also tasty, with almonds in a rich chocolate base. There are occasional specials, such as **strawberry Oreo** and **blueberry cheesecake.**

For **nonfat yogurt,** Dick & June's has one of those makes-a-million-flavors machines that blends plain yogurt with your choice of ingredients. They list a variety of fun combinations, from **Red Ape** (strawberry-banana) to **Cherry Cordial** (chocolate and black cherry).

Scoops

642 Hale Street, Beverly, MA 01915   (508) 927-7778
Hours: Memorial Day–Labor Day, daily 11 A.M.–10 P.M.;
   closed September–May

Scoops is owned by Christopher Flynn who also owns Prides Crossing Confections across the street (see "Sweet Indulgences," page 341). This is 15 percent butterfat ice cream—very good. Most of the flavors are standard, but the **milk chocolate** is especially tasty. To make it, Flynn melts pounds of chocolate and stirs it into an ice-cream base. He also chops up some of his own **candies** and adds them to make various flavors.

DANVERS

Cherry Farm Creamery

210 Conant Street, Danvers, MA 01923   (508) 774-0519
Hours: March–November, daily 11 A.M.–10 P.M.;
   closed December–February

Cherry Farm offers a variety of flavors of their homemade ice cream. Steve Jones, the father of three girls, says he test-markets a new flavor first on his family, then as a "flavor of the week" for the general public. Thus was born one of the stand's best flavors, **Kahlua chip,** and the popular-among-kids **Cotton Candy.** It really tastes like cotton candy, in ice cream form. "We had trouble selling it at first," Jones recalls. "Then we called it 'Barney' [the flavor is a pale purple color], and it went flying out the door. We changed the name back to Cotton Candy to avoid problems with rights, and now people know what it is." The **coffee,** unfortunately, is sadly lacking in flavor: if you tasted it blind, you couldn't tell it was coffee. Among the better flavors is a wonderful **chocolate–peanut butter.**

The stand also sells **sandwiches, burgers,** and **hot dogs.** There are several picnic tables in back, next to Cherry Farm's driving range. It's a way to burn off those ice cream calories, albeit slowly.

Putnam Pantry. See "Sweet Indulgences," page 342.

Treadwell's Ice Cream

30 Hobart Street, Danvers, MA 01923   (508) 777-3858
Hours: daily 10 A.M.–10 P.M.

1025 Osgood Street, North Andover, MA 01845   (508) 686-2051
Hours: daily 10 A.M.–10 P.M.

46 Margin Street, Peabody, MA 01960   (508) 531-9430
Hours: daily 10 A.M.–11 P.M.

Brad Treadwell's father Russ started Treadwell's in 1946. "He went to UMass and studied dairy technology," Brad says. "Ice cream interested him the most." Brad grew up in the business and got involved full-time in 1977. Treadwell's is one of the few places that makes their own base—with 16 percent butterfat. This is *rich* ice cream. Treadwell's makes about forty-five flavors and offers about thirty-six at any one time.

The basic **vanilla** is very good here, and the homey **Grape-nut** is surprisingly popular in the summer. Some flavors are to be avoided, like the artificial-tasting bright yellow **banana** and the bright green **pistachio,** which is made with walnuts. But other flavors are to be sought out. The **Girl Scout Cookie** is available during Girl Scout cookie season; it has a hint of mint and is laced with finely chopped mint cookies. Although the basic **coffee** is very mild, the **mocha** flavors are nice at Treadwell's. They are more coffee than chocolate. I like the **mocha-almond fudge,** made with Treadwell's own **hot fudge sauce,** and the excellent **mocha chip. Mochaccino** is a new flavor—a more chocolatey mocha with a cappuccino swirl, a ripple of cinnamon-coffee syrup. It tastes like a sundae. The chocolate flavors are very good, from the basic **chocolate** to **chocolate walnut fudge** and **chocolate marshmallow.** The **Heath Bar crunch** is particularly good; the candy is chopped fine and melts into ripples of flavor in the ice cream.

There are five **sherbet** flavors, all fruit. I find these to be more refreshing in the summer, since they are lighter than regular ice cream. I like **raspberry** best, then **watermelon.**

Treadwell's also makes **frozen yogurt**—and has been doing so longer than almost anyone in the area, since 1974. It comes in **low-fat, nonfat,** and **sugar-free;** the hard nonfat sells best. The **French vanilla** isn't bad, and the **chocolate** is okay. The **nonfat, sugar-free ice cream** comes in two flavors—a decent **coffee** and **chocolate** that tastes like a Fudgsicle.

The stores, all of which are open year round, have become distinguishable in recent years by their purple-painted roofs. There is no indoor seating.

IPSWICH

White Farms
266 High Street, Ipswich, MA 01938   (508) 356-2633
Hours: April–October, daily 10:30 A.M.–10 P.M.;
   closed November–March

White Farms has been making ice cream since 1953. In the early 1990s the shop took a turn for the worse when the original owners sold it. The new owner ran the place into the ground, doing things like not making his own ice cream and damaging White Farms' good reputation. The original owner bought it back and then sold it in 1993 to Laurene and Chris Clark, who have an ice-cream operation in Gloucester. The Clarks have done their best to restore the shop's reputation, and they have succeeded in making excellent ice cream.

This is very rich ice cream—16 to 18 percent butterfat. Chris Clark has created a variety of fun flavors, in addition to the usuals. My favorite here is **key lime pie**—a flavor worth driving for. It tastes exactly like excellent key lime pie—creamy, citrusy, with a swirl of graham-cracker crust. Kudos to Chris for creating this flavor. The **banana** flavors were less successful. When I visited, both plain **banana** and **banana swirl,** with a ripple of fudge, were icy. However, **Funky Monkey** was creamier. This has a banana base studded with chocolate chips and walnuts. Another terrific, popular flavor is **Coco Jamocha Chip,** a coffee-mocha base spiked with Jamaican rum and laced with toasted coconut and chocolate chips. **Carmel Cow** is vanilla ice cream with white-chocolate chips, chocolate chips, and a caramel swirl.

The more mundane flavors are also quite good. The **maple-walnut** is delicious. The **coffee** is very creamy, and the **pistachio** is loaded with pistachios.

When the Clarks took over White Farms, they did major renovations, including putting in an inside dining area. They also serve their own very good **roll-up sandwiches,** and sell muffins and breakfast pastries.

At this writing, White Farms closes for the winter; the dates above are estimates. They hope to be open year round within the next few years.

MIDDLETON

Richardson's Ice Cream

156 South Main Street (Route 114), Middleton, MA 01949
    (800) 698-5450 or (508) 774-5450
Hours: June–Labor Day, daily 9 A.M.–11 P.M.;
    September–May, Mon.–Fri. 10 A.M.–9 P.M.; Sat. 9 A.M.–10 P.M.;
    Sun. 9 A.M.–9 P.M.

Paul Richardson is the eighth generation of Richardsons to be operating a dairy in this location; his family started here in 1690. They have their own cows and produce their own milk: **skim, 1 percent,** and **whole milk,** as well as **cream.** The dairy was once the primary business, but now it is ice cream, which Paul's father and uncle started making in 1952. "They weren't sure it would do well," Richardson recalls. "But it has done *very* well. We've had to keep expanding.

The family has had a driving range next to their ever-growing stand for about thirty years, and they added a second one, along with miniature golf in 1990, and a batting cage in 1994.

But these entertainments are just toppings on the ice cream. Richardson's produces a tremendous amount of ice cream, and they supply a large percentage of the ice-cream stands throughout eastern Massachusetts. Many places that sell "home-made" ice cream sell Richardson's. And this is not a bad thing, because Richardson's ice cream is very, very good. It has a high butterfat content—16 percent. Since it is a dairy, Richardson's makes their own base, and the result is a fresher tasting ice cream.

The ice cream kitchen is impressive; pipes running along the ceiling carrying pasteurized milk to giant mixing tanks where the white base and the chocolate base are mixed. These bases in turn are pumped through more lengths of pipe into the ice-cream makers where the dozens of flavors are made. "The main ingredient is the mix," Richardson says. "No matter what the flavoring, the mix is most important." I've found that the flavoring matters too, and many of Richardson's flavors are quite good. Their specialty is candy flavors, and I liked these best. The **Milky Way** is a light chocolate ice cream with swirls of caramel. Richardson says he tried to create the flavor of the nougat in a Milky Way candy bar filling. The **Snickers** is vanilla-based, chock-full of stuff—caramel swirl, peanuts, and chocolate chips. The **Reeses Peanut Butter Cup** is a very good peanut butter ice cream with chopped Reeses candy throughout. Also good are the **maple-walnut** and the **pistachio.**

On your way out, pick up a gallon of milk or cream, pasteurized on the premises, and check out the cows grazing in the fields behind the dairy.

NORTH ANDOVER

Treadwell's Ice Cream. See Danvers, page 315.

PEABODY

Treadwell's Ice Cream. See Danvers, page 315.

SALEM

Puleo's Dairy
376 Highland Avenue, Salem, MA 01970   (508) 744-6455
Hours: June–August, daily 7 A.M.–9:45 P.M.;
    September–May, daily 7 A.M.–7 P.M.

Chuck Puleo's father started this dairy in 1928 when he was twenty years old; in 1940 the family opened a seasonal ice-cream stand using their own milk and cream. Today Puleo's offers a range of delicious ice creams year round.

Puleo's no longer has cows, but it is still a dairy; they get milk from area farmers and pasteurize it themselves. They make their own ice-cream base, and, naturally, use their own milk and cream. The ice cream here is great—extremely fresh-tasting. They make a good **vanilla** and a light **chocolate,** like a milk chocolate. Of the thirty or so flavors offered, my favorites are **mocha Heath Bar** and **Funky Monkey,** made with fresh bananas, walnuts, and chocolate chips. The **cappuccino** is also very tasty.

Puleo's makes the best **frappes** (milk shakes to the rest of the world) I've ever had—creamy and incredibly thick. They use four scoops of ice cream and their own milk, and the resulting concoction has the consistency of soft-serve ice cream—you can hardly slurp it. I recommend two scoops of mocha Heath Bar combined with two scoops of coffee, and coffee syrup. Sublime.

The store is also a diner-style restaurant, with a counter and booths, serving breakfast and lunch. The base of each counter stool is made from old milk cans. Opposite the counter are refrigerators and freezers. You can take home prepacked quarts and half-gallons of ice cream, and Puleo's milk in glass bottles.

This is great **milk.** I never liked **skim milk,** but theirs is actually palatable and creamy tasting; Chuck Puleo says that theirs tastes better because they heat it slowly, over a longer period of time, which keeps the milk from turning that undesirable watery blue I usually associate with skim milk. The **whole milk** is a rich indulgence, and the best treat is the **Cream Line whole milk,** which has the cream floating to the top of the milk. Puleo's is a real find, a dairy-lover's delight.

Sweet Scoops

13 Washington Square West, Salem, MA 01970   (508) 741-1548
Hours: April–November 15, daily 9 A.M.–10 P.M.;
        November 16–March, Sat. only, 9 A.M.–10 P.M.

Sweet Scoops is owned by Bob Colombosian, whose parents started Colombo Yogurt. From 1929 until 1950, they made their yogurt in the back of their house in Andover and sold it locally, primarily to the Armenian community, and to immigrants who were familiar with yogurt. In the 1950s there was an article in *Reader's Digest* extolling the health benefits of yogurt, and the national demand for yogurt began. Colombo was the only yogurt available on the East Coast, until Dannon entered the picture. Star Market was the first to carry Colombo yogurt, and the Colombosians eventually established a large plant in Methuen in 1970.

Bob Colombosian tinkered with frozen yogurt as early as 1968, and sold soft-serve frozen yogurt from a truck in 1971. But it didn't catch on then the way it has now. In 1976 he sold the Colombo Yogurt Company but stayed on as a consultant for a few years.

He opened Sweet Scoops in 1981. "I started this as a hobby," Colombosian says. "I wanted to stay active." The store has always made both **frozen yogurt** and **ice cream,** and Colombosian called the product "yogurt-ice cream" when he started, because people were unfamiliar with hard frozen yogurt. The yogurt is **low-fat** and is among the best frozen yogurts I've tried. While it is not as low-calorie as nonfat yogurt, it is significantly less caloric than ice cream.

The first yogurt flavors I tried I thought were ice cream —the frozen yogurt is that good, smooth, and creamy. The flavors are often creative, such as the subtle, wonderful *tiramisù,* which has a mild coffee favor and tiny bits of chocolate. The **pistachio** is quite good; Colombosian and his daughter Robin, who manages the shop, apologize for the fact that it is green. "People want pistachio to be green," they shrug. It still tastes great and is loaded with the nuts. The **peanut butter chip** is also excellent—full of flavor.

Not everything tasted terrific, however. I was disappointed with the fruit flavors—both the **peach** and the **black raspberry** are too sweet. But the **cookie dough,** a flavor I am not usually enamored of, is quite good. Colombosian uses Toll House cookie batter and actually blends it into the yogurt as it is being made, so the yogurt tastes like chocolate chip cookies.

The **ice cream** is very good as well. The **Sludge** is a winner, especially if you like stuff in your ice cream. It is studded with nuts, Oreos, Heath bars, and chocolate chunks. The **Oreo** is the best rendition of this flavor. Colombosian blends in the cookie while the ice cream is being mixed, so the bits of cookie are pulverized into the ice cream, infusing it with an Oreo flavor. He also stirs in chunks of the cookie afterwards, for those who like bigger pieces. The **maple-walnut** is also tasty.

The store also sells **breakfast pastries, bagels,** and **Toll House cookies,** all baked on the premises.

WAKEFIELD

Meletharb Ice Cream
393 Lowell Street, Wakefield, MA 01880   (617) 245-4946
Hours: daily 10 A.M.–10 P.M.

Don "Bart" Barthelemy was working as a manager at a Brigham's store in the early 1970s, when, according to his son Don, "He got the urge to have his own thing." He bought a new place and started from scratch, making premium ice cream. The name of the place comes from spelling *Barthelemy* backwards, sort of.

Today, Don works with his father; they are the ice-cream makers for Meletharb. They have a roster of a hundred different flavors, with about thirty-five available at any one time. The **strawberry** is particularly good, made with frozen strawberries, not a syrupy mix. I also like the very simple **sweet cream.** It has a clean flavor, and with hot fudge I prefer it to regular vanilla. It is used as the base for a very good **chocolate chip,** which has both tiny specks and larger bits of chocolate. The **coffee** is very pale in color, but with a good coffee flavor. I especially like the **cappuccino,** which has an assertive cinnamon flavor. Another coffee flavor, **mocha chip,** is good, too. It is a tad more chocolate than coffee, but it is a mild chocolate, and the coffee flavor comes through. The **peanut butter fudge**—peanut butter ice cream with a chocolate swirl—is very rich. Try it in a cup with **banana** —very good here, with a natural, fresh banana flavor.

Meletharb is located in a small shopping center and has several tables. It is very kid-friendly. Don offers regular tours to preschool kids, and a wall of the store is covered with Polaroid photos of kids eating ice cream.

SOUTH

DEDHAM

Maddie's Ice Cream
565 High Street, Dedham, MA 02026   (617) 461-1715
Hours: Mon.–Sat. 11 A.M.–11 P.M.; Sun. noon–10:30 P.M.

686 Washington Street, Norwood, MA 02062   (617) 255-0074
Hours: Mon.–Sat. 11 A.M.–11 P.M.; Sun. noon–11 P.M.

Donna D'Entremont started Maddie's Ice Cream, named for her mother, in 1983. "I like the business," she says. "It's fun. Ice cream is a happy thing. Everyone that leaves my store, leaves happier."

The ice cream is good, with 14 percent butterfat. Noteworthy flavors are **Coconut Almond Joy,** coconut with chocolate chips and roasted almonds; **pumpkin-raisin-nut,** which tastes like creamy pumpkin pie and unfortunately is only seasonal; **Ernie's Grape-nut;** and **butter 'n' pecans.** The soft **yogurt** is all **fat-free** and isn't bad, but I prefer the **fat-free very berry sorbet.**

Both locations prepare **ice-cream cakes** and **pies** to order and also sell them off the shelf. There are several tables at each location, so you can eat your ice cream right there.

EASTON

Hilliard's House of Candy
316 Main Street, North Easton, MA 02356   (508) 238-6231
Hours: May–October, daily 9 A.M.–9 P.M.; closed November–April
Also: "Sweet Indulgences," page 351.

Hilliard's has long been known for its candies. In 1991 owners
Charlie and Judy (Hilliard) McCarthy added a line of premium
ice cream, to bring in business during the slow summer months.
They make excellent ice cream, and it is a shame that it is not
available year round. There are many creative flavors, such as **The
Swamp.** This popular flavor has a malted vanilla base and it
is loaded with stuff—nuts, M&Ms, brownies, chocolate chips,
everything. The **Cookies and Cookie Dough** is vanilla ice cream
with Oreos and vanilla cookies, as well as bits of cookie dough.
The **Colombian coffee** is a good coffee ice cream. It serves as
the base for **Coffee Brownie Madness,** filled with chunks of
homemade brownie; and for **Chewy Turtle Soup,** which is studded with the candy store's cashew turtles, chopped. They use
their own **buttercrunch** in the **vanilla-toffee crunch.** The **black
raspberry** is very good. Hilliard's uses real black raspberries, not
just a flavoring.

My favorite flavor here is a simpler one. Hilliard's makes
the best **chocolate chip ice cream** I've had anywhere. They call
it **Vanilla Chunky Chip.** While the ice cream is stirring, they
add melted bittersweet chocolate and it freezes on contact, break-
ing into tons of tiny bits. Then they add thin chocolate chips, so
there are larger pieces of chocolate as well.

Hilliard's makes their own **waffle cones** and **sauces.** The
caramel is too sweet, but the **hot fudge** is terrific. Some of the
toppings for ice cream include Hilliard's **candies.**

NORWOOD

Furlong's Cottage Candies and Ice Cream Co. See "Sweet
Indulgences," page 356.

Maddie's Ice Cream. See Dedham, page 321.

QUINCY

Purdy's Ice Cream Parlor

68 Billings Road, North Quincy, MA 02171   (617) 472-8558
Hours: Sun.–Wed. 8 A.M.–10 P.M.; Thurs.–Sat. 8 A.M.–11 P.M.

Lynne Forti describes her father as an entrepreneur. He had a submarine shop next door to Purdy's, and he wanted to open an ice cream shop, too. When Lynne graduated from college, she worked with him to start Purdy's in 1985. Her husband Kevin joined the business in 1991. In 1995 they doubled the size of the shop, opening for breakfast and adding entertainment—story time for the kids in the afternoon, live jazz in the evening. It is a kid-friendly place, with a blackboard for drawing on one wall, next to a mural of a flying cow and a smiling moon.

The ice cream is 15 percent butterfat. The Fortis make over a hundred flavors, with about twenty available at any one time. After **vanilla,** the most popular flavor everywhere, **Oreo** is popular here, and they get a lot of requests for **Swiss chocolate-orange** and **white pistachio,** which has an almondy flavor and is made with real pistachios. I like the **Oreo,** which has both chunks and pulverized cookie crumbs blended into the ice cream. I also like the **chocolate,** which is light. Kevin notes that they have many Asian customers, who make the **green tea** ice cream disappear quickly. They also favor the **ginger,** which is very good —my favorite flavor here. The **maple-walnut** is good, containing a secret ingredient that, Lynne says, "you don't usually find in maple walnut." But they aren't telling what it is. The **mint chip** is too strong on the mint, and the **coffee** has a slight bitterness.

Purdy's offers a couple of nondescript **frozen yogurts,** as well as **soft-serve ice cream,** popular with kids. A **Whizard** is the soft serve blended with any of some two dozen candies, nuts, and cookie crumbs. Purdy's also offers several fun beverages, including a variety of **Italian sodas.** These consist of flavored Italian syrups, ice, and soda water. The **cream sodas** are the same, with half-and-half drizzled in. When I visited, the store had just started offering **Frappuccinos** and **Mocha Glaciers,** odd concoctions using a powdered mix, ice, water, and flavored syrups. I prefer a straightforward **frappe** made from Purdy's ice cream.

RANDOLPH

The Ice Creamery
25 Memorial Parkway, Randolph, MA 02368   (617) 961-1345
Hours: summer, daily 11A.M.–midnight;
    winter, Mon.–Thurs. 11 A.M.–9:30 P.M., Fri., Sat. 11 A.M.–10 P.M.;
    Sun. noon–9:30 P.M.

The Ice Creamery has been in business since 1984; in 1995 current owners Jay and Debbie Vara bought it. It is located in a shopping center near downtown Randolph, and the shop offers a decent premium ice cream. Flavors are organized into whimsical categories. Basics includes a light **chocolate** and a custardy **French vanilla.** Chips covers a tasty **mocha chip** and **rocky road.** Nuts includes everything with nuts. The **maple-walnut** isn't bad, and **Swiss chocolate–almond** is pretty good. My favorite, under the Fudges, is **peanut butter fudge.** This is a flavorful peanut butter ice cream with ripples of fudge. Several of the Exotics are bland, including **Kahlua** and **rum-raisin,** although the **strawberry-cheesecake** is very nice. The Candies include **peppermint stick, bubble gum,** and a too-sweet **buttercrunch.**

The Dairy Barn
892 N. Main Street, Randolph, MA 02368   (617) 986-4456
Hours: February–October, daily 11:30 A.M.–10 P.M.;
    closed November–January

Dairy Barn looks like a Dairy Queen, and that's what it started out to be. But then it changed to a homemade ice cream stand. Current owner Linda Bourasso, a former accountant, has had the stand since 1989.

There are about sixteen flavors. The ice cream, which I tasted off season, is on the sweet side, and a little granular in texture. But some flavors are very good. Noteworthy flavors include **white pistachio,** which is loaded with pistachio nuts; **Grape-nut; Almond Joy,** which is coconut ice cream with almonds and chocolate chips; and **pineapple sherbet,** which is lower in fat than the other flavors.

The **soft-serve ice cream,** which has less fat than the hard ice cream, comes in a decent **chocolate** and **vanilla;** the **coffee,** which was a daily special, had no flavor.

Dairy Barn uses their soft-serve ice cream to make various novelty items, such as a **peanut-fudge bar,** which is ice cream on a stick with peanuts and fudge; and a **Chippywich,** an ice cream sandwich made with chocolate chip cookies.

SHARON

Crescent Ridge Dairy

355 Bay Road, Sharon, MA 02067   (617) 784-5892
Hours: March–November, daily 10:30 A.M.–8:30 P.M.;
    December–February, daily 10:30 A.M.–6 P.M.

Crescent Ridge Dairy is a dairy farm, complete with cows, started by Stanley Parrish's father in 1932. Parrish started making premium ice cream in 1968. The 14 percent butterfat base is made for Crescent Ridge, according to their specifications, using milk and cream from their herds. They have about thirty-five **ice cream** flavors, and some **low-fat yogurt** flavors. They don't make any of the sauces, but the homemade **whipped cream** is made using their own cream.

The ice cream is good and fresh tasting. The **vanilla** has a pleasant, mellow flavor. The **chocolate** is a dark chocolate, rich and flavorful. It is better than the chocolate base used for the **toasted walnut fudge,** which tastes watery. Parrish says that **butter-pecan** is their slowest flavor, but I thought it was very good; it's not too sweet and has a generous amount of nuts and a subtle butterscotch taste. I also like the **buttercrunch,** even though it is very sweet. It has a flavor like very good buttercrunch candy. The **rum-raisin** is a good version. There is rum in the ice cream, and the raisins are also soaked in rum. Parrish says he was reluctant to make rum raisin, since they already offer **frozen pudding,** a flavor popular in New England. Frozen pudding contains rum and a mix of candied fruits. I don't care for it, but ice-cream makers tell me it is popular among older customers. Parrish added rum raisin in 1993 at the repeated request of customers, and it sells well. Another comfort flavor is **Grape-nut,** and it very good here. I like the **ginger** as well; it's studded with bits of candied ginger.

Cresent Ridge Dairy sells their own **milk (skim, whole, 1 percent,** and **2 percent),** in half-gallon glass bottles. The refrigerators at the ice cream stand are full of their milk, and the freezers hold prepacked quarts and half gallons of their ice cream. The diary also has a twenty-truck home-delivery service that brings their products to much of the Boston suburban area.

WEYMOUTH

Welcome Farm Ice Cream

1478 Main Street, Weymouth, MA 02190   (617) 337-1972
Hours: Mon.–Thurs. 9 A.M.–10:30 P.M.; Fri.–Sun. 9 A.M.–11 P.M.

Jim and Joan Dwyer opened Welcome Farm in 1961. Jim had
worked in a dairy, in the ice-cream division, and liked it, so he
decided to open his own place. Several of the Dwyers' adult
children now work there, too.

There are about two dozen regular flavors, and a handful
of seasonal flavors, such as a tasty **pumpkin** and a refreshing
peach. From the beginning, Welcome Farm has made **ginger,**
with candied ginger in syrup, which gives the ice cream the palest
pink color. I like it very much, but it is a strong flavor. Also
strong is the rum in the **frozen pudding,** a flavor that tastes
almost like eggnog. The brandy in the **brandied coffee** dominates the ice cream. I prefer the milky regular **coffee. Toll House
cookie** is a newer flavor, and I hope that they will make it a
regular. Toll House cookies are mixed into chocolate chip ice
cream, and the resulting blend is terrific.

The stand also offers **sandwiches** and **burgers,** and provides both indoor and outdoor seating.

WEST

BELMONT

Rancatore Ice Cream

283 Belmont Street, Belmont, MA 02178   (617) 489-5090
Hours: Mon.–Fri. 7 A.M.–11 P.M.; Sat., Sun. 7:30 A.M.–7 P.M.

Joe Rancatore worked at his brother Gus's Toscanini's Ice Cream
shop for a few years before opening his own place in November
of 1985. "Not the best time of year to open an ice-cream store,"
he laughs. But business picked up the second year, probably
owning to the fact that he makes very good ice cream. Good
picks are the **Callebaut milk chocolate,** a lighter chocolate, and
bittersweet chocolate, as dark and rich as a candy bar. I also like
the simple **sweet cream,** which is like vanilla without the vanilla,
simply the ice cream base. The **butter pecan** is beige from the
butterscotch used in the ice cream, and **ginger-pineapple** is great
—tangy, with a juicy sweetness and a hot kick. The **frozen**

yogurt here is pretty good, especially the **coffee-toffee** and the **almonds and chips.**

For **ice-cream drinks,** I'm happy with a **coffee frappe** (or milk shake, as the rest of the world calls it), but Rancatore's offers a variety of choices, all blended with vanilla ice cream, including **ice-cream sodas** such as the **Philly Freeze** (with Pepsi), the **Boston Cooler** (with ginger ale), and the **Brown Cow** (with root beer). The homemade **hot fudge** and **butterscotch sauces** are delicious.

CARLISLE

Kimball's at Bate's Farm. See Westford, page 329.

CHELMSFORD

Skip's Ice Cream Stand
118 Chelmsford Street, Chelmsford, MA 01824   (508) 256-3201
Hours: March–November, daily 11 A.M.–10 P.M.;
    closed December–February

Sully's Ice Cream Stand
55 Graniteville Road, Chelmsford, MA 01824   (508) 256-5971
Hours: March–November, daily 11 A.M.–10 P.M.;
    closed December–February

Skip's Ice Cream Stand has been here since 1932. Ricky Sullivan was a customer, and he jumped at the chance to buy the place when it was up for sale in 1982. In 1986 he opened Sully's which his brother Robert "Larry" Sullivan runs. The ice creams in the two stores are very similar. There is an extensive list of flavors. Sully's makes several more; "He's always going off from the recipes," Ricky says of his brother.

The portions are large, and the flavors are creative in both places. The ice cream is 15 percent butterfat. I like the **butterscotch,** a flavor I've seen at few ice creameries. Also good is the **peanut butter fudge. Snickers** has a coffee-chocolate base, very light, threaded with caramel and peanuts; **Milky Way** is about the same without the nuts. The flavor of the plain **coffee** is too mild. There are several different chocolates. I like the lighter regular **chocolate. Swiss chocolate–almond** is more chocolatey; it tastes like a Fudgsicle.

They also offer frozen yogurt, not homemade. Both

stands are seasonal and provide no indoor seating. You come here for the ice cream, not the ambience.

SUDBURY

Herbie's Ice Cream
103 Boston Post Road, Sudbury, MA 01776   (508) 440-8557
Hours: Sun.–Thurs. 11 A.M.–11 P.M.; Fri., Sat. 11 A.M.–midnight

When he opened his ice-cream store in Framingham in 1980, Phil Lewis named the shop for his father. He moved the store to this Sudbury location in 1995. His recipe list includes about seventy flavors of 14 percent butterfat ice cream; thirty-five are available at any one time. The ice cream here is terrific—it's one of the top ten places in the Boston area.

Lewis often uses real ingredients to flavor the ice creams, not just extracts, as with the **White Chocolate Blizzard.** This white-chocolate ice cream laced with white-chocolate chips is perfect as a base for a hot fudge sundae. The **maple-walnut** contains real maple syrup, giving it a subtle and delicious maple flavor. Herbie's is one of only a few places I've found that makes a truly great maple-walnut. Lewis prides himself on his **Mud-Slide Chip,** a blend of Kahlúa, vodka, and Bailey's, studded with chocolate chips, inspired by the frozen mud-slide drink. He makes some of the best **rum-raisin** I've tried, both creamy and rummy from raisins that have soaked in rum for weeks. Lewis's favorite flavor is the **butter pecan,** and it is a good version, not too sweet. The **Oreo** is very good, with Oreos both blended into the ice cream and mixed in as chunks. Lewis says it is the top contender with **vanilla** for the shop's most popular flavor.

There are **chocolate ice creams** for fans of both light and dark. The regular **chocolate** is rich and chocolatey. It's also used as the base for **chocolate raspberry truffle,** which is laced with raspberry swirl and chocolate flakes. I like the lighter **chocolate mousse.**

WELLESLEY

White Mountain Creamery. See Newton, page 312.

WESTFORD

Kimball's Farm
100 Littleton Road (Route 110), Westford, MA 01886
   (508) 486-3891
Hours: April–October, daily 10 A.M.–9 P.M.; closed November–March

Kimball's at Bate's Farm
343 Bedford Road, Carlisle, MA 01741   (508) 369-1910
Hours: April–October, daily 10 A.M.–9 P.M.; closed November–March

Initially, Kimball's ice cream was a side business for a dairy farm. But the ice cream proved so popular that the Kimball family soon sold the farm. All the ice cream is made on the premises of this large seasonal ice-cream stand, and has been since 1939. Kimball's consists of a barn-size building with half a dozen windows where you place and receive your order. There is no indoor seating, and there are only a few picnic tables by the parking lot —not nearly enough to accommodate the masses that arrive at lunchtime from nearby Digital Equipment.

It's true that there is not much food-wise in the vicinity, but the ice cream here is great, old-fashioned ice cream. The prices are reasonable, and the servings are enormous; two scoops is roughly the equivalent of a pint. If you want a sundae, I recommend that you bring an extra bowl, since the sundaes are vertical: one scoop on top of another, topped by sauce and real whipped cream, all balanced in the same tiny dish, which can barely hold a single, naked scoop.

Kimball's makes about fifty-five flavors, with forty available at any one time. Peter Kimball says that his family likes coffee, and they make several coffee ice creams. The **Kahlúa Crunch** is coffee ice cream spiked with real Kahlúa and peppered with bits of chocolate toffee—my favorite flavor here. There is also **coffee Heath Bar, coffee Oreo,** and **mocha chip,** made with coffee. The **mocha almond** is a blend of coffee with a bit of chocolate, but the coffee flavor comes through. This is one of the better mochas around.

Kimball's started out making standard 12 percent butterfat ice cream, but during the early 1980s and with the advent of Steve's, they changed to a 14 percent premium ice cream. Among the noteworthy flavors are **vanilla–peanut butter cup,** a malted vanilla ice cream mixed with chopped peanut-butter cup candies; **German chocolate fudge,** a chocolate-coconut ice cream with bits of fudge; and **chocolate-mint Oreo,** which is unusual and refreshing.

You also have the option of ordering a couple flavors of Colombo frozen yogurt, but if you've come this far, why bother? Go for the butterfat.

The grounds around Kimball's are pleasant to walk around, and for golf fans, Kimball's in Westford operates a driving range located about a hundred yards behind the ice cream building.

THE BESTS OF THE BEST

Note: There are so many very good ice cream establishments that I also offer a best for each region.

Best ice cream overall: **Herrell's**
Best ice cream/Boston: **Herrell's** and **Ron's Gourmet**
Best ice cream/Metropolitan Boston: **Herrell's, Christina's,** and **Toscanini's**
Best ice cream/North: **White Farms**
Best ice cream/South: **Hilliard's House of Candy**
Best ice cream/West: **Rancatore's** and **Herbie's**
Best flavor selection: **Christina's**
Best chocolate: **Herrell's**
Best vanilla: **Legal Sea Foods Market Place**
Best strawberry: **Herrell's** and **Meletharb**
Best coffee: **Christina's** and **Herrell's**
Best Oreo: **Sweet Scoops**
Best pistachio: **Christina's**
Best chocolate chip: **Hilliard's House of Candy**
Best maple: **Herrell's**
Best Grape-nut: **Maddie's**
Best coconut: **Ron's Gourmet**
Best black raspberry: **Hilliard's House of Candy**
Best butter pecan: **Rancatore's**
Best rum raisin: **Ron's Gourmet** and **Herbie's**
Best unusual flavors: **White Farms'** key lime pie, **Toscanini's** gingersnap molasses
Best sorbet: **Toscanini's**
Best gelato: **Il Pastificio** and **Café Paradiso**
Best frozen yogurt, fruit flavors: **Tuesday's**
Best frozen yogurt, nonfruit flavors: **Sweet Scoops**
Best frappe: **Puleo's Dairy**
Best hot fudge: **Rancatore's, Toscanini's,** and **Herrell's**
Best butterscotch: **Putnam Pantry** and **Christina's**
Best marshmallow topping: **Christina's**

❖ C H A P T E R   N I N E ❖

SWEET INDULGENCES

Choices for chocolate truffles, almond bark, turtles, caramels,
buttercreams, peanut brittle, buttercrunch, and pounds of solid milk,
dark, and white chocolate.

*G*IVEN my sweet tooth, it is fortunate for my health that I am not a chocoholic. I do appreciate good chocolate in small quantities, and while working on this book I discovered many excellent opportunities to nibble my way through wonderful samples in and around Boston.

The Boston area has a long history of chocolate- and candy making. Baker's, the first chocolate manufacturer in the United States, was established in Dorchester in 1780. In Cambridge, the New England Confectionery Company (Necco) started producing candies in 1901. There were several other large candy factories in Cambridge during the early part of the century including Fanny Farmer. Baker's has since moved on, having been purchased by Kraft/General Foods, and Fanny Farmer is now based in the Midwest. But when you walk through Central Square you can still smell the Necco wafers and other candies being made in the Mass. Ave. factory.

In the early part of the century there were small candy shops on every corner in every town, but with World War II and a sugar shortage many small businesses were forced to shut down.

331

Before I started researching this book, I thought there was only a scant handful of such places still around. But in fact, there are still quite a few old-time chocolatiers and candymakers in the Boston area.

There is also a new crop of small chocolatiers. The 80s was a decade of specialization which saw the opening of many small chocolate shops offering distinctive truffles, toffees, and other sweets. Many of these yummy confections contain nuts, such as brittles and turtles—although technically, no candymaker can use the name *turtle* for the treat made with layers of chocolate, caramel, and nuts, because Nestlé has the rights to it. Some businesses play by the rules, calling their creations anything from *patties* to *tortoises*. Others figure they are small enough and local enough that it doesn't matter if they sell sweets called *turtles*.

When it comes to hard candies, many shops make peanut brittle and butterscotch, but there are only a few places that make old-fashioned sucking candies such as barley lollipops, horehound drops, and ribbon candy. During the holidays you can find homemade candy canes.

Of course, Boston has branches of national chain stores such as Godiva and Fanny Farmer. But once you know that there are local special chocolatiers who make their own chocolate, often on the premises (or at least nearby), you won't want to bother with the national chains.

In this chapter, I cover three types of shops. First and foremost are the chocolatiers and candymakers, people who make their own candies. Next are the nut roasters, shops that specialize in roasted nuts or confections made with nuts. Finally, there are stores that sell other people's candies. Since there are over a hundred in the Boston area, I include only a few of these—just those that offer something a little different from the typical mall candy store.

* Described in another chapter.

CANDYMAKERS

Bari & Gail Chocolatier	Newton
The Chocolate Box	Cambridge, Arlington
Chocolate by Design	Swampscott, Andover, Marblehead
The Chocolate Dipper	Boston, Natick, Newton

Furlong's Cottage Candies and Ice Cream Co.	Norwood
Gowell's Candy Inc.	Brockton
Harbor Sweets	Salem
Hebert Candies	Shrewsbury, Bolton, Framingham
Hilliard's House of Candy	Easton
*Kilvert & Forbes Ltd.	Boston
Melville Olde Tyme Candy and Products	Weymouth
Merckens Chocolate	Mansfield
Mrs. London's Confections	Concord
Mrs. Nelson's Candy House	Chelmsford
*Modern Pastry Shop	Boston
New England Confectionery Co.	Cambridge
*New Paris Bakery & Candy Shop	Brookline
Nichols Candies, Inc.	Gloucester
Philips Candy House	Boston
Prides Crossing Confections	Beverly
Priscilla Candy Shop	Concord, Gardner
Puopolo Candies	Hingham
Putnam Pantry	Danvers
Serenade Chocolatier	Boston, Brookline
Stowaway Sweets	Marblehead
Waldman Candies	Brookline
Winfrey's Fudge and Candy	Rowley, Stoneham
Ye Olde Pepper Candy Co.	Salem

NUTS

Carolyn's Pecans	Concord
Gourmet Nuts	Boston, Watertown
Mixed Nuts	Belmont
Squirrel Brand Company	Cambridge
Superior Nut Co.	Cambridge

CANDY STORES

Candyland	Revere
Dairy Fresh Candies	Boston
Jack Smillie Inc.	Woburn
Kendall Confectionery Co. Inc.	Cambridge
Pearl's Candy & Nuts	Framingham

❖ C A N D Y M A K E R S ❖

BOSTON

BOSTON

The Chocolate Dipper

200 State Street, Boston, MA 02109   (617) 439-0190
Mail order: available   Hours: Mon.–Sat. 10 A.M.–7 P.M.;
  Sun. noon–6 P.M.

Longwood Galleria, 350 Brookline Avenue, Boston, MA 02215
  (617) 731-4931
Mail order: available   Hours: Mon.–Fri. 10 A.M.–6 P.M.;
  Sat. 11:30 A.M.–5 P.M.; closed Sun.

278 Washington Street, Boston, MA 02109   (617) 227-0208
Mail order: available   Hours: Mon.–Sat. 10 A.M.–7 P.M.;
  Sun. noon–6 P.M.

Chestnut Hill Mall (Route 9), Newton, MA 02167   (617) 969-7315
Mail order: available   Hours: Mon.–Fri. 10 A.M.–9:30 P.M.;
  Sat. 10 A.M.–8 P.M.; Sun. noon–6 P.M.

Natick Mall (Route 9), Natick, MA 01760   (508) 647-4846
Mail order: available   Hours: Mon.–Sat. 10 A.M.–10 P.M.;
  Sun. 11 A.M.–6 P.M.

Joseph Pelligrino bought The Chocolate Dipper when it was just a year old, in 1987, when he was a few years out of college. He wanted his own business, and he knew something about the food business—his family started Prince Spaghetti. After he bought the State Street store, he went to business school, and a few years later he began to expand the business, fairly quickly; the Natick, Chestnut Hill, and Washington Street stores each opened within a month of each other, at the end of 1994 and the beginning of 1995.

The Chocolate Dipper makes a selection of the usual **creams** and **caramels,** which are pretty good, although not worth their extremely high price—$23 a pound, compared to $10 to $18 per pound at most other places. The **rocky road** candy, made with caramel, nuts, and crushed cookies coated in milk chocolate, sounded intriguing. Although the caramel is good, the cookie part tasted stale. The **truffles** are more expensive still: $28 a pound. I tried **raspberry** and **hazelnut truffles,** both of which were good, but not amazing. What the Dipper does best, and what makes it unique is the **chocolate-covered fresh fruit.** The fruit they use is of good quality, and they dip it in Merckens chocolate. They offer the expected **strawberries** and **bananas,** which are great. The unusual **cranberry cluster** is pleasingly tart and crunchy; a trio of cranberries is set in a disk of milk chocolate. The Chocolate Dipper does a similar treatment with **blueberries** and **grapes,** all in season. Surprisingly good were the **chocolate-covered fresh orange peels**—not candied, as is more usual, but fresh and soft. I expected that the pith would have a bitter taste, but it didn't.

Kilvert & Forbes Ltd. See "Everything Nice," page 230.

Modern Pastry Shop. See "Everything Nice," page 233.

Serenade Chocolatier. See Brookline, page 336.

DORCHESTER

Philips Candy House

818 Morrissey Boulevard, Dorchester, MA 02122   (617) 282-2090
Mail order: available   Hours: Mon.–Sat. 8:30 A.M.–8 P.M.;
   Sun. 9:30 A.M.–6 P.M.

Mary Ann Nagel's grandparents started Philips (named for her grandfather's first name) in 1925 in Belmont, initially as a wholesale business. They moved to the current location in 1952, and her whole family is involved in the business.

    With a shop assistant at your side, you can move around the display counters, picking out your choices of chocolates from dozens of options. There are many pieces common to all chocolate stores, such as **creams** and **jellies.** I'm not big on jellies, but Philips's **raspberry jelly** is nice and tart. The **caramel-based candies** are quite good here, and Philips has won accolades for their **turtles.** I prefer the more unusual **honey paws,** made with honey caramel. Another sweet with a pleasant honey flavor is the **nougatine,** studded with toasted almonds. A lighter, more crumbly nougat is used in the **pecan roll,** which is surrounded with caramel and pecans. This item disappears very quickly. The **tête-à-tête** is a yummy blend of caramel and chopped peanuts. Since the caramel is so good, their **caramel topping** for ice cream is also delicious.

    The **walnut truffle** is a buttercream center that is surrounded by milk chocolate, then rolled in walnuts. The **almond**

buttercrunch is good but not great, but I liked it crushed up in **almond–toffee crunch bark.**

Philips also makes their own **peanut brittle** and, harder to find, a delicious, buttery **cashew brittle.** And their **butterscotch** is excellent.

In addition to their own candies, Philips carries a selection of truffles, hard candies, and diabetic candies. They also have a wide variety of dishes and baskets on hand for making up attractive gifts.

METROPOLITAN BOSTON

BROOKLINE

New Paris Bakery & Candy Shop. See "Everything Nice," page 245.

Serenade Chocolatier

1393 Beacon Street, Brookline, MA 02146   (617) 739-0795
Mail order: available   Hours: Mon.–Fri. 10 A.M.–6 P.M.;
   Sat. 10 A.M.–5 P.M.; closed Sun.
2 South Station, Boston, MA 02110   (617) 261-9941
Mail order: available   Hours: Mon.–Fri. 7:30 A.M.–7:30 P.M.;
   Sat., Sun. 9 A.M.–7 P.M.

Serenade's secret ingredient is "Uncle Bill" Federer, who has made candy for forty-five years in Brookline. "I went to culinary school to learn about candy," owner Nir Kilic asserts, "but I learned much more from Uncle Bill."

The rich smell of tempering chocolate surrounds you as you enter this shop. Behind the display cabinet housing the various chocolates, Kilic and company are busily making chocolates in an open kitchen. Kilic makes some sixty varieties. I recommend **New England bark,** dark chocolate with a hint of lemon, studded with dried cranberries and macadamia nuts. The **raspberry creams** are made with fondant and real raspberries; the **florentines** are lacy cookies made with almonds, orange peel, and glacéed cherries, coated with chocolate. Kilic makes two kinds of **truffles:** the round, **chocolate ganache truffle** (quite good; it comes in several flavors) and the **Viennese truffle.** This confection, also called a *Figaro* elsewhere, is square, with layers of dark and milk chocolate blended with hazelnut paste. One of the best candies is the **marzipan ganache,** an intense layering of almond marzipan and rich chocolate cream.

The front of the store is devoted to displays, including a huge selection of novelty items—chocolate computers, toolboxes, telephones, and a selection of attractive boxes. For Valentine's Day, they have the best selection of heart-shaped boxes.

Waldman Candies

441 Harvard Street, Brookline, MA 02146   (617) 566-8086
Mail order: available   Hours: Mon.–Sat. 9:30 A.M.–4:30 P.M.;
closed Sun.

Elaine Cramer represents the third generation to make Waldman Candies. She started in the business when she was a teenager then worked elsewhere as a paralegal for several years. In 1990 she was looking for a change (she had just turned forty, and her parents wanted to retire, so she took over. Now her kids—the fourth generation—help out in the store.

The store's specialty is **dipped fruit,** and they use an excellent quality Australian glacéed fruit. The **apricots** are big, heavy, and almost juicy; dark chocolate is a natural complement to them. The dark-chocolate-dipped **Australian ginger** is truly sophisticated. In season, Cramer also dips **fresh fruit,** and does clusters of smaller fruits such as **cranberries.** There are also **barks** and **dipped nuts.** The **jumbo cashews** are particularly good.

Most of the filled candies are made for Waldman's by outside candymakers. Notable items include **coffee marshmallow,** which has marshmallow's spongy texture with a rich coffee flavor.

The prices are extremely reasonable. In 1995 everything was $10.99 a pound, and Cramer promises that the prices will stay the same as long as her landlord doesn't raise the rent. I've seen this same dipped fruit offered elsewhere at nearly double the price or more. But at Waldman's the company's slogan is "Where high quality and low prices are a tradition."

In addition to the chocolates, Waldman carries a line of no-longer-penny candy (would that be "penny-style" candy?) and colorful sweets that appeal to children. There is also a full line of sugar-free candies—chocolates, chews, and sucking candy.

CAMBRIDGE

The Chocolate Box

1768 Massachusetts Avenue, Cambridge, MA 02140   (617) 868-7575
Mail order: available   Hours: Mon.–Thurs. 8:30 A.M.–10 P.M.;
 Fri., Sat. 8:30 A.M.–11 P.M.; Sun. 11 A.M.–10 P.M.

1375 Massachusetts Avenue, Arlington, MA 02174   (617) 646-7575
Mail order: available   Hours: Mon.–Sat. 10 A.M.–6 P.M.; closed Sun.

Several years ago I was walking down Mass. Ave. in Cambridge when a sign in a store window caught my eye: "Free truffle." Naturally, I entered the store. Then, as now, there was no catch. The Chocolate Box offers a free sample truffle to those who have never had one before—based on the honor system. These are extremely fresh **truffles,** a sublime blend of butter and chocolate that melts in your mouth. There are now over two dozen flavors available. Joe Ballow, who bought the thirteen-year-old business in 1990, added a line of **white chocolate truffles.** Several of the flavors are **fruit** and **nut varieties,** containing chopped apricots, almonds, hazelnuts. I'm a purist when it comes to truffles; I don't really like lots of stuff in them. The three I like best are **bittersweet chocolate, coffee,** and **ginger–white chocolate.** The truffle trend these days is toward overwhelming, golf-ball- or egg-sized renditions; the Chocolate Box's is the more traditional (and manageable) bite-size morsels.

Another favorite of mine is the **tiny turtles:** caramel sandwiched between two pecan halves and coated with dark chocolate. For your own candy making, the store sells plain solid chocolate, including Merckens and Lindt, in small bulk amounts.

The store also makes their own **baked goods.** These include a variety of chocolate-oriented **cakes** and **cookies** that range in quality. The best are the **Sarah Bernhardts** and the **almond Bernhardts.** Sarahs are coconut macaroons covered with a mound of bittersweet chocolate truffle then dipped in chocolate. Almond Bernhardts use an almond macaroon and are excellent—chewy, with a marzipan flavor. There's also a **raspberry almond** version, made with chocolate-raspberry truffle; and if you're feeling less decadent, there's a plain **almond macaroon.** My other favorite cookie is the **ginger-pecan florentine.** It's a thin, crisp cookie with an assertive, sophisticated ginger flavor. The **chocolate chip cookies,** however, are bland.

Raisin scones are available, as well as a variety of creative

muffins, such as **pear-almond** and **mocha chocolate chunk** (I would call this a cupcake, but *muffin* makes it sound healthier and more acceptable for breakfast). The **individual cheesecakes** are also popular. The best is **Southern pecan.**

Sadly, Ballow passed away suddenly in 1995. His wife, Rosemary, is continuing with the business. There are two Chocolate Box locations, both on Mass. Ave., in Cambridge and in Arlington, near the Lexington border. The Cambridge store is also a café, serving coffee and providing half a dozen tables and a relaxed atmosphere—conducive to serious chocolate consumption.

New England Confectionery Co.

254 Massachusetts Avenue, Cambridge, MA 02139   (617) 876-4700
Mail order: not available   Hours: Thurs., Fri. 11 A.M.–1 P.M.;
      closed Sat.–Wed. and July–mid-August

The New England Confectionery Co., also known as Necco, has been in operation for a century and a half. According to Walter Marshall, vice president of logistics and planning. Oliver P. Chase came from England and started the Chase Candy Company in 1847, after inventing a lozenge-cutter candy machine, which was the machine used to make what would later be called Necco Wafers. In 1901 Chase and two other candymakers joined forces to become the New England Confectionery Company, then in South Boston; they moved to the current location in Cambridge in 1927. In 1963 United Industrial Syndicate bought the company.

Necco's most famous candies are **Necco Wafers,** thin discs that still come wrapped in the wax paper packaging they used when I was a kid. I never was crazy about Necco Wafers, but I appreciate the nostalgia factor they offer. And there is the fun factor: Necco Wafers produce sparks when you crack them. Necco also makes thicker mint-flavored sugar wafers called **Canada Mints.**

In recent years, Necco has bought a few other candy companies and expanded their line. They own Stark in Wisconsin, whose local branch, in Watertown, makes **Mary Janes,** peanut butter and molasses chews. Necco is now the only company in the country to make **candy buttons**—those drops of colored candy that come on sheets of paper. They are also the largest producer of **peanut butter kisses** in the world and make 80 percent of the **conversation hearts** (those heart-shaped candies with messages on them that are sold around Valentine's Day) made in the United States.

In chocolates, Necco makes a line of inexpensive **boxed chocolates,** under the brand name **Candy Cupboard;** these can be found at Kmarts and the like. There are three lines: The high-end **V.I.P.** assortment, the mid-level **Candy Cupboard,** and the low-end **Masterpieces.** None of these are great, although there are a few worthwhile flavors in the boxed assortment of the V.I.P. line—notably the **peanut crunch,** the **buttercrunch,** and the **coconut.**

The Candy Cupboard line is available in Necco's retail shop, which is open for a couple of hours twice a week. (You'll need to sign in.) In addition to the boxed chocolates, a full line of the company's candies is available, including ones made by Stark, such as **gummy bears.** You'll also find **Bolster,** a peanut crunch bar similar to a Clark Bar, that has been around for over sixty years. Necco also makes the **Sky Bar** four-in-one candy. In 1994 Necco bought Haviland, so the store also carries Haviland items. Everything in the store is sold at wholesale prices—a pound box of chocolates can be as cheap as $3.

NEWTON

Bari & Gail Chocolatier

1244 Chestnut Street, Newton, MA 02164   (617) 964-5306
Mail order: not available   Hours: not applicable

Bari & Gail's signature item is the **tortoise,** an excellent, attractive, and *huge* turtle-style candy; it's about three inches across. These are made in three styles, with **pecans, almonds,** and **macadamia nuts;** the latter, made with white chocolate, is my favorite. They also make boxes of **tiny tortoises.** The candies are characterized by decorative squiggles across the top in contrasting types of chocolate. Among the other pieces is the very good **chocolate mint cups,** a round of subtly minted dark chocolate with a seasonal decoration on top. There are also delicious (and pricey) half-dipped **Australian glacéed apricots** and half-dipped **cashews.** The **dark chocolate–coated Bavarian pretzels** are yummy.

Bari & Gail Chocolatier is strictly a wholesale operation,

but you can get their upscale chocolates in various candy and gourmet shops around town, including the Ritz Gift Shop in Boston, Barsamian's in Cambridge, and Confetti in Wellesley and Newton. The candies are all handmade, and expensive. Call the factory to find out which stores in your area carry Bari & Gail chocolates.

The Chocolate Dipper. See Boston, page 334.

NORTH

ANDOVER

Chocolate by Design. See Swampscott, page 349.

BEVERLY

Prides Crossing Confections
641 Hale Street, Beverly, MA 01965   (508) 927-2185
Mail order: available   Hours: Mon.–Sat. 9 A.M.–5 P.M.;
    Sun. 10 A.M.–5 P.M.

You're driving along Route 127 in Beverly, nary a store in sight, when all of a sudden, on the western side of the street, a tiny little house promises Prides Crossing Confections. Inside, behind the display case, owner and chocolatier Christopher Flynn may sit, bent over a machine dripping chocolate, preparing fillings to be covered in the stuff.

Flynn makes wonderful chocolates. He's among the best chocolatiers I've visited. "This profession makes people happy," he says, and Prides Crossing Chocolates certainly does its job. The **caramels,** in various forms, are simply great. I like them plain, wrapped in cellophane. The **caramel-pecan turtle** is a classic, loaded with nuts and gooey stuff. **Caramel-almond squares** are a variation on this theme; caramel filling sits between a layer of milk chocolate and a layer of toasted almonds. The **buttercrunch** is also excellent—buttery, not burnt tasting. The **chocolate fudge** and the **penuche fudge** are the best I've tried.

Although I'm not a fan of **jellies,** Flynn's **raspberry jelly** is pretty good. **Chocolate bark** is generally the same in most places, but Flynn makes a few unusual variations, such as **peanut**

butter bark, peanut butter swirled into chocolate. Even the plain **milk chocolate–almond bark** is better than most; it's thinner, and somehow that makes it taste better.

Flynn also owns Scoops (see "Frozen Delights," page 314), the ice-cream place across the street, and a few of the flavors have some of his candy mixed in.

DANVERS

Putnam Pantry
Route 1 North at the intersection of Route 62, Danvers, MA 01923
 (508) 777-1336
Mail order: available   Hours: Sun.–Thurs. 11 A.M.–9:30 P.M.;
 Fri., Sat. 11 A.M.–10 P.M.

The building housing Putnam Pantry has been in owner Galo Putnam Emerson's family since before the American Revolution. It started as a seventeenth-century shack on the property of the adjacent house, which was built in 1648 and is the birthplace of Emerson's ancestor, General Israel Putnam, known for his command, "Don't fire until you see the whites of their eyes."

The building remained a shack until 1948, when Emerson's father started the candy company. The nearby two-lane highway had just become a six-lane highway, and "It seemed like a good idea at the time," Emerson recalls.

Putnam Pantry's candies are simply excellent. They make some three hundred varieties of **creams, caramels, jellies, barks,** and **crunches,** and carry about another three hundred kinds of hard and soft nonchocolate candies. They also make an excellent **fudge.** The **maple-roll fudge,** made with real maple syrup and studded with walnuts, is coated with caramel and studded with more nuts. Wow. Also great is the **maple-caramel nut** candy. This is a finger-shaped maple caramel dipped in chocolate and nuts—a special item. The **peanut butter cups** are available in **milk** and **white chocolate,** which goes very well with peanut butter.

The **peanut butter log** is a gourmet Clark bar: a crunchy peanut butter center coated with chocolate and chopped peanuts. All the **caramels** are good, especially in the **turtle** form, with chewy caramel studded with **cashews, almonds,** or **pecans,** available sandwiched between **milk, dark,** or **white chocolate.**

The chocolates cost between $10 and $13 a pound—

"Too cheap," Emerson says ruefully—and generally are among the better candies I've sampled. Nearly all the ones I tried were delicious, and the variety available is overwhelming.

Over the years, Emerson has expanded the shack on all sides. In 1969 he opened his trademarked **Ice Cream Smorgasbord,** a make-your-own-sundae bar featuring a variety of traditional toppings. The real winner here is the homemade hot **butterscotch sauce.** It's fantastic, redolent of butter, cream, and sugar. The **hot penuche sauce,** made with brown sugar, is also very good. Tables and ice-cream-parlor chairs with heart-shaped wire backs fill the floor, seating over a hundred, and in the summer there are picnic tables outside. Enjoy a sundae, then bring home a box of candy.

GLOUCESTER

Nichols Candies, Inc.

1 Crafts Road (Exit 12 off Route 128), Gloucester, MA 01930
   (508) 283-9850
Mail order: available   Hours: Mon.–Sat. 9 A.M.–8 P.M.;
   Sun. 10 A.M.–6 P.M.

The address for Nichols Candies reads "Gloucester," and this is technically true, but the shop is actually located outside town, off Route 128, with an exit just for them.

The Nichols built their "candy house," as they call it; from the outside it looks like a house. It is perched next to a pond, and the surrounding grounds are pretty. Inside, chocolates cover several tables of varying shapes and sizes. Handwritten signs indicate the types of chocolates to be found on each table, such as **"home-style" (buttercrunch, pecan rolls, meltaways), "hard & chewy," (nougatines, caramels) "soft center" (creams, jellies).** Scales from various eras decorate the tables. Tell one of the staff which candies you want, and they'll put them together in a box for you.

Nichols candies are very good. They make many items found at most chocolatiers—creams, jellies, caramels—but there are some tasty original items too. The **tulip** is a Brazil nut wrapped in caramel and half-dipped in dark chocolate—by far the best use for a Brazil nut I've tasted. The **molasses coconut** is unusual; the assertive flavor of the molasses goes well with sweet coconut. Molasses also flavors the **Creole,** a chewy nougatine.

The **butterscotch chew** is odd, sticky with a hard-to-pinpoint flavor and an artificial aftertaste. Though not exactly my style, the **California** is an intriguing filling reminiscent of fruit cake. It's a green jelly, slightly dense, studded with candied fruit.

The **fudge** here is buttery and very good, and it's used in several pieces, such as the **velvet,** a treat made with a center of vanilla fudge that is coated in dark chocolate and rolled in chopped cashews. Similarly, the **pecan fudge roll** is a finger of chocolate fudge wrapped in caramel and nuts. The **chocolate-nougatine pecan roll** has a center of chewy nougatine with a subtle cocoa flavor.

The **creams** are not remarkable. I've had better elsewhere. Nichols' turtles are called **patties.** They are the coated style; that is, a round of caramel is studded with nuts **(cashews, pecans,** or **almonds)** and immersed in chocolate. The caramel is on the sticky side, but the flavor is good. I loved the **peanut butter meltaway,** a blend of white chocolate and ground peanuts. My favorite item actually has no chocolate: Nichols' **Pop-n-Jays.** Popcorn, almonds, and pecans are covered with an irresistible caramel coating. This is excellent caramel corn—the best I've tasted.

MARBLEHEAD

Chocolate by Design. See Swampscott, page 349.

Stowaway Sweets
154 Atlantic Avenue, Marblehead, MA 01945   (617) 631-0303
Mail order: available   Hours: Mon.–Sat. 9:30 A.M.–5:30 P.M.;
    Sun. noon–5 P.M.

Stowaway Sweets is located on the main street of Marblehead, but away from the main drag, in a converted wrought-iron foundry. The building is beautiful—and large. Owners Alicia and Michael Caniffe have five children, and they live behind the candy display room. You enter the building from the side and step into a wood-floored room with candies beautifully displayed in glass-boxed tables set into wrought-iron frames. These tables were made at the foundry, Alicia says. Candy making takes place down a steep flight of stairs, with a lot of handwork done on marble slabs and fillings cooled in large copper kettles. The chocolate used is Peter's (by Nestlé), very good, and the Caniffes make some 135 different pieces of candy.

There are several traditional pieces, but it is the untraditional ones that make Stowaway Sweets so interesting. **Glover's Grog** is an intriguing blend of raisins, rum, cinnamon, and nutmeg. I especially liked the **ginger penuche,** great penuche spiked with candied ginger. Pass on the **pistachio nougatine** though; everything else I tried was so good, but this one is unpleasantly artificial-tasting. The **mocha-cream meltaway** is soft and buttery, dipped in sugar for a little bit of crunch. I also loved the **praline,** ground buttercrunch folded into chocolate. The more common **turtles** are very good. The **caramel** items here are quite tasty. The basic **chocolate fudge** is rich and very fresh tasting. Although slightly chewy, the **buttercrunch** is tasty, with a terrific thick coating of toasted almonds. The **peanut butter truffle** is an appealing layering of dark and milk chocolate blended with peanut butter, with a slight, tasty saltiness.

ROWLEY

Winfrey's Fudge and Candy

40 Newburyport Turnpike, Rowley, MA 01969   (508) 948-7448
Mail order: available   Hours: Mon.–Sat. 10 A.M.–5 P.M.;
  Sun. noon–5 P.M.
41 Main Street (Route 28), Stoneham, MA 02180   (617) 279-7448
Mail order: available   Hours: Mon., Tues., Sat., Sun. 9:30 A.M.–6 P.M.;
  Wed.–Fri. 9:30 A.M.–9 P.M.

Chris and Stuart Winfrey started their business in Danvers in 1979 making **fudge,** and they offer twenty-five flavors. The best is the more traditional **chocolate walnut fudge,** but I also liked the plain **vanilla. Milk chocolate fudge** is delicious, a cross between fudge and milk chocolate. The seasonal (early summer) **strawberry** uses fresh strawberries from a local farmer. The **penuche** is too mild—I like a more assertive brown-sugar flavor. The **Kahlúa** is slightly grainy, with a very mild coffee flavor. Fun flavors include **Creamsicle,** vanilla with orange, **rum-raisin,** and **Heath Bar.** The company also makes their own **saltwater taffy,** which seems to be a traditional partner for fudge.

The **fudges** are good here, but the candy is actually better. The **caramel** is delicious, especially in items such as the **Brazil nut chew,** a Brazil nut wrapped in caramel and chocolate; **turtles;** and **pecan clams,** pecans covered with a layer of chocolate and caramel. I like the contrasting flavors in the **molasses-coconut chew. Swiss fudge** is a creamy cube of milk chocolate

345

studded with pecan bits. The taste and texture of the **peanut butter parfait** is very nice. The **buttercrunch** is a little soft but has a delicious flavor.

For a nominal fee, you can tour the Rowley facilities every Tuesday or Thursday at 10 A.M.; larger groups can schedule tours by appointment. You'll get a history of candy making and of the company and see the fudge and chocolates being made.

SALEM

Harbor Sweets
85 Leavitt Street, Salem, MA 01970   (508) 745-7648 or
   (800) 243-2115
Mail order: available   Hours: Mon.–Fri. 8:30 A.M.–4:30 P.M.;
   Sat. 9 A.M.–3 P.M.; closed Sun.

After years as a director of marketing for Schraft's, a now-defunct candymaker in Charlestown, Benneville Strohecker decided to test a marketing truism he had always been curious about: "If someone provides the best product, regardless of cost, are there enough people in the world who will perceive the value so it can prosper?" In 1972 Strohecker started developing recipes. His goal: "To make the best candy in the world." His basement hobby turned into Harbor Sweets, a good-size company that brings in $3 million a year.

These candies are not cheap; in fact, Strohecker says they are among the most expensive in the country, weighing in at about $26 a pound. But boy, are they good. The company only makes six different kinds of candy, all of which have a nautical theme. The flagship product, which accounts for half the business, is the **Sweet Sloop,** a sailboat-shaped piece of almond buttercrunch coated with white chocolate; the bottom is dipped in dark chocolate and toasted almonds. The other candies Strohecker makes are the **Marblehead Mint,** a thin round of minted bittersweet chocolate flecked with crystals of peppermint candy and decorated with a ship; the **Sweet Shell,** a scallop of dark chocolate flavored with orange and peppered with crushed orange candy; the **Barque Sarah,** dark chocolate studded with toasted almonds; the **Sand Dollar,** chocolate filled with caramel and a pecan; and the **Harbor Lights,** a raspberry-cranberry-chocolate truffle filling coated with dark chocolate set on a white chocolate base. The latter is my favorite; it has a fantastic truffle filling, sweet and rich, and the fruit flavoring gives this candy a surprise tartness.

In 1994 the company introduced a line of three equestrian-theme pieces. Ovals of dark chocolate filled with their existing centers are decorated with different horses sculpted onto them. The **Dressage Classic** has an almond-buttercrunch center, the **Grande Prix Jumper** has creamy caramel in the middle, and the **Peppermint Pony** is a variation of the Marblehead Mint.

Buttercrunch and **caramel** are also available as **candy bars,** called the **Sandbar** and the **Sand Castle,** available in **milk** or **dark chocolate.**

Harbor Sweets is primarily a mail-order and specialty-store business, but a visit to the factory's small shop is a treat in itself. A tray of Harbor Sweets greets you as you enter, and you are encouraged to sample the wares. The store area overlooks the factory, so you can watch all the candies being prepared by hand. The candies are even wrapped and packaged by hand. When asked why they don't use machines, president Phyllis LeBlanc says, "When you start using machines, they determine the size the nuts must be and how the chocolate should be formed. We prefer to control that. And besides, we like all these people!"

Are Harbor Sweets' candies the best in the world? I can't quite agree with that. But these are extremely good chocolates. Packaged in their attractive red boxes and gold foil wrapping, Harbor Sweets makes a great gift that will definitely be appreciated by anyone with a sweet tooth.

Ye Olde Pepper Candy Co.

122 Derby Street, Salem, MA 01970   (508) 745-2744
Mail order: available   Hours: daily 10 A.M.–5 P.M.

Ye Olde Pepper is perhaps the oldest continuously operating candy company in the United States. It was started by a John Pepper in 1830 and has been through various owners since then. Current owner Bob Burkinshaw's grandparents, who had worked for the company, bought Ye Olde Pepper around 1900. "It's had its ups and downs," Burkinshaw reflects. "Originally it was strictly wholesale, and then they also made shoe polish; once it was almost as big as Schrafts. When my father had it, it was a very profitable business. But then we lost it all in the depression. We started again from scratch and stayed with it."

The candy that launched the company in 1830, still

made today, is called a **Gibralter,** and, according to the wrapper it is "the first candy made commercially in America." The Smithsonian sells these candies as a bit of historical Americana. According to legend, in 1806 a Mrs. Spencer was shipwrecked and ended up in Salem, destitute. She received a donation of sugar and turned it into these palm-sized slabs of firm, chalky candy, flavored with lemon or mint, which she peddled from a horse-drawn wagon (now the company's logo). The business was successful, and in 1830 her son sold it to John Pepper, who went on to develop molasses **Black Jacks,** the first stick candy to be manufactured commercially.

Of the two historic candies, I prefer the Black Jack, with its assertive molasses taste. The Gibralters are more interesting for their story than for their taste. They are very sturdy candies; sugar, Burkinshaw says, lasts forever. In fact, the store has on display a large jar of 160-year-old Gibralters. They're still edible. Until only a few years ago, Burkinshaw would try one every now and then.

The fun part of visiting the store (aside from the obvious fun of buying candy) is watching the candy making. A large, wall-sized window offers a view of the candy kitchen, complete with copper kettles and marble slabs. You can see Burkinshaw, his son Craig, and other cooks stirring bubbling sugar mixtures for fudge, and cooling the fudge on slabs or stretching other mixtures against a heavy hook set in the wall or pouring hard candy mixtures into old-fashioned round or oblong molds.

Ye Olde Pepper is one of the few candymakers around that makes both **hard candies** and **chocolates.** Burkinshaw added chocolates when he took over the business some twenty-five years ago. They also make over two dozen flavors of cream-and-butter-based **fudges.** The best flavors are the traditionals: I liked the very good, creamy **chocolate-walnut** and the **peanut butter;** the more exotic ones, such as **Amaretto swirl** have an unpleasant, artificial aftertaste. Of the chocolate candies, I liked the **honey nougat,** the **butterscotch-caramel,** the **peanut butter cup** made with milk chocolate studded with Rice Krispies, and the very good **buttercrunch.**

Ye Olde Pepper also makes sugar-dusted **hard candies** in a variety of flavors, from **cherry** to **cinnamon,** to old-fashioned **horehound drops.** Burkinshaw prepares the horehound himself, steeping it in water. Horehound drops are soothing to a sore throat, but they are an acquired taste. The factory makes **barley pops** as well. Burkinshaw notes that at one point, so-called barley sugar once actually contained barley, but now the term refers to sugar that has been cooked to an incredibly high heat—hotter than usual for any other candy.

Ye Olde Pepper also sells Richardson's ice cream. There are a few sidewalk tables where you can sit and enjoy the treats.

STONEHAM

Winfrey's Fudge and Candy. See Rowley, page 345.

SWAMPSCOTT

Chocolate by Design

425 Paradise Road, Swampscott, MA 01907   (617) 598-2272
Mail order: available   Hours: Mon.–Sat. 10 A.M.–9 P.M.;
   Sun. noon–6 P.M.

16 Main Street, Andover, MA 01845   (508) 749-9969
Mail order: available
Hours: Mon.–Sat. 9 A.M.–6 P.M.; Sun. noon–5 P.M.

60-A Atlantic Avenue, Marblehead, MA 01945   (617) 631-7758
Mail order: available
Hours: October–June 1, Mon.–Thurs. 9 A.M.–5:30 P.M.;
   Fri., Sat. 9 A.M.–6 P.M.; Sun. 10 A.M.–5 P.M.;
   closed June 2–September

Chocolate by Design has a few specialties. First, as indicated by the name, they will design custom-molded chocolate for anyone. You pay for the molds ($200–$250), and tell them what you want. They also have a collection of literally thousands of molds, so if there is a shape you like, ask for it. The chocolate they use is very good.

Then there are the chocolate pieces themselves. All the candies are made completely by hand here—there are no enrobing machines—and owner Steve feels strongly that this is the way he wants to make chocolate. CBD specializes in fun, gooey candies. All the items are named after the owners' kids, friends, and family. The most popular item is **Katie's Krunch** (named for eldest daughter Katie), buttery toffee wrapped in caramel and dipped in milk or dark chocolate. **Twin Treats** (created when the couple's twins were in utero and anticipated) is an elaborate pair of doubles: a buttercrunch center surrounded by rich dark-chocolate truffle, a milk chocolate base, and dark-chocolate coating. Another truffle, the **Grand Sam,** is rolled in chopped pistachios and topped with a blob of milk chocolate.

Sometimes the actualization doesn't quite live up to the concept. **Nik-Naks** are caramels stirred with puréed Oreos and dipped in milk chocolate; the caramel is good, but you don't really taste the Oreos. There are also **chocolate-covered Oreos,** which on some occasions tasted stale. **Dan's Peanut Butter Fantasy** is a milk-chocolate rectangle filled with peanut butter on one side and caramel on the other; the peanut butter was too, well, peanut-buttery in texture—maybe it should be blended with a little white chocolate or something. Peanut butter *is* blended with white chocolate in the marvelous **Tiger Bark,** which is striped with milk chocolate—one of my favorite items here.

Another temptation is the **Peanut Butter Crunchies,** a delicious peanut butter filling mixed with Rice Krispies and coated in milk chocolate. Rice Krispie treats and caramel are at the center of the **ulTIMit** and **Double D's,** caramel and coconut dipped in milk chocolate then dark chocolate. Caramel appears in many pieces, and it's really good caramel. For my taste there wasn't enough caramel in the **turtle,** although they did have white chocolate on top and dark on the bottom, a combination I like. The **macadamia nut chewy** (caramel studded with macadamia nuts; it also comes in **pecan)** is just wonderful.

Presentation and service are important at Chocolate by Design. They want happy—and frequent—customers. The candies are placed in small wicker platters or baskets and shrink-wrapped.

Chocolate by Design offers birthday parties at their Marblehead store—a true treat for any chocoholic, adult or child. At the parties you get to experience making (and eating) your own chocolates.

SOUTH

BROCKTON

Gowell's Candy Inc.

727 N. Main Street, Brockton, MA 02401   (508) 583-2521
Mail order: available   Hours: Mon.–Sat. 9 A.M.–6 P.M.;
     Sun. 10 A.M.–6 P.M.; closed July

Gowell's makes a variety of very good **chocolates,** and they are also among the few companies to make **hard candies.** A stand near the door offers wrapped hard candies in eighteen flavors, including **ginger, cinnamon, honey horehound,** and **raspberry.** Another table displays boxes of homemade **ribbon candy.** There are a few filled hard candies: **Chicken Bones** are pinky-sized sticks of hard candy filled with chocolate, and **Peach Blossoms** are logs of hard peach candy filled with peanut butter. The **peanut brittle,** made with Spanish peanuts, is excellent—one of the two best I tried.

Peanut-based candies are actually Gowell's strong point, and they make several. I liked the peanut items best here. They roast their own nuts, so the candies have a particularly fresh flavor. **Peanut crunch** is a dense square packed with nuts. **Peanut butter pillows** are flakier and taste like a really good Butterfinger. **Peanut butter logs** are also flaky, but more brittle, with a slight coconut taste.

The **buttercrunch** is decent, with a good texture; the **creams** are nothing special. John Wayne was a fan of their **dark chocolate bark;** he ordered twenty-five pounds at a time during the last five years of his life, when he was a patient at Mass. General. For me, bark is bark—if the chocolate is good, the bark will be good, and Gowell's is good. The **caramel** is good stuff here, especially in the **half-dipped pecan turtles.** The **fudge** is also very good.

EASTON

Hilliard's House of Candy

316 Main Street, North Easton, MA 02356   (508) 238-6231
Mail order: available   Hours: daily 9 A.M.–9 P.M.
Also: "Frozen Delights," page 322.

In 1924 Perley and Jessie Hilliard started a candy company that eventually grew to fourteen stores. After Perley died in 1962, Jessie continued the company for another nineteen years with one of her daughters, Ruth.

Other Hilliards went into other businesses. One, Alan, picked up on some of his father's "tinkerings." Perley had been a carpenter, and he also liked to build machines. He developed some of the equipment he used for tempering chocolate. Alan further developed these machines and made a company out of them, Hilliard's Chocolate Systems, located in West Bridge-water. The company makes half a dozen different machines that are used by over 3,500 small candymakers across the country. In 1985 Alan retired and sold the business to Jim Bourne.

In 1981 Jessie was no longer able to keep the business going, and there were three shops left. The Hilliards wanted to keep the business in the family, and Perley's granddaughter Judy (Alan's daughter) and her husband, Charlie McCarthy, bought the primary store in Easton.

In the ensuing years, the McCarthys built up the business significantly, and added premium ice cream in 1991.

One of the candies I like best here isn't chocolate; it's the **molasses sponge.** This is weirdly appealing stuff: caramel-colored chunks that come in a big bag. When you bite down on a fluffy piece it gets compact. It almost tastes like molasses-flavored hard cotton candy. It's fun to eat because of its changing properties. The best chocolate piece is the **Jazz Square,** salty peanuts layered with caramel.

Hilliard's offers **truffles** in two sizes; they make their own large ones, steeped in alcohol, such as the **Grand Marnier truffle.** The **Irish Creme** is best; its alcohol flavor better complements the chocolate. The **chocolate-dipped Australian ginger** is very sophisticated—candy for grown-ups. I like the **buttercream,** with its fudgelike texture. **Brittles** come in an assortment of flavors, such as buttery **cashew brittle.** Most unusual is the **pecan lace,** essentially pecan brittle. The **pecan logs** are a tasty mix of caramel, nougat, and lots of pecan halves. The **buttercrunch** comes in two varieties. The **dark chocolate** version is broken into large pieces and sold by the box; I prefer the smaller pieces dipped in **milk chocolate.**

HINGHAM

Puopolo Candies
222 North Street, Hingham, MA 02043
(617) 749-6638 or (800) 749-6638
Mail order: available   Hours: Mon.–Sat. 10 A.M.–6 P.M.;
    Sun. noon–5 P.M.

Richard Puopolo made candies with his uncle Fred Levaggi for eighteen years. When his uncle died, Puopolo opened his own shop in Hingham with his wife, Debbie, in 1987.

The Puopolos have a roster of names to drop when they're asked who buys their candies. Michael Keaton orders all his Easter candy here every year, and Harrison Ford wrote them a letter saying that theirs is the best chocolate in the world.

The shop is small and friendly, and it looks like a house from the outside. Notable items include the **Hingham Drumstick,** a large pretzel stick dipped in caramel and rolled in nuts. They are also known for their **square turtles,** a square of caramel and nuts with the bottom dipped in chocolate. Their **Snowballs** are vanilla creams coated in white chocolate and rolled in coconut.

MANSFIELD

Merckens Chocolate
150 Oakland Street, Mansfield, MA 02048
Mail order: not available   Hours: not applicable

While there are hundreds of candymakers; there are only fourteen chocolate manufacturers in the United States; by *chocolate manufacturers* I mean companies that actually produce chocolate, starting from the cocoa bean. Merckens, located in Mansfield, Massachusetts, is one of those fourteen. When you drive through town, the smell of chocolate fills the air.

In 1993 I conducted a chocolate tasting, which I later wrote up in a small publication called *The Chocolate Report.* Six other judges and I tasted some eighty-five different dark, milk, and white chocolates. The tasting was blind, and one of the top raters in each category was made by Merckens. But who is Merckens? Most chocolate lovers have never heard of the company, largely because Merckens supplies candymakers; the company does not market any chocolate under its own name to the public.

One can learn a lot about chocolate by studying Merckens' chocolate works. The chocolate manufacturing process is fascinating and complex. A huge storeroom in the back of the building holds stacks of burlap bags filled with cocoa beans from South America, Indonesia, and Africa. Merckens uses eight to ten different kinds of cocoa beans, and each type is roasted separately. After a quick cleaning, the beans are transported into the main building, where they undergo an initial roasting. The initial, partial roasting is necessary to heat the beans enough so that the shells come off. (The discarded shells are then sent to gardening centers, where they are packaged as mulch; the landscaping around the Merckens plant is mulched with cocoa-bean shells.)

Once the shells are removed, the beans of each variety are roasted some more, then cooled and ground into a liquid state, called *chocolate liquor.* Different blends of chocolate liquor are then mixed with raw materials such as sugar and vanilla to make different varieties of chocolate. Sweetened dark chocolate is composed of chocolate liquor, cocoa butter, sugar, and vanilla; milk chocolate also has dry milk added. White chocolate is just sugar, milk, and cocoa butter, without the chocolate liquor. Merckens makes sixteen different milk chocolates (**Marquis** is the most popular); eleven dark chocolates (**Yucatan** is the most popular); and one white, called **Ivory.** Several different liquors may be combined to make one kind of chocolate. A computer determines the formula for each variety.

Merckens also makes what are called *compound coatings,* which are made with vegetable oil instead of cocoa butter and come in a variety of colors, as well as chocolate-flavored. Compound coatings are popular especially among home candymakers because they are easy to work with (they are also cheaper than real chocolate). Chocolate made with cocoa butter is very temperamental and difficult to *temper,* or melt, in the right way, so that when it hardens is will be crisp and shiny. If you melt the chocolate at too high a temperature, it whitens, or *blooms,* as it cools and then becomes slightly crumbly. This problem never occurs with compound coatings; they always *look* beautiful, and they come in all kinds of colors. But compound coatings generally do not taste very good. Merckens's are better than most, and if you're making chocolates just for decorations, these are worthwhile; otherwise, go with the Yucatan, Marquis, and Ivory.

After the chocolate liquor is mixed with raw materials, it goes through a two-stage refining process. The prerefining churns out blobs of chocolate, which drop onto a conveyor belt and look like piles of mud. This chocolate then gets carried down the belt to the second refiner, a set of machines that have a series of water-cooled metal rollers that keep the chocolate in a solid, as opposed to a liquid, form (chocolate has a low melting point of 92°F). The chocolate is then transported to the conching tanks. *Conching* is the process during which the chocolate is melted to a liquid and stirred as a thick mass, and the amount of time a chocolate is conched determines the mellowness of the flavor. Depending on the kind of chocolate, it may be conched anywhere from thirty minutes to a week.

After conching, the chocolate goes into tanks for standardizing to customer specifications; usually cocoa butter is added at this point to thin out the chocolate. The chocolate then goes through various machines, depending on what is needed to make the final chocolate product. There are machines for making buttons, quarter-sized drops of chocolate, the easiest size for small candy makers, and machines for making ten-pound slabs. Some large companies get their chocolate in liquid form, transported in huge tanks on trucks.

For **cocoa** and **cocoa butter,** which the company also makes, unsweetened chocolate liquor is pressed in a hydraulic press for about twenty minutes. When pressed, all the liquid, in the form of melted cocoa butter, runs out through pipes to a filtering system, then to a storage tank. The press then releases the cocoa, in solid, flat disks, about eighteen inches across; these disks are then ground into cocoa powder.

The Mansfield plant manufactures the special dark **Dutch cocoa** used in Oreo cookies and the chips for Chips Ahoy cookies.

Merckens does not have a factory outlet, but there are a few companies in the area that sell their chocolate. Several candymakers use Merckens, and both Furlong (Norwood, page 356) and The Chocolate Box (Cambridge, page 358) sell Merckens by the pound. The best deal on Merckens is from Jack Smillie Inc., a wholesaler in Woburn (see "Candy Stores," page 369).

NORWOOD

Furlong's Cottage Candies and Ice Cream Co.

1355 Providence Highway (Route 1), Norwood, MA 02062
  (617) 762-4124
Mail order: available   Hours: Mon.–Fri. 9 A.M.–8 P.M.;
  Sat. 10 A.M.–8 P.M.; Sun. noon–8 P.M.

Furlong's has been making candy for over seventy years, and current owners Gail Chelfi and Doris Thrasher, cousins, have been making traditional chocolates here since 1980. The former hairdresser and office manager wanted to go into business for themselves, and they soon found that the candy business was a male-dominated field. "Furlong thought women couldn't handle it. He was nervous because our husbands weren't involved," the owners recall. "But no one else would meet his price." The Shop's business has tripled since the cousins bought it.

As with many of the wonderful candy places in the Boston area, Furlong's candy is made the old-fashioned way. Fillings are made with various sugars and flavorings, melted in copper kettles and stirred and poured into molds by hand. The store specializes in **chocolates,** but also makes **lollipops** and, during the holidays, homemade **candy canes.**

A house specialty is **stemmed cherries;** chocolate-coated maraschino cherries with a filling that is both liquid and creamy —messy, but great for cherry lovers. The **buttercrunch** is among the best I've tasted, close to that of my friend K.C. Turnbull, who makes the best ever. The **pecan patties** (turtles) are oversized and loaded with nuts and very good chewy caramel; they come in **milk** or **dark chocolate.** I highly recommend the **peanut brittle:** it's thin, crunchy, overflowing with Spanish peanuts, and addictive—one of the two best I've tasted. And the hard **butterscotch** is buttery and incredible.

As old-fashioned chocolatiers, Furlong's makes a variety of creams. I am not big on creams; I find them to be overly sweet, with not much flavor. Nevertheless, Furlong's makes classic **creams,** including a **cream mint,** which is quite popular and comes in a few flavors. They use Merckens chocolate, which is very good, and you can buy plain Merckens here, too, for $7.50 per pound.

Furlong's also carries a selection of chocolates made by other companies, including a line of diabetic candies, as well as jelly beans and other hard candies. From April to October they offer ice cream made by Puritan in Jamaica Plain. Try some topped with Furlong's own **hot fudge.**

WEYMOUTH

Melville Olde Tyme Candy and Products

1654 Main Street, Weymouth, MA 02199   (617) 331-2005
Mail order: available   Hours: Mon.–Sat. 9 A.M.–9 P.M.;
   Sun. noon–9 P.M.

Gary Melville's family has deep roots in America. He says that the Melvilles came over on the boat after the Mayflower, and they brought the recipe for barley candy with them. Melville has candymakers on both sides of the family. Since 1980 he has been making barley **Sweetheart Pops,** lollipops made with barley liquid, which gives the candy a unique, subtle flavor. Melville claims that few companies still use actual barley.

Melville makes the **lobster pop** that you can find all over the place as a Boston souvenir. Originally, although it was red, it was not flavored; it was just a sweet lollipop with a unique flavor from the barley sugar. But people expected flavor from something red, so now the lobster pops are cherry flavored.

The current incarnation of the company opened in 1995, and I visited the store a few weeks before it opened. The inside is decorated with various replicas of old-fashioned memorabilia, all for sale, such as cast-iron banks, radios, and old newspapers. A forty-year-old Coke machine sells soda by the bottle. A few flavors of Howard Johnson's ice cream can be had by the cone.

Through a door on the side you can step into a small windowed room and watch the **barley candy** being made. In addition to the lobster pop there are all different shapes—holiday figures, animals, planes, trains, cars. These are all made by hand, using metal molds; the metal used is a trade secret. Some of the molds, Melville says, date back over 170 years.

One machine makes **Little Sweeties,** standard-size lollipops, also barley-based, in a myriad of flavors—**blueberry, green apple, strawberry cheesecake.** Another machine makes **barley pieces,** tiny rounds that also come in several flavors. The molded **barley pops** are the most fun. The shop makes a few other candies, including **peanut brittle** and **fudge.**

357

And is Gary related to Herman? "Could be," Melville smiles. "Melville's not a very common name."

WEST

ARLINGTON

The Chocolate Box. See Cambridge, page 338.

BOLTON

Hebert Candies. See Shrewsbury, page 361.

CHELMSFORD

Mrs. Nelson's Candy House

292 Chelmsford Street, Chelmsford, MA 01824   (508) 256-4061
Mail order: available   Hours: winter, Mon.–Sat. 9 A.M.–8 P.M.;
  Sun. 10 A.M.–4 P.M.; summer, Tues.–Fri. 10 A.M.–5 P.M.;
  Sat.–Mon. 10 A.M.–4 P.M.

Mrs. Nelson's was started by "Grandma" Nelson in 1920 and moved to Chelmsford in 1954; it is popularly referred to as the "Red House in Chelmsford." When Arthur Mapes bought the place in 1984 he carried with him the recipe for Bailey's hot fudge—the specialty of the now-closed and much-missed Bailey's of Boston—where he started as a candymaker and left as a vice president.

The shop is a good-sized space with tables laden with packaged candies on display, as well as cases of candies to buy by the piece. A few years ago Mapes developed **yogurt bark** as a summer item; it proved to be so popular that he now offers it year round. The yogurt barks are colorful fruit-flavored barks, such as pink **strawberry,** yellow **lemon, cranberry** (pink studded with bits of dried cranberries), and **orange.** I found them more intriguing than tasty; I prefer Mapes's other lighter line, **Ting-a-lings.** These are made with white chocolate mixed with crushed hard candies. They are very pretty candies, with a pleasing contrast in textures. When I visited, the Ting-a-lings came in four flavors: **clove,** which is spicy and weird-tasting; **orange,** which tastes like a crunchy Creamsicle; refreshing **lemon,** and minty **spearmint.**

The **raspberry jelly** is very good—Mapes uses real fruit. I would prefer it without the chocolate, but it has a very good flavor. The **raspberry creme** is interesting; it is actually black raspberry, and tastes like black raspberry ice cream. The **almond butter toffee** is excellent. I like the **coffee toffee,** which is more of a coffee-flavored caramel. **Molasses Smack** is a molasses-flavored caramel, also very good. Mrs. Nelson's is one of the few places that offers homemade **truffles,** and these are delicate and creamy, made with milk chocolate. The **mint soufflé** is one of the better mint creations I've tried. It is essentially a mint truffle, a blend of milk chocolate and dark chocolate with cream.

A Mrs. Nelson's tradition is the **corn cake and Old Fashioned;** Mapes doesn't know the source of the combination, but this item is much in demand. A popcorn ball shaped into a flat thick disk is packaged with an old-fashioned chocolate drop, which is a vanilla creme. Mapes explained that people eat this by smooshing the chocolate on top of the popcorn cake and then taking a bite. Interesting, different, and not particularly good. I like the seasonal (June–July) **coconut strawberry,** a citrus-coconut confection colored and shaped like a strawberry.

The store offers several **fudges.** The best is the **chocolate walnut fudge** and **maple fudge,** made with real maple syrup, and the slightly salty **peanut butter fudge** is also very good.

CONCORD

Mrs. London's Confections

50 Beharrell Street, Concord, MA 01742   (508) 371-3074
Mail order: available
Hours: September–May, Mon.–Fri. 10 A.M.–5 P.M.; closed Sat., Sun.;
    June–August, Mon.–Thurs. 10 A.M.–4 P.M.; closed Fri.–Sun.

Buttercrunch is probably my all-time favorite kind of candy. My friend K. C. Turnbull makes a homemade version (as an annual holiday gift), and I used hers as a standard of comparison when trying others for this book. The buttercrunch at Mrs. London's Confections measured up.

Berta London started her business in a Lexington church kitchen before setting up a more permanent operation in the space she now shares with Carolyn's Pecans (see page 366). The refrigerators in her small commercial kitchen are filled with pound cases of butter—the key ingredient to good buttercrunch —and boxes of imported chocolate line the walls.

London's "confections" consist of five flavors of **buttercrunch** (she is in the process of developing other flavors). Each kind is great and appeals to slightly different tastes. The candy has a perfect texture—not too hard or brittle, yet crunchy with a slight give. **English Toffee Crunch** is topped with a blend of milk and dark chocolate and sprinkled with walnuts. Frangelico flavors the **Hazelnut Lover's Crunch,** a buttercrunch coated with bittersweet chocolate. The **Milk Chocolate Peanut Crunch** has peanuts in the toffee center, and has a fun, less fancy feel to it. My favorite is **White Chocolate Macadamia Crunch,** probably because the toffee center is double thick. The newest flavor, my second favorite, is **Coffee Lover's Crunch.** Kahlúa flavors the toffee, which is coated with a blend of milk and dark chocolates stirred with ground espresso. The candy is then dusted with chopped espresso beans, cocoa, and chocolate sprinkles. Fabulous.

Mrs. London's wholesales and sells a lot of retail candy by mail. It's worth visiting the small store, if only to sample each flavor of buttercrunch. But beware: this toffee is truly addictive.

Priscilla Candy Shop

19 Walden Street, Concord, MA 01742   (508) 371-0585
Mail order: available   Hours: Mon.–Fri. 9:30 A.M.–5:30 P.M.;
   Sat. 9:30 A.M.–5 P.M.; closed Sun.

4 Main Street, Gardner, MA 01440   (508) 632-7148
Mail order: available   Hours: Mon.–Sat. 9 A.M.–5:30 P.M.;
   Sun. 10 A.M.–4 P.M.; June–August, closed Sun.

Priscilla's chocolates are quite good, and the **creams,** which use fresh fruit, are the best I've tasted. The **raspberry creams** taste like raspberries, and the **peach cream** is light and peachy—great with dark chocolate. The turtles here are called **croquettes,** and they're very good. The **toasted coconut brownie** is delicious; it's basically just milk chocolate laced with toasted coconut. Most places don't toast the coconut, but Priscilla does, and it adds a nice crunch to the chocolate. I also love the **peanut butter cup,** which has ground peanuts folded into milk chocolate. Another special item is the **pecan meltaway,** a very smooth blend of white and milk chocolates blended with ground pecans. The **butter-**

crunch is good, not quite perfect in texture, but with an appealing saltiness from the toasted almonds that stud the chocolate.

The **fudge** is good, although grainy. Manager and owner Maureen Gallant says there's an ongoing debate on whether fudge should be grainy or creamy. I liked the **penuche,** which has a strong molasses flavor, and the very peanut-buttery **peanut butter fudge.** During the holidays, Priscilla makes their own **candy canes,** which is a real family endeavor. "We need eight people to do it," she says, "and it takes the whole Thanksgiving weekend." They make over three thousand fifteen-inch canes for the holidays.

Both stores carry a selection of hard candies and sweets such as jelly beans, arranged in gift packaging. If you call ahead, you can arrange for tours of the Gardner factory.

FRAMINGHAM

Hebert Candies. See Shrewsbury, below.

GARDENER

Priscilla Candy Shop. See Concord, page 360.

NATICK

The Chocolate Dipper. See Boston, page 334.

SHREWSBURY

Hebert Candies
575 Hartford Turnpike (Route 20), Shrewsbury, MA 01545
   (800) 642-7702
Mail order: available   Hours: daily 9 A.M.–8 P.M.

Hamilton Plaza, 680 Worcester Road (Route 9 East),
   Framingham, MA 01701   (508) 872-3381
Mail order: available   Hours: Mon.–Sat. 10 A.M.–6 P.M.;
   Sun. noon–5 P.M.

Sugar Road (Exit 27 off Route 495), Bolton, MA 01740
   (508) 779-6586
Mail order: available   Hours: Mon.–Sat. 10 A.M.–6 P.M.;
   Sun. noon–5 P.M.

Hebert Candies has been in business, and operated by the Hebert family, since 1917. Frederick Hebert first established his candy shop in Worcester and then opened several stores before the sugar shortage during World War II forced him to scale back. In 1946 Hebert moved to what the company calls "The Candy Mansion" in Shrewsbury, an actual residence that was built in 1917. This building became the company headquarters and production facility. Over the past fifty years, the business has grown, and there are now eight stores in New England. The current owners are Frederick's grandchildren, siblings Ronald, Richard, Fred, and Diane, who have been working here since they "were old enough to hold a broom."

Hebert is a major candy-making operation—the largest of all the family-owned businesses I visited. During an eight-hour shift, they produce a thousand pounds of candy.

In 1990 the Heberts built an enormous addition to the mansion, expressly for making candy bars. When they started making candy bars, it was primarily for fund-raising purposes, and the wrappers had that slightly dated look to them. In 1994 the company decided to compete actively and nationally with upscale imported chocolate bars, such as the Lindt varieties. They came out with a line of **filled chocolate bars** with striking packaging. The dozen flavors include a **liquid raspberry,** which is good, but a little sweet and sugary; **peanut butter truffle,** which is delicious; and **hazelnut truffle,** which is good. The elaborate candy machines can churn out sixty thousand candy bars during an eight-hour shift.

Although there are several Hebert shops in the area, it's worth making a trip to the main facility. The building itself is beautiful; it really was a mansion and has gorgeous wood floors and paneling. At the retail area the candies are all prepackaged; that's one drawback of a larger company. (Most other places let you pick and choose individual candies.) The packages are all temptingly displayed on glass-topped tables with custom-made cast-iron bases. Along one wall is a window where you can see some of the candy making going on. Behind the main display room is a make-your-own-sundae bar, and behind that is a holiday room, a room filled with baskets, tins, and boxes of candies themed to the current holiday.

The candies themselves are good but not great, although the chocolate used is very good, Hebert's makes its own blend from three different manufacturers. Early on, they became known for their white-chocolate selections, and every candy type includes a white-chocolate version. The chocolates are prepackaged in **half-** and **one-pound boxes,** with themes. The most popular is the **Mansion Fancy,** a selection of each type of candy. Then there are **cremes** and **chews,** each available in **milk, dark,** or **white** packages, or **Trios,** a mix of all three.

The **caramel** pieces are pretty good, although I wanted more caramel in the **nut patties** (a.k.a. turtles). The **Geneva** is popular; it's simply a thick square of milk or white chocolate. The best offering is the **hazelnut meltaway,** which has a surprising, yet appealing saltiness. Also good is the **Coconut Dainty.**

Sold separately, in bags, is a yummy, buttery **peanut brittle.** The peanut taste is not that dominant, but the brittle itself is very good, almost like buttercrunch. I liked it better than the **buttercrunch** itself, which is too brittle. The **fudge** is also good. Other items include **chocolate-covered pretzels, animal crackers,** and **crackers.**

The Candy Mansion sponsors various events throughout the year. In October they create a haunted mansion, where, for a fee, kids can trick-or-treat through different "haunted" rooms. In the spring they have an open house and give tours of the factory.

The Framingham store is situated in a shopping center and sells just the candies. The Bolton store is a house (smaller than the Mansion), and also has a tempting ice-cream sundae bar.

❖ N U T S ❖

BOSTON

BOSTON

Gourmet Nuts
720 Atlantic Avenue, Boston, MA 02110   (617) 737-1915
Mail order: available   Hours: Mon.–Fri. 7 A.M.–8 P.M.;
    closed Sat., Sun.

32 Mt. Auburn Street, Watertown, MA 02172   (617) 923-2280
Mail order: available   Hours: winter, daily 10 A.M.–7 P.M.;
    summer, Thurs.–Sat. 10 A.M.–7 P.M., closed Sun.–Wed.

Avo Bedrossian is a third-generation nut roaster. His grandfather started a store in his native Lebanon, and Bedrossian continued in the business there. He moved to the States in 1981 and spent time in other businesses and learning English before opening Gourmet Nuts in Watertown in 1989.

The store offers all kinds of nuts roasted on the premises. *Chor chamich* is their version of trail mix, a toss of pistachios, peanut brittle, sesame brittle, raisins, chickpeas, sunflower seeds, dates, and dried apricots.

They also make their own **baklava,** which has a strong honey flavor.

METROPOLITAN BOSTON

CAMBRIDGE

Squirrel Brand Company
17 Boardman Street, Cambridge, MA 02139   (617) 547-1481
Mail order: available   Hours: Mon.–Fri. 8 A.M.–4 P.M.;
   closed Sat., Sun.

Squirrel Brand has been roasting peanuts since 1888. The company started sometime before that in Boston, that year, so the story goes. Three carpenters who had been engaged to do work for the company bought it. Eventually, one of them, Perley Gerrish, took it over. He moved the business to Cambridge, home of many candy factories, first to Main Street and then, in 1917, to the current location. The company added a line of **candies,** including the **chocolate** and **vanilla nut caramels,** which Squirrel still makes today. In 1928 Squirrel incorporated—and trademarked the name *Squirrel.* No other company can use the word for any nut, candy, or fruit product.

Today Squirrel is headed by Perley's son Hollis, who is now in his eighties. The company makes a handful of products, which you can find in supermarkets and candy stores. At the retail outlet they sell **peanuts** and a few chewy candies. The **saltwater taffy** comes in a myraid of colors and artificial-tasting flavors. I never was a fan of the stuff, but the kids like the pink, blue, and green colors. The item I like best is the **Zippers,** tiny squares of peanut-infused caramels. The trademark **nut caramels,** popularly known as Squirrels, are big and hard—the kind of caramels that lock your teeth together.

The packaging for all Squirrel's products looks as if it hasn't changed in eighty years and is oddly appealing.

Superior Nut Co.

225 Monsignor O'Brien Highway, Cambridge, MA 02141
   (617) 876-3808
Mail order: not available   Hours: Mon.–Fri. 9 A.M.–4 P.M.;
   closed Sat., Sun.

Superior Nut Company has been in business since 1933 and at their current location since 1979. It is owned by the reclusive Harry Hintlian (I was denied an interview), and members of his family are involved with various other nut businesses around town.

Superior is primarily a wholesale nut-roasting company, but they have a small retail office, which feels like an office. You can smell the peanuts roasting as you pull into the parking lot. The receptionist sits at her desk, and the nuts are displayed on bookshelves. You pay, in cash, at the desk.

The nuts are good, and quite inexpensive. The **pignoli** were $6 per pound here; elsewhere they were $10 to $14. There are raw and roasted **almonds, pecans, cashews, walnuts, blanched filberts,** a.k.a. **hazelnuts** (a plus, since it's always a pain to remove the skins from these nuts), shelled and unshelled **pistachios, macadamias,** and lots of **peanuts.** Superior makes their own all-natural **peanut butter,** as well as a **peanut butter topping** used by many ice creameries.

In addition to plain nuts, which are sold by the bag, Superior makes various **salted** and **honey-roasted nuts.** The **honey-roasted cashews** are very good. Their **butter-toffee peanuts** are individual nuts in a crunchy coating. **Peanut crunch** and **cashew crunch** are sold packaged or canned and are precut into even squares. These are like peanut brittle, but densely packed with nuts. You can also buy an assortment of **dried fruit,** such as **papaya, banana chips,** and **raisins.**

WEST

BELMONT

Mixed Nuts

203 Belmont Street, Belmont, MA 02178
   (617) 489-3022 or (800) 466-3022
Mail order: available   Hours: Mon.–Sat. 10 A.M.–7 P.M.; closed Sun.

Souren Etyemezian started Mixed Nuts in 1990, modeling it after similar nut shops in his native Jordan. He gets almost all his nuts raw and roasts them on the premises. The prices aren't cheap, but the nuts are very good. Most nuts, such as **pecans, almonds,** and **hazelnuts,** come either **salted** or **unsalted. Peanuts** come roasted several ways: **dry-roasted, oil-roasted, salted, unsalted,** honey-roasted (not done by Mixed Nuts, but they're popular), **sesame-roasted** (the peanuts are dipped in a slightly salty sesame-seed coating), and *Cri-Cri* (a crunchy flour coating). There are **roasted chickpeas,** including a spicy version with a strong after-kick, and several **roasted seeds,** including **watermelon, squash, sunflower,** and **long sunflower.** Etyemezian is happy to offer tastes of any nuts that intrigue you; I recommend trying a **mixed nut sampler,** which includes some of every kind of nut the store has. Mixed Nuts also carries several dried fruits and designs fruit-and-nut gift baskets. They recently started offering **chocolate nut clusters,** their nuts covered with milk, dark, or white chocolate, and **chocolate-dipped dried fruits. Sugarfree** chocolate versions are also available.

CONCORD

Carolyn's Pecans

50 Beharrell Street, Concord, MA 01742   (508) 369-2940
Mail order: available
Hours: September–May, Mon.–Fri. 10 A.M.–5 P.M., closed Sat., Sun.;
   June–August, Mon.–Thurs. 10 A.M.–4 P.M., closed Fri.–Sun.

Carolyn Harby Schaefer makes just one product, but with variations: incredible **spiced pecans.** Her pecans are an appealing mix of sweet and salty, perfectly crisp, and a bag of them disappears in seconds. She first made a batch, inspired by a Chinese recipe, for a catering client in 1984. He liked them so much that he ordered them as corporate gifts, and Schaefer has been making the nuts ever since. A few years ago she added **milk- and dark-**

chocolate dipped spiced pecans to her line, using delicious Merckens chocolate (see "Candymakers," page 353). She shares a kitchen with Mrs. London's Confections in a building located on a back street in West Concord. The nuts are available there (with free samples), in shops around Boston, such as Barsamian's and Duck Soup, and by mail.

WATERTOWN

Gourmet Nuts. See Boston, page 363.

Note: For additional sources for nuts, see "Going Organic." Some produce stores also carry a good selection; see "Earthly Delights."

❖ CANDY STORES ❖
BOSTON

BOSTON

Dairy Fresh Candies
57 Salem Street, Boston, MA 02113   (617) 742-2639
Mail order: available
Hours: Mon.–Thurs. 9 A.M.–6 P.M., Fri. 9 A.M.–7 P.M.,
   Sat. 8 A.M.–7 P.M., closed Sun.; Oct.–May, daily 10 A.M.–5 P.M.

Owner Joseph Matarra started selling candy in the North End from a pushcart, and in 1957 he opened this store. He has since doubled the space to two rooms packed from floor to ceiling with every manner of prepackaged and bulk candy imaginable. The entrance room displays **novelty candies** reflecting upcoming holidays—chocolate bunnies with pastel jelly beans, red foil-wrapped hearts, candy corn. Across from these are **nuts** and **dried fruit** in bulk, including harder-to-find items such as papaya and melon.

Glass cases in the second room display quality **chocolates**—almond bark, buttercreams, truffles, and such. None are homemade, but several come from small Massachusetts companies, such as the oversized peanut butter cups. You can buy premium chocolate in bulk amounts, in white, milk, and dark chocolate from Nestlé's Peters, Valrhona, Ghirardelli, Callebaut, and Lindt.

In addition to candy, the store sells high-end specialty items, many with an Italian theme, such as olive oils and vinegars, and imported cookies and panettone, a sweet yeast bread studded with candied fruit. The prices overall are very good, and discounts are available for larger purchases.

METROPOLITAN BOSTON

CAMBRIDGE

Kendall Confectionery Co. Inc.

27 Spinelli Place, Cambridge, MA 02140   (617) 661-6760
Mail order: not available   Hours: Mon.–Fri. 8 A.M.–4:30 P.M.;
    closed Sat., Sun.

Kendall, in business since 1921, is primarily a wholesaler, supplying stores around town with every manner of candy imaginable, from boxes of Hershey bars to cartons of gum. They have a front room that is open to the public, and it's a good source for significantly discounted **imported chocolates,** such as Lindt and Perugina. The display room is small, and the items on display are the fancier ones, but if you know what you want, the sales staff will be happy to go to their huge storeroom and get it. You can stock up on Juicy Fruit candy or Mars bars. You do have to buy small bulk amounts, but the prices are less than elsewhere.

NORTH

REVERE

Candyland

149-A Squire Road (Route 1A), Revere, MA 02151   (617) 289-0550
Mail order: not available   Hours: daily 10 A.M.–6 P.M.

Chris Drucus has been selling bulk candies here since 1981. Candyland is located in a small shack-like building on Route 1A. The candy here is penny-style, bagged in bulk—usually by the half-pound. There are also nuts, although the prices aren't as low as for the candies. The setup here is similar to that of Pearl's Candy & Nuts in Framingham.

WOBURN

Jack Smillie Inc.

15 Linscott Road, Woburn, MA 01801   (617) 935-1000
Mail order: not available   Hours: Mon.–Fri. 8:30 A.M.–4:30 P.M.;
    closed Sat., Sun.

Jack Smillie started this wholesale distribution company in the 1930s in Cambridge; his sons moved it to Woburn in 1979. The Smillies distribute primarily to gourmet stores and carry over six thousand items. They are the best source for individuals who want to buy chocolate. They carry Merckens chocolate, and you can buy it in small bulk amounts (the minimum is a ten-pound block) for very good prices. Prices change, but in 1995 a ten-pound block was $18.50; I've seen the chocolate by itself selling elsewhere for close to that amount *per pound*. They also carry a few other brands, including Nestlé's Peters, Van Leer, and Lindt.

The business is not really set up for retail. You can just walk in and buy, but it's best to call in advance to make sure Smillie has what you want.

WEST

FRAMINGHAM

Pearl's Candy & Nuts

371 Worcester Road (Route 9), Framingham, MA 01701
    (508) 875-7772
Mail order: not available   Hours: Mon.–Fri. 9:30 A.M.–5:30 P.M.;
    Sat. 9 A.M.–4 P.M.; Sun. noon–5 P.M.

Pearl's has an impressive selection of bulk candies. Much of the candy is penny-style, from Boston baked beans candies and fire balls to chocolate-covered almonds and Hershey kisses. Everything is prebagged, usually in half- or one-pound amounts. The prices are very good here for the candies; less so for the nuts, although there is a good selection. You can buy chocolate candies by the piece, although they aren't locally made. For homemade chocolates you'd do better to seek out local chocolatiers.

Pearl's has the largest selection of sugar-free candies around—some three dozen flavors of sucking candies. You can also get Jelly Belly jelly beans in a variety of fun flavors. There are also novelty candies, such as candy necklaces and good ole Pez.

THE BESTS OF THE BEST

Best chocolatier: **Prides Crossing Confections** and **Stowaway Sweets**
Best buttercrunch: **Mrs. London's Confections**
Second best buttercrunch: **Furlong's Cottage Candies** and **Prides Crossing Confections**
Best caramels: **Prides Crossing Confections**
Best turtles: **Prides Crossing Confections**
Best mint-chocolate candy: **Mrs. Nelson's**
Best creams: **Priscilla Candy Shop**
Most unusual assortment: **Stowaway Sweets**
Best peanut brittle: **Gowell's Candy** and **Furlong's Cottage Candies**
Best butterscotch: **Philips Candy House**
Best fudge: **Prides Crossing Confections**
Best maple candies: **Putnam Pantry**
Best truffles: **The Chocolate Box**
Best molded chocolates: **Chocolate by Design**

❖ C H A P T E R   T E N ❖

AN EPICUREAN
AGENDA

*Shops offering a world of gourmet foods—condiments, pâtés, oils,
preserves—plus producers of homemade cheese*

W HAT defines gourmet? Is it price? Is it quality? Is it
limited availability? If you go into a so-called gourmet
shop, these all seem to be accurate descriptions. But
what sets gourmet foods apart from regular supermarket items is
the care that is taken in preparing them. The cheesemaker
watches what the goats eat to ensure the best-tasting milk for
cheese; the fish farmer raises the trout carefully so that the
smoked trout will be moist and flavorful; the cook uses lots of
butter and fresh lemons so the lemon curd will taste heavenly. To
be gourmet, it has to taste good.

In a way, gourmet shops are sort of pan-ethnic markets
in that they usually offer goods from around the world. The
foods at these shops often come with high price tags—importing
preserves from England and cookies from Sweden can be expensive. But a food doesn't have to be imported to fit the gourmet
bill. And it doesn't have to be expensive, although invariably such
items are, because they tend to be made in small batches, using

more expensive ingredients. Read the ingredient list on a gourmet salsa and compare it to a supermarket brand, and you may understand the price difference.

The gourmet shops in the Boston area are diverse. Some are large, some small. Some offer prepared food such as salads and sandwiches in addition to the jarred and boxed goods. All offer prepared foods and ingredients to delight the epicurean consumer.

There are four businesses in the area that make fresh cheeses, and I've listed these separately at the end of the chapter.

* Described in another chapter.

GOURMET MARKETS

Barsamian's	Cambridge
*Berman's	Lexington
J. Bildner & Sons	Brookline
Boyajian Boston	Newton
The Butler's Pantry	Andover
*Cambridge Country Store	Cambridge
*Capone Foods	Somerville
Cardullo's Gourmet Shoppe	Cambridge
The Cheese Shop/The Concord Shop	Concord
*V. Cirace & Son	Boston
*Concord Spice & Grain	Concord
*Cremaldi's	Cambridge
*John Dewar & Co.	Newton
Duck Soup	Sudbury
*The Elegant Farmer	Chelmsford
Formaggio Kitchen	Cambridge
*Fruit Center Marketplace	Hingham, Milton
*Garden of Eden	Boston
*Homsy's	Westwood
*Idylwilde Farm	Acton
Le Saucier	Boston
Marty's	Allston, Newton
*Rustica	Belmont
*Savenor's	Boston
Salumeria Toscana	Boston
*The Syrian Grocery	Boston
*Truffles	Marblehead
Wasik's Cheese Shop	Wellesley
*The Wine and Cheese Cask	Somerville
*The Winecellar of Silene	Waltham

CHEESEMAKERS

Gigi's Mozzarella House	Everett
Giuseppe Cheese	Medford
Ipswich Goat Cheese	Ipswich
Purity Cheese	Boston

❖ G O U R M E T ❖ M A R K E T S

BOSTON

BOSTON

V. Cirace & Son. See "Libations," page 488.

Garden of Eden. See "Goodies to Go," page 195.

Le Saucier
Faneuil Hall Marketplace, Boston, MA 02109   (617) 227-9649
Mail order: available   Hours: Mon.–Sat. 10 A.M.–9 P.M.;
     Sun. noon–6 P.M.

Lisa Lammé started this unique store after she was laid off from the Zayre Corporation. Her father had been a caterer who specialized in large functions, and she knew she wanted to do something in the food business. She liked to cook, and, she says, "People would rave about the food. I always said, 'It's not the food. It's the sauce.' " Friends started to ask her to provide them with sauces that she had discovered, and she turned that interest into a mail-order business specializing in sauces. She opened her retail shop in 1990.

The shop is small and is located along one of the outside stretches of Faneuil Hall. There are over five hundred items here, from thirty-five countries. Salsas are a big seller, and that's what stands out. There's even a "shelf of death" for true chili heads. The featured salsas include Liquid Summer, a mild yet spicy sauce made from Datil peppers; and Doc's Special Hellfire, made with ultrahot Scotch Bonnet peppers (there is also a powder made from the same peppers). Condiments include an unusual Beyond Horseradish Jelly and Honeycup Mustard. There are also some oils and dry rubs, as well as a handful of New England-themed items. Lammé is very knowledgeable, and if you don't see the sauce you want in her store, she can likely order it for you.

Salumeria Toscana

272 Hanover Street, North End, Boston, MA 02113   (617) 720-4243
Mail order: available   Hours: daily 10 A.M.–10 P.M.

Salumeria Toscana is a beautiful store. It is also an expensive store: this is not the place for bargains, but it is the place for primarily Italian gourmet items. A deli case is packed with tempting meats and cheeses. All kinds of cured meats and salamis hang from the ceiling over the deli area. Across the store are wooden shelves displaying items such as Italian honey, olive oils, and vinegars. In the back a freezer case holds fresh-frozen pastas. The floor is decorated with an appealing black-and-white tile.

Salumeria is Italian for "sandwich shop," but Salumeria Toscana generally does not make sandwiches. They just supply the goods—meats, cheeses, breads—for making your own. Sometimes though, if you ask nicely, they will put together a sandwich for you.

Savenor's. See "Where's the Beef?" page 127.

The Syrian Grocery. See "The World in a Jar," page 426.

ALLSTON

Marty's

193 Harvard Avenue, Allston, MA 02134   (617) 782-3250
Mail order: available   Hours: Mon.–Sat. 9 A.M.–11 P.M.; closed Sun.
675 Washington Street, Newton, MA 02160   (617) 332-1230
Mail order: available   Hours: Mon.–Sat. 9 A.M.–11 P.M.; closed Sun.
Also: "Libations," page 490.

Much of the space at Marty's is devoted to wine and other alcohol, leading one to think, at first glance, that this is only a liquor store. And it is a very good liquor store, with helpful staff and great prices. But Marty's is much more. It is also a gourmet shop, with an extensive selection and nearly unbeatable prices. Hard-to-find items abound here. The aisles are filled with chestnut purée, chipotle peppers, Mexican Ibarra chocolate, tamarind paste, and more hot sauces than you knew existed. The reasonable prices are as striking as the choices. This is the place to check first when you're looking for gourmet items.

In the refrigerated section are a number of imported and domestic cheeses. Behind this is the oil and vinegar bar, a row of some two dozen olive oils and vinegars available for tasting. Choose a bottle that interests you, and someone behind the counter will give you a taste with a slice of French bread.

Next to the cheese is a deli counter offering a few dozen **salads,** some made on the premises, some made elsewhere. **Indian potato curry** is particularly good, as is the **olive antipasto,** made with six to twelve different kinds of olives. Fourteen kinds of olives are also available separately.

Marty's makes a variety of excellent **sandwiches,** including the **Parma Sub,** made with prosciutto, fresh mozzarella, roasted peppers, and extra-virgin olive oil; **chicken, chili, and cheddar,** with hot chicken breast; and **stuffed grape leaves on pita.**

The gourmet offerings here are really overwhelming. Coffee comes in the usual assortment of flavors, as well as raw, unroasted beans; Marty's sells coffee roasters and green coffee beans if you want to roast your own. The store sells over twelve hundred pounds of coffee every month.

There are all kinds of dried chilies—ancho, poblano, habañero, to name a few—and a wide selection of hard-to-find spices, which Marty's packages. The gourmet foods spill over into a small section of equipment and cookbooks, all of which are sold for 20 percent off the cover price.

METROPOLITAN BOSTON

BROOKLINE

J. Bildner & Sons

1317 Beacon Street, Brookline, MA 02146   (617) 566-6639
Mail order: available   Hours: daily 6:30 A.M.–midnight

In the mid-1980s J. Bildner's stores were popping up all over Boston faster than Starbucks. The theme seemed to be quality take-out foods and gourmet items as well as all the regular supermarket items, such as paper towels and canned soup. I remember being annoyed by the salads being priced by the quarter-pound.

But the stores grew too quickly and disappeared almost as quickly as they came. But, I discovered, they didn't disappear; they just regrouped, and the store still in operation has been running for a while.

Jim Bildner grew up in New Jersey, and his family owned the King supermarket chain there. Before opening his own establishment at the end of 1984, he was the vice president of operations for Store 24. Bildner says he looked at New York City's Balducci's as a model for his stores. When he opened, his goal, as he writes in the introduction to his cookbook (*J. Bildner & Sons Cookbook,* which, by the way, is very good; I especially recommend the recipes for Cocoa Muffins and Health Salad), was "to create a new kind of urban grocery store . . . that would combine convenience and a pleasing environment with premium groceries and produce . . . and an unusually broad selection of prepared take-out foods."

Bildner offers quite a broad selection of **prepared salads** and **entrées** (with prices listed by the full pound these days). You can taste most prepared salads before you buy. The service is generally helpful—although I've occasionally encountered cranky personnel. Popular and particularly good items include **Thai beef, Oriental green beans** flecked with sesame seeds, and **Asian cucumber salad**—a crisp, unusual side dish made with rice vinegar. Basic items such as **chicken salad** and **tuna salad** tend to be popular, but I wasn't impressed with these versions. The more unusual offerings tasted better. There are several potato preparations, and all I tasted were good, especially the lemony **Dijon potato salad.**

The **sandwiches** are very good; there are several set combinations, but the staff is accommodating, and you can create your own combinations, served on your choice from among several types of bread. The **Chef's Favorite** is made with *pâté de campagne* on pumpernickel, highlighted with Pommery mustard. Roast lamb and hummus, rolled in pita, go into the **Mediterranean.** The **No-Name** is a turkey salad made with cashews and grapes.

The baked goods sold here are not made by Bildner, although some muffins, from a mix, are made at the store. The desserts come from area bakeries.

Bildner is best for the take-out items, and for hard-to-find gourmet items. I wouldn't go here for one-stop shopping, though; items such as milk and soap cost significantly more here than at any supermarket.

CAMBRIDGE

Barsamian's

1030 Mass. Avenue, Cambridge, MA 02138   (617) 661-9300
Mail order: available   Hours: Mon.–Fri. 7:30 A.M.–10 P.M.;
  Sat. 9:30 A.M.–10 P.M.; Sun. 9:30 A.M.–8 P.M.

Ed Barsamian opened his eponymous store in 1987, originally intending for it to be a health-food store; he had just come from being director of retail operations at Erewhon, a health-food chain that was bought by the Nature Food Centres. That intention, which included a policy of no sugar products and all-natural ingredients "lasted about three months," Barsamian recalls. "I underestimated the Bread & Circus loyalty, and I needed to change the focus of the store. Cambridge has some of the most educated customers in the country, and they appreciate the international products I carry."

There is still an element of all-natural products here, but the emphasis is much more on international gourmet. The store is a good-sized market, with several departments, always overflowing with items. Although the aisles are well spaced, they tend to be crowded with boxes waiting to be unpacked.

Baked goods greet you as you enter. The fancy desserts come from Sweet Creations, a wholesale bakery, but all the **cookies** and **comfort treats** are made here.

The quality is mixed. There are a few fat-free items that are barely palatable, such as a **fat-free, sugar-free oatmeal-raisin cookie.** Like rubber. The **fat-free fruit bar** is also rubbery, but I grew to like it, especially the mix of dried blueberries and cherries on top. The **brownies** are pretty good and are offered in a variety of flavors, including **everything** (coconut, nuts, and chocolate chips) and **cream cheese.** The **chocolate chip cookie** is too soft, and the **lemon poppy cookie** has an artificial aftertaste. But the **cranberry-oatmeal cookie** is great. I vastly prefer dried cranberries to raisins, so this cookie is a special treat. It is also studded with toasted almonds.

The **sweet scones** are unremarkable, but the **savory scones,** which I've seen made by only a few bakeries, are quite good. The **cheddar-basil scone** is delicious.

There is a wide selection of breads from area bakers, including Clear Flour, Iggy's, and Panini (pages 15, 33, and 25). There are also a lot of sweets, packaged cookies, and candies from around the country. Barsamian will often buy from a manufacturer directly, so you may find products here months before they appear anywhere else.

The produce section includes a good **salad bar** with **prepared salads** such as **tabouli** and **three-bean.** The produce itself is mixed. Sometimes it's very fresh, with bargain prices; other times certain items look tired and on their way out.

You can find mainstream goods here, including cereal and sugar, as well as all kinds of oils and imported pastas, vinegars, sauces, cookies, crackers, jams, and condiments. Along one wall are bulk bins filled with grains, beans, and spices.

At the center of the store, toward the front, is a rectangle of refrigerated display cases. One side contains imported cheeses. The selection is not huge, but there is a variety of cheeses from several countries. One of the shorter cases holds seafood; it never looks particularly fresh, although there are some decent smoked items.

Two other cases hold **prepared foods.** One contains entrée-type items, such as **lasagne** and **stuffed chicken breasts.** The other case contains a myraid of **prepared salads.** The freshness of these items varies—some days some items had formed an unappetizing crust. But if the salad looks fresh, it is, and the choice is extensive. Most days there are at least two dozen **salads** available including six **chicken salads.** These include a rich **pesto chicken,** a tangy **balsamic vinegar and chicken,** and a **lemon tarragon and chicken.** There are also several vegetarian offerings, such as a spicy **Mexican corn salad** and a slightly oily **eggplant with roasted red peppers.** There are lots of pasta dishes too, from a rather bland **basil and ricotta pasta** to a more interesting **spicy Oriental noodles.**

The store menu describes both "classic" and "signature" **sandwiches.** Classic sandwiches include the expected **roast beef** and **chicken salad,** but you can also choose **smoked ham, Black Forest ham,** or **prosciutto, smoked turkey** or **roast turkey, salami, pastrami,** and **corned beef.** Signature sandwiches use these meats, with creative combinations, such as **roast turkey with chèvre and olive spread** or **smoked mozzarella with tomato basil mayo.**

At the front of the store near the cashiers, there is a small selection of wines to complete your meal.

Prices in general are not cheap here, but Barsamian's is a good source for hard-to-find items. They also do catering.

Cambridge Country Store. See "Liquid Refreshment," page 454.

Cardullo's Gourmet Shoppe

6 Brattle Street, Cambridge, MA 02138
 (617) 491-8888
Mail order: available   Hours: Mon.–Fri. 8 A.M.–8 P.M.;
 Sat. 9 A.M.–9 P.M.; Sun. 11 A.M.–7 P.M.

Cardullo's, in the center of Harvard Square, is one of the Boston area's oldest gourmet shops. Frank Cardullo's father opened the business in 1950. The prices here match the area rents, but the selection is impressive. The store stocks some six thousand items from over thirty countries. Only the sky-high prices prevent me from purchasing dozens of tempting products.

The aisles are narrow, long, and loaded. The goods are organized into various categories: fiery foods, with salsas and items such as chili peanuts and spiced chips; sauces; Thai foods; vinegars and oils, candy and chocolates; preserves; frozen foods; coffee and tea; and beer and wine.

There are a number of imported chocolates—Swiss, Belgian, French, Italian, Mexican—and preserves from all over the world. This is the one shop where I was able to find lingonberry jam. Cardullo says he has a strong collection of goods from Sweden and Britain. There is also an extensive choice of packaged teas, one of the best selections in the area.

In 1995 the store added a frozen food section, enabling them to carry frozen hors d'oeuvres and Out of a Flower sorbets. These are some of the best sorbets I've tasted. They come in a myriad of herbal combinations, such as chocolate mint and rose geranium.

In addition to the gourmet goods with their long shelf life, Cardullo's has a deli counter, and they make **sandwiches** using fresh breads from area bakers. You can also buy loaves of bread and focaccia. Sandwich offerings are basic—**ham, turkey, roast beef** and the like. The freshness of these items can be questionable—if it looks old, it probably is.

The service is mixed. When I pointed out a moldy chunk of cheese to the guy behind the deli counter, his response was, "So? It's natural." Other salespeople, however, have been very helpful.

Cremaldi's. See "Goodies to Go," page 173.

Formaggio Kitchen

244 Huron Avenue, Cambridge, MA 02138   (617) 354-4750
Mail order: available   Hours: Mon.–Fri. 9 A.M.–7 P.M.;
    Sat. 9 A.M.–6 P.M.; Sun. 8:30 A.M.–4 P.M.

To avoid confusion from the outset, Formaggio Kitchen and Formaggio's Deli in Harvard Square are two separately owned institutions, now unrelated. They started together in 1976, and current owner Ihsan Gurdal bought both of them in 1984, but then he sold the Harvard Square establishment in 1986. Now, the two shops are quite different (and the other one is in another chapter altogether; see "Goodies to Go," page 203).

Formaggio Kitchen occupies two storefronts, with the cheese and prepared foods on one side and the baked goods on the other. The cheese case is overflowing with intriguing wheels, slabs, and wedges. Employees will give you a taste of any cheese that has been cut into; also there are always cut-up samples on a marble board on top of the case. Gurdal is on the board of directors of the American Cheese Society, and he leads occasional cheese seminars around the city (he's also the coach for Harvard's volleyball team and is a former professional beach volleyball player.) He estimates that he carries three hundred to four hundred different cheeses. He tries to promote American cheeses; favorites include the pricey (around $17 per pound) Vermont Shepard cheese and Westfield Farms goat cheese, and other "artisanal" cheese. Gurdal defines these as cheeses made from a cheesemaker's own herds, handmade, scooped, washed, and ripened. He also specializes in rare meats, and carries several cured varieties including a number of hard-to-find salamis.

A large display case offers a selection of **cold prepared foods,** such as an excellent **lemon-pistachio chicken,** a spicy **chickpea and pepper salad,** and an intriguing **soy curry chicken salad.** Not everything is great; the **curry tuna,** while interesting, is on the dry side. But, as with the cheese, ask for a taste before you buy. There are also **hot entrées** to go, such as **lasagne.** The fresh pastas, made for Formaggio, are fair; a **caramelized leek ravioli** that fell apart when cooked was not worth the high price. This section of the store also houses condiments—all kinds of oils, vinegars, mustards, and preserves—as well as spices, various dried chilies, coffees, and Valrhona and Callebaut chocolate.

The other side of Formaggio Kitchen holds the **breads** and **baked goods.** They bake one yeast bread daily—popular flavors include **six-grain** and **cinnamon**—and carry other breads from several area bakers. Other baked goods are all made on the premises, and the quality varies. The **scones** come in unusual flavors such as **orange–poppy seed** and **tart cherry,** but they are much too dry. I like the **honey-raisin bran muffin,** which tastes like gingerbread. There are several cookies and bars; **cherry coconut** is unusual and quite good, but the **lemon bars** are too sweet and not lemony enough, although the crust is good and buttery. The **oatmeal-raisin cookies** are excellent, buttery, chewy, perfect. But the **chocolate chip cookies** are too soft and **almond macaroons** are too hard. The **spicy chocolate** is very good, an intriguing blend of chocolate, cinnamon, and other spices. The **coconut-almond** cookie, drizzled with dark chocolate, is also very good. Formaggio is one of the few places that offers **madeleines,** a sweet I know primarily from a high school French class version of Proust's *Le Petite Madeleine;* frankly, they aren't that exciting. Formaggio's comes **plain** or dipped in **white** or **dark chocolate.** Check when they were made, because they can have a refrigerator taste to them.

There are several **cakes,** both fancy layer and casual tea versions. The **chocolate layer cake** is good, chocolatey, and not too sweet.

In late 1995 Gurdal took over the produce store next door, so Formaggio now offers a variety of fresh fruits and vegetables in a third storefront.

NEWTON

Boyajian Boston
385 California Street, Newton, MA 02160   (617) 527-6677
Mail order: available   Hours: Mon.–Fri. 9 A.M.–5 P.M.;
    closed Sat., Sun.

Boyajian Boston is primarily a wholesaler, but the offices are open to the public. You may have some trouble finding the place. The offices are not located in a commercial area; there are no other stores nearby, and the corner building is not clearly labeled. But your trip will not be wasted. Come here for the best **smoked seafood** around and for marvelous **gourmet oils.**

John Boyajian initially made a name for himself as an importer of Russian caviar, and subsequently for his smoked seafood. He got into the caviar business after a chance meeting with the Petrossian family in Paris. At that time, he had been exporting lobster and asked them if they were interested. "Petrossian is *the* name in caviar," Boyajian explains. He visited the family in Cannes, had his first caviar, and was offered a job heading a New York branch of the company. "In December of 1980 I sold the first tin of caviar to the Ritz," Boyajian recalls. In 1987 Boyajian started his own business, buying caviar directly from Russia.

All his **caviar** is sturgeon roe. The three best, according to Boyajian (and most caviar fans) are Beluga, Ossetra, and Sevruga, which are found only in the Caspian Sea. Yes, caviar is extremely expensive. Is it worth it? You be the judge. I like it very much, but would I pay $25 to $50 for an ounce? Not yet. I prefer smoked fish; although it, too, is not inexpensive, you get more for your money. And Boyajian's is sublime. It is smoked to his specifications in New York, and the results are simply wonderful: the best **smoked salmon** I've tasted, excellent **smoked trout,** and wonderful **smoked bluefish pâté.**

In addition to the seafood, Boyajian carries amazing **roulades of foie gras** from the French Perigord region, and **fresh foie gras** from New York State. There is fresh Moullard duck and **rendered duck fat** as well.

Boyajian also produces a line of **oils.** Notable are the **citrus oils: lemon, orange,** and **lime.** These are not citrus-infused canola or olive oils; they are pure, concentrated oils from the fruits (it takes a few hundred of each fruit to produce a five-ounce bottle of oil), and a little bit goes a long way. When used in baking, a quarter teaspoon adds a truly fresh flavor to the food. There are also infused oils—among the best I've tasted. Noteworthy flavors include **garlic oil** and **chili oil.**

John Dewar & Co. See "Where's the Beef?" page 132.

Marty's. See Allston, page 374.

SOMERVILLE

Capone Foods. See "Lotsa Pasta," page 94.

The Wine and Cheese Cask. See "Libations," page 491.

NORTH

ANDOVER

The Butler's Pantry
7 Barnard Street, Andover, MA 01810   (508) 475-7121
Mail order: not available   Hours: Mon.–Fri. 8 A.M.–6 P.M.;
Sat. 8 A.M.–5 P.M.; closed Sun.

The Butler's Pantry is a charming shop in the center of Andover. They carry all sorts of gourmet items, such as imported cheeses, smoked Norwegian salmon, caviar, and frozen hors d'oeuvres. A chocolate section includes Godiva and Belgian Neuhaus chocolates, as well as Harbor Sweets from Salem (see "Sweet Indulgences," page 346). Gourmet items include oils and vinegars, salad dressings, Indian condiments, preserves, mustards, salsas and honey.

As you enter, a display case to your left offers a variety of **prepared foods,** as well as appealing **sandwiches.** Some are gourmet variations on classics, such as the **Southwest,** sourdough bread layered with smoked turkey, guacamole, lettuce, and tomatoes. **Ham What Am** is Black Forest ham and garlic-herb Alouette cheese on French bread. **Veggies and Grains** is made with red and green peppers, Danish Swiss cheese, and sprouts on seven-grain bread.

A bakery case includes some **cookies** baked on the premises, as well as items from area bakers. You can also buy coffee by the cup or by the pound.

Past the bakery case is a second part of the store, featuring cookware, table settings, and linens. Among the items displayed here are coffeemakers and Calphalon pots and pans.

MARBLEHEAD

Truffles. See "Goodies to Go," page 186.

SOUTH

HINGHAM

Fruit Center Marketplace. See "Earthly Delights," page 58.

MILTON

Fruit Center Marketplace. See "Earthly Delights," page 58.

WESTWOOD

Homsy's. See "The World in a Jar," page 424.

WEST

ACTON

Idylwilde Farm. See "Earthly Delights," page 67.

BELMONT

Rustica. See "Goodies to Go," page 190.

CHELMSFORD

The Elegant Farmer. See "Earthly Delights," page 59.

CONCORD

The Cheese Shop/The Concord Shop
25 Walden Street, Concord, MA 01742   (508) 369-5778
Mail order: available   Hours: Tues.–Sat. 9 A.M.–5:30 P.M.;
   closed Sun., Mon.

In the 1970s there was a franchise of stores called The Cheese Shop. Bill Barber, a high-school French teacher, decided to buy into the franchise with his wife Louise and take a few years off from teaching. Barber credits The Cheese Shop franchise with introducing Boursin to America. At one point there were as many as ninety stores across the eastern seaboard, of which Wasik's Cheese Shop in Wellesley was one. After a few years, the Barbers decided to buy out the franchise, and they gradually expanded the store to what it is today: a fabulous source for cheeses, wines, and all kinds of gourmet items, including a very good selection of **take-out items.**

The cheeses are the star here. There are over one hundred kinds at any one time. When I visited, there were four different brands of aged Gouda, my favorite cheese. Barber says, "I'm a sucker for anything made from goat's or sheep's milk," and the varieties of those cheeses are extensive.

The store is crowded, but organized. Every available shelf is filled with items, many imported from around the world. There are shelves of jams and jellies, boxes of cookies and candies, jars of salsas, spreads, and other condiments.

The food merges into the wine section of the store, which features a good variety of wines. The wines surround five tables. You can order dishes from the take-out counter and eat them here.

A freezer contains **frozen soups** and **appetizers,** such as **spinach triangles.** You can get good meaty **sandwiches** made to order on submarine rolls, using Boarshead deli meats. Another case displays **prepared salads.** Combinations vary from day to day but might include **couscous with almonds and dried fruit, sesame noodle salad,** or one of several **chicken salads,** including **cilantro mint** and **tarragon and grape.** The **chicken broccoli** is wonderful, with a roasted garlic dressing. You can also buy **heads of roasted garlic,** great for spreading on bread. There are always fresh **soups** and daily **hot entrées.** The Cheese Shop prints a calendar of the month's daily specials. **Soups** vary from a hearty **turkey noodle** to an exotic **saffron mussel bisque.** I tried a **lamb Navarin,** one of the best stews I've ever tasted. It has a deep, sophisticated red wine sauce, and you'll find yourself wanting to lick your plate clean. Other entrées include a cheesy **tamale pie, Cornish game hens,** and **jambalaya.**

For dessert there is a case of fancy pastries from area

bakeries, as well as the shop's own good **chocolate chip cookies, molasses cookies,** and **muffins.**

In 1985 the Barbers bought The Concord Shop next door and opened a passageway between the two stores. The Concord Shop specializes in cookware, and there is a marvelous collection of hard-to-find, exotic items here.

Concord Spice & Grain. See "Going Organic," page 444.

LEXINGTON

Berman's. See "Libations," page 487.

SUDBURY

Duck Soup
890 Boston Post Road, Sudbury, MA 01776   (508) 443-3825
Mail order: available   Hours: Mon.–Wed. and Sat. 9:30 A.M.–6 P.M.;
    Thurs., Fri. 9:30 A.M.–8 P.M.; Sun. noon–5 P.M.

Richard Ressler opened Duck Soup in 1971 in the Mill Village complex in Sudbury. The store offers a wonderful collection of both cookware and gourmet foods. Ressler and his staff, most of whom have been with the store for over fifteen years, travel the country looking for specialty items. Often they will buy items directly from a manufacturer; some local goods are not available through a national distributor. Rotel tomatoes are one such item. These wonderful spiced, diced tomatoes are made in Texas and are only available in some parts of the country, not including New England. The store carries close to three dozen kinds of mustard and seventy-five salsas, as well as jams, pastas, teas, and condiments from around the country and the world.

There is a coffee section, and Ressler relies on several sources for different roasts and blends. There is a Thermos of coffee to sample in small cups—nice if you need a little jolt of caffeine.

Duck Soup was one of the first places to carry Peter Breads (see "The Staff of Life," page 31), wonderful, unusual breads made by a local wholesale baker. There is a selection of imported cheeses, super Kalamata olives, and refrigerated dips and spreads. Samples of these items are often set out on a counter for customers to try.

Another section of the store is devoted to cookware. Duck Soup keeps up with trends—you can find bread machines, pressure cookers, coffeemakers, and pasta machines here.

The shop is not huge, but it is packed; you get the sense that Ressler and his staff have saved you the legwork of finding some of the best foods available.

WALTHAM

The Winecellar of Silene. See "Libations," page 491.

WELLESLEY

Wasik's Cheese Shop
61 Central Street, Wellesley, MA 02181   (617) 237-0916
Mail order: available   Hours: Mon.–Sat. 9 A.M.–6 P.M.;
    Sun. 9 A.M.–3 P.M.

Stephen F. Wasik was the vice president of The Cheese Shop company, a franchise of cheese shops that were popular during the 1970s. He moved to Massachusetts and bought The Cheese Shop in Wellesley in 1979. The store carries 200 to 350 different cheeses, depending on the season. Spring and summer are good for goat cheeses, and you can find some twenty varieties here.

When I visited, little cheese was on display. The current health inspector in Wellesley requires that all cheese be refrigerated so it is kept in the cases. But the staff is still more than happy to offer tastes. As one woman told me, "We prefer that our customers taste the cheese before they buy it. We want them to go home happy."

Around 1990 Wasik's wife, Carol, started developing a line of **chutneys** and **preserves,** which the store now sells under the Wasik name. These include **Yankee Chutney** (a peach chutney), **Harvest Chutney** (cranberry-apricot), **Nor'east Pepper Jelly,** and **Plum Rum Preserve.**

The Wasiks pride themselves on carrying hard-to-find gourmet items, and they stock a variety of foods such as olives, dried mushrooms, grains, smoked fish, and seasoned oils. They also carry a full line of bread and pastries from area bakers, as well as chocolates.

❖ CHEESEMAKERS ❖

Gigi's Mozzarella House
6 Cazenova Place (behind 355 Broadway), Everett, MA 02149
(617) 387-6810
Mail order: not available   Hours: Mon.–Fri. 8:30 A.M.–4 P.M.;
Sat. 9 A.M.–2 P.M.; closed Sun.

Gigi's is not exactly easy to find. The shop is located off a parking lot behind 355 Broadway. Go down the driveway, which opens into a parking lot. A rectangular white building is on one side, with a nondescript door on the right and a small sign. This is Gigi's.

The odor of sour milk greets you as you enter; don't be put off by the smell, because the cheese they make here is very good. Cheeses include an excellent **fresh mozzarella** and two kinds of ricotta. **American ricotta** is made from milk—creamy whole milk. **Italian ricotta** is made from the thin milky water left over from mozzarella making, and it is somehow creamier and softer than the American ricotta. The cheeses are very fresh. They have no added salt, so they have a very short shelf life. They are best consumed the day you buy them, although they may last for two or three days. There is also a **smoked mozzarella,** made with liquid smoke.

There is an aged cheese, *scamorze,* which is an elongated ball with a bulge on one end. This cheese is similar to provolone. Several rounds in the display case had spots of mold, which Gigi Cubellis said did not matter—you could just brush it off. I chose to buy a mold-free ball nonetheless. The *scamorze* is a good cheese, plain or melted on pizza.

Cubellis sells primarily wholesale, so it's best to call in advance to make sure that they have what you want.

Giuseppe Cheese
111 Bowen Avenue, Medford, MA 02155   (617) 396-0229
Mail order: not available   Hours: Mon.–Fri. 7 A.M.–4 P.M.;
Sat. 8 A.M.–noon; closed Sun.

Joseph and Philip Dragone's grandfather Giuseppe started a ricotta cheese company, Dragone, in 1926. This is *the* Dragone, the ricotta cheese sold in most area supermarkets. The family sold the business in 1972, then started Giuseppe, a smaller scale operation, in 1978.

Giuseppe's is the largest of the three area shops that make ricotta cheese, and their business is primarily wholesale. They have a small store at the corner of Bowen and Mystic Avenues, next to Maria's Ravioli, which is an exclusively wholesale operation. Giuseppe's makes three products: a very good **ricotta cheese,** made with whole milk; a **dry ricotta** used primarily by bakeries for cannoli filling; and for Christmas and Easter they make *formaggio frésco,* a cheese that is used to make the seasonal specialty *pizzagano.* Philip told me that at Christmas they sell about two hundred pounds of the stuff, but at Easter, the real *pizzagano* season, they sell fifteen thousand pounds. *Pizzagano* is a rich treat made with this curdlike cheese, eggs, a few other cheeses, and Italian cold cuts. Bob's Imported Food and Fine Catering (see "The World in a Jar," page 416) makes it, just during the weeks before Easter.

In addition to their cheeses, the wholesale outlet at Giuseppe's sells a few imported Italian pastas and tomatoes and some other cheeses. There are tubs of fresh mozzarella, waxed balls of provolone, containers of mascarpone, ground Romano cheese, and *reginito,* a hard cheese from Argentina. Joseph told me it was similar to Parmesan, but at half the price. I found the taste to be quite different from Parmesan, but I like this cheese very much. It's a hard cheese, though not as hard as Parmesan, with an appealing flavor.

Ipswich Goat Cheese

48 Turkey Shore Road, Ipswich, MA 01938   (508) 356-4473
Mail order: not available   Hours: by appointment

Alice Zawacki started making her **Ipswich goat cheese** rounds in the mid-1970s—long before chèvre became the rage. For years she made do with a two-goat herd of Nubian goats; now she has six goats and makes about twenty pounds of cheese a week. The size of these small rounds varies, as Zawacki makes them all by hand. The cheese is available in shops around the Boston area, including Formaggio Kitchen (see Cambridge, page 380) and Harvest Cooperative Supermarket (see "Going Organic," page 431). You can also buy from Zawacki directly; call to make an appointment to visit her cheese room.

Purity Cheese

55 Endicott Street, Boston, MA 02113   (617) 227-5060
Mail order: not available   Hours: Tues.–Sat. 7 A.M.–5:30 P.M.;
   closed Sun., Mon.

Peter Cucchiara's parents started Purity Cheese in 1938, and he has followed in their footsteps, making the best **whole-milk mozzarella** and **ricotta** cheeses around. Purity actually makes four cheeses, all in the back room behind the display area. The whole-milk fresh **mozzarella** has very little salt and a clean, pure taste (and a short shelf life—use it within two days). The other three cheeses can last up to a week, refrigerated. *Scamorze* is salted mozzarella, with a firmer texture; this is the cheese to use grated on pizza. The **smoked** *scamorze* is also terrific. The fresh **ricotta** is slightly drier than the kind you buy in tubs in the supermarket. Purity sells theirs by the slab, cut from a thick roll using a piece of string. They also supply most of the North End restaurants and pastry shops with ricotta, making about 2,500 pounds, and about 350 pounds of mozzarella daily.

In 1993 Cucchiara renovated the space into the airy display room it is now, expanding the space and adding a *salumeria,* Italian for **sandwich** shop. Various salamis and meats are available, as well as hard Italian cheeses, and the staff make a variety of sandwiches to order.

THE BESTS OF THE BEST

Best gourmet shop: **Duck Soup** and **Marty's**
Best cheese selection: **Formaggio Kitchen**
Best smoked fish: **Boyajian Boston**
Best fresh cheese: **Purity Cheese**

CHAPTER ELEVEN

THE WORLD IN A JAR

Ethnic markets covering the continents, from Asia to Europe, and from Africa to South America

*I*LOVE to cook foreign cuisines, and I'm always looking for new uncommon ingredients. But finding sources is not always easy. Some so-called ethnic markets carry only a few imported canned goods in addition to the usual milk and powdered soups you find in most convenience stores.

I like a market with atmosphere, with smells of unfamiliar spices and exotic ingredients, strange foods and brightly colored packages with foreign-language labels. I discovered that you *can* buy fresh lemongrass in Boston, as well as toasted watermelon seeds and mango pickles. You just have to know where to look.

There are ethnic markets representing over two dozen nationalities in Boston, including African, Armenian, Brazilian, British, Chinese, French, Greek, Haitian, Indian, Israeli, Italian, Jamaican, Japanese, Lebanese, Mexican, Portuguese, Russian, Spanish, Syrian, Thai, Vietnamese, and West Indian. This chapter is organized differently than most other chapters; rather than grouping stores by area, I have grouped them by regional cuisine, with establishments listed alphabetically under each heading.

* Described in another chapter.

AFRICAN

African Market	Roxbury

ASIAN

Ankor Watt Oriental Food Market	Revere
Bao-Viet	Chelsea
Cambodia Market	Chelsea
Chinatown	Boston
Cheng Kwong Seafood Market	
Chung Wah Hong	
The 88 Supermarket	
Ming's	
See Sun Co.	
*Choe's Fish Market	Weymouth
Ichiban Oriental Market	Framingham
J & K Oriental Market	Cambridge
Jin Mi Oriental Food Co.	Newton
Joyce Chen Unlimited	Acton
Kotobukiya Inc.	Cambridge
Lotte Market	Cambridge
M & M Market	Revere
Mai Oriental Store	Brockton
Oriental Groceries	Brookline
Reliable Market	Somerville
*Sandy's Market	Cambridge
Tam Loi	Allston
Tan Phanh	Chelsea
Truong Thin Market	Dorchester
Vien Dong Fareast Supermarket	Dorchester
Viet Huong Market	Dorchester
Yoshinoya	Cambridge

BRITISH

British Food & Imports	Plymouth, Southboro
Union Jack	Peabody

EASTERN EUROPEAN/RUSSIAN

Bazaar International Gourmet	Brookline
Berezka International Food Store	Allston
European Deli	Roslindale

| *J.P. Meat Market | Chelsea |
| Moscow International Foods | Allston |

GERMAN

| *Karl's Sausage Kitchen | Saugus |

HISPANIC/CARIBBEAN

La Economica	Chelsea
Hi-Lo Foods	Jamaica Plain
Mayfair Foods	Allston
Preparations	Dorchester
3-M Market	Roxbury
Tropical Foods	Roxbury

INDIAN

Framingham India Grocery	Framingham
India Foods & Spices	Cambridge
India Tea & Spices Inc.	Belmont
Madras Masala	Brookline
Shalimar India Food & Spices	Cambridge
Small Markets	
Annapurna Enterprises Inc.	Randolph
Eastern Food & Spices	Somerville
India Groceries	Brighton
Little India Groceries	Somerville
New Apna Bazar	Waltham

ITALIAN

*Alfredo Aiello Italian Pasta Store	Quincy
Bob's Imported Food and Fine Catering	Medford
*Cremaldi's	Cambridge
Imperial Grocery	Everett
*Nappi Meats & Groceries	Medford
*New Deal Fruit	Revere
J. Pace & Son Inc.	Boston
*Previte's	Quincy
Regina Food Store	Everett
*Salumeria Italiana	Boston
*Salumeria Toscana	Boston
Sessa's Italian Specialties	Somerville
*Tony's Meat Market	Roslindale
Tutto Italiano	Hyde Park, Newton, Wellesley

KOSHER

Beacon Kosher	Brookline
*The Butcherie	Brookline
*The Butcherie II	Canton
*Gordon & Alperin Inc.	Brookline

MIDDLE EASTERN

Arax Market	Watertown
*Blackstone Halal Market	Boston
*Cambridge Halal Meat Market &	
Grocery Store	Cambridge
Eastern Lamejun	Belmont
Homsy's	Westwood
*Kay's	Watertown
Lebanese Market	Roslindale
Massis	Watertown
*Near East Bakery	West Roxbury
*New Halal Meat & Grocery Store	Boston
Phoenicia Market	Brockton
*Roslindale Fish Market	Roslindale
The Syrian Grocery	Boston

PORTUGUESE/BRAZILIAN

*Court House Fish Market	Cambridge
*Fernandes Fish Market	Cambridge
International Market	Somerville
*New Deal Fish Market	Cambridge
The Portuguese American Market	Somerville

❖ A F R I C A N ❖

African Market

1023 Tremont Street, Roxbury, MA 02120   (617) 427-7131
Mail order: not available   Hours: Mon.–Sat. 9 A.M.–7:30 P.M.;
  Sun. noon–6:30 P.M.

African Market is a small market, but it is filled with fascinating foods. What is especially nice is that the owner, Hassan, is on hand to answer any questions, unlike at many ethnic markets, where you are left to guess what to do with an unusual ingredient. Hassan, who hails from Ghana, opened his store in 1991. There are goods here from several African countries: for example, a kola nut sauce from Nigeria and smoked shrimp from Liberia. A wooden bowl is filled with *shea* butter; also called *nkuto, ori,* and *okuma,* this is a firm, medicinal butter-colored fat that comes from a tree. A freezer is filled with a variety of smoked and dried fish and meat, pricey at $10 to $13 a pound.

❖ A S I A N ❖

Most Asian markets carry items from several different countries, but often they also focus on ingredients used by a certain cuisine. The countries most frequently represented include China, Japan, Korea, Thailand, Vietnam, and Cambodia. If one of the following markets focuses more strongly on foods from a particular country, I indicate this in the description. Certain areas have high concentrations of Asian markets, and I have highlighted the noteworthy markets. These include Boston's Chinatown, with the biggest Asian markets around. Chelsea has several smaller markets, and Dorchester Avenue in Dorchester seems to have a market with a Thai or Vietnamese focus every few blocks.

CHINATOWN

Chinatown is *the* place to go for Asian goods. It has the highest concentration of markets, some of which are quite large. There are two supermarkets, which are actually a bit removed from Chinatown proper: The 88 Supermarket and Ming's. I describe these in detail and also list other worthwhile markets in Chinatown.

Cheng Kwong Seafood Market
73–79 Essex Street, Boston, MA 02111   (617) 423-3749
Mail order: not available   Hours: daily 8:30 A.M.–7:30 P.M.

Chung Wah Hong
51–55 Beach Street, Boston, MA 02111   (617) 426-3619
Mail order: not available   Hours: daily 8:30 A.M.–7 P.M.

The 88 Supermarket

50 Herald Street, Boston, MA 02118   (617) 423-1688
Mail order: not available   Hours: daily 8:30 A.M.–7:30 P.M.

The 88 is very similar to Ming's right down the street, but for some reason it is much less busy, which can make it a more pleasant place to wander through. The staff here is no more helpful than at Ming's; it helps if you come with someone familiar with Asian ingredients. While Ming's emphasizes Chinese foods, The 88 carries many Thai ingredients. The 88 is one extremely large room, like a supermarket, with very long aisles. As you enter by the cashier, there is an aisle with bulk bins: walnuts are located next to teeny-tiny dried shrimp. The shelves include industrial-size containers of many items, such as water chestnuts, bamboo shoots, and coconut milk.

The produce section is located at the back of the store and includes a varied selection. Items that caught my eye include galangal (a type of ginger root often used in Thai cooking), instant soybean cheese, dried olives, and pickled young tamarind. The fish market runs along one wall here and includes live seafood.

Ming's

1102 Washington Street, Boston, MA 02118   (617) 338-1588
Mail order: not available   Hours: daily 8:30 A.M.–7:15 P.M.

Ming's is simultaneously fascinating and overwhelming. It is huge, the size of a small supermarket, and carries Asian goods, with the primary emphasis on Chinese foods. There is a Chinese-style bakery as you enter, followed by a case of cold drinks, such as grass jelly drink, black tea, and *lucozade* (a tropical barley drink). Aisle after aisle is filled with intriguing exotic items. Several have labels only in Chinese, but many have English translations, with explanations for what to do with items such as bird's nest or rock sugar flavoring or dried Chinese yam. Not much English is spoken here, so don't expect help from the staff; if you can go with someone familiar with Chinese cooking, you're in luck. But even if you don't, wandering through the aisles here may inspire you to try to make new dishes.

Ming's is quite similar to The 88 Supermarket in terms of what is offered, and just a block separates the two. The quality in both stores seemed similar to my eye, but Ming's was infinitely more busy on my visit. Both stores offer parking, and this area of town is easier to navigate in a car than Chinatown proper.

The store has roughly five sections. The first is where you enter. It includes aisles devoted solely to tea, as well as shelves featuring various medicinal herbs, spices, and sweets. Asian spices, oils, and vinegars are located in a space behind this area, along with hefty bags of rice. Through a doorway on one side is a room with sundries—woks, steamer baskets, and other cookware, tables and chairs—as well as American and Hispanic goods such as yam flour and tapioca.

A doorway on the other wall leads to the frozen and refrigerated aisles, which offer all kinds of Asian items, especially frozen dim sum dishes. There are lotus-seed moon cakes, yellow oak buns, and taro root popsicles.

Past this are the butchery, fish market, and produce aisles. The meats include many items foreign to Western palates, such as ox tendon, white spicy pork intestine, duck tongue, and goose feet. The fish market has several tanks of live seafood, including a bunch of bright green jumping frogs. There are dozens of fish on ice, which seem very fresh, and most are priced under $6 a pound.

Among the produce there are items such as Chinese okra, Japanese eggplant, banana flowers, and lemongrass.

See Sun Co.
25 Harrison Street, Boston, MA 02111   (617) 426-0954
Mail order: not available   Hours: daily 9 A.M.–7 P.M.

Ankor Watt Oriental Food Market
138 Shirley Avenue, Revere, MA 02151   (617) 286-2667
Mail order: not available   Hours: daily 8 A.M.–8 P.M.

Ankor Watt is very crowded. Boxes of produce greet you as you enter, topped with exotic-looking Thai prepared foods. Produce is the main attraction here, and the store features items such as fresh jackfruit. The displays are disorganized, especially if you are used to a supermarket's clearly delineated aisles. Dried fish is piled next to boxes of mangos. In the refrigerated section, which contains more produce, raw meat is unappetizingly placed right next to the vegetables. The aisles of canned goods are stacked with boxes waiting to be unpacked, so navigating can be difficult. You can find all kinds of Thai and other Asian items here, but the jumbled organization makes shopping a challenge.

Bao-Viet
365 Broadway, Chelsea, MA 02150   (617) 884-2277
Mail order: not available   Hours: Mon.–Sat. 9 A.M.–6:30 P.M.;
   closed Sun.

Chelsea is an ever-changing mix of ethnic neighborhoods. The current predominant cultures are Hispanic, Vietnamese, and Cambodian. Bao-Viet reflects the mixed neighborhood. The store carries primarily Asian goods, with a focus on Vietnamese foods. But the shop also stocks a handful of Hispanic products, such as canned beans and other items made by Goya. If you're lucky, Jin Trinh Hua will be working in the store. She is knowledgeable and helpful, and happy to tell you how to use various intriguing ingredients and food, such as *sweet mix,* an Asian dessert containing various beans, banana, and young coconut.

Cambodia Market
218 Broadway, Chelsea, MA 02150   (617) 884-8916
Mail order: not available   Hours: daily 9 A.M.–8 P.M.

Cambodia Market is a medium-sized market, densely packed with Asian goods. The produce here is in decent shape.

Choe's Fish Market. See "Some Things Fishy," page 122.

Ichiban Oriental Market
575 Worcester Road (Route 9), Framingham, MA 01701
   (508) 875-8830
Mail order: not available   Hours: Mon.–Fri. 10 A.M.–7 P.M.;
   Sat. 10 A.M.–6 P.M.; closed Sun.

Ichiban is a smallish Asian market with a Japanese focus. Not much English is spoken here, but the packages are generally well labeled. You can find items such as sesame oil, several types of soy sauces, rice crackers, and various fish preparations here. They also make **sushi to go.**

J & K Oriental Market
2376 Mass. Avenue, Cambridge, MA 02140   (617) 547-8723
Mail order: not available   Hours: Mon.–Sat. 10 A.M.–7 P.M.;
   Sun. 9:30 A.M.–8 P.M.

J & K is a small market with a variety of Asian and Korean items. The proprietor here speaks very little English. Just finding out the store hours was a challenge. However, if you're in the neigh-

borhood, this is a good place to find items such as canned water
chestnuts and lychees, ginseng tea, and several soy sauces.

Jin Mi Oriental Food Co.

313 Walnut Street, Newton, MA 02160   (617) 964-2668
Mail order: not available   Hours: Mon.–Sat. 10:30 A.M.–6:30 P.M.;
   Sun. noon–6 P.M.

A small market, Jin Mi has a very friendly, accommodating proprietor. Although the selection is not huge, it is varied. You can
find a good choice of Asian staples here, from green and jasmine
teas to rice vinegar and tamari. And lots of rice.

Joyce Chen Unlimited

423 Great Road, Acton, MA 01720   (508) 263-6922
Mail order: available   Hours: Mon.–Fri. 10 A.M.–6 P.M.;
   Sat. 9:30 A.M.–5:30 P.M.; closed Sun.

Joyce Chen Unlimited is both an extensive Asian market and a
source for Joyce Chen cookware, including a line of Chinese
items such as woks, Peking pans, wok utensils, and bamboo
steamers. The store carries several of the Joyce Chen **sauces** as
well.

   In addition to these products, there is a good selection
of items from China, Indonesia, Thailand, Japan, and Korea,
including coconut milk and rice-paper wrappers. The produce
section has items such as fresh lemongrass, Thai basil, and Thai
chili peppers. A freezer includes a variety of dim sum items.

   The staff here speaks English and can be very helpful in
explaining the uses of various products.

Kotobukiya Inc.

1815 Mass. Avenue, Cambridge, MA 02140   (617) 354-6914 or
   492-4655
Mail order: not available   Hours: Mon.–Fri. 10 A.M.–9 P.M.;
   Sat. 9 A.M.–9 P.M.; Sun. noon–7 P.M.

The Porter Exchange building, which used to be a Sears until the
mid-1980s, floundered around for tenants for several years before
it became a Japanese center. There are a few other shops here,
but those with a Japanese orientation dominate. There is a Japanese travel agency, a gift shop, several noodle restaurants, a pastry
shop, and Kotobukiya.

   Kotobukiya is a large Asian market with a Japanese focus,

and you can find all sorts of Japanese goods here. Many items are mysterious, even when the labels carry translations, since the foods are very foreign to the American palate. The canned and dry goods are best here. There is produce, but it never looks that fresh. Likewise with the fish: you'll do better at one of the area fishmongers.

The choice of canned and packaged goods, such as noodles, red-bean paste, and sweets, is quite extensive. Many staffers speak English and can answer questions about unfamiliar items.

Lotte Market

297 Massachusetts Avenue, Cambridge, MA 02139   (617) 661-1194
Mail order: not available   Hours: daily 9 A.M.–9 P.M.

Lotte is one of the newer markets. It opened in 1995 in the space of a former car-rental company. The market is a good size with space to move around in. The focus is on Japanese goods, and the items are nicely displayed.

The store is L-shaped. As you enter, the front of the store has baked goods, including items from Japonaise Bakery (see "Everything Nice," page 244). There is also cookware, including ricemakers and pots and pans.

Aisles of goods fill the rest of the store. There are packaged noodles, sweets, rice crackers, condiments, teas, and all kinds of dried fish. Along one wall there is a good choice of produce. The far wall includes **prepared foods** such as **tripe, long peppers in hot sauce,** and **whole marinated garlic.** Not every item includes an English translation, however. The fish department features sushi-quality fish such as tuna that is quite fresh and appealing. There are several meats as well, which are packaged and frozen.

M & M Market

157 Shirley Avenue, Revere, MA 02151   (617) 289-2834
Mail order: not available   Hours: daily 8 A.M.–8 P.M.

As you enter M & M Market, you'll be greeted by boxes of produce, with containers of prepared sweets and savory foods balanced on top. The front area of the store is narrow, but the space widens considerably at the back. The goods are Asian, with a concentration on Thai products. This is a decent source for Asian herbs, such as fresh lemongrass and Thai basil. There is an aisle of noodles and another one for canned goods. Meats and fish can be found in a refrigerated case along the wall and in freezers at the back of the store. Frozen items include banana leaves, grated coconut, and egg rolls. The organization at this end is somewhat haphazard, but the store is clean.

Mai Oriental Store

321 Belmont Street, Brockton, MA 02401   (508) 559-6336
Mail order: not available   Hours: Mon. 2 P.M.–6 P.M.;
   Tues.–Sat. 9:30 A.M.–8 P.M.; Sun. 11 A.M.–6 P.M.

Mai is a medium-sized market with an emphasis on Thai products. The prices are particularly cheap, and there is a good selection of items. I found a sweet coconut spread (delicious on pancakes) and a variety of Asian produce, including bitter melon, lemongrass, and eighteen-inch-long string beans. Duck eggs are displayed by the cash register. These are fertile eggs, with a half-formed duck inside—a popular Vietnamese and Chinese snack.

The proprietor speaks English and is very helpful.

Oriental Groceries

1617 Beacon Street, Brookline, MA 02146   (617) 232-0800
Mail order: not available   Hours: daily 10 A.M.– 8 P.M.

At first glance, Oriental Groceries appears small. But the room goes back farther than you think, and a passageway leads to a second room. This back room stocks several kinds of oil, including peanut and sesame, as well as rice wine and rice vinegar, soy sauce, and teas. There are also shelves of Korean videos and tapes.

Along the passageway to the front part of the store is a refrigerated case containing Korean **prepared foods** and some **fish dishes.** The main room has tall shelves overflowing with all kinds of noodles—rice, cellophane, ramen, and buckwheat. There are soup mixes and hot sauces, as well as packages of cookies and other sweets.

Reliable Market

52 Union Square, Somerville, MA 02143   (617) 623-9620
Mail order: not available   Hours: Mon. 10 A.M.–8 P.M.;
   Tues.–Sat. 9:30 A.M.–8 P.M.; Sun. 10 A.M.–7 P.M.

You can't really tell anything about Reliable Market from the outside, since the windows are filled with bags of rice and boxes. Inside, however, is a good-sized market, and a food-lover's paradise for Korean and other Asian products. An aisle is devoted just to ramen noodles, and another to all other kinds of noodles. The shelves are filled with various grains and beans, including at least four kinds of barely: steamed, peeled, split polished, and pressed. There are rows of condiments—black-bean paste, soy paste, hot pepper paste, and sweet rice paste—several brands of rice vinegars and sesame oils, and many kinds of dried mushrooms.

The store is very well organized, and most products include labels with English translations. I could spend hours here discovering new products.

There is also an aisle of fresh produce and homemade **prepared foods** such as **kimchee** and **pickled pellira leaves**.

Sandy's Market. See "Earthly Delights," page 55.

Tam Loi

485 Cambridge Street, Allston, MA 02134   (617) 782-1861
Mail order: not available   Hours: Mon.–Sat. 9:30 A.M.–8:30 P.M.;
Sun. 11 A.M.–7 P.M.

Tam Loi market provides an amazing selection of Asian goods, with a strong emphasis on Thai ingredients. The store is well organized with an extensive array of foods, and most products are labeled with English translations (although some of these translations may not mean much if you are unfamiliar with galangal or longan). The store is not much to look at from the outside —the display window is filled from floor to ceiling with fifty-pound sacks of rice. Inside, however, it is a haven for the adventurous food lover. I could spend hours wandering the aisles, reading the labels, discovering obscure ingredients called for in my Thai cookbooks. I initially came here searching for sticky rice (also known as glutinous rice), which costs only $2.50 for a five-pound bag. The prices in general are quite reasonable, if not cheap. Items that you can find in supermarkets, such as rice vinegar or sesame oil, are significantly less expensive here. And you have a choice of several kinds of each product; for example, there are at least half a dozen brands of bamboo shoots and curry pastes.

In the frozen foods section there are all manner of fish imported from Thailand—silver pomfret, octopus, spotted spiny eel, silver barb fish. In addition to fish, the freezer displays frozen produce, such as fresh-frozen grated coconut, young coconut juice, and rhizome and galangal, roots used in Thai cooking.

Fish make an appearance in the dried-goods section as well, with cellophane bags of pinkie-length anchovies and barracudas, dried river catfish pierced on a stick, and more. You'll also find bags of fried pork skins—huge pieces that actually look like what they are—and fried pig ears, as well as boxes of preserved duck eggs.

Although the cans, bags, and jars are all well labeled, the produce section is not. There is an impressive array of goods here, including bitter melon, fresh lemongrass, Thai basil, kefir lime leaves (which the store also sells dry), and several items I was unfamiliar with.

Among the canned goods are items you would never find at Star Market, such as shark's fin soup, palm sugar, braised gluten, bananas in syrup, jackfruit in syrup, coffee-coated peanuts, cuttlefish-flavored crispy fried green peas (called Greenuts), and rice-flour cookies flecked with black sesame seeds. The beverage refrigerator includes coconut soda, pennywort drink, and canned chrysanthemum tea alongside Pepsi and Sprite.

The noodle selection is impressive, with dozens of both fresh and dried wheat and rice noodles. On the counter by the cash register are stacks of Thai pastries, such as banana cake wrapped in banana leaves, and crunchy blocks of sweetened rice cakes.

Tan Phanh

434 Broadway, Chelsea, MA 02150   (617) 884-1993
Mail order: not available   Hours: daily 9 A.M.–8:30 P.M.

Tan Phanh is small, but it has a respectable number of Asian items. The produce offerings are good and fresh, and the staff is helpful.

Truong Thin Market

1051 Dorchester Avenue, Dorchester, MA 02125   (617) 436-5652
Mail order: not available   Hours: daily 9 A.M.–9 P.M.

English is barely spoken at this medium-sized Asian market. The produce selection is good, but I don't recommend purchasing fish from the live tank here—I noticed three dead fish in the water. The emphasis is on Thai goods, and there is a wide variety of noodles and various flours, including mung bean, rice, and tapioca. Canned goods include several curries of varying colors—red, green, yellow—preserved radishes, and bananas in syrup. Stacks of intriguing rice sweets are piled near the cashier.

Vien Dong Fareast Supermarket

1159 Dorchester Avenue, Dorchester, MA 02122   (617) 265-9131
Mail order: not available   Hours: daily 9 A.M.–9 P.M.

This is a medium-sized Asian market that includes fresh fish, meat, and produce, cleanly presented. No English is spoken so it helps to know what you want.

Viet Huong Market

1826 Dorchester Avenue, Dorchester, MA 02124   (617) 265-2553
Mail order: not available   Hours: daily 9 A.M.–8:30 P.M.

Viet Hong is a medium-small Asian market with a decent selection of goods, including fresh produce and meats. The people working here speak English. This is where I learned that the purplish, pointed oval thing I saw in several places is a banana flower, and how to prepare it.

Yoshinoya

36 Prospect Street, Cambridge, MA 02139   (617) 491-8221
Mail order: available   Hours: Tues.–Fri. 10:30 A.M.–7 P.M.;
    Sat. 9 A.M.–7 P.M.; Sun. noon–5 P.M.; closed Mon.

Yoshinoya was one of Cambridge's first Japanese markets, and they always have a good selection. It is like a small supermarket, with dry and frozen goods, produce, and fish. Yoshinoya was one of the first places where you could find sushi-quality tuna. They carry breads and baked items from Japonaise Bakery in Brookline (see "Everything Nice," page 244). You can also find things such as wonton skins and several kind of tofu (fresh, freeze-dried, pressed) here. The aisles contain shelves of noodles, condiments, teas, and sweets.

In addition to food, Yoshinoya carries several Japanese durables, such as cookware and lamps, as well as gift items.

❖ B R I T I S H ❖

British Food & Imports

1 Court Street, Plymouth, MA 02360   (508) 747-2972
Mail order: available   Hours: Mon.–Sat. 10 A.M.–5:30 P.M.;
    Sun. noon–5 P.M.

Brickyard Square, 216 Turnpike Road (Route 9), Southboro, MA 01772
   (508) 229-0878
Mail order: available   Hours: Mon.–Sat. 10 A.M.–5:30 P.M.;
   Sun. noon–5 P.M.

British Food & Imports carries a variety of British goods, with a strong emphasis on candies and other sweets. Owner Bruce MacLean supplies imports to several stores around the country as well.

The Plymouth store bakes a variety of English foods, including **sausage rolls; Cornish pasty,** a pastry filled with meat, potatoes, and vegetables; **steak and kidney pie; shepherd's pie;** and **bridies,** a triangular-shaped pastry filled with meat. These items are available, frozen, in the Southboro store, too, along with English sausage, Irish sausage, and black pudding. On Saturdays you can get **scones.** The pastries are sold both fresh and frozen; it's best to call in advance to see what is available.

The variety here is not overwhelming. I've been in many other ethnic markets with hundreds more choices. But this is one of two sources for British items, such as Lyle's Golden Syrup, an ingredient that makes a superb pecan pie; Marmite; several different brands of marmalade; and Heinz baked beans—the British version is different from the American version. MacLean says that the baked beans are one of his best-selling items, along with two candy bars by Cadbury, the Flake and the Crunchy.

Union Jack

134 Newbury Street (Route 1 South), Peabody, MA 01960
   (508) 535-6256
Mail order: not available   Hours: Mon.–Sat. 10 A.M.–5 P.M.;
   Sun. noon–5 P.M.

Union Jack has been supplying the North Shore with British goods since 1987. A sign proclaims that the store carries "British food and gifts," and gifts include teapots and tapes of Rowan Atkinson (a very funny comic actor) and other British television shows.

Much of the food is candy and cookies—or biscuits, as they are called in Britain. These include items such as treacle crumble cookies, Highland oatcakes, and Cadbury candy bars. Savory items include tiny jars of crab spread and tuna with mayonnaise, canned spaghetti ("made from fresh pasta"), brown-bread mix, and frozen items such as Irish bacon. British tea comes in huge packages (1,100 tea bags).

EASTERN
❖ EUROPEAN ❖
& RUSSIAN

People from the former Soviet Union have been immigrating to the Boston area for years. Brookline and Allston have the highest concentration, as reflected in the several markets in this area. These markets offer items from Russia, Poland, Ukraine, and other Eastern European countries. Some Western European items slip in too—I've seen a fair amount of Swiss chocolate in these places.

Bazaar International Gourmet

1432 Beacon Street, Brookline, MA 02146   (617) 739-8450
Mail order: not available   Hours: Mon.–Sat. 9 A.M.–9 P.M.;
   Sun. 10 A.M.–8 P.M.

Bazaar is located on Beacon Street in Brookline, at the very edge of Coolidge Corner. The shop offers a good selection of Russian and Eastern European items, including canned goods and refrigerated foods. A deli counter runs along one side of the store and contains smoked fish, salamis, and a variety of prepared foods, such as **chopped herring,** several **eggplant salads,** and **mushroom pâté.**

Berezka International Food Store

1211 Commonwealth Avenue, Allston, MA 02134   (617) 787-2837
Mail order: not available   Hours: Mon.–Sat. 9 A.M.–9 P.M.;
   Sun. 10 A.M.–6 P.M.

The layout of Berezka is somewhat odd; the store is on two levels. You walk up steps through a dark, though wide, entranceway, and are immediately greeted by dozens of sausages, primarily cured, in a display case and hanging above the counter to your left. Owner Inna Agron says that she carries about 140 boiled, half-smoked, and hard-smoked sausages. The cashier is by this counter, which runs into more steps. Another counter on your left is filled with all kinds of smoked fish—sturgeon, herring, sturgeon belly, several different varieties of smoked salmon. Across the way are shelves of sweets, chocolates wrapped in brightly colored papers.

The next display case features dozens of Eastern European pastries. Agron drives to the Kiev Bakery in Brooklyn twice a week to pick these up. Naturally, these are best if you can get them the day they come in. These include unusual sweets such as a **walnut cookie** with coffee cream. This consists of two large (four inches across) walnut macaroon cookies with a coffee-flavored, frosting-like filling. Similar is the **margarita,** made with almond meringue, slightly soft, yet chewy and crisp on the edges. The **potato** is so called because of its shape. It is a sphere of chocolate dough, like a cross between a brownie and fudge, laden with nuts and covered with chocolate.

Aisles in the back part of the store include all kinds of canned goods, including several varieties of canned mushrooms —bay bolete, oyster, *cèpes,* canary. There are jars of *lecso* (stewed tomatoes with peppers and onions), pitted sour cherries, rosehip preserves, and *tekemalli* (Russian plum sauce). Refrigerators hold butter from several countries, including France, Germany, Israel, and Russia. They carry Siberian *pelmeny*—ravioli filled with ground pork, beef, chicken, onions, and garlic. Breads here are from area bakers and are imported from abroad.

If you have any questions, it's best to come on a day when Agron is in. She's had the store since 1982, and she knows all about everything she sells. Note that you need to be assertive, even aggressive, when waiting in line here, as fellow shoppers often cut to the front.

European Deli

18 Corinth Street, Roslindale, MA 02131   (617) 325-7730
Mail order: not available   Hours: Mon.–Sat. 9 A.M.–10 P.M.;
    Sun. 11 A.M.–6 P.M.

The European Deli is a combination Russian deli and market that has been open since late 1994. The store carries a selection of Russian goods, including candies and jams and *protokvasha,* a thin yogurt that comes in a bottle. The deli offers a variety of cured meats and smoked fish, including the tough end pieces of smoked salmon, which are best used chopped finely and mixed with cream cheese. A lot of these items are available in **sandwiches,** along with more mundane **ham, roast beef,** and **turkey.**

J.P. Meat Market. See "Where's the Beef?" page 130.

Moscow International Foods

133 Harvard Avenue, Allston, MA 02134   (617) 782-6644
Mail order: not available   Hours: daily 9 A.M.–9 P.M.

Moscow International Foods is like a smaller-scale version of Berezka International Food Store, which is located around the corner on Commonwealth Avenue. The items are similar—sausages, smoked fish, and canned goods from Eastern European countries, as well as lots of chocolates and brightly wrapped candies.

❖ G E R M A N ❖

Karl's Sausage Kitchen. See "Where's the Beef?" page 136.

❖ H I S P A N I C & ❖ C A R I B B E A N

The Boston area has immigrants from South and Central America, and from Caribbean countries, and often there is an overlap in the markets catering to those cuisines. For that reason I've grouped these markets together here. The markets I list are some of the better, larger ones, but there are also dozens of small Hispanic markets around town. Multicultural Dorchester has several convenience stores with Hispanic and Caribbean leanings, as does Chelsea.

La Economica
164 Park Street, Chelsea, MA 02150   (617) 889-3529
Mail order: not available   Hours: daily 8 A.M.–10 P.M.

La Economica is a good-sized Hispanic market with an extensive array of items. They have one of the larger selections of Mexican chocolates, for example, with at least half a dozen brands, including Ibarra, Luker, and Corona. The selection here is great, and fortunately many items include English translations, because the staff is less than helpful.

Items that caught my interest include several drinks, such as cashew juice—cashews are actually seeds of a fruit, and this juice is made from the fruit—and *super horchata,* a mix that includes marrow seeds, rice, sugar, cocoa, peanuts, vanilla, and sesame seeds. There are several preserves made with tropical fruits, including guava, papaya, and passion fruit.

A refrigerator houses meats, fish, and dairy, including *tasajo*, salt-cured beef; baggies of tiny salt-cured fish; *Crema Salvadoreña*, a blend of sour cream, heavy cream, and cream cheese; and *queso la ricura*, a fresh cheese used in cooking.

Hi-Lo Foods

413 Centre Street, Jamaica Plain, MA 02130   (617) 522-6364
Mail order: not available   Hours: Mon.–Wed. and Sat. 7 A.M.–7 P.M.;
    Thurs., Fri. 7 A.M.–9 P.M.; Sun. 9 A.M.–6 P.M.

Hi-Lo is a supermarket-sized market that just happens to have a strong Hispanic focus. The choice of items is extensive, though not quite as specialized as the large Tropical Foods market in Roxbury. There are all the usual supermarket aisles, but they are filled with items from South America and the Caribbean. The dairy aisle includes *queso blanco,* a fresh white cheese. Condiments include sweet-potato jam with chocolate, Jamaican molasses, and twenty-six-ounce bottles of hot sauce. The produce section has stacks of plantains, chayote, and mangos, and the beverage aisle includes pear drinks, ginger beer, and mauby concentrate. Frozen goods include puréed guanábana pulp. There is the whole line of Goya canned beans, a brand found in most Hispanic markets as well as the larger generic supermarkets.

The store also carries meats, diapers, and other items you'll find in any supermarket.

Mayfair Foods

506 Cambridge Street, Allston, MA 02134   (617) 782-5539
Mail order: not available   Hours: Mon.–Sat. 7 A.M.–9 P.M.;
    Sun. 7 A.M.–8 P.M.

Mayfair is another store that shows little promise from the outside, but inside is quite a good source for Hispanic foods. Owner Omar Ocampo, a native of Colombia, has been running the store since 1982, and he tries to offer a wide selection. The store is clean, and items are easy to find. If you don't see what you want right away, the employees are helpful and glad to point things out. Unusual products include yerba mate tea, sold loose in large multi-pound packages or in tea bags, and Ibarra Mexican chocolate. You'll find tamale husks, guava paste, *dulce de leche* (a sweetened milk spread), jars of mole sauce (a savory sauce for meat and poultry, made with ground nuts, spices, and unsweetened chocolate), and all kinds of dried chiles.

Preparations

436 Blue Hill Avenue, Dorchester, MA 02121   (617) 445-5120
Mail order: not available   Hours: Mon.–Sat. 8 A.M.–10 P.M.;
    Sun. 10 A.M.–6 P.M.

Preparations is small and unassuming from the outside, but when you enter, you realize this is a better market than most. It is tiny, but everything is clean and beautifully displayed. The shop is owned by three brothers, Dexter and Cecil Wangoon (the primary proprietor), and Gino Victor, all originally from Trinidad. They also own a beauty salon by the same name, and a restaurant, Preparations Sea and Grill.

Cecil is knowledgeable and helpful regarding Caribbean cuisines; he'll give background information on the products he sells, such as the *root juices*. While I visited, several men came in and bought bottles of the juices, which are said to give you energy and improve virility. I tried a bottle; there's a slight buzz to the fermented drink, which tastes like a sweet beer. The fermented taste grew on me, and I kind of liked it, but my husband thought it was foul tasting. (I experienced no discernible change in energy.)

Preparations also sells fresh green coconuts. These do not look like the brown hairy spheres you see in the supermarket. They are larger—bigger than a honeydew melon. The proprietors will cut off an end and stick a straw in the coconut so you can drink the juice. Several customers came in for this as well. When you finish drinking the thin, refreshing liquid, they'll cut the coconut open, and you can eat the translucent jellylike meat —quite different from the firm white flesh of mature coconuts. Try the sugar cane. You chew it to extract the sweet juices, then spit out the fibrous pulp, which is indigestible.

All the produce comes from the New England Produce Center (see "Earthly Delights," page 55) and is beautifully displayed. The brothers also sell a homemade **fruit salad** made with their produce.

3-M Market

3114 Washington Street, Roxbury, MA 02130   (617) 522-8716
Mail order: not available   Hours: Mon.–Sat. 7:30 A.M.–9 P.M.;
    Sun. 8 A.M.–8 P.M.

As you enter 3-M Market, bear to your right. This is the section with the homemade **prepared foods,** some of which are quite good. Most are not for vegetarians; there are several trays of meaty stews, including **beef, chicken,** and **steak.** **Pastalo pie** is a tasty turnover filled with plantain, meat, and eggs. There is also **beans and rice,** popular as a side dish; **sausage soup;** and **plantain patties.** This section is the highlight of 3-M. Though the space here is large, there is not an overwhelming selection, but standard Hispanic goods are available.

Tropical Foods

2101 Washington Street, Roxbury, MA 02119   (617) 442-7439
Mail order: not available   Hours: Mon.–Sat. 7:30 A.M.–8 P.M.;
    Sun. 9 A.M.–6 P.M.

Tropical Foods is *the* place to go for Caribbean and South and Central American ingredients. Like all ethnic markets, I could spend hours here, studying the unusual ingredients.

The main part of the store carries a mix of Hispanic, Caribbean, and American goods; it is also where you'll find sundries such as paper towels. There are eight different canned Spam-like meats, a half-dozen nonalcoholic malts, six brands of sweetened condensed milk and eight of evaporated milk.

The second part of the store is the real tropical department. This is where you'll find items such as palm oil and coconut oil, kola nuts, and cream of palm fruit. South American countries have a variety of unusual drinks, many grain-based, and Tropical Foods has canisters of instant oat, barley, and other powdered drinks.

An aisle is devoted to canned and dried beans, all kinds —navy, yellow split pea, whole green pea, adzuki, cranberry, and more. There is also a variety of flours and another aisle dedicated to rice. Breads include a tasty coconut bread and Jamaican hard bread. This is a loaf of bread that is, well, hard. If you are not accustomed to it, as I am not, it is not that appealing.

The produce section is quite good, with well-labeled items—a switch from many ethnic markets. You may not know what to do with yucca or jicama, but at least you'll know what it looks like.

❖ I N D I A N ❖

Immigrants from India are settled mainly in Cambridge, Somerville, Framingham, and Waltham. Cambridge in particular probably has the area's highest concentration of Indian restaurants. Just two blocks of Central Square have half a dozen. The Indian markets range in size from tiny holes in the wall to medium-large; none are huge. Upon entering you are greeted with smells of incense and exotic spices.

Framingham India Grocery

185 Concord Street, Framingham, MA 01701   (508) 872-6120
Mail order: available   Hours: Mon.–Sat. 10:30 A.M.–9 P.M.;
    Sun. 10:30 A.M.–8:30 P.M.

Framingham India Grocery is by far the largest Indian market in the Boston area. Owner Minhaj Imtiazuddin says it is the largest Indian store in Massachusetts.

The number of items is impressive, and Imtiazuddin is happy to answer any questions, and to explain things, such as the difference between two seemingly similar vermicellis packaged in attractive patterned blue cardboard boxes (one is roasted, the other isn't). There are all sorts of intriguing canned vegetables, such as drumsticks (a kind of stalk) and Indian baby pumpkins. The front of the store also has fresh produce; inspect this carefully, as some items looked to be on the wrinkled side. Fresh turmeric may be hard to find, but you don't want it to be all shriveled up. The grocery also carries several items I've never heard of, either in Hindi and in the English translation.

One aisle is devoted to dals, which are all kinds of legumes, most the size of lentils or smaller, and flours made from those dals, such as *ladoo, jowar,* and *bajri.* Nearby are syrups for making drinks, such as *rooh atza,* a rose-flavored drink. You can find fresh *paneer* cheese here as well—a rarity.

Imtiazuddin and his wife, Imtiaz, have a table set up with savory **homemade pastries,** such as ***samosas,*** and **sweets.** They do also do catering.

In addition to food, there are several sundries, such as Ayurvedic soaps and creams, as well as clothing.

India Foods & Spices

80 River Street, Cambridge, MA 02139   (617) 497-6144
Mail order: available   Hours: Mon.–Sat. 10 A.M.–8 P.M.;
  Sun. noon–6 P.M.

Crammed into a tiny area smaller than the average living room
are numerous Indian goods, from tamarind chutney and *pappadam* (a cracker made from lentil and rice flours) to all the raw
ingredients you'll need to make every recipe in your favorite
Indian cookbook. There are nearly a dozen kinds of dal (prepared
lentils and split peas), as well as exotic spices you won't find in the
supermarket, such as *garam masala* (a mixture of spices, similar to
curry powder) and *asafetida*. The spices are ground on the premises, so they are fresher and stronger than spices you'll find elsewhere.

A few boxes hold produce used in Indian cooking, such
as mangos and bitter melon, but I've often found these items to
be in a rather unappetizing state—bruised and withered.

The store also sells **take-out Indian foods** made on the
premises or down the street at India Pavilion restaurant. Owner
Raghbir Singh's relatives own this and two other Indian restaurants. Take-out items include good *samosas* (potato and pea
turnovers), various **breads** and a **vegetable curry.** My favorite
item is *masala dosa,* a South Indian pancake made from ground
lentils and rice and filled with very spicy potatoes and chilies.
India Foods & Spices is one of only a few places in the Boston
area that makes *dosas,* and they do an acceptable job, creating a
filling meal that I like very much. The *dosa* is served with an
eye-tearingly hot soup called *sambar* and cooling **coconut-mint
chutney.**

A display case features over a dozen **Indian sweets,** most
of which you won't find on restaurant menus. They are all made
on the premises or, as with the savories, at India Pavilion.

Indian desserts are very different from American ones;
they are dense and sweet, fudgelike, and a small portion goes a
long way. The flavorings tend to be rosewater and cardamom,
distinctive tastes not always appealing to Americans. I like the
combinations, and I like Indian desserts, although I don't like all
the offerings here. Check when the item you are interested in
was made—most are best when freshest. Pass on the *balchai,* a
deep-fried patty that tastes mainly sweet and greasy. *Gulab
jamun,* a ball-shaped pastry deep-fried and soaked in a rosewater-

scented syrup, is a favorite, and India Foods' version is good, if slightly soggy. The *cutlass* is similar; it uses the same powdered-milk dough, cut into oval slices and colored pink and green in the center. I did not care for the *chamcham,* a milk-based dough with an odd chalky texture. Many of the desserts are milk-based, but the milk is evaporated to thicken it. My favorite sweet is the *pista burfi,* a kind of fudge made with milk that is slowly evaporated, stirred with sugar and ground pistachios. It is sweet but less sweet than American fudge.

Chickpeas are also used in several Indian desserts, and I've grown to like some of them (although initially I disliked them all). The taste is not unlike sesame halvah, the Middle Eastern candy. *Patasa* has an intriguing texture, flaky and crunchy, with a little bit of chewiness. *Besan burfi* is creamy and slightly crumbly, fudgelike in flavor and texture. I also like the **carrot halvah** (totally unlike sesame halva), which is a cross between a pudding and a candy, made with grated carrots, almonds, and cardamom seeds.

India Foods & Spices is small but it carries an extensive selection. Raghbir is helpful; this is my favorite Indian market.

If you want to end your Indian meal with a movie, you can rent one of several hundred made-in-India titles.

India Tea & Spices Inc.

453 Common Street, Belmont, MA 02178   (617) 484-3737
Mail order: available   Hours: Tues.–Fri. 1 P.M.–7 P.M.;
    Sat. 10 A.M.–6 P.M.; closed Sun., Mon.

India Tea & Spice is a medium-to-large space. It is the oldest store in the area, in operation since 1971. All the basic Indian items are here—spices, beans, rice. Basmati rice is available in both white and brown. Basmati is my all-time favorite rice, and I prefer the brown rice. It has a nutty flavor and smells like baking bread as it cooks.

Although the selection here is good, items are not always well labeled. This can present a challenge if you don't know exactly what you are looking for. But owner Niru Jinwala is knowledgeable and helpful. The store carries fresh produce—call to see when the latest delivery was made for the freshest pick. Choices include Indian items like *dhoodi* squash (a long green squash), *pappadam,* small eggplants, and curry leaves.

Frozen foods include several meat and vegetarian dinners, such as chicken curry and *palak paneer* (spinach with Indian *paneer* cheese). There are frozen dals (legumes) and prepared foods such as *kaman,* a chickpea puff.

Madras Masala

191 Harvard Street, Brookline, MA 02146   (617) 566-9943
Mail order: not available   Hours: Mon.–Sat. 11:30 A.M.– 8 P.M.;
   Sun. 1 P.M.–6 P.M.

Madras Masala is a medium-sized store with items nicely displayed along the walls and on tables in the middle of the store. They carry most Indian items, such as black mustard seeds, dried mango powder, a variety of mango pickles, and *pappadam.*

Shalimar India Food & Spices

571 Mass. Avenue, Cambridge, MA 02139   (617) 868-8311
Mail order: not available   Hours: Mon.–Sat. 10 A.M.–9 P.M.;
   Sun. noon–8 P.M.

Shalimar is a very long, very narrow store with an extensive array of Indian goods. You can find all kinds of dal here—beans, that is—which is required for Indian cooking, as well as a large collection of spices. The owners are helpful, if somewhat formal. A refrigerator includes prepared foods brought in from New York.

SMALL MARKETS

The following Indian markets are small, but worth a peek if you are in the neighborhood.

Annapurna Enterprises Inc.

1185 N. Main Street, Randolph, MA 02368   (617) 961-3740
Mail order: not available   Hours: Tues.–Fri. 2 P.M.–8 P.M.;
   Sat. Sun. noon–7 P.M.; closed Mon.

Eastern Food & Spices

233 Elm Street, Somerville, MA 02144   (617) 666-8721
Mail order: not available   Hours: daily 10 A.M.–8 P.M.

India Groceries

16 Tremont Street, Brighton, MA 02135   (617) 254-5540
Mail order: not available   Hours: Mon.–Fri. 2 P.M.–8 P.M.;
   Sat. noon–7 P.M.; Sun. noon–5 P.M.; closed Sun. in the summer

Little India Groceries
361-B Somerville Avenue, Somerville, MA 02143   (617) 623-1786
Mail order: not available   Hours: Mon.–Sat. 10 A.M.–9 P.M.;
    Sun. 11 A.M.–7 P.M.

New Apna Bazaar
395 Moody Street, Waltham, MA 02154   (617) 893-4816
Mail order: not available   Hours: Mon.–Sat. noon–8 P.M.;
    Sun. noon–7 P.M.

❖ I T A L I A N ❖

The Boston area is permeated with Italian influences. The North
End is the obvious Italian neighborhood, and it has its share of
excellent markets. But nearly every town has a small market with
an Italian bent, a source for imported Italian pastas and olive oils.
Following are some of the area's more worthwhile stops.

Alfredo Aiello Italian Pasta Store. See "Lotsa Pasta," page 98.

Bob's Imported Food and Fine Catering
324 Main Street, Medford, MA 02155   (617) 395-0400
Mail order: available   Hours: Mon.–Thurs. 9 A.M.–7 P.M.;
    Fri. 9 A.M.–8 P.M.; Sat. 8 A.M.–7 P.M.; Sun. 8 A.M.–3 P.M.

Bob's is a store that wears many hats. Bob DiGiorgio is the third
Bob in the business; his grandfather started the store in 1934, as
a basic grocery. Over the years the store has grown and changed.
Now it is more of a specialty foods store, with a concentration
on Italian goods. They make extruded **pasta** from semolina,
durum, and eggs, in a variety of shapes. No fancy flavors here,
although they will make **spinach pasta** to order, as well as their
own **tortellini** and **ravioli.**

A chef is on hand, cooking pasta to order for takeout,
in luscious-smelling combinations such as **chicken, ziti, and
broccoli.** Other take-out items include **prepared salads,** such as
grilled chicken Caesar salad and homemade **vinegared peppers.** Then there are the **sandwiches**—terrific. Their **grilled
marinated eggplant** is one of the best versions I've had of this
sandwich. When you order your sandwich, the cook removes the
eggplant from the flavorful marinade and grills it to order. Also
great is the **marinated lamb-kabob sub.** Bob says his favorite is

the **chicken Parmesan sub.** Sandwiches come in three sizes and prices. A medium, served on a French baguette, is a fairly generous portion.

Next to the sandwich counter, which is in the back of the store, is a meat counter, where you can buy fresh meats cut to order. Bob's makes their own **sausages,** including **sweet, hot,** and **fennel,** as well as an intriguing **roasted red pepper–provolone.** The also have **chicken sausage,** made to order only.

In the center of the store are aisles with imported Italian goods, including a range of dried pastas, tomatoes, and olive oils. There are also loaves of fresh bread, including a thick-crusted Italian round from New York.

Bob and his father (Bob number 2) both work in the store, and they are very helpful, as are all the staff. The shop also does catering.

Cremaldi's. See "Goodies to Go," page 173.

Imperial Grocery
82 Main Street, Everett, MA 02149   (617) 389-2412
Mail order: not available   Hours: Mon.–Sat. 8 A.M.–8 P.M.;
    Sun. 8 A.M.–1 P.M.

Imperial, located just off the rotary at the beginning of Everett, has a good inventory of Italian foods. There are several imported pastas, olive oils, and cookies, and the prices are decent. Owner Tracy Imbriano recently added a **sandwich** counter, with a variety of Italian and American cold cuts. They also make **espresso.** Imbriano has already enlarged the store three times, and she has plans for further expansion.

Nappi Meats & Groceries. See "Where's the Beef?" page 134.

New Deal Fruit. See "Earthly Delights," page 57.

J. Pace & Son Inc.
22 Cross Street, North End, Boston, MA 02113   (617) 227-9673
Mail order: available   Hours: Mon.–Sat. 8 A.M.–7 P.M.;
    Sun. 8 A.M.–5 P.M.

2 Devonshire Street, Boston, MA 02109   (617) 227-4949
Mail order: available   Hours: Mon.–Fri. 6 A.M.–8 P.M.;
    Sat. 8 A.M.–4 P.M.; closed Sun.

J. Pace & Son in the North End is a spacious, airy grocery. The store isn't huge, but the aisles are wide, and the selection of imported Italian goods is extensive. There are dozens of extra-virgin olive oils, ranging in both price and quality. There are also several other kinds of hard-to-find oils—grapeseed, walnut, hazelnut—in both tins and bottles, as well as several brands of balsamic vinegars. You have your choice of dried Italian pastas or durum and semolina flours in bulk if you want to make your own. Other bulk items include sun-dried tomatoes and peppers, nuts, and grains. Arborio rice, the rice of choice for risotto, was reasonably priced at under $2 a pound when I visited. Boston's Pastene brand of canned goods—beans and such—figures prominently here, as does the French Roland brand. There's a choice of Italian cookies and cakes, as well as brightly colored Italian stoneware on which to serve them.

The store also has standard convenience items such as soda and paper towels, and it has a deli section. The yeasty smell of baking bread comes from this corner—**focaccia** is made on the premises, in two flavors: **onion** and **potato-pesto.** If you ask (and if you're here at the right time), you can get one of these flat, rectangular loaves fresh from the oven; otherwise they're bagged in plastic, which tends to soften the crust. J. Pace also makes loaves of flavored bread. The **prosciutto** and the **sun-dried tomato breads** are unremarkable. However, the **olive bread,** made with both black and green olives, is delicious. The **sandwiches,** made on bread baked in a neighborhood bakery, are very good, and come with a variety of meats and cheeses.

In late 1995 Pace's opened a second store in Boston (after closing one in Beverly) at the former site of a J. Bildner. They make a lot of sandwiches here, catering to the business lunch crowd.

Previte's. See "Where's the Beef?" page 140.

Regina Food Store
203 Main Street, Everett, MA 02149   (617) 387-1655
Mail order: not available   Hours: Mon.–Sat. 7 A.M.–7:30 P.M.;
    Sun. 7 A.M.–1 P.M.

At first glance, you may think Regina Food Store is a typical convenience store—and you can get chips and soda here. But step in further and you'll find a very good choice of imported

Italian items. There are several kinds of pasta, as well as imported Italian tomatoes, oils, vinegars, and other items. The business card notes that they specialize in cold cuts, and there is indeed a good selection of these, as well as cheeses—more than just provolone.

Salumeria Italiano. See "Goodies to Go," page 197.

Salumeria Toscana. See "An Epicurean Agenda," page 374.

Sessa's Italian Specialties
412–414 Highland Avenue, Somerville, MA 02144   (617) 776-6687
Mail order: available   Hours: Mon.–Sat. 8 A.M.–6 P.M.;
   Sun. 8 A.M.–1 P.M.

Giancarlo Sessa has been operating this overflowing Italian market in Davis Square, Somerville, since 1979. The shop started as one storefront and has now expanded into the space of three stores. Aisles are packed with the expected Italian ingredients—olive oil, pasta, tomato sauce—only there is more variety of everything than you might expect. At last count, Sessa asserts, he carries some forty-three varieties of extra-virgin Italian olive oil. For dried pasta, all imported from Italy, I counted over a dozen brands, and Sessa says he carries every cut of four different brands. The *cut* is the size and shape of the pasta. Look at the packages and you'll see a number; this indicates the cut, from spaghetti to *tagliatelle* and beyond. Brands included Mennucci, Delverde, Igomitoli, and many others.

Other notable products include several mineral waters. In addition to the now more common San Pellegrino, there are brands such as Levissima and Galvanina. There is also a variety of Italian juices and sodas. The store carries a full line of Pastene and Progresso products—canned beans, tomatoes, and the like —as well as imported arborio rice (reasonably priced) and several kinds of balsamic vinegar.

Sessa sells fresh bread from three bakeries—two local and one in New York, which supplies crusty Italian Tuscan bread. A deli counter boast a variety of cheeses, including heavy wheels of Parmesan and Romano, fresh mozzarella, and cured meats. Sessa makes his own **tomato sauce,** which he keeps in the refrigerator.

Tony's Meat Market. See "Where's the Beef?" page 128.

Tutto Italiano

1889 River Street, Hyde Park, MA 02136   (617) 361-4700
Mail order: not available   Hours: Tues.–Sat. 9 A.M.–6 P.M.;
    Sun. 9 A.M.–1 P.M.; closed Mon.

1300 Centre Street, Newton, MA 02159   (617) 969-1591
Mail order: baskets available   Hours: Mon.–Fri. 10 A.M.–6 P.M.;
    Sat. 10 A.M.–5 P.M.; closed Sun.

568-A Washington Street, Wellesley, MA 02181   (617) 431-2250
Mail order: not available   Hours: Tues., Wed., and Fri., 10 A.M.–
    6 P.M.; Thurs. 10 A.M.–8 P.M.; Sat. 9 A.M.–6 P.M.; closed Sun., Mon.

Angelo Locillento opened his first Tutto Italiano store in Hyde Park in 1986. It is a combination Italian market and *salumeria,* or "sandwich shop"; the slogan on the front door claims, "The best sandwiches outside of Italy." While I'm not sure I would agree wholeheartedly, these are very good sandwiches. Locillento makes his own **panella bread** in the Hyde Park facility daily, from a two-hundred-year-old recipe, as well as his own **mozzarella cheese.** The bread is terrific, just the right firm texture for sandwiches. Great **sandwiches** are made with the simple mozzarella, tomato, and basil and the prosciutto, mozzarella, tomato, basil, and oregano. They also make a decent **focaccia.**

Locillento has high goals for his business; he hopes to turn it into a franchise with 144 stores. Why 144? He likes that number. As of this writing, he had just franchised the Newton store to Carol Stout, a longtime customer.

In addition to sandwich fixings, the stores also carries frozen and dried pasta, imported olive oils, olives, cookies, and other goods from Italy.

❖ K O S H E R ❖

Most kosher butchers also carry a few kosher foods, such as condiments and cookies. Some carry a more extensive choice of goods, including those listed below. Kosher butcheries are featured in "Where's the Beef?"

Beacon Kosher

1706 Beacon Street, Brookline, MA 02146   (617) 734-5300
Mail order: not available   Hours: Mon., Tues. 7:30 A.M.–8:30 P.M.;
    Wed., Thurs. 7:30 A.M.–9 P.M.; Fri. 7:30 A.M.–3 P.M.;
    Sun. 8:30 A.M.–3 P.M.; closed Sat.

Israeli music greets you as you enter Beacon Kosher. There is kosher meat here, but that is not the primary focus. The primary focus is kosher goods. Everything in the store is kosher, and there are many items imported from Israel: an excellent goat cheese, canned and frozen produce, pickles, olives, chocolates, and bubble gum. There is also a bakery that churns out fresh **challah, bagels, cookies,** and **cakes,** all of which are *pareve,* or dairy-free. This is the place to come for the widest selection of kosher-for-Passover items.

The Butcherie. See "Where's the Beef?" page 145.

The Butcherie II. See "Where's the Beef?" page 145.

Gordon & Alperin Inc. See "Where's the Beef?" page 146.

❖ M I D D L E   E A S T E R N ❖

There are immigrants in the Boston area from a myriad of Middle Eastern countries—Syria, Lebanon, Turkey, and Egypt, to name some of the more common countries. Watertown has one of the country's most prominent Armenian communities, and a high concentration of Armenian markets. Markets owned by immigrants from other Middle Eastern communities can be found scattered throughout the Boston area. Some of these shops are described in detail in other chapters, notably a few pita bakeries and halal meat markets that also carry Mediterranean items. (See "The Staff of Life" and "Where's the Beef?")

Arax Market
603 Mt. Auburn Street, Watertown, MA 02172   (617) 924-3399
Mail order: not available   Hours: Mon.–Sat. 8:30 A.M.–8 P.M.;
    closed Sun.

Arax is noticeable first as a produce market, with boxes of fruit displayed on the sidewalk. When I first saw the store several years ago, I wondered how they could stay in business, since they are located directly across the street from Kay's, which has many more fruits and vegetables. But Arax stays in business because they have something different to offer. Although there isn't as much produce, there are harder-to-find items, such as eggplant in several shapes and sizes, kumquats, a variety of chili peppers, and fresh herbs.

Furthermore, produce is only a small part of what the market carries. The crowded aisles are overflowing with Middle Eastern items and other foods. There are all kinds of nuts and dried fruit, including dried cranberries, cherries, and blueberries, as well as raisins, currants, and apricots. There are stacks of pita breads, from small pocket pitas to huge, cloth-thin breads folded over into a rectangular package.

Most of the time when you visit, Alice Setian will be behind the counter near the door. She owns the place with her husband and sister-in-law, Elizabeth Basnajian. She speaks five languages (English, French, Armenian, Arabic, and Turkish) and understands a smattering of several others. Any questions about Middle Eastern ingredients? Setian can help.

Exotic spices are abundant here. This is where I found *limoo amoni,* a dried Persian lime called for in Moroccan recipes. There are beans and grains—bulgur in various sizes, couscous, rice. In the refrigerator, which runs along one wall, and along the shelves opposite, are over a dozen kinds of olives. Setian and Basnajian make their own **pickles,** which are kept in large tubs by the shelves. Find a plastic container and help yourself. These are no ordinary pickles. There are **pickled cucumbers,** but then there are dozens of other **pickled** and **marinated vegetables**— **turnip, mushroom, cauliflower, eggplant, okra,** and **mixed vegetables,** to name a few.

A cheese case offers about twenty different cheeses, including Hungarian *kasseri* and three kinds of feta—Greek, Bulgarian, and French. There are also canned and jarred items, such as grape leaves, chili paste, and sour cherries.

Blackstone Halal Market. See "Where's the Beef?" page 141.

Cambridge Halal Meat Market & Grocery Store. See "Where's the Beef?" page 143.

Eastern Lamejun
145 Belmont Street, Belmont, MA 02178   (617) 484-5239
Mail order: available   Hours: Mon.–Fri. 8 A.M.–7 P.M.;
    Sat. 8 A.M.–6 P.M.; closed Sun.

Since 1944 Eastern Lamejun has been selling Middle Eastern specialties and making *lamejun,* a kind of Armenian pizza made on a cracker-thin crust and covered with spiced ground lamb. When Bedros Der Vartanian came here from Syria and bought the place in 1984 with his family, they continued the established traditions and added some of their own. Most of the Armenian bakeries in Watertown make *lamejun,* but I think Eastern's is the best. They also introduced **chicken** and **vegetarian** versions in the early 1990s, which proved popular enough that other establishments are making them as well.

The store carries a wide variety of goods, from canned grape leaves to pasta and olive oils. They are also a distributor of spices, carrying 105 different kinds, including sumac, a deep red spice with a lemony flavor, which is used in several Armenian dishes.

Through a door in the middle of the store is the kitchen, where several people are cooking throughout the day. Some of the women who prepare the *lamejun* by hand have been working here for more than two decades. In addition to the *lamejun,* Eastern makes excellent **stuffed grape leaves,** filled with rice and raisins. They make the now ubiquitous **tabouli, hummus,** and **baba ganoush** (all are very good), but they also make several other **dips** and **prepared foods,** including the absolute best *muhammara* I've tasted. This is an unusual dip made with walnuts, red bell peppers, sumac, and pomegranate molasses. It's rich and complex, and always a hit at parties. There's also an **eggplant dip** made with eggplants and tomatoes; as well as **olive salad, kidney-bean salad,** and *metch,* a blend of bulgur, tomatoes, and scallions.

Eastern makes a number of **frozen entrées,** including *kefta,* balls of dough made out of bulgur and stuffed with a meat or vegetarian filling, and **moussaka. Spinach pies** and **cheese pies** are available fresh or frozen. If you can get here when the cheese pies come out of the oven, you'll be in luck; they taste best this way, with the cheese still hot and melty. There are also several **Armenian pastries,** including *puklava* (same as baklava), made by Bedros's mother, **pistachio cookies,** and **raisin cookies.** The latter two are dry and not too sweet—good for dunking in coffee.

In addition, Eastern Lamejun carries a selection of olives (Alfonso, black Greek, Kalamata, oil-cured), Middle Eastern cheeses (*kefalotiry, vlahotiri, manyopi*—my favorite), and meats, including *pasterma,* a dried beef, the beef sausage *soujuk,* and the pork sausage *loganico.*

Homsy's
224 Providence Highway, Westwood, MA 02090   (617) 326-9659
Mail order: available   Hours: Mon.–Thurs. and Sat. 9 A.M.–6 P.M.;
    Fri. 9 A.M.–7 P.M.; closed Sun.

Laura George of Near East Bakery (see "The Staff of Life," page 43) told me about Homsy's, her other business. I thought, she owns the place, naturally she thinks it's wonderful. But when I visited I discovered that Homsy's *is* indeed wonderful. A large market and gourmet shop, it carries the specialties of several countries—many customers are Indian—although the dominant theme is Middle Eastern.

There are shelves of oils, including several olive oils, nut oils such as hazelnut and pistachio, and flavored oils such as garlic and chili. Lots of teas, preserves, salsas, pastes, and spices line the other shelves. An aisle at the back, next to the freezers, is filled with large bags standing open, containing rice and beans, including several different dals for Indian cooking.

Around the sides of the store, the Middle Eastern presence can be felt. The freezers contain homemade savory **filo pastries,** and the refrigerators have containers of homemade **hummus** and **baba ganoush.** A counter near the door has **prepared foods,** including an unusual **eggplant with yogurt, marinated olive,** and vegetarian **stuffed grape leaves.** The store carries most of Near East's pitas, but they make their own **meat pies** and **spinach pies.** The latter are terrific. The pastry used is a yeast dough, but it is rolled ultrathin, almost translucent. The spinach filling is cooked to the point where the spinach melts in your mouth, and it is heavily seasoned with lemon and sumac.

A case in the back contains homemade **pastries.** The *mamoul,* crumbly molded cookies filled with either walnuts or dates, is fair. The **pistachio baklava** is a real treat. Buttery layers of filo pastry are topped with a half-inch-thick layer of chopped, sweetened pistachio nuts. The **walnut baklava** is the same but with walnuts, and it isn't as tasty.

The other end of the counter offers six different kinds of halvah, rich cakes of sesame candy. Behind the counter is a vast array of spices—over a hundred different kinds. There are nine types of dried mushrooms, and hard to-find items like chestnut flour and arrowroot.

Kay's. See "Earthly Delights," page 60.

Lebanese Market

4640 Washington Street, Roslindale, MA 02131   (617) 469-2900
Mail order: available for orders over $100
Hours: Mon.–Sat. 9 A.M.–8 P.M.; Sun. noon–5 P.M.;
  closed Sun. in the summer

The Lebanese Market, located by a shopping center (so there's lots of easy parking), is a medium-sized Middle Eastern market that sells groceries and fresh produce. The store could be cleaner; the floor is grubby, and some of the pickled eggplants that weren't submerged in a display vat had mold growing on them. But it is a good source for olives, oils, grains, and condiments from the Middle East. The owners also make a selection of **prepared foods,** including **stuffed grape leaves, *kibbeh,*** and various **salads.** Some items looked fresher than others. Before buying their homemade items, ask when they were made, or go by your gut reaction to the way things look.

Massis

569 Mt. Auburn Street, Watertown, MA 02172   (617) 924-0537
Mail order: not available   Hours: Mon.–Sat. 7:30 A.M.–7:30 P.M.;
  closed Sun.

Massis is bright and roomy and stocks a good selection of Middle Eastern foods, such as dry-roasted chickpeas (eaten as a snack), black and green olives, and *labane* (yogurt cheese). The store's specialties are its **baked goods,** most of which are made on the premises. The sweets are average—baklava and other filo pastries (which they don't make), and a few dry cookies. What's best are the **breads** and **savory turnovers** (called *pies)* especially the **spinach pies.** These are triangles of thin yeast dough with a flavorful spinach filling. The key seasoning is deep-red sumac, which imparts a lovely lemon taste. Massis makes my favorite of all the area's spinach pies. Other fillings are **cheese, meat,** and **spinach and cheese.** They also sell an intriguing **tahini pastry,** a crisp, flaky flat dough flavored with tahini (sesame paste) and honey. The breads include O-shaped **sesame rings** and round **flat breads** with a variety of toppings, including **spicy red pepper** and *zaatar,* an oregano-like herb.

Near East Bakery. See "The Staff of Life," page 43.

New Halal Meat & Grocery Store. See "Where's the Beef?" page 142.

Phoenicia Market
469 Centre Street, Brockton, MA 02402   (508) 580-2494
Mail order: not available   Hours: daily 9:30 A.M.–11:30 P.M.

Phoenicia is a combination Middle Eastern market and take-out restaurant. The offerings are few but they provide the necessities, such as Beirut honey, carob molasses, and various olives.

Take-out items feature traditional Lebanese fare, including good **falafel,** and very good **tabouli.** Less common items include **raw *kibbeh,*** a dish made with bulgur and ground lamb, as well as *kibbeh kababs* and *bastorma,* an aged beef eaten as an appetizer. There is also a refreshing *labane* (yogurt cheese), **cucumber, and mint salad.**

Owner Nannette Ata makes all the food, and all the pastries, including both **pistachio** and **walnut baklava,** both of which are among the better baklavas I've tasted.

In 1995 Ata opened a full-service restaurant adjoining the market.

Roslindale Fish Market. See "Some Things Fishy," page 112.

The Syrian Grocery
570 Shawmut Avenue, Boston, MA 02119   (617) 426-1458
Mail order: available   Hours: Mon.–Fri. 10:30 A.M.–6:30 P.M.;
    Sat. 10 A.M.–6 P.M.; closed Sun.

The Mansour family has owned this store since 1967, and the store itself has been in operation since 1940. The three sons now run the store along with a wholesale business; they are distributors for several Middle Eastern products, including Athens filo dough and Sahadi tahini. Middle Eastern items in this store include grape leaves and *labane* (yogurt cheese), shelled pistachio nuts, halvah from New York, and pita breads and pastries from Near East Bakery. They also sell their own homemade **hummus** and **baba ganoush.**

The store is not exclusively Middle Eastern; they carry a number of gourmet items and ingredients for other kinds of ethnic foods, such as Indian chutneys, Italian balsamic vinegar, green French lentils, and Walker shortbread from Scotland.

❖ PORTUGUESE & ❖
BRAZILIAN

Cambridge Street in Cambridge is the place to go for Portuguese and Brazilian products. There are several bakeries and small markets along the stretch from the Court House to Inman Square, which also supports some excellent seafood. Union Square in Somerville also has a couple of markets.

Court House Fish Market. See "Some Things Fishy," page 114.

Fernandes Fish Market. See "Some Things Fishy," 115.

International Market
365 Somerville Avenue, Somerville, MA 02143   (617) 776-1880
Mail order: not available   Hours: Mon.–Sat. 9 A.M.–7:30 P.M.;
    Sun. 10 A.M.–5:30 P.M.

The International Market is small and crowded, but there is a worthwhile selection of Brazilian items, including *crotalara* leaves in brine, frozen conch meat, salted beef, and linden flower tea. They also have chipotle peppers, which can be difficult to find. There is some fresh produce, of mixed quality, though you can find unusual fruits such as bitter oranges. The store also carries a variety of Brazilian breads and pastries.

New Deal Fish Market. See "Some Things Fishy," page 116.

The Portuguese American Market
57 Union Square, Somerville, MA 02143   (617) 666-4532
Mail order: available   Hours: Mon., Tues. 8 A.M.–6 P.M.;
    Wed.–Sat. 8 A.M.–7 P.M.; closed Sun.

This is a very large, uncrowded space, with a small inventory of Potuguese goods, including salt cod. You'll find loaves of Portuguese sweetbread here, as well as various grains and dried beans. Their meat counter features several kinds of sausage.

THE BESTS OF THE BEST

Best Asian market: **Ming's** and **The 88 Supermarket**
Best British market: **British Food & Imports**

Best Eastern European/Russian market: **Berezka International Food Store**

Best Hispanic/Caribbean market: **Tropical Foods**

Best Indian market: **Framingham India Grocery** and **India Foods & Spices**

Best Italian market: **J. Pace & Son Inc.** and **Sessa's Italian Specialties**

Best kosher market: **The Butcherie** and **Beacon Kosher**

Best Middle Eastern market: **Arax Market, Eastern Lamejun,** and **Homsy's**

Best Middle Eastern dips: **Eastern Lamejun**

Best *lamejun:* **Eastern Lamejun**

Best spinach pies: **Massis** and **Homsy's**

Best Portuguese/Brazilian market: **The Portuguese American Market**

❖ CHAPTER TWELVE ❖
GOING ORGANIC

A survey of area health-food stores

*T*HE term *health food* can have various interpretations. These days, it seems health-food stores prefer to be called *whole food* or *natural food* markets. Whatever. I still think of a place that sells organically grown produce, tofu, and half a dozen kinds of brown rice as a health-food store.

Interestingly, Cambridge, which has lots of ice-cream establishments, also has the area's largest concentration of health-food stores.

I like health-food stores for the options they present. Many offer all kinds of grains and flours you can't easily find in a conventional market. Several establishments have bulk bins, from which you can measure out the exact quantity you want of items such as grains, beans, flours, granolas, pastas, and spices. These stores are usually very good sources for nuts, often sold in bulk. The nuts are fresher, and there is more variety than you would find in a supermarket. Bulk spices here are also fresher, and significantly cheaper than prepackaged varieties.

A health-food store is also the place to find products such as miso, vital wheat gluten (useful when making whole wheat bread), and barley malt, as well as various obscure ethnic products. Many offer vegetable juices, hormone-free meat, buck-

429

wheat noodles, and perhaps some culinary inspiration. It's always fun to explore and to purchase unknown products and experiment with them at home.

A lot of so-called health-food stores are actually natural vitamin stores. Sure, they have some token boxes of oatmeal and bags of brown rice, but the main focus is vitamins. I make no claims to be a vitamin expert. The stores included in this chapter focus primarily on food and offer a selection of natural products.

* Described in another chapter.

Arborway Natural Foods	Jamaica Plain
Arlington Food Co-op	Arlington
Arlington Health Foods	Arlington
Bread & Circus	Boston, Brighton, Cambridge, Newton, Wellesley
Cambridge Natural Foods	Cambridge
Cape Ann Food Co-op	Gloucester
Concord Spice & Grain	Concord
The Earth Food Store	Andover
Good Health Natural Foods	Quincy
Harvest Cooperative Supermarket	Allston, Cambridge
Lee Nutrition	Cambridge
The Natural Gourmet	Concord
New Horizons Health Food Store	Beverly
New Leaf	Beverly
Simple Enough	Westboro
Simply Natural	Southboro
*South End Naturals	Boston

BOSTON

BOSTON

Bread and Circus. See Cambridge, page 434.

South End Naturals. See "Liquid Refreshment," page 466.

ALLSTON

Harvest Cooperative Supermarket

449 Cambridge Street, Allston, MA 02134   (617) 787-1416
Mail order: not available   Hours: Mon.–Sat. 9 A.M.–10 P.M.;
   Sun. noon–9 P.M.

581 Mass Avenue, Cambridge, MA 02139   (617) 661-1580
Mail order: not available   Hours: Mon.–Sat. 9 A.M.–9 P.M.;
   Sun. noon–8 P.M.

I have been coming to the Harvest Co-op for years—before it was called Harvest. The two stores started out as two separate co-ops around 1974: the Boston Food Co-op in Allston and the Cambridge Food Co-op in Cambridge. When the Cambridge Co-op nearly went out of business, the Boston Food Co-op bought the Cambridge store and merged the two stores, renaming them Harvest.

Harvest is a *cooperative*, which means that it is member-owned. Anyone can shop here, and anyone can join. There are a few levels of membership, but the basic individual annual membership fee is $10, which gives you a 2 percent discount off marked prices. Members who work three hours a month get a 10 percent discount, and members who work two hours a week get a 20 percent discount.

Since I live in Cambridge, I prefer this location, but both are good stores. At my store there is a long, wide hall from the Mass. Ave. entrance, and it is filled with pushcarts selling anything from incense and embroidered imported clothing to jewelry and used books.

In the store itself there is a good produce section, with organic and conventional fruits and vegetables. The quality here can vary, as can the prices; seasonal is always best. Harvest prides itself on being a full-service market, and they do have some sundries such as paper towels and commercial products as well as all-natural ones. The meat and poultry are hormone-free, although they don't always look that great. The fish rarely appeals to me.

There is a very nice **salad bar** (Cambridge only), and the deli section has a variety of pleasing **prepared salads,** most of which are made at the Cambridge store, which is a little larger than the Allston store. The **Mediterranean quinoa salad** is terrific, light and refreshing in the summer with feta cheese,

431

cucumber, and tomato. There are several **pasta salads,** with combinations a little different from those commonly seen. **Poppy cheese pasta** is a rich, tangy dish made with cream cheese, yogurt, and poppy seeds, and it is tasty. I don't care for the **paprika pasta**—too much paprika. The **dilled tuna pasta,** bite-size shells liberally seasoned with dill, is quite good, and I also like the **pasta Asiago tofu,** macaroni with a light vinaigrette. **Tofu-fried rice** is a best-seller.

They offer some entrées made to be heated up, such as **grilled tofu and onions,** a slab of tofu served with a side of caramelized onions; **chicken Florentine,** with a bread and spinach stuffing; and **chicken seafood medley,** chicken breasts stuffed with seafood. The deli case prices are all strikingly low. Everything here is significantly cheaper than virtually any other take-out place I've visited. Most salads are about $2.99 a pound, and none cost more than $6 a pound. And they are good!

The deli section also sells smoked fish and about half a dozen kinds of olives and pickles. They make a variety of **sandwiches** to order. These aren't as cheap as the salads, but you have the option to get a half-sandwich. Appealing combinations include **Ol' Smokey** (smoked turkey and smoked mozzarella) and **Mother Earth,** marinated roast tofu, sautéed onions, and tahini–poppy seed spread. You can also design your own combination with a choice of meats, cheeses, and vegetables. The bread used is from Wheatstone bakery (see "Staff of Life," page 5).

My favorite part of the store is the bulk bin area. Harvest has one of the more extensive selections of items you can purchase from bins. There are over a dozen kinds of grains, lots of nuts (try the roasted almonds, unsalted), and all kinds of grains. There are several rices, including brown basmati, which has become my rice of choice. There is also a great selection of flours, including chickpea, rye, rice, cornmeal, and blue cornmeal. Other bulk items include snacks, such as carob-coated nuts and chocolate pieces, and over a hundred kinds of herbs, spices, and loose teas. You can also buy maple syrup and tamari sauce in bulk, and fresh-ground peanut butter.

Harvest makes only a few baked items, although they are hoping to expand their offerings. They currently sell cakes made by Rosie's Bakery (see "Everything Nice," page 251) and some local wholesale companies. The non-fat applesauce raisin cake is surprisingly good, and the low-fat almond cake is tasty as well.

Other aisles contain groceries, from canned goods to crackers and cereals. There is a variety of ethnic items, such as coconut milk, Indian pickles, and Asian noodles. The refrigerated section contains yogurt and dairy products, including bottled milk. I rarely get cheese here, though. There is a reasonable selection, but it is often poorly wrapped, and I've found chunks with mold.

The coolers also hold prepared foods—tabouli, hummus, and other salads—as well as sandwiches, including some made by Season's Harvest (see "Goodies to Go," page 206). There is a small section for vitamins, herbs, and alternative medicines, as well as health and beauty products. Sale items are usually displayed on shelves near the front of the store. Both stores have nice play areas for kids.

BRIGHTON

Bread and Circus. See Cambridge, page 434.

JAMAICA PLAIN

Arborway Natural Foods

57 South Street, Jamaica Plain, MA 02130   (617) 524-9210
Mail order: not available   Hours: Mon.–Sat. 8 A.M.–9 P.M.;
    Sun. 9 A.M.–7 P.M.

Arborway has been a source for natural foods in Jamaica Plain since 1979. They stock a variety of specialty foods, as well as staples such as tofu and tahini. A bulk section has grains and flours and some legumes. There is produce, with organic items; this section includes an appealing **salad bar.**

The seafood section includes a lobster tank. There are both red meat and chicken, and the store sells **cooked chickens** as well. The refrigerated section features a variety of natural yogurts and other dairy goods. There is also a small wine and beer area.

The store sells primarily food, but they do have what they call a nutrition center stocked with lots of vitamins and supplements.

METROPOLITAN BOSTON

CAMBRIDGE

Bread & Circus

115 Prospect Street, Cambridge, MA 02139   (617) 492-0070
Mail order: not available   Hours: Mon.–Sat. 9 A.M.–9 P.M.;
Sun. 11 A.M.–8 P.M.

186 Alewife Brook Parkway, Cambridge, MA 02138   (617) 491-0040
Mail order: available but limited   Hours: daily 9 A.M.–9 P.M.

15 Westland Avenue, Boston, MA 02115   (617) 375-1010
Mail order: not available   Hours: Mon.–Sat. 9 A.M.–10 P.M.;
Sun. 9 A.M.–9 P.M.

15 Washington Street, Brighton, MA 02146   (617) 738-8187
Mail order: available   Hours: daily 9 A.M.–9 P.M.

916 Walnut Street, Newton, MA 02161   (617) 969-1141
Mail order: not available   Hours: daily 9 A.M.–9 P.M.

278 Washington Street, Wellesley, MA 02181   (617) 235-7262
Mail order: not available   Hours: daily 9 A.M.–9 P.M.

Also: "The Staff of Life," page 20.

Bread & Circus is the ultimate health-food store. The prices aren't low, but the selection *is* impressive, as is the quality.

The stores have grown over the years, along with the number of products available. In 1992 the chain was bought by Whole Foods, a California-based company. Thus far, the quality of goods each store offers has not deteriorated, as some feared might happen. In fact, the company put money into the Bread & Circus operations, enabling them to build a huge bakery, with brick ovens for making hearth-style breads (see "The Staff of Life," page 20).

The layout of each B&C (as it is popularly called) is slightly different, since the stores are all different sizes. The Fresh Pond store (Cambridge on Alewife Brook Parkway) is the largest —it replaced a medium-sized Stop&Shop—and the commissary is here. At these kitchens they make the prepared salads and entrées sold at each store. My favorite store is the one in Central Square (Cambridge on Prospect Street) simply because that is the neighborhood B&C I have been going to for years.

Because B&C is such a large store, they are able to carry a huge variety of items. This is where I discovered *mochi,* a six-inch square made of pulverized rice. You cut it into smaller squares and bake it until it puffs up. I bought *essene* bread here; it is a dense, chewy loaf made from ground bean sprouts, ideal for those with wheat allergies.

The stores have many departments, so I describe each one separately.

Produce

B&C is known for their produce, which is always beautifully displayed. It ain't cheap, but it is invariably good. They carry a variety of organic produce, as well as eclectic items such as golden beets, *mesclun* (greens), and several fresh herbs. There is also a good selection of dried fruit; none of it is sweetened with sugar, though this may change. B&C's long-standing policy had been no refined sugar, but they are now selling some products made with white sugar.

Near the produce you can usually find the bulk bins, which contain several kinds of grains, beans, flours, and pastas.

Dairy

The dairy case contains a huge variety of cheeses from around the world, as well as several local brands. Fresh Pond has the largest selection. If you see a cheese you are curious about, ask someone in that department for a taste, and they will be happy to oblige. And if you see a cheese you like but you'd rather buy a smaller amount, they will open a package and cut a smaller piece for you. In general the staff at B&C are very accommodating and helpful, and usually knowledgeable about their department. If someone doesn't know the answer to your question, he or she will usually direct you to someone who does.

The dairy case also contains several different brands and types of yogurts. Honey, fruit concentrate, and maple syrup are used as sweeteners instead of sugar. There are even soy-based and goat's milk yogurts.

Refrigerated juices are also found here, including my current favorite brand, Fresh Samantha, which is a line of absolutely marvelous fresh juices, from a company in Maine. I especially like Strawberry Orange and Raspberry Dream (raspberry, orange, and apple juices).

The freezers contain various healthful frozen foods, including prepared meals and frozen organic vegetables.

Grocery

The aisles in B&C are like the aisles of a supermarket, but they contain only natural foods. No artificial ingredients are allowed. There are all kinds of cereals, including a line of kid-oriented products sweetened with rice syrup, barley malt, or fruit juice. Are they really healthier? I don't know, but I feel like I'm being a responsible parent by getting Fruitios for my kids instead of Froot Loops. Cookies are similarly sweetened. There are chips, juices, sodas, pasta sauces, salsas, jams, jellies, baking items. Another aisle is devoted to vitamins and health-care products, including medicinal herbs, tinctures, homeopathic medicines, aromatherapy items, and natural health and beauty aids, and health and cookbooks.

Meat and Seafood

Although B&C is immensely appealing to vegetarians, there are meat and seafood departments. The meat here is beautifully displayed and quite appealing. The meat and poultry come from animals that tend to be grain fed and chemical free; they led happy lives and taste better for it. The seafood is gorgeous to behold—always very fresh. Prices in these sections are high.

Bakery

The B&C bakery in Everett makes a pleasing variety of **breads** (see "Staff of Life," page 20), and they carry Iggy's breads as well. They also make a wide variety of **baked treats.** None of the baked goods contain refined sugar, but a few years ago the company okayed the use of Sucanat, which they call cane juice. I call it sugar, but it *is* unrefined. It tastes like dark brown sugar, with a strong molasses flavor. Sucanat is good for baking because it has sugar's chemical properties; however, it can sometimes impart a stronger taste than you might want. It gives an interesting, even appealing taste to B&C's **coconut macaroons.** These are made with unsweetened coconut and taste less sweet than macaroons usually do, with a molasses overtone. I like them.

My all-time favorite cookie here, and maybe anywhere (except for the elusive truly amazing chocolate chip) is the **maple cream pie.** Two tasty (although sometimes crumbly) oatmeal cookies sandwich the maple cream, a thick spread made of butter and maple syrup—essentially maple buttercream. It's this buttercream that makes the cookie. It has an assertive, delicious maple flavor, and I just want to eat these cookies constantly.

The **brownies** are okay, kind of cakey (I guess that makes them "okakey"). The **mint brownie** is too strongly flavored—it could knock you over. The best flavor is the **double chocolate brownie.** Several items are forgettable. The *rugalach* is disappointing. It's made with cream cheese, which gives it a good flavor, but it is much too heavy, undercooked, and low on filling. The **chocolate chip** and the **gingersnap cookies** aren't bad, but they have a "something-missing" flavor I associate with foods sweetened with barley malt. I prefer the flavor of the **vegan gingersnap.** There are a few other vegan cookies, that is, cookies made with no egg or dairy products. The best among them is the **jam drop,** which tastes buttery and is made with finely chopped almonds. I also liked the **tahini-oat cookie.** The ingredients are simple: oats, tahini, raisins, walnuts, rice syrup, and honey. They definitely taste healthy, but they also have an interesting nutty taste from the tahini, and a good chewy texture. The **vegan chocolate cookies** are, well, awful. I like the regular **peanut butter cookies,** which have a good peanut butter taste and a chewy texture.

The **muffins** are fair—too much good-for-you taste and not enough good taste. For breakfast pastries, the best is the **caramel nut roll.** It's made in a buttery croissant-like pastry. The pastry is made with whole wheat flour, which makes it a tad heavy, but it also gives the pastry some flavor. The butter taste comes through most pleasingly and goes very well with the caramelized pecans.

There is also a variety of **cakes** and **pies.** Whole versions are on display, but they will cut you a piece of any you like. Many items taste better when they are fresher, such as a **chocolate-walnut tart.** The one I tasted wasn't bad, but I had the sense that it had been sitting there for some time. The **Neapolitan cheesecake** is pretty good. These are individual cheesecakes; other flavors are available as well. The Neapolitan has a sticky brownie crust, a thin layer of vanilla, and a thicker layer of strawberry-flavored cheesecake. The strawberry is appealing, and the texture is light and creamy at the same time.

Deli

B&C carries all kinds of **salads** and **prepared foods.** They will be freshest at Fresh Pond, since that is where they are made. Individual stores make some items, such as the **barbecued chicken** and the immensely popular **teriyaki wings.** Other entrée items are **eggplant Parmesan** and **lasagne.**

Not everything is great. In the past I've been disappointed by promising-looking salads. Before settling on an item ask for a taste; you can sample anything you like. The **black bean and corn salad** can be good, although it is a little heavy on the oil, and sometimes the beans have not been cooked enough. In fact, several salads, including ones that tasted delicious, have more oil than seemed necessary. The *sag paneer,* an Indian creamed spinach dish, is overcooked to the point of loss of flavor, but the **spinach sautéed with garlic** is delicious. The **grilled tuna niçoise** is terrific, loaded with wonderful things: grilled fresh tuna, green beans, lettuce, green olives. *Ensaladilha* is a Brazilian dish of potatoes, carrots, peas, hard-boiled egg, and raisins, and tastes great. **Buffalo potato wedges** are spicy and good, best when reheated. The **three-mustard potato salad** is slightly tangy, slightly hot, totally delicious. I also like the **French lentils with fennel** and the refreshing **carrot-ginger salad. Chicken salad** is made at each store. There are several variations, including mayonnaisey **old-fashioned, Moroccan, Sonoma** (with a sour cream and poppy seed dressing), **curry, pesto,** and **fat-free** (made with yogurt).

There are also **burritos** and **sandwiches.** In some stores these are made to order; Central Square is a smaller store, so these items come prepacked, but they are still very good. Popular sandwiches include **smoked chicken, avocado, and cheddar.** The smoked chicken used is tasty, cut to order. I prefer it to any smoked turkey I've tried; it is much moister and more flavorful. Another of my favorites is the **Southwestern fire-roasted turkey with pesto mayonnaise.** This is a turkey breast laced with roasted chili peppers. There is also an **herbed turkey breast.** Other sandwiches include veggie offerings such as **grilled eggplant and roasted red pepper with fresh mozzarella, tofu salad,** and **grilled tofu.**

The deli case at Fresh Pond is huge. There is also a **salad bar** (all the stores have salad bars, except for Central Square).

Fresh Pond also has a **juice bar,** where they make fresh juices to order. You can get them to go, or drink them at the bar, or in one of the booths set up along the windows by the entranceway.

Of note, B&C has a "free trial guarantee." This means that you can try anything in the store, and if you don't like it, they'll give you your money back. And they really honor this policy.

Cambridge Natural Foods

1670 Mass. Avenue, Cambridge, MA 02138   (617) 492-4452
Mail order: available   Hours: Mon.–Sat. 9 A.M.–8 P.M.;
   Sun. 11 A.M.–8 P.M.

The first thing that catches your eye at Cambridge Natural Foods is the wide variety of politically correct T-shirts in the window. Inside, you can buy the shirts, and yes, food. The store is medium-sized, filling two storefronts. To the right as you enter are sale items; then there are two short aisles of cereals and bulk items, including grains, legumes, and granolas. The two aisles on the left side of the store are longer. The first has a small produce section, with some organic items, and refrigerated goods. The second aisle is vitamin city on one side, frozen goods on the other.

Harvest Cooperative Supermarket. See Allston, page 431.

Lee Nutrition

290 Main Street, Cambridge, MA 02142   (617) 661-9600
Mail order: available for vitamins only
Hours: Mon.–Fri. 8:30 A.M.–5:30 P.M.; Sat. 8:30 A.M.–3 P.M.; closed Sun.

Getting background details on Lee Nutrition is like pulling teeth, but I was able to ferret out some information. A large part of the company business is mail-order vitamins and natural supplements; when MIT took over this building in 1986, the company relocated the mail-order operations to Illinois but kept the store here. The back wall of this medium-large shop still stocks vitamins. The rest of the store has a surprisingly good selection of health-food items. The anonymous person on the phone said that they were moving away from exclusively health-food items, and there are items containing sugar (a health-food store no-no). But there are also many items that are sweetened with fruit juice and unrefined sweeteners.

Everything is prepackaged—no bulk bins here. The store feels like a combination convenience store/health-food store, or a health-food store run as a convenience store. You can get cleaning supplies and health and beauty items, chips, cookies, teas, and soda—but most edibles are made by natural-food manufacturers. Prices can be high, but sale items are reasonable. There are a large number of vegan impulse items (cookies and bars) by the register.

NEWTON

Bread & Circus. See Cambridge, page 434.

NORTH

ANDOVER

The Earth Food Store
28 Chestnut Street, Andover, MA 01810   (508) 475-1234
Mail order: not available
Hours: Mon.–Wed. and Fri. 8:30 A.M.–6 P.M.; Thurs. 8:30 A.M.–8 P.M.;
   Sat. 8:30 A.M.–5:30 P.M.; Sun. noon–5 P.M. (closed Sun. in summer)

The Earth Food Store, located in a basement of a very new shopping complex building, is a medium-sized store with a good selection of products, from grains and legumes to crackers and chips. They have a **juice bar** where you can get freshly prepared juices, such as **carrot juice** and **apple juice.** There is also a deli case with a variety of **prepared foods,** which are primarily macrobiotic. Most items are made on the premises. **Salads** and **entrées** change, but might include *upama,* an Indian grain dish with peas; prepared **tempeh;** and **marinated tofu and vegetables.**

The produce section is small here, but all the fruits and vegetables are organic.

BEVERLY

New Horizons Health Food Store

10 West Street, Beverly, MA 01915   (508) 921-0411
Mail order: not available   Hours: Mon.–Sat. 9:30 A.M.–6 P.M.;
   closed Sun.

New Horizons is a very small store. It's a good place to go if you
live in the neighborhood and want to pick up fresh bread, whole
grains, and more popular natural-food products.

New Leaf

261 Cabot Street, Beverly, MA 01915   (508) 927-5955
Mail order: available   Hours: Mon.–Sat. 9:30 A.M.–6 P.M.; closed Sun.

New Leaf is a small store, but it's a good local source for whole
foods such as grains, natural cereals, and legumes.

GLOUCESTER

Cape Ann Food Co-op

26 Emerson Avenue, Gloucester, MA 01930   (508) 281-0592
Mail order: not available   Hours: Mon.–Sat. 9 A.M.–7:30 P.M.;
   Sun. noon–5 P.M.

The Cape Ann Co-op is one of the larger natural foods stores on
the North Shore. They have a good-sized produce selection, and
they are probably the best source in the area for organic produce
—about 80 percent of the produce sold here is organic.

In addition to the produce, there is a variety of health-
food items—tofu, a wide selection of cheese, yogurt, frozen prepared food, grains, flours, and legumes.

When natural foods became popular in the late 1960s
and early 1970s, there were not many health-food stores. Co-ops
were often the only source for these foods. Many co-ops started
as buying clubs, in which a group of people would order foods
in bulk amounts to save on costs. Some of these developed into
storefront co-ops, which are member owned and operated. The
extent of member involvement varies among the different co-ops.

Membership in the Cape Ann Food Co-op costs $25 per
year; with membership you get a 2 percent discount. If you are a
working member (and, a staffer told me, most members of Cape
Ann are not), you get a 7 percent discount off the prices marked.

SOUTH

QUINCY

Good Health Natural Foods

1627 Hancock Street, Quincy, MA 02169   (617) 773-4925
Mail order: available   Hours: Mon.–Fri. 9 A.M.–9 P.M.;
   Sat. 9 A.M.–6 P.M.; Sun. noon–5 P.M.

965 Washington Street (Old Red Cider Mill), Hanover, MA 02339
   (617) 826-0808
Mail order: not available   Hours: Mon.–Fri. 9 A.M.–7:30 P.M.;
   Sat. 9 A.M.–6 P.M.; Sun. noon–5 P.M.

Good Health is a surprisingly large store. It has been around since 1980, and in the Quincy location since 1986. Every time I have visited in the last few years, it has improved. The first time I went there, I was struck by the large amount of *empty* space. Since then, they have managed to fill the shelves.

To your right as you enter the Quincy store are the bakery and deli case. (The second store, in Hanover, has no deli section.) This area had been languishing when I first came here, but then owners Ralph and Diane Maturo hired chef Wilma Bruining to spice it up, and she has done so with aplomb. The **bakery items** are generally made without refined sugar—a challenge for any baker. The **fat-free blueberry bran muffins** are one of the best healthful muffins I've tried. They are moist and tasty and are made with whole grains, so they are more healthful than the average fat-free muffins (which are usually made with lots of sugar). But beware—they are not low in calories.

Health-food baked goods are in a different category from fine pastries; they can't really compete, but Bruining does a good job. The **almond cookies** are nice. The **raspberry dots** also have a subtle almond flavor, with a circle of jam in the center. My favorite item here is the **maple-walnut bar;** it's moist and chewy. Bruining also makes **bread;** I tried the **whole wheat,** which is a good loaf for sandwiches. A yeast dough is used for the **apple puffs.** Although these are heavier than the name would suggest, they are very good. They consist of a ball of whole wheat dough filled with apples, walnuts, and cinnamon.

The deli case has a variety of **prepared foods,** primarily vegetarian, with some seafood and poultry. The **tuna salad** is surprisingly good, considering that it is made with tofu mayonnaise. Bruining tries to make products without eggs when possible. There are also **dairy-free items,** such as a very good **Jerusalem artichoke lasagne** made with herb tofu, soy cheese, and pasta made from Jerusalem artichokes. I also liked the **tofu fried rice,** a popular item.

They make a variety of **sandwiches,** most of which they package and keep in the refrigerated section; the store is too busy at lunchtime to make sandwiches to order. For a warmer dish, you can get a slice of whole wheat **pizza** or **calzones.** As *pizza,* Good Health's is okay; if you call it something like *vegetable bread,* it is very good. Most of their pizzas do not use tomato sauce, but are topped with a variety of vegetables, such as carrot, zucchini, and pepper or tomato, eggplant, and onion. The calzones are made with soy cheese.

Beyond the deli case is the rest of the store. The aisles are wide and easy to negotiate. They stock a good choice of cereals, fruit-juice-sweetened cookies, grains, chips and crackers, canned goods, teas, and condiments. They also carry honey made by a local beekeeper.

The produce section is in the back of the store, and the quality here varies. Sometimes the offerings are good; sometimes they are paltry. The nearby dairy case holds a variety of yogurts and a wide choice of soy cheeses.

Good Health also occupies a second storefront; this area is devoted exclusively to vitamins and homeopathic medicines.

WEST

ARLINGTON

Arlington Food Co-op
7-A Medford Street, Arlington, MA 02174
  (617) 648-FOOD (3663)
Mail order: not available   Hours: Mon.–Sat. 10 A.M.–9 P.M.;
  Sun. noon–6 P.M.

Arlington Food Co-op is a member-owned health-food store that has been in business since 1975. To join, you pay an initial $25, which is held as equity and returned to you if you leave. The annual membership fee is $7.50, and it entitles you to a 2 percent discount off marked prices. Members who work two and a half hours a month get a 10 percent discount, and members who work two and a half hours a week get a 20 percent discount.

The medium-large store is located in the basement of an older building. It has a funky '60s feel to it, slightly grubby and *very* laid-back. The selection of items is good, with a variety of produce, dairy, and dry goods. Co-ops are usually associated with vegetarianism, but Arlington, like other co-ops in the area, has a seafood and a meat department. The meat here is more appealing than the fish, which looks tired. There are bulk bins with grains, legumes, and flours. You can also buy spices in bulk; they are kept in large glass jars on a set of shelves.

Arlington Health Foods

14 Park Avenue, Arlington, MA 02174   (617) 643-6600
Mail order: not available   Hours: Mon.–Sat. 9:30 A.M.–6:30 P.M.;
    Sun. noon–5 P.M. (closed Sun. in summer)

Arlington Health Foods is a medium-sized store with a reasonable selection of grains and legumes, which are available in bulk. They also sell frozen foods and canned and boxed goods. There are a lot of vitamins here; new owner Craig Torres became Mr. Massachusetts in 1993 (a sort of male pageant), and he is interested in both the vitamins and healthful food.

CONCORD

Concord Spice & Grain

93 Thoreau Street, Concord, MA 01742   (508) 369-1535 or
    (800) 244-1535
Mail order: not available   Hours: Mon.–Wed. and Fri., Sat.
    9 A.M.–6:30 P.M.; Thurs. 9 A.M.–8 P.M.; Sun. noon–6 P.M.

When you enter Concord Spice & Grain, it seems more like a gourmet store than a health-food store. Teas and jams are on shelves to your left, along with various imported goods. But when you get past these shelves, the store gets wider, and you'll see the aisles of vitamins. Lots of vitamins. On the right side of the store are the aisles of food. Grains and such come prepackaged here. There is a good choice of items, though I found the goods to be a little more expensive here than elsewhere. Gourmet items are mixed in with the natural foods, such as mustards, imported soups, and all-natural soups. There is no produce. A refrigerator

case carries a choice of cheeses and prepared foods such as packaged sandwiches and salads made by area kitchens.

The choice of items is good here, but the responsiveness
of the staff can be mixed. Sometimes you'll get someone friendly
and knowledgeable; other times you won't.

The Natural Gourmet

98 Commonwealth Avenue, West Concord, MA 01742
  (508) 371-7573
Mail order: available   Hours: Mon.–Wed. and Fri., Sat. 8:30 A.M.–
  6:30 P.M.; Thurs. 8:30 A.M.–8:30 P.M.; Sun. noon–6 P.M.

I have a warm spot in my heart for The Natural Gourmet. The
store opened when I was working in West Concord in 1989.
Other than a sub shop, there was no place nearby for lunch.
Then Debra Stark opened The Natural Gourmet and started
dishing out the most wonderful, healthful soups. During the
time I was pregnant with my older son, Gabriel, I must have
eaten Natural Gourmet soups at least once if not two or three
times a week.

The Natural Gourmet is primarily a health-food store,
with a take-out counter in the back. Over the years, the store has
grown considerably, without actually expanding its square foot-
age. There is more shelving now, and the shelves are bursting
with good things. You can find all kinds of grains, including
several varieties of rice. Stark uses these items to make the take-
out foods. This is where I first had black Japonica rice, which is
truly black, with a slightly sticky texture.

The store is good as a source for natural foods, but I still
like it best for the **soups** and **salads.** These change daily, and are
primarily vegetarian. There are all kinds of **bean soups,** such as
a robust **wild rice, chickpea, and rosemary soup.** Fresh ginger
adds a kick to **red lentil soup with ginger.** The **corn chowder,**
made with milk, not cream, is lighter than chowders often are,
and is delicious. A favorite of mind is the rich **Indonesian peanut butter soup.** It is an unusual combination of ingredients—
spinach, onions, ginger, peanut butter—that work wonderfully
together.

The **salads** and **dips** are great here as well. You can buy
tubs of the homemade **black-bean dip,** which is flavored with
lemon, lime, and lots of salsa—a pleasing alternative to hummus.
This is also where I first had quinoa, in the **quinoa with pine**

nuts and apricots, and learned that it is pronounced *keenwa,* not *kwinoah.* The **Southwestern salad** is an appealing mix of corn, kidney beans, and peppers.

There will often be an **entrée** as well, such as **polenta pie,** a vegetable casserole with a cornmeal crust, or **lasagne.**

You can top off the meal with a healthful dessert. I like the chewy **ginger cookies,** which are large and very thin. A popular cookie is the **tahini keenies,** a sweet blend of tahini, honey, and oatmeal.

The store is probably best known for **Debra's Natural Gourmet Granolas.** Stark had been making the granolas in the store, but they proved to be so popular that she moved their production to a factory. The granola is now sold all along the East Coast, and stores such as Bread & Circus sell it in their bulk bins. It comes in three flavors: **maple-nut,** with almonds and coconut; **molasses-maple nutty,** with walnuts, pecans, and pumpkin and sunflower seeds; and low-fat **maple-raspberry-blueberry.** All are fantastic—the best granola I've tasted. It's actually addictive. Maple syrup is used as the sweetener, and I love the flavor it gives to the granolas.

Stark has written a cookbook, which includes recipes for many of the dishes she serves at the store; the title is *Round the World Cooking at The Natural Gourmet.* It's the next best thing to visiting The Natural Gourmet.

SOUTHBORO

Simple Enough
18 Lyman Street, Westboro, MA 05181   (508) 366-7037
Mail order: not available   Hours: Mon.–Fri. 10 A.M.–7 P.M.;
    Sat. 10 A.M.–6 P.M.; Sun. noon–5 P.M.

Simply Natural
Brickyard Square, Route 9, Southboro, MA 01772   (508) 481-7445
Mail order: not available   Hours: Mon.–Fri. 10 A.M.–7 P.M.;
    Sat. 10 A.M.–6 P.M.; closed Sun.

Simply Natural is a medium-sized store with a good selection of products. Henry and Helen Pietal opened the Westboro Simple Enough in 1985, and followed with the Southboro Simply Natural eight years later. There are bulk bins, a feature I like in health-food stores, since I like to be able to choose the exact amount of rice or bulgur I'm buying. Bulk granola and spices are available. It is especially good to be able to buy spices this way, because spices lose their flavor over time, so it is better to buy small amounts more frequently.

There is a wide selection of all-natural brands here for items such as soups, sauces, salsas, chips, and cereals.

WELLESLEY

Bread & Circus. See Cambridge, page 434.

WESTBORO

Simple Enough. See Southboro, page 446.

THE BESTS OF THE BEST

Best health-food store: **Bread & Circus**
Best bulk section: **Harvest Cooperative Supermarkets**
Best spice selection: **Harvest Cooperative Supermarkets**
Best produce section: **Bread & Circus**
Best take-out food in a health-food store: **The Natural Gourmet**

CHAPTER THIRTEEN

LIQUID REFRESHMENT

Featuring fresh-roasted coffee and imported tea,
fruit smoothies and fresh juices

G OOD coffee has long been available in the Boston area, but the 1990s has seen a coffee explosion. Coffeehouses abound in both the city and the suburbs; words such as *espresso, cappuccino,* and *latte* have become commonplace.

Of course, the spread of the Seattle-based Starbucks cafés has contributed to this. Starbucks arrived in Boston in 1994, but its reputation preceded it: when Starbucks arrives, it arrives with force. By mid-1995 there were fifteen Starbucks in the Boston area. Starbucks is an acquired taste. The style is to roast the coffee very dark; I find the coffee tastes burnt.

Boston's own coffee source has long been the Coffee Connection, headed by George Howell; coffee lovers, myself included, were saddened when Howell sold his company to Starbucks. Thus far, the coffees at Coffee Connection are still being roasted separately, and Howell is still the bean buyer for Coffee Connection, but I am not optimistic about the future.

For many years, there were only a couple of places, including Coffee Connection, that roasted their own coffee. Now, to distinguish themselves from the glut of coffee shops opening in the area, a few more shops are roasting coffee on-site. I include those places in this chapter.

The coffee roasters usually offer two dozen or more kinds of beans, both plain and flavored. The precise definitions of different types of roasts are actually somewhat controversial. For a good explanation, I recommend *The Joy of Coffee* by Corby Kummen. I'm a purist and don't care for flavored coffees. But if hazelnut or Bailey's strikes your fancy, the fresh-roasted versions are best (often flavored beans can be mighty stale or inferior). My bean of choice is Kenya AA, and that is what I sampled at various roasters.

Coffee roasters and coffee houses usually offer a full range of coffee drinks: standards now are espresso, cappuccino, latte (half steamed milk, half coffee), and regular American coffee. There are many variations, including cold and flavored coffees.

In coffeehouses I looked for the quality of the cup, the take-home coffee, and the atmosphere of the place.

I love tea, and interest in this beverage is growing, since it is the next logical step from coffee. Some coffee shops also sell a variety of loose and bagged teas, and a few hotels serve high tea. But two tea shops opened and closed while I was writing this book. The best source for quality teas is a mail-order company.

Beverages also includes juices. A few years ago there was a juicing craze: juice extractors sold in the millions, and infomercials proclaimed the healthful effects of drinking freshly extracted juice. There are, however, only a handful of juice bars in the Boston area. I include these, as well as places that specialize in juice drinks.

* Described in another chapter.

COFFEE ROASTERS

Beans	Brookline, Newton
Browse & Beans	Westford
Cafe au Lait	Boston
Cambridge Country Store	Cambridge
Coffee Connection/Starbucks	various locations
Green Mountain Coffee Roasters	Newton
Java Sun	Marblehead
Key West Coffee & Teas	Concord, Acton

*Marty's	Allston, Newton
Montego Bay Coffee Roasters	Needham
Polcari's	Boston

COFFEEHOUSES

Brewed Awakenings	Hingham, Weymouth
Café Coffee	Newton, Boston
Coffee Cantata Bistro & Beans	Jamaica Plain
Francesca's Espresso Bar & Café	Boston
The North End	Boston
Café Graffiti	
Café Paradiso	
Caffe Vittoria	
1369 Coffee House	Cambridge

TEA

Upton Tea Imports	Hopkinton

JUICE MAKERS

*Ali's Roti Restaurant	Mattapan
*Bread & Circus	Cambridge and other locations
*Emack & Bolio's	Cambridge, Boston
Harnett's Homeopathy & Body Care	Cambridge, Newton
Juicy Jack Patrick's	Cambridge
*Maryam's Famous Cuisine	Dorchester
The Other Side Cosmic Café	Boston
*Shawarma King II	Brookline
South End Naturals	Boston
Trident Booksellers and Café	Boston

❖ C O F F E E   R O A S T E R S ❖

BOSTON

ALLSTON

Marty's. See "An Epicurean Agenda," page 374.

BOSTON

Cafe au Lait
241 Washington Street, Boston, MA 02108   (617) 742-3434
Mail order: available   Hours: Mon.–Fri. 6 A.M.–6 P.M.;
   Sat. 8 A.M.–6 P.M.; Sun. 8 A.M.–5 P.M.

Cafe au Lait is located near Downtown Crossing. Pedro, the roaster, hails from Brazil. He prides himself on his **dark roasts.** I am not crazy about darker roasts, so I find Cafe au Lait's beans too dark for my taste, but they are fresh. There are about a dozen types of coffee available, including Colombian and Kenya AA, as well as flavored beans.

   The store is also a take-out spot for breakfast and lunch, and they make most of the items they sell. There are **muffins** and **sconewiches,** savory scones with fillings such as **ham and cheese with scallions** and **turkey and cheese with herbs.** The **cookies** are okay, such as a candylike **chocolate caramel cookie** and a **toffee cookie.** The **sandwiches** are very good and are made with some more unusual fillings. I like the **smoked tuna,** with plum tomatoes, sprouts, and a peppery vinaigrette. The baguette for the **Casalingo salami and provolone** sandwich is drizzled with extra-virgin olive oil, then covered with watercress. There are several **salads,** including **German-style leek and potato salad** and various **pasta salads.**

Polcari's
105 Salem Street, North End, Boston, MA 02113   (617) 227-0786
Mail order: available   Hours: Mon.–Sat. 8:30 A.M.–6 P.M.; closed Sun.

Siblings Maria and Ralph Polcari run this corner store, which offers a tantalizing selection of coffees, spices, legumes, and grains, as well as various Italian appliances. The store was started by their father in 1923, in the same location. Polcari's was always primarily a coffee store, and when they first opened, they used to

451

roast the coffee themselves; there are photographs on the wall of their former roaster. Although they no longer roast the coffee themselves, Polcari's sells a variety of very good coffees. They also offer green beans for home roasting.

The store is crowded with barrels of bulk goods, a joy for any food lover. A narrow aisle runs between the counter and the side of the store, leading to the back, by a case of salamis and cured meats. Every time I go there, I find another unusual item, from exotic spices to great prices on pine nuts. The siblings work behind the counter, and Maria in particular is happy to talk about the store and its history, bringing out pictures from fifty years ago.

SOUTH BOSTON

Coffee Connection/Starbucks
6 Drydock Avenue, South Boston, MA 02210   (617) 261-4800
Mail order: available

There are currently twenty Coffee Connections and fifteen Starbucks in the Boston area. The beans are roasted at the above address in South Boston and sent to each store; at this writing, the Coffee Connection beans are roasted separately from the Starbucks beans. I prefer Coffee Connection's **"full-flavor" roast** to Starbucks' **extradark full-city roast.** I don't know how long the two will remain separate entities. Starbucks plans to open another ten stores in the next year; call the above number to find out the location nearest you.

From September through June, the company offers free coffee classes at its headquarters. These are fun tasting events. Classes are offered once or twice a month, both evenings and weekends. There are three regular classes: Coffee 1, Coffee 2, and Espresso/Cappuccino.

METROPOLITAN BOSTON

BROOKLINE

Beans

1655 Beacon Street, Brookline, MA 02146   (617) 277-5282
Mail order: available   Hours: Mon.–Thurs. 7 A.M.–9 P.M.;
    Fri., Sat. 7 A.M.–11 P.M.; Sun. 7 A.M.–8 P.M.

199 Boylston Street, Newton, MA 02167   (617) 244-4468
Mail order: available   Hours: Mon.–Fri. 8:45 A.M.–9:30 P.M.;
    Sat. 8:45 A.M.–8 P.M.; Sun. noon–6 P.M.

Victoria Wallens worked for Bank of Boston, in commercial real estate, for several years before she made the transition to the coffee business. After an unsuccessful try at a coffee cart, Wallens, fortunately for coffee lovers, opened a shop where she roasts the beans on the premises. There are two stores, in Brookline and in the Chestnut Hill Mall in Newton. Each site has its own roasting machine, and the smell of roasting coffee fills the air on Beacon Street in Brookline and entices shoppers at the mall.

The beans are roasted in small batches, ten to forty pounds at a time. The coffee here is very good, and fresh. Most varieties come in a choice of roasts: **full-city, Viennese,** and **French,** the darkest roast. Beans has thirty coffees available, including a few flavored coffees (**hazelnut, macadamia,** and **French vanilla**); they flavor the beans themselves during the roasting process.

Beans is also one of the area's better sources for loose teas. Wallens gets all her teas from Upton Tea Imports (see "Tea," Hopkinton, page 463), and carries thirty-five different varieties.

Beans carries pastries made by various local bakeries, including Carberry's and Dancing Deer (see "Everything Nice," pages 17 and 242). The truffle brownie is particularly good, and I also liked the Coolidge Corner, a triangle of almond cake. Good cookies are the peanut butter–honey and the mocha-walnut.

Beans has a wonderful selection of other things that go with coffee, including cups, mugs, and plates, as well as teapots —items from all over the world. There are commercial brands, as well as one-of-a-kind pieces by area artists. This section of Wallens's establishment has become so popular, that she offers a bridal registry. The atmosphere in both places is pleasant, and relaxed.

CAMBRIDGE

Cambridge Country Store

1761 Mass. Avenue, Cambridge, MA 02140   (617) 868-6954
Mail order: available   Hours: Mon.–Fri. 10 A.M.–7 P.M.;
   Sat., Sun. 10 A.M.–6 P.M.

Cambridge Country Store has been in this location for over thirty years and has been offering roasted-on-the-premises coffee since 1979. Current owner Sandra Duckett has been roasting the coffee here since 1989, and she does a nice job. There are eighteen kinds of coffee, as well as ten flavored coffees, which she also roasts. There is always a coffee of the week offered at a special price. The store also sells coffee equipment and bulk teas. Duckett brews coffee by the cup, but more as a courtesy; the brewed pot may have been sitting there for a while, so you should probably seek a freshly brewed cup elsewhere. The beans for taking home, however, are very fresh—Duckett roasts beans daily.

Near the register there are cookies and chocolates from various sources. The chocolate toffee pistachios, in a jar behind the counter, are noteworthy. Duckett makes her own pretty good **fudge** with a fudge machine, offering fun flavors such as **M&M** and **Butterfinger fudge.** The store also carries gift items and gourmet foods, such as condiments and preserves.

NEWTON

Beans. See Brookline, page 453.

Green Mountain Coffee Roasters

88 Needham Street, Newton, MA 02159   (617) 332-4575
Mail order: available   Hours: Mon.–Fri. 6 A.M.–6 P.M.;
   Sat. 7 A.M.–6 P.M.; Sun. 9 A.M.–5 P.M.

Green Mountain is a mail-order coffee company based in Vermont, in business since the early 1980s. They have since branched out, opening stores throughout New England, in which the coffee is roasted on-site. The Massachusetts store opened in the fall of 1994.

My first encounter with Green Mountain was not positive: I received a sample of their roasted, ground coffee in a vacuum-sealed pack. It wasn't bad, but it wasn't great either; it was fine to use in cooking.

However, I was impressed with the coffee roasted in the store. Most of the coffee sold here—60 percent—is roasted on-site by coffee roaster Dave Belson, who worked at Coffee Connection for several years. Green Mountain calls their roasting level **appropriate roast;** Belson says this is just under **full-city,** or **medium.** On his recommendation I tried the **Hawaiian Kona Coffee,** roasted four days before, and it was great. Green Mountain dates their roasts and sells beans within seven days of roasting. They offer some twenty-five to thirty varieties of beans roasted in the store, and carry five to twelve flavored coffees roasted at company headquarters.

The coffee here is fresher than you will get by mail from Vermont. They sell the vacuum-packed ground coffee at the store, but there is no reason to buy it, when you can get the beans freshly ground to order. They also brew a decent cup of coffee and sell the usual cappuccino and other variations. There are tables and a variety of pastries available as well.

The shop borders the same parking lot as New England Mobile Book Fair, the best source for cookbooks in the country.

Marty's. See "An Epicurean Agenda," page 374.

NORTH

MARBLEHEAD

Java Sun

35 Atlantic Avenue, Marblehead, MA 01945   (617) 631-7788
Mail order: available   Hours: Mon.–Fri. 6 A.M.–6 P.M.;
   Sat., Sun. 7 A.M.–6 P.M.

Java Sun has been roasting beans on the premises of their Marblehead store since 1991. Roaster Mark Corday was trained by master roaster Jim Cleaves, who has been roasting coffee for over twenty years. Both Corday and his wife, Christine, the store manager, are very knowledgeable about beans, and they discuss special arrivals with excitement.

Java Sun roasts the best coffee in the Boston area. The coffee I tried was perfectly roasted to bring out the best flavor of the beans. They offer thirty-one kinds, including a wonderful

Estate Kenya AA. Most are varietals; five are blends. Most of the beans are **full-city** roasts, not too dark, and there are half a dozen **French roasts** for fans of darker beans.

The store has a full coffee bar as well. You can enjoy **coffee drinks** and pastries and then buy the beans. In addition to coffee, Java Sun sells about fifteen kinds of loose and bagged teas.

WEST

ACTON

Key West Coffee & Teas. See Concord below.

CONCORD

Key West Coffee & Teas

12 Walden Street, Concord, MA 01742   (508) 369-6636
Mail order: available   Hours: Mon.–Fri. 7 A.M.–6 P.M.;
　Sat. 8:30 A.M.–6 P.M.; Sun. 8:30 A.M.–5 P.M.

342 Great Road, Acton, MA 01720   (508) 264-4647
Mail order: available   Hours: Mon.–Wed. and Fri. 6 A.M.–6 P.M.;
　Thurs. 6 A.M.–8 P.M.; Sat. 8 A.M.–6 P.M.; Sun. 8:30 A.M.–5 P.M.

David Beardsley opened Key West Coffee & Teas in Acton in the fall of 1990. Previously this area west of Boston had no good source for fresh coffee. They roast their own beans, offering some twenty different varietals, as well as six blends. Roaster Francisco Diez has been with the company since the two stores opened, and roasts beans daily in the Acton store. The Key West **house blend** is the best-selling coffee. Beardsley favors a high-end **Celebes Kalossi** and a **Mexican Custepec.** Key West also has the largest selection of **flavored beans,** which they flavor themselves, including about five **hazelnut** variations.

Beardsley calls their roast a **Key West roast,** but says it is essentially **full-city.** Because they roast their own coffee, they can make adjustments to suit the particular bean; some taste better a little lighter and some a little darker.

Both stores have a full coffee bar, but minimal seating. This is not much of a lingering place. But Key West is a great source for very good, very fresh coffees.

The Acton store is located in a strip mall. The Concord shop has more charm, though it is a little tricky to find. It is located behind some stores in Concord Center, down a driveway leading to a public parking lot. The store has two parts. One room has all the coffee beans, displayed in glass jars. This room also has several teas, bagged, but none loose. A door leads to the second room, with a display case filled with pastries. This is where you get brewed cups.

NEEDHAM

Montego Bay Coffee Roasters

970 Great Plain Avenue, Needham, MA 02192   (617) 449-0144
Mail order: available   Hours: Mon.–Fri. 7 A.M.–6 P.M.;
    Sat. 8 A.M.–5 P.M.; Sun. 8 A.M.–2 P.M.

Cathie and Mike Hyatt opened Montego Bay in 1993. After working for over a decade in high-tech jobs at Digital, both were ready to go into business for themselves. "We came across the coffee idea," Cathie says. "Then we went on a trip to the Caribbean and visited this out-of-the-way bar that was light and fun. We wanted to re-create that atmosphere, but with coffee."

The theme here is tropical: the walls are decorated with painted palm trees and colorful birds. When you enter this large corner store, you'll walk by several tables and burlap bags of coffee beans on the way to the counter where you place your order. There are bags of beans because Cathie and Mike roast their own coffee, right there behind the counter. The shop smells wonderful. Their roster is capable of handling small batches— they can roast as little as one pound—so if a bean you like is currently not available roasted, they can roast it to order. They roast the more expensive beans to order so that they will remain fresher longer.

My standard coffee of choice is **Kenya AA,** and it is very good here. Cathie recommends **Yauco Selecto,** and **Colombian** is the best-seller. Most coffees here are roasted **city roast,** which is not too dark and is good for flavor. I find that Vienna and darker roasts can mask the flavor of the bean.

Montego Bay offers about sixty different coffees. This includes **decaf** and **blends,** which Mike has created from the beans they roast. There are about forty varietals, ten blends, and ten flavored coffees; the Hyatts flavor their own beans.

The shop also sells about two dozen kinds of loose teas, as well as tea bags. Opposite the counter are shelves with boxed teas and gourmet items, such as preserves and other condiments, and a variety of Caribbean foods.

The display counter features salads and **baked goods;** the Hyatts make some of their own, such as a decent **Reeses cookie**—like a chocolate chip cookie but made with chopped Reeses Peanut Butter Cups. They also carry some of Boston's best pastries, such as Meri Bond's Sticky Wicked Buns (see Buns of Boston in "Everything Nice," page 258).

WESTFORD

Browse & Beans
174 Littleton Road, Westford, MA 01886   (508) 692-8609
Mail order: available   Hours: Mon.–Wed. 6:45 A.M.–7 P.M.;
    Thurs., Fri. 6:45 A.M.–9 P.M.; Sat. 8 A.M.–6 P.M.; Sun. 8 A.M.–5 P.M.

Browse & Beans roasts about fifteen to twenty different coffees and has been in business since 1992. The **house breakfast blend** is good, a nice balance of beans from around the world: Kenyan, Colombian, Sumatran, and Guatemalan dark. In general Browse & Beans roasts their beans a little **dark**—not as dark as Starbucks, but a shade darker than **full-city.** They also roast their beans for flavoring, selling about sixteen flavored coffees. Among the flavors are **hazelnut** and **French vanilla,** as well as ridiculous flavors such as **Rain Forest, Snickerdoodle, eggnog,** and **chestnut.**

The store is also a full coffee bar, serving espresso, cappuccino, and the like. They carry various pastries and make **sandwiches** at lunch.

❖ C O F F E E H O U S E S ❖

BOSTON

BOSTON

Café Coffee. See Newton, page 461.

Francesca's Espresso Bar & Café

564 Tremont Street, Boston, MA 02118   (617) 482-9026
Mail order: not available   Hours: Mon.–Thurs. 8 A.M.–11 P.M.;
   Fri., Sat. 8 A.M.–midnight; Sun. 9 A.M.–9 P.M.

This is owner Francine D'Olimpio's second coffee bar; her other one is in Provincetown and is open seasonally. Francesca's opened at the end of 1994. The atmosphere here is lovely. The room is wide and shallow, with French windows decorated with tiny lights. The overhead lighting is mellow and soft. A beautiful buffed stainless-steel bar counter curves along from the pastry cases to one wall.

The coffee here comes from three sources: the whole beans are from Chicago Roasters, the Costa Rican coffee is from Café Britt, and the **espresso** is Le Vazza.

There are tables and café-style food—**light entrées, soups, salads,** and a number of **baked goods.** Francesca's carries muffins and cookies from Bentonwood Bakery and Café and Biga Breads, and bakes several of their own desserts, such as **pecan pie, fruit tarts,** and **carrot cake.**

THE NORTH END

Espresso, cappuccino, latte—these are all Italian terms and methods of preparing coffee. Long before Starbucks came to Boston, before Coffee Connection even opened, you could get a fine demitasse of espresso in the North End. The North End is still the best place to come for espresso. There are dozens of cafés brewing Italian coffee here; I recommend the following places. *Note:* Since these are places to go for a cup of coffee, I do not include mail order information.

Café Graffiti

307 Hanover Street, Boston, MA 02113   (617) 367-2494
Hours: Mon.–Sat. 6 A.M.–midnight; Sun. 8 A.M.–midnight

Café Paradiso
255 Hanover Street, Boston, MA 02113   (617) 742-1768
Hours: daily 7 A.M.–2 A.M.
Also: "Frozen Delights," page 296.

Caffe Vittoria
296 Hanover Street, Boston, MA 02113   (617) 227-7606
Hours: Sun.–Thurs. 8 A.M.–midnight; Fri., Sat. 8 A.M.–1 A.M.

JAMAICA PLAIN

Coffee Cantata Bistro & Beans
605 Centre Street, Jamaica Plain, MA 02130   (617) 522-2223
Mail order: not available   Hours: Mon.–Thurs. 7:30 A.M.–9 P.M.;
    Fri. 7:30 A.M.–10 P.M.; Sat. 8:30 A.M.–10 P.M.; Sun. 9 A.M.—3 P.M.

Coffee Cantata is a lovely, pleasant café. Eric Kamen, a professional pianist, started the shop in the fall of 1994 with his wife Cynthia Bell. The name is an homage to Kamen's musical roots: the *Coffee Cantata* was a piece written by Bach in 1734, as coffee became popular in Europe. The small space is filled with several appealingly mismatched tables and chairs. It is a corner shop, with windows on two sides, so it is bright and sunny. A square wooden column, lined with mirrors on three sides, is decorated with twirling vines painted by Bell, who is a calligrapher.

The coffee is a good brew. You can also get beans to go, about half a dozen varieties, including a **decaf blend.** Pastries are displayed in a case and on a transplanted fireplace mantel. The **pecan pie** is so-so, and the crust on the **apple crisp tart** was underdone. The **coffee cake,** with a cinnamon-walnut streusel top, is tasty, as is the rich yet light **Queen of Sheba** chocolate cake, made with decaf espresso and hazelnuts. Coffee Cantata makes one of the best **nonfat** baked goods I've tried, the **cranberry-banana bread.** It's not too sweet, with a delicious flavor and decent texture.

The place is open for lunch, and they offer a nice, simple assortment of **sandwiches** and **salads.** Since I visited, they have started serving dinner six nights and a weekend brunch.

METROPOLITAN BOSTON

CAMBRIDGE

1369 Coffee House

1369 Cambridge Street, Cambridge, MA 02139   (617) 576-1369
Mail order: not available   Hours: Mon.–Thurs. 7 A.M.–10 P.M.;
   Fri. 7 A.M.–11 P.M.; Sat. 8 A.M.–11 P.M.; Sun. 8 A.M.–8 P.M.

757 Massachusetts Avenue, Cambridge, MA 02139   (617) 576-4600
Mail order: not available   Hours: Mon.–Thurs. 7 A.M.–10 P.M.;
   Fri. 7 A.M.–11 P.M.; Sat. 8 A.M.–11 P.M.; Sun. 8 A.M.–8 P.M.

The 1369 offers one of the best cups of coffee in town—owing, I'm convinced, to the fact that they clean their equipment regularly. Coffee goes rancid quickly, and if the brewing equipment isn't cleaned frequently, freshly brewed coffee will have an unpleasantly bitter aftertaste. Not so at the 1369. Their coffee comes from Coffees Without Compromise, distributors for Shapiro's Coffee of New York. They sell half a dozen coffees by the bag, either whole bean or ground.

In addition to coffee, the 1369 offers a variety of baked goods, including Buns of Boston sticky buns and savory scones. Although the muffins aren't made from scratch, they are baked on the premises; **sour cream–poppy seed** and **hazelnut pumpkin** are noteworthy. The **pecan pie,** made on an experimental basis during the holidays by owner Gerry Wolf, is excellent; I hope it becomes a regular item.

The coffeehouse offers a limited selection of **sandwiches, salads,** and **soups,** all of which are fine—not worth a special trip, but good for a quick lunch. The coffee, tea, and pastries are the bigger draws here.

The atmosphere in both locations is comfortable, inviting you to linger.

NEWTON

Café Coffee

244 Needham Street, Newton, MA 02164   (617) 527-2233
Mail order: not available   Hours: Mon.–Sat. 7 A.M.–9 P.M.;
   Sun. 10 A.M.–5 P.M.

100 Huntington Avenue, Copley Place, Boston, MA 02116
   (617) 236-2236
Mail order: not available   Hours: Mon.–Thurs. 7 A.M.–9 P.M.;
   Fri., Sat. 7 A.M.–10 P.M.; Sun. 11 A.M.–6 P.M.

The Guarenti family owned the New England Athlete's Foot franchise. A few years after they sold it, patriarch William Guarenti decided to pursue the specialty coffee business. He hired coffee guru Bill Trull as coffee consultant and buyer. The Newton store opened in 1991, and at present the company has four other stores: one at Copley Place and one each in Rhode Island, Connecticut, and New Hampshire.

The store carries some thirty-five coffees, including nine flavored beans, from the most popular **hazelnut** to **chocolate-raspberry** and **Southern pecan.** The coffees are listed on a board according to regional source: **Central and South America, Africa and Arabia, Indonesia and Pacific Islands,** and **blends. Guatemalan Dos Marias** is a bean exclusively carried by Café Coffee, and it is very good. The beans are roasted to the company's specifications at a coffee roaster in Connecticut.

Atmospherically, there is not much to the stores, especially the one in Newton; it has a Formica counter and a florescent-lighting fast-food feel to it. There are a couple of tables with stools, and various pale-looking pastries are for sale.

But the coffee they brew is very good, especially the **ice coffee,** which is the best I've tried anywhere. Trull is a coffee expert, and he will happily explain his method. The ice coffee, made with Café Coffee's **breakfast blend,** is made using cold water, in a cold-water extractor. The ground coffee essentially steeps for twelve to fourteen hours, producing a smooth concentrate; five pounds of coffee produces three quarts of concentrate. Trull says that this method keeps the bitter acids and oils out of the coffee, making for a very smooth cold cup. The concentrate is then diluted with water to produce a cup of ice coffee. If you take it black, it's half water and half concentrate; with milk it's one third each of milk, water, and coffee concentrate. Trull adds a little vanilla from New Orleans, which gives the coffee a smooth, creamy taste.

SOUTH

HINGHAM

Brewed Awakenings

19 Main Street, Hingham, MA 02043   (617) 741-5331
Mail order: not available   Hours: Mon.–Sat. 6:30 A.M.–9 P.M.;
  Sun. 7 A.M.–5 P.M.

4 Union Street, Weymouth, MA 02190   (617) 340-0732
Mail order: not available   Hours: Mon.–Fri. 6 A.M.–7 P.M.;
  Sat.–Sun. 7 A.M.–5 P.M.

Brewed Awakenings is a pleasant coffeehouse, located right in downtown Hingham in a corner building. There are several tables where you can sit and enjoy the view. The Hingham store opened in 1993, and they added the Weymouth location in 1995.

The shop carries nine coffees, and ten flavored coffees. You can order from a full selection of coffee drinks. They also make **fruit drinks** and carry several teas. You can accompany your beverage with pastries from area bakers or with lunch items such as **quiche, calzones,** and **sandwiches.**

WEYMOUTH

Brewed Awakenings. See Hingham above.

❖ T E A ❖

Tea shops should not be confused with tearooms. The latter stress psychic readings and tea leaves; the former sell specialty teas. Sadly, the only two tea shops in the Boston area opened and closed within a few years. A few hotels offer high tea, but the best source for loose tea is by mail.

Upton Tea Imports

231 South Street, Hopkinton, MA 02148   (508) 435-9922 or
  (800) 234-8327
Mail order: strictly a mail-order business
Hours: Mon.–Fri. 9 A.M.–5 P.M.; Sat. 9 A.M.–3 P.M.; closed Sun.

Upton Tea Imports is strictly a mail-order operation, but I'm including them here because Upton is absolutely the best source for loose teas in the Boston area, or anywhere, really. Tom Eck started the company in 1989 as a career change; he had been in the high-tech business. "I am a tea drinker," he says. "In Europe you would see tea shops offering 150 to 300 varieties of tea. I wanted to mimic that concept of variety, selling tea all over the United States."

Eck carries loose teas only, over 150 varieties in 125-gram packets or tins. The teas are described in his quarterly catalog/newsletter, where they are categorized by country. Teas are available from India, Africa, Nepal, Formosa (Taiwan), Ceylon (Sri Lanka), Japan, and China. He also has blends, flavored teas, and decaffeinated teas. When Coffee Connection stopped carrying loose teas, they referred customers to Upton.

When you order by mail, the teas arrive within a few days. Beans in Brookline and Newton (see "Coffee Roasters," page 453) carries about thirty-five of Upton's teas.

❖ JUICE MAKERS ❖

BOSTON

BOSTON

Emack & Bolio's Ice Cream. See "Frozen Delights," page 306.

The Other Side Cosmic Café
407 Newbury Street, Boston, MA 02115   (617) 536-9477
Mail order: not available   Hours: Mon.–Wed. 10 A.M.–midnight;
  Thurs.–Sat. 10 A.M.–1 A.M.; Sun. noon–midnight

Sean Collins hails from Seattle originally. He first came to Boston in 1989 to work for what he describes as an avant-garde shoe designer on Newbury Street. "I noticed the lack of places to get a good cup of cappuccino," he says, explaining what catalyzed his desire to open a café. Cappuccino soon merged with other liquids, and juices became central—so much so that wheatgrass, popular among juice fans, inspired the café's name. Collins explains it as "where the grass is always greener." Coincidentally, the place he and partner Valerie Lausier found is on the "other" side of Newbury Street. You might think Newbury Street ends at Mass. Avenue. Not so. It continues for another block, and this is where you'll find the Other Side Cosmic Café.

This is a great place. The space had stood empty for several years, and Collins and Lausier did modest initial renovations to turn it into a café, and they opened for business in 1992. When I visited in the summer of 1995, they were in the process of doing further renovations, including installing a full kitchen in the basement. The decor was pure "Salvation Armani," as Collins calls it: mismatched everything—tables, chairs, plates, cutlery. The food, however, is a perfect match.

The menu is split between **Liquids** and **Solids. Liquids** is divided into four categories. **Pharmacy Drinks** include a variety of fruit and vegetable blends; although this choice is not listed, you can create any combination you like, or order a single item juiced. There are several creative combinations of fruits and vegetables, some of which are surprisingly good. I've never been a fan of carrot juice, but I like the **carrot-apple-celery-lemon** blend. It's refreshing and tasty. Other combos include **pear-lemon-ginger** and **pineapple-mint-wheatgrass.** Wheatgrass is one of those acquired tastes that I think I won't acquire; it tastes, well, green. Like grass. It comes in a dose or a double dose. A dose is very small—about an ounce—but it is more than enough. It's not so bad mixed with other items.

Next there are **Smoothies,** a blend of fruit, yogurt, honey, and ice. Some combos work better than others here. **Banana-orange-ginger** is more interesting than tasty; I like fresh ginger, but it overpowers the drink here. I prefer the more straightforward **banana-orange-strawberry.** Another intriguing blend is **peanut butter–banana.**

Cold Fluids include the mundane soda and milk, as well as **strawberry lemonade** and **Mochaccino,** a frozen espresso drink with chocolate syrup, and the vanilla syrup counterpart, **Vanillaccino. Hot Fluids** are very good cups of coffee, from regular **coffee** to **espresso** and **cappuccino.** The Other Side does not have flavored coffee beans, but they do have a couple of syrups for flavoring your brew—**almond, chocolate,** and **vanilla.** These are used to flavor hot steamed milk, as in the **Almond Moo,** topped with whipped cream.

The **Solids** side of the menu includes a terrific array of **sandwiches.** I love the **Brie cheese,** a generous portion of Brie layered with sliced apples, pears, onions, lettuce, and tomatoes, on a baguette spread with honey mustard. **Prosciutto red pepper** includes provolone cheese and the café's **special sauce,** made with puréed roasted red peppers, cilantro, and mayonnaise. The menu will expand considerably once the kitchen is built; they are planning to start serving breakfast.

A display case is filled with **baked goods,** including excellent **pies.** They offer **cherry, apple, blueberry, pumpkin,** and **pecan** throughout the year. The **pecan** is good, a tad sweet, with an excellent crust. There are **cheesecakes** in several flavors, **chocolate layer cake,** various **cookies,** and **carrot cake,** with a cream-cheese frosting laced with Amaretto.

South End Naturals
517 Columbus Street, Boston, MA 02118   (617) 536-2119
Mail order: not available   Hours: Mon.–Fri. 8 A.M.–8 P.M.;
   Sat. 8 A.M.–6 P.M.; Sun. 11 A.M.–5 P.M.

Prior to coming to Boston, Mark Aznavourian lived in New York City and had enjoyed frequenting juice bars there. He and partner Tim Ticehurst noticed the lack of similar establishments in Boston, so they moved here to open South End Naturals in June of 1994.

This is a lovely store on the corner of Greenwich Park and Columbus. There is a nice selection of health-food items, including vitamins and bulk grains, legumes, nuts, and granolas. The main attraction, though, is the **made-to-order juices.**

The juice counter is to your left as you enter. There are a number of fruits and vegetables to juice, including **apples, grapefruit, kiwi, oranges, lemons, various melons, carrots, celery, beets, spinach,** and **parsley.**

Juices use a lot of fruit: it can take a pound of carrots to make a 16-ounce cup of juice. Prices per serving range from $2.50 to $3.50, depending on the size and number of ingredients. You can get healthful add-ins, such as **wheatgrass,** a "detoxifier." According to Aznavourian, an ounce of wheatgrass juice is the equivalent of eating twelve pounds of leafy greens. "It's like a RotoRooter for your system," he says. In other words, it's a diuretic. Other add-ins include **wheat germ, ginger, garlic, bee pollen,** and **super blue-green algae.**

You can create your own combo or choose one of South End Naturals'. I like anything with strawberries in it, such as the **orange-banana-strawberry** blend. **Natural lemonade** is a blend of apples and lemon. The **smoothies** here are generally **nondairy,** made with soy milk, and come in nice blends, such as **Blue**

Banana (with blueberries, bananas, and apple juice), and **Dunes of the Cape** (with pineapple, banana, and coconut nectar).

Trident Booksellers and Café

338 Newbury Street, Boston, MA 02115   (617) 267-8688
Mail order: not available   Hours: daily 9 A.M.–midnight

I discovered Trident about a year after they had opened, in 1984, when I used to work in Back Bay. At that time there was not much in the way of food on this end of Newbury Street, and Trident became a welcome haven offering a simple menu of excellent soups, salads, and coffee drinks. The bookstore part was and is extensive, specializing in New Age material, and there were a handful of tables separated from the books by potted plants.

The place has changed a bit in the past decade. Several more tables have been added, the menu has been expanded considerably, and the café now serves freshly extracted **juices.** Trident offers the basic juicing produce—**carrots, celery, tomatoes, beets, cucumbers, apples,** and **oranges,** with some combinations, such as the **V4,** made with carrots, celery, apples, and parsley. You can add bee pollen, soy protein, or wheat germ to any juice.

There are also tasty **coffee drinks.** The **plain coffee** is good, but I like to come here more for the fun items, such as **chocolatino,** espresso with steamed chocolate milk, topped with whipped cream and shaved chocolate. If you like flavors, Trident has a selection of Italian syrups to add to your cup. There is also **hot white chocolate,** which is okay: it tastes like sweet, oily milk. I prefer the **steamed milk** and **hot mulled cider.**

DORCHESTER

Maryam's Famous Cuisine. See "Everything Nice," page 237.

MATTAPAN

Ali's Roti Restaurant. See "Goodies to Go," page 169.

METROPOLITAN BOSTON

BROOKLINE

Shawarma King II. See "Goodies to Go," page 200.

CAMBRIDGE

Bread & Circus. See "Going Organic," page 434.

Emack & Bolio's Ice Cream. See "Frozen Delights," page 306.

Harnett's Homeopathy & Body Care
47 Brattle Street, Cambridge, MA 02138   (617) 491-4747
Mail order: available   Hours: Mon.–Sat. 10 A.M.–8 P.M.;
    Sun. noon–8 P.M.

Anthony Harnett, founder of Bread & Circus, opened Harnett's Homeopathy & Body Care in 1993, a year after he sold B&C. The store offers a range of alternative health-care products, and includes a bulk section with medicinal herbs. They also have a **juice bar,** with thirteen choices available, including the ubiquitous carrots and wheat, and you can create our own combos as well. The vegetables used are all **organic,** and the fruits are organic in season and whenever possible. Pleasing combos include **carrot-apple-beet** and **green apple–ginger-parsley**

Harnett's **smoothies** are nondairy. The base is orange or apple juice, blended with frozen fruits; freezing the fruits gives the smoothie a thicker consistency. You can create your own blends or choose from among the available combinations, such as **Negril Sunset** (pineapple, kiwis, and bananas with orange juice) or **Mardi Gras** (strawberries, blueberries, and bananas with apple juice). **Mix-ins** include **royal jelly, spirulina, brewer's yeast,** and **wheatgrass.**

For hot drinks, Harnett's offers **Chinese herbal elixirs.** The key ingredients are herbal tinctures, alcohol-based herbal preparations. The tincture is then mixed with hot water. I cannot vouch for the actual effects of these elixirs, but the menu is intriguing. **Yang tonic** is described as a "quick pick-me-up, . . . regarded for its strengthening effects upon muscles and mind." **Perfect Harmony** is "for peak creative flow and an overall sense of well-being."

Juicy Jack Patrick's

1815 Mass. Avenue, Cambridge, MA 02140   (617) 354-6677
Mail order: not available   Hours: Mon.–Fri. 7 A.M.–10 P.M.;
Sat., Sun. 8 A.M.–8 P.M.

Jack Isaacs and Patrick Fabrizio had been working as fitness counselors at Holiday Health when they decided to open Juicy Jack Patrick's in 1989. "We knew there was a need here," says Fabrizio. The place is located in the basement of the Porter Exchange building, right next to Holiday Health. The shop offers a variety of juices extracted to order, such as **carrot, orange, apple,** and **grapefruit.** "We used to have set combinations," Isaacs says, "but people kept coming up with their own, so that's what we make." Add-ins include **ginseng, royal jelly,** and **wheatgrass.**

Their **smoothies** are made with frozen yogurt blended with fresh fruit, any type of juice, and milk or water. There are also **protein shakes,** essentially smoothies with either Mete-RX or Metavolol II protein powders added. Juicy Jack Patrick's also sells frozen yogurt.

THE BESTS OF THE BEST

Best coffee roaster: **Java Sun**
Best cup of coffee: **1369 Coffee House**
Best ice coffee: **Café Coffee**
Best espresso: **The North End**
Best tea source: **Beans** for in-store; **Upton Tea Imports** for mail-order
Best juice bar: **The Other Side Cosmic Café**

❖ CHAPTER FOURTEEN ❖
LIBATIONS

Area wineries, breweries, suppliers for home brewers and winemakers, and stores that sell beer and wine

*M*ASSACHUSETTS has thirteen wineries, six of which are located within an hour and a half of Boston. The climate in New England is not ideally suited to most kinds of wine grapes, and most of the nearby wineries specialize in fruit wines. You can visit each winery for tours or tastings.

When it comes to beer, the past decade has seen an explosion of microbreweries. Originally, this term referred to a brewery that produced less than 5,000 barrels of beer annually. As microbreweries became more successful, this definition was changed to 15,000 barrels. Some microbreweries, such as The Boston Beer Company, exceeded that number as well. Nowadays the term refers to brewers that produce relatively small quantities of beer; such brewers are also called *craft brewers*.

There are a few kinds of microbrewers. There are those companies that brew their own beer and sell it in kegs to bars. Then there are those that both sell kegs and bottle their own beer, which is available in liquor stores. Finally, there are brew pubs: bar/restaurants that brew their own beer on the premises and sell it only on tap. The latter are not covered in this chapter.

Before Prohibition, there were thirty-one breweries in

Boston, mostly located in Jamaica Plain. Five survived Prohibition, including the original Boston Beer Company, which was founded in 1828. The brewery was later bought out by the Haffenreffer Company, which closed in the 1960s. By the 1980s, there were no breweries in Massachusetts. The new Boston Beer Company, makers of Samuel Adams beer, changed all that, paving the way for microbreweries around the country to flourish. As of this writing, there are thirteen microbreweries in the Boston area: one keg brewer, seven bottle brewers, and five brew pubs. Several more are in the works.

Many of the microbrewers started their businesses after years of home brewing. For the amateur brewer, the Boston area offers several sources for brewing equipment and courses in home brewing. Winemaking supplies are also available. I list beer- and winemaking supplies later in the chapter.

There are hundreds of liquor stores where you can find Massachusetts wines and beers. If you're interested in wine or beer from other states and countries, there are a handful of stores worth a special trip.

The chapter is organized into four sections. Wine comes first, with descriptions of nearby Massachusetts wineries. I then describe the area breweries, some of which offer tours. Next is a section on places that sell equipment and supplies for making your own beer and wine. Finally, I include descriptions of noteworthy liquor stores. Because there are not many entries in each section, the establishments are listed alphabetically, rather than geographically.

A final note: It is technically illegal to ship alcohol (although some stores do), so you won't find any mail-order information in this chapter.

* Described in this chapter under "Brewing and Winemaking Supplies."

WINERIES

Goodale Orchards	Ipswich
Nashoba Valley Winery	Bolton
Plymouth Bay Winery	Plymouth
Plymouth Colony Winery	Plymouth
Via della Chiesa Vineyards	Raynham
Westport Rivers Vineyard and Winery	Westport

BREWERIES

Atlantic Coast Brewing Co.	Charlestown
The Boston Beer Co.	Jamaica Plain
Ipswich Brewing Co.	Ipswich
Lowell Brewing Co.	Lowell
The Mass Bay Brewing Co.	Boston
Middlesex Brewing Co.	Wilmington
Old Harbor Brewing Co.	Hudson
Ould Newbury Brewing Co.	Newburyport

BREWING AND WINEMAKING SUPPLIES

Barleymalt & Vine	Newton
Beer and Wine Hobby	Woburn
Boston Brewers Supply	Jamaica Plain
Boston Brewin'	Beverly
Brewer's Market	Haverhill
The Modern Brewer Co. Inc.	Somerville
Stella Brew	Marlboro
The Wine Co.	Hingham
The Witches' Brew	Foxboro

LIQUOR STORES

Bauer Wines, Ltd.	Boston
Berman's	Lexington
V. Cirace & Son	Boston
Federal Wine & Spirits	Boston
Martignetti Liquors	Boston, Brighton, Chelsea
Marty's	Allston, Newton
Merchants Wine & Spirits	Boston
University Wine Shop	Cambridge
The Wine and Cheese Cask	Somerville
The Winecellar of Silene	Waltham
* The Wine Co.	Hingham

❖ W I N E R I E S ❖

There are thirteen wineries in Massachusetts. I visited the five that are within an hour's drive of Boston, and one a little farther, and I describe them here. All wineries offer tastings, and most have tours of their facilities. Massachusetts wines are also available in wine shops in the Boston area; call the winery to find out where their products can be found.

Goodale Orchards

123 Argilla Road, Ipswich, MA 01938   (508) 356-5366
Hours: April, Sat., Sun. 9 A.M.–6 P.M.; closed Mon.–Fri.;
   May–December, daily 9 A.M.–6 P.M.; closed January–March
Tours: not available
Also: "Earthly Delights," page 64.

Goodale Orchard (pronounced *g'dale*) has been in business as a
farm since 1920. The Russell family bought the farm in 1979,
and Max Russell started making hard ciders and fruit wines in
the mid-1980s. I prefer the ciders to the fruit wines. There are
four **ciders: dry,** one of my two favorites, with a subtle apple
flavor; **slightly sweet; sweet;** and **sparkling,** my other favorite,
made with a Champagne yeast. Then there is **perry,** a hard
ciderlike drink made from pears *(perry* is an official name, deter-
mined by the Department of Alcohol, Tobacco, and Firearms*).*
The perry is sweeter than cider, with an appealing flavor. I also
liked the **cider and perry blend.**

I was less enamored with the **fruit wines,** although they
are intriguing. Goodale's **dandelion wine** is a strong, fruity wine,
very assertive. Other fruit wines include **strawberry, raspberry,
sweet blueberry, dry blueberry,** and **rhubarb.** I liked the rhubarb best; it is drier, with more complicated flavors. The other
wines I found to be too, well, fruity, and somewhat acidic. And
definitely sweet. The sweet blueberry, for example (which I prefer
to the dry) is best as a dessert wine.

The fruit wines are all made from fresh fruit, most of
which Goodale grows or purchases from local farmers. The afore-
mentioned fruit wines are the ones Goodale makes regularly, but
Russell is always experimenting with new fruits. When I visited
they also had a **currant wine** and a **strawberry-rhubarb.**

Goodale is fun to visit even without the wines. It is a
working farm, with a variety of pick-your-own options (see
"Earthly Delights," page 64). Produce and other items, including
the wine, are sold in an ancient barn. The wine is in one corner.
The winery is located in the basement of the barn and the nearby
house and is not set up for tours, but the staff is happy to let you
taste any wine that interests you.

There is also a bakery, where they make yummy **cider
donuts,** a gingerbread color from the cider and molasses. They
also make **apple pies** and **apple pie rollups,** a cross between a
turnover and a piece of pie. These are very good.

Nashoba Valley Winery
100 Wattaquadoc Hill Road, Bolton, MA 01740   (508) 779–5521
Hours: Wed–Sun. 11 A.M.–5 P.M.
Tours: Sat., Sun. 11 A.M.–4 P.M.

Nashoba Valley Winery makes the best fruit wines I've tasted, by far. These are very good wines, in their own right. The winery was started by Jack Partridge in the late 1970s. Because of family health issues, he sold it in 1995 to move to Arizona.

Nashoba offers three categories of wines: **dry, semisweet,** and **dessert.** The **dry whites** are made from apples and pears. My favorite is one that is less popular, the **Gravenstein.** It is quite dry, crisp, and clean, with a subtle apple aftertaste. When I visited, the staff said this item may be discontinued; I hope not. I prefer it to the **Baldwin,** although that is also good, just not as dry. The **dry pear** is sweeter, with a more assertive fruitiness.

The reds are blueberry-based. **Dry blueberry** is aged in oak barrels for two years and has a definite oaky flavor, along with a pleasing blueberry aroma. Other blueberry wines I've tasted elsewhere are both sweeter and more acidic. The **blueberry-pear** is also strong-tasting, but slightly more mellow and fruity from the pear.

Although it has a stronger tannin taste than other Nashoba wines, I enjoy the **cherry** wine, which is made with sour cherries and has a faint cherry-pie aroma. The **Maiden's Blush** is less interesting, despite the intriguing name. This is a 99 percent apple wine with 1 percent elderberry. I did not care for the **strawberry-rhubarb,** although it has a delightful aroma. I must conclude that strawberries just don't make good wine; this one had a plasticky aftertaste. The **Cyser** is more pleasant, a Colonial wine traditionally made from apples and honey. It is not too sweet, with a honey taste that lingers after you swallow. The most popular wine is the **cranberry-apple.** It goes with New England: every winery I visited makes a cranberry wine, and it's the best-seller for each one. Others I tried are made with a grape-based wine, or entirely cranberry. The cranberry-apple is fruitier, without being overly sweet. The cranberry flavor comes through after you swallow.

There are a few dessert wines. I tried the popular **After Dinner Peach.** It is dry, yet richly sweet, with a honey aftertaste.

Nashoba Valley is also a pick-your-own farm, with raspberries, blackberries, peaches, plums, and apples. The apples are noteworthy because there is a huge variety to choose from, including several antique heritage apples.

Plymouth Bay Winery

170 Water Street, Plymouth, MA 02360   (508) 746–2100
Hours: September–June, Mon.–Sat. 10 A.M.–5 P.M., Sun. noon–5 P.M.;
    July, August Mon.–Sat. 10 A.M.–9 P.M., Sun. noon–5 P.M.
Tours: not available

Winemaker John LeBeck has been making wines his whole life, he says. He worked in New York State before coming to Massachusetts to make wine at the nearby Plymouth Colony Winery. After several years at Plymouth Colony, he decided to go into business with Tim Cherry, who opened Plymouth Bay in 1994 in the Village Marketplace Landing, a group of shops in quasi-charming buildings, down the street from Ocean Spray's Cranberry World. They don't offer tours, but they do tastings. Indicate your interest, and John or Tim will pour you a cup.

There is no vineyard or farm here; Plymouth Bay makes their wines from fruit juices and concentrates. There are three **grape wines.** I prefer the **Drydock white,** a dry white wine made from Chenin Blanc and Aurora grapes. It has a clean flavor. I'm not big on sweet wines, so I don't like the **Widow's Walk,** a sweet white wine made with Cayuga grapes. The **Pinot Noir** is dry but very acidic; it made even my teeth pucker.

The best is the winery's best-seller, **Cranberry Blush,** which is white wine and 10 percent cranberry juice. The wine is made with Seyval grapes, and it has a clean taste and is not too sweet. Also popular is the **Cranberry Bay,** a 100 percent cranberry wine. This fruit wine is sweet and tastes like a wine cooler with a cranberry aftertaste.

Other fruit wines include a very sweet **peach,** with honey undertones; a slightly dry **Raspberry Bay;** and a sweet yet dry **Blueberry Bay.** Plymouth Bay wines are more for the tourist than the purist.

Plymouth Colony Winery

Pinewood Road, Plymouth, MA 02360   (508) 747–3334
Hours: May–December, Mon.–Sat. 10 A.M.–5 P.M., Sun. noon–5 P.M.;
    February–April, Sat. 10 A.M.–4 P.M., Sun. noon–4 P.M.; closed January
Tours: available

A. Charles Caranci, Jr., started his winery in 1983, when a business colleague suggested that he make a cranberry wine. This wine is **Cranberry Grandé,** the winery's flagship wine and an ongoing best-seller. It is a fruity wine, reminiscent of a wine cooler. I prefer the **Bog Blush,** which is 90 percent Cayuga white wine and 10 percent cranberry wine. It is dryer and less sweet. I also prefer the dryer white **Bog Blanc,** made from Seyval Blanc grapes, to the popular **Whale Watch White.** The latter does have a catchy label, but it is *very* sweet and fruity. Caranci's son, also named Charles, is now the winemaker, and he recently added a **Whale Watch Red,** which is a sweet red wine. All the wines are made from juices or concentrates.

Other fruit wines are **peach,** which tastes like a semi-sweet white; a tannic **raspberry;** and a smooth, sweet **blueberry,** best consumed as a dessert wine. All of these will be more appreciated by the casual wine drinker than by the connoisseur.

The winery is situated off Route 44 on a residential road in a small building in the middle of ten acres of cranberry bogs. The setting is quite pleasant, and you may see geese wandering down the road. The shop next to the winery sells wines and various cranberry-based products, such as cranberry saltwater taffy and cranberry cookies.

Via della Chiesa Vineyards

Church Street off Route 44, Raynham, MA 02767   (508) 822–7741
Hours: daily 11 A.M.–5 P.M.
Tours: available

Robert DiCroce was in his sixties when he decided to start his winery in 1986. "My father, like all the Italian and Portuguese immigrants, made wine in his basement," DiCroce says. The amateur winemakers used to buy grapes from California because the Massachusetts climate was hostile to the grapes they grew in Europe. DiCroce planted Cayuga grapes, which grow well in Massachusetts, and hired Matyas Vogel, a winemaker from Hungary, to make his wines. DiCroce named the winery for the street it's on: *Via della Chiesa* is Italian for "Church Street."

The winery is an appealing, open building built in front of the vineyards. Inside, wines and various souvenirs are displayed on long tables that are vertical slices from the same 181-year-old oak tree. (A horizontal circle of the same tree is illustrated with a timeline of events that happened during the tree's life.) Tables are set up inside and outside on a porch overlooking the gorgeous vineyards and woods along the Taunton River, and you are welcome to bring your own meal (the winery has no license to sell food). You can taste the wine in the large entrance room.

Via della Chiesa makes three wines with grapes from the vineyards. The **Cayuga Supreme semi-dry** is popular, but it is too sweet for my taste. I prefer the **Cayuga Supreme dry,** which has a slight fruit flavor without being cloying, and a clean taste. The **Cranberry Delight,** which DiCroce is pushing as a Cape Cod souvenir, is a blend of the Cayuga wine and cranberry concentrate.

The building's second, larger room contains the winery. A rectangular walkway overlooks the actual winemaking para- phernalia. You can take a self-guided tour of the winemaking process. The backdrop for this room is that wonderful view of the vineyards.

The shop sells glasses and other souvenirs, and the win- ery offers a custom-labeling option. They will make a wine-bottle label with your greeting on it; they even have a device to print pictures such as family photographs on the labels. Not for wine purists, but a fun touch.

Westport Rivers Vineyard and Winery

417 Hixbridge Rd., Westport, MA 02790   (508) 636–3423
Hours: April–December, daily noon–5 P.M.;
    Jan.–March, Sat., Sun. noon–5 P.M.; and by appointment
Tours: Sat., Sun. noon–5 P.M.

Long before they produced their first wine, Bob and Carol Rus- sell planned to make wine. They had lived in Dighton for twenty- five years, and decided to start a vineyard. They considered moving to Oregon, California, and even New Zealand before settling on Westport, in coastal Massachusetts, with its temperate climate. They bought this former dairy farm in 1982, ordered the grapes in 1984, planted them in 1986, and started making wine in 1989. The first bottle was available for sale in 1991.

These wines are in a class above the other wines pro- duced in the state. As Carol Russell says, "We are an estate winery —98 percent of the wine we make is made from grapes we grow." With fifty acres of Chardonnay, Riesling, Pinot Noir, and Pinot Meunier, Westport is New England's largest vineyard.

It's worth a trip down to this very southern part of the state, a good hour and a half from Boston, because the area is so beautiful. The winery sponsors a festival a month in June, July, and August; these are not cheap ($30 to $60), but they offer a chance to sample excellent wines and food from some of the state's best chefs. You can also sample the wine during tours of the winery. **Cuvee RJR Brut sparkling wine** is pricey, but very good, and the **Chardonnay** is lovely. Definitely the best winery in Massachusetts.

❖ B R E W E R I E S ❖

Beer is essentially made from four basic ingredients: malted barley, water, hops, and brewer's yeast. The type of ingredient is what can affect the flavor. For example, barely malt comes in a variety of roasts, and there are many strains of hops, a kind of flower. Sometimes additional ingredients are added, such as other grains or fruit, to achieve different flavors.

There are essentially two kinds of beer: ale and lager. They use different kinds of yeast and different fermentation techniques. Ale is aged at warmer temperatures, about 60°F, and is ready in about three weeks. Lager is aged at cooler temperatures, about 48°F, and takes six to eight weeks before it is ready.

Atlantic Coast Brewing Company
50 Terminal Street, Charlestown, MA 02129   (617) 242–6464
Hours/tours: Fri. 4 P.M.; and by appointment

The Atlantic Coast Brewing Company was founded in 1993, and owners Chris Lohring and Alex Reveliotty brewed their first **Tremont Ale** in the spring of 1994. This ale was recommended to me by several beer lovers as a true British-style ale. And it is excellent. The equipment is imported from England, and the ale is fermented in open vessels (most other breweries use closed vessels for fermentation). They also make **Tremont Best Bitter,** which is cask-conditioned. The company is starting to make seasonal beers as well, including **Tremont India Pale Ale.**

At this writing the beers were available only on tap at bars around town; a few liquor stores also carry quarter- and half-kegs. Lohring and Reveliotty hope to have Tremont Ale available in bottles soon.

The Boston Beer Company

30 Germania Street, Jamaica Plain, MA 02130   (617) 522–9080
Hours/tours: Thurs., Fri. 2 P.M.; Sat. noon, 1 P.M., and 2 P.M.

Several people were quick to tell me that, in fact, the Boston Beer Company's Samuel Adams beer is *not* brewed in Boston. This is true. When Jim Koch, a sixth-generation beer brewer, started his company in 1985, he based it in Boston but contracted out his great-great-grandfather's beer recipe to a Pittsburgh brewer. Initially the beer was available only in Massachusetts; it then became the first American beer to be sold in Germany.

Over the next decade, Samuel Adams beer experienced enormous popularity, and the Boston Beer Company experienced enormous growth. In 1988 Koch opened his own brewery in Jamaica Plain, in the former Haffenreffer brewery, so finally the beer was living up to its name. But demand soon exceeded capacity, and the beer is once again contract-brewed at breweries in Pittsburgh, New York, and Oregon as well. But wherever it is brewed, Samuel Adams is great beer.

Boston Beer makes six beers that are available throughout the year, all part of the **Samuel Adams** line. Koch named his beers for Adams, a fellow Harvard alumnus (class of 1748) and brewer, as well as the organizer of the Boston Tea Party and one-time governor of Massachusetts. The flagship **Samuel Adams Boston Lager,** along with **Boston Lightship,** the company's light beer, and **Samuel Adams Boston Stock Ale** have all won gold medals in beer competitions. The other regulars are **Honey Porter,** which is fermented with honey, giving the beer an unusual sweetness; **Cream Stout,** a rich, flavorful beer; and my favorite, the relatively new **Scotch Ale,** a dark, flavorful, almost thick beer made with malted barley that has been both roasted and smoked.

There are also six seasonal beers; the most interesting is wintery **Cranberry Lambic,** which contains wheat, cranberries, and maple syrup. I didn't care for the summer **Cherry Wheat,** which tastes like cough drops. Most intriguing (and delicious) is the **Triple Bock,** a highly alcoholic "beer." It has an alcohol content of over 17 percent (compared to the usual 2 to 6 percent in most beer) and is almost syrupy and sherry-like. It is designed to be served at room temperature and comes in an attractive cobalt-blue bottle with simple gold lettering.

The Jamaica Plain location is the company's headquarters and R&D facility; they do brew beers here that are occasionally offered on tap at local bars. You can come here for tours and tastings for a nominal fee. The tour of the facilities is fun—very informative about the brewing process, and about Koch's family history. Crunch on the malted barley and sniff dried hops before entering a mock saloon for beer tasting. You can keep the small souvenir glass you'll use. The tour guides are knowledgeable and friendly.

Ipswich Brewing Company

23 Hayward Street, Ipswich, MA 02138   (508) 356–3329
Hours/tours: by appointment and Sat. 1 P.M. and 3 P.M.

Jim Beauvais, brewer and co-owner of Ipswich Brewing Company, started home brewing ten years before he left his job in computer programming and opened his company in 1992. His brewery is located in an office park; it helps to call for directions if you are planning a visit.

Ipswich brews three beers. I liked the **Ipswich Pale Ale** best; it's a nice, refreshing, and mild beer. Beauvais's favorite is the **Ipswich Dark Ale,** which is more complex, with a roasty aftertaste. The third beer is a thick **Oatmeal Stout,** made with seven grains. The texture is almost syrupy, and the taste creamy. The company also contract brews **Dornbusch Gold Lager,** which tastes more alcoholic than the ales.

The beers are all unfiltered. Beauvais says, "Leaving the yeast in the beer enhances the flavor dramatically." Consequently, the beer must be kept refrigerated; it has a shelf life of about three months. The beers come in reusable half-gallon jugs, and the stout and lager come in brown 1-liter bottles.

You can buy Ipswich beers at the brewery, or at several local liquor stores. It's fun to visit the brewery, and Ipswich has several other worthwhile foods stops, so this is a good town to walk around.

Lowell Brewing Company

199 Cabot Street, Lowell, MA 01854   (508) 937–1200
Hours/tours: Mon.–Fri. 9 A.M.–5 P.M.

Lowell Brewing Company opened for business in January of 1994 and began selling their first beer a few months later. They are situated in a converted turn-of-the-century mill building, which also houses a restaurant, the Brewhouse Café and Bar, which serves their beer on tap. The brewer here is Paul McErlean, one of the area's more credentialed brewers. McErlean started home brewing in 1980 and then attended the intense one-year master's brewer's program at the University of California at Davis.

Lowell's **Mill City** beers are good, with slightly more carbonation than others I've tried. My favorite two are their newest beers. The **Mill City Oatmeal Stout** is the best of this genre I've tried; it's thick and creamy, with a distinctive coffee flavor. I also like the **Mill City Vienna Lager,** a very smooth, clean beer.

The best-selling **Mill City Amber Ale** is complex and slightly bitter. The **Mill City Lager** is clean, tangy, and mild. In addition to these four core beers, Lowell brews seasonal beers, as well as a popular **root beer,** which takes a week to carbonate. Lowell is one of the few bottle breweries to use both 12-ounce and 22-ounce bottles.

Adjacent to the brewery and restaurant Lowell operates a pub where you can buy the beer on tap or in bottles. You can also order food from the restaurant menu. The room is pleasant and fun, with high loft ceilings, brick walls, and wide windows. The decor is clublike—mismatched tables and desks, chairs in all sizes, including armchairs and couches. Books for perusing are piled on shelves and the corners of tables.

In 1995 Lowell sponsored a home-brewing competition and had over fifty entries. The winner got to have his beer brewed and bottled at the brewery, with a special label. The company plans to make this an annual event.

The Mass Bay Brewing Company

306 Northern Avenue, Boston, MA 02210   (617) 574–9551
Hours/tours: Fri., Sat. 1 P.M.; Harpoon 5:30 Club,
   Tues.–Thurs. 5:30 P.M.–7 P.M.

The Mass Bay Brewing Company grew out of a Harvard MBA thesis written by Rich Doyle and two colleagues. They incorporated in 1986 and produced their first beer, **Harpoon Ale,** in 1987. Their initial marketing strategy was to play up the fact that their beer is brewed and bottled in Boston (as compared to Samuel Adams, which isn't; see "Boston Beer Company," page 479). But the company grew and exceeded their space. Now all Harpoon beer on tap is made in the Boston location; the bottled beer is brewed in a facility in Utica, New York.

Mass Bay gives the impression of being a fun-loving company. The tour starts with a tasting; they always have three beers on tap. The best is **Harpoon India Pale Ale (IPA),** which started as a summer item; it proved so popular that Mass Bay now makes it year round. Other regular beers include **Harpoon Golden Lager,** a forgettable **Harpoon Light,** and **Harpoon Dark.** They also make seasonal beers.

The tour takes place in the tap room, overlooking the brewery. After you've tasted a few beers, the tour begins. It consists of looking down into the brewery as the guide explains the beer-making process. I found this tour to be less informative than some others; the guide knew his routine, but he was unable to answer many questions. After the brewing talk, it's time to taste more beer. In addition to the tours, there is the Harpoon 5:30 Club. Groups can reserve time for a free tasting after work; reservations are necessary.

In the fun-loving vein, Mass Bay hosts several beer festivals throughout the year, featuring both beer and food, and often live music.

Middlesex Brewing Company
844 Woburn Street, Wilmington, MA 01887   (508) 657–8100
Hours/tours: Sat. 2 P.M.–4 P.M.

Brian Friguliette was working as an optician when he started home brewing as a hobby in 1987. He quit his job and started Middlesex Brewing Company in 1992. When I spoke with him, his beers were bottled in 22-ounce bottles, but he was in the process of moving his operation from Burlington to Wilmington, where he plans to offer tours and both 22- and 12-ounce bottles and kegs. The beers here are slightly unusual. You can get a dark **Oatmeal Stout,** a chocolate **Brown Ale,** and a fruity **Raspberry Wheat.** The beers are bottle-conditioned and contain live yeast, so they must be kept refrigerated. They are available at area liquor stores.

Old Harbor Brewing Company
577 Main Street, Hudson, MA 01749   (508) 562–6992 or
    (800) 303–2333
Hours/tours: by appointment and Sat. 1 P.M. and 3 P.M.

Partners Lou Amarotti and John Monro met while working at Ipswich Brewery. Initially they started their brewery at that site, but they later moved to their own space in an industrial park in 1994. Before visiting it's best to call in advance for directions. When I visited, Old Harbor made three regular beers under their Pilgrim label. **Pilgrim Brown Ale** is their flagship product. **Pilgrim ESB** (Extra Special Bitter) is indeed bitter, but very refreshing. I like the **Pilgrim Cream Ale** best; this is a lighter beer, very smooth. The brewery also makes seasonal beers, such as a **Raspberry Wheat** in the summer and a **Pilgrim Stout** in the winter. They are in the process of developing a **Pilgrim Pale Ale** to add to their regular repertoire.

Old Harbor beers are all unfiltered and nonpasteurized, which means that they must be kept refrigerated.

Ould Newbury Brewing Company

50 Parker Street, Newburyport, MA 01950   (508) 462–1980
Hours/tours: by appointment and Sat. 1 P.M.

Joe and Pamela Rolfe started brewing beer out of their home in 1992, and in 1994 they moved into industrial space. They make four beers, all of which are bottle-conditioned. They leave the yeast in the beer, and it is unfiltered, so keep the beer refrigerated. **Yankee Ale** is an amber ale, slightly hoppy. The **Plum Island Extra Pale Ale** is golden and very light. There is also **Old Newbury Porter** and a ruby **Rye Ale.** The beers are sold in 22-ounce bottles and are available at area liquor stores.

BREWING AND ❖ WINEMAKING ❖ SUPPLIES

The three best, most extensive stores for beer-brewing and winemaking supplies are Barleymalt & Vine, Beer and Wine Hobby, and The Modern Brewer Co. But there are some other sources for home-brewing materials.

Barleymalt & Vine

26 Elliot Street, Newton, MA 02161   (617) 630-1015
Hours: Tues.–Fri. 11 A.M.–8 P.M.; Sat. 10 A.M.–5 P.M.; Sun. noon–5 P.M.

After owner David P. Ruggiero had been a home brewer for twelve years, he observed the growing interest in the field and decided to cater to it, opening his store in 1989. You can find a complete line of brewing supplies here, including hops, malted barley, and yeast. In 1995 the company opened a You Brew facility, similar to that of The Modern Brewer. That means you can come to the store to brew your own beer. The staff will help you choose a recipe and ingredients. You spend a couple of hours preparing the ingredients, leave it to ferment for a few weeks, then return to bottle it and cart it home.

The store also carries winemaking supplies, such as several grape juices and concentrates, and fresh grapes when they are in season—usually late summer and early fall.

Beer and Wine Hobby

180 New Boston Street, Woburn, MA 01801
  (617) 933-8818 or (800) 523-5423
Hours: Mon.–Wed. 9 A.M.–6 P.M.; Thurs. 9 A.M.–8 P.M.;
  Fri., Sat. 9 A.M.–5 P.M.; Sun. noon–5 P.M.; June–August, closed Sun.

Beer and Wine Hobby is the largest and oldest continually operating beer and wine supply store in New England. They do a significant mail-order business, so they are located in a huge warehouse. (It's not in a retail district and may be a little hard to find, so call for directions.)

When Beer and Wine Hobby opened in 1972, home brewing was still illegal, thanks to a law left over from Prohibition. Winemaking, according to store owner Karin Banker, was legal, provided you were the male head of the household. In the beginning the store specialized in winemaking supplies, and established itself first in that area. They carry a wide selection of grape concentrates and grapes in season. When home brewing became legal in 1978, the beer end of the business picked up, and the store now does "a tremendous amount of beer business," according to Banker.

Banker is knowledgeable about both home winemaking and home brewing. When I spoke with her, she was in the process of opening a microbrew pub in Merrimack, New Hampshire.

Boston Brewers Supply

48 South Street, Jamaica Plain, MA 02130   (617) 983-1710
Hours: Mon. and Wed.–Sat. noon–7 P.M.; Sun. noon–6 P.M.;
  closed Tues.; July and August, closed Sun.

This store carries a wide selection of grains, yeasts, and hops for beer making. The store, which opened in 1993, also carries winemaking supplies.

Boston Brewin'

281 Cabot Street, Beverly, MA 01915   (508) 921-1559
Hours: Mon.–Fri. noon–9 P.M.; Sat., Sun. noon–5 P.M.

Boston Brewin' was in Danvers for a few years before the store merged with Boston Hobby and moved next door in Beverly. They carry a selection of beer-making supplies.

Brewer's Market

651 Broadway (Route 97), Haverhill, MA 01832   (508) 372-6987
Hours: daily 7 A.M.–9 P.M.

Brewer's Market is part of a convenience store that has been in business for several years. In 1993 they started carrying a small selection of brewing supplies. An aside: they also carry dart supplies, and recently they started carrying winemaking kits.

The Modern Brewer Co. Inc.

99 Dover Street, Dover Plaza, Davis Square, Somerville, MA 02144
   (617) 629-0400 or (800) SEND-ALE (736-3253)
Hours: Mon.–Thurs. noon–9 P.M.; Fri. noon–8 P.M.;
   Sat. 11 A.M.–7 P.M.; Sun. noon–6 P.M.

A college course in micology, Our Moldy Earth, inspired Jeff Pzera to experiment with beer making. He tried it, he liked it, so he decided to set up a place where people could buy supplies to brew their own beer. He opened The Modern Brewer Company in 1990. In 1995 he moved to larger facilities and opened a Brew on Premises facility, similar to that of Barleymalt & Vine. You choose your recipe from the store's list, or come in with your own, and the staff will take you through the brewing process. Modern also has a wine press, so you can make your own wine on the premises as well.

When I spoke with Pzera in the summer of 1994, he was in the process of obtaining his brewer's license and had hopes of microbrewing beer.

Stella Brew

197 Main Street, Marlboro, MA 01752   (508) 460-5050 or
(800) 248-6823
Hours: Tues., Wed. 11 A.M.–6 P.M.; Thurs., Fri. 11 A.M.–8 P.M.;
Sat. 11 A.M.–6 P.M.; Sun. 1 P.M.–5 P.M.;
July and August, closed Mon., Tues.

Owner Bruce Susel is a true beer enthusiast. He will give beer-making demos in his store; he'll even come to your house to demonstrate how to make your own beer, for a home brewer's version of a Tupperware party. The store carries a wide selection of beer-making supplies, along with a smaller selection of wine-making paraphernalia.

The store's name, by the way, is a variation on a song by the Grateful Dead, "Stella Blue." Before running his business occupied all his time, Susel was a Deadhead.

The Wine Co.

100 Derby Street, Hingham Plaza, Hingham, MA 02043
(617) 749-1147
Hours: September–May, Mon.–Fri. 10 A.M.–9:30 P.M.,
Sat. 10 A.M.–7 P.M.; June–August, Mon.–Thurs. 10 A.M.–9 P.M.,
Fri., Sat. 10 A.M.–7 P.M.; closed Sun. year round

The Wine Co., according to Bill Stuart, was one of the first stores on the South Shore to carry fine wines. They stock over a thousand wines and several beers. In 1984 the store began stocking supplies for home brewing and winemaking. Stuart is knowledgeable about both wine and beer.

The Witches' Brew

25 Baker Street, Foxboro, MA 02035   (508) 543-2950
Hours: by appointment and Tues.–Fri. noon–6 P.M.; Sat. 10 A.M.–5 P.M.;
closed Sun., Mon.

The Witches' Brew carries supplies primarily for beer making, as well as for making homemade soda and wine. The store has been in business since 1985.

❖ L I Q U O R   S T O R E S ❖

There are hundreds of liquor stores in the Boston area. I asked Sandy Block, one of the country's few Masters of Wine, and the first on the East Coast, for his recommendations. (Master of Wine is a title granted only to those who have passed an elaborate, multi-day written exam.) Block also teaches courses on wine at the Boston Wine Center. The following stores are good sources for wine and microbrew beers. Different stores have different attributes. All have knowledgeable staff who can answer most alcohol-related questions. Some establishments sell their products at particularly good prices. Many offer regular wine tastings. Call in advance to find out what the featured wine will be.

Bauer Wines, Ltd.

337 Newbury Street, Boston, MA 02115   (617) 262-0363 or
   262-0083
Hours: daily 10 A.M.–11 P.M.
Number of wines in stock: 700
Number of beers in stock: 100
Wine tastings: Sat. 4 P.M.–6 P.M.

Bauer Wines has been in business since the 1950s. Wine buyer Howie Rubin is extremely knowledgeable and helpful; he does a weekly radio bit on WFNX called "The Wine Report" and also hosts occasional live shows on the station.

Bauer offers a big selection of California wines, and they are also strong on wines from Spain and Italy. Despite the upscale-seeming Newbury Street location, the prices here are quite competitive.

Berman's

55 Massachusetts Avenue, Lexington, MA 02173   (617) 862-0515
Hours: Mon.–Thurs. 8 A.M.–9:30 P.M.; Fri., Sat. 8 A.M.–10 P.M.;
   closed Sun.
Number of wines in stock: several hundred
Number of beers in stock: 15
Wine tastings: Sat. noon–5 P.M.

Joel Berman is the third generation to run Berman's; his grandfather started the business in 1909. Around 1990 the business began to go into importing, and they look for wines from small vineyards. The shop specializes in wines from California, Italy, and France, with a focus on southern France. The staff is very knowledgeable, encouraging you to try new and less familiar wines. Manager Marc Sachs conducts the wine tastings and also teaches courses in wine at the Learning Center in Boston.

In the late 1980s the store began carrying gourmet and specialty items. They offer breads from Iggy's and Biga (see "The Staff of Life," pages 33 and 6), as well as a selection of gourmet items.

V. Cirace & Son

173 North Street, Boston, MA 02109   (617) 227-3193
Delivery: available
Hours: Mon.–Thurs. 9 A.M.–8 P.M.; Fri., Sat. 9 A.M.–9 P.M.; closed Sun.
Number of wines in stock: 1,000
Number of beers in stock: 100
Wine tastings: Fri. 5 P.M.–7 P.M.

V. Cirace is now operated by Cirace's son Jeff and daughter Lisa; in 1906 their grandfather opened the shop as a wholesale grocery and tobacco business. Their father went to law school, but was drafted for World War II before he ever practiced, and when he came home, he took over the business with *his* sister. He developed the store into what it is today, an elegant and extensive liquor store. Jeff joined the business in 1972, and Lisa followed in 1978.

The space is extensive but cozy, consisting of several adjoining rooms. The purchasing counter is to your right as you enter, and is made up of wooden wine cases carefully fitted together and varnished—built by Jeff Cirace.

The selection of wines is impressive, especially the Italian wines. In 1988 the Italian Wine and Food Institute listed V. Cirace as the number one Italian Wine Shop. They have the best grappa selection I've seen. It's kept under glass and sold in gorgeous hand-blown glass bottles that sell for $60 to over $100.

In 1983 Lisa started designing gift baskets, and the store now displays beautiful wine-based arrangements. They also carry a number of gourmet foods—pasta, cookies, preserves, and condiments. In 1988 Jeff started a brokerage business representing several Italian wines.

Throughout the year the store sponsors wine tastings, usually on Friday afternoons. Call for a schedule. There are also occasional free seminars, during which a winemaker will come in to discuss his or her wine.

Federal Wine & Spirits

29 State Street, Boston, MA 02109   (617) 367-8605
Hours: Mon.–Fri. 9 A.M.–7 P.M.; Sat. 11 A.M.–6 P.M.; closed Sun.
Number of wines in stock: 700
Number of beers in stock: 50
Wine tastings: Wed. 4:30 P.M.–7 P.M.

Federal has been in business since 1946, and Len Rothenberg has owned the store since 1985. The wine collection is particularly strong in wines from Burgundy, Bordeaux, and the Rhône in France.

Martignetti Liquors

1650 Soldier's Field Road Extension, Brighton, MA 02132
    (617) 782-3700
Hours: Mon.–Thurs. 9 A.M.–10 P.M.; Fri., Sat. 9 A.M.–11 P.M.;
    closed Sun.
Number of wines in stock: 2,000
Number of beers in stock: 50–65
Wine tastings: Sat. noon

64 Cross Street, Boston, MA 02113   (617) 227-4343
Hours: Mon.–Thurs. 9 A.M.–10 P.M.; Fri., Sat. 9 A.M.–11 P.M.;
    closed Sun.
Number of wines in stock: 2,000
Wine tastings: yes, but not regularly scheduled

1020 Revere Beach Parkway, Chelsea, MA 02150   (617) 884-3500
Hours: Mon.–Thurs. 9 A.M.–9 P.M.; Fri., Sat. 9 A.M.–10 P.M.; closed Sun.
Number of wines in stock: 300–500
Wine tastings: September–December, Sat. 2 P.M.–4 P.M.; occasionally
    during the rest of the year

Martignetti's is best known for their great bargains, and for their terrific Italian wine selection. The North End location was the first store in Boston to obtain a liquor license. The center aisle of this location, as you enter, features the bargain specials. The prices in general are very good, and the staff is knowledgeable and helpful. The Brighton store is the largest of the three, with the most extensive selection of wines.

Marty's
675 Washington Street, Newton, MA 02160   (617) 332-1230
Hours: Mon.–Sat. 9 A.M.–11 P.M.; closed Sun.
Number of wines in stock: 5,000
Number of beers in stock: 450
Wine tastings: Fri. 5 P.M.–7 P.M.; Sat. noon–2 P.M.

193 Harvard Avenue, Allston, MA 02134   (617) 782-3250
Hours: Mon.–Sat. 9 A.M.–11 P.M.; closed Sun.
Number of wines in stock: 5,000
Number of beers in stock: 450
Wine tastings: Sat. noon–4 P.M.

Also: "An Epicurean Agenda," page 374.

Marty Siegal's father had a liquor store, Macy's, for several years at the Allston location. When Marty bought the Newton store, he changed the focus of the store. With wine, as with food, Marty's goal is to provide the widest selection at the best prices. In 1986 the Allston store had a fire, and Marty renovated it and turned it into a second Marty's. The wine selection is tremendous, and the staff is knowledgeable and helpful, more so than you might expect in a store this size. According to Sean Siegal (Marty's son and the vice president of the company), they have the largest selection of microbrews in the state. The choice is impressive. They also have an extensive selection of German wines.

Merchants Wine & Spirits
6 Water Street, Boston, MA 02109   (617) 523-7425
Delivery: available within suburban Boston
Hours: Mon., Tues. 10 A.M.–6 P.M.; Wed.–Fri. 9 A.M.–6:30 P.M.;
    Sat. 11 A.M.–5 P.M.; closed Sun.
Number of wines in stock: 900
Number of beers in stock: 45
Wine tastings: Thurs. 4 P.M.–6 P.M.

Merchants is located in the site of the old Federal National Bank, which went under in the crash of 1929. They specialize in wines from Germany, and in red and white Burgundies. Owner Bill Friedberg also has a wine importing business. The store is notable for its wine vault: the French wines are kept in an actual bank vault. The store logo is a vault door surrounded by grapes.

University Wine Shop

1739 Massachusetts Avenue, Cambridge, MA 02140   (617) 547-4258
Delivery: available in the Boston area
Hours: Mon.–Thurs. 10:30 A.M.–10:30 P.M.;
    Fri., Sat. 10:30 A.M.–11 P.M.; closed Sun.
Number of wines in stock: 900
Number of beers in stock: 450
Wine tastings: Sat. 10:30 A.M.–3 P.M.

University Wine Shop has been open for over forty years. They have a good selection and specialize in wines from California and Italy. Their beer selection is impressive: they carry almost every beer available in the United States.

The Wine and Cheese Cask

407 Washington Street, Somerville, MA 02143   (617) 623-8656
Hours: Mon.–Thurs. 10 A.M.–10 P.M.; Fri., Sat. 10 A.M.–10:45 P.M.;
    closed Sun.
Number of wines in stock: 2,000
Number of beers in stock: 130
Wine tastings: not available

The Wine and Cheese Cask has been in business since the mid-1960s. The wine selection is extensive, with a strong section of wines from Spain. California, France, Germany, and Australia are also well represented. The staff is knowledgeable and usually helpful; occasionally I've encountered a knowledgeable but surly staff person. The store publishes and distributes a free monthly newsletter describing current specials.

As the name implies, the store also provides a good selection of imported and domestic cheeses, about fifty to seventy-five varieties. They carry a variety of gourmet items, including olive oils, condiments, and breads. You can also get basic submarine-style **sandwiches** made to order.

The Winecellar of Silene

475 Winter Street, Waltham, MA 02154   (617) 890-2121
Delivery: available inside Route 495
Hours: Mon.–Sat. 10 A.M.–9 P.M.; closed Sun.
Number of wines in stock: 800
Number of beers in stock: 150
Wine tastings: Fri. 5 P.M.–7 P.M.; Sat. 2 P.M.–4:30 P.M.

The Winecellar of Silene has been in business since 1971. The focus of the wine selection here is Italian and United States wines. The beers are primarily microbrews. In 1993 the store began carrying specialty food items as well, including cheeses, sausages, condiments, and, on weekends, fresh breads from local bakers.

The Wine Co. See "Brewing and Winemaking Supplies," page 486.

THE BESTS OF THE BEST

Best winery: **Westport Rivers Vineyard and Winery**
Best fruit wines: **Nashoba Valley Winery**
Best beer on tap: **Atlantic Coast Brewing Company's Tremont Ale**
Best oatmeal stout: **Lowell Brewing Company's Mill City**
Best pale ale: **Ipswich Brewing Company**
Best dark ale: **The Boston Beer Company's Samuel Adams Scotch Ale**
Best lager: **Ipswich Brewing Company's Dornbusch Gold Lager** and
    Lowell Brewing Company's Mill City Vienna Lager
Best brewery tour: **The Boston Beer Company**

INDEX

Foods, beverages, and types of markets are set in **boldface**. Names of establishments are set in plain face.